Business and Agricultural Property Relief

Fifth Edition

CW01082999

Business and Agricultural Property Relief

Fifth Edition

Toby Harris LLB CTA TEP

Bloomsbury Professional

Bloomsbury Professional Ltd, Maxwelton House, 41–43 Boltro Road, Haywards Heath, West Sussex, RH16 1BJ

© Bloomsbury Professional Ltd 2011

Bloomsbury Professional, an imprint of Bloomsbury Publishing Plc

A CIP Catalogue record for this book is available from the British Library.

ISBN: 978 1 84592 344 0

Typeset by Phoenix Photosetting, Chatham, Kent

Printed and bound in Great Britain by Hobbs the Printers Ltd, Totton, Hampshire

Preface

This book is for the busy practitioner, not the academic, so each chapter contains a 'headnote' to guide the reader to the relevant section. In reviewing contentious areas I have quoted at length from the decided cases, giving the practitioner with a limited library enough detail to decide whether it is worth reading the actual report before advising. Many of the worked examples are drawn from life. I am grateful to colleagues for bringing to me specific situations that illustrate points in the legislation. Some of the knowledge in this book has been won the hard way.

If I had made a chargeable transfer on the day the last edition of this book went to press, it would by now have fallen out of account. That has been too long an interval but has given time for some developments that seemed dramatic at the time to fall into perspective. I have cut down the analysis of the older cases to make way for newer ones. In writing, we try to hit a moving target: I understand, for example, that an appeal is contemplated in the Swain Mason case.

In examining legislation I have, where appropriate, paraphrased the text or broken it up into 'bite-sized' portions, following the example of Blackburne J in Starke, or have repeated words to help explain the meaning. References to HMRC include their predecessors.

Carol, Geoff and Melissa

In the worked examples, as in earlier editions, I have introduced imaginary advisers whose relative skill in tax matters will quickly be apparent to the reader. Carol is an accountant, Geoff a solicitor and Melissa his new assistant, a Registered Trust and Estate Practitioner who has qualified under the Diploma route. More can be learned from cases that go horribly wrong than from the well ordered files that the practitioner aspires to. In the examples, as in life, there may be details that are not absolutely essential to the points in issue.

Teamwork

My thanks are due to my wife Penny, for her patient support during the writing process; to Heather Saward at Bloomsbury Professional for her encouragement and to Peter Smith for his meticulous reading of the text, which has made this a much better book than its predecessor.

Norwich, May 2011

Contents

Contents

Contents

Contents

Contents

Contents

Contents

Contents

Table of statutes

*[References are to paragraph numbers and appendices. Paragraph numbers in **bold** indicate where the material is set out in part or in full]*

xxiii

Table of statutes

Table of statutory instruments

[References are to paragraph numbers and appendices]

Table of statutory instruments

Table of cases

C

F

G

Chapter 1

Introduction

THE PLACE OF BPR/APR IN IHT

1.1   Agricultural property relief (APR) and business property relief (BPR) are amongst the most significant reliefs from IHT and have attracted much attention from tax planners. The reason is simple: the owner of valuable assets has often worked hard to build up, or at least to preserve, family assets; late in life, this concern for the protection of assets is augmented by worry about having enough to live on in old age; couple this with an irascible disposition, and you have an almost total argument for not making any kind of lifetime gift. Property is power within certain family situations, a power that is not lightly given up.

The advice of the IHT planner will often be to give early and to give generously (and certainly to give without reservation), but 100% APR and BPR offer the ageing Croesus exactly what he wants: an excuse to retain control, until his death, of the assets of which he is so fond. The adviser who can demonstrate that, in the particular circumstances of the case, one or other of these reliefs will be available at 100% will be popular. **Chapter 16** asks how long that situation may last and what the prudent family involved in business or agriculture should do to protect itself.

HISTORY OF BPR/APR

1.2   We can learn from the history of the relief: it is often set out in disputed cases to explain the current meaning of obscure legislation. Farming was treated kindly under estate duty. Anyone could qualify for agricultural relief by purchasing agricultural property late in life, without the need for a qualifying period. The concept of the 'working farmer', which is discussed in some detail in **Chapter 3**, came in with *FA 1975*. Even then, the definition of the working farmer was wide enough to include farmers who had retired and full-time students. There were limits to that relief as to acreage and to value. There is a trend in recent cases to try to import some of the spirit of 'working farmer' into tests such as relief on farmhouses.

Agricultural relief was not extended to let farms, which were generally worth much less than land with vacant possession, except where farmers let their land to companies which they themselves controlled or to partnerships of which they were partners. Naturally, many farmers found it convenient to enter into partnership with one or more of their children and let the land to the firm. This produced the 'double discount', in that the land itself was devalued and 50% (as it then was) agricultural relief was available.

That generous situation was curtailed by *FA 1981, s 96* and *Sch 4*, by which agricultural landlords gained some relief and the 'working farmer' limits were removed, except for what was then described as transitional relief (even though the period of transition has been very long indeed).

The history of BPR is more recent. There was no relief under *FA 1975* except that tax could be paid by interest free instalments. *FA 1976, s 73* and *Sch 10* gave additional relief at 30% for transfers after 6 April 1976, with multiple reliefs being introduced in October of the following year. From 10 March 1992 onwards, the reliefs were increased further. There was a difficult period of transition during which, if a lifetime transfer was chargeable when made, the new more generous rates of relief which had been introduced with effect from 10 March 1992 applied only for the purpose of the 'top up' charge which arose by reference to the death of the transferor. The value for cumulation stayed the same.

From 6 April 1996, matters were simplified by amending *IHTA 1984,s 105(1)* so as to make available 100% relief on all shareholdings of unquoted shares of any size transferred on or after that date, a change that also applied to any charge to tax on an earlier transfer which arose as a result of an event occurring on or after that date.

The former Capital Taxes Office, long known to practitioners as the CTO has, indirectly, become HM Revenue and Customs, Charity Assets and Residence, Inheritance Tax. In this book, it is referred to as HMRC: that means the CAR Division, unless the context otherwise requires.

OUTLINE OF THE SCOPE OF THIS BOOK

1.3   APR is considered before BPR in this book because of the priority afforded to APR within the legislation. We look first, in **Chapter 2**, at the kind of property in respect of which the relief can (and cannot) be given. In the following chapter, there is an examination of the value in respect of which the relief may be given and of the rate of the relief. **Chapter 4** brings together a number of difficult areas of concern.

Broadly the same pattern follows in relation to BPR, considering first in **Chapter 5** the kind of property that now qualifies for the relief, with a passing reference to those categories which were important until 5 April 1996 and will still be relevant to those practitioners with estates in administration which date back to that time. **Chapter 6** identifies the most important conditions for eligibility for relief and the factors that will exclude that relief, a theme continued in **Chapters 7 8** and **9**which cover not only the treatment of liabilities, which can reduce the relief but, in excepted assets and in 'wholly or mainly holding investments', two of the areas where the relief has frequently been denied. There follows in **Chapter 10** an examination of another difficult area, the clawback of relief.

Included in **Chapter 11** is a description of the relief available on woodlands, which is very closely related to APR and BPR and sometimes takes second place to those reliefs.

In **Chapters 12** to **16**, the book takes a different direction, looking at what the taxpayer may properly do to minimise the tax burden. When the first edition of this book was planned, the outlook for owners of farms and businesses seemed bleak from a taxation point of view. It now seems perhaps slightly worse: many businesses are struggling, and the State's need to gather taxes is more urgent than it was. The present coalition government cannot as easily ignore the 'politics of envy' as might a single political party, and the recent denial of electoral reform will stiffen political resolve to achieve redistribution of wealth but perhaps the need for consensus may prevent the introduction of extreme measures.

Chapters 17 to **20** examine the reliefs conditionally available in respect of heritage property, and **Chapter 21** examines the (rather rarefied) world of maintenance funds. **Chapter 22** outlines the requirements for compliance, and finally **Chapter 23** looks at facilities for payment of tax or, in the case of heritage property, use of this property itself to satisfy the liability to tax.

TERRITORIALITY

1.4   This is considered at **2.29** in relation to APR, and at **5.3** in relation to BPR. In broad terms, APR and woodlands relief were, until 2009, restricted to property in the United Kingdom, the Channel Islands or the Isle of Man, whereas BPR was never so restricted. The position was relaxed by *FA 2009, s 122*. There are, however, strict territorial aspects to relief on heritage property.

INTERACTION WITH OTHER RELIEFS

1.5   BPR applies to the value transferred by a transfer of value which is attributable to business property. The relief is applied before other reliefs. Where a gift is made of property qualifying for 50% relief, the unrelieved value may thus be sheltered from taxation by other exemptions. Thus a gift of property qualifying for 50% BPR and having a value of £500 would take effect after relief as a gift of £250 which might thus be exempt as a 'small gift' under *IHTA 1984, s 20*. Note, incidentally, that the value transferred is not grossed up for this purpose. Care should be taken to avoid the use of *s 20* where it is not appropriate, since a transfer of £251 is not exempt at all under *s 20*. Likewise, HMRC may refuse relief under *s 20* where the gift is made into settlement, since *s 20(1)* makes it clear that the transfer must be 'by outright gifts'.

At a more realistic level, the same principle applies in relation to the combination of the use of APR or BPR and relief under *s 21* (normal expenditure out of income) and *s 19* (annual exemption). Occasionally, in order to test the value of an asset from the point of view of a larger proposed gift, a transferor would make a gift which deliberately exceeded by a small margin, after relief, the available exemption. Where the resultant gift is a PET, this does not achieve agreement of value with HMRC, since the possibility that the transfer might not be chargeable robs the exercise of financial utility, from their point of view. The same holds true even where the transfer is a chargeable one falling within the nil rate band of the transferor. Valuation may be in point for the purposes of CGT in such a circumstance, but that is a matter to be regulated by self-assessment and, probably, the CG34 procedure for post-transaction valuation checks. If the issue is the availability of BPR, it may be possible to get a non-statutory ruling, as is explained later.

The interaction of APR, BPR and woodlands relief is complicated. The priority of APR over woodlands relief, and of BPR over that relief, are considered in **Chapter 11**.

There is some interaction between APR and BPR, on the one hand, and heritage relief, on the other. Here, the relationship is not so much between legal rules as a practical consideration.

Example 1.1: fudging the issue

A transfer on death includes agricultural land comprising a working farm and some let lands together with a substantial house with good quality contents. At some distance from the main house, there is another good quality house that has been occupied by one member of the family who also acts as farm manager. It is the surviving parent of the farm manager who has died.

The executors might initially claim BPR on the whole estate, perhaps claiming the kind of relief that was allowed in the case of *Farmer* (examined in **Chapter 9**) and encouraged by elements of the recent decision in *McCall* (as to which, see below and in **Chapter 5**). A claim might also be made that the principal house qualifies for APR on the ground that the deceased was, say, in partnership with the son who is the farm manager.

It is quite possible, applying the tests that are examined in **Chapter 2**, that the application for APR on the principal house might fail because it is really the other house, where the son/farm manager lives, that is the 'farmhouse'. It might, therefore, be appropriate, if the principal house is sufficiently grand, to seek relief on it as heritage property, particularly if the farmer is happy living in his present circumstances and does not want to move up to the main house. As will be seen in **Chapter 18**, a provisional or protective application for heritage property relief may be made even before the issue of APR or of BPR has been concluded.

HOW THE RELIEFS APPLY COMPUTATIONALLY

1.6 We always start with the full, open market value because relief may not be allowed, or not in full. The value transferred by a transfer of value is reduced by the appropriate percentage of the relief: see, for example, *IHTA 1984, s 116(7)*. This applies equally to 'straight' transfers and those occasions on which tax is chargeable under the relevant property trusts regime. APR and BPR are given before deduction of the annual exemption and before taking into account any other basis of exemption and, where the transferor pays the tax, before grossing up.

Where the percentage of the relief has in the past been increased, for example from 30% to 50% and from 50% to 100%, those increases apply both to:

● transfers of value made after the dates on which the increases became effective; and

● charges, or further charges, to IHT that arise on a death that occurs after the effective date of the increase in respect of any transfer made before 10 March 1992.

The treatment of liabilities differs slightly between agricultural property and business property. If liabilities are charged on agricultural property, they are deducted from the value of that property. If the value is only partly agricultural, it becomes necessary to apportion the liabilities between the part of the value that qualifies for APR and the part that does not. The situation is slightly different where the liabilities are not charges on the agricultural property. This is discussed in greater detail in **Chapter 8**. Special rules apply to disregard both APR and BPR in a clawback situation: this is more fully explained in **Chapter 10**.

Particular complications apply to relief in respect of qualifying property held by a relevant property trust. Note, in particular, that:

- a reference to 'a transfer of value' in relation to such a trust can include an occasion of charge on the settled property;

- a reference to 'the value transferred' is treated as being a reference to the amount on which IHT is actually chargeable; and

- a reference to 'the transferor' in such a situation can include a reference to the trustee.

As a result of this, BPR may be available by treating the trustees as the owners of such part of the trust fund as might qualify for the relief.

However, the way that the charging rules for relevant property trusts work can have the effect that sometimes BPR will reduce the amount on which tax is charged but not the rate at which that tax is charged. On other occasions, depending on the circumstances, the effect is to reduce the rate of tax but not the amount on which that tax is charged. A detailed exposition of the charges to IHT on discretionary trusts is outside the scope of this book: the reader may like to refer to *Inheritance Tax 2010/11* (Bloomsbury Professional), chapter 8 and the many worked examples there set out.

In general, on an exit charge where APR or BPR is in point, the relief will affect the value but not the rate of tax. There is one exception, where the settlement was made before 27 March 1974 and the exit charge arises from an event that occurred before the first ten-year anniversary.

On the other hand, the periodic charge is concerned with an imaginary transfer made up of:

- the sum of the amount in respect of which the charge is now made; and

- the value, immediately after that property first became comprised in the settlement, part of which is subject to discretionary trusts and which has not since become 'relevant property' within the discretionary trust tax regime; and

- the value of property comprised in any related settlement immediately after that settlement commenced.

APR or BPR on the relevant assets could therefore reduce the tax rate. By contrast, there is no reduction for BPR or APR where:

- there has been property in the same settlement which was not 'relevant property' (or such property in a related settlement); and

- the value of such property has to be taken into account in order to arrive at the rate of tax.

There is a planning point here. Where the periodic charge is reduced because BPR or APR applies, that will also serve to reduce the exit charge during the next ten-year period, whether or not that exit charge relates to property which qualifies for BPR or APR.

INTERACTION WITH INSTALMENT RELIEF

1.7   Under estate duty, there was relief for 'industrial hereditaments' by way of a reduction of 55% in the rate of tax (*FA 1954, s 28*) but there was no relief for business assets as such under capital transfer tax until *FA 1976*, except for the option of paying tax by interest-free instalments. At a time of inflation, that facility was of considerable value, giving the family a breathing space. It was not always wise to use the facility of paying tax by instalments, as the lawyer executor found to his acute cost in *Howarth's Executors v IRC* [1997] STC (SCD) 162, an account of which is included at **23.9**. A particular example of the value of the instalment facility is the business rich in assets, which are either intangible or not readily realisable but which are growing in value. High technology businesses might once have been thought to fall into this category.

THE DISTINCTION BETWEEN BPR AND APR

1.8   The same property may qualify both as agricultural property and as relevant business property. APR is subject to the notable restriction that the value qualifying for relief is the agricultural value only. There may be circumstances, such as the existence of valuable mineral rights, where BPR is available in respect of part of the value of property not covered by APR. The development value of land encouraged the claim to BPR in *McCall and another (Personal representatives of McLean Deceased) v HMRC* [2009] NICA 12. Another distinction examined in the book is the 'use' or 'occupation' test. In general terms, APR may be available in respect of land which is occupied for agriculture, whereas BPR is limited to assets actually used for the purpose of a business.

In respect of transfers before 10 March 1981, it could be beneficial not to claim agricultural relief but to take advantage of business relief. One reason might be to avoid the 'working farmer' limits. That facility was removed by *IHTA 1984, s 114(1)*, under which APR applies automatically in preference to BPR such that BPR is not available on any value which has been reduced by APR. See **Chapter 12** for examples of overlap of the reliefs and of situations where BPR is available in the absence of APR.

A more fundamental difference between the two reliefs is that APR is given on specific items of property whereas BPR is given on the business itself. This gives rise to a series of cases, noted in **Chapter 5**, determining whether property in respect of which relief is claimed is an interest in a business or a 'mere asset'. However, this has been called into question by the ingenious (and successful) arguments of the taxpayer in *Nelson Dance v HMRC* [2009] EWHC 71 (Ch). This distinction also has knock-on effects in relation to the disposal of specific assets (but not the business itself) for the purpose of clawback: see **Chapter 10**.

WHY DO WE HAVE TWO CODES?

1.9   At a time when the government recognises the need to simplify tax, a strong argument can be made for simplification of the law by extending BPR and repealing APR. Farming as an industry is undergoing serious difficulties. Rural employment is as scarce as ever. Diversification should be encouraged, for instance into the holiday and leisure trades. Julie Butler in her book *Tax Planning for Farm and Land Diversification*, 3rd Edn (Bloomsbury Professional), has done excellent work in exploring the possibilities here. Holiday cottages qualify for no APR and will only rarely qualify for BPR. There is scope here to help a beleaguered community, and at the same time to save the administrative cost of two parallel tax codes

Chapter 2

Agricultural property: qualifying property

QUICK GUIDE

This chapter defines the property that will qualify for APR. The 'big issue' is whether a farmhouse qualifies: see the discussion at **2.8** onwards. Next, issues arise as to what actually constitutes farming and whether any is being done. Broadly, the relief relates to land rather than to buildings. The other major problem area concerns farming companies. APR is available only to controlling shareholders.

Some specific assets do not qualify for APR: see **2.30**.

2.1   *IHTA 1984, s 115(2)* seems straightforward at first sight. 'Agricultural property' means and includes:

- agricultural land or pasture;

- woodland (if occupied with agricultural land or pasture and that occupation is ancillary to, ie does not dominate, the occupation of the agricultural land or pasture);

- any building used in connection with the intensive rearing of livestock or fish (if that building is occupied with agricultural land or pasture and the occupation is ancillary to that of the agricultural land or pasture);

- such cottages together with the land occupied with them as are of a character appropriate to the property;

- such farm buildings together with the land occupied with them as are of a character appropriate to the property; and

- such farm houses together with the land occupied with them as are of a character appropriate to the property.

The scope of *s 115(2)* is extended by *s 115(4)* in relation to horses, and further extends to short rotation coppice (see **2.25**) and land in conservation schemes (see **2.27**).

9

AGRICULTURAL LAND OR PASTURE

2.2 'Agriculture' is defined in *Agricultural Tenancies Act 1995, s 38(1)* as including 'horticulture, fruit growing, seed growing, dairy farming and livestock breeding and keeping, the use of land as grazing land, meadow land, osier land, market gardens and nursery grounds, and the use of land for woodlands where that use is ancillary to the farming of land for other agricultural purposes'. It is not enough merely for property to be of a type which might qualify for agricultural land. It must, under *IHTA 1984, s 117*, be occupied for the purposes of agriculture (or deemed to be so occupied under a 'set aside' or similar agreement).

The leading farmhouse case, *Starke and Another (Executors of Brown Deceased) v IRC* [1995] STC 689, which is considered in detail at **2.16**, actually tells us relatively little except that a building is not itself 'agricultural land or pasture'. That expression means bare land, fields or land which is used either for the grazing of animals or for the cultivation of crops. Thus, 'agricultural land' has a more restricted meaning than 'land'. Except where specifically amplified by the wording of *s 115*, 'agricultural land or pasture' means bare land, fields or land which is used either for the grazing of animals or for the cultivation of crops.

WOODLAND

2.3 The relief for woodland in its own right is discussed in **Chapter 11**. Woodland may also attract BPR, as to which see **Chapter 5**. For an account of an attempt to treat a plantation as woodland, see *Jaggers (t/a Shide Trees) v Ellis* [1997] STC 1417, discussed in greater detail in **Chapter 11**. For the occupation of woodland adjoining pasture, see comments *obiter* in *Williams v HMRC* [2005] SpC 500, discussed below.

BUILDINGS USED FOR INTENSIVE REARING OF LIVESTOCK OR FISH

2.4 It will be noted later in this chapter, in the discussion of farmhouses, that there may be careful scrutiny of a claim to APR in respect of a farming business which occupies less than 20 acres. Earlier editions of this book suggested the example of that could be an estate consisting of several pig units or of several poultry units, each separated from the other by a cordon sanitaire (literally) for protection from the spread of disease. *Section 115(2)* will not allow APR in respect of such land unless the building used as the pig or poultry unit is occupied with agricultural land and that occupation is ancillary to the occupation of the agricultural land.

Almost exactly that scenario came before the Special Commissioner in *Williams v HMRC* [2005] SpC 500. Mrs Williams owned Wells Farm, 7.41 acres spread across four parcels: about half an acre on which the residence stood; a paddock of a third of an acre; grazing land of just under four acres; and, most important to the case, 2.99 acres on which stood three broilerhouses. Mrs Williams owned the business that was run from the broilerhouses, until a few years before her death, but was losing money. She was advised to sublet, which she did. But for that, her personal representatives could simply have claimed BPR. As it was, they were forced to try to claim APR. It was agreed that the buildings were used for the intensive rearing of livestock within *s 115(2)*.

The claim to APR failed because the buildings dominated the land they stood on. There was detailed examination of the meaning in *s 115(2)* of 'occupation is ancillary to that of the agricultural land and pasture', both as to the relevant land and the nature of the occupation. The taxpayer argued that few, if any, broilerhouses would qualify for APR if tested by reference only to the parcel of land on which they stood; which could not have been the intention of Parliament. HMRC argued that the relief had been appropriate for 'smaller working farmers' rather than for factory farms and had worked well.

The decision of Commissioner Hellier merits detailed review because, after consideration of many legal sources, it contained several propositions which, though not binding on others, may be useful when advising on borderline situations:

- 'Occupation', as shown by earlier case law, exists where four elements are present, namely:

    - physical possession;

    - control of use;

    - power to exclude others; and

    - some form of right to enjoyment of the land.

- The tenant occupied the broilerhouses.

- The other land was not relevant to the 'ancillary' test, because the same person must be in occupation of the land and the buildings to satisfy the test.

- The *nexus* for this part of *s 115* is occupation rather than ownership.

- The occupation of the broilerhouses was not ancillary to the occupation of the land on which they stood.

- 'Ancillary occupation' requires that the use of buildings be ancillary to the use of the land.

11

- Occupation of woodland, for example, could be ancillary to occupation of land where there was a common purpose, as where the woodland provided shelter, for instance, for grazing cattle.

- The buildings need not be used only for purposes ancillary to the use of the land (so, in the case of woodland, it might also produce timber or support wildlife).

- 'Intensive' buildings within *IHTA 1984, s 115(2)* are to be considered as one with the land on which they stand and do not on their own qualify as agricultural land or pasture.

- Ancillary control does not require any test of the area of the land.

- The right to exclude others did not decide the issue here.

- Minor rights of enjoyment did not decide the issue here.

- The 'character appropriate' test is to be applied to farm buildings, namely:

  - size, content and layout by reference to the farmland;

  - size proportionate to farming use;

  - overall impression;

  - the 'educated rural layman' test; and

  - the history of the building.

Having summarised these principles, the Commissioner reviewed the legislation and *Hansard*, but gained little help from either. The broilerhouses would be ancillary only if occupied as an 'add-on' to larger agricultural enterprises on the other land, here meaning only the 2.99 acres. They failed that test.

Fish farms, or stew ponds may be treated as farm buildings in certain circumstances.

Example 2.1: raising trout and carp for the table

Isaac Walton is the owner of the Compleat Estate, through which runs a natural stream giving a very high-quality water supply. Isaac excavates near the stream, extracting gravel, and turns the excavations into a series of stew ponds. In pond A, he rears rainbow trout, in pond B brown trout and, in an off-lying pond, he breeds mirror carp. He offers within the estate in pond D some 'easy' fly fishing for rainbow trout and operates a kiosk from which, apart from selling fishing permits and the like, he sells fresh and smoked rainbow trout to passing trade, and carp to members of the Polish community nearby.

An analysis of the eligibility of the estate for APR would show that all of the river and pond complex is occupied with the agricultural land that constitutes Compleat Estate. Subject to the comments below, the stew ponds may be treated as farm buildings. The brown trout and carp are mainly sold to specialist angling clubs. Strictly, a fish farm which rears fish only for sport is not agricultural.

The part of the business which rears rainbow trout and carp may be able to show that, essentially, they are reared for food because they are sold as such at the farm gate. A purist might well argue that fishing for rainbow trout in an overstocked pool is so predictable as to be not sport but merely a delayed means of eating the fish in question. The fish breeding tanks or ponds will qualify for APR where the fish are reared for food, but pool D and the stream that feeds the whole farm will not, though *de minimis* unless the fishing rights in respect of the stream are valuable, the value, if any, of pool D and the stream itself may be 'lost' in the valuation of Compleat Estate as a whole.

The distinctions are, actually, academic. Isaac has run the whole operation on business-like lines. Despite his famous name, he is not an angler himself; no part of the operation is excluded as an excepted asset under *s 112*. Insofar as APR is not available, Isaac secures BPR at 100%.

It is not every kind of fish farm that is considered to be 'farming'. The traditional type of trout farm could be said to have a dependence on the land and therefore to come within the meaning of 'husbandry'. HMRC have indicated (see BIM55105), in the context of other taxes, that fish farming in natural lakes or rivers will be farming, whereas fish farming where the stock are kept entirely separate from the land, as in artificial tanks or in the sea, and fed entirely on purchased feed, will not. For BPR the difference is immaterial since, in either case, the operation may be a business regardless of its linkage to land. In any case, the brief summary in BIM55105 does not sit easily with *s 115(2)* and makes no reference to it, and all the cases there referred to pre-date *IHTA 1984*. The Business Income Manual would be more helpful if it addressed all taxes.

For APR, which is an asset-based relief, the linkage with land is explicit in the wording of *s 115(2)*, as interpreted in *Williams*. The exclusion of sea-borne activities may be consistent with the exclusion from relief of oyster bed (see *Gunter v Newtown Oyster Fishery* (1977) 244 EG 140). However, the exclusion of conventional 'onshore' fish farming from relief does seem hard to justify. A 'building' used for the intensive rearing of fish is specifically within *s 115*, so, in an appropriate case, argument might turn on the meaning of 'building'. The Concise Oxford Dictionary defines it as 'permanent fixed thing built for occupation (house, school, factory, stable, etc)'. Although a building commonly has a roof, that may not be an essential ingredient, and a tank constructed specifically for the rearing of fish, no doubt with inbuilt protection, even from the air, from predators ought to fall within the definition. It does not appear that a case specifically on this point has come before the courts. In any event, in the light of the decision in *Williams*, the installations relating to fish would have to be part of a larger overall establishment.

Ancillary occupation

2.5   The issue of occupation of buildings has just been discussed. The same issue arises in relation to woodland. There was, until *Williams*, little direct authority on the interpretation of *s 115(2)(b)*. *Williams* did take note of the House of Lords' decision in *Farmer (Valuation Officer) v Buxted Poultry Ltd* [1993] AC 369, where the meaning of the expression 'occupied together with', a phrase from rating law, was considered.

To succeed in the dispute, Buxted Poultry Ltd had to show that a poultry processing factory was 'occupied together with' buildings used for the keeping or breeding of poultry. As is the custom for the industry, the buildings were scattered over a very wide area. The House of Lords held that the factory was not an agricultural building and that, for one building to be 'occupied together with' another building (or land), the following tests must be satisfied:

- the buildings must be in the same ownership at the same time and jointly managed or controlled; and

- the buildings must be occupied together so as to form a single agricultural unit in a real sense. Evidence that the buildings are close together may well show that they are so occupied. If they are separated, that may indicate that they are not.

Woodland often adjoins farmland. The fact that it offers the farmer a degree of privacy and may form habitat for birds not reared as livestock, namely pheasants, partridges and the like, may be of great personal advantage to the farmer. Fortunately for him, that does not cause APR to be denied, because there is in the APR code no precise parallel to the 'excepted assets' rule for BPR. All the farmer must show is that the shelter belts are occupied with the land that they shelter, that such occupation is ancillary to that of the farmland, and that such occupation is, in fact, not for the purpose of an annual shoot but is for the purpose of agriculture. Again, this was confirmed in *Williams*.

FARM COTTAGES

2.6   The provision in *s 115(2)* relating to farm cottages is extended by ESC F16. That Concession provides that, on a transfer of agricultural property which includes a cottage occupied by a retired farm employee or by the widow or widower of such an employee, the condition as to occupation for agricultural purposes is regarded as satisfied with respect to the cottage if one of two conditions is satisfied, namely:

- the occupier is a statutorily protected tenant (for example, under the *Housing Act 1988*, the *Rent (Agriculture) Act 1976* or similar legislation in Northern Ireland or Scotland); or

- the occupation is under a lease granted to the farm employee for his or her life and the life of any surviving spouse as part of the contract of employment of the employee. That contract of employment must be by the landlord for agricultural purposes.

The first of these situations arises where someone employed in agriculture for the previous two years has occupied a dwelling-house provided by the employer. Depending on the date when the tenancy licence or occupancy began, that employee's right of occupation is normally protected under the *1976 Act* or is protected as an assured agricultural occupancy under the *1998 Act* or, in Scotland or Northern Ireland, under other legislation giving similar results. That protection can extend to any surviving spouse following the death of the employee. The second situation will arise where there is a similar result from any other lease granted to an employee as part of his or her terms of employment for the purpose of agriculture.

The following principles emerge relating to cottages:

- there is no relief if the cottage is not 'of a character appropriate';

- 100% relief is available if the tenancy began on or after 1 September 1995 and is an unprotected service tenancy or an assured shorthold tenancy; this is however subject to certain qualifications and is examined at **3.18** below;

- APR will be limited to 50% of the tenancy in an assured agricultural occupancy, unless it can be shown that suitable alternative accommodation is available, or that the tenant is in breach of the tenancy such that vacant possession could be obtained at the time of transfer, albeit after court delays; see again at **3.18** below.

Attempts are made from time to time to test the boundaries of the definition of 'agricultural property', even in relation to quite small parcels of land. An example is *Wheatley's Executors v CIR*, considered at **2.23** below. In *Dixon v IRC* SpC 297, [2002] SWTI 43, a Special Commissioner had to consider a claim for APR on a small residential property and applied the test of 'the educated rural layman'. The property was an interest in a cottage, garden and orchard of which the total area was 0.6 acres. It adjoined a nursery garden and orchard where vegetables, fruit and flowers were grown commercially. The orchard included damson trees whose fruit was picked by the neighbour and sold with his own. The proceeds, some £70 per annum, were not included as income on the tax returns of the owner of the cottage. Evidence showed that, under these damson trees, there had grazed geese, a goat that was kept for milk, chickens kept both for their eggs and for the table and, for a period of three years, a neighbouring farmer was allowed to graze six ewes and lambs. The consideration for that grazing did not appear on a tax return either; in return for the grazing, the farmer's wife did some household chores for the owner of the land.

By 2001, this rural idyll had deteriorated somewhat: the orchard was overgrown and the crop of damsons was not pickable commercially (but there was potential if the orchard could be cleared). On the death of a part-owner of the property, the Revenue determined that the property was not 'agricultural property' within *s 115(2)*.

The Special Commissioner agreed. Fruit growing and grazing could be agriculture, but it was a question of fact and of degree which must be determined in the light of the purposes of the *Act*, which was designed to give relief for land and pastures used for agriculture but not for a private residence. On the facts, the activities were consistent with the use of the property as a residence and garden, not for agriculture. The issue was not whether the cottage was appropriate to agricultural land, but rather whether the orchard and garden were appropriate to the cottage. There was no history of agricultural production. The property consisted primarily of a cottage used for domestic and residential purposes, with a garden and orchard that were of a character appropriate to such a cottage. The appeal was dismissed.

FARMHOUSES

2.7 Few difficulties arise, in practice, over claiming APR on a house which is modest in size and which has for generations been owned and occupied by farming families together with adjoining land. Many claims are well made and succeed. The problems, as always, arise at the margins of what is reasonable. One problem here is that the claim to APR is all or nothing; although, in practice, where it can be argued that part of the house is the farm office, a claim to BPR may give some scope for 'fudging the issue', since such a claim is for a proportion of the open market value of the house, not the agricultural value. Even so, a substantial amount of value may remain subject to tax.

Tests of a farmhouse: historical background to the current law

2.8 Advocates in farmhouse cases often refer back to the old law. In view of the way that agriculture is changing, perhaps that approach may no longer be justified, though background is set out below. This area of the law is hotly contested both in the courts and in the political arena. For example, the Institute for Public Policy Research, in its review a few years ago of IHT 'Fair Dues', included in its catalogue of exemptions and loopholes all the reliefs described in this book, but singled this subject out:

> 'The Agricultural Relief also provides an exemption for farmhouses, which anecdotal evidence suggests provides a cover for a large number of country cottages [or], "fake farmhouses" to be passed on tax free. At the least, it may be desirable to tighten the definition of agricultural property to close this loophole.'

For a more academic expression of those ideas, see the observations of the Lands Tribunal in *Lloyds TSB Private Banking plc (PR of Rosemary Antrobus Deceased) v Peter Twiddy (Inland Revenue Capital Taxes)* [2002] STI 1398, discussed in detail below and better known as *'Antrobus Number 2'*. There, the Lands Tribunal were not considering as such the availability of the relief so the comments were *obiter* but, in order to arrive at a value for the purposes of the relief, they did consider what house should qualify for the relief in the first place. They concluded that:

> 'A farmhouse is the chief dwelling house attached to a farm, the house in which the farmer of the land lived. There is, we think, no dispute about the definition when it is expressed in this way. The question is: who is the farmer of the land for the purposes of the definition of *s 115(2)*? In our view it is the person who lives in the farmhouse in order to farm the land comprised in the farm and who farms the land on a day to day basis ... We do not think that the house occupied with the farm is a farmhouse simply because the person living there is in overall control of the agricultural business conducted on the land; and in particular we think that the lifestyle farmer, the person whose bid for the land is treated by the appellant as establishing the agricultural value of the land, is not the farmer for the purposes of the provision.'

The fact that those comments were *obiter* never seems to dissuade HMRC from relying on them.

The historical context of the law and of the subject dwelling

2.9   Busy practitioners will skip this section and go straight to **2.20** and the leading case, *McKenna*. Insofar as history is still relevant, we can see farmhouses in the historical context not merely of the building but of the legislation. In 1975, the concept of the 'working farmer' (discussed in greater detail in **Chapter 3**) was of much greater importance than it is now. The farmhouse was seen to be of a character appropriate to that 'working farmer' test. The classification of rural residences included mansion houses, farmhouses and farm cottages. Of these, only the latter two qualify for relief. Mansion houses have not qualified for relief since 1975. The test of the house was not necessarily an economic one. The feasibility of farming was not relevant.

17

There were then, and may still be, many holdings in parts of the United Kingdom of between 25 and 50 acres which were centred around a substantial house. It is arguable that no-one in their right mind would try to carry on farming on such a small scale, yet farming families continue to do so. This is not necessarily to suggest that, historically, farmers are not in their right minds, though the willingness of some families to continue that way of life in the face of recent difficulties may nowadays seem truly remarkable. In this kind of farming operation, the farmhouse would qualify for relief whilst the owners continued to try to eke out a living from the land.

Suppose, however, that some change of economic circumstance, such as urban growth, were to cause the family to give up farming and to sell the house and the entire acreage to the family of a successful conveyancing solicitor. Whilst it may be imagined that the acreage would remain the same, and the solicitor and his family might succumb to the charms of rural life to the extent of arranging, through a team of contractors, to work the land, such that it might appear that substantially the same acreage was still put to the same use, it is much less certain that APR would be available to the lawyer than it was to the original owners. The building would be a farmhouse by virtue of historical association, but the failure of the lawyer's family to rely upon the land wholly for their livelihood would weaken the case for relief. It is also very possible, in such a situation, that proximity to urban development might have given a substantial house standing in open land a premium value well above straightforward agricultural value. That premium would not in any event qualify for APR: see **3.1** relating to agricultural value, and the commentary on valuation at **4.22**.

Mansion houses and big farmhouses

2.10   Is there an upper size limit of building, above which, no matter how large the estate, no relief will be given in respect of the principal residence on the estate? Probably: even when let land is taken into account, in addition to farms in hand, so as to demonstrate that the estate is large, a house with, say, 13 bedrooms (all en suite) plus staff flats and a full range of leisure facilities may be too grand to qualify for APR as a farmhouse. It will not help the claim that, as may well be the case, the true centre of the farming operations is an estate office situated in or near the residence of the farm manager, and the owner of the estate goes to that office to supervise farming and estate matters. On this point, see *McKenna*, reviewed at **2.20**.

Tests applied in earlier cases

2.11   Traditionally, there were three tests as to whether a house was 'of a character appropriate to the property': historical association; geographical comparables; and financial viability. For a time, it seemed that the last of these tests was the most important, the question being whether:

- the income of the enterprise actually was, at the time of the relevant transfer, sufficient to support the farmhouse or farmhouses for which relief was claimed and to provide a livelihood for their occupants; or

- the activities of the enterprise could be so arranged as to produce such a result.

An unpublished decision of the Special Commissioners in Autumn 1994 rejected the traditional indicia. The Commissioners stated, 'whether or not one can make a living from a given acreage of land cannot be determinative of the question whether a building is a farmhouse'. Subject to what follows, this view is now reflected in the treatment of claims for APR on farmhouses: HMRC clearly prefer a functional test (see IHTM24036).

The starting point was laid down by Blackburne J in *Starke v IRC* [1994] STC 295, when he held that:

'cottages, farm buildings and farmhouses ... will constitute "agricultural property" if used in connection with agricultural land or pasture provided that they are of a character appropriate to such agricultural land or pasture (that is, are proportionate in size and nature to the requirements of the farming activities conducted on the agricultural land or pasture in question).'

Earlier editions of this work considered tests such as 'primary character', 'local practice' and 'financial support', but recent cases, especially *McKenna* considered in detail below, have produced a better checklist to work from, making the older cases less important. One such, *Executors of John Sydney Higginson v CIR* [2002] STI 1400, now serves mainly to illustrate an extreme principle, namely whether a farmer would buy this particular house in order to farm from it.

Higginson: an extreme case

2.12   Mr Higginson's home had been Ballyward Lodge, set in a landed estate of 134 acres of which 63 were agricultural land, 3 acres were garden and 68 acres were woodland and wetland. The house was not a typical farmhouse. Sales particulars showed it to have 'enormous potential as a charming family home or as a small active farm'. The deceased had bought the property in 1954 and farmed it himself until 1985. After that, he let the farmland. In 1990, the woodland and wetland were made areas of nature conservation. The heir to the estate had wished to farm the land in principle but (which proved fatal to the claim) he realised that it was not economically viable, and the estate was sold for £1,150,000.

The Commissioners considered that the object of APR was to allow families to continue farming. There was no precondition that the deceased should have been farming but it was a very significant factor. Land and house together must be an agricultural unit. Within that unit, the land must be the dominant element. Farm buildings and farmhouses must be ancillary to the land. That was not the case here: the single most significant fact was the price for which the family were able to sell the property. A figure of around £1,000,000 for the property as a whole was beyond the means of many who might otherwise be interested in farming. It would represent 'an appalling investment in terms of yield' from a farming perspective. APR was refused on the house.

This case is helpful in illustrating another point, addressed at **3.1** and **4.23** below, concerning the restriction of APR to the agricultural value of the relevant asset. The comments are clearly *obiter*, but the Commissioner did say:

> 'It seems to me that the notional restrictive covenant would have much less of a depreciatory effect in a case where the property has a value greater than ordinary, not because of development potential but rather because of what I might call "vanity value" on account of its site, style or the like.'

That means, in effect, that (subject to the discussion below) one does not simply discount the open market value of a farmhouse by 30% to arrive at the agricultural value. In the light of *Higginson*, the practitioner must now ask, in relation to a dwelling for which APR is sought, whether a purchase of it and its land would, at today's values, be 'an appalling investment in terms of yield'.

Antrobus No 1: lifestyle farming

2.13 *Lloyds TSB as personal representative of Rosemary Antrobus Deceased v CIR* [2002] STC (SCD) 468 concerned Cookhill Priory, enjoyed with 126 acres of freehold land and 6.54 acres of tenanted land. The father of Miss Antrobus, the deceased, had purchased the property in 1907. It had 6 bedrooms and dated to the mid 16th century. An extension had been added in about 1765. The original nunnery had been founded in 1260. In 1785, the chapel of the nuns was rebuilt. In 1910, the Georgian extension to the property was again extended. The father had farmed the land until 1942, dying the following year. His widow died in 1959. Miss Antrobus had a tenancy of 104 acres of other land and a licence over 20 acres. She acquired the property from relatives in 1959. It was then listed Grade II*, not because it was particularly attractive but because of its history.

Although Miss Antrobus showed losses in her accounts from time to time, she had made profits in 1993 and 1994. She was clearly a farmer, working with both arable and stock. On her death, it was agreed that the land and buildings were agricultural property, but APR was disputed in respect of two let houses and Cookhill Priory itself. An expert witness described the property as a working farm and produced much evidence of comparable buildings in that part of England. The Revenue acknowledged that this was not 'a rich man's considerable residence', but that it had a dual purpose. It had become the dwelling of a prosperous person and was surrounded by parkland. It was a family home of some distinction. The holding was not an economic one.

Before the Special Commissioners, it was acknowledged by both parties that Cookhill Priory was a farmhouse. The Special Commissioner accepted the expert advice that Cookhill Priory was not a gentleman's residence. It had been a working asset integral to the farm for at least 100 years. It was relevant that visual impact of the Georgian front was somewhat impaired by large corrugated iron farm buildings not too far away. It was also relevant that the property was in a poor state of repair. Even if, at one time, this had been 'a family home of some distinction', it had become, by the date of death, both in appearance and in use the farmhouse of a working farm. That was enough to decide the matter in favour of the taxpayer.

The Antrobus checklist

2.14   Dr Brice, the Commissioner deciding *Antrobus*, very helpfully summarised the relevant principles for deciding the test in *s 105(2)*. Decisions of the Special Commissioner are not binding on the High Court, but the principles in *Antrobus,* as further amplified by Dr Brice in *McKenna*, now form the checklist for any enquiry.

(1) Is the house appropriate, by reference to its size, content and layout, to the farm buildings and the particular area of farmland being farmed?

This test is derived from *Korner and others v CIR* (1969) 45 TC 287, an income tax case. It was not considered to be directly relevant because, by the time that particular case reached the House of Lords, the Revenue had conceded that the house in question was a farmhouse. The second issue arising out of the *Korner* test is, however, that of comparables. Practitioners will do well to marshal expert evidence concerning the size of the dwelling, the way it is set out and how the farm buildings compare with other landholdings. In that case, Lord Upjohn required the dwelling to be judged by 'ordinary ideas of what is appropriate in size, content and layout, taken in conjunction with the farm buildings and the particular area of farm land being farmed, and not part of a rich man's considerable residence'.

(2) Is the house proportionate in size and nature to the requirements of the farming activities conducted on the agricultural land or pasture in question?

This is the test from *Starke and Others (Executors of Brown Deceased) v IRC* [1996] All ER 622. It was noted in *Antrobus* that most farmers were now making less profit than previously.

21

(3) Is the subject property 'a family home of some distinction'?

Although one cannot describe a farmhouse which satisfies the 'character appropriate' test, one knows one when one sees it. This is the test in *Dixon* [2002] SWTI 43. The Commissioner was guided by the expert evidence that Cookhill Priory was a farmhouse of a character appropriate. This is the 'elephant' test referred to below.

(4) Would an educated rural layman regard the property as a house with land or as a farm?

This has been described as 'the man in the rural Volvo Estate test'. The Commissioner heard the evidence, looked at photographs and considered that the whole use and visual presentation of Cookhill Priory supported the view that it was a farmhouse.

(5) How long has the house in question been associated with the agricultural property? Was there a history of agricultural production?

These are also tests from the *Dixon* case. Can the taxpayer point to 95 years of agricultural production within the same family, as could the family of Miss Antrobus? If not, what period can be shown, bearing in mind the relaxed time scales that may apply in rural communities?

The 'elephant' test

2.15   These are not the only criteria that had earlier been described by Mr Twiddy on behalf of HMRC when describing his approach to the issue. HMRC would also consider whether there has, for example, been a large reduction in the area farmed from the house. An example of this is mentioned below. Having applied the test of the rule equivalent of the reasonable man on the Clapham omnibus, 'we should then stand back and take a balanced view in the round, and that may be described as the elephant test – difficult to describe, but you know one when you see one'.

It follows that each case will turn on its own facts. Thus, *Harrold (executors of Harrold deceased) v CIR* [1996] STC (SCD) 195 served to identify a six-bedroomed farmhouse as appropriate for the substantial acreage of the farm with which it was 'enjoyed' (if that is not an exaggeration in respect of a house that was not fit for occupation). That case, however, turned on another issue, as is explained at **3.15**.

Review of s 115(2) in Starke

2.16   One difficulty for the practitioner is that HMRC rely, for the starting point in considering farmhouse relief, on the decision of Blackburne J in *Starke* *v IRC* [1994] STC 295. However, that decision is subject to two limitations. First, the judgment of Blackburne J was reconsidered by the Court of Appeal. Second, there were particular circumstances in that case which will rarely apply. Some aspects of the judgment can very usefully be studied. First, it was not disputed that *s 115(2)* may conveniently be divided into three parts or 'limbs' (separately numbered in the extract below):

The text of the section, with the subdivisions adopted in *Starke*, reads:

'In this Chapter "agricultural property" means

[limb 1] agricultural land or pasture; and

[limb 2] includes woodland and any building used in connection with the intensive rearing of livestock or fish if the woodland or building is occupied with agricultural land or pasture and the occupation is ancillary to that of the agricultural land or pasture; and

[limb 3] also includes such cottages, farm buildings and farmhouses, together with the land occupied with them, as are of a character appropriate to the property.'

The difficulties in the subsection arise from the following questions:

- Does 'land' mean not merely land but any buildings on it?
- Does the requirement that woodland etc be occupied 'with agricultural land or pasture' mean with any such land or pasture, or must that land or pasture belong to the owner of the woodland or building?
- Must cottages, farm buildings and/or farmhouses with their land be of a character appropriate to the agricultural land in limb 1?
- Is it sufficient if cottages etc are generally of an agricultural type, or must they be appropriate to other agricultural land that is in the same occupation?

Notwithstanding the limitations of the *Starke* case mentioned below, it is relevant to consider the arguments that were put on behalf of HMRC in the High Court. These were that 'agricultural property' is effectively bare land, and that land with buildings can qualify for relief only under limbs 2 and 3. Further, property within limbs 2 and 3 qualifies for no relief on its own, but must be occupied in conjunction with agricultural land or pasture that already qualifies for relief within limb 1 *and is owned by the transferor* (emphasis added).

This highlights a particular difficulty of the *Starke* case. For reasons that were particular to that case, the taxpayer was able to proceed with the appeal only by giving an undertaking that the land in question should be judged by reference to limb 1 of the subsection and not, as the taxpayer might well have preferred, under limb 3. As a result, the meaning of limb 1 of *s 115(2)* was considered in isolation. As will be seen below from the review of the Court of Appeal decision, the case went against the taxpayer by applying the *Interpretation Act 1978*, which confirmed that the definition of 'agricultural land' should take account of the definition of 'land' in *Sch 1*, but that the *Act* should apply only where no contrary intention appeared. A contrary intention did so appear in the present case, and the relatively small area of land retained by the transferor, a house and small garden on a 2.5-acre site, was not 'agricultural land and pasture' within limb 1. In a nutshell, *Starke* just tells us that buildings are neither pasture nor bare land. It would be wrong to try to get much more out of the decision.

Subject to those limitations, there are some useful, if *obiter*, propositions from the judgment in the High Court of Blackburne J. Five points in particular arose:

(1)   Limb 1 is a composite one but broadly it describes bare land.

(2)   If limb 1 was intended to describe not merely bare land but other types of land, including any that had buildings standing on it, there would be no need for limbs 2 and 3. Limbs 2 and 3 are not mere illustrations of limb 1. They extend the definition to property that would not necessarily qualify under limb 1.

(3)   A building as such is neither land nor pasture.

(4)   Cottages and farmhouses must be of a character appropriate if limb 3 is to have any meaning at all. They are therefore not comprised within limb 1. They will qualify for relief only if used with agricultural land or pasture and are of a character appropriate to such agricultural land or pasture.

(5)   A stud farm may be agricultural land, and the provision in *s 115(4)* would not be needed if limb 1 could include all agricultural land and buildings.

Commenting on farmhouses, Blackburne J considered that they could constitute agricultural property 'if used with agricultural land or pasture provided that they are of a character appropriate to such agricultural land or pasture – that is, are proportionate in size and nature to the requirements of the farming activities conducted on the agricultural land or pasture in question'. Interestingly, Blackburne J did not expressly agree with the argument for HMRC that the connection or *nexus* between property in limb 3 and property in limb 1 must be common ownership.

The Court of Appeal decided the case on the fairly narrow ground that the property in question did not fall within limb 1. The interest of the decision in the Court of Appeal for the practitioner in the more usual case, who may rely on limbs 1, 2 and 3 of *s 115(2)*, is the observation of Morritt LJ. He said:

'Thus the question whether the property with which this appeal is concerned is excluded from part 3 because there is no other property in the same ownership to which its character may be appropriate does not arise for decision. Counsel for the Crown indicated that the official view is that there must be some nexus between the property alleged to fall within part 3 and other agricultural land or pasture and that such nexus must be derived from common ownership as the structure of Inheritance Tax legislation deals with the diminution in value of the estate of the transferor. The alternative view might be that the nexus, which must surely be required, may be provided by common occupation without common ownership thereby recognizing the reality of the agricultural unit of which, as in this case, the buildings evidently formed part.'

Rosser v IRC

2.17   The specific issue discussed above came before the Special Commissioner in *Rosser v IRC* SpC 368, [2003] STI 1152. The decision is perhaps limited, as will be seen from the analysis below. The deceased and her husband set up a farming partnership in the 1930s, later buying a farm comprising 41 acres of agricultural land, a house and a barn. In 1989, they gave 39 acres to their daughter, retaining on a two-acre site the house which was their home and a barn. The daughter and her husband farmed the 39 acres and, from 1990 onwards, also farmed the two-acre site that had been retained by the deceased and her husband.

In 1996, the farming partnership of the deceased and her husband was dissolved. The only agricultural activities carried on at the retained property were the provision of refreshments for those working on the farm and the storage of farm tools and pesticides. The barn was still used for agricultural purposes in connection with the adjoining two acres of land and served the needs of the 39 acres that had been given to the daughter, the appellant in the case, Mrs Rosser.

Following the death of the deceased and of her husband, a notice of determination was issued that the house and barn did not fall within the definition of 'agricultural property' in *s 115(2)*, not being 'of a character appropriate' to the agricultural land and pasture that remained in the estate of the deceased. The case is interesting because it considers many of the tests of a farmhouse that are mentioned in the following sections of this work.

The first issue was whether the house and barn were agricultural land within limb 1 of *s 115(2)*. The husband of the appellant represented her and argued that the house and barn were agricultural land but the Special Commissioner considered that he was bound by the specific decision of the Court of Appeal in *Starke* to the contrary.

The Commissioner considered the issue that the courts had not considered in *Starke*, namely whether the farmhouse and/or the barn might be considered by reference to the two acres of agricultural land that were retained at the time of death, or to the original 41 acres. He acknowledged that there was no decided authority on the nature of the *nexus* between the buildings and the property, quoting the extract from the judgment of Morritt LJ set out above. The Special Commissioner heard argument from Mr Peter Twiddy for HMRC that the *nexus* must be derived from common ownership, not common occupation.

This argument was that IHT is charged on the value transferred by a chargeable transfer which is itself a transfer of value made by an individual where not exempt. That transfer is defined as a disposition as a result of which the value of the estate of the transferor is reduced. *Section 4(1)* charges tax as if there were a transfer of the value equal to the value of the estate immediately before death. The common connection is the word 'estate' and, on that basis, the only *nexus* acceptable for the interpretation of *s 115* is common ownership.

The Special Commissioner agreed, stating that the 'alternative view that the farm buildings are in the estate that the property to which they refer is not is untenable. This view would seriously undermine the structure for Inheritance Tax and create considerable uncertainty about when tax is chargeable and the amount of the value transferred'.

Review of 'limb 3' in Rosser

2.18   The Commissioner in *Rosser* was free, unlike the court in *Starke*, to consider whether the house in question was a farmhouse in accordance with limb 3 of *s 115(2)*. He considered that this was a two-stage process, involving, first, a decision as to whether the house was in fact a farmhouse and, if it was, whether it was of a 'character appropriate'. In this, the Commissioner was guided by the arguments of Mr Twiddy which, although persuasive, did not refer to specific authorities. He argued that the dwelling must be 'the centre of operations or the headquarters for the farming activities' to qualify as a farmhouse. The justification for that proposition was reference to the Oxford English Dictionary, Collins Concise Dictionary and Chambers English Dictionary.

On the facts in *Rosser*, it was acknowledged that the dwelling had provided a home for generations of farmers and their families, but the test was whether the dwelling was actually in use as a farmhouse immediately before the death. The facts showed that it was not. By then, the deceased had retired. Instead, the land that might support the dwelling in the application for APR was managed by the daughter and her husband from another farm not far away. The IACS certificate and some of the invoices for the land were in the name of the daughter at the other farm. The deceased and her husband, until his death, had kept an eye on things from the dwelling, but it was the son-in-law who would deal with any problems. The only activities clearly associated with the farming at the material time were the provision of early morning refreshments and the midday meal and the storage of agricultural equipment and pesticides.

The Commissioner concluded that those activities were incidental to the prime function of the house as a retirement home and were of themselves not enough to characterise the dwelling as a farmhouse. Thus, the dwelling failed the primary test and it was not necessary to consider whether it was of a character appropriate. The case is, however, useful because the Commissioner did then consider whether the barn, rather than the house, might be of a character appropriate to the property, and applied the checklist approach that was adopted in *Antrobus*.

The nexus between the land and the house

2.19 Following the decision in *Rosser*, HMRC took note, and legal advice, as to the alternative possibility mentioned by Morritt LJ that sufficient *nexus* might be established for farmhouse relief even where the house and the land were not in the same ownership. They have, in particular, considered:

- whether an interest in land that was let to a third party should be considered when judging whether a farmhouse satisfied the character test; and

- whether the financial viability of the farm was material consideration, here distinguishing 'financial viability' in some way from 'economic viability'.

This is still 'work in progress': we do not have an authoritative statement of the law from any decided case.

The leading case: McKenna

2.20 *Arnander (Executors of McKenna Deceased) v HMRC* [2006] STC (SCD) 800 is a valuable and very thorough examination of the issues outlined above, to which this summary can barely do justice.

Rosteague House, Cornwall, overlooked the sea. It was in poor condition but nevertheless listed Grade II* and 'at the very top end of the size of a farmhouse in Cornwall', even in the context of many Grade I, Grade II* and Grade II farmhouses in the district. It stood in, or in front of, 187 acres which included 52 acres of coastal slope (from which at one time seaweed was collected as fertiliser) and over a mile of sea frontage. Its origins went back perhaps as far as the 13th century, the present house back in part to 1597, according to contemporary maps. It was a very substantial house with extensive and impressive gardens. There were farm buildings.

The farming history could be traced back to 1365, though recently it had been conducted by agents. The gardener also briefly engaged for a time in pig breeding for the owner. From 1984 onwards, there were contract farming arrangements. The woodland area was extended with the help of a planting grant. The contractor would have grown maize, but Mr McKenna disliked that and prevented it. The farm buildings were little used as such, but did house garden implements.

There were good farm records etc which took the owner perhaps an hour a day to prepare but, from 1995 onwards, illness prevented him from inspecting the land. In 1997, he put all the property then remaining into joint names with Lady McKenna, his wife. She was then in poor health. He died in January 2003, she in June of that year. The estate was sold, but not as a farm, for £3,050,000. Later evidence showed that urgent repairs would cost the purchaser nearly £200,000.

Against that background, Dr Brice found as follows:

- It was not a farmhouse. She quoted with approval the decision in *Rosser v IRC*. She approached the views of the Lands Tribunal in *Antrobus No 2* 'with some caution' as *obiter*, but held that the principle that 'the farmer of the land is the person who farms it on a day-to-day basis rather than the person who is in overall control of the agricultural business conducted on the land is a helpful principle'. After a review of all the cases, she derived the following principles:

  - A farmhouse is a dwelling for the farmer from which the farm is managed.

  - The farmer is the person who farms on a day-to-day basis, not the manager.

  - The purpose, not the status, of occupation is what matters.

  - If the premises are extravagantly large, then even though occupied for the purpose of agriculture they may have become something more grand.

  - Each case turns on its own facts, judged by ordinary ideas of what is appropriate in size, content and layout, taken in context with the buildings and the land.

  Based on this, Dr Brice found that the actual farming was not done from the house, which was too grand for the much-reduced farming operations carried on.

- It was not of a 'character appropriate' anyway. After referring to the *Antrobus* principles and to *Higginson*, Dr Brice reviewed the elements as follows:

  - There were many fine farmhouses in Cornwall, some quite large and with very pleasant gardens.

  - Rosteague House was large and, despite its condition, had 'an interior of grace and charm'.

  - The farm buildings were not really used as such.

  - There was not enough land.

  - A layman would think of it as a large country house; it was in effect marketed as such.

  - On sale, 65% of the price realised was for the house, part for tenanted properties and only 12% for the agricultural land. It would not attract commercial farmers needing to make a living from the land.

- It was not occupied for the purposes of agriculture. Neither Mr McKenna nor Lady McKenna had been able to farm actively during the relevant two-year period.

- Most of the farm buildings were not occupied for the purposes of agriculture. One was a dung stead, latterly use in connection with livery, but livery of horses is not an agricultural purpose. On the facts, however, some were used for agriculture.

This decision makes a claim for a 'lifestyle' farmer in respect of a charming country house that much harder to pursue.

Example 2.2: find the farmhouse

Richard is, by any measure, a successful man. His home, somewhat inappropriately called 'The Lodge', is a Grade II listed building comprising: ten bedrooms, several of which, notwithstanding the listing, are now en suite; spacious reception rooms; more than adequate ancillary rooms; and coach houses that have been adapted tastefully to accommodate cars. The Lodge is set in 75 acres of land, mainly woodland with some parkland immediately adjoining the house.

Richard's farming enterprises are basically three in number. The 'home' farm is 400 acres. This lies only three miles from The Lodge. Richard controls the enterprise himself and has long since sold off the Victorian pile that was the farmhouse as being surplus to his requirements. Home Farm therefore consists of some farm buildings but otherwise bare land.

Low Farm is 30 miles away in the next county. It is 'carrot' land: there is irrigation but there are no buildings. Richard uses contractors to farm this land, saving himself the need to have either employees or farm buildings for the effective management of the land.

Top Farm is a 450-acre holding lying 100 miles from The Lodge. Before BSE, Richard ran a successful stock enterprise with help from a farm manager and other staff. They occupied the various cottages and the substantial Dales farmhouse. Government compensation following BSE was applied partly in paying off the various farm workers when Richard decided to terminate the risks of maintaining his own stock. The farm manager received the house in which he was living as part of a compensation package. Some vacant cottages are now in the hands of a holiday letting agency.

In this context, The Lodge may well be the centre of operations, but is it really the farmhouse in relation to any of the more distant acreage? Richard cannot farm the other land from it on a day-to-day basis. It is a substantial property, exceptionally well maintained and comfortable. It neither looks nor smells like a farmhouse. However, parts of the property are quite clearly devoted to the administration of a farming business. Richard is the farmer. He does not live anywhere else. None of the farms now has a building with any better claim to be regarded as the farmhouse.

The question that has not yet properly been examined by recorded cases is the size of property that is appropriate in relation to a large and successful farming operation. It is probably unfair to deny Richard APR on The Lodge simply because he has so ordered his farming arrangements that he does not, each morning, step into his gumboots by the kitchen door and walk across a 30-foot courtyard to tend his stock.

The courts have accepted evidence that, these days, farming can be viable only with the benefit of certain subsidies. It is perhaps not an exaggeration to argue that farming success lies as much in the successful management of paper as of crops and stock. We should not expect every farmer to conform to some 'romantic' image of a rotund middle-aged male of cheerful disposition with mud on his boots and a straw in his mouth who constantly lives close to the land. That is not what farming is now about.

The fine house with 'a bit of land'

2.21   *McKenna* shows us that substantial houses will struggle to qualify for APR, certainly if enjoyed with relatively small acreage, on none of which stand any farm buildings, where the land is occupied under a grazing licence. Even where the transferor can meet the 'character appropriate' tests in relation to the mansion house, he faces a further hurdle in relation to the land. So long as he has the right to obtain vacant possession within 24 months, he may qualify for APR at 100%. If he grants a farm business tenancy then, in relation to the farmhouse, he is no longer a farmer but a mere landlord. He is not occupying the mansion for the purpose of agriculture. He loses APR on the house. His alternative is to grant a right of herbage to a grazier. Unless the owner of the house personally undertakes work on the land it seems that, however much pasture he owns, he will get no relief on the house. HMRC and the First-tier Tribunal are, arguably, introducing a form of 'working farmer relief' by the back door.

In any case, the landowner must take care. He must ensure that, under any contract, the responsibility for any manuring, seeding and fertilising the land are retained by him and that he himself, or someone living in his house, does the actual work. Following *IRC v Forsyth-Grant* (1943) 25 TC 369, the owner will be considered to be occupying the land for the purposes of husbandry and will be accepted as such both for the purposes of income tax and IHT, qualifying for 100% on both farm and farmhouse. The income will be taxed as farming income under Schedule D, Case I. The taxpayer will preserve any entitlement he already has to roll-over relief for CGT and, insofar as other tests are satisfied, entrepreneurs' relief.

The Country Land and Business Association, commonly known as the CLA have prepared a recommended form of deed to grant a 'right of herbage'. The form has been approved by HMRC. Detailed reference should be made to Country Landowner, March 1997, and to an article by N S Murray at page 24. In brief: Not all owners of mansion houses are expert in the arts of fertilising or of hedging or ditching. It would be fatal to the APR claim to employ, as a contractor for these purposes, the person who is also party to the agreement as grazier. Taxpayers should note the observation of the Financial Secretary to the Treasury on the terms of such agreements, in the context of Schedule D, that 'owners wishing to enjoy the generous tax reliefs that trading status brings should take care to ensure that they comply with the statutory definition of farming'. Thus:

(a)   the owner must cultivate for, sow and establish the grass crop;

(b)   the owner must harrow and roll the grass as necessary;

(c)   the owner must fertilise the grass crop in the Spring and through the season as necessary;

(d)   the owner must cut or spray all weeds to prevent seeding;

(e)   the owner must do any mowing that may be required for whatever reason or purpose on the ground to be grazed;

(f)   the grazier must covenant 'not to mow or cut the grass'; and

(g)   the owner must do any hedging, fencing and ditching needed and any other work of a proprietorial nature.

From the point of view of income tax, *ICTA 1988, s 832* provides that farmland is that which is occupied wholly or mainly for the purposes of husbandry. The person farming is the person who is 'paramount occupier'. It is thus only if the owner shows that he is in paramount occupation that he will be regarded as the trading farmer. Only then will his grazing income be accepted as farming income under Schedule D rather than under Schedule A. For IHT purposes, the agreement should not exceed 24 months. The longer the agreement runs, the more likely the grazier will be regarded as 'paramount occupier'. It is understood that HMRC will look behind the wording of a legal deed to judge the actions of both the owner and the grazier where that is material for tax purposes.

Land and farmhouse not in identical ownership

2.22 The discussion of the decision in *Starke* shows that, ideally, house and land should be in the same ownership. There may be some 'wiggle room', as the next example illustrates.

Example 2.3: shared ownership of the family farm

Roger and his wife Stephanie own Bridge Farm, comprising 300 acres, at the centre of which stands the farmhouse and buildings. They have taken their two daughters into the farming partnership and wish to transfer into the names of the four partners the bulk of the acreage, retaining for themselves only the farmhouse (which they wish to continue to occupy). After the transfer, Roger and Stephanie remain the joint owners of the farmhouse and retain 20% between them of the value of the remaining land.

APR is probably not lost by reason of the transfer. It is understood that, if the ownership by Roger and Stephanie together (and of the survivor of them) were to fall below 10% of the farmland, APR on the farmhouse would be seriously at risk.

Farmers who fall ill

2.23 Even though a dwelling might in other respects qualify as a farmhouse, it will not qualify for APR unless occupied for the purposes of agriculture. Given the current HMRC view that the farmhouse must be the centre of farming operations, there must be a difficulty where, on the facts, the farmer is no longer well enough to look after the land. The various possibilities are considered in detail at **3.23** and **3.24**.

HORSES

2.24   It had been held in *Hemens v Whitsbury Farm and Stud Ltd* [1988] AC 601 that the breeding and rearing of horses was not, under the general law, 'agriculture'. For the purposes of IHT, that rule is specifically amended by *s 115(4)*. A stud farm can apparently qualify within *s 115(4)* even if there is no stallion permanently present at the farm. That section allows the breeding and rearing of horses on a stud farm, and the grazing of horses in connection with such breeding and rearing, to be taken to be agriculture. Any buildings used in connection with those activities can be treated as farm buildings. With any other horses, it is important to establish the agricultural connection, because livery is not agriculture (though it may be a business). The guidance to inspectors (see IHTM24068) is to carry out the following checks before allowing relief for a stud farm:

- age of taxpayer at the time of purchase of the farm and at the time of transfer, eg death;

- period of ownership of the stud;

- number of horses and breeding record;

- advertising and publicity;

- accounts of the business, showing purchases and sales; and

- where the horses pass into the food chain, evidence from the horse passport scheme.

Naturally, HMRC are looking to see a viable business. That is appropriate for BPR, where *s 103(4)* excludes hobby enterprises, but there is no statutory parallel in the APR code.

In *Wheatley's Executors v CIR* SpC 149, [1998] STC (SCD) 60 a meadow used for grazing horses failed to qualify for APR. Although the meadow had been owned by the deceased throughout seven years prior to his death, subject during all that time to a grazing agreement and as such constituted 'pasture' within *IHTA 1984, s 115(2)*, it was not 'occupied for the purposes of agriculture'. On the evidence, the horses which grazed the meadow were not connected with agriculture but were used by their owner for leisure pursuits. The horses were not 'livestock'. The grazing by horses would only fall within the provisions of *s 117* if the horses were connected with agriculture, which was not the case in this appeal.

The decision of the Special Commissioner has been criticised for concentrating on the nature of the animals that graze rather than on the main purpose of occupation of the land. Where land is used for grazing, the issue is whether the landowner is growing a crop of grass. If the landowner is treated as being in

33

occupation of the land, and if his profits are assessed under Case 1 of Schedule D, it really makes no difference what eats the grass.

Example 2.4: exotic grazing

Samantha's farm includes pasture and several stands of willow. She pollards the willow as feed for giraffe at a nearby zoo and supplies hay for its bison. The land is occupied for agriculture because Samantha is producing a crop of feed. It would be different if the wild animals visited Samantha's farm to graze.

There is an issue here for landowners keen that their acres should qualify for APR. In practical terms, the farm business tenancy may contain a covenant by the tenant to occupy only for agricultural purposes; but the taxation of the landlord's asset will be based on what actually happens on the ground, not what the landlord stipulated should happen. An action might lie against the tenant, but it is easy to imagine that the extent of the claim might be substantial and that the tenant might not have the resources to meet it.

SHORT ROTATION COPPICING

2.25   By *FA 1995, s 154(3)*, 'short rotation coppice' means a perennial crop of tree species planted at high density, the stems of which are harvested above ground level at intervals of less than ten years. *Section 154(2)* allows land on which short rotation coppice is cultivated to be regarded as agricultural land, and buildings which are used in connection with the cultivation of short rotation coppice to be regarded as farm buildings. Examples of this activity are trees harvested regularly where the branches are used as a renewable fuel, for certain types of power station.

Section 154(2) is expressed to be 'for the purposes of the *Inheritance Tax Act 1984*'. Its application is therefore more general than that of the relief for horses set out above, which is expressed to be 'for the purposes of this chapter', and of the 'set aside' relief of *s 124C* which, again, is expressed to be 'for the purpose of this chapter', ie the APR Code.

MILK QUOTA

2.26   Milk quota is now of little practical importance in the context of IHT. It is the specific quantity of dairy product which a farmer may produce without creating liability to pay a levy for over-production. It cannot arise on any date earlier than 2 April 1984. Quota is not an interest in land; it is a licence that may be sold with freehold land, and with certain tenancies, and which may be leased. Its ownership can change involuntarily on the termination of a tenancy and on certain other grants, assignments and transfers of interests in land. Its value is commonly treated as if part of the land (see below).

In *Faulks v Faulks* [1992] 1 EGLR 9, it was held that milk quota should not be included among the assets of a partnership. It was available to a deceased's partner in his capacity as a tenant of land, not as a partner *per se*. Quota was not, as such, an asset; it was the elimination of a liability. *Faulks* was a case on partnership law rather than on revenue law. For IHT, it thus becomes important to identify the precise interest of the transferor. The value of milk quota can be regarded as included in the value of land transferred. That helps owners of tenanted land who accordingly qualify for APR on the value of the milk quota, assuming the land itself qualifies for APR.

Although milk quota can be regarded as included in the value of land transferred by an owner-occupier, this clearly cannot apply where a tenant's share of milk quota is disposed of by the landlord on termination of a tenancy. In these circumstances, the quota will be regarded as a separate asset and should fall to be treated as included in the value of the farming business. The value will be a matter for BPR rather than APR.

LAND WITHIN CONSERVATION AND SIMILAR SCHEMES

2.27   Farmland and related buildings which have been dedicated to wildlife habitats on or after 26 November 1996 qualify for 100% APR where the normal ownership tests have been satisfied. Land used in such a scheme must be managed in accordance with the scheme. The effect of *s 124C* is, notwithstanding precisely the fact that land is taken out of agricultural use, to satisfy the occupation test. Where land is farmed, for example, in an organic way, the occupation test is satisfied without the need for *s 124C*. The extension of the relief under *s 124C* to buildings used in connection with management of the land as a habitat scheme is helpful, in that those buildings are to be regarded as farm buildings. Given the test of use for the purposes of agriculture as examined in *Harrold (Executors of Harrold Deceased) v CIR* [1996] STC (SCD) 195, which is considered in **Chapter 3**, it may be that the test under *s 124C* is easier to satisfy than the test that was appropriate in *Harrold*.

The relevant habitat schemes are:

● *Habitat (Water Fringe) Regulations 1994, SI 1994/1291, reg 3(i)* as amended by *SIs 1996/1480* and *1996/3106*.

● *Habitat (Former Set-Aside Land) Regulations 1994, SI 1994/1292* as amended by *SIs 1996/1478* and *1996/3107*.

● *Habitat (Salt-Marsh) Regulations 1994, SI 1994/1293* as amended by *SIs 1995/2871, 1995/2891, 1996/1479* and *1996/3108*.

35

- *Habitats (Scotland) Regulations 1994, SI 1994/2710, reg 3(ii)(a)* as amended by *SI 1996/3135.*

- *Habitat Improvement Regulations (Northern Ireland) 1995, SR(NI) 1995/134, reg 3(1)(a).*

From 1988 to 2008, farmers could enjoy set-aside payments in respect of land that was lying fallow, either on a permanent or rotational basis; or woodland; or occupied for other approved use, such as camping, game reserve, riding school or the like. IHTM24064 allows fallow to be treated as occupied for agriculture, but is less positive about the other uses, which will each turn on their own merits. This issue has been complicated by the 'Mid-term Review' described more fully at **3.19** which has introduced the single farm payment (SFP) and which, apart from requirements as to keeping the land in good agricultural and environmental condition, separates the subsidy from actual production. The SFP takes the place of many earlier entitlements. A farmer who has not kept his machinery up to date may decide simply to keep the SFP and to grant a licence at modest cost to a contractor. As discussed, that approach is fatal to a claim for APR on the (former) farmhouse. The land will still be occupied for the purpose of agriculture, but perhaps not by the owner; so, as will be seen in the next chapter, the ownership period required for relief is longer. The Manual (at IHTM24064) recognises that this is a fluid situation.

FARMING COMPANIES

2.28 *Section 122* allows APR on the value of shares in, or securities of, a company if and only if:

- the agricultural property forms part of the assets of the company, and part of the value of the shares or securities can be attributed to the agricultural value of that agricultural property; and

- the shares or securities gave the transferor control of the company immediately before the transfer.

The definition of 'control' for *s 122* provides (see *s 122(2)*) that there is no control if:

- the shares or securities would not have been sufficient, without other property, to give the transferor control of the company immediately before the transfer; and

- the value of the shares or securities is taken to be less than the value previously determined under the related property provisions of *s 176*, ie where there is a sale within three years after the death of the transferor.

It is actually rare for control to be achieved by owning securities other than shares. To calculate the value on which APR is allowable, it is necessary to deduct any debts which are secured on property from the value of that property and to spread unsecured debts, or debts which are secured only by a floating charge, across all the assets of the company, whether agricultural or not. That calculation reveals the part of the value of the shares or securities that is attributable to the farm and qualifies for APR. Where the rest of the company is engaged in trading rather than investment, the exercise is of little practical value, since BPR will usually be available on that part of the value which does not qualify for APR.

The operation of *s 176* is considered in **Chapter 4** and, in the context of BPR, at **5.31**.

Section 116 is modified by *ss 122(3)* and *123*. The result is that it becomes necessary to examine whether the interest of the company in the land carries the right to vacant possession (or to obtain it within 12 or 24 months). If the company could obtain that possession, 100% relief is available on the shares of the company (or the agricultural proportion of them). Likewise, that relief is available if the company can satisfy the 'working farmer' test.

To satisfy *s 123* (minimum period of occupation or ownership) the company must show:

- that it has occupied the farm for the purpose of agriculture throughout the last two years before the date of transfer, or

- that it has owned the farm throughout the last seven years before the date of transfer, and that either the company or someone else has occupied the farm for that purpose throughout that period.

Even that is not enough to satisfy the substituted test as to ownership and occupation. By *s 123(1)(b)*, the transferor must have owned the shares or securities throughout the same period. As will be noted in **Chapters 3** and **4**, a company is treated as having occupied a farm which it owns at any time when that farm was occupied by a person who subsequently controls the company: see the example of Feargus at **4.11**, Example 3. There are provisions as to replacement of property in relation to farming companies in *s 123(3)*, which are considered in the examination of replacement property in **Chapter 4**.

TERRITORIALITY

2.29   With effect from 22 April 2009 and by virtue of *FA 2009, s 122*, APR is available on the transfer of agricultural property in:

- the UK, the Channel Islands and the Isle of Man; or

- any EEA State (as defined by the *Interpretation Act 1978*).

There is thus a distinction between APR and BPR since, as will be seen in **Chapter 5**, a business may qualify for BPR if it is situated anywhere in the world. This is specifically provided by *s 115(5)*. Pub quiz hosts will wish to know that there are currently 30 EEA territories, namely Austria, Belgium, Bulgaria, Cyprus, Czech Republic, Denmark, Estonia, Finland, France, Germany, Greece, Hungary, Iceland, Ireland, Italy, Liechtenstein, Latvia, Lithuania, Luxembourg, Malta, Netherlands, Norway, Poland, Portugal, Romania, Slovakia, Slovenia, Spain and Sweden, as well as the United Kingdom. *Finance Act 2009, s 122* introduced provisions requiring equivalence, in local law, to certain UK rules: see *s 116(8)*. If tax was paid under the old rules which is no longer payable, a claim for repayment had to be lodged by the later of the normal repayment deadline and 21 April 2010.

The normal, statutory deadline for repayment claims was six years from the payment of the tax, or of the last instalment; but, in line with many other time limits, that is being reduced, with effect from 1 April 2011, to four years under *FA 2009, Sch 51, para 13*, which amends *s 241(1)*. See the 'appointed day' provisions of *SI 2010/867, para 2*.

WHAT DOES NOT QUALIFY FOR APR?

2.30   The restrictions on APR will be apparent from the discussion in this chapter of its limitations, and the identification of further problems in **Chapters 3** and **4**.

It is not necessary, which is perhaps just as well for many farmers at present, for the carrying on of agriculture to be profitable. *Section 115* does not contain a restriction parallel to that for BPR in *s 103(3)*. The restriction for income tax purposes on relief in respect of farming and market gardening contained in *ICTA 1988, s 397* does not rob a farming enterprise of APR.

Chiefly, APR will be lost in what might otherwise have seemed to be 'likely situations' where, when viewed as a whole, it cannot be said that there is an agricultural enterprise being carried on. This was the case in *Dixon v CIR* and in *Wheatley's Executors v CIR*, considered earlier in this chapter. We in England 'rather like' farming as an activity: it is considered to be 'a nice thing to do' (via a farm manager, of course). If the profits of the farming enterprise are low and a claim is made to APR, it may be necessary to examine just why the transferor is (or was) in business. It may very well appear, by rigorous examination, that the enterprise taken as a whole is really an investment. This point is considered again in the context of BPR.

The distinction between what does and what does not qualify for APR is examined at various points in this and the next two chapters. In brief, particular attention should be given to the following areas:

- woodland not occupied with agricultural land;

- buildings used for rearing birds or fish for sport;

- farm cottages neither used nor occupied by farm workers nor former farm workers nor their dependants;

- mansion houses occupied with small let acreages;

- farmhouses, the ownership of which is separated from that of the land, where the land is not held by a company controlled by the owner of the house;

- paddocks for ponies used for riding;

- 'unusual' property, for example oyster beds (see *Gunter v Newtown Oyster Fishery* (1977) 244 EG 140); and

- farms which, for whatever reason other than set-aside, are not occupied for agriculture.

Chapter 3

Agricultural property: agricultural value, the rates of relief, occupation and other aspects

QUICK GUIDE

Relief is mainly at 100% on the true farming value of the asset. The agricultural property must be occupied for farming. Various rules extend occupation, particularly in the context of trusts: see **3.5**. A very important issue is whether land is let on a 'new' tenancy, ie one beginning on or after 1 September 1995, because land let under older tenancies will usually attract relief at 50% only.

There is a large body of law concerning the old 'working farmer' relief. Fewer and fewer cases fall precisely within this relief but, where it is relevant, see **3.6**. The material is retained because there is much about it that suits the current political climate. We have seen in CGT the re-use, for entrepreneurs' relief, of concepts that were relevant to retirement relief: perhaps we might one day go back to the idea that agricultural relief is 'really' for those few people who make their sole living from working the land.

AGRICULTURAL VALUE

3.1   APR is limited by *IHTA 1984, s 115(3)* in the UK to 'the value which would be the value of the property if the property were subject to a perpetual covenant prohibiting its use otherwise than as agricultural property', and elsewhere within the EEA to what it would be if subject to an equivalent provision. Insofar as the market value of agricultural property exceeds the agricultural value, there may well be scope for a claim to BPR.

Sporting rights may have considerable influence on the value of agricultural land. Shooting rights were considered in *Earl of Normanton v Giles* [1980] 1 All ER 106. That was a case concerning the *Rent (Agriculture) Act 1976* in connection with a gamekeeper's tenancy. The House of Lords considered that pheasants reared to be shot for sport were not kept for the production of food. Eating the shot pheasants was merely an incidental result of the shooting. The case has since been relied on, in the context of APR, to show that the use of land for sport is not agriculture. It may therefore be necessary to examine the conduct of the shoot to see whether it has been managed as a business. That was the issue in *Customs and Excise Comrs v Lord Fisher* [1981] STC 238, a case on whether Lord Fisher had conducted a sporting shoot with such efficiency from a financial point of view that it was a business in respect of which VAT should be charged.

Probably, therefore, the landowner must choose: he will not secure APR on the value of sporting rights, although he may succeed in claiming BPR if the exploitation of those rights amounts to a business, as to which any evidence that the business has been treated for VAT will be very helpful.

Crops growing on the land at the date of transfer are legally part of that land until severed. IHTM23180 shows that the Valuation Office should include pasture, cultivations and unexhausted manure but exclude the value of growing crops from the valuation report. If the taxpayer has included the value of growing crops without a separate figure, enquiries will be made as to the separate value. Trees and underwood are included within 'agricultural value'. The definition of that value which applied for working farmer relief was similar to that now applied in *s 115(3)*. For working farmer relief, the value would include trees, underwood and growing crops, even though they might be subject to a contract for sale. The important point for working farmer relief was not the sale but whether the crops had been severed from the land.

Example 3.1: loss of farming status

The Arlington Estate originally comprised a five-bedroomed house, with barns, stockyard and implements sheds adjoining, three cottages and 450 acres; but tax and school fees have taken their toll and the best 100 acres have been sold off. Not much farming is now being done. The disposition of the remainder is now:

- house and garden: 0.75 acre;
- farm buildings still used as such: 1 acre;
- redundant farm buildings: 1.25 acres;
- meadows and paddocks: 5 acres;
- pasture subject to grazing licence and (trout) stream: 25 acres;
- arable land subject to a contract farming agreement: 275 acres;
- woodland parcels adjoining pasture: 5 acres;

- woodland subject to a sporting lease that will soon expire: 35 acres;
- cottages let to commuters: 1 acre; and
- roadways: 1 acre.

Much of the value lies in the situation of the land, with good rail links to London, the house and its amenity land, fishing and shooting. Agricultural value will be severely restricted. If the house qualifies for APR at all, we can expect agricultural value to be no more than 70% of open market value. APR may be available on the five acres of woodland, as explained in **Chapter 2**, but not the 35 acres of woodland. The cottages are no longer occupied for the purpose of agriculture, so APR is not in point. The farm buildings no longer used as such do not qualify for APR.

The valuation of farmhouses for the purpose of APR raises special considerations (see **4.22** below).

THE RATES OF RELIEF

100% APR

3.2 APR is allowed at 100% under *s 116(2)* if basic conditions referred to below are satisfied as to ownership and occupation. Where a beneficiary of a trust has an interest in possession under *s 49(1)*, he is regarded as the beneficial owner of the settled property; the applicability of APR in trust situations is examined at **3.5** below.

The ownership or occupation test

3.3 By *s 117*, no relief is available unless:

- the property was occupied by the transferor for the purposes of agriculture for two years ending with the date of transfer; or
- the property was owned by the transferor throughout the period of seven years ending with the date of the transfer and was, throughout that period, occupied for the purposes of agriculture, whether by the transferor or by some other person.

The meaning of 'occupation' for this purpose is considered at **3.14** below and, in the case of partnerships, at **4.3**. The occupation of land under mere licence is discussed at **4.27**. Ownership may be deemed under the succession provisions of *s 120* (see **4.11**).

The test determinative of the rate of relief

3.4   100% relief is now, and has (with an exception mentioned later in this section) in respect of deaths (and other chargeable events) occurring since 10 March 1992 been, available where (author's numbering):

(*a*)   (i)   the transferor had, immediately before the transfer, the right to vacant possession of the property; or

(ii)   the right to obtain it within the next 12 months; or

(iii)   the right to obtain it within the next 24 months; or

(iv)   the property is valued at an amount broadly equivalent to vacant possession value, notwithstanding the terms of the tenancy;

(*b*)   the transferor has been entitled to his interest in the property since before 10 March 1981 and the 'working farmer' conditions are satisfied (see below); or

(*c*)   the property, not falling within (*a*) or (*b*) above, is let on a tenancy beginning on or after 1 September 1995.

Of the conditions just set out, those in (*a*)(iii) and (iv) are not statutory. They are contained in ESC F17 which extended the condition in *s 116(2)(a)* in two circumstances: where the transferor's interest carried a right to vacant possession within 24 months of the date of the transfer, or where the interest of the transferor in the property is valued at an amount broadly equivalent to the vacant possession value of the property, notwithstanding the terms of the tenancy.

Situation (*a*)(iii) will commonly arise in *Gladstone v Bowers* situations, ie where there is a tenancy which lasts for more than one year but less than two years, as was the case in *Gladstone v Bowers* [1960] 3 All ER 353. Alternatively, the (*a*)(*iii*) situation may arise where the landlord, whilst having the right to serve notice on the tenant to vacate the property within 12 months, cannot actually obtain vacant possession for a further 12 months after the termination of the agreement, owing to the provisions of the *Agricultural Holdings Act 1986*.

The (*a*)(iv) situation will apply where, for example, land is let to a company which is controlled by the transferor. In HMRC's Shares and Assets Valuation Manual, this situation is called a 'packaged' valuation (see SVM108210).

The increased rates of relief, as has been noted, are generally applicable from 10 March 1992 onwards. If a lifetime transfer was chargeable when made, and was made before 10 March 1992, the higher rate of relief applies only for the purpose of calculating the 'top up' tax charged by reference to the death of the transferor. There is no change to the value for cumulation purposes. That is calculated at the time of the transfer by reference to the rate of relief which applied at that time. This principle of 'locking into' the rate of relief which is applicable at a particular time is examined again in **Chapter 16** where, for planning purposes, it might operate to the advantage of the taxpayer.

FARMING TRUSTS

3.5   The 'old-style' (pre-*FA 2006*) tenant for life of settled property is treated, as already noted, as being its owner. The termination of his interest, in whole or in part, is thus a transfer by him of the settled property, which forms part of his deemed transfer immediately before death. Wherever the claim to APR is in respect of shares in, say, the family farming company, we must refer to *IHTA 1984, s 269(3)* to establish whether the tenant for life had control of the company. By virtue of that section, voting powers on trust shares or securities are treated as being given to the tenant for life, except where the trust is discretionary.

The tests as to ownership or occupation, mentioned at **3.3**, therefore apply to the situation of the 'old-style' tenant for life. 100% relief is available where, in his capacity as the beneficiary, the tenant for life can obtain vacant possession or where the 'working farmer' relief provisions described in the next section of this book can be applied to his situation as a beneficiary. Since the introduction of *FA 2006*, we have situations where a person may, for the purposes of trust law, income tax or CGT, have a life interest and yet not have an interest in possession for IHT, perhaps because his interest is not an IPDI. For clarity in this section, the beneficiary of a relevant property trust who does not enjoy an interest in possession is called a 'life beneficiary'. This situation must be approached with care: if the trust under consideration is a relevant property trust, it will be the trustees, and not the life beneficiary, who own and are deemed to own the underlying assets.

For the purpose of satisfying the test as to control of shares in the family farming company, the holder of an interest in possession may take account not only of the shares in which he has an interest in possession but also his personal shares and any related property. The tests as to ownership and occupation of company land are then applied.

Must the holder of an interest in possession himself be the farmer?

3.6   It was long thought that the occupation test was satisfied only where such a person himself farmed for his own benefit, such that what he received was his 'earned' income rather than trust income. The position is now less clear. A life tenant who farms personally is obviously in occupation of the land.

He may also be the occupier where he is not personally involved and where the trustees employ a farm manager and merely pay the tenant for life any profit made. Certainly that would be consistent with the situation of the outright owner of land: he is still in occupation even where he employs a manager.

Many permutations will be encountered in practice. Taking first the clear-cut cases where the land has been held by the trust subject to the interest in possession of the tenant for life for more than seven years, APR will be available either:

- because the tenant for life himself has farmed; or

- because the trustees have owned the farm for the requisite period and it has been occupied for the purposes of farming during the whole of that time.

Equally, where the ownership period exceeds seven years, it ought not to matter who is employed to do the farming: that could equally be the tenant for life himself.

Where the period of ownership is less than seven years and the trustees employ the tenant for life to do the farming, he is almost certainly treated as being in occupation and qualifies under the two-year rule. This will equally be so where the tenant for life is merely allowed to farm the land on an informal basis, he being entitled to the profits, because he is in occupation.

Where the trustees have owned the land for less than seven years and a manager is employed to do the farming, the life tenant does not automatically qualify for 100% relief because he has not occupied it for long enough. If the manager is employed by the trustees, and the trustees do the farming, it is they who occupy the land, which should be valued on the basis of vacant possession and relief will be allowed at 100%.

Another possible scenario is the grant by the trustees of a lease to the life tenant who then either himself farms the land or employs a manager. The life tenant occupies the property and therefore qualifies for 100% relief after two years. This is because, on the one hand, he is deemed to be the owner of the freehold of the land and, on the other, he is personally entitled to the lease. The interests together comprise a value equal to that of vacant possession.

Trustees of discretionary trusts must apply slightly different rules. If they themselves farm the land or appoint a manager, they will qualify after two years for 100% relief, because they have the right to vacant possession. If they let the land, they suffer two disadvantages: first, the relief falls to 50% only; and, second, the relief is available only after the trustees have owned the land for seven years. Even if they have owned the land since before the 'working farmer' rules first applied, they cannot claim the 'double discount', because they do not have vacant possession of the land and could never have qualified for working farmer relief.

WORKING FARMER RELIEF ('DOUBLE DISCOUNT CASES')

3.7   Most of the time, this subject is of academic interest only, and busy readers should move straight to **3.15**. Before 10 March 1981, 'working farmers' had the benefit, where they let their land before 10 March 1981, of gaining two advantages: partly that the value on which it could be applied was less, because the land was let; and partly that relief was available on agricultural property. Although the relief is described as 'transitional', it is still highly relevant and the practitioner must, unfortunately, have a working knowledge of the rules.

The conditions for working farmer relief are that:

(*a*)   the transferor has owned his interest in the land since before 10 March 1981; and

(*b*)   the transferor would on that date have been entitled to the old relief; and

(*c*)   at no time between that date and the transfer has there been a right to vacant possession; and

(*d*)   the transferor did not fail to obtain a right to vacant possession by any act or deliberate omission.

The limits to the relief are, generally, the greater of £250,000 and 1,000 acres. 1,000 acres equals 4,046,856.4224 square metres of land: see the *Units of Measurement Regulations 1995 (SI 1995/1804)*.

Stud farms do not come within working farmer relief because *s 115(4)*, which extended APR to stud farms, was not in force prior to 10 March 1981. The tests for the relief are set out in *FA 1975, Sch 8*.

The further detailed conditions for the relief are set out in *FA 1975, Sch 8, para 3*. They are that:

(*a*)   the transferor was wholly or mainly engaged in the United Kingdom in one of the capacities set out below in not less than five of the seven years ending with 5 April immediately before the transfer, and

(*b*)   (i)   the agricultural property was, at the time of the transfer, occupied by the transferor for the purposes of agriculture; and

      (ii)   was so occupied by him throughout the two years immediately preceding the transfer; or

(iii)   replaced other agricultural property and was so occupied by him for a period which, when added to any period during which he so occupied the replacement property, made up at least two years in the five years immediately before the transfer.

The favoured capacities required for the relief are:

- farming as a trade, alone or in partnership;

- being employed in farming as a trade by someone else;

- being a director of a company carrying on farming in the UK (which includes, for this purpose, the Isle of Man and the Channel Islands) as its main activity; or

- in full-time education.

'Wholly or mainly engaged'

3.8   *FA 1975, Sch 8, para 3(3)* helpfully defines the main (but not exclusive) test of 'wholly or mainly engaged'. The test is satisfied where at least three-quarters of the relevant income of the transferor was derived directly from his engagement in agriculture in the United Kingdom. The extension to APR in *FA 2009, s 122* does not affect this relief. The 'relevant income' is the aggregate of income in any five of the last seven years of assessment immediately preceding the transfer, including unearned income but excluding income from a pension, superannuation, other allowance, deferred pay or compensation for loss of office. For this purpose, the rules as to aggregation of a wife's income which were in force in 1981 are to be disregarded.

Where a transferor failed the '75% test', he might still show by other means, such as time spent and the other sources of income, that he was a working farmer. In certain situations (see below), a farming widow or widower enjoyed the benefit of 'transferred years' to help satisfy the seven-year test.

The occupation test for working farmers

3.9   There is further help in satisfying the occupation test mentioned above. Where the agricultural property had been occupied by the transferor for the purposes of agriculture by a member of the transferor's family throughout the 'gap period', linking the transferor's own occupation to the date of the transfer, the conditions in *FA 1975, Sch 8, para 3(1)* are treated as satisfied if they would have been satisfied had the transfer occurred at that time.

Difficulties could arise where the transferor occupied agricultural property at the time of transfer but had not occupied that property throughout the two-year period immediately before the transfer. If that was replacement property, and the earlier agricultural property had had a lower value than the replacement property, taking the value at the time that the replacement property was first occupied, the relief was reduced to the fraction of the agricultural value of the replacement property represented by the agricultural value of the earlier held land (see *FA 1975, Sch 8, para 3(5)*).

Working farmer relief also contained provision, in *para 3(6)*, for the situation where the transferor inherited agricultural property, providing that the occupation by the transferor of the agricultural property was deemed to have begun on the death of the person from whom he inherited it. Where:

● that person was actually the spouse of the transferor; and

● at the time of the death of the transferor's spouse

● the working farmer conditions were satisfied,

those conditions are treated as being satisfied in respect of the inheritor who is now the transferor.

By an unfortunate quirk of the legislation, which few practitioners will now need to remember, the date on which a person was deemed to have become entitled to a farm for the purposes of working farmer relief was not the same as it is now. This is because the legislation, which now forms *IHTA 1984, s 91* and which is discussed at **6.11** in relation to extending the period of ownership, did not apply to cases falling within *FA 1975, Sch 8*.

Instead, the old rule applied, drawn from *Sudley v A-G* [1897] AC 11, that a residuary legatee became 'entitled' to a specific asset which formed part of residue only when the estate had been administered. Situations may be imagined where, through delay in administration followed by the early death of the residuary beneficiary, relief under the working farmer relief rules might have been lost through no fault of the relevant transferor.

Other difficulties and restrictions relating to working farmer relief

3.10   A farmer could not increase the amount of working farmer relief by 'trading up' shortly before the event, such as death, constituting the transfer. A restriction applied. The part of the value of the new farm which qualified for relief was the proportion which the value of the previous farm bore to the value of the new farm when acquired.

The relief was, by contrast, quite generous in the situation where the working farmer retired. Relief was not denied merely because he no longer qualified as the occupier of the farm. As long as he had previously occupied the farm for the purposes of agriculture, relief was still available if the farm was now occupied by a member of his family from the time that he last occupied it up to the time of transfer. This was so, even if members of the transferor's family in succession occupied the farm. Strikingly, if the farmer found that retirement did not suit him and again took occupation, the relief which he had previously enjoyed was lost until he had completed two years of reoccupation.

A further relief was available where, for example, the recipient of agricultural property himself died within two years. Relief was available on the recipient's death, provided the conditions as to 'working farmer' and 'occupation' were satisfied. By a deeming provision, those conditions were satisfied where:

- there had been a transfer of value not more than two years before the later transfer, and one of those transfers was on death;
- the value transferred related to the same farm;
- the working farmer and occupation conditions were satisfied on the first transfer;
- the farm was being farmed at the time of the later transfer, either by the recipient of the land or by the personal representatives of the first transferor; and
- the farm became the property of the recipient (or of his spouse) as a result of the earlier transfer.

Slightly different rules from those just set out applied before 29 July 1976. From and after that date, a restriction applied, relating, in particular, to the situation where the recipient of the land had in part purchased it from the earlier transferor. *FA 1975, Sch 8, para 1(2A)* worked in much the same way as is now provided by *IHTA 1984, s 121(3)* in relation to successive transfers so as to restrict the relief.

Transfers made by the same person on the same day were treated as one transfer for working farmer relief. Where those transfers, taken together, exceeded the limits, the excess was spread across the farms according to agricultural values or areas. That difficulty could, of course, be avoided by making the transfers on different days, with the result that the first transfer would have priority over the second or later transfers: see *FA 1975, Sch 8, para 5(3)*.

Working farmer relief and companies

3.11   Occupation by a company which is controlled by the transferor is treated as occupation by the transferor himself. Occupation of property by a Scottish partnership is treated as occupation by the partners.

Limitation of working farmer relief by value or by acreage

3.12   The conditions for relief under *FA 1975, Sch 8, para 4* were:

- the farm must form part of the assets of the company, and part of the value of the shares or debentures of the company must be attributable to the agricultural value of the farm;

- the transferor must have control of the company through its shares or debentures immediately before the transfer;

- the main activity of the company must be farming and must have been farming for the last two years;

- the farm must be in the United Kingdom, Channel Islands or Isle of Man; and

- the farm concerned must be occupied at the time of the transfer for farming and must have been so occupied throughout the last two years before the transfer or must have replaced another farm giving the company, over the five years before the transfer, two periods of occupation together making up at least two years.

The limit described below relating to value or acreage applied to a company so as to reduce the relief proportionately in respect of the excess over the 1,000-acre limit.

Where the shares or debentures of the farming company were related property, relief might be lost where, as a result of a sale within three years after a death, the value was reduced. If, notwithstanding the relevant sale, the holding of shares or debentures gave the deceased control of the company without relying on the related property provisions, relief was preserved. Otherwise, it was lost.

As with agricultural property generally, working farmer relief was affected by the existence of a binding contract for sale. A form of relief applied where the death of the vendor occurred between contract and completion. Similarly, if the purchaser died between contract and completion, relief might be available (if other conditions were satisfied) on the amount which the purchaser, at the date of his death, had paid, ie normally the deposit. The rules were different in Scotland: where death occurred between missives of sale and the delivery of a disposition, the rule used to be that relief was available to the buyer rather than the seller; that changed for the short period from 1978 to the expiry of applicability of the rules in March 1991, during which time the seller might secure working farmer relief even if he had received the purchase money.

Highly technical rules applied for a time, ie until the coming into force of *FA 1976*, to compute the part of the value eligible for relief for working farmers.

These complicated rules applied under *FA 1975, Sch 8, para 9(1)* but ought not now to trouble practitioners dealing with estates in administration.

The limitation to £250,000 or 1,000 acres for working farmer relief is not absolute. By *FA 1975, Sch 8, para 5(2)* (inserted by *FA 1976, s 74(6)*), the area of any rough grazing land was to be counted as one-sixth of its actual area, at least in relation to chargeable transfers made after 6 April 1976.

Where the restriction bites, the percentage of APR available is:

- 100% in respect of the unrestricted portion; and

- 50% in respect of the remainder (see *s 116(4)*).

Section 116(5) provides that *FA 1975, Sch 8, para 5* must be interpreted as if the references to relief given in *FA 1975, Sch 8* in respect of earlier chargeable transfers included references to relief given by virtue of *IHTA 1984, s 116(2) (b)* or *(4)* or by *FA 1981, Sch 14* as far as the earlier chargeable transfers were concerned. This means that the farmer entitled to double discount, who would have benefited from the old relief, will get 100% on the unrestricted portion of the transfer and 50% on the rest. He may not claim BPR instead of the 50% APR.

Working farmer relief: successions

3.13   *IHTA 1984, s 120(2)* extends working farmer relief. Where a person became entitled to an interest on the death of a spouse on or after 10 March 1981:

- the survivor is deemed, for the purposes of *s 116(2)(b)*, to have been beneficially entitled to the agricultural property for any period in respect of which the spouse had been entitled to it;

- if (and only if) the condition in *s 116(3)(a)* (that the earlier holder would have qualified for the relief) is satisfied, then that condition is satisfied in relation to the surviving spouse; and

- the condition in *s 116(3)(b)* (no recovery of vacant possession) is treated as satisfied only if there was no opportunity of recovering vacant possession available either to the original holder or to the spouse.

What this means in practice is that, if the original holder, the deceased spouse, could have claimed working farmer relief, then so can the survivor, provided that neither of them could have recovered vacant possession of the land after 9 March 1981. This relief is available only where one of the spouses has died.

51

It does not apply to lifetime gifts between spouses: there is, thus, scope for negligence through advising accidentally on a transfer between spouses which causes the relief to be lost.

Example 3.2: an unwise gift

Judith's father had been a full-time working farmer. On his death in 1977, Judith inherited from him the Grange Farm extending to 600 acres of hill land in Wales. Prior to her marriage to Henry, Judith farmed the land herself. From Michaelmas 1979 onwards, the land was let and was thereafter occupied for the purposes of agriculture.

In June 1983, Judith and Henry consulted Geoff (see Preface to this book), Judith then being dangerously ill. In the course of his advice, Geoff considered that it would be helpful, for a number of reasons, to equalise the wealth of Judith and Henry. He recommended a lifetime transfer to Henry of the tenanted farm. Judith had other assets not qualifying for relief which, it was proposed, should form part of a gift of her nil rate band. Six months later, Judith died, leaving an estate that was fully exempt, passing, except for the nil rate band, to Henry. The fact that Geoff had advised wrongly was not obvious at the time.

By virtue of Geoff's negligent advice, the extension provisions of *s 120(2)* cannot apply to Henry. He was concerned that, on his own death, APR will be available only at 50%. He consulted Carol (see Preface) who, with some care, negotiated with the tenant a variation of the lease, the effect of which is to constitute a new lease created after 1 September 1995. Henry has owned the land in his own right for 12 years, during all of which it has been occupied for the purpose of agriculture. By virtue of Carol's work, he is entitled to APR at 100%.

Restrictions on working farmer relief

3.14   The relief was applied by way of reducing the value of the 'part eligible for relief'. That part might be less than the agricultural value if not all of the property had been transferred. Such a situation could arise where the agricultural property was sold at an undervalue or where the transfer was partly exempt. The result was a complicated multi-stage calculation. First, the value transferred had to be established without working farmer relief and as if no tax were chargeable on it. That was the value after exemptions and before grossing up: the 'unreduced value' in *FA 1975, Sch 8, para 1(3)*. Relief was available on such part of the value so found as was attributable to the agricultural value. It was that figure that qualified for 50%.

The way the sums worked, by deducting exemptions before applying 50% relief to the agricultural value, was less favourable than the rules under APR and BPR as we now have it, where the reliefs apply before deducting exemptions. This has made working farmer relief less valuable than the new reliefs in certain circumstances. As time passes, these factors become increasingly academic.

LAND LET ON NEW TENANCIES

3.15   The straightforward case of a transfer of land subject to a new farm business tenancy will give little difficulty. More interesting is the situation where there is an existing tenancy under the *Agricultural Holdings Act 1986* which gives no right to vacant possession within either 12 months or 24 months. To secure 100% APR, the tenancy should come to an end. There must be a clear surrender of the old tenancy and a grant of the new. Interestingly, a tenancy which begins on or after 1 September 1995, only because the statutory succession rules apply, will not for that reason be excluded from full relief. For the purposes of IHT, the commencement of the new tenancy is taken to be the date of death of the tenant who is succeeded: see *s 116(5A)*. *Section 116(2)(c)* applies to all agricultural tenancies throughout the United Kingdom which began after 31 August 1995. It is thus not limited to tenancies under the *Agricultural Tenancies Act 1995*.

Section 116(5B) covers the situation where the tenant, or the last surviving tenant, of the property dies on or after 1 September 1995 and, as a result:

● a person obtains the tenancy of that property under statutory rules; or

● a person is granted a tenancy in circumstances where he is already entitled statutorily to obtain that tenancy, except that the tenancy to which he is entitled under statute takes effect at a later date; or

● a person is granted the tenancy who is, or who has become, the only (or only remaining) applicant or the only (or only remaining) person who is eligible to apply for such a tenancy under a particular enactment.

In any case covered by these circumstances, the tenancy is treated as beginning on the death of the tenant, except *s 116(5C)* where the property is situated in Scotland.

The effect of this is that *s 116(5B)* relates to a situation where the property is outside Scotland and, although the point is not expressed within the legislation, *s 116(5A)* deals with a similar situation where the property may be situated in Scotland. *Section 116(5A)* provides that:

● on the death on or after 1 September 1995 of the tenant (or last surviving tenant) of any property;

- where that tenancy becomes vested in a person as a result of beneficial entitlement under the will of the deceased tenant or under other testamentary disposition; and

- the tenancy becomes binding on the landlord and the inheritor respectively as landlord and tenant;

s 116(2)(c) is treated as having effect as if that inherited tenancy had begun on the date of the death of the tenant.

A special deeming provision, *s 116(5D)*, applies where the transferor dies on or after 1 September 1995 and, before the death:

- a tenant has given notice of an intention to retire in favour of a new tenant; and

- that retirement in favour of a new tenant takes place after the death but not more than 30 months after the giving of the notice.

In these circumstances, the tenancy granted or assigned to the new tenant is treated as if it began immediately before the deemed transfer on death. By way of interpretation, 'the new tenant' in *s 116(5D)* means the person or persons who are identified, in the notice of intention to retire in favour of a new tenant, as the person or persons who it is desired should become the tenant of the property to which the notice relates. Alternatively, 'the new tenant' may mean the survivor or survivors of the persons identified in the notice, either alone or with others. The notice must be in writing.

Section 116(6) provides that, for the APR code, the interest of joint tenants is taken to carry the right to vacant possession of the land if, taken together, all the joint owners have vacant possession or the right to obtain it within 12 months. The section has wording to accommodate Scottish equivalents.

'RENEWING' THE TENANCY TO SECURE 100% RELIEF

3.16   In a learned article in *The Conveyancer*, under the title 'Variation of lease or a new tenancy', Dr Allen Dowling considered cases both for the proposition that there was a variation and against it, in respect of several different possible changes. On one view, which appears to carry some authority, it is possible to secure 100% APR without losing the protection of the *Agricultural Holdings Act 1986* if a small piece of land can be added to the holding or if a small extension can be made to the term of the contract. It is not easy to extend the term of an annual tenancy, but it might be relatively easy to add a small area of land. The addition of a new party to the tenancy has been regarded merely as a variation. For technical reasons, it would appear that the addition of land or the extension of a term must cause a surrender and re-grant.

New rules were introduced by *FA 1995, s 155* increasing the rate of relief for transfers of tenanted farmland from 50% to the present rate of 100% where the tenancy commenced on or after 1 September 1995 'in relation to transfers of value made *and other events occurring*, on or after 1 September 1995'. The reference (author's italics) to 'other events occurring' covers the situation where the landowner has made a PET of tenanted land before 1 September 1995 and dies thereafter in circumstances where the previous tenancy has been replaced by a new tenancy commencing after 1 September 1995. In these circumstances, APR which would previously have been available only at 50% will be available at 100%. This makes the practical effect of the failure of the PET a non-event, subject of course to problems of clawback and reservation of benefit.

This situation can perhaps be exploited where the practitioner can identify PETs of this nature made within the last seven years, ie those cases where the donor and donee are still on risk. The donee should take steps to bring the old tenancy to an end and to grant a new one. Not only will this mean the donee is in the position of having 100% relief himself in respect of any transfer made by him, but it will also avoid a charge to IHT if, on the death within seven years of the gift of the donor, the PET should fail.

The interaction of IHT and CGT is relevant here. A simple surrender of lease is a disposal by the tenant, and can give rise to a chargeable gain. That is recognised by ECS D39, which provides that the extension of a lease will not be regarded as a disposal or part disposal of the old lease where the transaction meets the following conditions:

- it is on arm's-length terms, even if between connected persons;
- it is not part of a larger transaction;
- the lessee does not receive a capital sum;
- the same area of land is let; and
- the lease terms are substantially the same, except for duration and rent.

To this list should be added two provisos when dealing with Concessions:

- that they are of general application only, so might not relieve a particular case; and
- that the transaction is not entered into for tax avoidance.

In the situation described, which is for the benefit of the landlord, it would be reasonable for the tenant to ask for a tax indemnity before agreeing to the variation.

Where a tenancy is granted for full consideration, *s 268(2)* provides that a gift of the freehold reversion more than three years later shall not be taken to be associated with the earlier grant. (That section also provides, though this will now be of academic interest in most cases, that no operation effected after 27 March 1974 shall be taken to be associated with an operation effected before that date.) It follows that care should be taken not to make a gift within the three-year period, since the transfer of value will be treated as taking place at the date of the later of the associated operations. Only where, for example, the rate of relief had become more valuable in the interim would the taxpayer score an advantage.

OCCUPATION FOR THE PURPOSES OF AGRICULTURE

Agricultural purposes

3.17   The 'farmhouse' cases discussed in **Chapter 2** illustrate the principles now applied. Refer to the cases of *Dixon*, *Williams* and *McKenna* for analysis of the law. The meaning of 'agricultural purposes' was first considered in connection with rating cases. A useful summary of earlier principles in Scottish law is *Assessor for Lothian Region v Rolawn Ltd* 1990 SLT 433, 10 STNR 158. In that case, the company grew and sold turf. The Assessor argued that this was not an agricultural purpose. The local valuation appeal committee disagreed. The land valuation appeal court approved the decision of the appeal committee.

As a result of that case, some principles appear:

- Is the land being cultivated? That may be an end to the matter, unless cultivation is for the purposes of horticulture or forestry.

- Is the crop an unusual one? The decision whether the land is occupied for agriculture may depend on the general impression gained from the evidence as a whole.

- If the land is not being cultivated, is it used to support livestock? If so:

    – does the livestock produce or contribute to producing the means of human sustenance?

    – are the animals of the kind found on an ordinary farm?

- Agriculture has its ordinary meaning, which is to be decided by the tribunal of first instance rather than the court, especially where the members of the tribunal are drawn from an agricultural community and understand agricultural questions.

- How is the land treated for rating purposes? An IHT appeal would lie to the Special Commissioner who might not be an expert in agriculture. The treatment of land for rating purposes would be relevant.

It may be necessary to look at the use of the land from more than one standpoint. Land of poor quality may yield no more than sustenance income for much of the year, but may be capable of producing extra revenue from occasional use.

Example 3.3: diversification into the provision of rock music

Peregrine was the owner for many years of a small sporting estate in Scotland. The land supported small-scale sheep farming and, more important to Peregrine, had the benefit of excellent shooting and, years ago before certain commercial and environmental changes along the coastline, one of the finest runs of sea trout on the West Coast of Scotland. At the time of his death, it was argued successfully that occasional use of the land for shooting (not an agricultural purpose) did not rob the land of its essential quality as grazing for the sheep. However, the part of the value of the estate as a whole that related to the sporting rights so greatly exceeded the agricultural value that APR was severely restricted.

Peregrine's son established a rock band of some notoriety after leaving agricultural college. He brought new wealth (and much besides) to the glens of his father's estate, establishing a three-week summer festival, part of which, to the annoyance of his neighbours, extended past 12 August in each year. On his early demise (not, as it happens, at the hands of his neighbours but through self-administered poisons), it was again argued that APR should be available in respect of the estate.

Evidence was available, however, that, quite apart from the three-week duration of the 'rock fest', the land was taken out of use for agricultural purposes for a much greater period so that it could be prepared for the annual influx of visitors. Considerable alterations had been made to the estate to provide the necessary facilities for the visitors. The entire character of the estate had changed to such an extent that the income from the grazing of sheep was insignificant compared with the rock fest income. The use of the land for grazing had been interrupted so much that the land was not occupied for the purposes of agriculture. Similarly, whereas farm cottages had been occupied by retired farm workers or their surviving spouses, annual noise pollution prompted them to seek council accommodation in the nearby town, with the result that relief was not available in respect of any of the cottages, now occupied by recording engineers for the period of the festival and by holiday makers at other times.

The land was no longer being used for the purposes of agriculture so as to qualify for APR, though an argument might (just) be made that part of it should qualify for BPR.

Diversification

3.18   The question of occupation for 'agricultural purposes' was examined, though not in a fiscal context, by the Court of Appeal in *Jewell v McGowan* [2002] EWCA Civ 145. The tenant of land in Gloucestershire was bound by his agreement to use it 'for agricultural purposes only'. He ran an 'open' farm which the public could visit. A good deal of the tenant's income was derived, not from the farming activities as such, but from the open farming. The landlords objected. The tenant initially complied but later sought a declaration from the court that he could continue open farming without being in breach of the agreement.

For the purposes of *s 1(1)* and *(2)* of the *Agricultural Holdings Act 1948*, an agricultural holding is 'land used for agriculture'. The tenancy of such land is an agricultural one if the land is let for use as agricultural land, but subject to such exceptions as do not substantially affect the character of the tenancy.

At first instance, the court thought that open farming was agricultural, partly on the ground that it was essential for the financial viability of the farm. The Court of Appeal disagreed. 'Agricultural purposes only' in the agreement was not intended to refer exclusively to the definition in the *1948 Act*. The wording of the particular agreement, to use the land 'for agricultural purposes only', prevented the tenant from enjoying any exception to that agricultural use, even where such exception did not affect the character of the tenancy. The open farming was a separate commercial enterprise. Its purpose was to educate the public and to promote both organic farming and organic farm produce. Whilst that might direct the agricultural activity, it did not comply with the terms of the agreement. The open farming activities were not agricultural in nature and did not become agricultural merely because they enabled farming to be carried on on the holding.

That case turns on its own particular facts and, at a time when it seems that the continuation of farming in many parts of England and Wales is dependent on diversification, it is to be hoped that the less restrictive interpretation of what constitutes occupation for the purposes of agriculture will prevail when tax is in issue. HMRC are certainly alive to the issues: see their Rural Diversification Project (more fully described, with commentary, on the website of CLA) which urges landowners to comply with their obligations as to income tax, VAT, the intricacies of incorporation, PAYE and the correct treatment of overheads.

The Common Agricultural Policy Mid-term Review

3.19   There is a trend, noted at **2.8**, for HMRC to examine closely the nature of farming activities when deciding whether or not to allow APR on the farmhouse. The argument is sometimes seen that what the farmer is doing amounts only to what a landlord would do, rather than to 'real' farming. We do not yet know how that approach to farming will be affected by the CAP Mid-term Review. The range of subsidies that used to apply is replaced by a single farm payment (SFP). Since the SFP is payable not only to 'working farmers' but also to those who just happen to own land that was once farmed, there may be political pressure to treat the SFP more in the nature of investment income than trading income.

BIM55130 sets out some principles for the tax treatment of SFP. There are implications not only for IHT but also for income tax and CGT in respect of reliefs. The most serious effect of the new regulations may be the loss of APR wherever the farmer (here nicknamed the 'SFP banker') decided that it was simply not worthwhile attempting to farm the land and that he should in effect take early retirement by selling all, or nearly all, of his live and dead stock and keeping only such equipment as is necessary to comply with the conditions for the SFP, which will require him to keep the land in good condition but not actually to farm it. BIM55130 argues that, in the SFP banker situation, there is:

- no agricultural production; so
- no occupation for the purposes of husbandry; so
- no farming trade.

HMRC recognise that a new trade could arise of managing the land on a commercial basis with a view to profit, but that would not be farming. Just receiving the subsidy does not make you a farmer.

Who is the occupier?

3.20   An owner of land, who lets it to a tenant farmer under a full agricultural tenancy, is not in occupation. A farm manager does not occupy the farm: it is the employer, who benefits from profits or suffers losses, who is the occupier. The person who holds an interest in possession in settled property does not occupy it, where the farm is operated exclusively by the trustees on behalf of the trust. This might also occur where the trustees form a company for the purpose or employ a manager. The trust takes the profits or suffers any losses. The result is that, when the tenant for life dies, he has not been in occupation under *s 117(a)*.

On the other hand, the person who actually farms the land for his own benefit is in occupation. He is also in occupation if he farms under an agricultural tenancy, even a farm business tenancy. The farmer is treated as occupying not only the house in which he lives but also the houses or cottages in which his farm manager and employees live. The question of farm cottages is considered later in this chapter. Similarly, where the farming is carried on in partnership, each partner is treated as occupying the property. This rule can be very useful in certain circumstances: see *Atkinson* below.

Where the land is settled and the farming is carried on not by the trustees as was described above but by the holder of an interest in possession, that person for life will, by virtue of *s 49(1)*, be an occupier. His farming profits, if he makes any, are for consistency to be treated as his earned income and not as trust income. Where the trustees join in the farming operation, perhaps as limited partners, the two-year occupation test is not satisfied as to the trustees. *Section 49(1)* relates to the tenant for life, and not to the trustees. They will become entitled to relief only under the seven-year ownership rule.

Occupation in partnership situations

3.21   A common situation is the family partnership of mother, father and son, where mother and father take son into partnership not only as to the profits or losses from year to year but also ownership of the farmland itself. Where mother and father retain sole ownership of the farmhouse, and give the son an interest in the farmland only, the complications arise that have been examined in relation to *Rosser v IRC* at **2.17** above. On the other hand, in the event of the sale of the farmhouse, main residence relief from CGT will shelter the whole of any gain.

Where, as an alternative, the son acquires a one-third interest in the residence but does not live there, no CGT shelter will be available to the son under *TCGA 1992, s 223*. The family will probably accept that restriction: it is unlikely that the farmhouse will be sold. Does the son occupy the farmhouse for APR purposes? Much will no doubt depend on the evidence. Although the son no longer lives there, does he visit his parents' house every day? Is there a farm office at the house? What is the pattern of working: does the father still work the land, or is his involvement more akin to that of a landlord? Matters of family relationships could be relevant: does the daughter-in-law resent the time that her husband spends at the farmhouse? If the case came before the First-tier Tribunal, evidence that father and son did not get on and spent virtually no time together could have a significant effect on a claim for APR in respect of the son's share in the house.

Most farming families put the farm before the family, and put the farming members of the family before the non-farming members. Most farming families will therefore be happy to confirm, in the situation described above, that the son does indeed occupy the farmhouse on a daily basis because it is from there that he and his father run the farm. It may be difficult to show that all the partners take an active role in managing the farming enterprise. Care should be taken to avoid the suggestion that in fact neither mother nor father has any active role, since that would play into the hands of HMRC to employ the argument in *Rosser v IRC*.

Occupation of the farmhouse for agriculture

3.22 Proving the occupation of the house for the purposes of agriculture can give rise to problems. One principle is clear: where the occupier of a farmhouse lets the land that he previously farmed, APR on the farmhouse is lost. This is because the farmland becomes, in many respects, a mere investment enjoyed by a person who just happens to live in what was previously recognised to be a farmhouse. The occupier of the farmhouse is not occupying in his character as a farmer, because he is no longer farming. HMRC's Inheritance Tax Manual urges further investigation where the deceased is described as retired (see IHTM24013).

Assuming that the hurdle of occupation of the farmland can be overcome, the question is whether the taxpayer was occupying the farmhouse itself. Occupation is a matter of fact. If a person farms land for his own profit, he is in occupation. His employees and contractors are not in occupation. It is the person who owns the business, and not the manager who runs it, who is in occupation. This is true whether the owner of the business is in physical occupation or not. It is thus possible for the owner to occupy the entire farm, including the tied cottages of employees. However, as was explained in *McKenna,* this will not help a claim to APR since, for farmhouses, the test is of the person who actually does the work, rather than merely supervising it.

Allowing other people to use the land for part of the year on seasonal grazing or mowing licences can be compatible with retaining occupation for the purposes of agriculture, although it can depend on the terms of the licence. Certainly, as a general principle, you can distinguish between physical occupation and a legal right to occupy, but it is not reasonable, in the context of APR, to limit the meaning to physical occupation.

The farmer who falls ill

3.23 It is argued by Julie Butler, see *Tax Planning for Farm and Land Diversification*, 3rd Edn (Bloomsbury Professional, at para 4.35, that APR will not be lost where the farmer is not in physical occupation of the farmhouse at his death, through ill-health, but had every expectation of returning to the farmhouse were it not for his intervening death. Back in 2003, at a Countryside Tax Conference, the late Mr Peter Twiddy (before his retirement from IRCT) noted that *IHTA 1984, s 117* applied a test of occupation, which includes legal rather than actual occupation, making the intention of the farmer relevant. He considered that the requirements of *s 117* could still be satisfied where, for example, family members could be regarded as acting as agents of the farmer in continuing to run the business from the farmhouse on his behalf.

This is a difficult area on which, so far, there is only one decided case, *Atkinson*, discussed below, which turns on specific facts. Where, for example, the farmer suffers ill-health and effectively gives up living at the farmhouse and moves to a nursing home or hospital, it will be relevant to examine exactly how the farming is carried on. In the absence of help from family members in the way described by Mr Twiddy above, it may be possible to show that there is a contracting agreement in place. All too often, in the difficult circumstances that apply to farming generally and especially where the farmer is ill, and perhaps even reluctant to accept advice from close relatives, the arrangements will be informal. The key to the analysis is that 'occupation' does not strictly mean 'residence', although the requirements set out in *McKenna* virtually take us to that point.

It may be possible to argue that a neighbouring farmer, under an unwritten but settled relationship, looks after the land and for that purpose has access to the farmhouse and uses part of the farmhouse for managing the land. On this basis, an argument that the business of the farmer includes part use of the farmhouse may form the basis for a modest BPR claim where the full claim for APR is strenuously disputed by HMRC. This may not actually be as poor a substitute as it sounds: the claim to APR would only ever have been in respect of the agricultural value of the farmhouse, whereas a BPR claim in respect of the 'business part' of the house will be on the appropriate proportion of the full value of the house. That may form the basis of a compromise that will allow the executors to wind up the estate.

In these cases, much will turn on the specific evidence. What is the extent of the farming operations? When did the farmer last direct farming operations from the farmhouse? Has anyone else occupied the farmhouse as a mere residence since the farmer went into the nursing home or hospital? How often is attendance at the property required for the running of the business? Is this a business which, following the illness, is progressively run down?

Atkinson: special case or loophole?

3.24   In *Executors of Atkinson Deceased v HMRC* [2010] UKFTT 108 (TC), the Tribunal had to consider the issue outlined above. The farmer's health had deteriorated to the point that he was, at the time of his death, living in a care home. The deceased had been in partnership with his son and daughter-in-law from 1980. He granted a tenancy of the farm to that partnership. The partnership was increased in 1994 when the grandson joined, but reduced the following year when the son died. In 1996, the deceased, his daughter-in-law and grandson agreed that they farmed in partnership and that the earlier tenancy was a partnership asset; and the tenancy was assigned to the deceased, his daughter-in-law and grandson. A bungalow had been built in 1966 and was occupied by the deceased. He became ill, moving first to hospital and thence to a care home. The bungalow remained furnished; his personal things were left there.

The tribunal held that the bungalow was 'occupied for the purpose of agriculture' within *IHTA 1984, s 117*. It, like the whole farm, was occupied by the partnership. For 22 years, the bungalow had been the residence of the deceased. For the last four years of his life, it was not, but he remained a partner, taking an interest in the business of the farm, visiting the bungalow occasionally and keeping his possessions there. The tribunal noted that the facts were broadly the reverse of those in *Harrold v IRC* [1996] STC (SCD) 195, considered below, where a farmhouse had not been brought into use and was not therefore occupied for agriculture. Here, the bungalow had been so occupied and nothing was done to disturb that.

The most important lesson for practitioners here is to get the paperwork right. It greatly helped the taxpayer's case that there was a formal written agreement, both as to farming in partnership and as to the tenancy of the land. A cynic might conclude that, on that basis, few farming cases 'in the real world' will succeed.

Occupation of dwellings for agricultural purposes

3.25   Difficulty may arise where a farming company owns a farmhouse and other residential property occupied by members of the family. By *s 119(1)*, occupation by a company controlled by a transferor is regarded as occupation by the transferor himself. Under *s 122*, APR is allowed on shares in a company only if the transferor controlled the company. Under *s 123(1)(a)*, (author's numbering):

(1)   the property must have been occupied either by the company for agricultural purposes throughout the previous two years; or

(2)   the property must have been owned by the company throughout the seven-year period and occupied throughout (by the company or another) for agricultural purposes; and

(3)   the shares must also have been owned for the corresponding period.

The test in each case is whether the occupation is accepted as being for agricultural purposes. Clearly, a contract of employment requiring occupation of a particular dwelling is helpful in negotiations with HMRC to support a claim that occupation, perhaps by a member of the family, has indeed been for agricultural purposes. If the occupier does not have a controlling holding, relief will be under BPR rather than APR. This is one of the areas of overlap of the reliefs considered in **Chapter 6**.

The issue of occupation was considered in *Harrold (executors of Harrold deceased) v IRC* [1996] STC (SCD) 195, SpC 71. A Norfolk farmer and his son bought a farm which included a six-bedroomed farmhouse, then much neglected and in need of substantial renovation. This was destined to be the home of the son when ready for occupation. Following initial running repairs, a major renovation was carried out. It was not until 64 months after the purchase that the son took up residence. Two years prior to taking up residence, the father assigned his share of the farm to the son, dying some 18 months later. APR was claimed on the whole farm. That was disputed by the Revenue on the grounds that such part of the value transferred by the deed of gift as was attributable to the farmhouse:

- was not agricultural property within the meaning of *s 115(2)*; or alternatively

- having regard to *s 117(a)*, was not agricultural property occupied by the assignor for the purposes of agriculture throughout the period of two years ending on the transfer.

The Special Commissioner held that the farmhouse did indeed fall within the meaning of 'agricultural property': it passed all the tests. *Section 117*, however, required the property actually to be occupied for the purposes of agriculture. An intention to occupy at a future date was not enough: the owner was not in occupation until he moved in. The judgment relied in part on the test as to future intention in *Arbuckle Smith & Co Ltd v Greenock Corpn* [1960] AC 813. On this evidence, the Commissioner could not find that either the father or the son occupied the farmhouse for the purposes of agriculture before the date on which the son took occupation.

It was considered, prior to the enactment of *s 124C*, that land lying fallow within a conservation scheme might be regarded as not occupied for the purposes of agriculture. *Section 124C*, considered at **2.27**, sets out the relevant habitat schemes.

Occupation by a partnership or company is considered at **4.9** below.

Farm cottages: the rate of relief

3.26   100% relief will be available (provided the two-year occupation/ seven-year ownership conditions have been satisfied) if:

- the occupation began on or after 1 September 1995; or

- the tenancy began before 10 March 1981 and the 'working farmer' tests are satisfied.

Relief may therefore be available in the case of an occupier with no protected service tenancy, perhaps a partner or an occupier with the benefit of an assured agricultural tenancy, such as a farmworker employed on the farm or an occupier who has an assured shorthold tenancy. HMRC have confirmed that a person with the benefit of an assured shorthold tenancy will normally be regarded as occupying the cottage for agricultural purposes.

The difficulty arises in relation to cottages first occupied after 10 March 1981, ie without the protection of the old working farmer relief and before 1 September 1995 (when the new rules began to operate). In these cases, the nature of the occupation determined the rate of the relief. Where there is an unprotected service tenancy or an assured shorthold tenancy, 100% relief is available. Where there is an assured agricultural occupation, whether by a farmworker or by a retired farmworker or by the surviving spouse of a farmworker, the rate is 50% only. Thus the farmer-landowner can be in a worse situation than, for example, the owner of a forestry business whose estate includes a woodman's cottage. That cottage will attract 100% BPR.

There is one exception, noted in IHTM24034: if, at the date of transfer, there is evidence that suitable alternative accommodation was available for the tenant, relief may be claimed at 100%.Where the tenant was in default of the terms of his occupation, then 100% relief may likewise be available, because the landlord can recover possession. Where the tenant was not in default the rate of relief will depend on whether possession may be obtained by another route, as for example under the *Agricultural Holdings Act 1986, Sch 3*.

The 50% relief applies where the landlord is unable to obtain vacant possession within 24 months. Thus where, for example, a cottage had been part of a farm but was let temporarily to an outsider before being returned to farm use and was transferred within less than two years after such resumption of farm use, APR would not be available.

Farm cottages must be valued on the basis that there is a planning tie restricting occupation to agricultural use only (see *s 169(1)*). The law in this area is not entirely satisfactory but the values involved may, in the context of whole landed estates, be marginal, such that litigation, even before the First-tier Tribunal, is unlikely.

Share farming and contract farming

3.27   Ever fewer farmers now keep and maintain the equipment needed for even quite basic farming operations. Partly, perhaps, the earlier generation were content with lower-powered machinery and would wait for the weather to work in their favour, whilst now people want to get on with the year's work regardless, which may be possible with modern tractors. As a result, we now often find that the farm buildings stand idle because all the heavy gear is owned by the contractor. Under a share farming arrangement, the landowner provides the land, buildings and fixed equipment and pays a share of other costs. The working farmer supplies the labour and working machinery and also pays a share of the other costs. Profits are divided between the landowner and the working farmer according to an agreed formula.

Until July 1991, the Revenue had, both in practice and in correspondence with the Country Land and Business Association ('CLA'), agreed that the landowner had the tax status of a farmer and could benefit from APR (and from roll-over and retirement reliefs for CGT). The Revenue had argued in writing that the working farmer was not a farmer, although in practice they regarded him as a trader. In July 1991, the Revenue stated that they regarded the working farmer as a farmer but that the landowner would not be in occupation of the land for the purpose of husbandry and thus would not qualify for the various reliefs from capital taxation. A press release issued by the CLA on 3 September 1991 confirmed the Revenue argument for their new position, namely that, where persons do not have qualitatively the same occupation rights, only one can be regarded as occupier of the land in receipt of farming income for tax purposes. In share farming, it would be the operator who is treated as being in receipt of the income, being the one with the greater presence and control over the land. The CLA submitted an alternative construction of the law. From July until December 1991, an uneasy situation prevailed, with a measure of relief being given by the Revenue.

Happily, the position was eventually resolved, to a large extent in favour of the position adopted by the CLA. The Revenue agreed that, under an agreement based on the model set out by the CLA, the landowner may establish trading status. He must show that he concerns himself with the details of farming policy. He must go onto the land for a 'material purpose', eg to inspect crops or stock and to decide the farming policy in the light of that inspection. There was, in the hearing at first instance of *McCall (Personal representative of McClean) v HMRC* [2009] NICA 12, some discussion of farming operations, but APR was not disputed there: it is a case on BPR and is examined at **5.6**.

50% APR

3.28   *Section 116(2)* allows relief at 50% in any case where the conditions for 100% relief are not met. This mainly means land let under an *Agricultural Holdings Act* tenancy.

One specific situation where 50% relief will apply is in relation to working farmer relief where the £250,000/1,000 acres test cannot be met (see *s 116(4)*). In these circumstances, relief is at 100% for the part of the value which qualifies for the old relief and 50% for the remainder. There is a complication at the point of overlap between APR and BPR arising from *s 116(5)* (noted at **1.8**) and discussed more fully in **Chapter 12**. That subsection requires *FA 1975*,

Sch 8, para 5 to be construed as if references to working farmer relief included references to relief given under *IHTA 1984, s 116(2)(b)* or *(4)* or under *FA 1981, Sch 14* by virtue of *FA 1981, Sch 14, para 2(ii)(b)* or *(iv)*. The effect is that a transferor who would have been entitled to working farmer relief secures the new 100% relief up to the limit of the qualifying value or acreage, and 50% on the balance. There can be no claim to BPR as an alternative to the 50% APR.

Chapter 4

Agricultural property: areas of particular concern

QUICK GUIDE

APR is lost if there is a contract to sell the asset at the time of the transfer.

For trusts and partnerships, there are quite complicated rules as to occupation of land so as to qualify for APR: see the examples at **4.4**.

There are two circumstances in which the two-year ownership rule is varied. These concern:

- the replacement of qualifying property by other qualifying property: see **4.6** onwards; and

- the replacement of one qualifying owner by another under the rules relating to successive transfers: see **4.11** onwards.

Briefly, a spouse acquiring APR property from a spouse on death automatically acquires the period of ownership that the deceased spouse had.

Complicated rules affect replacement property in order to limit APR to the value of property that has been held for the two-year period.

Valuation of agricultural estates is intricate. There are several rules built around decided cases including *Buccleuch*, *Baird*, *Ellesmere*, *Lady Fox* and *Alexander*. Each of those cases is summarised in this chapter. If a value is properly agreed, it will not normally be reopened, even where the land is later sold for a higher figure. The rules as to hope value are considered at **4.21**.

The impact of APR on sales of shares within 12 months of death, and of land within four years of death, is examined in detail at **4.24** and **4.25**. A problem applies with the interaction of the related property rules: see **4.26**.

NO CONTRACT FOR SALE

4.1   *IHTA 1984, s 124(1)* provides, quite clearly, that APR is lost if, at the time of the transfer, the transferor has contracted to sell the property. The only exception is where:

- the sale is to a company; and

- the consideration is wholly or mainly shares in or securities of the company; and

- those shares or securities give the transferor control.

Similarly, APR is withheld under *s 124(2)* (which allows APR in respect of farming companies) if, at the time of the transfer of the shares or securities, the transferor has contracted to sell them. Again, there is an exception where that sale is for reconstruction or amalgamation of the farming company.

The treatment of sales for APR and BPR is different. The two reliefs differ over the treatment of sales, because APR is related essentially to particular assets from or by which farming is carried on, whilst BPR tends to look at the business entity rather than at the underlying assets. Thus APR may be given in respect of the shares of a farming company which is in liquidation in the situation where the farm itself is not being sold. That contrasts with the BPR position in *s 105(5)*. APR will be denied where the sale of the asset giving rise to the relief takes place before the transfer, whereas under BPR the exchange of one business asset for another does not as such jeopardise the relief: it is only necessary to show that the business continues and that the new asset is used or, if cash, that it is required or will be required for the purposes of the business. In the case of farmland, the replacement provisions may help. Where a growing crop is sold, the crop itself no longer qualifies for APR, but BPR will usually be available on the proceeds.

Section 124(1) refers to agricultural property and excludes relief 'if at the time of the transfer the transferor has entered into a binding contract for its sale'. A refined argument, which has not been tested before the First-tier Tribunal, takes the definition of agricultural property as meaning not a mere interest in an asset, but the asset itself. This is because *s 115(2)* defines such property as 'agricultural land' etc, and not as a mere interest in such land or in the other categories of asset identified in *s 115(2)*.

Based on this argument, it is suggested, in the case of a partnership, that the vendor does not agree to sell the land itself but merely to sell an interest in it, such that there is no binding contract that excludes relief under *s 116*. This argument, if it works, will apply only to partnerships and not, for example, to direct ownership of assets such as the land itself or a controlling shareholding in a farming company. Equally, this argument is not appropriate to BPR, because that relief relates not to the underlying asset but to the interest in the business itself.

JOINT OWNERSHIP

4.2   *IHTA 1984, s 116(6)* provides that, for the APR code, the interest of one of two or more owners of land, whether they hold as joint tenants or as tenants in common, carries the right to vacant possession if the interests of all of them carry that right. The same applies, in Scottish estates, to joint owners or owners in common.

PARTNERSHIPS

4.3   There is no specific statutory rule to this effect, but occupation of land by an English partnership is treated as occupation by the partners. This is so in relation to each partner, however active or inactive that partner may be. That was partially illustrated in *Atkinson's Executors v HMRC* [2010] UKFTT 108, discussed in detail at **3.24**. This rule is helpful where reliance is made on *IHTA 1984, s 117(b)*.

Example 4.1: occupation test

James bought Bridge Farm many years ago. In 1996, he took his wife Mary into partnership with him. The freehold of the farm remained in his name. He was suffering from ill health and in 1997 he retired from the partnership, at the same time that their son Charles became a partner. In 1998, James transferred the land, three-quarters to Mary and one quarter to Charles. *Section 117(a)* would not be satisfied in relation to the transfer to Charles (being irrelevant to the other transfer) because, at the time of transfer, he was no longer occupying the land for the purposes of agriculture, but *s 117(b)* would be satisfied by virtue of the occupation by Mary and Charles together.

A Scottish partnership is a legal person in its own right. Notwithstanding that, *s 119(2)* provides that occupation by any such partnership is to be treated as occupation of the land by the partners irrespective of *s 4(2)* of the *Partnership Act 1890*.

There is a link, though not expressed, between *ss 119* and *120* (successions). This allows successive ownership to 'earn' occupation.

Example 4.2: occupation of successive properties

In 2000, John, an accountant, bought Manor Farm. It adjoined the Manor itself, in which he lived, and was subject to a long-term agricultural tenancy. There was no link in occupation between the Manor and the farm at John's death in 2003. It was occupied for the purposes of agriculture, but not by him. He had not, at that stage, owned the land for seven years so as to comply with *s 117(b)*.

John's will left the house and the farm to his widow Sarah for life, giving her an 'old-style' interest in possession. The will contained power to 'trade down' and, at Sarah's request, the trustees sold both the house and Manor Farm. They bought, for about the same money, Low Farm, comprising a smaller house but larger acreage, the acreage again being let but producing a greater income. Sarah died in 2008.

Is APR available in respect of Sarah's interest in Low Farm? She did not satisfy *s 117(b)* because, although she was treated as the owner of the land by virtue of her interest in possession, she had not owned the property for seven years. The replacement provisions of *s 118(2)* are not satisfied because, in her capacity as tenant for life, it could not be shown that she had owned the land for seven years. The situation is saved by the operation of *s 120,* as Sarah is deemed to have owned Manor Farm (but not the Manor itself) from the date of its purchase by John within *s 117*. As a result, Sarah does qualify under *s 118(2)*.

There then follows a nice argument as to whether, in applying the proceeds of the Manor as well as Manor Farm in the purchase of Low Farm, *s 118(3)* comes into play so as to restrict APR. It is arguable that the Manor was never occupied for the purposes of agriculture, simply being the residence of a retired accountant. On that basis, only the proportion of the value of Low Farm which relates to the proceeds of Manor Farm will qualify for APR.

TRUSTS

4.4   It was noted in **Chapter 3** that the tests as to occupation give rise to problems in relation to trusts.

Example 4.3: farming by trustees

Wayne is 21. Under the will of his father, Stephen, he has an immediate post-death interest in the 500-acre family farm. Wayne is no scholar nor even, yet, a competent farmer. Stephen's will appointed as his trustees the family lawyer,

Geoff, and accountant, Carol. Geoff is very concerned that Wayne should have time to learn his trade and that the farming assets should not be put at risk. He therefore suggests that, for the next few years at least, the farming operations should be conducted or supervised by Carol and himself, employing a manager for the purpose.

Carol observes that, since Wayne has an interest in possession, the arrangement which Geoff proposes will mean that, for the time being at least, the condition in *s 117(a)* will not be satisfied, though she recognises that, barring accidents, Wayne is likely to live for many years yet. It is therefore agreed, subject to suitable indemnities, that the farming operations be conducted as Geoff proposes. The trustees, in the exercise of the power given them by the will, take out term assurance on Wayne's life for an amount which they consider will compensate the fund for a charge to IHT made in the event of Wayne's death within the next, say, ten years.

Where property is held in a settlement created before *FA 2006*, such that a beneficiary has an interest in possession, the land can qualify for relief since, by *s 49(1)*, the person beneficially entitled to an interest in possession in settled property is to be treated for the purposes of the *Act* as being beneficially entitled to the property in which the interest subsists. That rule does not extend to all trust interests. For example, an interest in reversion does not benefit from APR during the time in which there is another person enjoying the benefit of a life interest, but that does not usually matter because a reversionary interest is excluded property anyway.

Since the coming into force of *FA 2006*, newly created *inter vivos* trusts, unless created for certain narrow categories of beneficiary such as the disabled, will be relevant property trusts. The trustees of such trusts qualify for APR as the legal owners of the land rather than the beneficiaries. By holding the land continuously, these trustees will escape ten-year charges on the fund; and by distributions only in specie they will escape exit charges once they have held the land for seven years (or two years if they do the actual farming).

More specifically, *IHTA 1984, s 115(1)* provides that, for the APR code, references to a transfer of value include references to an occasion on which tax is chargeable under the relevant property code of *Chapter III* of *Part III* of the *Act*. However, *s 115(1)* excludes the rare situation where *s 79* (exemption from the ten-yearly charge where there has been conditional exemption for heritage property) applies. The value transferred by a transfer of value includes the amount on which tax is chargeable. The transferor includes the trustees of the settlement. Where the whole or part of the value transferred by a transfer of value is attributable to the agricultural value of agricultural property, *s 116(1)* provides that the value (or part of the value) so transferred is reduced by 'the appropriate percentage', subject to the general provisions of the APR code.

Occupation by more than one beneficiary: Woodhall v IRC

4.5   Who holds the interest in possession, when the trust instrument allows a class of beneficiaries to occupy? That issue was tested by the Special Commissioner in *Woodhall v IRC* [2000] STC (SCD) 558.

A will provided a trust for sale of residue with power to postpone, but there was to be no sale of the family home for as long as any of the children of the testator wished to live there. There were three children: Annie, Alan and Eric. The will provided that, until any sale, the trustees (two of whom were children of the deceased) should allow any of the children to occupy the house, on the basis that the occupier paid ten shillings per week rent and all outgoings, and kept the house in good repair. Following a sale, the three children would share the proceeds equally.

By the time the testator died, in 1957, Eric had already left home. The following year, Annie married and also left. She died in 1971. Alan lived on in the house until his death in 1997. Eric was the personal representative of Alan. Eric, as personal representative, argued that, for as long as the house was settled property, Alan was not entitled to an interest in possession in it, because the trustees under the terms of the will had a discretion to give an interest in possession to any one of the three children. What was more, if Alan did have an interest in possession, it was in respect of only half the house, within *s 50(5)*, because Eric in his personal capacity was entitled to the other half. The Revenue disagreed, on the grounds that Alan was entitled, at the time of his death, to an interest in the whole property as settled property.

The Special Commissioner considered that the trustees had no discretion as to who occupied the house. The purpose and effect of the will was to give each of the children a determinable life interest. Annie having died, Alan at the date of his death held a determinable life interest in one half only. The trustees did not have a dispositive power which allowed them to decide that any one child should occupy the house alone. They had only an administrative power to allow any child to occupy it. If more than one had wanted to live there, they could have done so. The appeal, therefore, was partly successful.

For an interesting commentary on this issue, consider *Brian Maxwell Cook and Elaine Margaret Dawn (Executors of Joyce Elizabeth Watkins Deceased) v IRC* [2002] STC (SCD) 318. The deceased had left a house, the former matrimonial home, to her husband to occupy for as long as he wished. The issue was whether the widower took an interest in possession in all or part of the house. After his wife's death, the widower stayed with his daughter. He fell ill and died. He never went back to the property (which was in fact divided into two flats, one of which was let).

The Special Commissioner could find nothing from the facts to show that the widower never again intended to live at the flat. There was no proper disclaimer of the life interest, by conduct or in writing. He held that the widower did acquire an interest in possession in the former home, but did not take such an interest in the flat that was let.

REPLACEMENT PROPERTY

4.6   The occupation condition of *IHTA 1984, s 117(a)* is extended under *s 118(1)* where, on the date of transfer, the agricultural property occupied by the transferor replaced other agricultural property. In certain circumstances, there may be a link between the replacement property rules and the rules for successive transfers; this is considered later in this chapter.

Test of replacement property as to occupation

4.7   The occupation condition is treated as satisfied if the agricultural property transferred, the property which it replaced and any agricultural property directly or indirectly replaced by that other property were occupied by the transferor for the purpose of agriculture for periods which, taken together, comprise at least two years falling within the five years which end with the date of transfer.

Test for replacement property as to ownership

4.8   *Section 118(2)* is concerned with satisfaction of the ownership test under *s 117(b)*. Where the agricultural property owned by the transferor at the date of the transfer replaces other agricultural property, the ownership test is satisfied if:

- that agricultural property;
- the other property which it replaced; and
- any agricultural property directly or indirectly replaced by that other property

were, for the periods which together comprised at least seven years falling within the ten years ending with the date of transfer, both owned by the transferor and occupied (by him or another) for the purposes of agriculture.

In neither case can relief exceed, in relation to new property, the relief that would have been available on the old property: see *s 118(3)*. For the purpose of this particular restriction on relief, any changes which result from the formation, alteration or dissolution of a partnership are to be disregarded: see *s 118(4)*. The farmer is not to use the replacement property rules to circumvent the normal two-year/seven-year rules of *s 117*. This is achieved by looking at the agricultural values at the date of the death (or of the transfer) of respectively the old farm (in respect of which the *s 117* test was satisfied) and the new farm. APR is limited to the lower of:

- the agricultural value of the old farm, if it were still owned by the transferor; and
- the agricultural value of the new farm.

It may be difficult to value the old farm. The land may have been broken up and may now be put to different uses. The attitude of HMRC may well be influenced by evidence (or the lack of it) that the transferor sold the old farm and bought the new one in order to exploit APR.

The point may be academic. BPR may be available in respect of value which does not qualify for APR. A fundamental difference, noted elsewhere, between the two reliefs is that BPR applies to the value of the business, and not to underlying assets. It is possible, within the context of BPR, for there to be the sale of one asset and its replacement by another, which may be of a different nature or of a different value, even though it is employed in the same business.

Example 4.4: farm move

John's farm adjoins a new town development, the extension of which results in the sale of the whole farm to New Town Development Corporation for development. It had an agricultural value of £1,000,000, although the sale price was £6,000,000. After gifts to the non-farming members of his family, John applies £3,500,000 in buying a new farm further away from the town. £3,000,000 is the true agricultural value. His death occurs within two years of the purchase of the new estate, at which time the new farming business is worth £4,000,000.

An assumption can be made that, at the time of the sale of the original land to New Town Development Corporation, the farming business run by John was worth £6,000,000. Following the gifts and the repurchase, the value of the remaining farming business is £4,500,000. Of this, £1,000,000 qualifies for APR and £3,000,000 for BPR as replacement of the business assets.

CONTROLLED COMPANIES

4.9   Occupation by a company which is controlled by the transferor is, under *IHTA 1984, s 119(1)*, to be treated, for the purpose of the rules relating to minimum period of ownership or occupation or replacement, as being occupation by the transferor.

SCOTTISH LIMITED PARTNERSHIPS

4.10   By *s 119(2)*, as has been noted earlier in this chapter, occupation of any agricultural property by a Scottish partnership should be treated as occupation for the purposes of satisfying the tests as to minimum period of occupation or the test as to replacement property, notwithstanding the provisions of *s 4(2)* of the *Partnership Act 1890*.

SUCCESSIVE TRANSFERS AND INHERITED OWNERSHIP

Successions

4.11   Aspects of *IHTA 1984, s 120*, which deals with successions, have already been considered in this chapter in relation to the tests which relate, for example, to partnerships in respect of occupation. *Section 120* provides a means of extending the minimum period of occupation or ownership under *s 117*. A somewhat similar situation is addressed in both *ss 120* and *121* (successive transfers). *Section 120* is considered first.

Where the transferor of property became entitled to it on the death of another person, his ownership runs from the date of the earlier death. The general rule, in the administration of an estate, is that a residuary beneficiary cannot claim any particular asset until the administration is complete. That rule is overturned by *s 120(1)(a)*. By the same provision, the transferor of land is deemed to have occupied land from the date of death if he later occupies it.

In addition to that relieving provision, which can apply where the transferor has inherited property from any person, *s 120(1)(b)* extends the relief in the case of transfers between husband and wife. By *s 120(1)(b)*, if the earlier owner of the property was the spouse of the inheritor/transferor, the transferor is deemed to have occupied the land for the purposes of agriculture for any period for which the spouse so occupied it. The inheritor/transferor is also deemed to have owned the land for any period for which the spouse owned it. As will be seen in **Chapter 6**, there is, parallel to this, a rule in *s 108* relating to business property.

The relief in *s 120(1)(a)* is valuable, and the requirements of the section must be strictly complied with.

Example 4.5: career switch

Hugh occupied Top Farm for many years, and lived and worked on the farm right up to the date of his death. He bequeathed it to his brother Alec, a

76

solicitor, at his death in 2006. Alec, who lived 75 miles away, made immediate arrangements for the farm to be managed. Following the loss of his legal aid franchise, Alec made all his staff redundant and sold his high street practice, intending to enjoy the spreading acres.

In fact, it was 14 months before he could take up residence in his brother's house. Sadly, through inexperience, his death occurred as a result of incorrect use of farming machinery two months later.

The conditions of *s 120(1)(a)* are satisfied. The occupation of the farm by Alec was for agricultural purposes and, though transient, it was his intention to live at the farm for the rest of his days, as indeed he did. Further, the farm was not occupied for any non-agricultural purpose at any time between the earlier death and the later transfer on death. The situation would have been otherwise had Alec immediately wound up the farming trade with a view, for example, to a sale of the land for some non-agricultural purpose. In that situation, he would not have satisfied the requirements of *s 120(1)(a)*.

Example 4.6: occupation by widow

George farmed in partnership with his sons Robert and Tom. He owned the land. The partnership has run since April 2000. By his will, George, who died in November 2006, left the farm house and land to his widow Katherine on IPDI trusts. Robert and Tom carried on farming. In April 2007, they asked Katherine to join them as a partnership to occupy the land. She died in June 2008.

At the date of Katherine's death, the farm qualifies for APR. By virtue of *s 120(1)(a)*, she has occupied the farm since George's death. By *s 120(1)(b)*, she is deemed to have occupied the farm ever since George bought it. In her own right, she has occupied it as a partner for only 15 months, but that does not matter in view of the alternative qualifying periods.

Example 4.7: technical occupation

Feargus is 'something in the City'. When he inherits his father's farm, he immediately lets it to one of his father's neighbours, who farms it through a private company which shortly afterwards suffers financial decline. Feargus is one of the few to enjoy a bonus. Anxious to avoid conspicuous consumption, he applies it in buying a controlling interest in the farming company. Soon afterwards, having no real interest in farming, he transfers the farm to a discretionary trust, recognising that this will be a chargeable transfer and can give rise to an immediate tax charge. Although farming is bad, at the time of this transfer the company is still operating the land.

Is the requirement of *s 117* satisfied at the time Feargus transfers the farm to the trust? He cannot rely on *s 117(a)*, not having set foot on the farm for many years, nor on *s 117(b)*, since his period of ownership is just short of the seven years required by that section. However, by the deeming provision of *s 119(1)*, the occupation by the farming company which he controlled at the time of the transfer is regarded as being his own occupation. Examination of *s 120(1)(a)* shows that Feargus is deemed to have owned the farm from the date of his father's death and, although there was a gap during which he did not actually occupy it, ie until he purchased the controlling interest, he is deemed to have occupied the farm from the date of his father's death. The farm has actually been occupied throughout, however unprofitably, by the company for agricultural purposes. It therefore seems that, in fact, APR will be allowable in respect of the transfer into the trust.

Successive transfers

4.12   The rules in *s 121* as to successive transfers relate to a slightly different situation from those in *s 120*. By *s 121(1)*, relief is available, where the conditions of *s 117* as to the minimum period of occupation or ownership would not otherwise be satisfied, if (all of the) four conditions are complied with, namely:

- The property concerned qualified for APR (or would have done had APR been available at the time of the transfer). This applies where the condition is satisfied as to the whole or part of the value transferred.

- The whole (or part) of the property qualifying for APR under the earlier transfer became, as a result of that transfer, the property of a person (or spouse) who transfers that property on a later transfer and is, at the time of that transfer, occupying the land for the purposes of agriculture. That occupation may either be in person or through the personal representatives of the earlier transferor.

- The property, or part of any replacement property, would qualify for APR on the later transfer, but for the 'minimum period' of *s 117*.

- One of the transfers was made on death.

Although the legislation does not specifically say so, a tenant for life of farmland can, it is believed, come within the second of these conditions by virtue of the deeming provisions: the property is that of the tenant for life for the purposes of satisfying *s 121(1)(b)*.

Complicated situations may be imagined where farmland is occupied by a company controlled by the second of the two transferors. There is no direct reference within *s 121*. It would be awkward if *s 121*, which is apparently intended to extend *s 117*, did not benefit from the kind of extension to the rule which has been examined already in relation to *s 119*. This could result in a situation where the treatment, for example, between English and Scottish partnerships might be different: a partner in an English partnership might satisfy the condition of *s 121(1)(b)*, whereas the partner in a Scottish partnership might not.

Section 121 'should' apply to replacement property, although there is no decided case on the point. This is clear from *s 121(2)*, which provides that, where property qualifies for relief under *sub-s (1)*, that relief is not to exceed what it would have been if the replacements had not been made. If there is replacement property, how is the occupation requirement in *s 121(1)(b)* satisfied? It seems that the occupation test should apply to the replacement property. *Section 121(3)* restricts the relief where, under the first of the transfers to be considered, APR was available on only part of the value. There will be a proportionate restriction on the relief on the second transfer.

Example 4.8: limited relief

David had occupied Loam Pit Farm for three years when, in January 1992, he wished to transfer it to his son Tom. He did not feel that he could afford to make an outright gift, so he sold it to Tom for £400,000 at a time when it was worth £600,000, ie there was a gift of £200,000. At that time, APR was available at 50%, with the result that APR of £100,000 is available.

Tom died in July 1993 when the farm was worth £650,000. On his death, the basic condition in *s 117* could not be met. Relief was available under *s 121(1)*, but restricted under *s 121(3)*, to 650,000 × (200,000 as a proportion of 600,000) 1/3, ie £216,667.

Replacement property

4.13   If shares or securities owned at the date of transfer replace other property qualifying for APR, ie a farm itself, or shares or securities of a farming company, then *s 123(3)* comes into play. The effect is that the condition in *s 123(1)(b)* as to ownership which qualifies the transfer for relief under *s 116* is satisfied if the replacement property and the property which it replaces (directly or indirectly) were owned by the transferor for periods which, taken together, comprised:

- at least two years within the five years ending with the date of transfer, where the situation falls within *s 123(1)(a)(i)* and the agricultural property was occupied by the company for the purposes of agriculture throughout the two years ending with the date of transfer; or

- at least seven years within the least ten years up to the date of transfer, where the agricultural property was owned by the company throughout the period of seven years ending with the date of transfer and was throughout that period occupied either by the company or by someone else for the purposes of agriculture.

This relieving provision is itself subject to the restriction contained in *s 118*, which prevents relief from being extended by virtue of replacement: replacement does not increase the relief that would have been available had there been no replacement.

PROBLEMS ARISING OUT OF SUCCESSIVE *GLADSTONE V BOWERS* AND GRAZING AGREEMENTS

4.14 A mere casual 'letting' of land does not destroy the qualification of the owner of the land to be regarded as the occupier. This much appears from *IRC v Forsyth-Grant* (1943) 25 TC 369 and *Mitchell v IRC* (1943) 25 TC 380. A problem may arise where there is a significant interval between one casual letting and another. Is the land 'occupied for the purposes of agriculture' in the interval? Probably; where it can be shown that the casual letting was for the part of the year when the land could effectively be used for agricultural purposes, and the gap occurred during a time when the land could not well be so used, the existence of a gap will not be grounds for showing that the land has not been occupied for the purposes of agriculture.

A problem arises where one grazing agreement after another, or one *Gladstone v Bowers* agreement after another, has been entered into over a period of time. Where it appears, from an examination of the conduct of the parties over a period of time, that it was always understood that the agreement would be renewed, it may well be argued against the taxpayer that effectively the land is let. That will not create too much of a problem where it can be shown that the letting began after 1 September 1995, since 100% relief will be available. The difficulty will arise where the situation has existed since before that date, as it will become arguable that the relief should be available at 50% only. Again, this will be a problem where the land in question falls within the circumstances described in **Chapter 2** relating to 'the fine house with a bit of land' and the existence of a long-term letting demonstrates that the occupier of the mansion does not occupy the land.

VALUATION OF AGRICULTURAL PROPERTY

General considerations

4.15 A full discussion of valuation principles is outside the scope of this book, but the general rule is that a value at any time of any property, for the purposes of IHT, is the price which the property might reasonably fetch if sold on the open market at that time. The price is not to be reduced on the ground that, if the whole of the property to be valued were placed on the market on the date of valuation, the price would be depressed: *IHTA 1984, s 160*. The comments of Charles McNicol (recorded in **Chapter 22** in relation to the valuation of chattels) should apply to land also: an 'adversarial' valuation only provokes enquiry; a 'probate' valuation, showing on its face that the value is depressed below market value, will provoke not merely enquiry but the risk of imposition of penalties.

The general rule is varied both in relation to certain circumstances and in relation to particular forms of property. Among the circumstances which will concern the practitioner in connection with APR and BPR are the rules relating to transfers within seven years before death and those relating to the valuation of land sold within four years after death.

Among the other situations where the general rule does not apply, the practitioner will be concerned with:

- any restrictions on freedom to dispose of the asset;

- the valuation of related property;

- the situation where a lease is treated as a settlement;

- the treatment of debts;

- farm cottages; and

- unquoted shares and securities.

The 'open market' is, to some extent, hypothetical. The courts envisage a market with certain ideal attributes. Some of these are best replicated in an auction, although sales by private treaty or by tender may be the best available guides where there has been a sale of similar property at similar date. For example, the sale of small parcels of agricultural land by tender can throw up quite exciting sale values, where farming neighbours compete with each other to secure land that will not come up for sale again within 50 years. The court assumes that there has been adequate publicity or advertisement before the sale and that the market envisaged is one in which the property is offered for sale to the world at large, so that all potential purchasers have an equal opportunity to make an offer as a result of it being widely known what is being offered for sale: see the observations in the House of Lords in *Lynall v IRC* [1972] AC 680.

Certain restrictions, notably pre-emption clauses in the articles of association of a company, have been considered in relation to IHT valuation. In *IRC v Crossman* [1937] AC 26, the House of Lords decided what assumptions are to be made in relation to the hypothetical sale. What is valued is the interest in the hands of the transferor at the relevant time. Restrictions that would prevent or hamper a sale are not taken to do so in considering what a purchaser would have paid for the asset. It is assumed that the purchaser would be subject to those restrictions after he had made his purchase, and that the price he would pay would take into account the fact that those restrictions would then apply to him.

The principle was summarised by Lord Guest in the later case of *Duke of Buccleuch v IRC* [1967] 1 AC 506:

'It is not necessary to assume an actual sale; a hypothetical market must be assumed for all the items of property at the time of death. The impossibility of putting the property on the market at the time of death or of actually realising the open market price is irrelevant. In other words, you do not have to assume that the property had actually to be sold; the assumption is that it is sold at the moment of death.'

That comment should perhaps be read in the light of the earlier observation in *Re Sutherland, Winter v IRC* [1960] Ch 611, that it need not be assumed that the sale has occurred. The question is, 'if it were sold today on the open market, what would this asset fetch?'.

It is fair, particularly when considering the valuation of a control holding in respect of a company, to consider the best price that a purchaser might get on liquidating the company immediately after purchase. Such a buyer would take account of liabilities to tax within the company that would crystallise on liquidation and would allow for that in the price that he offered. In completing Inland Revenue Accounts, a nominal value should not be used for unquoted shares. A reasoned value should be shown, noting if appropriate that it is an estimate. As and when more reliable figures are available, they should be notified to HMRC, particularly where the adjustment increases the tax by £1,000 or more: see the observations on compliance at **22.8–22.12**.

Expenses of sale may not be deducted in arriving at the value for IHT on death. The principle was established in the case of *Tapp v Ryder* [2008] TMA/284/2008 and confirmed in *Price v HMRC*, considered at **4.23**. In *Tapp*, a house had been occupied by the deceased, Mr Atkinson, from 1974 until December 2005 when, aged 83, he went into hospital. The house was filthy and stank; most of the night storage heaters did not work; the toilet did not work properly; and the wiring was defective. Mr Atkinson's niece thought that Social Services might not let her uncle move back there; besides, the property was unsaleable in its present condition for anything over £150,000. She therefore arranged essential repairs, the cost of £15,000 being funded partly by Mr Atkinson and partly by the niece and her husband. Mr Atkinson died in April 2006. The niece was losing enthusiasm for the project and, in June, had the house valued with a view to sale. Even though much of the finishing was still to be done, it was now worth between £210,000 and £220,000. The niece and her husband carried on renovating the property and, by October, the house was ready for sale. It was sold in November 2006 for £267,000.

For IHT purposes, the niece assumed straight line growth from £150,000 to the sale, and valued the house at April 2006 at £195,000. She also asked the tribunal to take into account the costs of sale. The value was challenged by HMRC; based on comparable properties, they put the value at between £230,000 and £250,000.

The tribunal considered that work was less advanced in April than the Valuation Office may have thought. The valuer saw the property only long after the work had been done. Even so, the value reached by the Valuation Office had been heavily discounted. The tribunal fixed the value at £230,000, allowing no discount for the costs of sale, relying both on *s 160* and on the principles set out in the 'Red Book'[.

Tenancies: Baird's Executors v IRC

4.16   It is rare for an agricultural tenancy to be assignable. Tenancies established before 1 September 1995 nevertheless are regarded as having a value, even though the tenant cannot sell because of the security of tenure provisions which apply. Certainly, the fact that the tenancy cannot be assigned does not prevent it from having a taxable value. Applying the principle in *Crossman*, the tenancy is valued on the assumption that it is capable of being sold notwithstanding the restriction. The assumed new tenant will be subject to the same restriction.

This was considered in *Baird's Executors v IRC* 1991 SLT (Lands Tribunal) 9, where George Baird had relinquished the tenancy of an agricultural holding in favour of his daughter-in-law and grandson. The tenancy had been granted in July 1921, and the transfer of it took place on 9 December 1977 with the consent of the landlord. Mr Baird died in 1985. The Revenue determined that the transfer of the lease was a chargeable transfer for capital transfer tax under *FA 1975, s 20(2)*.

The Lands Tribunal in Scotland had to decide whether the interest of a tenant in these circumstances was capable of valuation. It determined that the value of the interest assigned is the price which the interest might reasonably be expected to fetch if sold on the open market at the date of the transfer. In applying that test, the tribunal disregarded the fact that the tenancy could not be assigned, but assumed that the assignees would be subject to the same restrictions. The District Valuer had taken note of four factors in concluding that the interest of the tenant in the lease was equivalent to 25% of the vacant possession value of the land itself. The factors that influenced him were:

(1)   the price that a landlord might pay to a tenant to recover vacant possession;

(2)   the price that a prospective tenant might accept from a prospective landlord in a sale and leaseback transaction;

(3)   the price paid to a tenant where there was compulsory acquisition of part of an agricultural holding; and

(4)   the rents commanded by equivalent holdings when let in the open market on terms similar to those of the lease in question.

Having come to a figure of 25% of the vacant possession value, the District Valuer did indicate that the value could be as high as 50% of vacant possession value, but for the uncertainty in the hypothesis he was applying. That approach was largely accepted by the tribunal.

The result of the decision in *Baird* is that the right of a tenant in an agricultural lease is an asset which can have a value. That value is not necessarily 25% of the vacant possession value of the land itself. However, under *IHTA 1984, s 177*, which applies to Scottish agricultural leases such as that considered in *Baird*, it is provided (see *s 177(1)*) that, where any part of the value of a person's estate immediately before his death is attributable to the interest of a tenant in the unexpired portion of a lease for a fixed term of agricultural property in Scotland, any prospect that that lease might be renewed by 'tacit relocation' is to be left out of account in determining the value of the lease.

Further, where any part of the value of a person's estate immediately before his death is attributable to the interest of a tenant of agricultural property in Scotland which is held by virtue of tacit relocation and which is, on the death, acquired by a new tenant, in general the estate is valued without including the value of that tenancy. That is provided by *s 177(2),* except that neither *sub-s (i)* nor *(ii)* is to apply unless the deceased had been tenant of the property in question for at least two years continuously preceding the death or had become a tenant by succession. The part of the value to be left out of account does not include compensation to a tenant for improvements. It would seem that the upshot of this is that there is no value transferred where there is no new tenant by succession.

Section 177 applies on the death of individuals. If the tenancy is held by a partnership which continues or by a company, *s 177* will not apply. In those circumstances, it will become necessary to value the lease.

The situation becomes more complicated where the same person has an interest both in the tenancy and in the freehold, as will be seen in the next section.

Gray (surviving executor of Lady Fox) v IRC

4.17   This was a decision by the Lands Tribunal which was subsequently considered by the Court of Appeal and reported at [1994] STC 360. Lady

Fox owned a substantial agricultural estate farmed by a partnership in which she was a partner. The partnership had an agricultural tenancy. Lady Fox was entitled to 92.5% of the partnership profits. On her death on 27 March 1981, the Revenue assessed the CTT on the basis that both the land and the share in the partnership could be valued together, with the vacant possession value being discounted in a number of ways. That produced a much higher figure than merely taking the investment value (if the partnership share was disregarded). Although the Lands Tribunal disagreed with the Revenue on this point, the Court of Appeal reversed the tribunal on the question of principle. The tribunal had already considered what should be the method of valuation if it was permitted to lot the two together, the method which was approved by the Court of Appeal.

It had been agreed that the vacant possession value of the land was £6,125,000. From that figure, the Cambridge District Valuer deducted his estimate of what the partners (other than Lady Fox) would accept to sell their share of the tenancy. He reckoned that figure was £100,000, based on valuing the tenancy as a whole at nearly one quarter of the vacant possession value. He took 45% of the difference between vacant possession value and tenanted value (which had been agreed at £2,751,000), based on comparables that were available to him. Having arrived at a value, he discounted it by 7.5% of the vacant possession value to compensate for the risk and delay in obtaining vacant possession of the whole after a purchase of the freehold. This gave him a figure of £5,565,000 for the two interests taken together, namely the freehold and the partnership share.

In considering the evidence, the tribunal felt that there was no guarantee that the minority partners would accept £100,000 nor that they would come to the table quickly. It seemed to them that 7.5% discount was not enough, but the valuer for Lady Fox gave no evidence on that particular point, so the tribunal had no better evidence than that of the District Valuer.

Each valuation is likely to turn on its own facts. On another occasion, there might be a strong argument for a greater discount than that applied in the *Lady Fox* case. Further, where the agricultural tenancy is held by trustees or by executors in their own right and not merely because they are trustees or executors, and yet they hold the freehold in that fiduciary capacity, there is no obligation to dispose of the tenancy with the freehold so as to get a better price for the trust. In these circumstances, only a tenanted valuation would apply. The effect of ESC F17 (Relief for Agricultural Property) was noted earlier, in considering the rates at which APR is allowed. On a transfer of tenanted agricultural land, 100% relief will be allowed where the interest of the transferor in the property is, notwithstanding the terms of the tenancy, valued at an amount broadly equivalent to the vacant possession value of the property. That concession takes some of the sting out of the *Lady Fox* case.

Alexander v IRC

4.18   The deceased owned the long lease of a flat in the Barbican which had been bought under the 'right to buy' legislation. The price, net of discount, was £24,600. Under the terms of the lease, the discount was repayable, if the property should be disposed of within five years of the purchase, but on a sliding scale. The deceased died in January 1984, one year after the purchase. Had the flat been sold at the date of death, all of the discount would have been repayable. The Lands Tribunal ignored the discount and valued the flat at £63,000. The point came before the Court of Appeal ([1991] STC 112), which held that the charge in respect of the discount should be taken into account. It was an encumbrance on the property within what is now *IHTA 1984, s 164(4)*. The court referred the matter back to the Lands Tribunal to fix the amount that a purchaser would pay, even taking into account the discount to be repaid. As a result, the deduction from the full value of £63,000 was less than the actual discount of £24,600. The taxpayer wanted the full discount but did not get it.

Lotting for sale: 'natural units'

4.19   For the purposes of valuation, it must be assumed that the seller marketed the property in the way that would produce the best price, where appropriate dividing it into lots or assembling disparate items to sell them together. This may be particularly relevant (see **4.22**) in relation to farmhouses. In *Earl of Ellesmere v IRC* [1918] 2 KB 735, an estate was sold as a single entity after wide advertisement. The purchaser kept part of the land but sold the rest, making a profit (after allowing for the retained portion) of about 19% of the purchase price. The Revenue assessed the value for estate duty purposes at more than the sale price achieved by the executors. The court eventually reduced the Revenue figure to one which represented a premium of some 11% over what the executor had realised.

In *Duke of Buccleuch v IRC* [1967] 1 AC 506, the trustees did not dispute a basis put forward by the Revenue which divided an estate into 532 separate lots and which yielded a figure for the whole of £868,129. The trustees did, however, argue that, after taking out the readily saleable lots, amounting to about 9% in number, the remainder should be valued at the price that would be paid by an individual purchaser who would expect a profit (of 20% it was argued) for taking on the whole estate.

The House of Lords accepted that:

> 'We must take the estate as it was when the deceased died; often the price which a piece of property would fetch would be considerably enhanced by small expense in minor repair or cleaning which would make the property more attractive to the eye of the buyer. Admittedly that cannot be supposed to have been done: and I can see no more justification for requiring supposition

86

that natural units have been divided. This subsection applies to all kinds of property. A library was instanced by Wynn LJ. Generally there would be little difficulty, delay or expense in getting someone knowledgeable to pick out valuable books for separate valuation, and I would therefore regard such books as natural units. Suppose, however, that the deceased had bought a miscellaneous and mixed lot of surplus stores intending to sort out and arrange them in saleable lots. That might involve a great deal of work, time and expense, and I see no justification for requiring the supposition that that had been done and then valuing the saleable lots that would have emerged.'

The general principle to emerge from this is not that there must be lotting into 'natural units', but that the property would be marketed in such a way as to produce the largest price, provided that that did not involve undue expenditure of time or effort. The issue is particularly relevant to the farmhouse and garden. Practitioners should resist any attempt by the District Valuer to regard these assets as a separate valuation unit isolated from the farm as a whole, even though IHTM9711 urges the inspector to apply whatever lotting will yield the highest taxable value. The correct lotting must be a matter of fact in each case. A situation can arise where a unit which is uneconomic on its own is particularly valuable to two neighbouring owners, such that it may be natural to lot the farmhouse and garden separately from the land. It must not be assumed that this is the natural lotting. There is more specific consideration of the valuation of farmhouses at **4.22**.

Returning to the case of *Gray (surviving executor of Lady Fox) v IRC* [1994] STC 360, which has already been noted, the Lands Tribunal considered that the land and the partnership interest taken together must be a 'natural unit', as that expression was used in *Buccleuch*, if they are to be valued as if sold together. The tribunal did not think that the land and the partnership interest did together constitute a natural unit, but the court indicated in *Lady Fox* that the hypothetical vendor must be regarded as having done whatever was reasonably necessary to get the best price, including taking separate properties and selling them together, as had been done in the current case with the freehold and the partnership share. Certain technical objections had been raised by the tribunal, in that it had exclusive jurisdiction over questions as to the valuation of land but not of other kinds of property. The court held that the tribunal could consider the value of assets which were not land as part of the means by which the tribunal arrived at the value of the land itself.

Other aspects of valuation

4.20   The procedure for valuation is for the Valuation Office to negotiate with the taxpayer, either directly or, more rarely, through HMRC. Where no agreement can be reached, the Board may issue a notice of determination. The taxpayer can appeal, as appropriate, to the First-tier Tribunal. The tribunal, as has just been noted, may determine the value of the land, taking into account not only the value of assets other than land, where relevant, but also charges relating to contingent liabilities. Although there is no exact parallel to the CG34 procedure for CGT, the District Valuer can sometimes agree informally the value of land before delivery of the IHT account.

It is not the practice of HMRC to reopen a valuation where it has already been agreed, on the basis of full and accurate information supplied by the accountable persons, and HMRC have either confirmed that agreement and made an assessment of tax on the basis of that value, or issued a letter of clearance. This is so, even though the property may later be sold for a higher price. On the other hand, if the property is later sold for less than the agreed valuation, the taxpayer may have two bases on which to reopen the valuation. The first might be that he can show that the original valuation was based on inaccurate information. Alternatively, as is considered at **4.27**, the provisions of *IHTA 1984, s 190* may apply where the sale takes place within three years of death.

Let land is usually valued as a multiple of the net annual value, calculated by deducting from the gross rent the annual outgoings such as repairs, insurance, ground rent and the like. The expense of management is not deductible. If the property is vacant, it is usual to compare similar properties to arrive at a value. This is not easy where there are no comparables or where the situation of the property is in some respects unique. Where there is no formal tenancy, it becomes necessary to establish whether there is a reasonable prospect that vacant possession will be obtained in the not too distant future. It has already been noted that this is an aspect of valuation where land is let to a company which is controlled by the transferor.

Planning permission

4.21   The existence or prospect of obtaining planning permission will be taken into account. Here, the decision of the Lands Tribunal in *Prosser v IRC* [2001] RVR 170 illustrates the principles to be applied where there is hope value but no planning consent as yet. In that case, the deceased owned a house with a garden big enough for an extra building plot. There had been no application for planning permission by the date of death. The District Valuer proposed a figure of 80% of the value that the plot would have with such consent, allowing for the fact that no application for planning permission had yet been made. The executors did later get planning permission on the land.

The tribunal considered that there was, at the time of death, at least a 50% chance of obtaining planning permission and that a speculator would offer, in the absence of such permission, not 80% of the development value but 25% only. The effect of this was to reduce the probate value of the affected land from the District Valuer's figure of £44,000 to only £12,500. The tribunal observed:

'if a prospective purchaser was seeking a plot on which to construct a house for his own occupation, he would probably prefer to await the outcome of a planning application and, if appropriate, pay the full value rather than pay half of that value and run the risk of losing his entire investment. Similarly, a speculator would in my view not be interested in a purchase unless the potential profit resulting from a successful planning application were significantly greater than the potential loss if permission were not forthcoming.'

Farm cottages are valued without regard to any additional value that they might have if, instead of being occupied for agricultural purposes, they were available on the open market. This will be particularly relevant where a tied cottage is occupied by an agricultural worker. The extra value that might be available on the open market, if the restriction as to occupation did not apply, is to be disregarded.

The agricultural value of agricultural property is the price it would fetch if it were sold subject to a perpetual covenant confining its use to agriculture (or equivalent restriction where not situated in the UK). A freehold interest which is subject to an 'old' agricultural tenancy is clearly worth much less than vacant land, even though the tenant might well be a special purchaser. The discount to vacant possession value varies widely across the country. The profitability of farming must be a factor.

In *Willett v IRC* [1984] RVR 163, 264 EG 257, the Lands Tribunal valued a 48-acre arable farm in Staffordshire as at 30 May 1977. The issue was the value of the freehold reversion. The taxpayer's figure was £28,000 and that of the District Valuer £45,000. The tribunal fixed it at £39,000, slightly above the midway point between the two parties.

In that case, the tenant was thought to be in his late 60s. He had refused to surrender his tenancy at the time of the valuation date, although, about a year and a half later, he did surrender and the land eventually sold for over £126,000. As at the valuation date, it was considered unlikely that the family of the tenant could claim succession, so it fell to the tribunal to consider how soon the tenancy would fall in. The tenant might be likely to retire in eight years, and might live nearly four years after that.

The vacant possession value was fixed by the tribunal at £66,000. It then calculated the value of the freehold reversion by adding together a capitalisation of the existing rent, a figure for an increase in rent for the remainder of the term until possession might be acquired, and the value for the reversion discounted because possession could not be obtained immediately. These figures, taken together, produced a total of a little under £36,000. The tribunal considered that there had always been a possibility that the tenancy might fall in before the natural date of retirement or death of the tenant (as was indeed the case) and that the value of the reversion should be enhanced to allow for that by 10%. The resulting figure of £39,000 was 59% of the vacant possession value, as fixed by the tribunal.

Joint property: Arkwright v IRC

4.22   It is generally thought that the half share of a freehold property jointly owned by husband and wife must be equal to 50% of the value of the entirety. That view was challenged with ingenuity in two cases: *Arkwright v another (PRs of Williams deceased) v IRC* [2004] STI Issue 3 and *Price (Executor of Price, Deceased) v HMRC* [2010] UKFTT 474. They are worth detailed study. In *Arkwright v IRC*, Ashland Farm had been owned by Mr and Mrs Williams as tenants in common in equal shares. At the date of the death of Mr Williams, aged 83, Mrs Williams was aged 79 and in good health. Her husband had left her a life interest in the half share of Ashland Farm that he owned. Some months after the death, Mrs Williams and her daughters entered into a deed of variation that gave Mr Williams' share of the house to the daughters.

The value of that share of the house immediately before Mr Williams' death was the price that his interest might reasonably be expected to fetch if sold in the open market at that time. The parties agreed that, immediately before death, the house was worth £550,000. IRCT considered that the value of Mr Williams' share was £275,000. *IHTA 1984, s 171* provides that changes in the value of the estate of the taxpayer that occur by reason of the death and which fall within *s 171(2)* are to be taken into account as if they occurred before the death. *Section 171(2)* provides that a change falls within *s 171(1)* if it is an addition to the property comprised in the estate, or is an increase or decrease in the value of that property, unless the decrease arises from an alteration in the rights of shares within *s 98(1)*. However, *s 171(2)* specifically excludes from the operation of *s 171(1)* the termination on the death of any interest or the passing of any interest by survivorship.

As a separate argument, IRCT applied *s 161*, the related property provisions, the general effect of which is to deny the personal representatives any discount in respect of a share in joint property where the other share is owned by the spouse.

The executors took a different view. Immediately before the death of Mr Williams, a purchaser of his share of the property would have taken account of the fact that Mrs Williams owned the other half of the property and was in good health and had a right to occupy it. A purchaser would have recognised that he could not sell the property without the consent of Mrs Williams, and that would devalue the interest of Mr Williams.

IRCT regarded these arguments as being essentially arguments of value, that should go to the Lands Tribunal, rather than of statutory interpretation.

Dr Brice, as Special Commissioner, accepted the argument of the taxpayers that a purchaser would not pay full value for the share of Mr Williams but would discount it. Under the normal rules of valuation, the values of the shares owned respectively by Mr and Mrs Williams were not identical. Dr Brice then reviewed *s 171*. The proviso to *s 171(2)* had the effect that *s 171(1)* did not apply to the termination on death of any interest or the passing of any interest on survivorship but, in the present case, the interest of Mr Williams did not terminate on his death. It passed to his daughters. It passed to them not by survivorship but by the will, as varied. The value of his interest in the house would have changed by reason of his death, without regard to his actual death, because it would then have been a certainty and not merely a possibility that he would die before his wife. There was a decrease in the value of his interest, and his interest did fall within *s 171(2)*, so *s 171(1)* did not apply. As a result, the decrease in the value of his share that occurred by reason of his death should be taken into account in valuing his interest.

Next, Dr Brice considered the related property provisions of *s 161*. The scheme of *s 161* is, first, to fix the value of the entirety; and then to value each share in the property to establish a ratio. That ratio is then applied to the aggregate and, if the value of the share of the deceased is greater than the value of his separate share, the higher figure is taken. *Section 161(4)* provides a proportionate rule in relation to 'shares of any class', and applies similarly to stock debentures and units of any other description of property. IRCT argued that the shares of Mr and Mrs Williams were such units and that it followed that the ratio for the purposes of *s 161(3)* was one half. The personal representatives disagreed. Undivided shares in land were not 'units of property'. Dr Brice agreed with them, with the result that the value of the share of Mr Williams was not necessarily one half.

Dr Brice then considered the application by IRCT in respect of jurisdiction. Was this an appeal as to the value of land, that should have gone to the Lands Tribunal? Where an appeal had been brought to the Special Commissioners and included fixing the value of land, the correct procedure (see *s 222(4)–(4B)*) was not to strike out the appeal, as IRCT would have liked, but for the Special Commissioners to refer the matter to the Lands Tribunal. This arose from an amendment to *s 222* by *FA 1993* to correct a problem that had occurred in the past, in which an appeal must be made either to the Commissioners or to the Lands Tribunal. Under the new rules, it was no longer necessary, if the appellant picked the wrong tribunal, to start again with the other one. The Special Commissioners could accept the appeal, referring valuation questions to the Lands Tribunal, but all issues other than questions as to the value of land were properly to be determined by the Special Commissioners.

The Revenue appealed to the High Court, arguing that the Commissioner had exceeded her jurisdiction and that the case should be referred to the Lands Tribunal. Gloster J in part agreed with the Revenue. The Special Commissioner was entitled to conclude that the value of the deceased's interest in the property was not inevitably a mathematical one half because, in the circumstances, *s 161(4)* did not apply. Where the Special Commissioner had gone too far was in determining that, as a matter of fact, the value of the interest was less than one half. That was a matter for the Lands Tribunal.

Price (Executor of Price, deceased) v HMRC

4.23   The second case on this topic is *Price (Executor of Price, Deceased) v HMRC* [2010] UKFTT 474, in which the attitude of the taxpayer had great commercial reality and produced what many would consider to be a fair result. Mrs Price died in 1999, survived by her husband and four children, being at her death the owner with her husband of a house in London as tenants in common in equal shares. She gave her interest in the house to her children. The whole house was worth £1,500,000 but mortgaged for £364,164. The will was varied to leave the share in the house to the children, subject to the mortgage and to a charge of £260,000 in favour of residue, which went to the husband. It was agreed that half the house, valued on its own, would be worth £637,500. There was evidence that neither the deceased nor her husband contemplated a sale of the house.

Essentially, the case turned on the meaning in *s 161(1)* of the words 'the value of that and any related property'. The taxpayer argued that one should aggregate the two shares in the house, each being valued in isolation. HMRC said that one should value the whole as a single entity. The case was fully argued, the taxpayer being none other than Leolin Price QC, with Mr Ryder representing HMRC. Mr Price saw a distinction between shares in a house and units in a unit trust, and distinguished the *Arkwright* decision noted above. He also considered that the valuation of a share should take account of the notional cost of selling. He argued for a 15% discount.

Mr Ryder first argued that this was a matter for the Lands Chamber of the First-tier Tribunal the successor to, the Lands Tribunal referred to above, rather than the Tax Chamber, but that conflicted slightly with the statement of case. To interpret *s 161(1)*, one should, he said:

- fix 'the value of any property comprised in a person's estate'; then

- fix 'the value of the aggregate of that and any related property'; then

- fix the 'appropriate portion' of the latter value, using *s 161(3)*, ie the proportion which the value of the property in the estate bears to the sum of that value and the value of related property, but each being valued separately (in this summary, the 'last' value); and

- compare the values, taking the last value if higher than the first.

The shares must, Mr Ryder said, be aggregated before valuation, not after. As to the costs of sale, he (naturally) referred to *Tapp v Ryder* [2008] RVR 340, where he had persuaded the Lands Tribunal to disregard such items. That case was considered at **4.15**. He argued that deduction of one half of the mortgage debt should be a separate step, and that Mr Price's approach involved double counting.

The first part of the tribunal's decision concerned jurisdiction in the light of HMRC's review procedure and the reorganisation of tribunals, and concluded that it did have power to decide the case. Without feeling bound to accept the decision in *Arkwright*, and taking note of the comments of Hoffmann LJ in the Court of Appeal in *IRC v Gray (Lady Fox)*, the tribunal decided that it was right to value two assets held in the same estate on the basis that they would achieve a greater price if offered together, and applied that reasoning to *s 161*. Where *s 161* applies, the two items of property are to be valued as if offered for sale together and at the same time. There should be no deduction for expenses of sale. Debts are to be deducted separately. The detailed values, if not agreed, should be referred to the Lands Chamber.

THE VALUATION OF FARMHOUSES IN THE LIGHT OF *ANTROBUS NO 2*

4.24   Farmhouses pose special problems of valuation. In the same way that, for BPR, the recent case of *Hardcastle (executors of Vernede deceased) v IRC* [2000] STC (SCD) 532 applies a commercial basis and a 'relief' basis of valuation of the interest in a business, so the valuation of a farmhouse for general probate and IHT purposes may well be substantially different from its valuation for the purposes of APR. It is quite common for the District Valuer to argue that the agricultural value of a farmhouse represents no more than two-thirds of the value of the house on the open market.

The issues set out at **4.19**, relating to 'natural units' of valuation, are again relevant here. A situation may be imagined where the farmhouse, although occupied as such with a small acreage, does not in truth form part of a particularly viable agricultural unit and happens to adjoin a number of large and extremely viable farming units. In such a case, it might well be argued that almost any of the adjoining owners would be keen to add to their acreage but would not want the farmhouse which, like so many, is thus surplus to requirements. Such a situation might lead to lotting the house with, say, a paddock for Jennifer's pony, and to offering the land separately. This is indeed the assumption often made by the District Valuer.

There is some argument to support the idea that the value for APR should be as high as the open market value, on the ground that there is a ready market, in certain parts of the country, for a house with a sufficient cordon sanitaire of land to allow the owner both privacy and protection of attractive viewpoints. For many years, the law did not provide any administratively convenient rule of thumb. For example, different percentages applied for income tax and for VAT. However, the Lands Tribunal considered the issue of agricultural value of a farmhouse in *Lloyds TSB Private Banking plc (Personal representative of Rosemary Antrobus Deceased) v Peter Twiddy (HMRC Capital Taxes)* [2006] 1 EGLR 157, better known as *Antrobus No 2*. This was the sequel to the case discussed at **2.13**, where it was recognised by the Special Commissioner that the house in question, Cookhill Priory, was a farmhouse. This reference to the Lands Tribunal was on the issue of value, though the tribunal, in its decision, considered certain slightly wider issues. The open market value of the farmhouse and gardens was £608,475. HMRC argued that, of this amount, agricultural relief should apply to only £425,932.50, ie 70%. In the end, the tribunal fixed the agricultural value at the HMRC figure, but further decided that, if 'lifestyle' purchasers were included in the notional market, the right figure would be £517,203.75 or 85% of the open market value. Thus the outcome of the case is perhaps not far from what many people might consider reasonable, although the arguments and principles are important and, in the light of constant reliance by HMRC on the case, it merits detailed review here.

The taxpayer argued that the market for a farmhouse or farm that qualified for APR should include buyers who might be described as 'lifestyle' farmers with a career elsewhere. If 'lifestyle' farmers were excluded, the value of a house might be a great deal less because the other buyers would be farmers who were looking at the overall return on capital. There was evidence in this particular case of the people who might have been interested in buying the property. One offered £935,000, intending to refurbish the house and sell on for a profit. Others offered £1,000,035 and eventually got the property. There was another person, a chartered surveyor who was also a specialist farmer, who made an offer for the estate as a whole. This last person gave evidence that he would still have offered for the house provided that he was free both to farm the land and to carry on his business elsewhere; but that he would not have been interested if the property had been subject to a strict agricultural occupancy condition.

There was much expert evidence. On the one hand, Mr Beer of Savills argued that there was no other non-agricultural use of the property that would be in conflict with a perpetual covenant prohibiting its use otherwise than as agricultural property, so there should be no discount from market value. A covenant for agricultural use would have no adverse effect on the value, because the lifestyle buyer wanted privacy such as would be available where a farmhouse was surrounded by land. Such a buyer would actually welcome a restriction on use. However, it was clear from the evidence of Mr Beer that lifestyle farmers bid up the market, and that property which would eventually benefit from agricultural relief 'must top the lifestyle farm market, given the potential for 40% tax saving'.

Mr Swallow, for the Valuation Office, argued for a discount of 30%, on the basis that the agricultural covenant could never be lifted and that the effect of the law was to require 'the hypothetical purchaser to continue to occupy the house as a farmhouse, together with sufficient agricultural land or pasture to make the house of a character appropriate to the land'. He concluded that, for the purposes of discount, one should look at 'a working farmer, mainly engaged in agricultural operations on the land'. He therefore argued that a covenant in compliance with *s 115(3)* would have the effect of excluding lifestyle farmers from the market: 'Restricting demand to full-time working farmers would result in the price realised for the residence being significantly less than it would otherwise have been'.

Mr Swallow looked at the profit that could be earned from farming, the land that a non-farming purchaser would have to acquire and the cost of that acquisition. The return available from a joint farming venture would be extremely modest in relation to the investment involved. He produced evidence of discounts relating to properties subject to planning tie between 25 and 40%, and specific examples of discounts of 32.4% and 23.6%. What should be excluded from the agricultural value was the overbid for the farmhouse, with a small area of land adjoining it, from non-farming residential purchasers. The amount of that excess would depend on location, setting, views etc.

For the taxpayer, William Massey QC argued that a lifestyle farmer would satisfy the requirements of *s 115(3)*. There was no need for a farmhouse to be occupied by someone who was on the premises during the working day. There was no need for the occupier to be the person who was managing the farm on a day-to-day basis. Farming could be carried on in different ways, including short-term grazing lets, share farming, contract farming. The farmer could do the paper work but leave others to do the 'hands-on' work.

Phillip Jones, for HMRC, argued that the dwelling in question must be occupied by the person who was managing the farm on a day-to-day basis. Drawing an example from earlier legislation, he highlighted the distinction between a working farmer, who lived in a farmhouse, and a landed proprietor, who lived in a mansion house. Although the occupier of the mansion house might still technically carry on a farming business, that did not mean that his dwelling house was a farmhouse.

The tribunal preferred the evidence of the District Valuer and the arguments of the Revenue. It held that:

> 'a farmhouse is the chief dwelling house attached to a farm, the house in which the farmer of the land lived. There is, we think, no dispute about the definition when it is expressed in this way. The question is: who is the farmer of the land for the purpose of the definition of section 115(2)? In our view it is the person who lives in the farmhouse in order to farm the land

comprised in the farm and who farms the land on a day to day basis... We do not think that a house occupied with a farm is a farmhouse simply because the person living there is in overall control of the agricultural business conducted on the land; and in particular we think that the lifestyle farmer, the person whose bid for the land is treated by the appellant as establishing the agricultural value of the land, is not the farmer for the purposes of the provisions.'

In support of that, the tribunal considered various arguments, concluding that, 'the concept of the farmhouse is as the dwelling of a working farmer who requires a suitable house to support his working life'. The tribunal paid attention to the old legislation for 'working farmers'. Whilst Mr Massey had argued that the requirement of the working farmer conditions was removed when the law was changed, the tribunal did not feel that that changed the meaning of 'farmhouse'. It did not change what amounted to 'agricultural property'. The tribunal went further, so as to review the meaning of 'cottages' and to observe that buildings on a farm used to a minor extent for agricultural purposes but mainly for car repairs would not be agricultural buildings within *s 115(2)*.

The tribunal came back to the limitations commonly applied in planning restrictions, namely to restrict the occupation of the dwelling to a person solely or mainly working, or last working, in the locality in agriculture or in forestry, or the widow or widower or dependants of such a person. *Section 115(2)* is more restrictive than the planning tie because it will not do simply to be working 'in the locality'. The planning condition allows for people 'last working in agriculture', and again *s 115* is more restrictive. Finally, a planning restriction can be removed, whereas the restriction in *s 115(3)* is permanent. Taking these factors together, the tribunal concluded that the HMRC approach was right, even conservative.

The tribunal then reviewed the four cases of *Lindsay v CIR*, *CIR v John M Whiteford & Son*, *Starke v IRC,* and *IRC v Korner.* The conclusions that they drew from these cases was that the purpose of the legislation 'is to accord relief to the operational components of agricultural units'. On that basis, the agricultural value of a farmhouse fell to be determined on the assumption that the perpetual covenant would have prevented its use in any other way and would therefore exclude the 'lifestyle' purchaser. Based on that decision of principle, the tribunal reviewed specific examples.

The tribunal therefore accepted the argument of the District Valuer and fixed the agricultural value of Cookhill Priory at £425,932.50. Having done that, the tribunal then considered what the value might be if their interpretation of the legal position was incorrect, and if demand from lifestyle farmers might be taken into account when calculating the agricultural value. Based on the evidence, the tribunal considered that the lifestyle purchaser would still offer less for a property subject to a restrictive covenant than one that was not so subject. On that basis, they concluded that, if lifestyle purchasers were in the market, the agricultural value would be £517,203.75.

PLANNING EXERCISES RELATING TO TENANCY VALUATION

4.25   A landowner and a farmer might make arrangements which were designed to ensure that the farmer had no security of tenure. Such arrangements were put in place before the enactment of the *Agricultural Tenancies Act 1995*. One scheme involved the grant of a tenancy to an intermediary, who in turn granted a sub-tenancy to the farmer. The intermediary, on receiving notice to quit from the landowner, would fail to serve a counter-notice, thus losing his security of tenure. Under the common law, the sub-tenancy would fall with the tenancy. This scheme was reviewed by the House of Lords in *Barrett v Morgan* [2002] 2 AC 264. Lord Millett there also considered the situation where the intermediary surrendered the tenancy to the landlord. In such a case, ie surrender, he considered that there would be no automatic termination of the sub-tenancy, because surrender of the end tenancy is not the unilateral act of the landlord but occurs by agreement between landlord and tenant. The intermediary could not by this means prejudice rights that had been created in favour of the farmer sub-tenant.

Naturally the question arises, and it was considered by the Court of Appeal in *Barrett v Morgan*, as to whether these arrangements amount to collusion between the freeholder and the intermediary. That had been the view of the Court of Appeal in *Sparkes v Smart* [1990] 2 EGLR 245, but that earlier decision was overruled. Any agreement by the intermediary not to serve a counter-notice is void: that had originally been decided in *Johnson v Moreton* [1980] AC 37, a decision that Lord Millett affirmed in *Barrett v Morgan*. As a result, in pre-1995 Act cases, there must always be a risk that the intermediary will fail to serve a counter-notice, following service on him of a notice to quit by the freeholder. For as long as that situation applies, there must be a risk that the basis of valuation for APR is the 50% tenanted basis, on the ground that the freeholder is not entitled to vacant possession within 12 months, as required by *s 116(2)(a)*. As a result, and this will turn on the facts, 100% APR in such circumstances may be available only by reliance on ESC F17. Subject to the general point that a Concession cannot be relied upon where tax avoidance is in issue, F17 extends the period, within which the landowner must obtain vacant possession, from 12 months to 24 months.

Against this background, if it is essential for planning purposes to ensure that APR is available at 100%, it is probably not safe to rely upon an old 'intermediary'-style structure. It is probably better to bring to an end the existing sub-tenancy and create a new farm business tenancy direct to the farmer, bypassing the intermediary. In the light of the decision in *Barrett v*

Morgan, that the sub-tenant does not have security, it may now be easier than hitherto to persuade the farmer to cooperate. He must now accept that he no longer has the security that he may have thought he had. He should, therefore, be more ready to accept a new farm business tenancy, giving the landowner APR at 100%.

SALES OF SHARES WITHIN 12 MONTHS OF DEATH

4.26 There is a general rule, not specific to shares qualifying for APR or BPR, under *IHTA 1984, s 179* by which a claim may be made by 'the appropriate person' for relief so as to reduce the value of the estate for IHT by the amount of the loss suffered on selling shares within 12 months of death. It will be of limited application to APR cases. Where the loss arises because the securities are sold, it is the date of the contract which determines the availability of the relief. The rule relates to 'qualifying investments', defined by *s 178* as quoted shares or securities or holdings in unit trusts which, as is explained in the chapters on BPR, includes shares listed on the Unlisted Securities Market or, now, the Alternative Investment Market.

The difficulty of a claim lies in the fact that, if there is more than one sale of a qualifying investment, all the sales must be aggregated for the purposes of the relief: the taxpayer can 'cherry pick' his losses only by not selling, within the relevant period, those securities which stand at a gain. He may, however, 'cherry pick' in a different way. He may, as executor, transfer those securities which stand at a gain to the beneficiaries *in specie*, such that the gains are realised by the beneficiaries personally. He can then let the losses arise within the estate, where they may form the basis of a claim for relief.

There is a school of thought, prevalent amongst charities, that the executor should, wherever possible, appropriate assets to the charity-beneficiary 'in book form' (which is not a term of art and which may simply mean that no formal appropriation actually takes place) and then sell on the instructions of that charity (which will not be subject to CGT). In the opinion of HMRC, the personal representative must show that he has placed the asset at the disposal of the beneficiary, even if it remains in the name, but not in the control, of the executor. At times, this may simply not be possible or appropriate: the power of appropriation is generally available only at the discretion of the personal representatives (*Butterworths Probate and Administration Service*, vol 2, para 379). The beneficiaries have no power to demand its exercise. Often, executors will refrain from assenting to the vesting of property in order to save Land Registry fees. This may prove to have been false economy, where significant tax is in issue.

The relief relates only to sales effected by the 'appropriate person', who is the person liable for the tax. Where there is more than one person who falls within the definition in *s 178(1)*, the relief is available to the person who actually pays the tax. The relief is also restricted where new shares or securities are purchased by the appropriate person during a period which starts with the date of death and ends not within the 12-month period but within two months after the last sale in respect of which a claim is made: see *s 180(1)*. That is unlikely to happen where APR is claimed on shares in a farming company. There are special rules relating to capital receipts, payment of calls and changes or exchanges relating to holdings. For further particulars of this relief, the practitioner is referred to *ss 178–189*.

Note the unfortunate result of particular circumstances in *Lee and another (executors of Lee Deceased) v IRC* [2003] STC (SCD) 41. An asset was discovered long after the death and had, by the time of its discovery, fallen in value. The 12 months had expired. The Special Commissioner, although sympathetic, had no power to extend the period.

LAND SOLD WITHIN FOUR YEARS AFTER DEATH

4.27   Whilst the rule in *IHTA 1984, s 179* will seldom apply to property qualifying for APR or BPR, the similar rule in *s 191* may often be relevant. Originally, the rule allowed a claim in respect of land sold within three years of death but, from and after 16 March 1990, the period was extended: *FA 1993, s 199*. Where an interest in land forming part of the deceased's estate is sold by 'the appropriate person' within the period of four years immediately following the date of death and that person makes a claim (stating the capacity in which he makes it), the value of the interest in land, and of any other interest in land comprised in the estate which is also sold within that period by the person making the claim, is the sale value. That general rule in *s 191(1)* is qualified by *de minimis* provisions in *s 191(2)*. There is no relief where the fall in value is less than £1,000 nor where it is less than 5% of the probate value. Similarly, the relief does not apply (see *s 191(3)*) on the sale by a personal representative or a trustee to:

- a beneficiary; or

- the spouse, child or remoter descendant of the beneficiary; or

- trustees of a settlement under which a beneficiary (or spouse, child or remoter descendant) has an interest in possession in the property sold; or

- a sale under or by virtue of which either the vendor or any of the persons mentioned in the categories above obtains a right to acquire the interest in the land or any other interest in the same land.

These exclusions are absolute: there is no saving provision, even where the land in question is sold at market value. It will be noted that the restrictions apply neither to a sale to a parent of the beneficiary nor to trustees of a discretionary settlement. The 'appropriate person' defined in *s 190(1)* means, as in relation to the relief for shares, the person liable for the tax or, where there is more than one such person, the person who actually pays it.

An interesting attempt to exploit the relief was examined in *Jones (Balls' Administrators) v IRC* [1997] STC 358. In that case, the deceased died on 26 June 1988. He owned a farm. Letters of administration were granted to his son on 14 December in that year. On 25 June 1991, the son contracted to sell the property for £300,150. Completion was to take place a month later, but did not in fact take place. The son served notice to complete. Still nothing happened. On 22 August 1991, the son forfeited the deposit. He died only weeks later. On 23 December 1991, letters of administration were granted to the taxpayers in the matter, who found a new buyer for the farm. Contracts were exchanged on 28 January 1992 and completed on 25 February 1992.

On 17 May 1995, the taxpayers agreed the probate value of the farm with IRCT in the sum of £447,000, and purported to make a claim under *s 191* on the ground that there had been a sale in 1991. IRCT refused the claim, as did the Special Commissioners. The taxpayers were no more successful in their appeal to the High Court, which held that, for the purposes of the relief, a sale did not mean the exchange of contracts which did not proceed to completion. That would be inconsistent with the wording of *s 191(3)(b)*, which refers to the reduction of the value of an interest 'for any other reason'. The whole tenor of the code in *ss 191–198* pointed to a completed transaction. The draftsman clearly understood the distinction between a completed sale and a mere contract. The relief was refused.

Example 4.9: selling off the estate assets

Susan died on 20 December 2008. Her estate included three parcels of land. Low Cottage was valued for probate at £75,000 and sold in April 2009 for £74,100 realising a loss of £900. Top Pightle, valued for probate at £110,000, sold for £10,000 more than that in June 2009. Broadacres was valued for probate at £230,000 but proved difficult to sell, realising only £218,000 in September 2010, a loss of £12,000.

The loss of £900 is ignored under the *de minimis* provisions. The profit of £10,000 is set against the loss of £12,000 with the result that a claim may be made to reduce the estate overall by £2,000.

Is it possible to exploit *s 191* so as to achieve a beneficial result for the purposes of CGT? One learned commentator certainly used to think so, but the law has since been revised by the case of *Stoner (executors of Dickinson deceased) v IRC* [2001] SpC 288, [2001] SWTI 1501; see **14.21**.

SALES OF RELATED PROPERTY WITHIN THREE YEARS AFTER DEATH

4.28   *IHTA 1984, s 176* applies where, within three years after the death of the transferor, there is a qualifying sale of property which (author's numbering):

(*a*) (i)   was comprised in his estate immediately before his death; and

   (ii)   was valued in accordance with the related property provisions of *s 161*; or

(*b*) (i)   was valued in conjunction with property which was also part of the estate; but

   (ii)   has not at any time since the death been vested in the vendors.

Section 161 itself provides that, where the value of any property comprised in the person's estate would be less than the appropriate portion of the value of that property, if taken together with related property, the value of the portion of the property in the estate is to be regarded as the appropriate portion of the value of the entirety.

This related property valuation rule applies (see *s 16(2)*) so as to regard property as being related to the property in a person's estate where:

● it is part of the estate of the transferor's spouse; or

● it is, or has within the preceding five years been, the property of a charity or held on trust for charitable purposes only or has been the property of one of the bodies mentioned in *s 24, 24A, 25* or *26* (political parties, housing associations, national purpose gifts, public benefit gifts) and that property became the property of the charity or other public body on a transfer made by the transferor or his spouse after 15 April 1976 and was exempt to the extent that the value transferred was attributable to the property.

If a claim is made under *s 176*, the property may be valued, as at the date of death, without reference to the related property. The conditions for this treatment are:

● the sale must be by the persons in whom the property is vested immediately after the death or by the personal representatives;

● the sale must be at arm's length, the price freely negotiated and unconnected with the sale of any of the related property;

- no seller is to be connected with any purchaser, nor is any person having an interest in the sale proceeds to be connected with any purchaser nor, in either case, is there to be any connection with any person who has an interest in the purchase; and

- neither the vendors nor anyone having an interest in the sale proceeds is, in connection with the sale, to secure the property 'by the back door', by acquiring an interest in the property sold or an interest created out of that property.

A special rule applies to shares or securities of a close company. Relief under *s 176* will not apply where, between the death and the sale, the value is reduced by more than 5% and that reduction arises from an alteration in the share capital of the company, or its loan capital, or any rights attaching to either.

Finally, the *s 176* rules may also apply where the property was not part of the estate of the deceased, but was valued at his death in conjunction with other property which he did not devolve on the vendors. This might, for example, be property comprised in a settlement where the deceased was tenant for life.

VACANT POSSESSION OF LAND HELD OUTSIDE A PARTNERSHIP

4.29   Quite often, the owner of agricultural land will be a member of the partnership but will hold the land personally. The situation may arise where the partnership occupies the land on a mere licence, without any partnership agreement or any document setting out the terms of occupation. This will be a partnership at will. It follows that the partnership can usually be brought to an end on the next accounting date following the giving of notice. *Partnership Act 1890, s 32* relates to dissolution of a partnership by notice (see *Lindley and Banks on Partnership* (17th edn) at 24–19). Effectively, the dissolution occurs on the dates:

- specified in the notice; and
- on which the notice is communicated to all partners.

The basic rule, in *Partnership Act 1890, s 26* is that, subject to any contrary agreement between the parties (and often there will be none), retirement is achieved simply by notice.

Relying on *Harrison-Broadley v Smith* [1964] 1 All ER 867, HMRC argue that, until the partnership can be determined, the landowner does not have vacant possession. Under *IHTA 1984, s 116(2)(a)*, 100% APR might be denied in such a circumstance. The period of 12 months has been extended by ESC F17, as already noted, but that Concession relates to 'tenanted agricultural land' and not to land which is subject to a mere licence.

Clearly, where the practitioner is aware of the difficulty, it is relatively easy to put in place a partnership agreement which gives the landowner the right to vacant possession within 12 months. In practical terms, the difficulty may be in persuading families operating in an area not noted for its formality that they should have a partnership agreement at all. A full-blown partnership deed may not be needed: it may be enough to record an agreement as to what will happen in the event of the death of the owner of the land occupied by the partnership.

Chapter 5

Business property: property qualifying for the relief

QUICK GUIDE

There are six categories of property that may qualify for BPR: see **5.2**. Of these, the commonest are direct interests in a business, as a sole trader or partner, and unquoted shares in trading companies. Most businesses that are carried on with the prospect of gain will qualify for BPR. The exceptions are considered in later chapters.

It was long thought that relief attached to an interest in a business rather than a 'mere asset'. The CGT retirement relief definition was adopted (see **5.10**), but that view was successfully challenged. Special and detailed rules apply to Lloyd's Names and 'Namecos': see **5.13** onwards. With limited liability partnerships, there is scope to 'look through' to the owner.

Land and buildings, machinery and plant that are owned outside a business but used in it attract relief at 50%: see **5.28** onwards. The meaning of the word 'property' in this connection has been extended to suit changing circumstances.

INTRODUCTION: THE CONCEPTS

5.1   Over the years, two features characterised the treatment of BPR: the extension of BPR; and gradual simplification of the relief. *FA 1975* provided relief for business property only in the option to pay tax by instalments interest free. Reliefs were introduced at 30% for transfers after 6 April 1976, and at multiple rates from 27 October 1977. Overall, the reliefs were increased slightly with effect from 15 March 1983, and significantly from 10 March 1992 when *F (No 2) A 1992* increased the old 50% relief to 100% (except in the case of quoted shares) and the old 30% to 50%.

Simplification was achieved by *FA 1996, s 184* which amended *IHTA 1984, s 105(1)* so as to extend the 100% relief to all holdings of unquoted shares, however large or small. That change also achieved some administrative simplification, in that it applies to any transfer of value on or after 6 April 1996 and to any charge to tax arising on an earlier transfer which occurs by reason of an event which occurs on or after 6 April 1996: see *FA 1996, s 184(6)(b)*. The rules applicable after 6 April 1996 affect both the value of the estate charged on a death after that date and the calculation of cumulative transfers before the death.

The practical effect of this evolution is that many of the finer distinctions which characterised BPR are of interest only to practitioners who have old cases still unresolved. The regime seems quite stable: there has, so far, been little change under the present government, though there are no doubt pressures within the coalition on this as on other issues. If in doubt, 'bank' the relief.

RELEVANT BUSINESS PROPERTY: THE SIX REMAINING CATEGORIES

5.2   *Section 105* now provides that 'relevant business property' means:

(*a*)   property consisting of a business or an interest in a business;

(*b*)   securities of a company which are unquoted and which, either by themselves or together with other such securities owned by the transferor and any unquoted shares owned by the transferor, gave the transferor control of the company immediately before the transfer; and

(*c*)   any unquoted shares in a company.

(By virtue of *s 104*, property which falls into the above three categories qualifies for relief at 100%.)

Section 105 goes on to include as relevant business property:

(*d*)   shares in, or securities of, a company which are quoted and which, either by themselves or together with other such shares or securities owned by the transferor, gave the transferor control of the company immediately before the transfer;

(*e*)   any land or building, machinery or plant which, immediately before the transfer, was used wholly or mainly for the purposes of a business carried on by a company of which the transferor then had control or by a partnership of which he then was a partner, and

(*f*)   any land or building, machinery or plant which immediately before the transfer was used wholly or mainly for the purposes of a business carried on by the transferor and was settled property in which he was then beneficially entitled to an interest in possession.

(*Section 104* allows relief at 50% in respect of these three categories.)

Each category of relevant business property is examined below.

SECTION 105(1)(A): BUSINESS OR AN INTEREST IN A BUSINESS

5.3   'Business' is not defined and has its ordinary wide meaning. It need not be in the United Kingdom or the European Economic Area (in which respect, BPR differs from APR). Assets deposited with Lloyd's by individual underwriters qualify as business property (see later in this chapter). A business, to qualify for BPR, must be carried on for gain. It may include the exercise of a profession or vocation.

'Business' has a wider meaning than 'trade': see *Comr of Income Tax v Hanover Agencies Ltd* [1967] 1 AC 681, a case from Jamaica coming before the Privy Council. To calculate the chargeable income of a company, the Revenue rejected a claim for wear and tear in respect of one of the buildings occupied by a tenant of the company. The Court of Appeal found in favour of the taxpayer. The Revenue appealed. The word 'business', the Privy Council held, must be given its ordinary meaning unless the context otherwise required. Since the company was carrying on a business of negotiating leases and collecting rents from their properties for the purpose of *section 8(o)* of the *Income Tax Law 1954*, the profits on which they were assessed were profits arising from that 'business'. The court there distinguished the case of *Fry v Salisbury House Estate Ltd* [1930] AC 432, which had held that annual income from the ownership of land could only be assessed under Schedule A, and that the option of the Revenue to assess under whatever schedule they might prefer did not exist. The schedules were mutually exclusive.

Activities constituting a business

5.4   In *Land Management Ltd* [2002] SpC 306, a corporation tax case, the issue was whether an associated company of the appellant had carried on a business at certain times. To reach a conclusion, the Special Commissioner must decide whether the activities of that associated company constituted 'business', so this case offers a useful catalogue of situations, with the Special Commissioner's views set out below.

One activity was the management and letting of freehold property. The company paid for insurance, repairs and renewals and professional fees. Held, in each of four years of account, the associated company did carry on business in managing and letting of property.

The associated company also held and made investments. Held, the activities of a company whose income was mainly derived from the making of investments did constitute a business. The company paid administration expenses and distributed dividends. The making and holding of investments amounted to the carrying on of a business.

The associated company made a loan to the appellant company for which it charged interest. Held, whilst the making of a loan by an individual would not be a business, the associated company was incorporated in order to make profits and was therefore bound to make the best use of its assets, which in the present case included the making of loans. Making the loan amounted to carrying on a business.

The associated company placed money on deposit at the bank. Held, that on its own might not have constituted the carrying on of business by the company but, in the light of the other activities, it did constitute the carrying on of a business.

On all of these grounds, the associated company was in business in each relevant year, which was fatal to the appeal by Land Management Limited.

Non-investment businesses

5.5   In *Phillips' Executors v HMRC* [2006] SpC 555, a company lent to other family companies. A widow had held a majority shareholding on which, following her death, HMRC had rejected a claim to BPR on the basis, discussed at length in **Chapter 9**, that it was making or holding investments. Held, the company was the banking arm for in-house transactions. Few would regard the activities of a moneylender as investment. The company made the loans, but it did not invest in loans. The loans were not investments for their own sake, but the provision of finance for the other companies, so BPR was allowed.

In *Clark and another v HMRC* [2005] SpC 502, which is considered in greater detail in **Chapter 9**, it was held that management of properties was a business, albeit in that case it was 'swamped' by a business of holding investments.

DWC Piercy's Executors v HMRC [2008] SpC 687 concerned a property development company that owned land on which it had built workshops for letting. The executors of a major shareholder claimed BPR, but HMRC denied it on the ground that the company received substantial investment income and its business was therefore mainly making or holding investments, an issue examined in **Chapter 9**. The executors claimed that the company was still trading; it still held undeveloped land that it wished to develop for housing, but had to wait for uncertainty to be resolved concerning proposals for a new railway line. The Commissioner found that the land was still held as trading stock, not as an investment, and allowed the appeal.

Business, but of the wrong kind for relief: McCall v HMRC

5.6   *McCall and another (Personal Representatives of McClean deceased) v HMRC* [2009] NICA 12 concerned the taxpayer's attempt to secure BPR on farmland that had hope value. The agricultural value, at the date of death, was £165,000 but the market value was £5,800,000. The evidence was not entirely convincing as to how much time the son-in-law of the deceased spent on caring for the land, which lay on the edge of a town. Its boundaries were occasionally challenged, as when a van was driven into the fields and abandoned, resulting in a claim under the *Criminal Damage (Compensation) (Northern Ireland) Order 1977.*

The son-in-law walked the land, repaired the fencing, cleaned drinking troughs, cleared the drainage systems of mud and leaves, cut and sprayed weeds. For these purposes, he had a tractor and reaper and a knapsack sprayer. He probably worked no more than 100 hours per year. Some work was contracted out. The grazier fertilised the fields.

The Commissioner reviewed the authorities, including several mentioned above, and in particular the indicia noted by Gibson J in *C & E Commissioners v Lord Fisher* [1981] STC 238. He concluded that the son-in-law's activity of tending the land:

> 'was, just, enough to constitute a business ... The letting of the land was earnestly pursued, the work tending the land was modest but serious, the letting and tending were pursued with some continuity, the income was not insubstantial, the letting was conducted in a regular manner although the use of [the son-in-law's] time was something which is not a feature of an ordinary business, and the letting of land for profit is a common business. To my mind the Lord Fisher indicia point towards a business.'

An element of the case turned on ownership of the business, since the deceased had lost her mental faculties (this will frequently be in point but is not relevant to the present issue under discussion, of whether the business should qualify for relief). It was held in this case that the business was more than just the ownership of the land and receipt of its income. The deceased, despite her disability, owned the business constituted by the activities of her son-in-law and the letting of the land.

However, the taxpayers' case fell because the business consisted wholly or mainly of holding investments, within *s 105(3)*. After a detailed consideration of the nature of farming arrangements under the law of Northern Ireland, which may not be of general application, the Commissioner held that, 'The test to be applied is that of an intelligent businessman, not a land lawyer. Such a person would be concerned with the use to which the asset was put'. The deceased was making the land available, not to make a living on it but from it; the management activities related to letting the land; it was unlike 'hotel accommodation for cattle', as suggested by the taxpayer; nor was it like a:

> 'pick your own fruit farm, where after months of weeding, fertilising spraying and pruning, customers are licensed to enter to take the produce and pay by

the pound for what they take away; in the business of letting the fields there was less preparatory work, the fields were let for the accommodation of the cattle as well as for the grazing, and the rent was paid by the acre rather than by the ton of grass eaten.'

The Court of Appeal confirmed the decision of the Special Commissioner on the basis that the farmer whose animals grazed the land had exclusive rights, so could prevent others from using the land. The business of the deceased consisted in earning a return from grassland.

Quite apart from the concern that the decision caused in Northern Ireland, where the practice known as agistment of land is widespread, taxpayers everywhere will now worry that their farming arrangements will fail the *McCall* test. Often the practitioner will know his farming clients well and will have visited the farm occasionally. This is essential preparation for any dispute with HMRC, because all the cases show how the evidence is key to the decision. While it is not essential that the business should make a profit every year for it to fail the 'carried on otherwise than for gain' test in *IHTA 1984, s 103(3)*, the practitioner must be willing to see the set-up 'with through eyes', not of a friendly rural colleague, but of an educated businessman, or a potential purchaser.

Example 5.1: poor old chap needs help

Willows Farm has belonged to the Swallow family for three generations. From 1926 to 1950, grandfather ran cattle and sheep on the pasture, some of which, by the stream, was quite boggy, so grazed for only part of the year. His sons followed, replacing the heavy horses with second-hand tractors and farming without paid help. The elder son became disillusioned in 1970, so the business was split, and some of the better land and two cottages were sold off. The younger son, burdened with debt, carried on with (unpaid) help from his wife and daughter. From 1995 onwards, the greater part of the land was put into a contracting agreement, leaving the farmer with some of the pasture on which to fatten cattle; but even that became too much, the cattle were sold and a grazing agreement put in place. Only the single farm payment (SFP) now provides funds to service the outstanding mortgage, because the contractor in effect takes all the income from the land apart from the SFP. The daughter now lives with her family in the village nearby. Following the death of the wife, the farmer's house is both lonely and neglected; it is not really the centre of farming operations, even though the old man does still walk the land each day and supervises the animals for the grazier. He maintains the hedges and fences as far as the weather and his health allow.

How can the adviser help here? First, see how the accounts of the farm are presented. Ensure that any positive aspects are emphasised and income properly characterised, ie not shown as 'rent'. Check what records are kept of the work the farmer still does. Does the daughter visit regularly? Does she do the books? Would it be feasible for her and her family to move in with father? That, coupled with a gift of a share in the house covered by the rule in *FA 1986, s 102B(4)*, would compensate her family for having to live with granddad, and the proceeds of sale of her present house might finance renovation of the farmhouse, with provision of a good farm office as well as privacy for all. If she has teenage children, the extra space will be some compensation for living further out. If there is no local employment, even working on the farm is better than nothing. If the family can increase their involvement in farming operations, they may be able to save the business by increasing turnover and direct profit. They will also strengthen the APR claim on the house itself, where the tax may be significant. The big problem is likely to be investment in new machinery, the need of which was the spur for the contracting agreement in the first place, and learning the skills to use it. If the adviser can make a good case to a lender that the changes may save significant tax, finance may be available.

Authors, painters, sculptors

5.7   At one time, HMRC sought to exclude the businesses of authors and other professional persons such as musicians, painters and sculptors from BPR, perhaps on the grounds that the definition for IHT does not treat a professional vocation automatically as a business. There is a distinction here between IHT and VAT. For BPR, there has to be a business before relief can apply. This is discussed in greater detail at **5.13**.

Unincorporated business

5.8   There is an important distinction between the activities of an individual, or of partners, and those of a company. The mere receipt of rents by an individual from property is not regarded as carrying on a business, but for a company the rule is different: see *American Leaf Blending Co SDN BHD v Director General of Inland Revenue* [1979] AC 676. That was a Malaysian case where, after abandoning a tobacco business which had made losses, the company let a warehouse which was part of its business premises. Three years later, the remainder of the premises became empty and were also let. By the following year, five successive lettings of the premises had been made. The company was assessed to income tax in respect of the rents received. It claimed set-off of the earlier losses. That claim was disallowed on the ground that the lettings did not amount to the carrying on of a business. The company appealed to the Special Commissioners of Income Tax and thence to the Privy Council.

The Privy Council allowed the appeal on the wording of *s 4* of the *Income Tax Act 1967*, applying *Hanover Agencies Ltd* and distinguishing *Salisbury House Estate Ltd*. Where a company had been incorporated for the purposes of making profits, any gain from a use to which it put its assets *prima facie* amounted to the carrying on of a business. Although the fact that the letting of its premises was included in the objects of the company, that was not conclusive in deciding that the company was carrying on a business, since the only conclusion of fact which any reasonable Commissioners could reach from the evidence was that the company was carrying on a business of letting its premises for rent. Notably, it was observed that:

> 'the carrying on of "business", no doubt, usually calls for some activity on the part of whoever carries it on, though, depending on the nature of the business, the activity may be intermittent with long intervals of quiescence in between. In the instant case, however, there was evidence before the Special Commissioners of activity in and about the letting of its premises by the company during each of the five years that had elapsed since it closed down its former tobacco business.'

There is helpful guidance in the VAT case of *C & E Comrs v Lord Fisher* [1981] STC 238, where Ralph Gibson J found (at page 245) six factors to be considered, namely:

(1) Is there 'a serious undertaking earnestly pursued' or 'a serious occupation, not necessarily confined to commercial or profit-making undertakings'?

(2) Is there 'an occupation or function actively pursued with reasonable or recognisable continuity'?

(3) Has the activity 'a certain measure of substance as measured by the quarterly or annual value ... of supplies made'?

(4) Was the activity 'conducted in a regular manner and on sound and recognised business principles'?

(5) Is the activity 'predominantly concerned with the making of ... supplies to customers with consideration'?

(6) Are those supplies 'of a kind which, subject to differences in detail, are commonly made by those who seek to profit by them'?

These criteria have been relied on regularly in BPR and APR cases.

The restrictive effect of s 105(3)

5.9 Perhaps the most important provision to consider in defining 'relevant business property' is the exclusion contained in *IHTA 1984, s 105(3)* which applies 'if the business or, as the case may be, the business carried on by the company consists wholly or mainly of one or more of the following, that is to say, dealing in securities, stocks or shares, land or holdings or making or holding investments'. The subject is considered in greater detail in **Chapter 9**.

Exception to s 105(3)

5.10   A business or an interest in a business or shares or securities of a company escapes the denial of relief contained in *s 105(3)* where (see *s 105(4)*) the business is:

- wholly that of a 'market maker' or of a discount house, and in either case is carried on in the UK; or

- that of a holding company of one or more companies whose business does qualify.

'Market maker' means, by virtue of *s 105(7)*, a person who holds himself out at all normal times in compliance with the rules of the Stock Exchange as willing to buy and sell securities, stocks or shares at a price specified by him and is recognised as doing so by the Council of the Stock Exchange. By *FA 1986, s 106(4), (6)* and *(8)* the Board of HMRCmay make regulations to modify that definition. That power has been used (see the *Inheritance Tax (Market Makers) Regulations 1992, SI 1992/3181*) in relation to transfers of value and other events occurring after 22 March 1992. The effect of those regulations was to include, within the reference to the Stock Exchange, 'LIFFE (Administration and Management)', which had become a recognised investment exchange within the meaning of the *Financial Services Act 1986*.

Woodlands

5.11   Woodlands managed as a business qualify in the same way as other property for BPR. The relief, as is explained in **Chapter 11**, applies to the land and other assets used in the business, trees and underwood.

Sole proprietor's business

5.12   This category is the simplest form of property qualifying for the relief. Eligibility for relief will in part be determined by the ability of the taxpayer to demonstrate that there is actually a business, ie that the activities carried on have sufficient commercial purpose. As will be seen in the examination of the 'wholly or mainly' test, HMRC will argue that an unprofitable business falls foul of the test required by *s 103(3)* that it be carried on for gain. In practice, it may well be harder for the sole trader to resist a claim under *s 112(6)*, that particular assets are not used wholly or mainly for the purposes of the business, than might be the case with a larger trading entity.

This is a difficult area: the accounts may flatter the strength of the balance sheet by including significant assets that are not really much help in generating profit. The rules as to the general operation of *s 112* are considered in greater detail in **Chapter 7**. Equally, accounts of sole traders may be very conservative, recognising profit only when invoices are paid, and disregarding the value of any asset that cannot readily be liquidated, on the basis that 'cash is king'. That is fine from a commercial point of view, but it can restrict claims to BPR. After death, it may be hard to prove that a specific asset, perhaps a building, has been part of the business if it is not in the balance sheet. The courts have recognised that a sole trader 'is', in one sense, the business, seeing no distinction between work and play and between his various assets.

A special rule relates to the carrying on of a profession. If one spouse inherits the assets of the profession of the other spouse, and then carries on that profession, the successor spouse has, in the view of HMRC, started a new 'business'. The successor will not be able to count the period of ownership of the deceased spouse towards his or her own period of ownership.

Authors, artists, sculptors and musicians

5.13   Specific provisions apply to the treatment of authors, who will generally carry on business alone. BPR was refused by HMRC in the past because it was considered that the special nature of the business of an author was such that it ceased on the death of the author and could not be transferred during lifetime, being so personal. It was argued that the value of the business of the author lay in copyrights producing royalties, and that all that could therefore be given away was not a business but the mere copyright, holding of which was an investment. Therefore, the 'mere asset' test applied to deny relief, because it was impossible for the author to transfer the business as a whole.

The policy behind this was that BPR was intended to minimise the risk that the payment of capital taxation might disrupt or liquidate a healthy business which could otherwise have continued after the death of the owner. Such a policy consideration would not and could not apply to authors. Other creative artists might be in the same position. However, the attitude of HMRC in recent years seems to have relaxed slightly. The facts may support the BPR claim, as where, prior to the death, business accounts show that the royalties are actively managed. It may help if turnover is high enough to require VAT registration. Even though an artist may, in his or her later years, no longer do much painting (and this might be more true of sculptors), there may be a substantial body of work unsold which the artist promotes and sells from the studio.

Likewise, an elderly composer who no longer produces many new symphonies may be active in attending concerts of her works and in encouraging the young to perform any music, and preferably some of hers. The fact is that, sadly, many musicians and artists fade from the public awareness after death unless the catalogue is vigorously promoted. This may involve the cost of engraving works that previously existed only in manuscript: most musicians, and certainly most amateurs, much prefer to perform from 'proper' printed scores, so the expense may be essential to get the less well-known *oeuvre* into the public domain. 'Music isn't music until it's performed'. It will help a later claim to BPR that the composer, in her lifetime, actively managed her work.

BPR may be allowed in respect of 'personal copyrights' of a deceased or of a majority shareholding in a company which owns the copyrights. This does not help the gift of a copyright during the lifetime of the author, which will probably not qualify for relief, unless the decision in *Nelson Dance v HMRC* [2009] EWHC 71 (Ch) (discussed at **5.16**) can be extended. For an illustration of the difficulty of assigning royalties, see the income tax case of *Braithwaite v HMRC* [2008] SpC 674, where an attempt to transfer half the income from royalties on a dry powder inhaler failed to achieve its objective.

Partnership interest

5.14   The interest of a partner in a business is not an interest in the underlying assets but in the proceeds of the sale and division of the assets of the partnership. That argument is not used to deny BPR on the ground that it is an interest in the proceeds of sale. Instead, interest in a business does include the interest of a partner, provided that that interest is not merely by way of a loan. A loan, being a liability of a business, is not part of its net value (see **Chapter 8**). The interest may be in any joint venture, including foreign forms of association not recognised in UK law.

The 'mere asset' exclusion: review of the early cases

5.15   *IHTA 1984* appears to draw a distinction between an interest in a business and the underlying assets. The law has received a fresh interpretation in the *Nelson Dance* decision, analysed below. There is a strong similarity between the test applied here and that applied under the rules for CGT for retirement relief. An important distinction is that, in retirement relief, the relevant wording concerns the 'disposal of the whole or part of a business' rather than 'property consisting of a business or interest in a business'. Nevertheless, a knowledge of the principles which were relevant for retirement relief is helpful here (and will again be relevant for practitioners who have to advise on CGT entrepreneurs' relief).

Sale of a small part

In *McGregor v Adcock* [1977] STC 206, there was a disposal of five acres from a holding of 35 acres on which the taxpayer had been carrying on mixed farming. The taxpayer continued to farm the rest of the land, but claimed that the sale of the five acres, on which he had obtained planning permission, was a disposal of part of his business entitling him to retirement relief. It was held that nothing suggested that the sale had seriously altered the scale of the business or interfered with the farming which could be described as amounting to a disposal of part of the business. There was simply the sale of an asset, and not part of the business.

Was there a major change in the business?

Two appeals came before the Commissioners in 1988 on similar facts. In *Mannion v Johnston* [1988] STC 758, the Commissioners found on the facts that, after the sale, there had been a major change in the business of the taxpayer and, on that basis, there had been a disposal of part of the farming business. In *Atkinson v Dancer* [1988] STC 758, the various parts of the mixed farming business of the taxpayer depended on each other. Following the sale of part of the land, it was not possible to continue with the remainder. On appeal by the Revenue in both these cases, the principle emerged that a change in the activities of a business, or in the assets of the business occasioned by anything other than sale, was irrelevant. It was correct to consider the business activities before and after the sale. If the position after that sale was wholly different as a result of changes caused by the sale, then the sale might be regarded as of a business or of part of a business. Two separate disposals should not be taken together, as if a single transaction, unless both formed part of the same contract.

Nelson Dance

5.16   The main challenge to the 'mere asset' rule is in *Trustees of the Nelson Dance Family Settlement v HMRC* [2009] EWHC 71 (Ch), which is worthy of detailed review. Mr Dance, farming as a sole trader, transferred to a settlement land and buildings used in that trade. He died only two years later, so relief must be tested. Agricultural relief was not in issue: the taxpayer wanted business relief, because the land had development value. HMRC denied relief on the basis that what Mr Dance had transferred was not an interest in his farming business but a 'mere asset'.

The taxpayer argued that we must look not at the asset transferred, but at the transfer of value, and apply the 'loss to the estate' principle. The estate of Mr Dance was reduced by the transfer. What was reduced was the value of his farming business. He had been in farming for many years, so the transfer of value fell to be reduced by business relief. There was no policy reason to deny relief, since the business would be carried on, and not disposed of.

HMRC said that reference to the value of a business implied that the transfer was of a business (or of part of a business that could be separated from the remainder). The policy of the relief is to encourage business and the transfer of businesses, so it requires restriction to transfers of businesses or parts of them.

The Special Commissioner could see a distinction between those cases, such as spouse relief, where the identity of the recipient is important and that person must receive certain property, and the present situation, where the basis of relief is the transfer, and not the underlying asset. 'Value transferred' in *IHTA 1984, ss 3(1)* and *104(1)* must mean the same thing. Where the value was attributable to business property, the Special Commissioner said that all the taxpayer must show is that the value transferred should be attributable to the net value of a business, commenting (at para 16):

> 'All these form part of an overall scheme. Everything turns on the loss in value to the donor's estate, rather than what is given or how the loss to the estate arises, except where the identity of the recipient is crucial to a particular exemption.'

This differed from several textbooks that the Special Commissioner had consulted (and earlier editions of this one, though not mentioned). The Commissioner could not see how those authors had reached their conclusions. The phrase 'a business or an interest in a business' in *s 105(1)(a)* defines a category of property that qualifies for relief; the context of *Chapter 1* of *Part V* of the *1984 Act* implied that only property comprised in one of the categories set out in *s 104* was 'relevant business property'. The argument put forward by the taxpayer in *Nelson Dance* was ingenious but probably not what the draftsman envisaged.

On appeal, the High Court upheld the Special Commissioner's decision. It was enough for BPR purposes that the diminution in value of the transferor's estate by reason of the transfer was attributable to the value of relevant business property. The land had been used in the farming business. Its transfer could be attributed to the value of the business. BPR was therefore available. Sales J stated:

> 'For BPR to be available in respect of a transfer of value relating to a business there is no requirement that the property transferred should be a business which retains its character as a business in the hands of the transferee, or even that the property transferred should itself have the character of a business ... the simple issue in each case is whether the value of the transferor's relevant business property decreased as a result of the transfer of value; the issue is not as to the nature or value of the assets transferred, looked at in isolation.'

The decision opens up planning opportunities for sole traders and partners wishing to transfer business assets into trust with the benefit of BPR (and CGT holdover relief), whilst continuing to carry on the business. Particularly in the case of trading assets, the decision whether to transfer them into trust must be considered carefully, if the business interest would qualify for BPR 100% in any event. There is some limitation on the decision: it does not help investors. Mr Dance was clearly in business, and not merely the owner of a business asset. The new rule does extend BPR to the transfer by an investor of a 'mere asset', save where it falls within the 50% categories in *s 105(1)(d)* or *(e)*.

Disposal of part of a partnership share

5.17   Relief under *s 105(1)(a)* is in respect of 'a business or interest in a business': that does not, it is argued, mean '*the whole of* a business or *the whole of an* interest in a business'. Thus, as will frequently happen in practice, BPR may be allowed where a sole proprietor of a business takes another person into partnership and transfers to that person part of the capital, ie a share both of the assets and liabilities as identified in the balance sheet of the business, as the capital of that sole trader. By extension of that principle, one partner among many may (doubtless only with the consent of the others) divide his existing interest, as identified by his capital account in the balance sheet of the partnership, between himself and another person and claim BPR on that transfer.

What may be less certain is whether a mere book entry is enough.

Example 5.2: movements in capital account

Ellen farmed in partnership with her sons Fred and George. The capital account showed, at Michaelmas (this was a traditional firm) 2002:

Ellen	20,000
Fred	10,500
George	8,000
	38,500

By Michaelmas 2003, the balances were:

Ellen	24,000
Fred	12,000
George	7,000
	43,000

During 2004 ,the farming merely broke even, but a road widening scheme yielded to Ellen £100,000 in respect of farmland held outside the partnership. She paid the compensation into the farm account and instructed her accountant to transfer £80,000 of the capital to Fred and George equally. He showed the balances at Michaelmas 2004 as:

Ellen	44,000
Fred	52,000
George	47,000
	143,000

On Ellen's death in 2005, her executors wished to claim BPR on the £80,000 gift. The claim failed as to £60,000, because Ellen's capital from the two-year period prior to transfer had been £20,000. As to the £20,000, the claim succeeded. It was helped by the fact that there was a clear instruction to make a gift, which was promptly acted on. Ellen had in fact signed off the 2004 accounts. It was not merely a case of writing up the books after her death with the benefit of hindsight.

For a case that crossed the boundaries between partnership, quasi-partnership and a company, see *Rahman v Malik and others* [2008] EWHC 959 (Ch), concerning interests in a restaurant. The son of one of the founders of the business, having been thrown out by his uncle, four years later petitioned under *Companies Act 1986, s 459* alleging that his exclusion, the non-payment of dividends and under-declaring of profits all amounted to unfair prejudice. The court agreed, notwithstanding the nephew's delay, and ordered the uncle to buy the nephew's shares.

One business or several? What is the interest?

5.18   It is quite possible that a person may own more than one business, keep one and give away the other. In relation to farming, attempts are frequently made to distinguish one farming enterprise from another, especially in order to claim retirement relief on the disposal of one such enterprise. For BPR, it will be a question of fact whether the transfer is truly of a business in its own right or is merely a gift of a bundle of assets. If mere assets, the gift will qualify for the relief if it can be brought within the terms of *Nelson Dance*. Whilst the test is not the same as the transfer of 'a trade', as that expression is employed in *ICTA 1988, s 213* in relation to demergers, the kind of situation in relation to identification of separate trades for the purposes of demerger legislation may also serve to identify what is 'a business' rather than 'a mere asset' for the purposes of BPR.

The exact nature of an interest arose in *Oakley and another (PRs of Jossaume Deceased) v IRC* [2005] SpC 460. The case may not be of general interest or application, but it does show how important are the basic principles of land law and the law of trusts to the tax analysis. The issue was whether a building yard was to be treated as part of the estate of the widow of the deceased on the basis that she had an interest in possession. It was held that the trusts of a will (as substituted by deed of variation on the earlier death of the husband) came to an end on the death of the widow. The substituted will curiously gave an interest in possession to the family company, and not to the widow, even though on the earlier death the husband's estate had been taxed as if there had been a spouse-exempt transfer to the widow. The case turned on whether the direction in the substituted will that the company need pay no rent was dispositive or merely administrative. It was dispositive: this may in future be relied upon by HMRC, in circumstances such as non-payment of rent for occupation of a residence.

Lloyd's underwriters: the assets that qualify for BPR

Premium income deposit fund; special reserve fund

5.19   The premium income deposit and the special reserve funds of a Lloyd's underwriter qualify for BPR. Commonly, assets are deposited with Lloyd's as security for any obligations in respect of underwriting business. The assets so deposited will qualify for BPR provided that they are not excessive in value compared with the risks underwritten. Any excess will be regarded as an excepted asset under *IHTA 1984, s 112* (see **Chapter 7**). Here a distinction is made between sums in respect of which accounts are closed and sums deposited to support open years.

Bank guarantees

A shareholder in an underwriting company at Lloyd's may provide collateral to support the activities of that company, the 'Nameco'. Originally, HMRC considered that 100% BPR was available on the collateral assets themselves. They now consider that no BPR is available on the collateral, but that the valuation of the collateral assets for IHT purposes must take account of the negative value to the estate of the fact that those assets are provided as security for the underwriting.

The formula is complicated. First, value the open years and the possibility that the collateral assets will be drawn on. Then discount the value of the assets to take account of the period for which they will be subject to the collateral guarantee. These factors will together provide the value for BPR purposes.

Assets securing both Nameco and personal underwriting

The arrangements are different where assets secure not only collateral security for the Nameco but also for the personal underwriting by the shareholder. These assets are known as 'inter-available funds at Lloyd's'.

There was a transition affecting such assets, with different rules applying in respect of deaths that occurred on or before 31 December 2004 and those on or after 1 January 2005.

Deaths occurring on or before 31 December 2004

For deaths to which these rules apply, Names that had converted to underwriting through a Nameco could, within certain limits, attract BPR on the value represented by third party assets put up as funds at Lloyd's. If a shareholder put up his own assets to support the company underwriting, BPR would, generally speaking, be available on those assets, including amounts guaranteed under bank guarantees. However, there was a cap on the relief: it was only allowed on the level of funds that were needed for 2002. Further, relief was not given in respect of funds that greatly exceeded the level of underwriting as a whole. Full BPR was allowed on inter-available funds at Lloyd's up to the level needed for 2003.

Deaths on or after 1 January 2005

The new rules allow BPR on the value represented by the inter-available funds as needed for the underwriting of the individual Name. The funds will qualify for BPR only insofar as they are proportionate to the unlimited liability underwriting. No BPR will be given on assets put up as third party funds at Lloyd's. The valuation of those assets for the purposes of IHT must take account of the negative value of the arrangement for the estate of funds at Lloyd's. However, BPR will be allowed on inter-available assets if they are held as funds at Lloyd's, including the amount of bank guarantees, insofar as those inter-available funds are not disproportionate to the unlimited liability underwriting of the Name.

Where BPR is refused, because there is no personal unlimited liability underwriting, the valuation of the assets for IHT must take account of the negative value of the funding arrangement. This will involve a difficult valuation exercise. It will be necessary to value the open years and the likelihood that the assets will be drawn on, and then to discount the value of the relevant assets to allow for the fact that they are not freely disposable but are held as funds at Lloyd's.

The result of this change may be that it is attractive to hold assets within Nameco because the shareholder in a Nameco can effectively get relief on the value of assets held within that company by the ordinary BPR route of holding shares in an unquoted trading company. The difficulty, however, is that a Name who wishes to transfer assets to Nameco may incur a CGT charge on the transfer in.

Lloyd's Name losses

5.20   Clarification of the treatment of losses, in relation to BPR claims on behalf of the estates of deceased Names, emerged in *Hardcastle (Executors of Vernede deceased) v IRC* [2000] STC (SCD) 532, although HMRC consider the case to be one decided on its own particular facts (see below).

At the date of his death, Mr Vernede belonged to 11 Lloyd's syndicates. His estate protection plan policy, with an excess of £251,900, indemnified his estate against losses arising in respect of underwriting results not notified before death. The executors completed the Inland Revenue account so as to show that the net value of the interest in the business was £265,507. That was the amount of the funds held at Lloyd's. That was also the sum in respect of which the executors claimed BPR.

As a separate item, the executor showed in the Inland Revenue account that there were underwriting losses for years prior to death which amounted to £301,301. These were certain deferred losses and the excess under the estate protection plan policy. No demand had been received for payment of the deferred losses at the date of death. The executors claimed to offset the losses not against the value of the interest in the business, but against the estate as a whole. The Inland Revenue thought that to be the wrong treatment. The executors appealed.

By the time of the hearing before the Special Commissioner, the dispute concerned only the amounts owed by the deceased in respect of years that were open at the date of his death. By virtue of the insurance policy, the amount in issue was therefore £251,900. The question was whether the money owed on these open years was, within *s 110(b)*, 'a liability incurred for the purposes of the business'. The Inland Revenue had argued that the deceased's trading contracts, which might have given rise either to profits or to losses, were choses in action. They were assets because they were the means by which the business was carried on. It followed, their argument went, that, if the contracts were profitable, those contracts would increase for BPR purposes the net value of the interest of the deceased in the business. It should also follow that, where a trading contract went the other way, it gave rise to a liability incurred in the course of carrying on the business, and it was therefore incurred for the purposes of the business.

The Special Commissioner disagreed. Two tests were to be applied here: first, one must calculate the valuation of a business for general IHT purposes; and, second, one must calculate the value of the business for the purposes of BPR. The first basis of the valuation (described below as the 'commercial' basis) is to be determined by reference to *s 5*, which defines the meaning of 'estate' for IHT. The commercial basis includes not only assets and liabilities but trading profits or trading losses.

The second basis of valuation, which we describe as the 'relief' basis, is the more restricted one, and is concerned only with the assets used in the business and the liabilities incurred for the purposes of the business. It had been agreed both by the executors of Mr Vernede and by the Revenue that trading losses were not liabilities incurred as such for the purposes of the business. The question was whether the trading contracts that gave rise to those losses were assets used in the business.

For the purposes of the relief basis of valuation, some help could be drawn from the distinction, in income tax, between expenditure which brings into existence an asset for the enduring benefit of the trade and ordinary commercial contracts. In that context, insurance contracts in which a result has not been notified are ordinary commercial contracts made by the deceased in the course of carrying on his underwriting business. They are contracts for the disposal of his 'product'. The product dealt in is the assumption of a risk in return for a premium. Seen in that light, a contract which produced a loss was not a liability incurred for the purposes of a business. On that basis, the Special Commissioner found for the executors.

It was reported subsequently in *Lloyd's Market Bulletin* that HMRC considered the *Hardcastle* case to have been reached on its own particular facts and thus not to illustrate a principle of general application. They will, therefore, continue with the practice that existed before *Hardcastle*, ie open year losses will be deducted from other Lloyd's assets, and BPR will be allowed on open year profits. This was the basis for which HMRC had argued in *Hardcastle* but which the Special Commissioner did not accept. The point that seemed to have been established in *Hardcastle* was that ordinary liabilities incurred in the day-to-day running of the business would not reduce the value of the business for BPR. The implications, if that were to be a general principle, could affect the valuation of all businesses. In light of that, it is perhaps understandable that HMRC should wish to limit the effect of *Hardcastle*.

There are implications for the drafting of wills leaving business property (see **15.10**).

Assets supporting the underwriting business

5.21   Generally, the assets deposited will be stocks and shares. Occasionally, underwriters deposit letters of credit or bank guarantees instead, because the underwriters may wish to use their personal capital in another way or do not wish to realise certain assets such as gold. HMRC are willing to accept as qualifying for BPR assets taken by way of collateral security or bank guarantees or letters of credit. This is, however, subject to the requirement that the asset in question is restricted in use and cannot be used for personal benefit. The usual conditions as to the period of ownership must be complied with.

Where an individual Lloyd's Name provides a guarantee as part of his funds, 100% BPR is allowed up to the amount of the guarantee that is used or required as funds at Lloyd's. There has been a change of practice by HMRC, as noted at **5.19** above. The amount of BPR is no longer restricted by reference to the nature of the underlying asset. This was the case where assets backing the guarantee were not used wholly or mainly for the purposes of the Lloyd's business (see below). This restriction also used to apply if a guarantee was secured on a main residence the value of which was greater than the amount of the guarantee itself.

The value of an underlying asset is reduced by the amount of the guarantee for the purpose of giving any other reliefs or exemptions.

HMRC offer two examples.

Example 5.3: guarantee in place

N is an individual Member and Lloyd's Name. He is a farmer. The farm is worth £1 million. The other assets are £1,250,000. The farm qualifies for APR at 100%.

There is a bank guarantee of £400,000 secured on the other assets.

The calculation of APR and BPR on death is as follows.

The valuation of the Lloyd's interest, which qualifies for 100% BPR, is ignored for the purposes of this example, as are any other reliefs.

Farmland	1,000,000
Other assets	1,250,000
	2,250,000
Less BPR (£400,000 on bank guarantee)	(400,000)
APR on farmland	(1,000,000)
Net estate after reliefs	850,000

There is no reduction in the value of the farmland, because the bank guarantee is not secured on it.

Example 5.4: guarantee secured on the land

A similar example, but the guarantee is secured on the farmland. The IHT calculation, ignoring valuation of open years and other reliefs, is as follows:

Farmland	1,000,000
Other assets	1,250,000
Total	2,250,000
Less BPR (on bank guarantee)	(400,000)
APR (on farmland)	(600,000)
Net estate after reliefs	1,250,000

This issue was examined by the Special Commissioner in *Mallender (Executors of Drury-Lowe deceased) v IRC* [2001] STC 514.

The deceased had a personal reserve of quoted shares. There were also bank guarantees of £100,000 in all. These guarantees were based on an indemnity which the deceased had given to the bank against all liabilities. That indemnity was in turn secured by a charge over freehold property which the deceased owned. The property itself, 'the Denby land', which had been worth £1.2 million in May 1991, was worth about £1 million in July 1993 when the deceased died. It was subject to a coal mining lease. The rent was £170,000 per annum but British Coal was the only realistic operator. The lease itself was a depreciating asset. The executors considered that the value of the freehold should qualify for BPR, but HMRC determined that, for the purposes of *s 110*, the value of the property itself should be excluded. The relevant business asset for the purpose of relief was simply the guarantee. The executors appealed.

The Special Commissioner took a realistic approach. Banks do nothing for nothing: no bank guarantee would have been forthcoming without security. The minimum security in the circumstances would have been £142,858 but, in fact, security was provided of over £1 million. That was enough to satisfy the Special Commissioner that the land itself was one of the assets used in the business and that the net value of the freehold should be included for the purposes of relief.

On appeal to the High Court, HMRC succeeded. The Denby land was not used in the underwriting business. In calculating net value, the liabilities must be set against assets used in the business. It did not matter that the guarantee was supported by a charge on the land.

Where the value of the assets forming the collateral security exceeds the maximum amount payable under the guarantee, BPR will apply only to that proportion of the collateral security which is needed to meet it. There can be no more relief than the value of the assets used as security at the time of transfer.

Succession

5.22 Is there succession to the business of a Name? The point is uncertain. Underwriting as a profession is, in many respects, personal to the Name. The succession provisions in *ss 108* and *109* (see **Chapter 6**) do not in general apply. Inheriting the assets which a Name used for underwriting is not an automatic inheritance of the underwriting capacity and business. That is not to say, however, that the personal representatives of the Name cannot continue the underwriting business in succession to the Name during the administration period.

The right to a share in the profit of the syndicate is an asset of the business qualifying for BPR. The business of corporate Lloyd's Members may likewise qualify for the relief. The taxation of Lloyd's Names is a specialised subject. It is dealt with at HMRC through Shares Valuation Division at Fitzroy House, PO Box 46, Castle Meadow Road, Nottingham, NG2 1BD.

Limited partnerships and limited liability partnerships (LLPs)

5.23 Under the *Limited Partnerships Act 1907* a partner may contribute a defined amount of capital to the partnership and his liability may be limited to that amount. The partnership must be registered with the Registrar of Companies showing the details of the amount of the capital of the limited partners. Such a partnership must contain at least one general partner whose liability is not so limited.

As to LLPs, *s 267A* was inserted into *IHTA 1984* by the *Limited Liability Partnerships Act 2000 (LLPA 2000)* with effect from 6 April 2001 and provides that, for the purposes of *IHTA 1984* and of any other enactment relating to IHT:

• the property of the limited liability partnership is treated as the property of its members and that property used by such a partnership is treated as being used by its members as partners; and

• the business carried on by the partnership is treated as carried on in partnership by its members; and

• incorporation of the partnership, or any change in its membership, or its dissolution, is treated as the formation, alteration or dissolution of a partnership; and

• any transfer of value made by or to a limited liability partnership is treated as being made by or to the members of that partnership and not by the partnership itself as such.

Whilst a full consideration of *LLPA 2000* is outside the scope of this book, it should be noted that LLPs will be governed by certain provisions that are imported from company law rather than from partnership law: the participators will be members rather than partners; there must be two members but there is no upper limit; and certain members will be designated in a way similar to the directors and secretary of a company.

Accounts and formalities

5.24 The LLP will have to prepare accounts in a style which is similar to that of companies. They must be true and fair, published and filed. The requirements will be different according to the size of the partnership. There is provision in *LLPA 2000* for audit. The limited partner is not allowed to take any part in the management of the firm's business or to bind the firm. He may give advice to the other partners. Importantly for tax purposes, a limited partner is treated in the same way as a general partner, except that, for the purposes of income tax, there is a restriction on the amount of loss for which he may claim relief.

The interest of a member in an LLP may be capital or a loan. The capital may attract BPR but the loan will not, any more than a loan to an unlimited partnership would, unless for some reason it is 'an interest' in the business, but that will be rare. That accords with the SORP *Accounting by Limited Liability Partnerships.*

Jersey LLPs

5.25 It is not known whether a Jersey LLP should be regarded for tax purposes as a partnership or as a company. This was the point in issue in *R v IRC, ex p Bishopp* [1999] STC 531. In that case, PricewaterhouseCoopers wanted confirmation from HMRC that such a partnership would be regarded as a partnership rather than as a company. HMRC would not comply. The same point was troubling Ernst and Young. Again, HMRC would not answer. Both firms therefore applied for a declaration that, if they registered as Jersey limited liability partnerships, they would continue to be partnerships for the purposes of UK tax law. The accountants wanted certainty in their business affairs, and sought a judicial review to ascertain their true tax position as a matter of law before being assessed on a particular basis.

The court also refused to answer the question. Parliament provided certain clearance procedures and certain rights of appeal or challenge. That was an area where the taxpayer could examine the conduct of the Revenue. Parliament did not allow, except in those limited circumstances, clearance before transactions. It would open the floodgates to answer hypothetical questions.

The present dispute was based on hypothetical facts. It was not certain that either firm of accountants would register as a Jersey LLP even if it secured the ruling it wanted. Neither HMRC nor the court would, normally, answer abstract questions. The applicants were not entitled to an answer on the point and the court would not give it. The applications were dismissed.

Transition to LLP

5.26   Tax Bulletin issue 50, December 2000, clarified issues somewhat in relation to the incorporation of a partnership as an LLP. Periods of ownership will continue for APR and BPR (see also **6.9** onwards).

IHTA 1984, s 94, which relates to the charge on participators where a transfer is made by a close company, will not apply because transfers of value are treated (see *s 267A(d)*) as being made not by the partnership but by its members. Thus the reliefs available to the 'old' partners are available to members of the LLP. This will be relevant where a disposition occurs which is not intended to confer any bounty. *Section 10* will apply.

The position as far as Scottish partnerships are concerned is slightly clearer. A Scottish partnership is a separate legal person distinct from the individual partners. But for the saving rule in *s 119(2)*, a difficulty could therefore arise for a member of a Scottish partnership, whether limited or otherwise, as to occupation of land, since it would be the partnership that occupied the land rather than the individual. That would flow from *Partnership Act 1890, s 4(2)*. As a result of *s 119(2)*, this difficulty is removed, and occupation of any property by a Scottish partnership is treated as occupation by the partners.

SECTION 105(1)(B): UNQUOTED SECURITIES GIVING CONTROL

5.27   This heading mainly refers to securities such as loan stock which, either by themselves or with other securities or with unquoted shares, gave the transferor control of the company immediately before the transfer. It is not necessary, except where clawback of relief is in point, for either the transferor or the transferee to have control after the transfer has taken place. Since 6 April 1996, when 100% BPR became available to this category of asset, the reference to control applies only to securities under this heading and not to unquoted shares themselves.

Assets in this somewhat specialised class qualify for BPR only if they have votes attached to them and form part of a controlling holding. Therefore, whilst the 1996 changes made the issue of control much less important in relation to shareholdings, it is still necessary to examine the subject for the purpose of unquoted securities. In *I C McArthur's Executors v HMRC* [2008] SpC 700, a valuation case, the taxpayer held shares in three family investment companies and had lent money to two of them. The loans carried rights to acquire further shares, like convertible loan stock. The Special Commissioner rejected the taxpayers' argument that those rights had little value.

To qualify for BPR, the securities in question must give the holder control of the company immediately before the transfer. It follows that, where a transferor has, quite independently of the securities within *s 105(1)(b)*, enough ordinary shares to have control, the securities do not attract BPR because they do not give him control. It is the shares that give control in their own right.

Example 5.5: wise use of classes of shares

Druckmaschinen GmbH is a fairly typical middle-sized German company, part of the *Mittelstand*. The shares are held by the founding family. There are in issue 1 million 'A' shares, carrying ten votes each, and 5 million 'B' shares carrying one vote each. 'A' shares and 'B' shares in other respects carry the same rights, particularly as to dividends. Helmut, now aged 78, holds 700,000 'A' shares and the same number of 'B' shares, giving him 7,700,000 votes. Helmut is domiciled and resident in Germany and BPR is of little concern to him.

The remainder of the 'A' shares are held by Helmut's daughter, Elke, who also holds 2 million 'B' shares. The remaining 2,300,000 'B' shares are held by employees of the company and by trusts for the benefit of employees. Elke, married to an Englishman, has lived in the United Kingdom for so long that she is deemed to be domiciled here. She appreciates that her 'A' shares qualify for BPR because they are unquoted. There is, however, a listing on the Frankfurt Stock Exchange for the 'B' shares, so Elke is at risk of a charge to IHT on the value of her 'B' shares, as matters now stand.

Taken together, her shares give her only 5 million votes. Elke consults Geoff, who is keen to persuade Helmut to hand over the bulk of his shareholding to Elke, on the general principle that it must be a good idea to pass value down the generations. Helmut is not yet ready for such a drastic move. Fortunately, Geoff refers the detail of the matter to Melissa, who does the sums. Melissa is able to advise Elke that, if Helmut can be persuaded to release some of his shares, a substantial saving can be achieved. Elke needs only 2,500,001 more votes to have control. If Helmut is willing to give Elke 250,000 'A' shares and one token 'B' share, Elke will have control and Helmut will still retain, for the purposes of dividends, a great deal of his original holding. The saving will arise because Elke's 'B' shares will now, when taken with her 'A' shares, qualify for BPR at 50% under *s 105(1)(b)*.

The meaning of 'control'

5.28   The definition of 'control' is set out in *IHTA 1984, s 269*. The basic test is that a person has the control of powers of voting on all questions affecting the company as a whole which, if exercised, would yield a majority of the votes capable of being exercised on those questions. By *s 269(2)*, the related property rules of *s 161* (described more fully in **Chapter 8**) operate so that securities are deemed to give a person control of a company if they would be sufficient to give control if taken together with related property. Where shares or securities are comprised in a settlement in which there is an interest in possession, the tenant for life is deemed to have the powers of voting which the shares or securities give to the trustees of the settlement. This does not apply (see *s 269(3)*) to a discretionary trust.

A limited rule applies where shares or securities have powers of voting limited to the question whether the company should be wound up, or a question which primarily affects shares of securities of that particular class. In those circumstances, *s 269(1)* is treated as meaning a reference not to all questions affecting the company as a whole but to all questions other than any in relation to which those powers are capable of being exercised. In other words, the fact that a company has one or more classes of shares with restricted voting rights will not prevent a person from having control.

Certain questions of fact may arise here. For example, two unconnected persons may each hold half the shares of a company, with the chairman of the meeting having the casting vote. It is quite possible that one of those shareholders may, for most of his life, act as chairman. Suppose that person suffers an illness leading to death, during which, naturally, the other shareholder carries on the business and acts as chairman of meetings. At the time of the death, it cannot be said that the first shareholder has been exercising control of the company through his position as chairman. He does not have control at the time of his death.

This was substantially the issue in *Walker's Executors v IRC* [2001] STC (SCD) 86. The deceased owned land used for the purpose of a company of which she held 50% of the shares. She was chairman of the board of directors and, by virtue of the articles of association, enjoyed a casting vote at general meetings. To secure BPR, her executors must show under *s 105(1)(d)* that, at the date of her death, the deceased had control of the company. HMRC determined that she did not.

On appeal to the Special Commissioners, the executors argued that the casting vote gave control, because the deceased had control of powers of voting on all questions affecting the company as a whole which, if exercised, would yield a majority of the votes capable of being exercised on them. HMRC had argued that, when exercising her casting vote as chairman, the deceased owed a fiduciary duty in her capacity as an officer of the company. Had there been any conflict between her personal interest and that of the company, she could not have used her casting vote.

The Special Commissioners found for the taxpayer. The mere fact that the deceased might be trustee of the casting vote did not mean that she did not have control of the powers of voting. *Section 269(3)* makes no reference to fiduciary duties. The deceased, therefore, did control the company and was entitled to 50% BPR on the value of the land it used.

Occasionally, shareholders will have special voting rights, in particular enough extra votes to outvote all the other shareholders on the question whether that person be removed as a director. Such rights were considered in *Bushell v Faith* [1970] AC 1099. The existence of such additional rights effectively dilutes the voting control of a shareholder who, on all other issues, has a majority holding of voting shares. This is because that majority shareholder will not have a majority on all questions affecting the company as a whole.

Walding v IRC [1996] STC 13 again illustrates the point that the capacity of a shareholder to exercise votes does not affect control. There, the deceased held 45% of the voting share capital of the company, and her four-year-old grandson held 24%. On her death, her executors argued that the deceased had control of the company because the grandson could not exercise votes attached to his shares. The executors failed.

Where, as noted above, shares are held in a relevant property trust, the related property rules cannot apply. Unless the trustees hold more than 50% of the company, they will not qualify for BPR. This is an interesting and awkward planning point. Suppose that two majority shareholders jointly settle substantial holdings on the same trustees on relevant property trusts. Although the trustees are the same, there are actually two separate settlements. To exercise control, the trustees need to control more than 50% of the votes of the company. It is arguable that they hold two separate holdings, neither of which gives control.

The issue of control also arises in relation to quoted securities (see **5.30**). Securities which form part of an estate which has not yet been fully administered may qualify for the relief, and may count towards control, to the extent that the transferor of them was beneficially entitled under the rules in *s 91* (see **6.12**). This is also true of unquoted shares in an unadministered estate. Control need not be direct. This is examined in relation to quoted shareholdings below.

SECTION 105(1)(BB): UNQUOTED SHARES

5.29   50% BPR was available prior to 6 April 1996 on small (ie less than 25%) holdings of unquoted shares. The relief was not available in respect of loan stock. From 27 October 1977 to 14 March 1983, the relief was available at 20%, then increased to 30% until 9 March 1992, and 50% thereafter until the sweeping away of these smaller classes of shares by the *FA 1996* amendments with effect from 5 April 1996. Here the benefits of the simplification in the regime for BPR are most apparent. It is no longer necessary to consider the rules as to detailed voting rights which applied before 6 April 1996. From that date, all unquoted shares qualify for BPR at 100% regardless of the size of the holding. The meaning of 'unquoted' has been discussed earlier in this chapter and is considered at **6.19**. The expressions 'quoted' and 'unquoted' remain in the wording of *s 105(1)* even though, in the changes introduced by *FA 1996*, the expression 'listed' was generally used: see the frequent use of that term in *FA 1996, Sch 38*, creating an annoying anomaly. Shares listed on AIM, ETHEX and some on PLUS are unquoted for this purpose.

The legislation does not limit relief to ordinary shares as such. It just refers to 'any unquoted shares in a company'. Whilst loan stock is not 'shares', preference shares and/or redeemable shares are not specifically excluded from BPR. Some planning centres on this point, but may be seen by some advisers as provocative.

Unquoted shares will not qualify for BPR if the company is an investment business nor, generally, if the company is in liquidation nor if there is, at the time of death, a binding contract for sale. For an 'inspector's view' of the basic tests of companies for BPR, read the flowcharts in IHTM25022, 25023 and 25024.

SECTION 105(1)(CC): CONTROLLING HOLDINGS IN A QUOTED COMPANY

5.30   Among the categories of property qualifying for BPR at 50% is a holding which is listed or quoted on a recognised Stock Exchange and which gave the transferor control of the company immediately before the transfer. For a commentary on the meaning of 'quoted' and of 'recognised Stock Exchange', see **Chapter 6**.

SECTION 105(2): RESTRICTION ON RELIEF

5.31   The meaning of 'control' takes in the whole of the aspects mentioned in relation to unquoted securities set out above, with one additional consideration. This arises from *s 105(2)*. Shares in or securities of a company do not fall within *s 105(1)(cc)*, the category of security now under consideration, if:

- those shares or securities would not have been enough, without other property, to give the transferor control of a company immediately before the transfer; and

- their value is taken to be less than the value previously determined by reliance on *s 176*.

Section 176 is a specific rule concerning related property where, within three years after the death of the transferor, there is a qualifying sale of any property comprised in the estate of that person immediately before death ('the property concerned') and valued in accordance with *s 161* (related property rules), or valued in conjunction with property which was also comprised in the estate but which has not at any time since the death been vested in the vendors of the property. Put another way, if the shares were part of a control holding at death and qualified for BPR at 50%, that relief is lost if those shares are sold and revalued as part of a minority holding. As a result, it will now seldom be worth claiming the revaluation relief of *s 176*.

Originally, *s 105(2)* was wider in its effect, applying also to shares or securities within old *s 105(1)(b)*. *Section 105(2A)* was repealed by *FA 1996*. As a result, the point is now only of interest to practitioners with old, unresolved cases.

Preference shares: effect on control

5.32   The effect on the definition of control of the existence of preference shares is contained in *s 269(4)*, the background to which was considered in greater detail at **5.28** and **5.29**. In brief, where a company has a class of shares with limited voting rights, the definition of control, which requires powers of voting on 'all questions affecting the company as a whole', is regarded as a reference to all questions except those contained in the specific class rights of preference shares.

Clearances for BPR

5.33   Whilst it is generally very difficult to know in advance that property qualifies for BPR, HMRC introduced a clearance procedure. It was described in HMRC Brief 25/08 and is non-statutory clearance as to the application of tax law to a specific transaction or event. HMRC indicated in January 2009 that the BPR clearance service would be continued and extended. The purpose of the service is '… to provide certainty for businesses operating in the UK, as a useful practical service at a level whereby speed of response from HMRC can be reasonably assured'. As part of the service, HMRC will also give their view of the tax consequences of a transfer of value that involves a change of ownership of a business (succession) where this transfer, leaving aside the application of BPR, would result in an immediate IHT charge. HMRC states: 'Evidence must be provided that the transfer is commercially significant and is genuinely contemplated'. Clearances in this area will only remain valid for a limited period of six months.

There are various limitations to the procedure:

- Applicants cannot use the clearance service for general confirmation of the business property relief position where no commercial transaction is contemplated.

- There must be material uncertainty over the interpretation of the law.

- If the issue relates to anything older than the last four *Finance Acts*, the uncertainty must concern an issue that is commercially significant.

- The transfer of value must be a chargeable one, not a PET.

The limitations suggest that clearance would not be available, for example, to a farmer wanting to give away a two-acre field that might have hope value for development.

HMRC's guidance on the clearance service (www.hmrc.gov.uk/cap/ clearanceiht.htm) lists various circumstances in which a clearance application will not be accepted. These include:

- requests for tax-planning advice, or comments on such advice;

- where HMRC take the view that the arrangements are primarily to gain a tax advantage rather than primarily commercially motivated;

- where there is not considered to be any uncertainty (eg where the point is covered in HMRC's published guidance); or

- in cases where the disposition of property under a will is conditional on the availability of BPR.

HMRC's guidance sets out specific circumstances in which clearances given will not be binding, including (unsurprisingly) if incorrect or incomplete information is given when the clearance application is made. The writer's experience of the official but informal clearance facility is very good indeed. Application is initially by e-mail, but paper confirmation is given, usually very promptly. It seems to be recognised that the availability of BPR can often be, if not wholly uncertain, at least just enough dependent on the facts of each case for practitioners to worry about it. The clearance allows transactions to proceed that might otherwise be stalled over tax worries. Basically, the procedure does exactly what it sets out to achieve. It cannot help where a PET is contemplated because of the limited duration of the clearance letter itself.

This, then, is a case of 'don't spoil it for other people': here is an initiative that really helps the practitioner and that could be withdrawn in the name of achieving cost savings. Practitioners should not just take the lazy view that HMRC can do their legal research for them, and abuse the facility by putting in applications for clearance that are not properly prepared. Drafting the application for clearance properly can take considerable time, since it should take account of anything relevant in the statute, HMRC's IHT Manual and case law. However, that may often be enough for the practitioner to resolve the issue, so it is not time thrown away.

Situations not covered by the clearance procedure

5.34   Where no IHT is presently in point, HMRC will not adjudicate on the availability of BPR: they are not resourced for that. That makes it difficult for executors to know with certainty what assets to appropriate to the trusts of the nil rate band, where so directed by the terms of the will. If residue passes, say, to the surviving spouse exempt, HMRC will adjudicate on BPR only on the second death. If too much value has been transferred to the trust, because BPR turns out not to be available, that is treated by HMRC as a transfer by the residuary beneficiary. HMRC argue that the executors had power only to transfer such value as would be within the nil rate band, so any excess was not a transfer by them and must have been by the surviving spouse.

It is difficult to get round the problem. With acknowledgement to Emma Chamberlain, the executors might try the following:

- a will could be drawn (or varied by deed of variation) so as to include a discretionary trust;

- a provision of the will or variation specifically gives the target asset to a discretionary trust (the specific gift takes it outside *s 39A*, considered in detail at **15.12** onwards);

- then include a gift of the nil rate band to the discretionary trust, being defined as such sum as would not attract IHT, but for this purpose ignoring the prior gift of the target property.

The result should be that there is IHT as stake that requires an adjudication of the BPR issue, because the mere existence of the gift of the nil rate band makes any other transfer on the same occasion a chargeable one. If the target asset is worth, say, £200,000 before relief, the structure will 'top up' the trust to the nil rate band, if that is desired. If BPR is found to be available, the asset can be appointed out to chargeable beneficiaries, such as children. If BPR is refused, and if a decision can be reached within two years of death, the trustee still have the option of appointing the asset to the spouse, in reliance on *s 144*, so as to avoid the immediate payment of IHT.

The difficulty is, of course, in getting everything done quickly enough that a decision is reached well within 24 months from the death. The procedure could easily be frustrated by hesitation within the family or pressure of work on the adviser (as was seen in slightly different circumstances in *Vinton v Fladgate Fielder* [2010] EWHC 904 and its preceding litigation at **6.7**).

SECTION 105(1)(D): LAND AND BUILDINGS ETC USED IN THE BUSINESS

5.35   Relief under this head is available (see *s 105(1)(d)*) only where two conditions are satisfied. First, the asset concerned must be used wholly or mainly for the purposes of a business; second, that business must be carried on by:

- a company of which the transferor had control at the time of transfer; or

- a partnership of which the transferor was at the time of transfer a partner.

A further condition is engrafted onto the requirements of *s 105(1)(d)* by *s 105(6)*. Land, a building, machinery or plant owned by the transferor, and used wholly or mainly for the purposes of the business carried on in compliance with *s 105(1)(d)*, will not qualify for the relief unless:

- the business; or

- the transferor's interest in the business; or

- the shares or securities of the company carrying on the business;

are relevant business property in relation to the transfer immediately before the transfer takes place. In practice, this means that the owner of, say, a valuable printing press used in a business in which he is neither partner nor, if incorporated, a shareholder cannot obtain relief on his deathbed by buying a controlling interest in the company which operates the press or by joining the partnership which operates it. The minimum period of ownership in relation to that company or partnership would not be satisfied.

Where the relevant asset is used by a company, it is important for the transferor to have control, that expression having the meaning already examined. This was the point in issue in *Walding v IRC* [1996] STC 13 (see **5.28**). The estate of Mrs Walding included the shares in the family trading company and the factory units used by that company. No relief was available in respect of the factory units under *s 105(1)(d)* because, as noted, it was held that the deceased did not control the company.

Notwithstanding the general rule in partnership law that each partner has an interest in the proceeds of the division of partnership assets, rather than an interest in specific assets, many partners can see a distinction between their interest in the partnership as a whole and their interest in a specific asset, for example the premises from which the partnership business is carried on. Tax law recognises this distinction, in that BPR is available either on the transfer of land held outside the partnership but used by it, or on the transfer by a partner of his interest in a specific asset owned by the partnership.

Relief on property used in a partnership is at 50% only. It is therefore likely that, in the second category of gift, the transfer of an interest which is an asset of the partnership, the transferor would seek to argue that what is given is in fact a proportionate share of the transferor's interest in the business as a whole, thus bringing the gift within the 100% category of *s 105(1)(a)*. There is scope here for fine argument: see the consideration below of *Featherstonehaugh v IRC*.

To supplement the 'two-year rule' in *s 105(1)(d)*, *s 112(3)* provides that an asset within the class now under consideration will qualify for no relief unless:

*   it was used for the purposes of the business throughout the two years immediately preceding the transfer of value; or

*   it replaced another asset which was so used, and both it and the other asset (and any asset directly or indirectly replaced by that other asset) were used for the purposes of the business for periods which together made up at least two years falling within the five years immediately preceding the transfer of value.

A common problem for farmers is that buildings may become unsuitable for modern machinery or farming practices. If let, relief may be denied because, perhaps, rent received is greater than farming income. The buildings are mere investments. Suppose that, instead of letting the buildings, the farmer enters into a limited liability partnership with the proposed occupant of the premises, rather like a farm contracting agreement. The occupier agrees to pay the farmer a fixed profit share, plus bonuses according to the success of the venture. The resulting income will, in the hands of the farmer, be derived from a trade or business and the buildings should qualify for BPR at 50%. The ownership period may already have been satisfied: it is a 'snapshot' test and does not require the buildings to have been occupied for the purposes of the business for two years.

Machinery and plant

5.36   These terms are not specifically defined for IHT. The capital allowances definition is used in practice, qualified slightly so as to exclude items which would qualify for capital allowances only on the renewals basis. However, that rule is not absolute; some latitude may be given (see IHTM25227). Thus, plant includes anything (see *Yarmouth v France* (1887) 19 QBD 647) which the businessman uses to carry on his business other than his stock in trade. It will include goods and chattels, fixed or movable, live or dead, which he keeps for permanent employment in his business. It does not just mean 'machinery'.

Animals

5.37 The relief is available on working animals and production livestock kept for the purposes of a business, and includes live animals kept for permanent employment in farming and which serve to produce saleable products. HMRC Capital Allowances Manual, at CAM21220, accepts that a horse used in a school or show jumping business is plant, as is a guard dog or circus animal; but, in the main, farm animals are not plant unless they work. That would include, for example, a sheep dog or a heavy horse used for ploughing.

Animals which are kept mainly for sale, or to provide a saleable product after slaughter, are outside the description. Thus there is a distinction between dairy cattle, which do qualify as 'production livestock', and beef cattle, which do not. Laying poultry are plant, but not broilers. Young animals not yet ready for use as production livestock do not qualify. Farm animals are normally trading stock such that their cost is a revenue item, thus barring a capital allowances claim.

The function test

5.38 The case of *Yarmouth v France* in fact concerned a vicious horse (which was plant because it was used for haulage). A full consideration of what constitutes plant for capital allowances is outside the scope of this book, but reference should be made to the following leading cases:

- *IRC v Barclay Curle & Co Ltd* [1969] 1 WLR 675 (examined in greater detail below): a dry dock;

- *IRC v Scottish and Newcastle Breweries Ltd* [1982] STC 296: light fittings, bagpipes and deerskins; and

- *Haigh v Charles W Ireland Ltd* [1974] 1 WLR 43: *not* a safe; it was stock; *Benson v Yard Arm Club* [1979] 1 WLR 347: *not* a ship used as a restaurant.

The durability test

5.39 In the cases listed above, the issue of whether an asset might be plant was concerned with identifying the function of the asset concerned. A separate line of cases has considered whether the item is of long-term or short-term use. The principle has emerged that articles with a working life of two years or more may qualify as plant if they are of the right type. In *Rose & Co (Wallpaper and Paints) Ltd v Campbell* [1968] 1 WLR 346, wallpaper pattern books failed to pass the 'durability' test which had previously been established in *Hinton v Maden and Ireland Ltd* [1959] 1 WLR 875, which rejected as plant

137

articles which might be consumed quickly or worn out after only being used a few times.

Intellectual 'tools' and property

5.40   Machinery and plant is not confined to assets such as lathes, lifts and cows. It can include books, as in the case of the law library of a barrister (*Munby v Furlong* [1977] 2 All ER 953), and computer software. Software itself was considered for the purposes of Cases I and II of Schedule D in R1 56 (November 1993). That interpretation summarised the thinking of the Revenue at that time on the treatment of expenditure on computer software in the computation of taxable profits from a trade, profession or vocation, noting that most software is acquired under licence and that payments may be regular, similar to a rental, or by way of lump sum. Where the payments are like a rent, they will attract revenue treatment and be outside the scope of this discussion as to what might, as a result, be relevant business property for BPR.

Where the payment for software is a lump sum, it is necessary to decide whether the licence is a capital asset in the trade of the licensee. R1 56 states: 'In broad terms a licence is a capital asset if it has a sufficiently enduring nature'.

It appears that Shares Valuation Division of the Valuation Agency have refused BPR on patent royalties, even though, when paid to an inventor, they are earned income. They have commented that 'it might be different if the individual invented the product, registered the patent and then engaged in the manufacture'. For an instance of defective drafting which failed to transfer half the benefit of royalties (on a dry powder inhaler) to a spouse, see *Braithwaite v HMRC* [2008] SpC 674. The original 1991 deed created or recognised intellectual property rights. The taxpayer entered into a declaration of trust of those rights. In 1997, he entered into a new deed that superseded the 1991 deed. The Commissioner held that the effect of the deed and associated documents was that the royalty income under the replacement deed belonged to the taxpayer alone.

Equipment, not 'the setting'

5.41   Plant includes the equipment by which or with which a trade or profession is carried on, but not the place where the business is carried on. This distinction has been argued in many cases and notably in:

- *IRC v Barclay Curle & Co Ltd* [1969] 1 All ER 732: the machinery of the dry dock was plant, but not the cost of excavating the dock itself.

- *ESC 26.2.97*: a caravan provided on a holiday site for holiday lettings, but not on residential sites.

- *Attwood v Anduff Car Wash Ltd* [1997] STC 1167: at a car wash plant, the items of washing equipment were plant, but the wash hall as a whole was not.

- *Bradley v London Electricity* [1996] STC 1054: not an electricity substation itself, although the switch gear was plant.

- *Bestway (Holdings) Ltd v Luff* [1998] STC 357: not the premises in which a company operated cash and carry wholesale supermarkets.

- *Family Golf Centres Ltd v Thorn* [1998] STC (SCD) 106: not three new putting greens, which were part of the golf course.

New categories of 'property'

5.42   Tax law adapts to changing conditions in trade. Even the understanding of what constitutes 'property' may be stretched to include new categories of asset. Is 'potential' taxable? This may be relevant to artists, sportsmen and entertainers.

Example 5.6: assignment of royalties

Sir Frederick, an eminent musician now in his 78th year, still spends two days a week teaching promising young string players. He regularly adjudicates at music festivals, at which some of his compositions are used as test pieces. He assigns to a friend (see Example 5.7) the right to receive royalties in recordings of some of his work. Following the decision in *Nelson Dance*, business relief may be claimed under *s 105(1)(a)* because, although he has disposed of a mere asset of the business, this will be taxed as a diminution in the value of his estate to which BPR will apply.

Example 5.7: holding royalties

Dame Sarah, a sculptress, is the friend to whom Sir Frederick in the previous example had given the recording rights. They are not part of her business and she has now retired anyway; she has sold most of her work and does not consider that she is still in business. On her death, the recording rights are a mere asset qualifying for no relief.

HMRC originally denied relief on the copyright of an author in his books on the death of the author, on the ground that the business had come to an end by virtue of the death or was so personal that it could not be transferred. That was to take too narrow a view of the matter. As is reported in *Carson v Cheyney's Executor* [1959] AC 412: 'It is only by exploiting the work of his brain and his pen that he can make any professional income … it would be absurd to treat his professional activity as merely turning property to gain'.

How far is the ability of, say, a sportsman to be taxed? He protects his name and endorses products. When he does so, does the endorsement agreement have a capital value to be included in his estate at his death? Is such an agreement an interest in his business as a sportsman qualifying for 100% relief under *s 105(1)(a)*, or is it machinery or plant qualifying for only 50% BPR under *s 105(1)(d)*? For many, the doubt may be resolved by incorporation, so that the asset in the sportsman's estate is a shareholding within *s 105(3)(bb)*.

A soprano so captures the hearts and minds of her public that her endorsement of a product carries a Midas touch, and the mere signature of an agreement either to record a work or to perform at some stadium has a value before the release of the recording or the occasion of the performance. She takes steps not only to develop and protect her voice (and looks) but also her name. She assigns to a friend the benefit of a future recording. Is that Midas touch 'property' within *s 105(1)(a)* or does it take more of the character of plant as being the 'apparatus' used by the soprano for the carrying on of her business? *Section 110(b)*, which is considered in **Chapter 8**, requires that value to be recognised under the heading of goodwill.

The meaning of 'property' in relation to a share of an unadministered estate has been clarified by the case of *Daffodil (Administrator of Daffodil Deceased) v IRC* [2002] STI *issue 20*. The case is considered in greater detail at **22.8** below.

Bookmakers' pitches

5.43   A fairly new category of property, identified by the Inland Revenue in Tax Bulletin 43, October 1999, is the pitch of a bookmaker. This arose from a change in the administration of on-course betting introduced with effect from 8 October 1998 when the National Association of Bookmakers, which had previously allocated pitches, lost control of racecourse betting rings to the National Joint Pitch Council (run by the Horse Race Betting Levy Board). As a result, bookmakers who gave up a pitch could auction their 'seniority' amongst bookmakers wishing to take it over. The right to occupy a pitch is now regarded by HMRC as an asset for CGT purposes and as property to which the deceased is beneficially entitled for IHT within *s 5(1)*. Where the right to occupy the pitch forms part of the deceased's business, its value may qualify for BPR at 100%, subject to compliance with the other statutory conditions.

There is an anomaly, somewhat similar to that applying to quota. Pitches which were acquired before October 1998 had no book value or cost. The new rules give those pitches a value with the result that, for CGT purposes, the disposal proceeds will have to be regarded as wholly gain. Where a pitch has been acquired by inheritance after October 1998, the pitch will have a value so that, on its disposal, *s 62(1)* will apply to provide a book value against which the sale proceeds can be measured. Naturally, if a member of a family acquires a pitch through inheritance then, where its value has been 'ascertained' for IHT purposes, that will also be the book value for CGT by virtue of *TCGA 1992, s 274*.

SECTION 105(1)(E): LAND AND BUILDINGS USED IN THE TENANT FOR LIFE'S BUSINESS

5.44   The wording of *s 105(1)(e)* follows quite closely that of *s 105(1)(d)* in allowing BPR on 'any land or building, machinery or plant which, immediately before the transfer, was used wholly or mainly for the purposes of a business carried on by *the transferor and was settled property in which he was then beneficially entitled to an interest in possession*' (italics supplied). It would therefore appear that the whole of the discussion of the meaning 'machinery or plant' set out above would apply with equal force to a claim under this heading as it does to a claim under *s 105(1)(d)*.

The meaning of 'interest in possession'

5.45   Considerable uncertainty had existed as to the meaning of 'interest in possession' until the House of Lords' decision in *Pearson v IRC* [1980] 2 All ER 479, where Viscount Dilhorne observed:

'The first [possible conclusion] is that the power of appointment under clause 2 not having been exercised, the three sisters on reaching that age acquired interest in possession defeasible should the trustees decide to exercise their power to accumulate income. They were then entitled absolutely to the capital and income of the trust fund in equal shares subject to the exercise of that power. The second is that they never secured an interest in possession for they never acquired on reaching that age the right to enjoyment of anything. Their enjoyment of any income from the trust fund depended on the trustees' decision as to the accumulation of income. They would only have the right to any income from the trust fund if the trustees decided it should not be accumulated or if they failed to agree that it should be or if they delayed a decision on this matter for so long that a decision then to accumulate and withhold income from the sisters would have been unreasonable.'

The House of Lords took the second view. Whilst the form of interest as it appeared in the settlement document was different from that of a discretionary beneficiary, in substance there was not much difference. The trustees had a discretion as to whether any of the daughters received income. That particular settlement contained a power for the trustees to apply income towards the payment of duties, taxes, fees and outgoings which would be payable out of, or charged on, the capital of the trust fund. The Revenue argued that the existence of that power also showed that there was no interest in possession. That argument was rejected on the ground that an administrative power does not affect the existence of an interest in possession.

The result of *Pearson* is that a trust to accumulate or a power to accumulate will destroy the existence of an interest in possession. In the light of the *Perpetuities and Accumulations Act 2009*, which removes the limitation on the length of the accumulation period, new trusts may postpone for the entire trust period of 125 years (the new perpetuity period) the date on which beneficiaries will attain vested interests in income. The test is whether, when income arises, the beneficiary can claim it. The existence of an overriding power which could be exercised to take away future income did not affect the existence of an interest in possession.

Prior to the decision in *Pearson* there was, in Revenue Statement of Practice 12 February 1976, an expression of the view of the Inland Revenue which has been confirmed by the House of Lords' decision. Since that decision, the Statement of Practice has been withdrawn, as being redundant, but (subject to the fundamental changes introduced by *FA 2006* which affect virtually all new trusts) it remains a neat summary of the point:

> 'An interest in possession in settled property exists where the person having the interest has the immediate entitlement (subject to any prior claim by the trustees for expenses or other outgoings properly payable out of income) to any income produced by that property as the income arises; but [that] a discretion or power, in whatever form, which can be exercised after income arises so as to withhold it from that person negatives the existence of an interest in possession. For this purpose a power to accumulate income is regarded as a power to withhold it, unless any accumulations must be held solely for the person having the interest or his personal representatives.

> On the other hand the existence of a mere power or revocation or appointment, the exercise of which would determine the interest wholly or in part (but which, so long as it remains unexercised, does not affect the beneficiary's immediate entitlement to income) does not in the Board's view prevent the interest from being an interest in possession.'

In the light of the *FA 2006* changes, this explanation is now chiefly important in fixing the way that income of trusts will be taxed unless the interest in question arises on death and may be an immediate post-death interest.

History of relief under s 105(1)(d)

5.46 This relief applied to transfers after 9 March 1981. Before that date, settled property could qualify for BPR only if used for the purposes of a business carried on by a company controlled by the life tenant or by a partnership of which he himself was a member, but not of a business carried on solely by the life tenant. The new relief is available only if the business of the life tenant is itself relevant business property. It is subject to exceptions and restrictions. The fundamental changes to the taxation of trusts in *FA 2006* will bear on this relief. In future, interests in possession may arise as immediate post-death interests, but will not, generally, arise on the creation in lifetime of any settlement. Lifetime transfers into trusts, unless for the disabled or for certain other restricted purposes, are characterised as being to relevant property trusts, and the transfer is a chargeable one.

Timing

5.47 The use of the property for the purposes of a business is to be tested at the time of the transfer. The transferor need not, therefore, have used the land or other asset concerned for business purposes at any other time. Specifically, *s 112(3)* excludes the operation of *s 112(2)* from claims under *s 105(1)(d)*.

Example 5.8: old man, old books

John and Helen, who are not related, are in partnership as chartered tax advisers and trust and estate practitioners, each working from home. Each has a fully equipped home office with safe storage facilities for wills and trust deeds, hardware and software, and library (both electronic and hard copy). They take over the business of an elderly colleague. This includes his cherished but elderly library, which actually duplicates some of their own books but will soon be out of date; and his substantial will bank, which was the real attraction of the practice.

The old books fall within *s 112(2)* on general principles: they will not be used for the business either now or in the future. That does not matter for a claim under *s 105(1)(d)* on, say, a transfer by either John or Helen, because of the rule in *s 112(2)*, but the effect will soon run off because *s 112(3)* prevents any claim on the value of the old books unless they were used continuously during the two years preceding the transfer. There are succession provisions in *s 112(3) (b)*, but they would not apply in this example.

The meaning of 'assets used in the business'

5.48   The meaning of this phrase was tested in *Finch v IRC* (otherwise *Featherstonehaugh v IRC*) [1985] Ch 1. The tenant for life of settled land carried on a farming business as sole trader. He farmed some of the settled land, but all the other assets of the business belonged to him in his personal capacity.

On his death on 8 September 1977, the trustees and the settled land executors claimed BPR in respect of the charge to CTT arising on his death. At that time, APR was subject to a limit of 1,000 acres, and in this case that limit had been used up on other land. The only scope for claiming BPR was under the provision now represented by *s 105(1)(a)*. Had the business been carried on in partnership, *s 105(1)(d)* would have applied. The trustees succeeded in the Court of Appeal.

Whilst the main argument concerned valuation of the business on the 'net' basis in relation to liabilities, and is considered in **Chapter 14**, the relevance of the case to situations now falling within *s 105(1)(e)* was the ruling by the Court of Appeal that distinguishes sole traders from partners. In determining the value of the business of a sole trader, every asset in the business is to be taken into account and included in the transfer of value. In valuing the interest of a partner in a business, on the other hand, only partnership assets are to be taken into account. Thus the assets owned by the transferor as his own separate property and used by the partnership business do not count towards the value of the interest in the partnership business. As a result of this, personal assets used by the partnership qualify for 50% relief under *s 105(1)(d)*, and not 100% relief under *s 105(1)(a)*.

The statutory fiction (see *s 49(1)*), that the life tenant owns land in which the interest in possession subsists, has to be applied in deciding the value of the assets of the business for the purposes of BPR. The result of this, the Court of Appeal held, is that the assets of the business included the life interest in the land which was used for the purposes of the business. On that basis, BPR applied to the value of the land.

The decision in *Featherstonehaugh* does create intellectual problems. The test in *s 105(1)(e)* is use 'for the purposes of a business'. That does not sit easily with the expression 'used in the business' in *s 110(b)*, the main section on valuation. Do these two expressions have different meanings? *Featherstonehaugh* left that particular issue open.

The main thrust of *s 110* in relation to liabilities is to set them against the value of the assets used in the business. Here the statutory fiction exposes certain impracticalities. Why should liabilities be deducted from assets which are not charged or mortgaged in respect of them? Suppose that, as will often be the case, the land is held by the trust and is free of mortgage in the commercial sense, whereas recurrent losses from farming have pushed the tenant for life into bankruptcy. In commercial terms, the trustees and the land will usually be safe from the claims of creditors. An earlier edition of this work suggested that it might be helpful to the taxation of the estate of the tenant for life to be able to set his liabilities against the value of the trust, but that it was certainly not logical. That view was upheld by the decision of the High Court in *St Barbe Green and another v CIR* [2005] STC 288, where the deceased held two life interests but was himself insolvent. The personal liabilities reduced the value of the free estate to nil, but the excess could not be set against the value of the trust funds.

The applicability of the lower rate of relief

5.49   Following the decision in *Featherstonehaugh* the question arose whether relief would be available under the more generous provisions of *s 105(1)(a)* or the restrictive provisions of *s 105(1)(e)*. The Financial Secretary to the Treasury wrote, in October 1985, to confirm that the more generous relief was available 'when the circumstances accord with those in the *Finch* case'. Thus the land and the business in such a case are to be included in the same transfer of value. This would normally happen on the death of the tenant for life.

This leaves the applicability of the lower rate of relief to those situations where the transfer of value does not include the business itself but only the trust asset.

Example 5.9: giving up lifetime interest

Philip farms, partly on trust land and partly on land that he has bought personally. The trust is an 'old style' interest in possession one, the fund passing to Philip's daughter Rachel on his death. The trust land includes a substantial house occupied by Rachel free of charge. She helps on the farm. Philip gives up his life interest in the house so that Rachel can own it (and mortgage it to pay for its renovation).

Philip's interest under the settlement comes to an end during his lifetime. That is a PET. If Philip dies within seven years, it will become a chargeable transfer under *s 52(1)* on the house but not on the business itself.

Other conditions

5.50   The normal restriction, that there must be no binding contract for the sale of the asset, applies to claims under this head. Similarly, the property must not be an excepted asset. Land or a building of which part only was used for the business may be apportioned between business and non-business use. This is discussed in **Chapter 7** when considering the whole subject of excepted assets.

The practitioner may therefore be faced with three somewhat similar situations:

- the tenant for life keeps both the land and business right through to death;

- the tenant for life gives up the land but keeps the business until death; or

- the tenant for life gives up the business but keeps the land until death.

In the first of these situations, a transfer of the settled property and of the business occurs at the same time. 100% BPR is available. In the second situation, assuming the land is held by the trustees and the business by the tenant for life, the release by the tenant for life of his interest in, say, the factory will qualify for 50% relief only. In the third situation, the tenant for life is disposing of an interest in a business which he owns in his own right and the income of which has been taxed on him as his personal income, not as trust income. 100% relief is available on the business. The trustees are left with land which is no longer used for the purposes of a business carried on by the transferor. It is probably, as a result, a mere investment qualifying for no BPR at all.

Chapter 6

Business property: the rates of relief, limitations to the relief

QUICK GUIDE

Business property must generally be held for two years before BPR can apply but, as with APR, there are rules to extend a period of ownership by reference to another holder. There are also rules to allow the effective rolling over from one qualifying asset to another: see **6.8**.

As with APR, the existence of a contract for sale, or for example provisions in a partnership agreement that amount to a contract for sale, will prevent BPR from being available. There is a detailed examination of this topic at **6.15**. The rules as to successive transfers, that were seen earlier in connection with APR, have a parallel in BPR which is examined at **6.17**.

Difficulties can arise when it is not certain whether shares in a company are 'quoted'. The categories of shares that are treated as quoted change from time to time, but the current position as to recognised stock exchanges is set out at **6.20** onwards.

THE RATES: MANNER OF APPLICATION

Interaction with quick succession relief

6.1   The relief applies to the value transferred by a transfer of value which is, wholly or in part, attributable to business property. The reduction in value allowed by *IHTA 1984, s 104* is applied before the claim to any exemption which might make the transfer of value wholly or partly exempt. Similarly, BPR is applied before quick succession relief.

Example 6.1: accumulated profits held as cash

Fred and George together run a successful company specialising in the production of theatrical costumes and fancy goods with a magical theme based

147

on a well-known children's book. On Fred's death on 6 June 2009, his estate includes shares in their unquoted trading company worth £100,000 which he leaves to George. Profits have been accumulated in cash within the company, and 25% of the net worth of the company is represented by cash and near-cash assets that are not needed for trading and are excluded property under *s 112*. Assume that Fred's estate is exactly double the available nil rate band, so that the effective rate of tax on his estate is 20%.

The tax charge on Fred's death is:

Value of shares	100,000
Value of shares less excepted assets (say)	75,000
Chargeable transfer (100,000 – 75000)	25,000
IHT thereon at estate rate of 20%	5,000

The business continues to prosper and, by 28 February 2011, when George dies, the holding that George inherited from Fred is worth £120,000. Of that value, only 20% is now represented by excluded property, with the result that 80% of the value, £96,000, is sheltered by BPR and £24,000 is chargeable, subject to any other relief.

The appropriate percentage under *s 141(3)(b)*, for a death more than one year but less than two years after the first, is 80%. We can now calculate the quick succession relief under *s 141(1)(a)*:

Increase in George's estate(the 'first transfer')	£100,000
Tax charge on the first transfer	£5,000
Reduction, per *s 141(3)*, of that tax	80%
Quick succession relief (5,000 × 80%)	£4,000

Interaction with other reliefs

6.2   *Section 104* interacts with *s 165*, which is concerned with tax on capital gains. Note that this is not a reference to *TCGA 1992, s 165* which allows relief from tax on gifts of business assets: by coincidence, *IHTA 1984, s 165* also affects a 'gains' situation. Under *IHTA 1984, s 165(1)*, tax may reduce the value transferred by a transfer. This may occur where a chargeable transfer is, or includes, the disposal of an asset and on that disposal a gain accrues to the transferor for the purposes of *TCGA 1992*. Commonly, the donor will pay the CGT and, in such a case, there will be no relief except that the estate of the donor is further reduced by having to pay that tax. Where, however, either the whole or part of the gain is a chargeable gain and the whole or part of any CGT chargeable on the gain is borne not by the person making the gain but by the donee within the meaning of *TCGA 1992, s 282*, then the CGT so suffered is treated as reducing the value transferred. However, BPR is applied before applying the reduction available under *IHTA 1984, s 165*.

Example 6.2: tax thrown away

Continuing the previous example, George, who had made transfers that exhausted the nil rate band then available to him, gave his brother Ron on 25 December 2009 a block of shares in the family trading company worth £100,000. As already noted, *s 112* excluded from BPR 25% of the value of the shares in the company at that date. The gain, which attracted no reliefs from CGT, on the shares was £40,000. Although a claim might have been made under *TCGA 1992, s 165* on the grounds that the shares qualified for holdover relief, under *TCGA 1992, s 165(2)(b)* no claim was made immediately and senile dementia, thereafter, prevented the parties from making one. Accordingly, the gain became chargeable. George did not pay the tax on the gain within 12 months, so that tax became recoverable from Ron under *TCGA 1992, s 282*.

The tax to be suffered by Ron of £40,000 would, under *IHTA 1984, s 165(1)* in the case of an asset not qualifying for BPR, reduce the value of the gift from £100,000 to £60,000. However, BPR of £75,000 first reduces the chargeable transfer to £25,000. That value is eliminated by the tax that Ron has (unfortunately and unnecessarily) paid. There is a right of recovery of such tax under *TCGA 1992, s 282(2)*. (It should be noted that the expression 'close relative' in *IHTA 1984, s 165(3)* does not include a brother. That expression is defined in *FA 1984, Sch 14, para 1(1)* to include only the spouse, children and remoter descendants.)

Grossing up

6.3   The effect of *IHTA 1984, s 104(2)* is also to apply BPR before any grossing up. There are complications in applying BPR where claw-back applies under *s 113(a)*: these are discussed below.

Example 6.3: simple grossing up

Alice and John were in partnership as motor engineers. On her death on 9 March 2001, Alice, who had made lifetime transfers in excess of the nil rate band, left to her brother, John, free of tax her interest in their business, then worth £120,000. Examination of the accounts of the business shows that 25% of its value is represented by investments not in use for the purposes of the business, with the result that BPR is restricted to £90,000. The unrelieved portion of the gift, £30,000, must be grossed up. The rate on the net fraction is two-thirds. The tax chargeable is, therefore, £30,000 × $^2/_3$ = £20,000.

BPR is available in appropriate circumstances to trustees of relevant property trusts. *Section 103(1)* includes within the definition of 'transfer of value' an occasion on which tax is chargeable under *Chapter III* of *Part III* of *IHTA 1984*, ie the relevant property trust regime, except for *s 79* (exemption from ten-yearly charge). Thus, *s 103(1)(b)* includes references to the trustees of the settlement concerned within the meaning of 'transferor'. In practical terms, this could give rise to the allowance of an exemption before BPR. This would occur on a partly exempt occasion of charge within the relevant property trust regime but outside the scope of the ten-yearly charge under *s 79*. This will be a rare occurrence.

The rates of relief

6.4   In relation to transfers of value made and other events occurring after 5 April 1996, the 100% relief applies to:

- unincorporated businesses;
- unquoted shares which either by themselves or with such other securities or unquoted shares gave the transferor control; and
- any unquoted shares in a company not listed on a recognised stock exchange, but including those traded on AIM, ETHEX or PLUS.

The 50% relief applies to:

- shares or securities giving control of a quoted company;
- land, buildings, machinery or plant in a partnership or in a controlled company; or
- land in a settlement (subject to the restrictions as before).

PERIOD OF OWNERSHIP

6.5   *IHTA 1984, s 106* provides, with admirable clarity and brevity, that 'property is not relevant business property in relation to a transfer of value unless it was owned by the transferor throughout the two years immediately preceding the transfer'. Ownership includes beneficial entitlement. If the asset is owned by trustees and there is an interest in possession, property in which the transferor has such an interest can qualify for relief. Where there is no such interest in possession, it is enough that the trustees have legal ownership.

Where the asset is a shareholding that has been added to from time to time, HMRC will ask for evidence that the shares actually transferred are derived from a holding that satisfies the two-year rule. It is best to number the shares and to be consistent in identifying which shares are involved in each transaction. Usually, first in, first out will give the best result.

Difficulties may arise where, in an unincorporated business, there has been substantial change in the value of a partnership interest shortly before transfer.

Example 6.4: acquired interest

Henry and Ian together operate a printing business. Trade is poor and Henry retires on 31 December 2007, selling his interest to Ian. Ian remains a partner until his death in June 2008. BPR is allowable at Ian's death on the whole of the value of his 'old' interest in the business, but on none of that part of the value which is represented by the share purchased from Henry.

Example 6.5: organic growth

Donald and Evelyn trade together as computer software engineers. In June 2006, the value of the interest of each of them in the business is no more than £20,000. Astute marketing in relation to the worldwide credit crunch secures lucrative contracts such that, by June 2008, the value of the capital held by each partner is £300,000. There has been no change in profit sharing ratio over the two-year period. All the growth has been organic. Even though, in real and commercial terms, much of the growth in value has arisen only in spring 2008, on a transfer of an interest in a business by either partner in July 2008 BPR is allowable on the entire value.

From the point of view of administrative convenience, it is preferable for husband and wife in a family business to have separate partnership capital accounts, so that ownership of a particular share in the business can be shown in order to prove the requirements of *s 106*.

An attempt to circumvent the two-year rule failed in *Executors of Mary Dugan-Chapman Deceased v HMRC* [2008] SpC 666, considered in detail at **6.7**. The aftermath of that case was a claim in negligence by the family against the lawyers: see *Vinton v Fladgate Fielder* [2010] EWHC 904 (Ch), which suggested that, if the scheme had been more precisely executed, relief might have been secured.

Modification of the two-year rule

6.6   The ownership of a mere business asset without business activity does not qualify for BPR; but, once it is established that a business is being carried on, a change in the precise nature of that business will not affect the requirement under *s 106* as to a minimum period of ownership. A change in the use of a business asset from one ('qualifying') trade to another will not prevent the value of that asset, if part of a business, from satisfying *s 106*. This is recognised in the positive language of IHTM25303.

REPLACEMENT PROPERTY

6.7   A more fundamental change, from the ownership of one business asset to another, is regulated by *s 107*, under which property satisfies the condition where it replaces other property and both the new property and the old property (and property which directly or indirectly replaces the old property) are owned by the transferor for periods which together amount to at least two years in the last five years before the transfer. Replacement may be in whole or in part.

For the replacement provisions of *s 107(1)(a)* to apply, any other property concerned in the exchange must be such that, had the transfer of value taken place just before the replacement of that other property, it would have qualified for BPR (except insofar as the period of ownership of the other property did not satisfy the test in *s 106*). *Section 107* is concerned with the replacement of property which consists of:

- a business or an interest in a business;

- unquoted company securities giving the transferor control;

- unquoted shares;

- quoted shares giving the transferor control;

- land or buildings, machinery or plant used for a business carried on by a company controlled by the transferor by a partnership of which the transferor was a partner; or

- land, buildings, machinery or plant used for a business carried on by the transferor but belonging to a settlement in which he had an interest in possession.

Dymond is authority for the proposition that *s 107* does not apply to the replacement of other property, for example mere assets of an unincorporated business. This is consistent with the wording of *s 105(1)*. It is important that the acquisition of the replacement property takes place after the disposal of the original property. The guidance in the old version of the Manual, which was criticised in an earlier edition of this work, has been revised and updated to reflect recent changes (see IHTM25314). See also the helpful flowchart at IHTM25312. The useful point is made that this is anti-avoidance legislation; so, unless the inspector feels that the taxpayer has attempted, by business changes, to bring value or property within the relief that was not there at least two years before the transfer, he should adopt a reasonable approach.

The reasonableness of the approach of the taxpayer was partly in issue in *The Executors of Mrs Mary Dugan-Chapman & Anor v Revenue and Customs Commissioners* [2008] SpC 666. It had been hoped by the taxpayer that the use of a rights issue to capitalise a loan might effectively sidestep the two-year ownership rule by deeming the shares acquired to be, in effect, part of an existing shareholding which had been owned for the requisite period. This relied on the reorganisation provisions of *TCGA 1992, s 126* when read with *IHTA 1984, s 107(4)*. The case turned on its own, very special, facts which are much compressed here but illustrate several principles.

Counsel had advised the family that a rights issue in the family trading company would have the result that new shares acquired under it would be identified with shares already held, so that the new shares would be deemed to have been held for as long as the shares in respect of which the rights arose. That would help Mrs Dugan-Chapman, who had a cash balance of £300,000 with the company and who was recently widowed, elderly and might not live two years.

The company had been inactive, which might prejudice a claim to BPR. There were worries that voting balance would be disturbed if only Mrs Dugan-Chapman took up shares. It was possible that the executors of Mr Dugan-Chapman might also take up shares. The company sold a painting, easing cash flow requirements, but was considering fresh purchases. There were issues over pre-emption rights. There was delay, during which the health of Mrs Dugan-Chapman deteriorated. Shares were issued to capitalise her £300,000 loan account but, in addition, documents were prepared for a further investment of £1,000,000. Mrs Dugan-Chapman, through an attorney, was to subscribe for £1,000,000 shares. There was no mention, second time round, of any offer to other shareholders. She died only two days after the second issue of shares.

There was confusion: the paperwork did not match the original concept. There were two versions of minutes for the same meeting; and two versions of the letters of application for shares, one marked 'wrong' and another 'This one was substituted'. There were errors in the increase of capital needed.

Section 107(4) allows BPR where shares would be identified with other shares under the 'paper for paper' CGT rules in *TCGA 1992, ss 126–136*. Judith Powell, as Special Commissioner, noted the doubts as to whether BPR would be available in respect of an inactive company. That was relevant to the motivation for the transactions. It was accepted by HMRC that the 300,000 shares did qualify for BPR. It was also accepted by the taxpayer that some shares renounced by a family member and taken up by Mrs Dugan-Chapman did not qualify for BPR because they were not issued in respect of her holding on that date.

Ms Powell held that the final investment no longer had the nature of a rights issue: 'there was confusion about the effect of a rights issue throughout the process'. Actions taken under extreme time pressures did not achieve the effect that had been hoped for. Relief would be available only in respect of new shares that represented a pro rata entitlement based on an existing shareholding, not just any shares issued as part of a rights issue, such as those renounced by other members of the company. Some informality in company dealings can be tolerated, but only where the shareholders are aware of all relevant facts (see the judgment of Neuberger J in *re Duomatic Ltd* [1969] 2 Ch 365). They were not so aware here. Relief was denied.

The general principles that practitioners may draw from the case are long established:

- shares issued as part of a rights issue can qualify for BPR immediately; but

- get the paperwork right;

- keep only one (correct) record of the transaction, not two conflicting notes; and

- get on with it.

Period of ownership of unquoted shares: capital reconstruction

6.8   The deemed period of ownership of unquoted shares may be governed by *IHTA 1984, s 107(4)*. This is without prejudice to *s 107(1)*. Where unquoted shares (falling within *s 105(1)(bb)*) are owned by the transferor immediately before the transfer, and (in a situation such as a paper for paper exchange) those shares would be identified with other shares previously owned by the transferor by virtue of the rules in *TCGA 1992, ss 126–136,* the period of ownership of the 'old shares' counts towards the period of ownership of the 'new shares' for the purposes of satisfying the two-year test in *IHTA 1984, s 106.*

The effect of *s 107* is only to 'save' periods of ownership which have already been earned in respect of the assets which have now been replaced, and not to increase the relief. By *s 107(2)*, the relief is not to exceed what it would have been had the *replacement* of any one or more of the *replacements* not been made. For this purpose, changes which result from the formation, alteration or dissolution of a partnership are to be disregarded. Similarly, changes arising from the acquisition of a business by a company controlled by the former owner of the business may be disregarded. See below as to how *s 107(4)* affects transfers on or after 6 April 1996.

Example 6.6: late incorporation

In February 2007, Roger transfers a business, which he has owned for many years and which is then worth £100,000, to a new company (formed for the purpose) in consideration of all the shares in that company. On 13 April 2008, he dies. The shares are then worth £150,000. Relief is available on the larger amount, notwithstanding that the shares have been owned for only 16 months.

A difficulty may arise in reconstruction situations where, for example, a taxpayer holds both 60% of the shares in a holding company and 20% of its subsidiary and becomes entitled, through a reconstruction, to extra shares in the holding company. If that augmentation of the holding in the top company increases the total value held by the shareholder in respect of which a claim is made to BPR, HMRC may require evidence of the prior value of each holding so as to prove that (as may well in fact not be the case) the limitation in *s 107(2)* has not been breached.

A similar point may arise in connection with employee share schemes. Supposing the original proprietor of shares both in a holding company and in its trading subsidiary, at a time when only 50% BPR was available in respect of minority holdings, transferred shares to an employee scheme and thereby lost some of the BPR that would otherwise have been available to him . On a reorganisation, the effect of which is to restore his holding to one qualifying for relief by the time of his death by transferring the shares in the subsidiary up to the top company, it will not be necessary to requalify for BPR by holding the new shares in the holding company for two years from the reconstruction.

Extending the period of ownership

6.9   The period of ownership for the purposes of *ss 106* and *107* is, on all inherited property, capable of being extended. The inheritor, ie the second owner, is treated as having owned the property since the date of death giving rise to that inheritance, ie the date of death of the person from whom the property is inherited. Where the previous owner was the spouse of the person so inheriting, any period of ownership of that previous owner counts towards the period of ownership of the person inheriting the property. *Section 108(b)* contains no limitation of this rule relative to the period of the marriage. The provisions of *s 108* are examined further at **6.16** in the context of successive transfers.

Example 6.7: no fool like an old fool

Arthur, an elderly bachelor, has run a manufacturing business for many years. In May 2007, he marries Bernice, many years his junior, revising his will to make her sole beneficiary of his estate. After a tempestuous relationship, he dies in July 2007. In September, Bernice, having meanwhile formed a relationship with Carl, makes a will in his favour. On her death in October 2007, BPR is available on the business notwithstanding that the period of ownership in her own right was two months, and that the period of ownership by Arthur, whilst her husband, was also only three months. Carl dies in August 2008. He is deemed, by *s 91*, to have been the owner of the property only since the death of Bernice in October 2007. No relief is due on his death.

New rules, extending the period of ownership, have been introduced by *s 267A* as a result of the enactment of *Limited Liability Partnership Act 2000, s 11* (see **5.23**).

PERIOD OF OWNERSHIP: DETAILED RULES

6.10   *Section 91(1)* provides that, where a person would have been entitled to an interest in possession in the whole or part of the residue of the estate of a deceased person had the estate been fully wound up, the same consequences follow under *IHTA 1984* as would apply if that person had become entitled to an interest in possession in the unadministered estate and in the property representing residue (or a corresponding part of it) on the date as from which the whole or part of the income of the residue would have been attributable to his interest, if the residue had been ascertained immediately after the death of the deceased person.

In brief, the legatee is treated as becoming entitled to his inheritance on the day of death. For the purposes of *s 91*, 'unadministered estate' means all the property in the hands of the personal representatives other than:

- property which passes to them otherwise than as assets for the payment of debts; and

- property which is specifically given to a beneficiary.

Due allowance has to be made for any charges on residue and for any adjustments as between capital and income that have to be made during the administration.

Definitions for s 91

6.11   *Section 91(2)* sets out three definitions for the application of *s 91(1)*.

'Ascertained residue' means residue proper, no longer held by the personal representatives to meet debts.

'Charges on residue' means (see *ICTA 1988, s 701(6), (7)*), in relation to the estate of a deceased person, the following liabilities, provided that they are payable out of residue and interest in respect of those liabilities, ie:

- funeral, testamentary and administration expenses and debts;
- general legacies, demonstrative legacies, annuities, and any sum payable out of residue to which a person is entitled under the law of intestacy of any part of the United Kingdom or any other country; and
- any other liabilities of the personal representatives 'as such'.

'Specific disposition' means (see *ICTA 1988, s 701(5)*) a specific devise or bequest made by a testator. The phrase includes the disposition of personal chattels made by *Administration of Estates Act 1925, s 46* (the widow's legacy), and any disposition which has an effect similar to that of the specific devise or bequest under the law of England and Wales, by virtue of any enactment or by the operation of a law of another country which has a similar effect. In many cases, the provision for a widow at the new rates will 'swamp' the estate. Real estate which is included in a residuary gift, either by a specific description or by a general description, is deemed to be part of the residue of the estate and is not deemed to be the subject of a specific disposition.

Cautious draftsmen of wills may consider that the ownership period of the beneficiary can best be put beyond doubt by making property which qualifies for APR or BPR the subject of a specific gift, rather than of a gift of residue. This is because, in relation to BPR, *s 108* treats the transferee as being entitled as from the date of death if he then 'became entitled to any property'. It is arguable that no such entitlement exists, immediately at any rate, in relation to certain forms of residuary gift.

TRANSFERS AFTER 6 APRIL 1996: SPECIAL RULES

6.12   The effect of *FA 1996, s 184* was to achieve some simplification. Conditions had been imposed for relief on lifetime transfers (and other events occurring) on or after 18 March 1986 and within seven years of the death of the transferor. These were contained in *FA 1986, Sch 19, para 21*, but did not apply to charges under the rules relating to gifts with reservation. It was *para 21* which inserted the claw-back charge of *IHTA 1984, s 113A*.

Section 113A does not affect the rate of relief, nor does it affect the amount on which that relief is given. In relation to transfers before 10 March 1992 (where the death occurred after that date), the relief was normally increased and shares that were traded on (what was then) the Unlisted Securities Market might be treated as if they had been unquoted at the time of transfer. The present arrangements, applying where the transfer was made before 6 April 1996 and the death occurred thereafter, allow the amendments enacted by *FA 1996, s 184* to apply to tax which is charged by reference to the death. The example below illustrates the point but, by now, such cases should long since have been resolved.

Example 6.8: no loss of relief

Jenny owns 12% of the shares in Tumble Limited, an unquoted trading company, which she gives to her son on 1 April 1996. That gift is a PET. BPR is available at 50%, the shares being relevant business property within *s 105(1)(c)* (since repealed). Jenny dies in July 1996, as a result of which the PET becomes chargeable. The shares have not been disposed of in the meantime and the claw-back conditions of *s 113A* are satisfied in full. By virtue of *s 184(6)(b)(ii)* the gift qualifies for BPR at 100%. Following the repeal of *s 105(1)(c)*, the gift falls within the more generous category of *s 105(1)(bb)*.

In such a case, does the 100% reduction apply for the purposes of cumulation as well as merely for the purpose of taxing the failed PET? In relation to a failed PET, it would seem that the 100% relief applies, although the situation might have been otherwise if the gift had been immediately chargeable. It is considered that, where the gift is a chargeable transfer, say because it is made by way of relevant property trust, the value for cumulation is undisturbed. That value is fixed by the tax charge at the time. If this view is correct, it does not always work to the disadvantage of the taxpayer, who may wish to 'lock into' a given level of relief for fear that it may be cut down by a later enactment.

Example 6.9: mixed relief

John owns 15% of the shares in Phizz Limited, an unquoted trading company. In December 1993, he settles the shares on (what were then known as) discretionary trusts, having previously made other chargeable transfers which exhausted the nil rate band applicable at that time.

At the time of the transfer, the shares are worth £150,000. Relief is available at 50%. On John's death soon afterwards, the value for cumulation is £75,000. That will, of course, affect the tax charge on the remainder of his estate, although the charge which would normally apply to uplift from the lifetime rate to the death rate in respect of the gift qualifies for the 100% reduction by virtue of *FA 1996.*

NO CONTRACT FOR SALE

6.13   The general rule under *IHTA 1984, s 113* is that, even where property would otherwise qualify for BPR in relation to a transfer of value, no BPR is available if a binding contract has been entered into for the sale of the property at the time of transfer.

What is 'a binding contract for sale'?

6.14   For a short time it appeared, following the authority in *Spiro v Glencrown Properties Ltd,* that the expression might include the situation where terms had been agreed for a sale although contracts had not been exchanged. This interpretation was vigorously opposed and formally excluded from the operation of *s 113* by the Capital Taxes Office (as it then was), as evidenced in correspondence published in the *Law Society's Gazette* of 6 May 1981 and 4 November 1982. For a somewhat similar review of the issue, but in a different context, see *Jones (Balls' Administrators) v IRC* [1997] STC 358, discussed at **4.27**.

Part performance

There has been, in *Yaxley v Gotts* [2000] Ch 162, some comment on the doctrine of part performance as it affects the requirement of *Law of Property (Miscellaneous Provisions) Act 1989, s 2(5)* that a contract be 'made in writing' rather than, as was previously the rule, 'evidenced by writing'. *Section 2(5)* does not, it seem, remove the force of all the old cases on the subject, although it might be difficult to show the precise date on which the deemed contract took place.

'Buy and sell' agreements

HMRC do, however, consider that there is a binding contract for sale where partners or shareholder directors of companies enter into an agreement under which, in the event of death or retirement of one of them, the personal representatives of the partner or director so dying are obliged to sell, and the survivors are obliged to purchase, the interest of the deceased in the business or company. These arrangements, known as 'buy and sell' agreements, are specifically referred to in SP12/80. In the view of the Board, such an agreement, requiring as it does a sale and purchase and not merely conferring an option to sell or buy, is a binding contract for sale within *s 113*. As a result, BPR is not available on the interest or the shares, as the case may be. That said, IHTM25292 very fairly acknowledges that most arrangements will not constitute 'buy and sell' arrangements: you must look at each case on its merits.

Examine each case

Further addressing the issue, the ICAEW published memorandum TR557 on 19 September 1984 giving guidance which reproduces correspondence between the Revenue and the accountancy bodies concerning the availability of BPR in these circumstances. This memorandum noted the table, published on 6 May 1981 in the *Law Society's Gazette*, summarising the position in various circumstances, which is examined in **Chapter 14**. The Revenue (now HMRC) regard each situation as individual, requiring careful scrutiny of the agreement in each case. It was generally considered that *s 113* was intended to deny relief where the transferor, having decided to cease trading, entered into a binding contract for the sale of his business and later died or gave away his interest before completion of the sale. BPR was not to be available on, in effect, the cash realised from the proceeds of sale of a business. The statement of practice extends the application of *s 113*. By inference, it is assumed that BPR will be denied to lifetime transfers, even where there was no intention to cease trading.

Cross-options

On 5 July 1982, the Revenue had confirmed that the purpose of *s 113* (as it became) was to limit BPR to transfers of property and to exclude from BPR the transfer of, in effect, the proceeds of sale of a business. The Revenue confirmed that, where, for example, on the death in service or retirement of a partner, the surviving partners have an option to buy and the retiring partner (or his personal representatives) have an option to sell, the share in the partnership relief will be available. That relief will also be available where there is no provision in the partnership deed for the purchase of a partner's share and that partner by his will directs that, if he dies in service, his interest in the partnership is to be sold. The key is whether there is freedom to retain the asset and, for example, sell elsewhere or give it away. Thus, where the provision in the partnership deed is more specific and the surviving partners 'shall purchase' the share of the deceased, no BPR is available. If the contract for sale is not to operate during the lifetime of the partner, such that the partner can give away his interest and that interest continues as an interest in the hands of the donee, BPR will be available.

Accrual/annuity provisions

In the situation where the partnership deed provides that, on the death in service or retirement of a partner, his share is to accrue to the surviving partners who are obliged to pay an annuity to the partner (or to the spouse of the partner as appropriate), BPR will be available on the lifetime transfer of that interest if the accrual/annuity provision does not then come into operation. If that provision does, on the occasion of the transfer, come into operation, then spouse exemption may be due to the extent of the value of the annuity. On death in service, there would be no BPR but exemption would be due on the widow's annuity. In such a case, it is also relevant to consider the Statement of Practice of 17 January 1975, in that any chargeable gains accruing to a retired partner would be computed by comparing the consideration received (including the capital value of the annuity) with the CGT 'cost' or the market value at the date of death for personal representatives of a deceased partner.

Agreements that failed

Further correspondence between the accountancy bodies and the Inland Revenue in 1983 highlighted the different views of the interpretation of *s 113* (as it became). *Section 113* excludes from BPR property which is subject to a binding contract for sale 'at the time of the transfer'. The accountancy bodies had argued that the legislation was authoritative for the view that, for the purposes of the tax, the time of a transfer on death is immediately before that death. Building on that argument, it was asserted that a buy and sell agreement in a partnership deed which comes into operation only at the moment of death could not be taken to fetter the interest of a partnership immediately before that death, such that it could not amount to a binding contract for sale at the time of the transfer with the result that the interest of the partner would qualify for BPR.

HMRC did not accept this approach. They considered that the combined effect of what are now *ss 3(4)* and *4(1)* is that the event, namely death, is an occasion of charge and requires a valuation to be made by reference to a hypothetical transfer before death. Effectively, under *s 3(4)*, the death is itself a transfer of value. Thus, when a binding contract for sale exists at the time of death, ie at the time of the statutory transfer of value within *s 3(4)*, BPR is excluded by *s 113*.

Expiry date of cross-options

Whilst cross-options do not constitute a binding contract for sale, care should be taken to ensure that the options do not exist over precisely the same period. This is because HMRC consider that such arrangements do, in effect, between them amount to a contract. The call option should therefore expire before the put option can be exercised.

Exception to the rule in s 113: underlying assets

6.15   The rule in *s 113* applies to the relevant business property, ie that falling within *s 105(1)*. It does not apply to the underlying assets. Thus, where contracts have been exchanged for the sale of an asset which is used for the purpose of a business, and relief is sought in relation to the business as a whole, BPR may still be available on the value of the business, including that portion which is represented by the right to receive the proceeds of sale, if it can be shown that those proceeds are required at the time of the transfer for future use in the business. This will be the case where the vendor was in the process of buying other assets to replace the property sold. This situation is considered in greater detail at **7.1**.

SUCCESSIONS AND SUCCESSIVE TRANSFERS: THE RULES IN SS 108 AND 109

6.16   The period of ownership for the purposes of *ss 106* and *107* may be extended on a 'succession' by operation of *s 108*, which by its brevity and clarity might seem to need no further elucidation. For a chart to navigate the requirements, see IHTM25332. This was noted at **6.9** and Example 6.7 but will bear restating, if only to distinguish successions from successive transfers. Thus, for succession:

- the person now making the transfer ('owner no 2') must have acquired the property from the original holder of the asset ('owner no 1') on the *death* of owner no 1;

- on the transfer in respect of which relief is now claimed, ie to owner no 3, the period of ownership by owner no 2 starts running from the date of death of owner no 1; and

- if owner no 1 was the spouse or civil partner of owner no 2, the period of ownership by owner no 1 is attributed to owner no 2.

Section 109 extends BPR in certain circumstances where the operation of *s 106* would deny the relief. The requirements are as follows:

- the whole or part of the value transferred by a transfer of value, 'the earlier transfer', must have been eligible for BPR or must have been of a nature which would have been eligible for BPR if that relief could have been given in respect of transfers of value made at the time of that earlier transfer; and

- the whole or part of the property which was relevant business property in relation to the earlier transfer must become, by virtue of that transfer, the property of the person (or of the spouse of the person) who is the transferor on the subsequent occasion, 'the later transfer'; and

- the property, or part of it, or property which directly or indirectly replaces it, must either have been relevant business property in relation to the later transfer, or capable of so being, except that the two-year period required by *s 106* is not satisfied; and

- either the earlier transfer was, or the later transfer is, made on the death of the transferor.

Section 109 cannot operate to increase the amount of BPR but only to preserve the BPR which, by virtue of *s 106*, would otherwise be lost. In this, *s 109(2)* finds a parallel in *s 107(2)* in relation to replacement property.

Where, under the earlier of the two transfers, the amount of the value transferred which was attributable to that property was only part of its value, that restriction will apply to the claim to BPR on the second transfer. This might arise on a transfer for less than full consideration.

Example 6.10: restricted relief (1)

Roger, a legal aid practitioner, was made redundant when his firm lost its franchise in September 2006. He set up in business as a willwriter. He did well and, by the time of his death in March 2009, the business was worth £70,000:

Cash	£30,000
Debtors	£4,000
Recurring income from storage fees of £4,000, for which an offer has been received of	£20,000
Other goodwill	£16,000

Roger, who had used all the nil rate band available, left all his estate to his partner Sally who had worked in the business and continued to run it with their daughter Gemma while Gemma was gaining appropriate qualifications. To encourage Gemma, Sally gave her a half share in the business in October 2010. In October 2010, the business has much the same value as in March 2009. It is considered that ownership of a part of this business is worth 90% of ownership of the whole, ie Sally's retained share is worth £31,500, so the gift to Gemma is a transfer of 70,000 – 31,500 = £38,500.

Applying *s 109*: the 'earlier transfer' qualified for relief in part. Roger had owned the business for over two years. It was carrying £15,000 more cash than it needed, but £55,000 of business relief was available, or nearly 80% of the transfer. The transfer to Gemma takes place before Sally has 'earned' BPR by two-year ownership, but the requirements of *s 109* are met. Relief is allowed on the transfer by Sally of 38,500 × 78.57% = £30,250.

Example 6.11: restricted relief (2)

Jennifer has owned a business for many years and agrees to sell it to her nephew David in April 2006. The price is £80,000, reflecting all of the value except goodwill, which is worth a further £20,000 and which also passes to David. David dies within 18 months of the purchase. The effect of this transaction will be to regard the sale by Jennifer as comprising in part a gift of £20,000. BPR is available. When David dies, *s 109(3)* operates so as to restrict the relief. Supposing the business to have fallen in value to £80,000, relief will be available only in respect of one fifth, being the fraction of the interest held by David which falls within the requirements of *s 109*. Relief is therefore £16,000.

For a time, specifically between 17 March 1987 and 5 April 1996, an additional rule was imposed by *s 109A*. The rule related to minority holdings of unquoted shares which did not qualify for the higher rate of relief unless the transferor held 25% of the votes throughout the two years immediately before the transfer.

LIQUIDATIONS AND RECONSTRUCTIONS

6.17   *IHTA 1984, s 113* specifically excludes, from its general rule, property in respect of which a binding contract for sale has been made where the property concerned is shares in, or securities of, a company and the sale is made for the purposes of reconstruction or amalgamation.

Under *s 113A*, relief is available only where the relevant business property disposed of by the transferor under a lifetime gift is kept by the transferee as business property in the hands of the transferee and remains so. A strict rule would be harsh where the original property had been replaced. To mitigate this, *s 113A(6)* allows relief where shares owned by the transferee immediately before the death of the transferor would qualify to be identified with the subject matter of the original gift under the CGT rules contained in *TCGA 1992, ss 126–136*, or where those shares were issued to the donee in consideration of the transfer of a business, or of an interest in a business, which in either case represented the original subject matter of the gift (or part of it). For *s 113A* to apply, the replacement must be of the whole asset.

A detailed examination of *TCGA 1992, ss 126–136* is outside the scope of this book but, in general terms, the relevant provisions concern reorganisation or reduction of share capital. For this purpose, 'reorganisation' means a reorganisation or reduction of a company's share capital; and, in relation to that reorganisation, 'original shares' means shares held before and concerned in the reorganisation, and 'new holdings' means the shares in and debentures of the company which represent the original shares as a result of the reorganisation

(TCGA 1992, s 126(1)). The effect of *TCGA 1992, s 127*, subject to the general code as to reorganisation, is to treat the original shares (taken as a single asset) and the new holding (likewise taken as a single asset) as being the same asset acquired as the original shares were acquired. See the detailed examination of *Executors of Dugan-Chapman deceased v HMRC* [2008] SpC 666 at **6.7** above.

A related subject, the relaxation of *s 113A* where the original property is sold, and other qualifying property is purchased, is described in **Chapter 8**. Apart from these specific exceptions, a liquidation of the company in which shares are held which would otherwise have qualified for BPR has the same effect as the sale of other categories of relevant business property. The relief is lost.

THE MEANING OF 'QUOTED'

6.18   The meaning of 'quoted' and 'unquoted' is explained in both *ss 105(1ZA)* and *113A(3B)*. The definition in *s 105(1ZA)* defines the availability of BPR on first consideration of the transfer rather than in relation to claw-back. The key is whether the relevant security is 'listed' rather than whether, from day to day, investors can see the price at which shares are traded. Thus, 'quoted' means 'listed on a recognised Stock Exchange' whilst 'unquoted' means 'not listed on a recognised Stock Exchange'. *Section 105(1ZA)* was inserted by *F (No 2) A 1992, Sch 14, paras 2* and *8* in relation to transfers of value made, and other events occurring, after 9 March 1992, but is subject to *F (No 2) A 1992, Sch 14, para 9*, though by now surely the specific qualifications of *Sch 14* must have run their course.

The existence of a market for unquoted shares does not automatically cause the loss of BPR. 'Unquoted' means and includes shares dealt in on the unlisted securities market and alternative investment market. It can also include shares traded on PLUS, a trading facility for dealing in unquoted shares, but take care: PLUS is, in effect, a partly regulated market: some shares are quoted and others are not.

Recognised stock exchange

6.19   The phrase 'recognised stock exchange' occurs throughout the *Taxes Acts*, for example in the definition of a close company in *ICTA 1988, s 415*. The definition itself occurs in *Income Tax Act 2007, s 1005* which is an improvement on the earlier, slightly unhelpful formula and means (with effect from 19 July 2007):

- any market of an investment exchange which is designated as a recognised stock exchange by an order of HMRC; or

- any market outside the UK which is so designated.

'Listed' means:

- admitted to trading in an exchange and included in the official UK list; or

- officially listed on a recognised exchange in a qualifying country outside the UK in conformity with provisions that correspond generally to what applies in EEA states;

and, by a circular definition, a 'qualifying country' is any country in which there is a recognised stock exchange. HMRC issued guidance on 29 March 2007 to answer questions that arose from Budget Note 37. The guidance was not primarily directed to IHT situations but does not exclude them. It notes that AIM is part of the London Stock Exchange and that the main exchange is recognised, so AIM shares are traded on a recognised exchange, but they are not 'listed' because they are not on the Official List maintained by the Financial Services Authority, which is the UK listing authority. The remainder of the AIM guidance concerns taxes other than IHT. It then draws a distinction between 'recognised investment exchanges' and 'recognised stock exchanges', noting that the investment exchanges will not automatically be designated as recognised stock exchanges. Such designation will be possible but not a foregone conclusion.

Securities traded in the Neuer Markt in Frankfurt, the Nouveau Marché in Paris and NASDAQ Europe (formerly EASDAQ) are not 'listed' by the relevant competent authority. Thus, shares on the Neuer Markt, Nouveau Marché and NASDAQ Europe benefit from the reliefs for unquoted securities that will qualify for BPR. This change does not affect NASDAQ because it is a recognised stock exchange.

Each situation should be examined carefully: for example, the Swedish exchange, OM, runs two lists, one for major companies and another for smaller entities. Swedish tax law favours the smaller companies, giving them special status, but that does not affect the English position. Since, in each case, the shares are 'listed', the only test to be satisfied is whether the shares in any given company are admitted to trading. If they are, the shares are 'quoted' for the purposes of BPR.

Other trading exchanges

6.20   Shares dealt in on the unlisted securities market (USM) used to be regarded by the Revenue as unquoted. For transfers after 16 March 1987, such shares came to be treated for all purposes as quoted shares. This was by virtue of the definition of 'quoted' contained in *IHTA 1984, s 272*, meaning listed on a recognised stock exchange or dealt in on the USM. However, for transfers after 9 March 1992, shares dealt in on the USM again came to be treated as unquoted for the purposes of BPR and for the purposes of instalment payment. Thus the significance of USM shares is now mainly concerned with valuation, as discussed in **Chapter 8**, where *s 168* is in point. The acceptance by the Revenue, in SP 18/80, that USM shares are unquoted was reversed by legislation. However, insofar as still relevant, the practice on the valuation of USM shares has probably not changed.

The present position is thus that BPR is available on a fairly wide range of securities, listed and 'quoted', in the sense that there is in the financial press a regular record of the prices at which deals have been struck. The nature of the PLUS (formerly OFEX) market is discussed at **13.7** below. HMRC's IHT Manual contains a history of the previous position but only an outline of which exchanges are recognised (see IHTM25191).

It is not to be assumed that all AIM and PLUS shareholdings qualify for BPR. The 'wholly or mainly' test in *s 105(3)* applies, and the accounts of an AIM or PLUS company will be examined to see if it qualifies as a trading company. Also, a company may have a secondary listing overseas which may be on a recognised exchange, robbing the shares of relief.

Which stock exchanges are actually recognised?

6.21   For an up-to-date view but, as will be seen, not quite the full picture, consult the HMRC website at www.hmrc.gov.uk/fid/table1-rse.pdf. Table 6.1 below, setting out those exchanges now designated by Order under *ICTA 1988, s 841(1)(b)* and *ITA 2007, s 1005*, recognises the following, from the dates shown. What follows is an adaptation of the table. As will be seen, HMRC have not been swift to recognise new or reconstructed exchanges, so some tracing may be needed to see if an entity now trading is part of what was previously recognised. This is, frankly, unnecessary and unacceptable and, with the growth of cross-border trading by sophisticated investors, will become more and more of a problem. Table 6.2 below sets out the exchanges that are recognised by country rather than by market.

Table 6.1

Athens Stock Exchange	Securities Market and Derivatives Market	14.6.1993
Australian Stock Exchange and any of its Stock Exchange subsidiaries	following its 2006 merger with Sydney Futures Exchange, known as Australian Securities Exchange; but only that part of the new exchange that can be identified as the original Australian Stock Exchange is recognised	22.9.1988
Bovespa	see Sao Paulo below	
Bermuda Stock Exchange		4.12.2007
Bond Exchange of South Africa	the whole market except the over-the-counter market, which is not listed	16.4.2008
Cayman Islands Stock Exchange		4.3.2004
Colombo Stock Exchange	this is difficult, because not every platform may meet the HMRC definition of 'listed', so practitioners should contact HMRC with details to see if the platform is listed	21.2.1972
Copenhagen Stock Exchange	see OMX	22.10.1970
Helsinki Stock Exchange	see OMX	22.10.1970
Iceland Stock Exchange	see OMX, as to the main market; the Alternative Market is not recognised	22.10.1970
Johannesburg Stock Exchange	Main Board; not the Alt-X, VCM or DCM markets	22.10.1970
Korea Stock Exchange	as with Colombo (see above), not all trading is recognised, so contact HMRC	10.10.1994
Kuala Lumpur Stock Exchange	as with Colombo (see above), not all trading is recognised, so contact HMRC	10.10.1994

London Stock Exchange	the Main Market is recognised, as is the Professional Securities Market, but not the AIM nor the Specialist Fund Market; 'listed' means securities included on the official list maintained by the FSA as listing authority. See also the Plus-listed market below.	Main Market has long been recognised, but specifically so designated on 19.7.2007
Malta Stock Exchange		29.12.2005
Mexico Stock Exchange	as with Colombo (see above), not all trading is recognised, so contact HMRC	10.10.1994
New Zealand Stock Exchange	the NZSX Market (Main Board) but not the NZAX (Alternative Market); but, since the renaming as New Zealand Exchange Ltd, HMRC are reviewing which market will meet the definition of 'listed'	22.9.1988
OMX Nordic Exchange	the stock exchanges of Stockholm, Copenhagen, Iceland and Helsinki are all part of OMX, which in turn is part of NASDAQ OMX Group. Only that part of the new exchange that can be traced back to the exchange that was originally designated as a recognised exchange can now be treated as recognised	the date of recognition is shown against the original exchange in this table
Plus-listed market	note that only the Plus-listed market is recognised, not the Plus-traded nor the Plus-quoted markets; the Plus-listed market is recognised, which admits to trading securities that are on the UK official list (see London above)	19.7.2007
Rio de Janeiro Stock Exchange	as with Colombo (see above), not all trading is recognised, so contact HMRC	17.8.1995

San Paolo Stock Exchange	the Main Market, but only insofar as traceable to the old Sao Paulo Exchange following the 2008 merger with the Brazilian Mercantile and Futures Exchange and now known as Bovespa; and not the over-the-counter market	11.12.1995
Singapore Stock Exchange	securities officially listed on the Main Board of the new market, SGX, that resulted from the merger with two earlier exchanges that were not recognised; only the part traceable to the original exchange is recognised	30.6.1977
South Africa	see Bond Exchange of South Africa above	
Stockholm Stock Exchange	see OMX	16.7.1985
Stock Exchange of Thailand	as with Colombo (see above), not all trading is recognised, so contact HMRC	10.10.1994
Swiss Stock Exchange	Main Market and EU Compatible Market; renamed Swiss Exchange in 2002	12.5.1997

Table 6.2

Any stock exchange is designated as a recognised stock exchange in the following countries which is a stock exchange within the meaning of the law of the particular country relating to stock exchanges (or as specified below). Listing is noted separately.

Austria	Vienna Stock Exchange, the Amtlicher Handel (Official market) and the Geregelter Freiverkehr (semi-official market): 22.10.1970
Belgium	NYSE Euronext Brussels, formerly the Brussels Stock Exchange; and Le marché hors bourse des obligations lineares, des titres scindes et des certificats de tresorerie: 22.10.1970; but the NYSE Alternext is unlisted

Canada	Toronto Stock Exchange, Montreal Stock Exchange and Toronto Venture Exchange: 22.10.1970; of t hese, all of the Toronto and Montreal Stock Exchanges, but only Tiers 1 and 2 of the Venture Exchange, are listed, leaving Tier 3 of the Venture Exchange unlisted
France	NYSE Euronext Paris, formerly the Paris Stock Exchange; MATIF and MONEP: 22.10.1970; all listed, that in Paris as NYSE Euronext France (though doubtless the location of that capital city is actually known to many Americans)
Germany	the regional history of the country lives on in its exchanges, in that, although Frankfurt may dominate, there are 'Amtlicher and Geregelter' exchanges in Berlin, Dusseldorf, Hamburg, Hannover, Munich and Stuttgart; and that in Bremen is allied to Berlin, not (as one might assume) with its closer neighbour Hamburg; all these are known as the 'regulierter' markets and are recognised from 5.8.1971; also recognised are the Risk Management Exchange of Hannover and the European Energy Exchange; the unlisted markets are the Freiverkehr markets and entry markets at these various centres
Guernsey	Channel Islands Stock Exchange: 10.12.2002
Hong Kong	Hong Kong Stock Exchange: 26.2.1971; the Main board is listed, but the Growth and Enterprise Market is unlisted
Italy	The Italian Stock Exchange (Borsa Italiana) is listed as to: its Electronic Share Market, MTAX Market, Expandi Market, MOT, ETF-Plus, SeDex and IDEM; also the MTS, MTS Corporate and the Bond Vision TLX market
Ireland (Republic of)	Irish Stock Exchange, Main market and Alternative Securities Market: 22.10.1970; the Irish Enterprise Exchange is unlisted
Japan	Tokyo Stock Exchange, Main board and Mothers market; the Main market of Nagora and Osaka Stock Exchanges; the Sapporo Securities Exchange and JASDAQ. JASDAQ was originally an over-the-counter market but became recognised from 3.12.2004

Luxembourg	Luxembourg Stock Exchange (Bourse de Luxembourg), Main market and EURO MTF
Netherlands	NYSE Euronext Amsterdam, formerly the Amsterdam Stock Exchange, Endex; MTS Amsterdam: 22.10.1970; the listed markets are NYSE Euronext, Amsterdam Cash Market, Derivatives Market, Endex and MTS; the NYSE Alternext is unlisted
Norway	Oslo Stock Exchange, Nord Pool, Imarex, Fish Pool and Fishex: 22.10.1970; the listed markets are Oslo Bors, Oslo Axess and Oslo Alternative Bond Market
Portugal	NYSE Euronext Lisbon, formerly the Lisbon Stock Exchange; Mercado de Futures e Opcoes; MEDIP: 21.2.1972
Spain	Bolsas de Valores of Barcelona, Madrid and Valencia; Mercados oficiales de Productos Financieros Derivados, MFAO de Futuros del Aciete do Oliva, AIAF Mercado de Renta Fija; Mercados de Deuda Publica en Anotaciones: 5.8.1971
USA	Any exchange registered with the Securities and Exchange Commission of the United States as a national securities exchange: thus the Main markets at the American Stock Exchange, Boston Stock Exchange, Chicago (both Board Options and Stock Exchanges), International Securities Exchange, National (formerly Cincinnati) Stock Exchange, New York Stock Exchange, NYSE Arca (formerly Pacific Exchange), Philadelphia Stock Exchange and NASDAQ. The NASDAQ stock market, as maintained through the facilities of the National Association of Securities Dealers Inc and its subsidiaries, is recognised and, of it, NASDAQ Global, Global Select and Capital Market are listed

The list of recognised stock exchanges is updated periodically. Copies may be obtained direct from Financial Institutions Division, Second Floor, West Wing, Somerset House, Strand, London WC2R 1LB (tel. 020 7438 6262).

THE WINDING-UP EXCLUSION

6.22   The concept, that BPR will be denied where the business property is subject to a binding contract for sale, is defined in most respects by *IHTA 1984, s 113*, which was considered at **6.13** above. It is thus possible for a person to own an interest in a business and to keep the benefit of BPR, notwithstanding the sale of one of the assets of the business and replacement of that asset by cash or other asset used in the business. The situation is different where the asset qualifying for BPR is a shareholding in that, where the shareholding is retained but an order is made to wind up the company, BPR is lost.

Section 105(5) excludes from BPR shares in or securities of a company if, at the time of the transfer:

- a winding-up order has been made in respect of the company; or

- the company has passed a resolution for voluntary winding up; or

- the company is otherwise in the process of liquidation;

unless the business of the company is to continue to be carried on after a reconstruction or amalgamation, and the reconstruction or amalgamation either is:

- the purpose of the winding up or liquidation; or

- takes place not later than one year after the transfer of value.

In effect, therefore, BPR on a shareholding is lost either where the shares themselves are sold, under *s 113*, or where the underlying business is terminated or disposed of under *s 105(5)*.

Chapter 7

Relevant business property: exceptions to the relief: excepted assets

QUICK GUIDE

Excepted assets cause problems. To see whether the rules apply, go to the flowchart on page 175 . If the rule applies, first value the business entity as a whole to establish the potentially taxable value, then revalue the business without the excepted assets to establish the amount available for BPR.

There are endless permutations, especially with a group of companies or with a 'hybrid' company: see **7.5**. The leading case on excepted assets is still *Barclays Bank Trust Co Limited v IRC*, examined at **7.11**.

EXCEPTED ASSETS

7.1   The provisions of *IHTA 1984, s 112* give rise to many difficulties (and disappointments) in practice. Any assets which are 'excepted' within the meaning of *s 112(2)* are left out of account in calculating BPR. The relief is, after all, so valuable that there is a strong incentive either to place within a business assets which do not relate to it or to leave within that business surplus cash. The problem can arise by stealth where, over a period of time as a business matures, the nature of the business changes and the balance sheet strengthens.

Example 7.1: organic development of a business

James, a farrier, served the proprietors of canal barges used to haul goods in the early stages of the Industrial Revolution. His son Nathaniel expanded the business to include repairs to horse-drawn vehicles, for that purpose buying larger premises with house and meadowland with the facility for the horses of customers to be stabled whilst awaiting attention and for vehicles to be repaired. He lived in the house. His son Allan substituted petrol vehicle repair for the equine side of the business, which was discontinued.

174

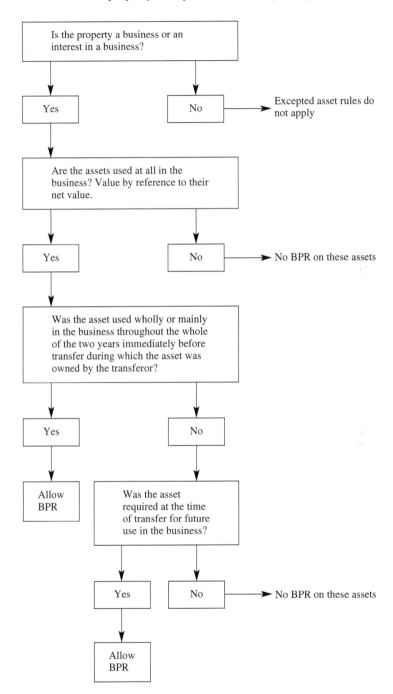

Allan's children now have a transport operator's licence where the stables and yard used to be, and have residential planning permission on the part of the old paddock which they have not already developed. Grandfather's cottage is vacant, being used only for the storage of old business records and memorabilia. The stabling was demolished when Allan and his children developed the site so as to incorporate the administrative offices of the haulage business, the ground floor being divided between a coffee bar, a small estate office from which the family's portfolio of let properties is managed, and an amusement arcade. All the freeholds and improvements are still in the partnership accounts at cost. The building work has been paid for and there is now a sum on deposit equal to two years' turnover. The cottage and estate office are not used for the purposes of the business(es). They are excepted assets. Almost certainly, some of the cash is an excluded asset also: see the case law commentary below.

Section 112(2) defines as an excepted asset any asset if it was neither:

- used wholly or mainly for the purposes of the business concerned throughout the whole (or the last two years) of the 'relevant period' (see below); nor

- required at the time of the transfer for future use for those purposes;

but with a saving where the business itself is carried on by a company (see the reference to *s 111* at **8.14**).

Group structures

That saving allows the use of an asset for the purposes of a business carried on by another company which, at the time of use and immediately before the transfer, was a member of the same group to be treated as use for the purposes of the business concerned, *unless* the membership of the group of that other company falls to be disregarded under *s 111*. Where a group contains dormant companies, it is submitted that the existence of such companies within the group does not prejudice BPR on the group: the dormant subsidiaries are disregarded under *s 111*. The value of their assets attracts no relief.

The test period for excepted assets

'The relevant period' in *s 112(2)* means, by virtue of *s 112(5)*, the period immediately preceding the transfer of value during which the asset was owned by the transferor. If the relevant business property is an interest in a business, the relevant period is that which precedes the transfer of a corresponding interest in the asset. This is one of the few occasions when the BPR code (necessarily) looks at the underlying asset, rather than at the actual interest held. If the business concerned is carried on by a company, the relevant period is that immediately preceding the transfer of value during which the asset was owned by that company or any group company (here meaning another company which, immediately before the transfer of value, was a member of the same group).

Where the excepted asset rule does not apply

The exclusion of an asset from BPR under *s 112(2)* as an excepted asset does not apply (see *s 112(3)*) in relation to an asset which is relevant business property in its own right under *s 105(1)(d)*. This was noted in **Chapter 5** in considering property falling within that section. An asset is not relevant business property by virtue of *s 105(1)(d)* unless either:

- it was used throughout the two years immediately preceding transfer of value which falls within *s 105(1)(d)*; or

- it replaced another asset which was used in that manner, and both it and the replacement asset or its replacement were used for periods which together comprise at least two years within the five years immediately preceding the transfer of value.

The rule in *s 112(3)* is further qualified by *s 109* (successive transfers) so that the rule in *s 112(3)* is treated as being satisfied if the assets or the replacement assets were used:

- throughout the period between 'the earlier and the subsequent transfer', as defined in that section; or

- throughout the part of that period during which the assets were owned by the transferor or the spouse of the transferor.

Applying the test

The strict view, for which IHTM25341 is the main authority, is that there is a two-stage process. This is explained in the flowchart on page 175. HMRC include a flowchart at IHTM25362 that fits their cross-referencing to other paragraphs in the Manual.

Although there is no formal Concession to this effect, some latitude is allowed in the particular situation where a business is transferred by a sole trader to a company which he controls, and the trader retains land or buildings, machinery or plant which are used in the business. Strictly speaking, if the transferor dies within the two-year period following the transfer to the company, those assets have not been used by the company for at least two years, as required strictly by *ss 112(3)* and *105(1)(d)*. In practice, the relief is allowed.

Use versus ownership

7.2   The test of two years' ownership in *s 106* stands alone, and must be satisfied independently of the test as to use in *s 112*. It is necessary to comply with both sections to qualify for BPR. An asset held for many years, but not used in the business, will not qualify for relief except under the 'future use' test in *s 112(2)(b)*. The extent of that test is considered in the case law commentary below.

Some apportionment is allowed under *s 112(4)* for assets of mixed use. Where part of any land or building is used exclusively for the purposes of the building, and the remainder is not so used and, but for *s 112(4)*, the land would be regarded as an excepted asset, or where, under *s 112(3)*, the land would not qualify for BPR, it is possible to divide the premises. The part used for the purposes of the building qualifies for BPR, and the remainder does not. The division is on a just and reasonable apportionment of the value. This rule can help when considering farmhouses that do not, for some reason, qualify for APR. If debt is secured on the asset or premises, it must be apportioned. Insofar as attributable to the part used for business, that debt reduces the relief otherwise available.

Personal use

7.3   An asset does not qualify for BPR when it is used wholly or mainly for the personal benefit of the transferor or of a person connected with the transferor. This provision is intended to catch luxury assets such as houses, virtually no part of which are a business premises, caravans, yachts and similar assets. In practice, the 'excepted assets' argument is easier to resist when considering a company than in relation to a partnership or a sole trader. Within a company, all assets tend to be regarded as held for the purposes of the trade unless, as in the case of a yacht, that simply cannot be justified. Basically, if a company passes the 'wholly or mainly' tests examined in **Chapter 9** below, most of its value will usually attract BPR.

Valuation principles applied where there are excepted assets

7.4   To fix the value qualifying for relief, *s 112(1)* requires that the part of the value of relevant business property which is attributable to the excepted assets be left out of account. Usually, the effect will be to reduce the value that qualifies for relief, either by the whole of the value of the excepted asset, in the case of a sole proprietor, or by a proportion where the business is a partnership. As a result of the double test mentioned above, an asset which is required for *future* use in an unincorporated business will not qualify for relief unless it is being used in the business at the time of the transfer: see the flowchart. That is the strict view: in practice, BPR may occasionally have been allowed (or at least an erroneous claim not challenged) in respect of assets which are 'required' for use, within *s 112(1)(b)*, but which may not in fact have been used much in the past for the purposes of the business.

The value of shares or securities otherwise qualifying for BPR must be adjusted for the purposes of *s 112*. First, it is necessary to consider the entire value of the assets of the company, including the excepted assets; and then, having established that figure, to fix the value being transferred, it is necessary to revalue the shares after taking out the excepted assets in order to compute the BPR. Where the holding to be valued is an influential one and where, under general valuation principles, it is more appropriate to look at the net asset value of the company than at the income those assets produce, the effect of *s 112* may be quite marked. Where, on the other hand, the transfer is of an uninfluential minority holding, it may be that there is little difference in value after stripping out the excepted assets.

Section 112 applies not merely where the company owns assets which are, to all intents and purposes, irrelevant to the carrying on of the business, such as the chairman's holiday home, but also to assets which are excluded from BPR by virtue of *s 105(3)* such as investments, investment properties and excess cash.

Example 7.2: examination of the business in Example 7.1

In Example 7.1 concerning James and his family, the family carry on separate trades of a haulage business, a coffee bar, the management of an amusement arcade, and the administration of a portfolio of let properties. Of these, the management of the let properties is an activity within *s 105(3)* and, as such, excepted under *s 112*. Had the family traded through the medium of a company, it would be necessary to determine, by looking at turnover, assets and the main activities of the company, whether it was engaged mainly in haulage or in property management.

A common case is of a company which has a genuine building trade and also retains certain properties as investments. If it can be shown that, on the whole, the company is trading as a builder rather than engaged in property management, all of the assets of the company will qualify for BPR. *Section 112* does not apply so as to exclude the investment properties from the relief. *Section 112* will operate to exclude from BPR only those assets which are not used by the company either for its building trade or as investments.

Valuation where assets used in part for business purposes

7.5   *Section 112(4)* provides a useful rule where land or buildings are not used wholly or mainly for business purposes, but in part constitute 'excepted assets'. The value of any part of the property that is used exclusively for the purposes of the business will qualify for BPR, and it is only the value of the part that is not so used that fails to qualify for relief by virtue of *s 112*. Exclusive use for this purpose will include use by another member of the group, provided that:

• the company using it is a member of the group at the time of the use and immediately before the transfer; and

• that separate company is not excluded by the rule in *s 111*.

Earlier versions of IHTM contained advice that practitioners should still heed: 'This is a difficult area as there is a subjective element involved. You must not become involved in serious disputes on this topic [without consulting Appeals Team via your Team Leader]'.

SPECIAL RULES FOR CORPORATE STRUCTURES?

7.6   It is argued by many that the rules as to excepted assets work differently on companies than on partnerships and sole traders. Although the argument has probably existed for years, it was given greater prominence by the comments of that specialist in this area, William Massey QC, in June 2003. Other contributors have been Malcolm Gunn, writing in *Taxation* magazine, and Roger Jones, writing in STEP Journal. The issue is whether a company that is otherwise considered to be trading may hold assets that are not used for the main trade but which may be considered to be held for a subsidiary part of the business of the company.

The argument can be highlighted by considering the cases that clearly fall one side of the line or the other. Where the investment activities of the company predominate, the rules as to excepted assets do not apply, because the company is not a trading company within *s 105(3)*. Where, by measuring the turnover, profit, capital and use of human resources, the investment content of a trading company is minimal, say 1% or less, *s 112* will have no effect, because the valuation principles described at **7.4** above are sufficiently imprecise that the value of the shares will be the same, whether or not the company holds assets that are not used for the purposes of its trade.

Example 7.3: Spanish villa

A company trades, for example providing plumbing and heating installations. It owns two special assets: a villa in Spain that is used by employees who are closely related to the managing director; and a portfolio of quoted investments. The villa will be an excepted asset on the 'personal use' test described at **7.3** above. It is the investments that are the subject of the discussion initiated by William Massey QC.

Mr Massey argues that, provided a company is not wholly or mainly an investment company, the fact that, alongside its trade, it may own an investment property has no adverse effect on the availability of BPR for the shares, and claims that this has traditionally been accepted by HMRC, with one possible exception: excess cash on deposit, for which the authority is *Barclays Bank Trust Co Ltd v IRC*, considered in detail at **7.11** below. That much is not contentious. However, Mr Massey would go further. He argues that the decision in *Barclays Bank Trust Co Ltd v IRC* is unsatisfactory because it was not argued there for the taxpayer that, by being put on deposit so as to earn interest, the cash was being presently used at the date of the death of the shareholder for the purposes of the business of the company within the decision in *American Leaf Blending Co v Director-General of Inland Revenue (Malaysia)*.

HMRC have revised their guidance. They used to recommend a practical approach to the problem, under which the Inspector should consider the nature and extent of the business operation and whether the investment interests are part of a 'hybrid business activity'. If the company was mainly trading, ie did not fail the 'wholly or mainly' test of *s 105(3)*, the Inspector was not to apply *s 112* to investments in the company. *Section 112* can apply only to assets which are not used either for the main trade of the company or for its investment business. That may still be their approach, but the Manual, at IHTM5342 *et seq*, is no longer so forthcoming.

THE MEANING OF 'BUSINESS'

7.7   One difficulty is to identify 'business' for this purpose. In the context of corporation tax, it was established in *Jowett v O'Neill and Brennan Construction Ltd* [1998] STC 482 that a company was not carrying on a business merely because it held a bank deposit and received interest. Another rule from corporation tax is Statement of Practice SP5/94, concerned with associated companies and small companies' relief. HMRC consider that a holding company which does not carry on a trade, but which holds shares in one or more companies which are its 51% subsidiaries, may or may not be carrying on a business in respect of that holding. The Revenue considered, in SP5/94, that a company would not be regarded as carrying on a business if:

- it had no assets other than shares in companies that were 51% subsidiaries;
- it was not entitled to a deduction for management expenses in respect of outgoings;
- it had no income or gains other than dividends which were franked investment income received by the company, and
- the 51% subsidiaries qualified as such under *ICTA 1988, s 13ZA* and related legislation.

Put more simply, SP5/94 states that, under *ICTA 1988, s 13(4)*, a company that does not carry on a trade or business in an accounting year is disregarded for the purposes of small companies' relief.

The problem is that, until a case comes before the Special Commissioners, which is argued with the thoroughness that characterises the work of advocates such as William Massey QC, we simply do not know whether the concept of carrying on a business should be lifted from corporation tax and carried across to be applied to BPR. *American Leaf Blending* was considered at **5.8** and must be the starting point for the debate. However, it sits uneasily with *Jowett v O'Neill*. The VAT case of *C & E Commissioners v Lord Fisher*, also considered at **5.8**, is a helpful summary of pointers towards the carrying on of a business.

However, *Rashid v Garcia* [2003] STC (SCD) 36 is a pointer the other way. That case concerned the liability of the appellant to pay class 2 National Insurance contributions in respect of 'earnings' from property letting. The Special Commissioner held that, whilst it was not free from doubt, the arrangements did not amount to a business. Rather, it was an investment which, by its nature, required some activity to maintain it. The issue whether a trade was being carried on was again considered in *Manzur v Revenue and Customs Commissioners* [2010] UKFTT 580(TC) in relation to share dealing losses. A retired surgeon managed a share portfolio, engaging in rapid trading, but made losses which he wished to set against other income. HMRC argued that:

- the trading volume was low;

- there were no customers;

- the taxpayer had no qualifications and was not regulated by the FSA;

- trading was done within a two-hour window in the afternoon;

- some investments were held for months, not days; there were fewer than 300 deals in a year; so

- the activity was consistent with speculative investment.

The First-tier Tribunal agreed. The taxpayer was not trading. The transactions were the management of an investment portfolio, with some holdings being retained for longer periods. The case should perhaps be seen in the context of a time when widespread share losses were being sustained by private investors, such that offset against income might cost the exchequer dear. It might be exploited in better times by canny families of savers who consistently make gains from 'day trading', but take care not to exceed the exempt amount for gains of each family member.

THE LEADING CASE: McCALL V HMRC

7.8   The nature of a business was considered in *McCall v Revenue and Customs Commissioners* [2009] NICA 12, in which Mr Massey appeared for the taxpayer on a claim to BPR on 33 acres of farmland that had development value. The decision of Mr Hellier as Special Commissioner in that case followed the well-trodden path which is also adopted in this work, noting that 'business' means more than 'trade' and quoting many of the authorities noted here. By a narrow margin, the work done by the relative in *McClean* did amount to a business; but it was held to be an investment business, so the taxpayer failed to secure valuable relief on development land.

On appeal, the Court of Appeal in Northern Ireland had to consider a sensitive issue, because much land there is held and enjoyed in the way that applied in this case. The court did not upset the Commissioner's findings of fact or the conclusions derived therefrom. The test is that of the intelligent businessman, who would be concerned as to the use to which the land was put, something that turns on the facts of each case. As a general rule, a landowner who derives income from land holds an investment, even though, to earn the income, he may carry out maintenance and management work. The work in this case was within that description. The graziers had occupation that was sufficiently exclusive, even of the landowner, so that the land was an investment. The landowner could not, during the currency of the grazing agreement, use the land for anything else.

HMRC commentary

7.9   As is right, the guidance is practical and purposive, stressing (see SVM111220) the use by valuers of their discretion. The legislation is targeted at significant and conspicuous assets. The specific guidance in relation to a mixed business is that 'the excepted assets rules can only apply to assets which are not used in either part of the hybrid's business'.

This attitude is reinforced in SVM111220, although not without reservation. It points out that 'a degree of activity is required to constitute a business, and whether investments involves sufficient activity must depend on their nature and the particular facts'. It is important how matters are viewed by the directors and shareholders of the company, and how the business is described in the report of the directors that accompanies the annual accounts.

SVM111220 goes on to set out specific guidance on surplus cash and on shares and securities. As to cash, there are five tests to apply, because the holding of cash cannot be regarded as a separate investment business nor as part of the hybrid business: 'It requires no effort and involves no activity'. The tests are:

- Was the cash used for the business?
- Was the cash used to finance the business carried on by the company?
- How much cash did the company use regularly?
- What were its short-term cash requirements?
- Does the amount of cash fluctuate?

In relation to shares and securities, there will be many factual considerations, such as the size of the holdings, the time spent on managing them, and the reason they are held.

Hybrid company

7.10   A practical approach is appropriate.

Example 7.4: mixed development

A claim is made to BPR in respect of the shares of James Benjamin Holdings Ltd. The annual report and accounts disclose that the group of which that company is the top holding company includes the following subsidiaries:

- Jim's Music Ltd – retailer of CDs and DVDs;
- Benjamin Nursing Homes Ltd – operator of nursing homes;
- Benjamin (Elbingerode) GmbH – property trading and development; and
- Benjamin Heritable Securities Ltd – property investment.

It appears from the accounts that about two-thirds of the profit of the group is earned from selling CDs or DVDs and from the nursing home, and one-third from the property redevelopment activities in the area of the Harz Mountains in Germany and the ownership of estates in Scotland. Examination of the payroll shows that only 5% of employees are engaged in property development or investment, the remainder working at selling CDs and DVDs or in the nursing homes.

Seen from the perspective of the employment of capital, the emphasis is rather different. Jim's Music trades almost exclusively from rented pitches in high street stores and has no freeholds. The nursing home freeholds amount to about one-third of the value of all properties held by the group, one quarter of the total being the German redevelopment scheme and the remainder the estates in Scotland. Of this last category, the jewel in the property crown is almost certainly an interest in one of the finest beats on the Tweed. Although this factor is not declared in the accounts of the company, the game book shows that, of the salmon grassed in the previous season, 75% were taken by James Benjamin or members of his party.

The issue here is, first, whether the business of James Benjamin Holdings Ltd taken as a whole qualifies for BPR; and, second, if the taxpayer succeeds on that point, whether *IHTA 1984, ss 110(c)* and *112(2)* will operate to restrict relief. Probably, taken as a whole, this hybrid company is mainly trading. The exception is Heritable Securities, the operations of which fall entirely within *s 105(3)*. The value of Heritable Securities should therefore be excluded from the claim under *s 110(c)*.

What about the development in the Harz Mountains? The observations of Joel Barnett MP, then Chief Secretary to the Treasury, in 1976 in a reply to a question in Standing Committee E may still be relevant: 'BPR should apply on the transfer of a property dealing business provided that the business includes building construction or land development'. He gave a further assurance that the housing stocks of a building company would qualify for BPR if those stocks were regarded in the accounts of the company as stock in trade. VAT will often be in point here. If, on the facts, it can be shown that Elbingerode is actually developing land and involved in the construction of properties, BPR may be allowable, as it was in *DWP Piercy* examined below.

What about the company as a whole? Quite a strong argument can be made out that this hybrid company is mainly trading, particularly after excluding Heritable Securities. The fact that, within the balance sheet, there may be some investments should not cause the 'excepted assets' rules to apply, with one exception: the salmon fishing. That asset is, however, held by the company to which *s 110(c)* applies, so BPR in respect of that asset is no longer in issue.

CASE LAW COMMENTARY

Barclays Bank Trust Co Ltd v IRC

7.11   This case proceeded only as far as a decision of the Special Commissioner, of which the report is refreshingly brief. In *Barclays Bank Trust Co Ltd v IRC* [1998] STC (SCD) 125, the deceased died in November 1990. She held half the shares in a company, and her husband, who had at times been a general dealer, held the remainder. The company dealt, inter alia, in bathroom and kitchen fittings, mainly to the trade. The company did not tie up working capital either in premises (which were owned by the husband) or in stock. The company's cash at bank and in hand in 1990 was rising, culminating in a balance of over £450,000. Cash was invested for periods of up to 30 days. The turnover was about £600,000; less in the final year. Although this analysis is not set out in the report, cash relative to turnover was as follows:

Year 1986–87   31.25%
Year 1987–88   42.43%
Year 1988–89   56.96%
Year 1989–90   68.87%
Period 1990–91   92.90%

It was accepted on behalf of the Crown that the company needed cash of £150,000; seen as a fraction of turnover, that was a fair, even a generous, concession to make and one that is relevant to cases now. On turnover averaging £600,000, it represents 25%.

About eight months before the death of the deceased, the company had approached a similar company with a view to buying the properties of that company. There was no reply. The other company was later liquidated. In 1997, the company spent over £355,000 purchasing goods which were imported from China.

The Revenue issued a notice of determination that £300,000 of the cash deposit at the time of the death was not required for the purposes of the business under *s 112(2)(b)*. The executors appealed.

The Special Commissioner, holding that the case turned on a question of fact, decided on the evidence that the £300,000 was not required for the purposes of a business. In view of his finding that this was a question of fact, later litigants may have little difficulty in distinguishing it. They should take some notice, however, of the guidance of the Special Commissioner that an asset does not cease to be an excepted asset merely because, at the time for determining the question, that asset might be required at any time in the future. 'Required' in *s 112(2)(b)* did not include the mere possibility that the money might be required should an opportunity arise in two, three or seven years' time for the purposes of the business. The wording of *s 112(2)(b)* implied some imperative that the money would be used on a given project or for some 'palpable business purpose'.

In the particular facts in *Barclays Bank Trust Co v IRC*, there was no evidence that the company would, at the date of death, be the purchaser of the assets of the other company. The money was not 'required'.

Whether an asset is required for future use is a matter of fact, to be decided, as in *Barclays Bank v IRC*, at the time of the transfer. Seasonality in a business will be relevant: the cash balances required by farmers at certain times of year are far greater than at other times, and this is a factor to be argued where the date of the transfer happens to occur at a time when cash resources are high. SVM11230 notes that travel agents may hold high balances at certain times

186

of year. That trade, in particular, relies on cash balances to avoid the need for very expensive trading bonds that are otherwise required by airlines and holiday operators. Of particular relevance at the time of writing is the attitude to difficult trading conditions; again, see SVM11230:

> 'Similarly in times of recession a company may hold significant amounts of cash and/or other investments and in a period when that company is making losses the income stream could be considered as supporting the company's main trading activity.'

There is some interrelation between treatment for income tax and inheritance tax. For example, where a private use proportion of 50% has been agreed for income tax in relation to vehicles used in a business, that same proportion of the value of those vehicles may be disallowed under *s 112*, although it seems that HMRC do not always take this point. There will be cases where this aspect has only a marginal effect on value overall. The value of a building in multiple use can be split and treated as two assets, part being used exclusively for the purposes of the business and qualifying for relief, and part being excepted assets. That would apply, in the case of Allan in Example 7.1, to the part of the new building occupied as administrative offices for the haulage business, and to the parts from which the family carried on the separate trades of a coffee bar and an amusement arcade.

Salaried Persons Postal Loans Ltd v HMRC

7.12   The issue in this case, reported at [2006] EWHC 763 (Ch), was whether an associated company carried on business by receiving rent. The company had carried on a 'trade' until 1995 but not thereafter; but what was relevant, for *ICTA 1988, s 13*, was whether it carried on a 'business'. It had vacated its freehold premises back in 1966 and let them to a third party. Once the company ceased to trade, the rent was its only income. The letting had been to the same tenant for over 30 years, involving little activity, so when HMRC restricted the small companies' relief, on the grounds that this was an associated company, the company appealed.

The Special Commissioner held that the company had not carried on a business in the years in point, and that the letting was independent of the trade of the company. That view was upheld on appeal: the company had not bought the premises as an investment. When the company ceased to trade, the rent was the only income left. It merely received rents and authorised review of those rents, but there was no active participation in the management of the property. There was no artificial arrangement to take advantage of the small companies' rate.

Clearly, there may be circumstances where a taxpayer may hope for the interpretation of similar facts to go the other way where BPR is in point.

The meaning of 'group' for BPR

7.13   In *Grimwood-Taylor and Mallender v IRC* [2000] STC (SCD) 39, a case which turned on the interpretation of *s 103(3)*, the 'wholly or mainly' exception which is discussed elsewhere in this book, the Special Commissioner had to determine the meaning of 'group' for BPR. It is also relevant when considering excepted assets (see IHTM25342).

The taxpayer had died in September 1986, holding investments in a number of companies. The Inland Revenue determined that his holdings in N Investments and BB Estates Company ('BB') did not qualify for BPR.

N Investments was incorporated in Eire. The deceased owned all of it. He owned 28.99% of BB, which was incorporated in England but resident in Jersey. The rest of BB was in trust for his children. He also owned NH Farms Ltd and C Ltd, which were English companies. The reports of the directors showed that N Investments had not traded during the year ended 5 April 1983. BB had as its principal activity the holding and management of property estates. NH Farms Ltd farmed. C Ltd was an investment company. There were accumulated losses in N Investments and in BB, as well as in the other companies.

The executors argued that N Investments, C Ltd and NH Farms Ltd should all qualify for BPR as part of a group. They acknowledged that C Ltd and N Investments were involved wholly or mainly in holding land and buildings, but these were occupied by NH Farms Ltd, which did qualify for BPR.

The tribunal looked at the report of the directors, which the executors might have wished that it would ignore. IRCT argued that, as the land had been bought for occupation by the shareholders, the business of the non-trading companies was carried on otherwise than for gain. The businesses therefore fell outside the rules for BPR because of *IHTA 1984, s 103(3)*.

The Special Commissioner would accept that BPR applied only if the companies were a group. 'Group' is not defined in *IHTA 1984*, save that *s 103(2)* indicates that 'for the purposes of this Chapter a company and all its subsidiaries are members of a group'. Whilst the deceased owned all the shares in NH Farms Ltd and in C Ltd and in N Investments, the fact that he owned those shares did not make them members of a group.

The executor had referred to VAT legislation, but the latest and most helpful version of it was not in force when the taxpayer died. Various arguments were tried including that, since the settlement was for the children of the deceased, the directors 'shared a common purpose' with the deceased.

What was fatal to these arguments was that BB was incorporated in England but resident in Jersey. There was no evidence that it had an established place of business in the UK. Its investments were run by Chase Bank in Jersey. The company was non-resident.

The Special Commissioner therefore decided that the various companies were not members of a group for the purposes of *IHTA 1984, ss 111* and *112*: see *Grimwood-Taylor and Mallender (as executors of Mallender deceased) v IRC* [2000] STC (SCD) 39.

Use of pension funds

7.14   Surpluses arise when the cash spun off from trading exceeds the amount on which the directors are prepared to pay income-related taxes. Difficulties arise where an elderly family member has given away shares but does not want the donees to enjoy any income from the gift. One tactic is to pay funds to an employee benefit trust. The trust must be for all employees of the company but, in a family-run business, that may not matter too much. Once in the trust, the money is lost to the business.

Interaction of excepted assets and debt

7.15   An apportionment is required to set debt against taxable assets.

Example 7.5: debt reducing relief

Donald practises as an optician, originally working from home. The balance sheet of the business comprises:

Premises	300,000
Other business assets	800,000
	1,100,000
Less liabilities:	
Mortgage	(100,000)
Unsecured loans	(400,000)
	600,000

Although the house was formerly part of the business, it is no longer used or needed for the trade and is merely a residence. The mortgage is set against its value as required by *s 162*, leaving net value not qualifying for BPR of £200,000, which is 20% of the remaining gross value, ignoring the unsecured debt. That debt reduces the value of the business under *s 110* and is set against the remaining assets according to value, so 400,000 × 20% = £80,000 reduces the value of the house, and the balance of £320,000 reduces the value qualifying for relief. The claim is therefore:

Gross value of the business	1,100,000
Net value of the business	600,000
Less relief claimed	(480,000)
Chargeable estate	120,000

The scope for saving tax by the placing of debt is examined at **14.9**.

Chapter 8

Relevant business property: aspects of valuation and the treatment of liabilities

QUICK GUIDE

The valuation of unquoted shares has been reviewed recently: see especially **8.8**. Where the shareholding represents an interest in a 'quasi-partnership' company, there is some argument for suggesting that there should be no discount for a minority holding, although some learned commentators argue to the contrary.

Where the asset to be valued is an interest in property, the case for arguing that a discount should apply is much clearer: see **8.13**.

The existence of debt within a business has profound relevance to valuation for BPR. As will be seen in **Chapter 14**, moving debt can in certain circumstances significantly improve the availability of BPR.

Do not forget the related property rules in *IHTA 1984, s 161*. They are considered at **8.16**, with an extended example.

BASIC PRINCIPLES

8.1   Some general principles of valuation were considered in **Chapter 4**, which are equally relevant here, and which are therefore not repeated in full. In particular, the principles in *IRC v Crossman* [1937] AC 26 apply to business property and to shares in unquoted companies where there will be restrictions that would prevent or hamper a sale.

QUOTED SHARES AND SECURITIES

8.2   The terms 'quoted securities' and 'recognised stock exchange' were considered at **6.19–6.22**. There is, curiously, no special statutory basis of valuation for quoted securities for IHT. This is in contrast to the basis for CGT set out in *TCGA 1992, s 272(3)*: the 'quarter up' rule in *s 272(3)(a)*, and the alternative rule in *s 272(3)(b)* of halfway between the highest and lowest bargains struck (other than those at special prices) recorded in the shares for the relevant date. In practice, the CGT rules are widely applied, as if *IHTA 1984* contained an equivalent section to *TGCA 1992, s 274*, but vice versa. Difficulties arise where the valuation must be made on a date when the stock exchange is closed. Then the valuer may, in relation to each item to be valued, elect either for the prices ruling on the last day on which the exchange was open or for those on the next day when it is open, whichever suits the taxpayer better.

Markings in the Stock Exchange Official List are observed, such that, where the price is quoted ex-dividend, the whole of the net dividend or interest payment must be accounted for separately in valuing the transfer. There can be problems where a security is in fact still ex-dividend but no longer marked as such, because the shares went ex-dividend some considerable time before. The same principle will apply where a security is quoted 'ex-rights'. The rights themselves must then be valued. Sometimes, they carry a separate quotation.

UNLISTED SECURITIES MARKET

8.3   Particular difficulties surrounded holdings quoted on the unlisted securities market (USM), as were noted in **Chapter 5** when considering the categories of property qualifying for BPR, and as will be seen in the special rules for clawback described in **Chapter 10**. USM shares are now treated as quoted shares for events after 16 March 1987. The rule considered below, as to what information might be assumed to be available to a prospective purchaser of unquoted shares, now no longer applies to USM shares. There may not be many transactions in USM shares, but such bargains as there are form the starting point for the valuation.

UNQUOTED SHARES

8.4   The valuation of unquoted shares is a subject in its own right and is outside the scope of this book. A key problem is to determine the information that would be available to a purchaser of unquoted shares. It is assumed (see *IHTA 1984, s 168*) that a prospective purchaser would have available to him all information which a prudent prospective purchaser might reasonably require if he were proposing to purchase the shares from a willing vendor by private treaty and at arm's length. Some of the tension between taxpayers and HMRC has occurred, not in the field of valuations for IHT, but in CGT, notably where a minority shareholding was held at 31 March 1982 which is subsequently sold.

The taxpayer will, for CGT purposes, seek a fairly full valuation as at March 1982 so that the price then fixed, with indexation, will reduce his gain. HMRC, on the other hand, will argue that an uninfluential minority holding should be valued on the basis of a very substantial discount. The issue of how much information might be available to the prudent purchaser of a small shareholding was considered in the 'Yorkshire Switchgear' cases where, on the same day, the Special Commissioners heard arguments from the point of view of CGT, where the taxpayer urged acceptance of a relatively high value for a minority holding, and contrary arguments for income tax in support of a low value.

Caton's Administrators v Couch

8.5   For IHT, the more interesting of the 'Yorkshire Switchgear' cases is *Caton's Administrators v Couch* [1995] STC (SCD) 34, which examined several important aspects of valuation and procedure.

Mr Caton died on 7 September 1987, being at that time the owner of 2,495,552 ordinary shares in Yorkshire Switchgear Group Ltd, 14.02% of the issued share capital. On 15 April 1988, all the shares in the company were sold, the executors receiving £3,269,173. The taxpayers were assessed to CGT in the sum of £494,430.25 and appealed in respect of the value. In arriving at the appropriate level of discount, the Special Commissioner had in mind that the holding was 14.2% only and that its owner could not insist on a sale. The company was trading successfully at the relevant date and it was not inevitable that it would be sold. Information about a sale was that one letter had been received 'requesting discussions leading to the acquisition of an equity interest'. There were very many uncertainties. The discount should be 50% or even more.

The Commissioner had taken the worth of the company to be £20 million or £1.12 per share (which was discounted to reach a figure of 56 pence per share). That was more correct than the figure of 45 pence, which would have been reached on the basis that no information about a sale was in prospect.

There were actually three issues for determination:

* When determining the value of the shares at the date of death, should it be assumed that unpublished information relating to the trading profits and budget forecasts of the company, and unpublished information relating to a possible sale of the company, would be available to a purchaser?

* What was the value of the shares on 7 September 1987? Was it 35 pence per share, as proposed by the Inland Revenue, or 50 pence per share, as proposed by the taxpayers on the basis that no information about a proposed sale of the company was available? Or was it 88 pence per share as proposed by the taxpayers on the basis that information about a proposed sale was available? Or some other figure?

- Were the professional costs incurred by the taxpayer, up to and including the hearing of the appeal, 'incidental costs' of the disposal and thus an allowable deduction in computing the chargeable gain?

The Commissioner observed that *Dymond's Capital Taxes* stated that the amount of information required will depend on the size of the purchase. If 25% or more of the issued capital is up for sale, the buyer will want to know the figures for sales and profits up to the latest date, with corresponding figures for the previous year and the board's view on trading prospects. He will also want to know the dividend prospects and the directors' dividend policy. *Dymond* further observed that, where the holding is less than 25%, it may be that the buyer will expect less information but that this is a matter for expert evidence.

The size of the company is important, and a buyer investing £200,000 would obviously be entitled to know more than one investing £2,000. Where the holding was small, say less than £50,000 and less than 5% of the capital, the buyer would not normally be expected to have more than the information which was published or which he could find out without questioning the directors.

On the subject of the costs, the decision of the Special Commissioners was later overturned by Rimer J: see [1996] BTC 114, which incorporates the report of the earlier decision on value.

Hawkings-Byass v Sassen and related appeals

8.6   These principles were examined for CGT in *Hawkings-Byass v Sassen and related appeals* [1996] STC (SCD) 319, again a case before the Special Commissioner, which considered the value at 31 March 1982 of shareholdings in Gonzalez Byass, the sherry and brandy producer. The report is itself a fascinating study of the family politics of that company and worth reading for that alone. Although some of the factors must be regarded as special to that case, similar situations must occur in relation to many private companies. It was noted that certain family groups could have secured control of the entire company by the purchase of one or more of the holdings to be valued in the case, and that multinational companies might have been interested in a purchase despite the restrictions that would apply to the holding once acquired. The dividend history of the company was patchy and the accounting information somewhat sketchy. Notwithstanding that, the Special Commissioners did take account of the 'political' factors and, in respect of one of the minority holdings being considered, allowed a premium because the acquisition of that holding would have given control to one or other of the families. That premium was fixed at 20%.

Denekamp v Pearce

8.7 A similar issue was considered in *Denekamp v Pearce (Inspector of Taxes)* [1998] STC 1120. The taxpayer there owned a minority of an unquoted company. It was liquidated in 1988, giving rise to an assessment to CGT and the need to value the holding at 31 March 1982. A part of the case, which need not concern us here, was the issue whether a letter from Shares Valuation Division constituted an agreement enforceable by the taxpayer. The remainder of the argument concerned the appropriate level of discount for a minority shareholding.

When the matter came before the Special Commissioner, it was noted that the question of discount was a difficult one and that a great deal depended on the information available to the hypothetical purchaser at the time. That purchaser must be assumed to hold all the information available to the directors and, in this particular case, the purchaser would have known that dividends had not been paid for many years and were not likely to be paid in the future. A purchaser would also know that the vendor was the 'key man' and that, if he left, profits would probably suffer. The majority shareholders might want to liquidate. A purchaser, therefore, would have been considering whether the company might trade on or be liquidated or sold.

The purchaser would know that the company had been up for sale without much success; he might have known, in that particular case, that there had been some interest in 1982. All in all, a purchaser in 1982 might well have concluded that, sometime in the future, the company would be sold. The Commissioner then reviewed the decision in *Caton's Administrators v Couch* [1995] STC (SCD) 34. There, in considering a holding of 14.02%, a discount of 50% was applied, as has been noted, to a company which was successful and profitable. In the present case, the holding amounted to 24% of a company which was unsuccessful. The Special Commissioner concluded that a discount of 55% was appropriate to recognise the status of the 24% holding.

The taxpayer had represented himself before the Special Commissioner but appealed to the Chancery Division, arguing that there was goodwill value in the company and that that should be reflected in the price also. The High Court were unsympathetic. If there was evidence of goodwill, it should have been adduced before the Commissioner. In the light of the evidence before the Commissioner, it could not be argued that the valuation should have proceeded by reference to a higher figure than that which was put forward. The court did not intervene.

CVC/Opportunity Equity Partners Limited and Another v Demarco Almeida

8.8   This case has called into question the basis of valuation of shares in unquoted companies, although commentators are unsure whether it will affect valuations for IHT. Opportunity had engaged four 'deal makers' as employees and directors. Each held one share in a company, the remaining 96 shares being held by Opportunity. Opportunity carried on business as general manager of a venture capital limited partnership established in the Cayman Islands. The limited partners expelled one of the directors, Mr Demarco, and wanted to exercise a call option over his one share.

The issue was what price they should pay. The case went as far as the Privy Council, where Lord Millett identified as 'quasi partnership companies' those companies where the parties possess rights, expectations and obligations which are not part of the structure of the company. In such companies, the legal, corporate and employment relationships do not tell the whole story: behind them, there is a relationship of trust and confidence similar to that of a partnership. He identified three possible bases on which to value a minority holding. These were:

- a value pro rata the total value of the company as a going concern without discount;

- a value pro rata the total value of the company, but subject to a discount; or

- a value pro rata the net assets of the company at break-up or liquidation value.

The right basis depended on all of the circumstances, but the choice must be fair. He could find no justification for adopting a break-up basis of valuation where the purchaser intended to carry on the business. If, then, a going concern basis was appropriate, he had to decide whether or not there should be a discount. He noted that, in the present case, Mr Demarco did not want to dispose of his shares. He was being thrown out. He commented that '... to require Mr Demarco to submit not only to his exclusion from the company, but to the acquisition of his shares at less than their going concern value by a purchaser which intends to carry on the business, is hardly less unfair'.

The Privy Council then decided that, in the case of a quasi partnership company, the majority can exclude the minority only if they offer to buy them out at a fair price. Fairness should be judged by reference to what will happen if the offer is accepted, not if it is refused. In the case of a quasi partnership company, the interest of the shareholder cannot be determined by a sale of his shareholding to his co-venturers unless the price reflects his share in the underlying business: 'The subject matter of the notional sale which forms the basis of valuation is, therefore, not the petitioner's minority holding, but the entire capital of the company'.

As a result, Opportunity must pay a going concern price without discount.

This decision fits with that in *Hawkings-Bias* and with *Caton's Administrators* and with *Lady Fox* (which was considered at **4.17** in the context of APR rather than BPR). The price to be found in the market is one 'which the evidence shows that various people would have been likely to pay, reflecting, for example, the fact that one person had a particular reason for paying a higher price than others ... The valuation is thus a retrospective exercise in probabilities, wholly derived from the real world'.

The learned comment of Robin Mathew QC on the case (see *Taxation*, 30 January 2003) provoked an equally learned but alternative view from Jenny Nelder in the same publication (at p 465). She could find nowhere in the legislation concerning tax valuations any reference to the management position of the shareholder or to the word 'fair'.

Phoenix Office Supplies Limited v Larvin

8.9   The contrary view to that in *Demarco* may appear from *Phoenix Office Supplies Limited v Larvin* [2003] BCC 11 and the observations of Jonathan Parker LJ when considering English legislation rather than that applicable to the Cayman Islands. His concern was to interpret *Companies Act 1985, s 459*. Did that section give a member of a quasi partnership company the opportunity to 'put' his shareholding onto the other members at its full undiscounted value, even when he had no contractual right to do so, when he wished to sever his connection with the company for his own reasons?

Jonathan Parker LJ commented, 'I can for my part see no basis for concluding that section 459 can have such a Draconian effect'. Nevertheless, in summarising the judgment of Lord Hoffmann in *O'Neill v Phillips* [1999] 2 BCC 600, Jonathan Parker LJ did note that ordinarily a fair value should represent an equivalent proportion of the total issued share capital, that is without discount for it being a minority holding. The offer should provide for equality of arms between parties: both should have the same right of access to information about the company which might bear upon the value of the shares.

It would therefore seem that, on the death of a quasi-partner shareholder, the shares may be valued subject to a discount. This is on the basis that, in the absence of a shareholders' agreement to the contrary, there is no means of forcing the other shareholders to pay more.

SO WHICH BASIS APPLIES?

8.10   There have been a couple of neat attempts to draw the threads of this argument together. John Tallon QC argues that the determining factor is that there is actually someone in the market who has his or her own special reasons for buying. The nature of those reasons is irrelevant.

David Collison agreed: the valuer should consider whether there is, in the circumstances of the particular company, another shareholder who would be prepared to make an offer for the shares that are being valued with a view to obtaining an undiscounted value. This might be either in winding-up proceedings or under the terms of a shareholders' agreement. That could make a difference to the valuation, but the difference would be marginal only. The purchaser would not have to offer the full undiscounted value, even though he might hope eventually to realise the shares without the discount. The profit is his. That view is certainly consistent with the comments (see **8.11**) on the case of *Re Courthorpe*.

Commentary

8.11   It is only with hesitation that any author questions a work of such authority as *Dymond*, not least when quoted with approval by the Special Commissioner. Nevertheless, even where relatively small sums are in issue, a prudent buyer of an illiquid asset would make, or cause to be made, fairly searching enquiries. Now that so many businesses keep their financial records electronically, it must be rare that the directors do not have management accounts for very recent trading: in a recession, that becomes even more important, so a purchaser would seek reassurance that accounts were up to date and would want to see them. Any seller of a minority holding would 'set his stall out' and would produce all the information he could lay his hands on that might serve to enhance the price he could get for the shares. Very often, minority holdings are held by close relatives of majority shareholders; in real life, the minority shareholder is often fully aware, or can be so aware, of the company's prospects and the chance of any sale of the whole company that would provide an exit route. To ignore these factors discredits the entire system of valuation in the eyes of the lay taxpayer, leading to a search for 'an alternative solution' of some kind, ie probably a solution that a prudent tax adviser would not countenance. The realism shown in *Hawkings-Byass* and *Caton* is to be encouraged.

The accuracy of a valuation, whether professional or the opinion of the directors, can have serious implications. For example, in the field of CGT, an incorrect return submitting a value for a business or for a holding of unquoted shares may give rise to a levy of a penalty where later the value is set aside and a different figure subsequently agreed. It will be the Inspector, in CGT matters, who will have the final say on the valuation, but he will not normally proceed without consulting Shares Valuation Division. The difficulty arises where more than one view of the value is tenable but, at the end of the day, the value agreed is much nearer the SVD figure than the figure put forward by the taxpayer. If the practitioner felt that the Inspector was pursuing penalties unjustifiably, the right course would be to approach SVD for some support. The whole issue of the use of estimates in preparing accounts for IHT is considered in **Chapter 22**; see especially **22.9**.

Although the practitioner is referred to specialist works on detailed matters concerning the valuation of unquoted shares, he should be aware of certain principles which will be relevant. There are two main factors which will always be relevant, namely the value of the assets of the company, and the ability of the company to put those assets to good use. One difficulty for the practitioner is that the value of the company assets is, on the whole, easier to discover than the earning potential. There is, therefore, some natural willingness to regard the value of the assets as the starting point. That willingness will, of course, be encouraged by HMRC where it is likely to yield a valuation which is more favourable to them than one prepared on an earnings basis.

Too much notice should not, however, be taken of the value of the assets. *Re Courthorpe* (1928) 7 ATC 538 is authority for the argument that, even in relation to the shares of a company whose assets are all easily valued, a purchaser would apply some discount on the ground that he would not buy the shares except with a view to making some profit on resale or on liquidation. Thus, the liquidation basis of valuation will take into account not only that profit, but also all the expenses of running the business down and the tax charges which, having been deferred whilst the company was trading, now 'come home to roost'. For example, on the disposal of assets realising gains, he will wish to provide fully for the tax on those gains, whilst HMRC will resist full provision on the basis that 'it might never happen'. Other additional tax charges may apply on cessation of trade which should be provided for. Equally, the valuation on a liquidation basis would have to take account of such matters as redundancy payments, costs of sale and of the liquidation itself.

A basis for discounting?

8.12   Is there any rule of thumb as to the discount that may be applied? In a bold suggestion which was recorded in *Taxation* (19 June 1997, p 322), it was suggested that no discount should apply in relation to a 100% holding (which is inconsistent with *Courthorpe*), and that:

- 2.5% is appropriate at 90% or more,

- 5% to 10% from 75% to 90%,

- 10% to 15% discount on holdings from 51% to 75%, and
- 20% to 25% for holdings over 25% but under 50%.

The same commentator observed that SVD will attempt to value minority holdings, even when no dividends are paid, by reference to price/earnings ratios for comparable companies, applying then a discount because the shares are not as marketable. That approach does indeed seem wrong: where there is no dividend flow, the basis for a price/earnings ratio is not supported. Most practitioners will hope to achieve lower valuations than are implied by the discounts set out above.

What is more generally accepted is that the valuation of an unquoted shareholding must proceed, first, by considering the value of the company as a whole, taking account of the current market value of the assets, usually on a going concern basis unless, as was observed in *Denekamp*, liquidation can reasonably be expected or assumed. Then one should consider the capital value of the future maintainable profits, starting, with a reasonably stable business in a reasonably stable market, by applying a multiple of 4. These are, however, only general observations and are not endorsed by any HMRC statement. Valuation of unquoted shares is an art, not a science, as can be seen from the discussion above of the issues in *Demarco*.

Minority interests in property: what discount?

8.13   It was long considered standard practice that a discount of 10% or even 15% was appropriate in valuing the interest of a joint owner in investment property. The decision of the Lands Tribunal in *Charkham v IRC* is important and should be seen in the light of the earlier decision of *White v IRC* (1982) 264 Estates Gazette 935. In *White*, a discount of 15% was considered allowable for certain residential properties where a view could be taken on how likely it was that a court would exercise its discretion in favour of one of the joint owners to order a sale.

Charkham

In *Charkham*, that principle was taken rather further. It concerned the valuation for IHT of undivided shares in a portfolio of investment properties. It became necessary to value the interests at various dates. The matter was further complicated by the fact that the size of the share in the property portfolio was different at different dates, varying from as little as 6% to over 24%.

The taxpayer's valuer looked at the income produced by the share in question. He took the view that a minority owner could not easily obtain an order for the sale of the properties as a whole and therefore, starting with the income, applied a multiplier (derived from the investments market) to value the holdings. The tribunal did not approve of that approach entirely, but did exercise its discretion to consider how likely it was, at any given time, that the minority owner of property might obtain an order for sale. What mattered was not so much the percentage owned by the taxpayer at any given time, as the purpose for which the property was held jointly and, if within a trust, whether the purpose of that trust had come to an end. In the light of that principle, the tribunal decided that a purchaser of a minority interest would know that it was not easy to obtain an order for sale. He would therefore discount the open market value of the property itself, since he would not be able to force a transaction through.

Second, the tribunal decided that that principle would apply approximately equally to a holding of 6% of the value or 24%. On the other hand, other factors, such as the obtaining of planning permission, which might affect the likelihood of an early sale could be taken into account, reducing the discount that might be applicable. On the particular facts, this resulted in a discount of 15% in relation to some of the properties, and of between 20% and 22.5% on others.

In the light of this, the practitioner should not accept a discount of only 10% without question. He should look at any possibility of redevelopment of the property, and should look at the other co-owners to see whether there is an obvious special purchaser, since the existence of such a purchaser would probably cause the discount to be reduced.

Arkwright and Price

These cases were reviewed at **4.22** and **4.23**, and the principles apply here also.

Effect of partial ownership on reliefs

Beware the situation where a business owner does not hold 100% of an asset that he uses for trade: the writer has seen it argued, for example in relation to farmland, that, where the farmer does not own the entirety, his entitlement to relief may be compromised because others may restrict or interfere with his farming activities.

Chattels

For an interesting foray into issues of discount in relation to chattels, see the work of Peter Vaines in *TAXline*, January 2006. He argues that HMRC are wrong to apply a discount to a 95% share of an asset on the ground that the existence of a 5% owner imposes a clog on sale: Peter thinks that, in the absence of a power for the 5% owner to frustrate a sale, a 95% share is worth

95%. The point here is that *LPA 1925, s 188(1)* is uncertain of application to assets other than land: we simply do not know if *s 188* gives joint owners of chattels the same rights as it does to joint owners of land.

GENERAL RULES APPLIED IN SS 110 AND 111

8.14   One aspect of valuation for BPR has already been considered in the examination of *Finch v IRC* (otherwise *Featherstonehaugh v IRC*) [1985] Ch 1. The main valuation provision is *IHTA 1984, s 110*, setting out three basic principles, namely:

- the value of a business or of an interest in a business should be taken to be its net value;

- the net value of a business is the value of the assets used in the business (including goodwill) reduced by the aggregate amount of any liabilities incurred for the purposes of the business;

- in ascertaining the net value of an interest in a business, no regard should be had to assets or liabilities other than those by reference to which the net value of the entire business would fall to be ascertained.

These rules are supplemented by additional principles concerning shares and securities contained in *s 111* which provide that, where a company is a member of a group and the business of any group member company is excluded from BPR on the ground that it consists wholly or mainly of dealing in stocks or shares etc or of holding investments, the value of the shares or securities in the company are taken for the purpose of BPR to be what they would be excluding that group member, unless either:

- the business is that of a market maker etc within *s 105(4)*; or

- the business fails to qualify for BPR because it consists wholly or mainly of holding land or buildings, and that land or those buildings are wholly or mainly occupied by other group companies whose business qualifies for BPR, ie the business of those group companies is not excluded under *s 105(3)* as holding investments or, if it is such a business, it qualifies for BPR under the 'market making' exception in *s 105(4)*.

Section 111 operates where the transferor has control of a company which is a member of the group. 'Holding company' and 'subsidiary', where those expressions are used in relation to BPR, have the meanings given to them by *Companies Act 1985, s 736*. A by-product of the rule in *IHTA 1984, s 111* is that the value of group companies may be affected by the exclusion of one member of the group. This might be the case where a non-qualifying group member gives guarantees which support the trading activities of the qualifying members.

Executors of Eighth Marquess of Hertford, deceased v CIR

8.15   The meaning of *IHTA 1984, s 110* was considered in relation to Ragley Hall for the purposes of a BPR claim in *Seymour Ninth Marquess of Hertford and others (executors of Eighth Marquess of Hertford, deceased) v CIR* [2004] SpC 444. Ragley Hall is a Grade I listed historic house. In 1991, the whole of the exterior of the building was accessible to the public to view, and 78% by volume of the interior was open. The remainder of the interior was occupied by the Eighth Marquess and by the then Earl of Yarmouth, subsequently the 9th Marquess and their families, as living quarters. In November 1991, the Eighth Marquess gave his son a business of opening a historic house to the public comprising: Ragley Hall; its contents; the goodwill of the opening business; copyrights in the catalogues and brochures; book debts; cash in hand and at the bank; and the benefit of contracts, motor vehicles, foodstuffs, beverages and all other chattels used in the business. After the gift, part of the hall was let to the Eighth Marquess as his living quarters at a rent of £10,000 per annum.

The Eighth Marquess died just over six years later, so the potentially exempt transfer became chargeable, except insofar as BPR applied. The executors argued that the part of the value of the business that related to the freehold of Ragley Hall qualified for 100% relief under *s 104*, because the building as a whole was one of the assets used in the business and its value was an ingredient of the net value for the purposes of *s 110(b)*. IRCT argued that relief should be restricted to the value of the part of the building that was open to the public. It was agreed that the excepted assets rules in *s 112* were not in point, and that the case turned on the meaning of *s 110*.

The Special Commissioner, Judith Powell, noted from the plans of the hall those areas that were or were not on display to the public, and that the exterior of the building was unaffected visually as a consequence of its occupation by members of the family. William Massey QC had argued for the taxpayers that, where an asset is used mainly for the purposes of a business, there is no provision for apportionment in the legislation. Mr Twiddy for IRCT considered that Ragley Hall was not physically all used in the business. At the date of his death, the deceased enjoyed a lease in his favour of living quarters. Under the claw-back provisions of *s 113A(3)*, the conditions for BPR must be satisfied both at the time of the transfer and at the time of death. Part of the hall occupied by the deceased could not, without his consent, be used for the business, which he no longer owned. The asset of the business within *s 110* was the area to which the public had access.

An interesting aspect of the case, as noted, is that it was agreed there were no excepted assets involved. *Section 112(4)* would appear at first sight to be directly in point, in that it deals with the situation where part but not the whole of a building is used exclusively for the purposes of a business. However, *s 112(4)* is directed at the situation where that building would qualify for no relief at all, being an excepted asset, except for the part that is used for the business. A common example, which was mentioned in correspondence, is the farm office in part of a farmhouse.

Careful reading of the judgment of Oliver LJ in the appeal in *Finch v IRC* [1985] Ch 1 showed that the legislation adopted 'the only practicable test – were they assets which were "used in the business"?'. There is a fine distinction between the situation of a sole trader, where the assets do not belong to the business but to the sole trader himself, and the partnership situation, where it is easier to suggest that the assets belong to the partnership rather than the individuals who have an interest in the business. (This issue is examined in greater detail below.)

The Special Commissioner also considered the arguments in *IRC v Mallender* [2001] STC 514 (discussed at **5.21**) where, applying the dictum of Oliver LJ, the court held that what was there used in the business was a guarantee rather than the underlying asset. However, *Finch* may be seen as an argument that *s 110* merely deals with valuation and looks at commercial reality rather than technical concepts. Although in *Finch* the assets owned by the trustees included land, some of which was and some of which was not the subject of the BPR claim, the issue whether the land comprised one or more assets was simply not discussed. On balance, the Special Commissioner found the *Finch* case unhelpful. It supported the idea that assets used in the business qualify for relief even if owned by a third party, but does not help to decide the meaning of the word 'asset'.

The taxpayer's arguments as to the meaning of *s 112* were quite detailed and are worth quoting here. An asset might fall within *s 112(2)* because it was not used wholly or mainly for the purposes of the business throughout the whole or the last two years of the relevant period; but, by way of relief, if part of that land or building was used exclusively for the purposes of any business, that part might be treated as a separate asset under *s 112(4)*. *Section 112(4)* would be unnecessary if the 'wholly or mainly' test was irrelevant to identifying the asset for the purposes of *s 110*. That is because the part used in the business would be the *s 110* asset. If, as IRCT argued, the correct approach is first to identify the asset, then to decide which part is used in the business, and treat that part as the asset for the purposes of *s 110*, there would be no need for *s 112(4)*.

IRCT argued that the correct approach, when dealing with a sole trader, is to identify the assets in the estate of the trader, and then consider what part of them in each case is used in the business. *Section 112* applies not only to sole traders but also to companies and partnerships, where it is necessary first to identify the assets that belong to the partnership or company, and then consider whether *s 112* applies. Thus, possibly, *s 112* has no relevance to sole traders.

The Special Commissioner concluded that, if an asset is wholly or mainly used for the purposes of business, there is no procedure for apportioning relief. That was enough to decide the case in favour of the taxpayer, but she then considered the second argument for the taxpayers, which was that the entire building had a business function. It was not appropriate to divide Ragley Hall into two assets. The business consisted of exhibiting a historic house and most of its contents. The public could see the whole of the exterior and most of the interior. Whilst there was no separate business of showing the exterior, the exterior was on show. The brochure showed the whole building. The lease was merely an exploitation of the asset that was used in the business. It was difficult to see where the dividing line could be drawn to separate the private quarters.

IRCT had argued that the asset of the business in respect of which relief could be allowed was part of the freehold of Ragley Hall, and that BPR should be allowed in respect of that part only. The Special Commissioner did not find the earlier decided cases particularly helpful but, on balance, concluded that the freehold of Ragley Hall was, in the normal sense of the word, a single asset; and that it was simply not possible to divide the hall in any sensible way so as to exclude part from relief. It was plainly important as a single structure, and the whole building was a vital backdrop to the business carried on. The appeal was allowed.

THE TREATMENT OF LIABILITIES

8.16   Where a debt is charged on an asset used in the business, it would seem that the value of the asset is reduced by the amount of the debt, whether or not that debt was incurred for the purposes of the business. This would seem to follow from the simple statement in *IHTA 1984, s 162(4)* that a 'liability which is an encumbrance on any property shall, so far as possible, be taken to reduce the value of that property'. There is thus scope for deathbed tax planning, although the rescheduling of debt may not have as great an effect in relation to businesses as a whole as it does in the specific area of farming. Examples of this are shown in **Chapter 14**.

HMRC practice is to treat property qualifying for BPR as primarily liable only for liabilities charged on it (see *s 162(4)*). Liabilities not so charged, and not taken into account under *s 110*, are deducted against property not qualifying for relief. Only if the value of that other property is not sufficient will the balance of the liability be set rateably against the value of all the property qualifying for relief. The important point here is that there is no requirement in the statute for the liability to have been secured on a particular asset for any particular length of time. Moving non-business debt off business assets can increase BPR. This form of planning may, therefore, be one of the few options open in 'death-bed' situations.

The operation is not a PET requiring the expiry of seven years for full effectiveness. The other specific advantage of this situation is that, save for the expense of advice and of disposals, there need not be other substantial tax costs. In the examples in **Chapter 14**, the investments are such as could be realised without crystallising a chargeable gain. In suitable circumstances, the same result might have been achieved by the rescheduling of mortgages: merely to pay off one mortgage and take out another does not lead to a disposal for the purposes of CGT. There may well be expenses in respect of Land Registry fees, legal fees and the like, but stamp duty will not be involved.

Liabilities of sole traders

8.17   The rules are different for sole traders than for partnerships or companies, and may actually work against the sole trader. Where a partner borrows on the security of his house to introduce capital, that borrowing is incurred not 'for the purposes of' the business but, in effect, to buy a further share in it. Where, however, a sole trader borrows, he in effect *is the business*. That was recognised by Oliver LJ in *Finch v CIR*:

> 'Now, in the case of a partnership, there is not generally very much difficulty in ascertaining what the partnership assets are, for this will be apparent from the accounts, but in the case of a sole trader who may have been carrying on business from his private residence and employing in it property which is not segregated from his other property, there may be considerable difficulty in ascertaining what is and what is not part of "the business" …

> The first part of [paragraph 14(2) Schedule 4 Finance Act 1975, the wording of which is now substantially the same as section 110(b)] is directed … to the case of the decedent who is a sole trader and where what has to be ascertained is not the value of some interest less than the whole but the value of "the business". In such a case there is no such thing as an asset "of" the business. All the assets of the estate, to the value of which the tax is attributable are assets "of" the decedent and in order to identify which of the decedent's assets can be taken into account in assessing the value of the business the legislator adopts the only practicable test – were they assets which were "used in the business" – it being, as [the judge] pointed out, necessarily postulated that the assets are assets, the value of which forms part of the value transferred and therefore which belonged to the decedent. Thus the "assets and liabilities" referred to in the subparagraph are not at this stage identified as assets or liabilities "of" the business. They are simply assets, the value of which is included in the transfer of value, and are to be identified as business assets for the purposes of the ascertainment of the net value by reference to whether they were used by the deceased in his business, just as those of the deceased's liabilities which are to be allowed as a deduction are to be ascertained by asking whether they were incurred by him for the purposes of his business.'

Thus, the debt that is incurred by the sole trader, however and on whatever asset it is secured, operates to reduce BPR. The effect of *s 110* with *s 162*, illustrated in **Chapter 14**, is limited to property of the type in the illustration. For holders of other kind of property, the scope for reducing IHT by moving debt is slightly greater (see also **Chapter 14**).

The situation is different where farming interests are concerned. This is because *s 110* is limited by the opening words 'for the purposes of this chapter' to the BPR code. It therefore has no relevance to the APR code. APR takes precedence over BPR by virtue of *s 114*. In the absence of the rules contained in *s 110*, the application of debts under *s 162* follows in an unrestricted way, ie a liability which is an encumbrance on any property is, as far as possible, taken to reduce the value of that property. This means that APR is reduced only by liabilities charged on the land, and not by liabilities which were incurred to buy that land but which were secured on other property.

Guarantees by business owners

8.18   A difficulty regularly encountered, where HMRC practice does not seem to match commercial reality, is where a business owner has entered into a guarantee, offering perhaps his home as security, to secure lending to his business. In practical terms, as his executors will soon find out, there is no way that the lender will release the house from the guarantee until the loan is repaid. HMRC, on the other hand, look at the likelihood that the guarantee will be called upon: so, unless the lender actually enforces the guarantee, it will not be allowed as a deduction from the value of the estate. The statutory basis is *IHTA 1984, ss 5(5)*, that no liability be admitted save where incurred for consideration, and *162(1)*, that no debt be admitted where there is any right to reimbursement. The HMRC view is set out at IHTM28353–28355. For the practitioner, the difficulty lies in fixing and in valuing the possibility that the guarantor might be reimbursed. It is difficult, in these cases, to negotiate a compromise.

THE RELATED PROPERTY RULES

8.19   One of the more important valuation rules is that contained in *IHTA 1984, s 161*, by which an artificial assumption is made in order to determine the value of property for tax purposes. The rule operates in general to increase the valuation. Where a person holds, for example, a minority shareholding and other shares qualify as 'related property', the minority shareholding falls to be valued as part of an imaginary larger holding comprising both the individual holding and the related property. The same principle will relate to the marriage value of holdings of interest in land (see Example 8.1).

Section 161(2) defines related property. Such property is related to that which is held by the transferor if:

(*a*)   it is comprised in the estate of the spouse or civil partner of the transferor; or

(*b*)   it is, or has within the preceding five years been,

   (i)   the property of a charity and became the property of that charity on a transfer of value made by the transferor, or his spouse or civil partner, after 15 April 1976 which was exempt to the extent that the value transferred was attributable to the property; or

   (ii)   the property of certain other bodies which became so in the same circumstances as have just been set out in (i) above. Those other bodies are: political parties, housing associations, bodies receiving gifts for national purposes and bodies receiving gifts for the public benefit.

By *s 161(3)*, a two-stage calculation is needed, first fixing the value of each parcel of related property in its own right to establish their relative value, then valuing the combined asset, then attributing part of the value of the combined asset to each of the components in the proportions first established.

This rule is refined, in relation to shares, so as to exclude value differentials which would be appropriate for different sizes of holding. The proportion which the value of a small number of shares of any class bears to the value of a greater number is to be taken to be the same as the number of shares, despite the fact that valuation of each holding in isolation might produce a very different result. That rule applies equally to shares, stock, debentures 'and units of any other description of property'. This rule applies where the shares are listed on a recognised stock exchange as being of the same class or would be if they were listed. These principles were examined in the context of real property in *Arkwright v CIR* (discussed at **4.22**).

The related property rules are of wide application. The practitioner must constantly bear in mind the possibility that the rules might apply when giving his advice. It was noted, in relation to valuation of shares sold within three years of death, that the relief in *s 176*, at first sight quite attractive, may often simply not be worth claiming because, although the sale of shares at a value lower than probate value might make an election for the lower value seem attractive, that is no help if, as a result of the sale, separation of the holding from the larger imaginary holding under the related property rules causes the loss of other reliefs. As in so many tax planning situations, it pays to do the sums before giving the advice.

Example 8.1: ransom strip never quite given away

The Diocese agreed that St John's, Untwood, should form the centre of a team ministry and that the Rectory lying immediately to the north of the parish church, with certain glebe land, should be sold to finance the building of a vicarage that would be more suitable for the ministry. Andrew and his wife Helen bought the whole of the property, inserting into the name of the house 'Old' in accordance with the requirements of the Diocese. The northern portion of the Old Rectory garden was laid out to orchard, and adjoined a separate eight-foot driveway to the meadow, which lay behind old developed property facing Church Road but gave an open view of countryside to the west. A plan of Untwood and of the property appears on page 210.

In January 1996, Andrew and Helen jointly transferred to an accumulation and maintenance trust ('the 1996 Trust') a strip of land along the northern boundary of the Old Rectory garden about ten feet in width (shown hatched on the plan). In 1998, with the benefit of local knowledge that the land to the west of Glebe Meadow would be developed, Andrew and Helen transferred the Glebe Meadow to a discretionary trust for their children ('the 1998 Trust') and severed their joint tenancy in the Old Rectory and the remainder of the land enjoyed with it.

On Andrew's death in January 2008, valuation advice was obtained. Glebe Meadow extends to 3.2 acres. By now, it is surrounded by developed land, but the eight-foot driveway is not sufficient for access to Church Road for a development site. Without planning permission, Glebe Meadow is worth £25,000. The 'ransom strip' that was given to the 1996 Trust is sufficient to create an access from Church Road to Glebe Meadow and sight-splay, and thus holds the key to the development value of Glebe Meadow which would be of the order of £880,000. The ransom strip is worth one-third of the development value, ie £290,000. The Old Rectory, minus Glebe Meadow and without the ransom strip, would be worth £250,000. If the title to the Old Rectory still included the ransom strip, the Old Rectory would be worth £600,000. The share in the Old Rectory passes to Helen under Andrew's will.

There is evidence that, since 1998, the trustees of the 1998 Trust have let Glebe Meadow on a commercial basis to the daughter of the proprietor of the filling station (see plan) to graze and exercise her horses. There is also evidence that the ransom strip was never fenced off. There is no evidence that the trustees of the 1996 Trust *bona fide* assumed possession and enjoyment of the ransom strip within the meaning of *FA 1986, s 102(1)*. Rather unfortunately, an eagle-eyed District Valuer, when inspecting the inside of the Old Rectory to establish its probate value, noticed a large-scale aerial photograph of the Old Rectory and its orchard, which appears to show the deceased and his family relaxing in front of a summer house which is clearly on part of the ransom strip. Even less

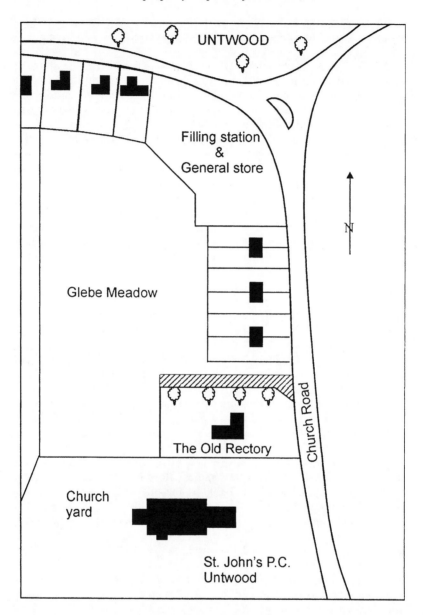

fortunately for the family, it is clear that the photograph was taken at or about the time of Andrew's 80th birthday in June 2005, judging from the caption to the aerial photograph incorporated within its frame.

Section 161 requires any valuation of Andrew's half share in the Old Rectory to be made without discount for a half share, because the other half share is owned by Helen. Whilst there is no need to consider the value of Glebe Meadow in relation to the Old Rectory, because it was fully and effectively given away 12 years before Andrew's death, a problem does arise in relation to the ransom strip, because the working of the gift with reservation rules has the result that, under the *Inheritance Tax (Double Charges Relief) Regulations 1987*, HMRC have the opportunity of disregarding the gift in 1998 and treating the ransom strip as if it were still part of the estate of Andrew (and of Helen) as at the death of either of them.

Andrew's estate, therefore, includes half the value of the Old Rectory, valued without discount for a half share, because the other half share is owned by Helen, plus half the value of the ransom strip. The £600,000 value is split between house and strip – £250,000 : £290,000 – giving a value for the house of £277,800 and for the land retained within the 1996 Trust of £322,200. Thus, the exempt transfer to Helen is £138,900, ie slightly greater than the actual value that she receives. The trustees of the 1996 Trust cannot set against the transfer to them of £161,100, such part of the nil rate band as was available to Andrew in 1996 because, for the purposes of the *Inheritance Tax (Double Charges Relief) Regulations 1987*, the gift in 1996 is ignored (see example 1 in relation to *reg 5*).

Valuation of shares and loan notes

8.20   In *McArthur's Executors v HMRC* [2008] SpC 700, the issue was whether certain option rights must be valued or whether, as the executors argued, they had little or no value. The shareholder had lent money to a family company on terms that gave him a right to subscribe for more shares. The Special Commissioner found that the terms of the documents (the 'writs of the debtor') gave the shareholder rights to repayment and to conversion into shares. Those rights must be valued. The actual unit of valuation was the shareholding in the company, plus the relevant conversion rights.

Chapter 9

Relevant business property: exceptions to the relief: 'wholly or mainly holding investments'

QUICK GUIDE

All of this chapter is concerned with case law. The dispute with HMRC concerns, mainly, the argument that certain land-based activities demand so much time and effort from their owners that they should be regarded as trading businesses whilst, in the view of HMRC, the income of the entity really only results from the exploiting of interests in land. Arguments turn on the nature of income in each example and, for that reason, this chapter reviews some of the cases in considerable detail.

INTRODUCTION

9.1   There is a distinction, which is becoming clearer as cases are heard (mainly before the Special Commissioner or, now, the First-tier Tribunal), between what the layman might regard as a business and what will qualify for BPR. As can be seen in the commentary on the cases which follow, the distinction is sometimes academic and has in the past apparently taken little notice of the effort put in by the taxpayer over the years to generate the wealth that is now to be taxed. Fortunately, recent cases have reversed that trend somewhat.

The distinction, which can serve to exclude from relief certain undertakings that might be considered to be businesses, is contained in *IHTA 1984, s 105(3)*, which excludes from relief a business, or an interest in the business, or shares in, or securities of, a company where the business which is the subject of the relief:

> 'consists wholly or mainly of one or more of the following, that is to say, dealing with securities, stocks or shares, land or buildings or making or holding investments.'

Most of the cases turn on whether a given activity has concerned the last-mentioned phrase, 'the making or holding of investments'.

Whilst there is some similarity of legislative purpose between the exclusion of certain assets from BPR under the excepted assets rule described in **Chapter 7**, and the exclusion of businesses from BPR which are in the nature of investments, there is usually more for the adviser to play for where the 'wholly or mainly' argument is advanced by HMRC. This is because, in the case of an excepted asset, the remainder of the business will normally qualify for relief – especially where it is unincorporated and the excepted asset simply never enters into the valuation.

The application of the 'wholly or mainly' test is however 'all or nothing'. Where the business is incorporated, the entire value of the shareholding is excluded from relief. For the sole trader, the application of the rules can be less harsh.

Example 9.1: mixed trade

Percy and Maureen own a tailoring business in the West Midlands carried on from freehold premises which they own as partnership property. One flat over the shop is let to a longstanding employee at a nominal rent, as part of the terms of his employment. A second flat is let to students. Percy and Maureen share an interest in restoring, and especially upholstering, period furniture from other premises adjoining the cutting room. They do not carry on this activity for full commercial returns. Mainly they supply family and friends.

The accounts of the separate elements of these activities show that the tailoring business, which is very well established, is profitable. The income from the student lettings is, owing to the location of the premises, only moderate. The furniture renovation activities just about break even.

On taking on Percy and Maureen as new clients, their adviser, Carol, reviews the business from the standpoint of all taxes. She concludes that the furniture restoration should be regarded as entirely separate from the other activities. There is no likelihood of a charge to income tax, because the activities are not carried on for gain, they currently yield no gain, and they have yielded no great gain in the past. The premises from which that activity is carried on are, it turns out, inconvenient, ill-appointed and of moderate value only. As a result, it matters little that no BPR will be available in respect of them.

On the other hand, Carol concludes that the student lettings should be treated as part of the overall business activity of the tailoring shop. The rents received are small, both in relation to overall turnover and profit. On examination, it appears that the accommodation available to a student at any one time is small, both in area and in value, by comparison both with the accommodation occupied by the old retainer and with the value of the premises otherwise occupied and used for the tailoring business.

Seen in the round, the undertaking carried on at the premises is mainly that of a very successful tailoring business: the rental income is merely incidental. Carol therefore concludes that the receipt of rents from the intermittent student lettings should be included within the turnover of the tailoring business, though naturally identified for what it truly is. By this means, Percy and Maureen stand a more than reasonable chance of securing BPR on the whole of that undertaking, including the value of its premises, relying in part on the ruling in *Farmer (Farmer's executors) v IRC* mentioned at **9.12** below.

THE MOORE CASE

9.2   In *Martin and another (Executors of Moore Deceased) v IRC* [1995] STC (SCD) 5, the Commissioner heard how Mr and Mrs Moore had run nine industrial units in Leicester in partnership, mainly on three-year leases. Mr Moore died in November 1989. Mrs Violet Moore carried on, though at a lower level of activity, until her death in June 1991. On appeal on the issue of eligibility of the letting business for BPR, Stephen Oliver QC considered what Mrs Moore actually did in relation to the properties. There were three aspects of the work:

- finding tenants, negotiating rents, granting leases, and deciding whether to accept surrenders or allow assignments of leases;

- keeping the outside of properties painted and in good repair and generally complying with her obligations as a landlord; and

- managing the estate as a whole, keeping properties tidy, secure and in good repair.

The Special Commissioner held that the first two of these categories were clearly attributable to the holding or making of investments. The third category were incidents of the business of holding investments. The money that resulted from these activities was the net rents and nothing else. The properties as a whole were an investment in the estate of Mrs Moore for the purposes of *s 105(3)* and wholly failed to qualify for BPR.

THE BURKINYOUNG CASE

9.3   *Burkinyoung v IRC* [1995] STC (SCD) 29 was heard with the *Moore* case. Mrs Burkinyoung bought a house in west London in the 1940s, converting it some 30 years later into four flats, all of which, at her death in December 1989, were let furnished on assured shorthold tenancies. Mrs Burkinyoung did not deal with day-to-day management herself; she entrusted that to managing agents. She controlled and directed the way in which the property was let. The managing agents dealt with maintenance, repairs, looking after common areas, arranging and supervising the lettings, collecting rents, insurance and paying rates. All of these aspects of management were considered by the Special Commissioner to be natural and necessary incidents of holding property as an investment. All Mrs Burkinyoung received from the property was rent. The business was wholly one of making or holding investments for the purposes of *s 105(3)*. No BPR was allowable.

PRINCIPLES EMERGING FROM THE COMMENTS OF THE SPECIAL COMMISSIONER

9.4   Although *Martin* and *Burkinyoung* are decisions of the Special Commissioner only, they are seminal in the development of this area of the law and, by their application in the cases mentioned below, have acquired a considerable status as authorities. In particular, Steven Oliver QC made certain comments which have formed the basis of later decisions.

Argument for the taxpayer in *Burkinyoung* included reference to VAT cases which drew a distinction between business and 'mere investment'. That line of authority was rejected, as throwing no useful light on the application of *s 105(3)*.

In argument for the taxpayer in *Moore*, there was reference to judicial recognition of the difference between an intermediate landlord, who sublets 'passively', and one who, by virtue of what he does, can properly be described as an occupier entitled to protection under the *Landlord and Tenant Act 1954*. Again, the point was rejected by the Special Commissioner as not being an appropriate test for *s 105(3)*.

Is a business an investment business? The Commissioner considered the tests as to existence of a business put forward by Ralph Gibson J in *C & E Comrs v Lord Fisher* [1981] STC 238 (see **5.6**).

Over what period is the matter to be tested? The essential nature of the business is to be decided by reviewing the activities of the landlord over 'a sufficient period'. In *Moore* this included the time when Mr Moore was alive and the level of business activities was higher than after his death. In *Burkinyoung* the Special Commissioner referred to 'the length of her ownership of the property, and the way she has been letting out the property for a rental income'.

THE LEVEL OF ACTIVITY

9.5   An investment business does not cease to be such simply because the landlord is actively involved. It seems that the late Mr Moore was at the property on most days from 7am. What decides the availability of the relief is not merely how much work is done but the nature of that work. Activities which are no more than the natural and necessary incidents of holding the property as an investment in order to derive rental income from it are the activities of 'holding investments'. This principle has proved decisive in later cases.

Are income tax cases any help? In *Fry v Salisbury House Estate Ltd* (1930) 15 TC 266, a distinction was drawn between, on the one hand, what the landlord did under the terms of the lease such as repairs and improvements, and on the other hand, business activities of the landlord not required under the lease and not connected with nor incidental to the holding of that property as an investment. Into the second category might come heating or cleaning services for which a separate charge was made. Where activities are required by the lease and no separate consideration is paid, those activities concern 'holding investments'. That test was fatal in both *Moore* and *Burkinyoung*.

Is *Hansard* any help? *Moore* and *Burkinyoung* are among the earliest recorded authority on interpretation of *s 105(3)*. The Special Commissioner thought that the relevant part of that subsection was sufficiently obscure that he might look at *Hansard* (in reliance on satisfaction of the other tests in *Pepper v Hart* [1993] AC 593). The Special Commissioner therefore considered the statement by the Chief Secretary to the Treasury, that business relief would not apply to the letting of land. That was enough for the Special Commissioner.

SUBSEQUENT DECISIONS ON S 105(3)

Hall v CIR

9.6   A series of cases fell to be decided concerning caravan parks. Although the matter has been reviewed by the Court of Appeal, the decisions of the lower courts are still relevant because this is so much an issue of fact that the practitioner may find help from the earlier decisions. The first was *Hall (Executors of Hall deceased) v CIR* [1997] STC (SCD) 126. In about 1967 the deceased commenced trading as a caravan park proprietor, being joined, following the death of her husband, by her son in partnership on the terms of a formal deed. The partnership had 18 acres, on nine of which stood nearly 100 caravans. There was a separate 'zone' of about one acre on which there stood 11 wooden chalets let on 45-year leases. The rent was reviewable five yearly. The lessors covenanted to keep the site clean and tidy, maintain the road, car parks, hard standings and footpaths. They were obliged to supply water, electricity and drainage.

This was not a touring caravan park. The caravans were static. They were not owned by the business. The season was from 1 March to 31 October. There was no right to occupy them during the winter.

The deceased ran the business whilst her son did the physical work. There were no other employees. Under the terms of the site licence, they had to provide numerous facilities and services. Caravan tenants were not allowed to sell their vans save through the agency of the business, which charged 10% commission.

In recognition of the tests outlined above, argument before the Special Commissioner included an analysis of the total income of the partnership for the year ended 31 October 1993. Rents and standing charges totalled £30,754. Mains supplies were collected on a non-profit basis. Sales of bottled gas produced a profit of £216 and fishing rents £205, whilst the takings from coin boxes (not all profit) was £294. Commission from caravan sales totalled £5,492.

The Special Commissioner found it easy to decide that the chalets let on long leases were investments. The caravan pitches were a greater problem. 'Investment' in *s 105(3)* was a 'difficult, slippery word'. The Commissioner rejected the definition of 'investments' in *Tootle, Broadhurst, Lee and Co Ltd v IRC* [1949] 1 All ER 261. He was more attracted to the majority judgment of the Court of Appeal in *Croft v Sywell Aerodrome Ltd* [1942] 1 KB 317. There, land 'equipped with buildings and facilities' was assessable to income tax under Schedule A rather than Schedule D. A distinction was drawn between land which had been made more attractive, by the installation of amusements, and 'unimproved land'. The land which had been 'improved' should be regarded as producing trading income.

On balance, the Commissioner regarded the caravan park as being unlike the amusement park in *Sywell Aerodrome Ltd*, and relied on photographs and brochures for the caravan park, showing that it was situated in a very beautiful part of Wales.

Whilst the Revenue had agreed that the business of the caravan park did not consist *wholly* of the making or holding of investments, that was not the point at issue. The Commissioner had to decide whether that business consisted *mainly* of the making or holding of investments. Eighty-four per cent of the total income came from rents and standing charges. That was enough to deny BPR.

The Pearce case

9.7   In *Powell (personal representatives of Pearce deceased) v IRC* [1997] STC (SCD) 181 the issue already considered in *Hall* came before the Special Commissioners again, with one distinction, that the caravan park concerned had pitches both for long-term and short-term lettings. The deceased, those who became her personal representatives and other members of her family worked the site and lived there. There was evidence of the work done by the family: one was always in attendance to ensure continuous supplies of gas (through bottles), electricity and the like. Many of the residents were long term and many were retired. Social and medical visits were organised for which no charge was made. Maintenance of the park included meter reading, grass cutting, hedging, ditching, security, painting, cleaning and maintaining the caravans.

Twenty-three of the thirty-three units were owned privately, the owners paying a fee for their pitch. Three were on short-term lets. Income was assessed for tax under Schedule D. On appeal from the determination of the CTO that the business fell within *s 105(3)*, the Special Commissioners ruled that the tax status of the income of the business was irrelevant to considering IHT, which depended entirely on the provisions of *IHTA 1984*. All the deceased's income came from pitch fees. All fell on the 'holding investments' side of the line drawn in *Burkinyoung* and *Martin*. The activities carried out by the family were required under the terms either of the caravan licence or of the lettings. The social and medical visits, which might have fallen on the other side of the line, were made for no charge.

A distinction was drawn between the position of proprietors of caravan sites and of hoteliers, on the ground that hoteliers offered 'a high standard of service' to their clients and did not merely rent rooms. The services of hoteliers were business activities, not 'holding investments'. The Commissioners ruled that it was not relevant either that the business was carried on by the deceased and her family 'in occupation' of the site, nor that the deceased herself worked there. The facts were very similar to those in *Hall*, perhaps even less favourable to the personal representatives. There was little difference between the situation in *Pearce* and the position of the owner of long leases who received ground rents. The deceased was carrying on a business consisting wholly or mainly of the holding of investments. BPR was denied.

Furness: a victory for the taxpayer

9.8   The taxpayer fared better in *Brendan Peter James Furness* SpC 202, again a case concerning a caravan park and arising out of a determination under *s 105(3)*. There was evidence that the park was licensed for static caravans and touring caravans. At weekends the park held rallies. No permanent residence was permitted at the park. The appellant reckoned he spent 80% of his time looking after the welfare of the residents at the caravan park, maintaining it and its structures. He employed three people full time to help. There was much evidence of how much work, and what kind of work, they did.

There was also an argument that less than half of the net profit of the business came from pitch fees for static caravans. Alternatively, the sheer quantity of work involved in running the site was enough to take the business outside the scope of *s 105(3)*. The Special Commissioner examined the evidence of the source of net profit. Caravan sales for the years 1993 to 1996 inclusive produced more profit than pitch fees. Even if the net profit in respect of caravan sales were to be reduced in respect of tours and caravan rally charges, the sales still exceeded the pitch rentals for each of the years in question.

The source of the profit may have been sufficient to decide the matter in any event, but the Special Commissioner took into account the very considerable amount of work undertaken both by the appellant and by his employees. He considered that that level of activity did not correspond to what one would normally find in a business concerned wholly or mainly with the holding of investments, and therefore allowed the appeal.

Weston v IRC

9.9   The next examination of this problem on appeal was in *Weston (Executor of Weston, deceased) v IRC* [2000] STC 1064, where again the income from caravan sales was highly relevant. The company in which Mrs Weston held shares at her death in 1993 bought and sold caravans on commission and granted rights to pitches on the park run by it. It maintained the park and supplied electricity and bottled gas.

This was no holiday park: it lay near the M25. It was residential, for people aged 50 plus. There was no shop or social club, only a laundry and storeroom. The caravans were owned by their occupiers, purchased from the company or, if from another resident, through the company's agency. The company accounts showed that pitch fees usually exceeded fees from sales. There were few sales: much staff time went on maintenance of the park. (Three employees between them spent 111 hours per week on site maintenance and 37 hours on sales.) In every year from 1988 to 1994 (except 1989), profits from pitch fees were greater than those from sales.

On the issue of 'wholly or mainly', the Special Commissioner had decided that, on balance, the company ran a park, rather than a dealership in caravans. Sales were ancillary to pitch fees. It followed that BPR was not available, owing to the requirements of *s 105(3)*. The taxpayer appealed: an additional argument was that caravan owners paid for services by the company, not merely for rights of occupation.

In the High Court, this new argument was rejected: it could not be raised because new evidence would be needed to test it. The Special Commissioner had made the right decision: as a question of fact, the business consisted wholly or mainly of making or holding investments.

The moral must be to take especial care in presenting the appeal at first instance.

Stedman's Executors v IRC; CIR v George and Another

9.10   The leading caravan park case is *Stedman's Executors v IRC*, first reported at [2002] STI issue 33 when it came before the Special Commissioner. The issues that had been relevant in the earlier cases were aired in detail. Evidence was produced of the various business activities carried on. The issue was whether:

- the holding of land so as to produce a profitable return was incidental to the carrying on of some other business; or

- it was the very business that was carried on by the company.

Given the differences between the various activities, it was argued that each must be looked at in isolation before considering the business as a whole. There were eight elements to the business, of which three in particular were relevant.

(1) The residential homes park

The caravans were owned by the residents, not by the company. Site fees were paid that yielded the company a profit on the supply of services. There was lighting of the common parts. The roads were maintained, as were fire hydrants and a car park for visitors. Rubbish was collected weekly. The company took a commission on the sale of caravans on site and sold some caravans itself.

The Special Commissioner considered that the site fees were like rent: they were a return on investment. However, they were also similar to a service charge, reflecting work done by the company for the benefit of the occupiers. Much of the site fees went on the expenses of running the site. That level of expense suggested a non-investment type of business. The right approach was to say that the investment business was that of making a return on the licensing of the site and its facilities. The expenditure relating to the provision of services did not relate to the business of holding investments. 72% of the site fees went in overheads. The service element was greater than the investment element.

The provision of gas and electricity did not relate to the holding of land and was quite unconnected with making or holding investments. Equally, the earning of commission on sales of caravans was not related to the holding of land but was part of a business.

(2) The club for residents

It was agreed between the parties that running the club that the company had established was not an investment activity.

(3) Caravan storage

An area was set aside for winter storage, subject to agreements for periods of six months to a year. There was a security fence and a security guard. A good deal of staff time related to this part of the business. The main element of the supply was the security. Nevertheless, even taking account of these overheads of security, the nature of the agreement relating to a plot showed that it was mainly to generate income from holding land. Thus, in relation to this part of the enterprise, the business that was carried on by the company was the holding of land as an investment.

(4)–(8) Other property and sources of income

The company maintained an office from which the park was administered. It owned and let a warehouse and a shop. There were fields let on grazing licences. The company enjoyed income from insurance agency commissions and interest on cash balances. The Special Commissioner found that the income from letting the warehouse and the grazing land was clearly investment income. Interest was income from investing money belonging to the company. The commission, on the other hand, was not income from holding investments. The cash arose from all of the activities of the company together. The earning of interest was not a business in itself, so this income did not arise from the holding of investments.

Taking the business of the company in the round, 'investment-type' income for 1998 represented 40% of turnover, 20% of gross profit and 16% of net profit before the fees of directors. Those figures were not outweighed by other factors. They gave a good reflection of the nature of the business. The business of the company was not, in the opinion of the Special Commissioner, mainly that of making or holding investments.

The arguments of the taxpayer failed to persuade Laddie J in the Chancery Division, who considered the issue from the point of view of a businessman and concluded that the core investment was in land and that the other activities were merely incidental to it. The various trading activities and the receipts from them amounted to the holding of an investment that included the site fees from the park, the right to place vehicles on company land and the storage facility. The supply of water was ancillary to the investment business. The core activity of the company was that of holding investments.

The taxpayer appealed successfully to the Court of Appeal, which held that the overall approach of the Commissioner had been correct in law. *Section 105(3)* did not require the opening of an investment 'bag' into which might be put the activities that were linked to the caravan park simply because they might be regarded as 'ancillary' to the investment business. The court did not need to decide whether or not investment was 'the very business' of the company. That was not required by the statute. This was a hybrid business. The holding of property as an investment was only one part of the business and, on the findings of fact of the Commissioner, not the main part. It was difficult to see why an active family business, such as that comprised in the present case, should fail to qualify for BPR simply because one necessary component of making the profits was the use of land.

Review of the law in the light of George

9.11   The result in *George* may perhaps lead to another way of looking at the issue, by reference to a 'special skills' test. We might ask Laddie J's businessman, when considering a purchase of this particular business, whether any particular skills would be needed to run the enterprise. What is the level of service provided? For example, a 'pure investment' yields a return on capital *per se*; often the capital is in the form of land. On the other hand, the business of, say, a restaurant, whilst it may include freehold or valuable leasehold premises, demands culinary expertise if it is to thrive. The mere receipt of rents demands clerical skill, in asking for the money, but relatively little entrepreneurial skill.

HMRC have reviewed their approach since the *George* decision (see IHTM25279):

'The judgment in *George* is helpful in clarifying what is to be regarded as either investment or non-investment activity. It makes clear that the provision of services under the terms of a pitch agreement is a non-investment activity. This means that in cases where a large part of the business's activities (measured in both time and money) consists of providing services to residents, we would be more likely to consider that the business was neither wholly or mainly investment in nature. However, we need to be satisfied that the figures for pitch fees, for instance, are not artificially depressed in the accounts in favour of inflated figures for wages or other non-investment expenses.

The judgment in *George* also recognises that the time and money spent on maintaining amenity areas is in part designed to maintain the value of the owner's investment. It follows that the taxpayers are entitled to return a reduced level of investment income by offsetting against it part of the maintenance costs. As this could lead to the net investment income being, proportionally, a smaller part of the overall income of the business we might well conclude in a particular case that the business was neither wholly or mainly one of holding investments. On the other hand, we would also need to take into account the time spent by the owner and/or his employees in the maintenance work. When taken together with other work carried out in the business, the evidence might lead us to conclude that the majority of work done is involved in maintaining the value of the owner's investment. If so, then we would seek to deny the claim under Section 105(3) IHTA 1984.

The judgment in *George* also suggests that the holding of land as an investment is separate and distinct from the service element of the business. Finally, when looking at the facts "in the round", trading figures are only a part of the overall picture.

When dealing with a claim for business relief on a caravan park, you will need to obtain detailed business accounts, including breakdowns of both the income and expenditure between the investment and non-investment elements of the business. In addition, you should ask the taxpayers to state precisely what services were provided to the park residents and how long was spent by the deceased (as park owner) and his partners and/or employees providing those services.'

That extract is also a clear guide to the practitioner dealing with this issue. It is more likely that the taxpayer will secure the relief if the facts are well researched beforehand, better still if the family get good advice long before the chargeable transfer takes place and run the business with an eye to qualifying for the relief. The adviser should visit the park site and assess the extent to which it offers space in one or more of the following categories:

- chalets;
- mobile homes;
- pitches for touring caravans that are taken for the season; and
- pitches for 'pull-on tourers', ie holidaymakers who are just passing through.

Of all these categories, it is the last that makes the most work for the site owner. A pitch may be taken for only one night; people may arrive late but still expect the site shop to be open and to stock fresh (local) produce. It must sadly also be said that, whilst most tourers are careful and considerate, someone who is moving on the next day might be more tempted than a more permanent resident to skimp on care, and for example to let the grey waste drain onto the pitch! Undoubtedly, the letting of a pitch for a whole season is attractive, both in providing reliable cash flow and in securing goodwill for eventual sale of the site. To enhance his claim to BPR, however, the cases show that a site owner should cherish his 'pull on' customers and put up with the work they cause him.

Mixed use estate: Farmer v IRC

9.12   The availability of BPR was considered in *Farmer (Executors of Farmer Deceased) v IRC* [1999] STC (SCD) 321. The late Mr Farmer both farmed and let surplus properties. In the accounts of the business, there was no distinction between the two business activities. For most of the period of years up to Mr Farmer's death in 1997, the turnover from farming was greater than that of rents, although the net rental profit was greater than the net farming profit.

Of the total holding of 449 acres, farmland and woodland accounted for 441 acres. The balance of 8 acres was tracks and let properties. There were 23 tenancies, mainly shorthold or licences. The landlord was responsible for repairs and, as is common, supplied water for which the tenants paid. When the entire property was valued for probate, the farmhouse, farm buildings and farm land were valued at £2,250,000 and the let property at £1,250,000. IRCT considered that the business was not relevant business property. It was mainly making or holding investments within *s 105(3)*. One argument, resting on *s 103(3)*, was that a business must be carried on 'for gain', and that profits are therefore an essential test of the value of a business enterprise.

The Special Commissioner eventually found in favour of the executors. All relevant factors must be considered. Profits were not only the test. The business was a landed estate. Most of the land was used for farming. The let properties were subsidiary in two ways: they occupied a relatively small proportion of the total area and, being sited towards the centre of the land, would not have existed but for the connection with the farm.

The Special Commissioner concluded that the business consisted mainly of farming. Importantly, the let property was not excluded property under *s 112*: once it had been decided that there was a single business for the purposes of *s 105(3)*, all the relevant assets qualified for that relief.

The Earl of Balfour's case

9.13   In the Scottish case of *Brander (Representative of Earl of Balfour deceased) v HMRC* [2009] TC 00069, the Earl of Balfour entered into a farming partnership with his nephew in November 2002. In June 2003, he died. HMRC considered that BPR was not due, and the Earl's personal representative appealed. Two issues arose. The first was whether the requirements of *s 107* as to replacement property were satisfied. They were: this issue was considered in general terms at **6.7**.

The second issue was whether the business failed the 'wholly or mainly' test of *s 105(3)*. By a settlement created under the 1923 will of the first Lord Balfour (who had been Prime Minister during the Great War), the family estate was tied up with a view to preserving it intact. The taxpayer, in applying the various tests, noted in relation to capital value that it was not intended by the first Earl, nor by his successors, that the land should ever be sold. Although the deployment of capital is a relevant factor, here its value was less important than it might otherwise have been. The First-tier Tribunal considered that Lord Balfour had managed the estate the way most of his generation did: without a specific plan but as a unified business, where each part contributed to and supported the whole, being a traditional mix of: agriculture, both in hand and let; woodland and forestry management; sporting interests; and letting of cottages and other properties, either to estate workers or others. Where cottages were not let to estate workers, a prospective tenant who had skills that might benefit the estate would be favoured over one without, even if the rent commanded might be less. HMRC appealed, arguing that some particular circumstances had been ignored, especially the value of capital involved.

The Upper Tribunal disallowed the appeal. Various factors, none of which might be conclusive on its own, could be considered to decide whether a business was mainly investment. The Upper Tribunal might have allocated some of the values differently (this was a large and complicated estate), but the lower tribunal was right in law and was entitled to attribute little worth to the capital value of investment properties.

Moneylending: the Phillips case

9.14   In *Phillips and others (Executors of Rhoda Phillips Deceased) v HMRC* [2006] SpC 555, there was a company which made informal, unsecured loans to related family companies. That was the company's business, which, it was held, did not consist wholly or mainly of making or holding investments. The shares in the company were held to be relevant business property within *s 105(3)*.

Building and developing: Piercy

9.15   *DWC Piercy's Executors v HMRC* [2008] SpC 687 concerned a property development company that owned land in Islington on which it had built workshops for letting. The executors of a major shareholder claimed BPR, but HMRC denied it on the ground that the company received substantial investment income and its business was therefore mainly making or holding investments. The executors claimed that the company was still trading: it still held undeveloped land that it wished to develop for housing, but had to wait for uncertainty to be resolved concerning proposals for a new railway line.

The Commissioner found that the land was still held as trading stock, not as an investment. A land-dealing company will not qualify for BPR if it is a speculative trader or dealer, but all other land-dealing companies that actively develop land or build on land are outside the exclusion. For a company to be wholly or mainly holding investments, the Commissioner held that it must actually have investments; thus, holding the land as trading stock was highly relevant here. The Commissioner allowed the appeal.

Carrying on a business 'for gain'

9.16 In the *Mallender* case, decided 23 November 1999, the taxpayer failed on the preliminary issue over whether the companies concerned were even carrying on a business 'for gain'. This is a preliminary test. IHTM25253 notes the exclusion of businesses carried on otherwise than for gain, noting that stud farms may fall into this category.

HMRC will strongly resist the argument, which was almost advanced in the *Clark* case considered below, that an activity, merely by being vigorously pursued, can become a business, even though its true nature is the holding of investments.

It should be noted in passing that the principles that may serve to deny BPR are applied separately from the test as to whether a business exists. This has the important result that, where it is accepted that a business exists but it is argued that *s 105(3)* denies relief, the instalment option will still be available, as will the benefit of relief from interest on instalments unless the business interest is a company.

Property management as a business: Clark

9.17 The most recent contribution to this debate is *Clark and Another (Executors of Clark Deceased) v HMRC* [2005] SpC 502. A partnership was established in 1895 and later incorporated. In the 1920s, as a company it bought a large site and built homes. Later the company bought back many of the properties and leased them to the former purchasers. The properties needed much maintenance and refurbishment, and the company had its own workforce to deal with the building and maintenance. At the date of death of C, the company owned 92 dwellings, 4 shops, 4 offices, 2 industrial units and 20 lock-up garages. The Clark family owned 141 other properties. All of them required very active management. The directors spent 75% of their time on managing the rental activity and 25% of their time on building works. The company owned 42% of the total property portfolio.

In support of a claim to BPR on the shares of the company, the executors argued: that letting property was no longer an investment activity; that the accounts of the company did not show just how much work and effort was required by the management and staff; that the two elements of the portfolio should be treated the same, ie as non-investment activity; that it was irrelevant that rental income is investment income for income tax; that 'investment' could be something done by a trading company, for example 'investing' in plant and machinery; that the rental income was part of the business activities of the company and was not investment; and that the attitude of HMRC discriminated against letting compared to other active businesses.

HMRC argued that activities that produce a rent are necessarily investment. They also wished to distinguish some of the cases relied on by the taxpayer as being based on other legislation rather than the most recent Court of Appeal cases on IHT. This was a mixed business which included, on the one hand, investment and, on the other hand, building. Mainly, the business consisted of holding investments.

The Special Commissioner could see a distinction between managing properties owned by third parties and managing properties owned by the company. A management fee was not the same as a rent. The rents came from leases of company assets rather than from an active building trade. The balance sheet showed the land as 'fixed assets – investments', which was correct. The rents were income from the ownership of that property. They would still be rents, even if someone else managed the properties and maintained them. The maintenance work was inherent in ownership of the property. Thus the rental activity was itself a business of holding investments.

The test was whether the business of the company consisted 'mainly' of holding investments, for which the Commissioner must look at the business in the round, reviewing profit, the overall context, capital employed, time spent and turnover. He therefore analysed the profit and loss account according to the different activities of the company but applying a consistent basis. An estimate of time spent on investment activity was used to apportion administration and establishment expenses, being mainly salaries. However, the profit on building and management activities was too small to bear the proportion of management time that was spent on it. It therefore looked as if the rental activity was subsidising the other activity.

Investment activity produced more turnover and profit, but took less time. Apportioning the time spent on the basis of turnover and profit resulted in a large loss for the non-investment activities, so that basis of apportionment could not be justified. The main asset shown in the accounts related to investment activity. Looking at the position in the round, the Commissioner concluded that the business carried on by the company consisted mainly of holding investments. BPR must therefore be denied.

Holiday lettings

9.18   The attitude of HMRC has hardened a little (see IHTM25278). Whereas previously an actively managed business, with lettings at arm's length (rather than just to family and friends), would qualify, the focus of the test is now the level and type of services, rather than on who provides them. Cases of this type will go to the Litigation Department of HMRC at an early stage.

In particular, the practitioner can expect resistance to a claim in respect of BPR on a holiday letting business where:

- the lettings are longer term, including assured shorthold tenancies;

- there is little or no involvement with the holidaymakers, for example where the accommodation is a villa or apartment abroad;

- the lettings are only to friends and relatives; and

- especially where it is clear that the taxpayer provides no services to the holidaymakers.

This subject is reviewed at **12.18** in the context of diversification of farming activity.

The same principles apply to caravan sites (see IHTM25279). HMRC recognise that such sites may range from land, provided with minimal facilities, to a full-scale holiday camp 'where the recreation and social facilities are of primary importance and the accommodation is only secondary'.

OVERVIEW

9.19   The questions for decision in *Farmer,* which still serve as a good guide even though they were qualified in *Balfour,* were these:

- Was the business of the company run on a businesslike basis with the help of agricultural consultants, farm managers, business plans and budgets?

- Who administered the lettings and what proportion of total management time was taken up with them?

- What was the allocation of turnover between different activities of the business?

- What was the allocation of profit from the business?

- How is capital employed between farming and lettings?

- Is the business of the company carried on 'for gain'?

- The standing back test.

In the light of *George*, we have different questions:

- Is there investment activity?

- Apart from pure profit rental, is there any income which the company claims to be trading income which is, in truth, disguised investment income?

- In the view of the reasonable businessman, is this mainly an investment business?

Given the different tests as to the existence of a business for differing tax purposes, for example BPR, holdover relief, business assets taper relief, associated companies and the like, there would be a clear advantage to administrators of the tax to have one definition that applied across the board.

One particular structure that can give difficulty is the group of companies that participates in joint venture agreements, notably overseas. Often, local law will require the holding company to accept less than 50% of the joint venture. The relevant tests may be those in *s 105(1)(cc)* or *s 105(4)*. Arguably, however, there is comfort in such a situation from the result in *Farmer*: one looks at the business entity as a whole, and overlooks the fact that some subsidiaries are investments rather than group companies. In the farming context, where the claim is to BPR rather than to APR, one may perhaps argue for a distinction between 'original' farm buildings, now used for holiday lets, and 'new' units, such as those bought in by the business as investments over the years. The new properties may be treated less favourably than the original units. Where does a barn conversion stand in this analysis? The shell was perhaps original, but it now has a value and a purpose that together bear no resemblance to a farm building as one commonly thinks of one. It will be a matter of fact and degree; but, when the developing of farm assets goes too far, the claim to BPR is endangered.

Chapter 10

Clawback

QUICK GUIDE

The sheer complexity of clawback rules prevents any useful summary beyond this: there is a risk period, following any lifetime gift of property qualifying for APR and BPR, that runs for seven years. During that time, the donee would be wise to retain the property, since relief will be lost if the donor (or the donee) dies during that seven-year period.

This chapter is twice as long as might seem necessary, because the clawback provisions are considered first in relation to business property and then in relation to agricultural property. This allows a practitioner to find all of the provisions that he needs in relation to either property in one section, rather than having to cross-refer.

The clawback risk period lasts up to seven years. During that time, it is acknowledged that changes may occur to the actual subject matter of a gift, and yet either the asset is still fundamentally the same, in which case the identity rules will apply, or it has been exchanged for another asset in respect of which relief ought to be allowed. These permutations are examined in relation to each relief.

Clawback of the relief may be partial or total, depending on the circumstances: see the rules in **10.8** and following. Generally, clawback affects PETs: chargeable transfers are affected only as to the 'uplift' of the tax rate from the lifetime rate to the death rate.

A flow chart to help the practitioner to follow a course through the legislation is included at **10.24**. An extended example of the rules then follows.

The most important section of this chapter is a discussion of steps to be taken to avoid clawback. It begins at **10.27**. A significant problem is that the practitioner may be acting for the donor rather than the donee, and yet it is the donee who needs to be aware of the clawback rules and how they operate.

INTRODUCTION

10.1   The clawback provisions were introduced by *FA 1986* and modified by *FA 1987*, *FA 1992* and *FA 1996*. They were once among the most difficult rules in IHT for the practitioner to memorise for the purpose of giving advice. They were simplified by the changes (*a*) to a single 40% rate of tax, and (*b*) to the allowance of 100% BPR on all unquoted shareholdings. They apply both for BPR and for APR. The code for BPR is considered first in this chapter, followed by the APR code. This involves some repetition but allows the reader to find the main provisions of each code all in one place for reference. Transfers before 18 March 1986 are not affected.

CLAWBACK OF BPR: THE BASIC RULE

10.2   BPR may be lost where, following a transfer which would otherwise qualify for BPR, certain conditions are not satisfied. The rule, which is contained in *IHTA 1984, s 113A*, operates to claw back BPR which would otherwise have sheltered a transfer from tax. It applies where a transfer is made within seven years of the death of the transferor. To achieve this, *s 113A* introduces the concept of a 'notional transfer' made by the donee of property immediately before the death of either:

- the transferor; or

- if earlier, the donee.

Thus, under *s 113A(2)*, if the conditions set out below are not satisfied, BPR will be clawed back in the situation where there has been a transfer of value qualifying for BPR which is or becomes chargeable and which is made within seven years of the death of the transferor.

Subject to special rules relating to replacement property, the conditions set out in *s 113A(3)* are that:

- the original property was owned by the transferee throughout the period beginning with the date of the chargeable transfer and ending with the death of the transferor; and

- subject to an exception discussed below, in relation to a notional transfer of value made by the transferee immediately before the death, the property would qualify for BPR but for the operation of *s 106*.

231

Example 10.1: takeover intervening

Oscar, a widower whose late wife Norah had used the nil rate band available to her but who did not use his annual allowance, held 20% of the ordinary shares in Oscar Fabrication Ltd, worth £100,000, which he gave to his nephew Roger in June 2006. The shares qualify for business relief. In December 2008, the company was taken over and Roger received £225,000.

Oscar died in May 2011, ie within seven years. His estate, which he leaves to his niece Samantha, comprises his house worth £200,000 and cash of £50,000. Roger has sold the shares before Oscar's death, so no BPR will be available. Tax on Oskar's estate is as follows:

	£
House	200,000
Cash	50,000
Estate in hands of executors	250,000
Lifetime gift (no reservation of benefit) (less 3,000 × 2)	94,000
Estate for rate including failed PET	344,000
Part nil rate band used on Roger's gift	94,000
Balance of nil rate band (325,000 – 94,000)	231,000
Chargeable estate (250,000 – 231,000)	19,000
IHT thereon at 40% suffered by Samantha	7,600

Example 10.2: going public

Angela gives her friend David a 10% holding in Interserve (Norwich) Ltd in August 2004. The shares are unquoted at the time of that gift. In September 2007, the company acquires a full Stock Exchange listing. The shares qualified for BPR at the date of the gift but, even though David retains the shares, if they are still quoted at the time of Angela's death in December 2010, no BPR will be available.

Change of property held: the rule in s 113A(3)

10.3   Under *s 113A(3)(b)*, the original property must (apart from the two-year ownership rule) qualify for BPR in relation to the notional transfer of the transferee just before the death, but that property need not be within the same category of property under *s 105(1)*. For example, in the quite common situation where a person owns a control holding of unquoted shares, he might make gifts of small blocks of shares to his family which, at the time of gift, might be PETs. This creates few problems now, in that all unquoted shares qualify for 100% relief; but, supposing the gift to have been made before 5 April 1996, relief would nevertheless have been available under *s 105(1)(b)*. Seven years have now elapsed since 5 April 1996: this will no longer worry practitioners, save for those whose work is not up to date.

Had the death occurred before the simplification of categories of relevant property achieved by *FA 1996*, a problem would have arisen in that the holding of each donee would be only a small minority of the issued share capital, falling within a different category of property for relief. The notional transfer deemed to take place under *s 113A(3)(b)* would be of shares falling within the (now defunct) category of *s 105(1)(c)*. The effect of *s 113A(3)(b)* would have been to allow relief at 100%, being the rate that would have been appropriate for the property had it remained in the estate of the donor. Many practitioners will be glad to be relieved of this kind of fine distinction in administering the relief.

Transfers of shares before 17 March 1987

10.4   Further difficulties arose in relation to transfers of unquoted shares before 17 March 1987. Such shares, whether or not dealt with on the Unlisted Securities Market ('USM'), were treated as unquoted for the purposes of the notional transfer by the transferee for clawback purposes. This was so, even though the shares might be dealt in on the USM at the death of the transferor (or, under the substituted provision, on the death of the transferee if that happened earlier).

Difficulties arose where a transfer was made between 17 March 1987 and 10 March 1992, and where the death of the transferor occurred before 10 March 1992. In those circumstances, no BPR was allowable on USM shares unless part of a control holding.

Fortunately, again, this is a complication which has now been removed and, in relation to deaths on or after 10 March 1992, shares which were dealt with on the USM are treated as unquoted for the whole period between the transfer and the death. This simplification is achieved by *F (No 2) A 1992, Sch 14, para 9(2)(a)*.

The computational rule under s 113A(3A)

10.5   Originally, *s 113A(3A)(b)* was more restricted than it is now. It applied to shares or securities falling only within *s 105(1)(b)*, ie control holdings in the unquoted securities of a company. Again, this restriction gave rise to difficulties of administration for the practitioner, which were fortunately removed in relation to transfers of value on or after 6 April 1996. A situation may open up which can benefit the taxpayer (see **10.32**).

Example 10.3: technical advantage

Mary owned 24% of the shares in Welsford Ltd, an unquoted company. At Christmas 1995, she gave the holding to her son William. That was a PET. At that time, relief was available at 50% under the old category *s 105(1)(c)*. Mary died in July 1999, with the result that the PET became a chargeable transfer. William at that time still held the shares, thus satisfying the requirements of *s 113A(3)(a)*.

By the date of Mary's death, BPR was available, not at the old 50% rate but at 100%, because by this time the property fell within *s 105(1)(bb)* as unquoted shares. William got the benefit of the 100% rate in two ways: it cancelled the tax charges that would otherwise have been made on the PET becoming chargeable; and it took the gift off Mary's 'clock'. This, at least, is the apparent effect of the changes introduced by *FA 1996, s 184*.

The situation might not be quite the same if Mary had transferred the shares to a discretionary trust. That would have been a chargeable transfer, with the result that there would be no change to the 'clock'. The benefit of 100% relief would, however, apply to relieve the 'uplift' charge on death which would otherwise have applied.

COMPUTATIONAL PROBLEMS RELATING TO CLAWBACK

10.6   Where a gift of business property was a PET and, by reason of the death within seven years of the transfer, that PET becomes a chargeable transfer, the operation of clawback is to increase the donor's 'clock' in computing the estate of the donor when calculating the rate at which IHT will be charged. On the other hand, where the transfer which was originally relieved was a chargeable transfer, clawback operates to charge extra tax on the original gift, on the basis that no relief is available. In this circumstance, there is no change to the donor's 'clock'.

Where clawback applies, the additional tax chargeable on death must be calculated without the benefit of BPR, unless the conditions set out above are complied with. By *IHTA 1984, s 113A(3A)*, special rules apply to shares or securities which were quoted at the time of the chargeable transfer, or which were unquoted and qualified for BPR under *s 105(1)(b)* or *(bb)*, and remained unquoted throughout the period from the transfer to the death. For the purposes of *s 113A(3A)*, 'quoted' means listed on a recognised stock exchange, and 'unquoted' means not so listed.

Example 10.4: a highly technical situation

Stanley controlled a quoted company. In December 2003, he gave a small minority holding of shares in the property to his son Arthur, the shares qualifying for relief under *s 105(1)(b)*. Arthur kept the shares and still held them when Stanley died in June 2009.

The gift was of quoted shares within *s 113A(3A)(a)* rather than within *s 113A(3A) (b)*. The result of this is that the exception in the first part of *s 113A(3)(b)* comes into play so that, in relation to the deemed transfer by the transferee, it is not necessary to satisfy the test in *s 113A(3)(b)*. It is enough that Arthur retains the shares so as to satisfy *s 113A(3)(a)*. Arthur therefore succeeds in claiming BPR. His holding is a minority one. Had all this happened a few years earlier, relief would have been available in respect of the original gift at 50% only.

If the transferee has died before the transferor, then the time for satisfying the conditions is the date of death of the transferee. As will be seen, this has implications for the rules by which a taxpayer can 'get back into' relief.

Additional tax: changes to the rules on computation introduced in 1992

10.7   *F (No 2) A 1992, Sch 14* applies to transfers of value (and other events) occurring on or after 10 March 1992. *Paragraph 9(1)* is concerned with two situations occurring in relation to a death on or after 10 March 1992:

• the failure of a PET; and

• clawback in respect of a chargeable transfer;

and requires *ss 113A* and *113B* to be interpreted on the basis that the amendments in *Sch 14* came into effect at the time the transfer was made, and that so much of the value transferred as would have been reduced in accordance with Chapter 1 of Part V (ie as would have qualified for BPR), as amended by *Sch 14*, was in fact so reduced. The old example that follows is now mainly of academic interest.

Example 10.5: an old example to illustrate the rule

Samantha had made no previous gifts but, at Christmas 1991, she gave Gerald, to whom she was not married, £153,000. To celebrate her birthday in January 1992, Samantha set up a discretionary trust to which she transferred 100,000 shares in Hunters Ltd, those shares being dealt in on the unlisted securities market and being worth £2.25 each.

10.7 *Clawback*

Tax was calculated as follows:

	£
Gift to Gerald	153,000
Less annual exemption1991/92	3,000
Less annual exemption 1990/91	3,000
	147,000

To calculate the tax on the chargeable transfer (Samantha then being alive and the PET not having failed):

	£
Value transferred	225,000
Less nil rate band	140,000
	85,000
Tax at lifetime rate	17,000

Samantha died in July 1994, by which time the nil rate band had increased to £150,000, ie more than enough to cover the gift to Gerald. By virtue of *Sch 14, para 9(2)(a)* the benefit is available of relief not previously available at the time of the gift but assumed to be so available. As a result, it becomes relevant that *s 105(1)(c)* was then in force (although that provision was itself repealed in relation to transfers after 5 April 1996). The effect of that was to make available 50% BPR.

The effect of *Sch 14, para 9(2)(b)* is to make a further assumption, ie to apply BPR as changed by *F (No 2) A 1992*. The calculation then proceeds as follows:

	£
Transfer to the discretionary trust	225,000
Less relief	112,500
Balance	112,500
Less amount by which nil rate band exceeds PET	3,000
	109,500
Tax at 40%	43,800
Less tax already paid	17,000
Tax payable on death	26,800

This calculation follows the method set out by HMRC in other connections, ie that the extra tax is the difference between:

- tax at the death rates on the value without relief; and
- tax at half the death rates on the value with relief.

236

It is hard to find specific authority for this approach. Many practitioners will be relieved that some of the complexities of these situations apply only to transfers occurring before the simplification of BPR, which has been celebrated throughout this book.

PARTIAL CLAWBACK: THE OPERATION OF S 113A(5)

10.8   Situations can arise where, in relation to the original property, the conditions of *s 113A* apply to only part. Where that happens:

- in relation to a PET, only a proportionate part of the value transferred as is attributable to the original property qualifies for BPR; and

- in relation to a chargeable transfer, the extra tax is worked out as if only a proportionate part of the value transferred (as was attributable to the original property) had qualified for the relief.

Example10.6: partial clawback (1)

At Christmas 2005, Sarah made a simple gift to Tom of a holding of unquoted shares. That was a PET. The shares were worth £180,000, a value later agreed with Shares Valuation Division. The holding is within *s 105(1)(bb)*, so relief involved is at 100%. Sarah died in June 2009, so clawback may be in point. Tom still holds half the shares that he was given, so BPR shelters half the gift. The other half loses BPR and becomes chargeable as a failed PET.

Example 10.7: partial clawback (2)

In April 2008, Ursula, who had used her annual exemptions, set up a trust for her son Victor of shares in the family trading company worth £100,000. In November 2009, the trustees accepted a cash offer for 40% of their holding but kept the remainder. Ursula died in January 2011, so within three years of the chargeable transfer that set up the trust. Relief from the 'top up' tax charge under *s7(4)* is restricted to £60,000.

Interaction of reliefs: clawback and 'pre-death loss relief'

10.9   Not for nothing do the current discussions on the simplification of tax centre on reliefs, as the following discussion will illustrate. Relief, in a form that deserves to be better known, is allowed under *s 131* in respect of any property where, broadly:

- a PET fails and the subject matter of the transfer is sold at arm's length for less than it was worth when given; or

- tax at 20% on a chargeable transfer falls to be 'topped up' to 40% because death occurs within three years of the chargeable transfer.

Where the property transferred is still held by the transferee (or his spouse or civil partner) and has fallen in value by the date of death, that fall in value may reduce the transfer. Where the property is no longer held, but has been sold under a 'qualifying sale' (one at arm's length to an unconnected person where there is no 'buy back' term in the sale), the same reduction may apply. We must now apply those rules to the situation where BPR is reduced by clawback because part of the original gift has been sold. Before 100% relief on unquoted shares, this could give rise to serious complications because it was necessary to decide whether the original gift was, in effect, divisible into the part retained and that later sold. The following example necessarily uses old dates to illustrate the point.

Example 10.8: relief as a result of sale

Adapting Example 10.6, at Christmas 1991, Sarah gave Tom all her unquoted shares in a company, worth £180,000 as agreed with HMRC, which at that time qualified for relief at 50% only. Before Sarah's death, Tom sold one-third of the shares for £50,000, so realising a slight loss. That sale is at arm's length for a price freely negotiated at the time of sale within *s 131(3)(a)*. Further, within *s 131(3)(b)*, it is a sale to an unconnected person without provision (see *s 131(3)(c)*) for any right to buy back or similar right.

Sarah died in June 1995. The value of the entire holding of shares at the date of Sarah's death is agreed at £90,000. There can be no relief on one-third of the shares, because Tom sold them. First, review the original gift. The transfer was valued at £180,000 and, but for the later sale, BPR would be £90,000. In the light of the sale, BPR is partially clawed back and only two-thirds is now allowed, ie 180,000 × ⅔ × 50% = £60,000. In view of the fact that the entire shareholding would now be worth only £90,000, Tom seeks further relief.

	£
Market value of all the shares at date of gift	180,000
Less relief on two-thirds at 50%	60,000
Net value at A below	120,000

	£
Sale price of shares sold	50,000
Value of retained shares at date of Sarah's death	60,000
Deduct BPR at 50% on the retained shares	(45,000)
	15,000
Total value at B below	65,000
Relief (A – B)	55,000

There is an alternative basis of calculation, arrived at by comparing values of individual holdings with the original, larger, holding. This yields much lower relief. With the removal of the old category of shares in *s 105(1)(c)*, the problem is hardly ever met in practice.

Disregard of BPR: the rule in s 113A(7A)

10.10   A difficult technical point arises from the operation of *s 113A(7A)*, which requires the provisions of BPR to be disregarded when deciding, for the purposes of clawback, whether there is a PET or chargeable transfer in any particular case. The difficulty of this provision could arise where, for example, the nature of property has changed between the time of transfer and the later death, such as unquoted shares becoming quoted.

Example 10.9: clawback after flotation

John, a widower whose late wife had used her nil rate band, owned shares in a fledgling company, the shares of which were dealt with on AIM. He gave all the shares to his daughter Sarah in April 2009 when they had a value of £300,000. He made further chargeable transfers using up his nil rate band but, by virtue of the AIM status, 100% BPR was available.

This niche company was one of the few to float successfully on The Stock Exchange in June 2010. John died in December 2010.

By virtue of *s 113A(7A)*, the gifts are treated as PETs within the requirements of *s 113A(1)*. This is so, whether or not the value transferred in 2009 would have been covered by BPR. As a result, BPR will not be available. The conditions of *s 113A* apply to the tax charge on John's death. This is because, in relation to a notional transfer of value made by the transferee immediately before the death, the shares would no longer be relevant business property within *s 113A(3B)*.

ADDITIONAL CONDITIONS

10.11   *IHTA 1984, s 113A* has imposed additional conditions to the general conditions for BPR. The taxpayer must show:

- that the property transferred was relevant business property at the time of the transfer, if that transfer is a PET which fails; or

- that, if that transfer was a chargeable one, it qualified for the relief at that time.

Where this cannot be shown, the relief will be lost. There is then no relief on the PET. If the transfer was a chargeable one, additional tax is payable (see *s 113A(2)*) without the benefit of the relief. The additional tax payable is the difference between:

- the tax at the death rates without the benefit of BPR; and

- tax paid at half the death rates on the value, but with the benefit of BPR.

Example 10.10: an old example

To illustrate the point, this example dates from some time ago: as a result, the situation may seldom be encountered in practice. Jennifer had made no previous chargeable transfers. She was in partnership with her daughter and owned some land used by the partnership worth £200,000. On 10 April 1989, she gave the land to trustees on discretionary trusts at a time when restricted relief was available, ie at 30%. The trustees later appointed the land onto interest in possession trusts for Jennifer's son Andrew.

The tax on the chargeable transfer is calculated on the basis that the trustees pay it, viz:

	£
Transfer	200,000
Less 30%	60,000
	140,000
Less nil rate band	118,000
Chargeable at lifetime rates	22,000
Tax chargeable at 20%	4,400

On Jennifer's death in January 1991, the additional tax payable depends on whether Andrew is then a partner in the business. If he is, the additional tax payable is simply the amount needed to 'top up' to the death rate, ie £4,400.

On the other hand, if Andrew is not a partner at Jennifer's death, then, in relation to the notional transfer deemed to be made by him, the land is not relevant business property. There can be no relief. The additional tax is then calculated as:

	£
Transfer	200,000
Nil rate band	128,000
	72,000
Tax chargeable at death rates	28,800
Less tax already paid	4,400
Balance of tax now due	24,400

In this example, the additional tax bites on the transfer but, as already observed, does not affect Jennifer's 'clock'. The rest of the estate is unaffected, ie it is treated as if Jennifer had made a gift of £140,000. That point is somewhat academic, in that the nil rate band did not rise above £140,000 until rather more than two years after the death of Jennifer in this example. The situation would have been different if the gift to Andrew by Jennifer had been an outright one since, by the operation of *s 113A(1)* on failure of the PET, it would go onto Jennifer's clock. The reduction of multiple rates to a single rate of 50% in this situation has reduced the complexity of dealing with computations in this area.

Where the gift is of property within *s 105(1)(d)*, such as machinery used for a business in which the transferor is a partner, *s 113A(3)* requires that the property requalify for BPR in relation to the notional transfer of value by the donee. The asset comprising the gift does not so qualify unless the donee is a partner or (in a corporate example) controls the company concerned. In the latter case, relief will be lost, in the common case of a gift of land, from which the family business trades, to two children equally; so clawback may apply. The better solution may be a gift of the shares and the land together to a discretionary trust, where the land itself, after 50% BPR, is worth no more than £650,000, ie within the nil rate band overall. Then the trustees will control the company, and clawback may be avoided.

Further amendments to s 113A(3A): the changing definition of 'quoted'

10.12 This subsection took effect in relation to transfers of value made, and other events occurring, on or after 17 March 1987. It affects property acquired by the transferee before that date so as to disregard *FA 1987, Sch 8* in deciding whether the property would qualify for BPR in relation to the notional transfer where that arises as a result of events happening on or after 17 March 1987.

10.13   *Clawback*

This rule applies to clawback only. From 10 March 1992 the definition of 'quoted' for clawback purposes included only shares or securities listed on a recognised stock exchange. From 1 April 1996, the expression 'listed' was substituted in *s 113A(3B)*. This affects USM shares. They are now treated as unquoted for clawback purposes throughout the period under review, ie from the date of the transfer. This rule, in *F (No 2) A 1992, Sch 14, para 9(2)(a)* is varied (see *para 9(3)*) in relation to a control holding. Control holdings of USM shares are treated as quoted for clawback purposes (see below).

There is a valuable exception (but annoying for practitioners to have to remember). This arises under *F (No 2) A 1992, Sch 4, para 9(3)*. That paragraph provides that where, disregarding the other amendments made by *Sch 4*, any shares or securities transferred fell within *s 105(1)(b)*, ie were securities of a company which were unquoted and which, by themselves or together with other securities, gave the transferor control, in relation to that transfer, the amendments are to be disregarded in deciding whether *s 113A(3A)* applies to the shares or securities.

The kind of situation affected is now unlikely, through the passage of time, to be met.

Example 10.11: an unusual situation

The holder of 51% of a USM company qualifying for BPR makes a gift of the shares to two people equally. The company goes public in February 1993. The donor dies in March of that year, at which time the donees still hold the shares, which are of course now quoted.

Is BPR available? *Section 113A(3A)* is not satisfied because, under *s 113A(3A) (a)*, the shares were not quoted at the time of the transfer and, under *s 113A(3A) (b)*, the shares were not part of a control holding throughout the whole of the requisite period. No relief would therefore be available, and clawback would apply but for the effect of *F (No 2) A 1992, Sch 14, para 9(3)*, which allows the shares to be treated as quoted at the time of the transfer for the purposes of bringing the situation within the requirements of *s 113A(3A)*. It follows that the shares fall within *s 113A(3A)(a)*. The test in *s 113A(3A)* is satisfied because the shares are still held. The original relief is preserved, and clawback does not apply.

Definitions employed in s 113A: 'the original property' and 'the transferee'

10.13   *Section 113A(8)* defines 'the original property', an expression used in *s 113A(3)(a)*. This is the property which must, under that subsection, be owned by the transferee for the period beginning with the chargeable transfer and ending with the death of the transferor, if clawback is to be avoided. The definitions also apply to replacement property (see *s 113B(8)*).

'The original property' means property which qualified for BPR in relation to the chargeable transfer.

'The transferee' means either:

- the person whose property the original property became on the chargeable transfer; or

- the trustees of a settlement where, on the transfer of the original property, it became settled on discretionary trusts (as it almost always will do, after *FA 2006*).

The result of this can be to trigger clawback where the trustees make an absolute appointment to an object of the trust. See, however, some possibilities discussed at **10.32** below.

For this purpose, the tenant for life of an 'old-style' interest in possession trust is deemed to be the owner of the original property. This had the result, in relation to interest in possession trusts for as long as they lasted, that, if the gift of property qualifying for BPR was to a person for life who then released that life interest before the death (within the seven-year period from the original gift) of the donor, clawback would apply and BPR would be lost. The situation was different where the tenant for life became the absolute owner because, by virtue of the deeming provisions, the tenant for life was treated as the owner anyway. The changes introduced by *FA 2006* will usually remove this complication.

RELIEF FROM CLAWBACK

Problems of identification: the rule in s 113A(6)

10.14 It would be very harsh to apply the clawback rules where, in substance, the asset given has been retained but has, perhaps through matters beyond the control of the transferee, changed its identity somewhat whilst remaining the type of property for which the relief was designed. This is allowed for in *s 113A(6)* in two situations.

First, where the shares comprised in the transfer are no longer held by the transferee because, through a reorganisation of share capital or a conversion of securities, new shares are identified with the old shares under the rules set out in *TCGA 1992, ss 126–136* (reorganisation or reduction of share capital), those shares are treated as if they were the original property.

Second, where the subject matter of the original gift was a business or an interest in a business, and that interest is no longer held by the transferee because shares were issued to him in consideration of the transfer by him of the business, again those shares are treated as if they represented the original property. BPR is given pro rata where the subject matter of the original gift is only partly represented by the new securities.

Replacement property for the purposes of clawback (BPR)

10.15   There are provisions allowing for the requirements of *s 113A* to be satisfied, even though the transferee may have disposed of all or part of the original subject matter of the gift before the death of the transferor. Any replacement must (see *s 113B(2)(b)*) be by way of a transaction at arm's length or, if it is not at arm's length, must be on terms such as might be expected to be included in a transaction at arm's length. The requirement is that the transferee must apply all of the proceeds of the disposal in buying a replacement property within the 'allowed period' of the disposal. Nothing in *s 113B(1)(b)* would seem to allow partial relief where not all of the proceeds are reinvested.

Example 10.12: unfortunate bank condition

Fred gives to Victoria a small industrial unit qualifying for 50% relief under *s 105(1)(d)* which is subject to a mortgage. Victoria agrees to take the property subject to that charge. Four years later, the requirements of the business occupying the unit change, and it is agreed that Victoria will buy similar premises at a different location. The security requirements of the bank are such that, on the occasion of the new purchase, a portion of the proceeds of sale of the first unit are applied in discharging Victoria's debts. No BPR will be available under *s 113B(1)(b)*, because Victoria has not applied all of the proceeds of sale of the first unit in purchasing the second.

For replacement property to qualify, such that relief is not clawed back, it must be purchased within 'the allowed period' of the disposal. That period is (see *s 113B*) three years or such longer period as the Board may allow. The allowed period applied not only to transfers of value made after 29 November 1993, when the period was extended from one year, but also to changes or further changes arising on a death after that date in respect of a transfer made before that date. This was confirmed by the Revenue in reply to a query raised by the ICAEW Tax Faculty but, by now, the point must surely be academic.

Further conditions: s 113B

10.16   *Section 113B* sets out further conditions to preserve BPR from clawback. These are contained in *s 113B(3)* and are:

- the replacement property must be owned by the transferee immediately before the death of the transferor; and

- throughout the period beginning with the date of the chargeable transfer and ending with the death (disregarding any period between the disposal and acquisition), either the original property or the replacement property was owned by the transferee; and

- in relation to a notional transfer of value made by the transferee immediately before the death, the replacement property would (apart from the requirements of *s 106* as to ownership for two years) be relevant business property.

Example 10.13: buying suitable assets quickly

Assume that:

- the transferor dies before the transferee; and

- all or any part of the original gift has been disposed of before that death (or fails to qualify for BPR because it is subject to a binding contract for sale); and

- the donee acquires the replacement property (or contracts to do so) after the death of the transferor but within the 'allowed period' of three years after the disposal of the original subject matter of the gift (or part of it, as the case may be).

In these circumstances, the primary rule would be that the condition in *s 113B(3)(a)* does not apply, because the donee does not own the property at the date of death, so relief would be lost. However, by *s 113B(5)*, a reference to a time immediately before the death is instead regarded as a reference to the time when the replacement property is acquired. That disapplies *s 113B(3)(a)*, preserving the relief.

In just the same way that, under the main clawback provisions of *s 113A*, the death of the transferee during the 'clawback risk period' could cause the clawback conditions to be tested so, by *s 113B(4)*, if the transferee has died before the transferor, a reference to the death of the transferor within *s 113B* has effect as a reference to the death of the transferee.

Other provisions parallel with those in *s 113A* are the definitions of 'the original property' and 'the transferee', which have been noted above. The timing of transactions is important. By *s 113B(7)* a disposal is regarded for the purposes of *s 113B(2)(a)* and *(5)(b)* as taking place at the time of a binding contract for sale. Thus, it is the contract date which determines applicability of clawback, whether under *s 113B(5)(a)* on disposal or *s 113B(5)(b)* on acquisition. (Note, incidentally, that this rule is well drafted, avoiding the slight doubt which has arisen, in the field of CGT, as to the date of acquisition in the context of rollover relief under *TCGA 1992, s 152*, where the argument had been advanced that the time of acquisition and disposal for the purposes of *s 152* does *not* follow the general rule in *TCGA 1992, s 28*.)

Again, in a provision which is parallel in *s 113B* to that in *s 113A* in relation to identification of property, *s 113B(6)* provides that *s 113A(6)* shall apply in relation to replacement property as it does to the original property.

In just the same way as the reconstruction and amalgamation provisions of *TCGA 1992, ss 126–136* apply under the main clawback rule to save BPR from loss, they apply by virtue of *IHTA 1984, s 113B(6)* to replacement property to save the relief.

CLAWBACK OF APR: THE BASIC RULE

10.17   APR may be lost where, following a transfer which would otherwise qualify for that relief, certain conditions are not satisfied. The rule is similar to the rule already described for BPR. The code is found in *ss 124A* and *124B*, which were inserted into *IHTA 1984* by *FA 1986* and which have effect in relation to transfers on or after 17 March 1986. APR is lost in two situations where certain conditions are not satisfied. These situations are where:

- any part of the value transferred by a PET qualifying for APR fails; and

- part of the value transferred by a chargeable transfer qualifies for APR and the transfer is made within seven years of the death of the transferor.

In the second situation, the tax concerned is the 'top up' from lifetime rates to death rates. The value of the chargeable transfer for accumulation purposes is not affected; it stays the same as calculated at the time of the chargeable transfer.

The conditions which must be satisfied for clawback of APR not to apply are set out in *s 124A(3)* and are as follows:

- The original property must be owned by the transferee throughout the period from the chargeable transfer to the death of the transferor and must not, at the time of that death, be subject to a binding contract for sale.

● Generally, the original property given must be agricultural property immediately before the death and must have been occupied for the purposes of agriculture throughout the relevant period, either by the transferee or by someone else.

● The exception to the rule just set out arises where the original property consists of shares in or securities of a company. Here the condition is that, throughout the period from the gift to the death of the donor, the agricultural property qualifying for APR by virtue of the 'farming company' rules of *s 122(1)* was owned by that company and was occupied for the purpose of agriculture, either by that company or by someone else.

Example 10.14: costly health problems

In January 2005, Mary gives her son William her farm at Low Street, together with the house adjoining it in which William lives. In 2010, through ill-health, William has to give up farming. He sells the land, buying an insurance bond with the proceeds, and continues to live at Low Street Farmhouse. Mary dies shortly afterwards. The death within seven years brings the clawback provisions into play. APR is no longer available on the house, because it has been separated from the land; nor can it be claimed on the investments now representing the proceeds of sale.

By *s 124A(4)*, if the transferee dies before the transferor, the date at which retention of agricultural property is tested for the purposes of escaping clawback under *s 124(3)* is that of the death of the transferee.

Example 10.15: death before clawback event

In June 2007, Andrew gave his brother James a parcel of agricultural land to add to James' existing holding. At the date of his death in October 2009, James still held the additional land, which was sold by his executors. Andrew died in January 2011. The gift qualified for APR when made as a PET. Tax is payable on the PET with the benefit of APR, even though the land has now been sold, because it was held by James for as long as he could do so.

PARTIAL CLAWBACK: THE OPERATION OF S 124A(5)

10.18   As was noted in relation to BPR, the situation can arise for clawback where the conditions of *s 124A* apply to only part of the property. Where that happens:

- in relation to a PET, only a proportionate part of the value transferred as is attributable to the original property qualifies for APR; and

- in relation to a chargeable transfer, the extra tax is worked out as if only a proportionate part of the value transferred (as was attributable to the original property) qualified for APR.

Example 10.16: partial clawback

Samantha owns the Kingsnorth Estate, consisting of three basic elements: a sheep farming operation, an adjoining moor with sporting rights, and a number of estate cottages. She gives the estate in June 2007 to her brother Tom. That is a PET. APR, should it become relevant, is available in respect of the lowland sheep farm and, with some difficulty, on the moorland but (it appears) not on the cottages, none of which have for years been occupied by farm-workers or their dependants.

Tom keeps the lowland farm and cottages but sells the moor. Samantha dies in February 2011, with the result that the PET fails. APR is not clawed back in respect of the retained farm but is clawed back in respect of the moorland. The conditions of *s 124A(3)* are not satisfied in relation to the cottages, in respect of which APR was never available.

DISREGARD OF APR: THE RULE IN S 124A(7A)

10.19   This rule finds a parallel for BPR in *s 113A(7A)*. In deciding whether there has been a PET or a chargeable transfer, APR must be disregarded. The rule applies to transfers of value on or after 28 November 1995. The rule does not affect the rate of relief. It does not affect the amount in respect of which the relief is given. To understand the rule, it is necessary to look at the situation which existed before it was enacted. As a result of earlier amendments to IHT, it was not certain whether clawback could operate on a lifetime transfer where the value transferred was, by virtue of APR, reduced to nil or to a very small amount. This was because it could be argued that APR at 100% reduced the value so as to cause the transfer to be wholly exempt within the small gifts exemption or annual exemption. In respect of transfers after 27 November

1995, the disregard of APR, in deciding whether there has been a PET or a chargeable transfer, makes it possible for clawback to operate where a transfer is reduced to nil or a very small amount by APR.

Definitions employed in s 124A: 'the original property' and 'the transferee'

10.20 *Section 124A(8)* defines 'the original property'. It is the property which, in relation to the chargeable transfer for clawback was either agricultural property qualifying for relief under *s 116* or shares in a farming company qualifying through *s 122(1)* for relief under *s 116*.

'The transferee' means either:

- the person whose property the original property became on the chargeable transfer, or
- the trustees of a settlement where, on the transfer of the original property, it became settled on discretionary trusts.

These definitions apply equally to replacement property (see *s 124B(8)*).

The result of this, as was noted in relation to BPR, can be clawback where trustees make an absolute appointment to an object of the trust. The effect of this is examined in relation to trusts later in this chapter. Further, a seemingly innocent gift may have disastrous consequences.

Example 10.17: catastrophe avoided

Terence, at the age of 75, made an outright gift to his son Jeremy of the farmhouse in which, at that time, Jeremy was living with Susan, his wife, and their two children. It had been the family home, which Terence had vacated (after his wife had died a few years before), handing it over in, frankly, fairly dismal condition. Susan had used her accumulated earnings to refurbish the house, installing a modern kitchen, bathroom and central heating.

During an estate planning exercise carried out for Jeremy by Geoff, on somewhat similar lines to that described in Example 3.2, it was proposed that, to recognise Susan's contribution, the farmhouse should be transferred by Jeremy into their joint names. By this time, Terence was aged 81 and in poor health.

Jeremy mentioned the proposal in passing to his accountant, Carol. She immediately grasped the point missed by Geoff, namely that a transfer by Jeremy would cause him, as 'the transferee' within *s 124A(8)*, to no longer be the owner of 'the original property' as required by *s 124A(3)(a)*. It might well be argued that, after the transfer, Jeremy was still the owner of half the farmhouse. It could not be ruled out, however, that HMRC might maintain that Jeremy's interest in the proceeds of sale of the farmhouse was materially different from his original interest, ie that, if Terence were to die within the next year or so, clawback might apply at the very least to one half, and possibly to the whole, of the value of the farmhouse. Either way, with six years having already elapsed since the gift, it would be madness to risk clawback.

As a result, the transfer to Susan did not take place. There was no claim against Geoff, but he never received any more work from Jeremy.

The effect of clawback

10.21   Clawback operates differently according to whether:

- the clawback charge arises on the death of the transferor; or

- the clawback charge arises on the failure of a PET, the PET being the release of the benefit (as to which see **10.26**);

and according to whether the original transfer when made was a PET or was chargeable. Where that transfer was a PET, there is simply no APR. As a result, BPR could apply.

Example 10.18: clawback, but relieved

Roger gives Phillip a small farm in September 2004. Phillip develops part of it as a trout fishery, which he conducts on business-like principles entirely within the requirements of Ralph Gibson J in *C & E Comrs v Lord Fisher* (see **Chapter 5**). On the death of Roger in February 2011, APR is available in respect of the undeveloped portion of the land without clawback. Clawback of APR applies to the trout fishery, but that may qualify instead for BPR.

If the transfer when made was chargeable, rather than a PET, and qualified at that time only for APR with IHT being payable at the lifetime rate, on the death of the transferor within seven years the 'top up' tax charge is calculated as if APR had not been available at the outset. There is no effect on the tax paid at the time of transfer. The donor's 'clock' is unaffected. As a separate matter,

BPR is not available in the alternative to relieve the 'top up' charge to tax; this is the effect of *s 114(1)*.

Example10.19: no benefit from later rules

In January 2008, Cedric gives to trustees for his children equally a parcel of let agricultural land qualifying at that time for APR at only 50%. No benefit is reserved. The trustees take the land in hand and farm it. By the time of Cedric's death in December 2010, the trustees still own and occupy the land. Under the notional transfer deemed to arise immediately before Cedric's death, the land qualifies for relief by reference to the trustees at 100%. The trustees get no benefit from the higher rate of relief: the rate of relief is therefore 50%, which was the rate applicable for such property at the death of Cedric.

An exception to clawback

10.22   Where the value transferred exceeds *the value of the property transferred*, relief operates in an interesting way, as explained in the IHT Manual at IHTM24174 and the first example there set out, which is paraphrased below.

Example 10.20: house losing value

Jessica gives her son Tom her farmland but lives on in the farmhouse, which she keeps. The value transferred, estate before less estate after, is (*a*) the value of the land plus (*b*) the drop in the value of the house once separated from its land.

Tom keeps and farms the land, all of which qualifies for APR. Jessica dies within seven years of the gift. To what value does APR apply? Assuming all conditions are met for clawback *not* to apply, the relief is available on the entire 'transfer value' of the land, ie including the element representing the depreciation in value of the farmhouse even though, being now separated from its land, it no longer qualifies for APR.

This interpretation follows from the definition of 'the original property' in *s 124A(8)*: the conditions are satisfied in relation to that property. Whether in reality a farmhouse would, these days, be any less valuable if shorn of its land is perhaps open to doubt: the rule might, however, apply in other circumstances that could be imagined.

RELIEF FROM CLAWBACK

Problems of identification: the rule in s 124A(6)

10.23   As was noted in relation to BPR, it should be harsh to apply the clawback rules where, in substance, the asset which was given has been kept although its identity has changed slightly. By *s 124A(6)*, clawback is avoided where shares (in a farming company) now held by the transferee can be identified with the shares originally given because they are effectively the same company by virtue of the rules in *TCGA 1992, ss 126–136* (reorganisation or reduction of share capital). The replacement shares are simply treated as if they were the original property.

Second, where:

- the subject matter of the original gift was agricultural property; and

- on incorporation of the farming business, the donee now holds shares which were issued to him in consideration of the transfer to the company of the agricultural property;

the scheme of the legislation is for the shares to be treated as if they were the original property.

Actually, the specific wording of the legislation is that the period of ownership of the transferee of the original property is to be treated as including his period of ownership of the shares. This wording is intended to get round the conceptual problem of the original legislation, which provided that the shares should be treated as if they were the original property (or part of it). It was not clear how the shares in such a circumstance could qualify for relief from clawback under *s 124A(3)*. The deeming provision as enacted by *FA 1987, s 58* gets round this problem.

Replacement property: the conditions

10.24   The scheme of *s 124B* gives further relief. This rule is in addition to *s 124A*. *Section 124B* is directed at the situation where the original property has been sold and other property purchased. There is a four-stage test before replacement property relief may be given:

- *Disposal triggering clawback*: The donee of the property must have made a disposal, before the death of the transferor, of part or all of the original subject matter of the gift.

- *Purchase of new property*: Whether that disposal was of part or of all of the original subject matter, the entire proceeds from the disposal must have been applied in purchasing new qualifying property. *Section 124B(1)(b)* refers to 'the whole of the consideration received by him for the disposal', which one learned commentator has regarded as being the proceeds net of both fees on sale and of CGT.

- *New purchase made soon enough*: The new qualifying property must be acquired, or at least there must be a binding contract for that acquisition, within a specified period. Originally that period was 12 months, no excuses. Since 1 December 1993, that period has been three years, or such longer period as the Board may allow.

- *Everything at arm's length*: The disposal of the subject matter of the original gift and the purchase of the new qualifying property must be by transaction at arm's length, or must be on terms such as might be expected to be included in a transaction at arm's length.

When all these conditions can be met, the effect of *s 124B* is to relieve the situation from clawback by deeming the conditions in *s 124A(3)* to have been satisfied; but only provided that four new conditions are met, namely:

- *Donee retains asset*: the replacement property is still owned by the transferee immediately before the death of the transferor, and is not at that time subject to a binding contract for sale;

- *Old land always farmed*: throughout the period from the original transfer to the exchange of property, the original property was owned by the transferee and either he or someone else occupied it for the purposes of agriculture;

- *New land always farmed*: throughout the period from the exchange of property to the death, the replacement property was also occupied for the purposes of agriculture, either by the transferee or by someone else; and

- *New land still farmland*: the replacement property is, immediately before the death, still agricultural property.

It may help practitioners to follow this sequence of tests through a flowchart. Assume that 'T' is the transferor of the asset and that 'B' is the beneficiary or transferee. Two flow charts are necessary, which follow one from the other and are shown on pages 254 and 255.

As with BPR, if the transferee has died before the transferor, *s 124B(4)* provides that it is the death of the transferee which is to determine whether the provisions as to replacement property saving the transaction from clawback are to apply.

Clawback flowchart

Assume that 'T' is the transferor of the asset and that 'B' is the beneficiary or transferee

STAGE 1:

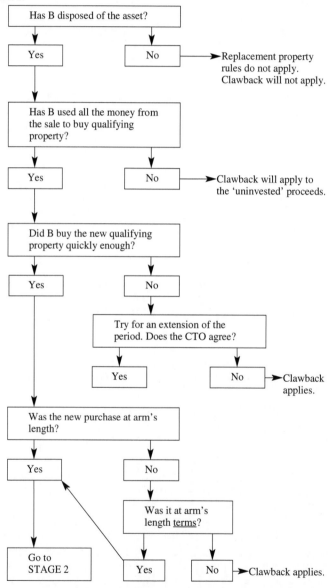

STAGE 2:

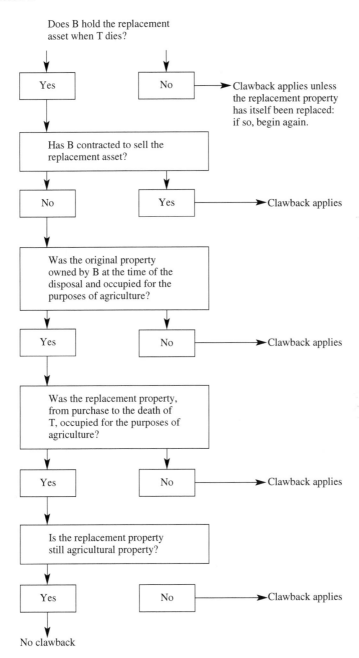

Replacement property: how the rules work

10.25   Without the benefit of *s 124B(5,)* the clawback provisions could be very restrictive where, for good farming or other reasons, the sale of the land which had been given and the purchase of alternative land was contemplated. That section provides that clawback may be avoided in a situation where all or part of the original property has been disposed of before the death of the transferor, or is subject to a binding contract for sale at the death of the transferor, and the replacement property is acquired, or there is in place a binding contract for the acquisition of replacement property, after the death of the transferor but within 'the allowed period' after the original disposal; and the transferor dies before the transferee. The purchase of the replacement property had, prior to 29 November 1993, to be made within one year. By virtue of *s 124B(8)*, 'the allowed period' is now three years or such longer period as the Board may allow. That is one element considered in the extended example that follows.

Example 10.21: rural village bypass

John bought Church Farm near Framlingham in Suffolk many years ago and farmed it until his death in December 2005, when the land passed under his will to his wife Sarah. Although she had been a great help on the farm all her life, much of the work was done to a greater or lesser extent by her five children. Andrew was now farming on his own account nearby at Rendham. Barbara had married a local builder and lived nearby. Celia worked in London as a hotel manager, David was farming at Saxmundham, and Edward had stayed at home on the farm and was now taken into partnership by Sarah to run the home farm.

Sarah, on 1 to 5 April 2007, made gifts in order substantially to reduce her estate. To Andrew she gave 12 acres near what passed, in that part of the country, for the main road. To Barbara, Sarah gave some redundant farm buildings which she thought Barbara and her husband might be able to make something of. There was a row of pretty but redundant cottages which seemed an appropriate gift for Celia, who could perhaps develop them into a holiday cottage business. David received a parcel of off-lying farmland. To Edward, Sarah gave a half interest in the remaining farmland.

In May 2007, there occurred a rare event for that part of East Anglia, a road widening scheme which was actually proceeded with, to the point that a strip of land was taken across the middle of the land which Andrew had received, leaving him with eight of the 12 acres; and to one side of the land that David had received, leaving him with six acres. In each case, the remaining parcel was no longer an economic unit. Meanwhile, Barbara and her husband, having carried out a feasibility study on the barns and having obtained planning permission for a development, decided that they would sell the barns in an undeveloped state but with the benefit of that planning permission.

The family solicitor was Geoff who dealt with all the conveyancing and who advised Andrew, Barbara and David that there was a risk, since Sarah was now elderly and might not survive the gifts that she had made by seven years, that clawback might apply to deny them APR. He explained that the sale to the council, even though it was not initiated by Andrew and David, could trigger the clawback and that they had (as he thought) only one year in which to make the situation good by putting the money back into farmland. By April 2008, Andrew, worried by the advice from Geoff and having found no land that was particularly suitable, made a hasty purchase at a slight overvalue of some land to reinvest the proceeds of the sale in May 2007. Barbara did not act so quickly. The property market was turning sour, so she and her husband kept the proceeds of the barns on deposit.

David was in something of a quandary: he did not want to ignore Geoff's advice, but there was no land near him immediately for sale. He did, however, understand that a neighbour of his would soon wish to retire and that extra land immediately adjoining David's land might therefore be on the market within a couple of years. He mentioned the problem to his accountant, Carol. She told David to wait. She explained that *FA 1994, s 247(2)* had extended the period within which he might make a purchase without risk of clawback. He should, however, make the purchase by April 2010 since there were, in her opinion, no circumstances that would give the Board reason to allow longer than three years. David duly made his purchase.

Sarah died on 10 December 2008.

Geoff was struggling with the administration of the estate. In terms of value, the 2007 gifts were substantial in relation to Sarah's remaining estate, the residue of which had been left to the five children equally. There was virtually no cash in the estate. Geoff was concerned that he would have to tell the children not only that there was nothing more to inherit but that they would have to find from their own resources any tax that might be payable in respect of the gifts. Having missed the point that Carol grasped, namely that the permitted period had been extended in relation to all deaths occurring after 29 November 1993, he was concerned from the human point of view that clawback would apply to Andrew's gift, and that, since it was the first of the five gifts, it would make a big hole in Sarah's nil rate band.

He considered, correctly, that the barns given to Barbara would not qualify for APR, because they had not been used for agriculture for many years. Similarly, the cottages, although of a character appropriate, had not been occupied by farm workers or retired farm workers or the dependants of farm workers and did not qualify for APR. He was, therefore, very glad to learn that, albeit through other solicitors, Andrew had made a purchase that would protect him from clawback. This freed up the nil rate band. Concern then focused on David, until Carol gently reminded Geoff that his tax knowledge was significantly out of date. Geoff had never been worried about the gift to Edward: he had stayed at home and was still farming the land which he had occupied in partnership with his mother since April 2007.

The effect of *s 124B(5)* is restricted in one particular circumstance, ie the requirement under *s 124B(5)(c)* that the transferor dies before the transferee. *Section 124B(4)* quite specifically allows substitution of the death of the transferee for that of the transferor only in relation to the replacement property provisions of *s 124B(1), (2)* and *(3)*. It is therefore possible to imagine situations where, as a result of deaths 'in the wrong order', clawback might bite.

The replacement property provisions of *s 124B* generally are wide enough to include shares in a farming company, by allowing *s 124A(6)* to apply to the replacement property as it did to the original property.

For timing purposes, it is the date of the contract that matters (see *s 124B(7)*).

It is not essential that agricultural property in the hands of the donee at the death of the transferor must qualify for relief at the same rate as the subject matter of the original gift. Provided that the property qualifies for relief, even if at a different rate, clawback can be avoided. Relief is awarded at the rate that was appropriate at the time of the lifetime transfer.

For example, the gift might be of farmland which, considered in the light of the circumstances at the time of the gift, qualified for relief at 100%. Whilst the land might be retained by the donee, circumstances might change such that, at the later death within seven years of the transferor, relief might be available at 50% only because there had been a change in the occupation of the land. In such a circumstance, there would not be clawback; relief would continue to be available at the full rate.

Gifts with reservation and the application of the clawback rules

10.26   Extreme complexity results from the interaction of the code for clawback and that for reservation of benefit. This is examined at **14.3** onwards. As was noted at **10.21**, the tax treatment depends on whether we are looking at the situation where some benefit was initially reserved, but later released, or where death intervened whilst the benefit was still enjoyed. This is examined in IHTM24201 and IHTM24202.

COUNTERING CLAWBACK IN RELATION TO BPR AND APR

10.27   It will perhaps be clear from this chapter that there are many circumstances, some of them perhaps unexpected, in which clawback can apply to defeat the tax planning efforts of the owner of relieved property. The complexity of the rules for clawback is such that it may be as difficult for the practitioner to explain the rules to his lay client as it has been for the author to set them out here. Members of the family may not have been privy to the detail of tax planning advice. As a result, the family may have imagined that 'all the tax was sorted out'. If the donee of property qualifying for APR or BPR disposes of it by sale, in ignorance of the rules of clawback, he or she will be very ready to blame the adviser for loss of the relief. If the situation is saved by *FA 1986, Sch 20, para 2(4)*, that will more likely be by accident than by design.

Countering clawback is therefore a combination of, in the first place, avoiding automatic loss of clawback and, in other circumstances, of ensuring that the family have a working knowledge of the particular aspects of the rules that apply to them and receive proper advice when circumstances change which could trigger the loss of the relief. It would seem, particularly in the light of comments in the judgment of Arnold J in *Swain Mason v Mills & Reeve* [2011] EWHC 410 (Ch) at para 197 as to the framing of letters of engagement, that it is not reasonable merely to expect the client to sign a letter acknowledging that he has studied and understands the effects of the clawback provisions. It will be prudent, though, for the adviser to have on his file some record that he advised not only the donor of the gift but that he advised the donee or urged the donee to take separate advice to avoid the risk of clawback.

Earlier in this chapter, when considering the definitions employed in *s 113A* for clawback of BPR, it was noted that clawback may be triggered where trustees make an absolute appointment to the object of a trust. Where the interest of a tenant for life under an 'old-style' interest in possession trust comes to an end during the lifetime of the tenant for life, in circumstances where the tenant for life becomes the absolute owner of property qualifying for BPR, there is no clawback. This is because, by virtue of the deeming provisions, he is treated as the owner of the property anyway.

Replacement of agricultural property by business property

10.28   The overlap between APR and BPR is considered in **Chapter 12**. RI 95 sets out the view of the Revenue (now HMRC) as to the availability of relief where agricultural property is replaced by business property (or the other way about) and considers the availability of the 'new' relief to the replacement asset.

There is an unfortunate mismatch in the provisions, as is noted in **Chapter 12**, concerning the operation of *s 124A(1)*.

Surrender of farm tenancies

10.29   If a tenancy itself is the subject matter of a gift attracting APR and that tenancy is surrendered, the death of the transferor within seven years must trigger clawback under *s 124A* because the asset which was the subject matter of the gift no longer exists. The parties cannot substitute a farm business tenancy in the hope of relying on *s 124B* because there is no 'consideration received by him for the disposal which has been applied by him in acquiring other property' within *s 124B(1)(b)*. It might be argued, inventively, that the new tenancy is derived from the old, by analogy with *TCGA 1992, s 43*, but really that analysis does not satisfy the requirements for replacement property.

Matthew Hutton some time ago suggested a solution to the problem. That is an indirect gift of the freehold reversion by the landlord to a nominee for the tenant. That would ensure that the asset, the tenancy, remained in existence insofar as it is possible (which might require careful arrangement) for the tenants to be their own landlords. To keep the tenancy in being, it would have to be transferred to a nominee. If, on examination of the values, there is no transfer of value, clawback will not be a problem. It may be necessary to re-examine the profit-sharing arrangements within the farming partnership to ensure that there is, commercially, no transfer of value.

The mention of surrender of a tenancy prompts the adviser to consider the possible impact of CGT on the disposal, but ESC D39 may be in point if the surrender is part of an arrangement that results in extension of the lease.

FURTHER HAZARD: DISCRETIONARY TRUSTS

10.30   Previous editions of this work examined problems for trustees of accumulation and maintenance trusts, which became academic with the *FA 2006* changes. Different considerations affect the practitioner in relation to discretionary trusts, where the trustees may decide whether or not to grant interests in possession. Clawback will not apply to a trust that has been running for several years, but can be triggered under *s 124A(2)* in respect of the 'top up' charge. The trustees should, therefore, be warned of the risk of clawback, so that their decision to advance funds is an informed one.

Example 10.22: tax on death within three years of transfers

Jonathan transferred to a discretionary trust in September 2005 ('the September Trust') a minority holding of unquoted shares in a trading company. In the seven years before that transfer, he had made chargeable transfers of £300,000. The 'estate before less estate after' calculation in relation to the September Trust placed a value on that transfer of £150,000.

In November 2006, Jonathan set up a second discretionary trust ('the November Trust'), having made no other transfers in the meantime. To the November Trust he transferred a 29% holding in the same company, which was then still trading. The 'estate before less estate after' calculation on the November Trust produced a value for the transfer of £175,000.

Jonathan paid the IHT on the transfer to the September Trust, and on the transfer to the November Trust.

In February 2007, the trustees of the September Trust appointed the entire fund to Rachel absolutely.

Jonathan died on 17 February 2008.

Tax on the September Trust (tax shown in italics) is as follows:

	£
Total of previous transfers (at the then rates)	300,000
Less IHT at current lifetime rates ('T')	*(5,000)*
Net equivalent of the total of previous transfers ('A')	295,000
Net transfer of first settlement:	150,000
Deduct BPR at 50%	(75,000)
Total net 'clock'	370,000
Tax on net clock (ie ¼ for excess over £275,000)	*23,750*
Deduct from (A) above the 'clock'	(295,000)
Deduct from (T) above	*(5,000)*
Present transfer is thus	93,750
Present IHT	*23,750*
Amount to carry forward:	
Total of previous transfers	300,000
Latest transfer	93,750
Tax on latest transfer	*23,750*
Total	417,500

10.30 *Clawback*

Tax on the November Trust (tax shown in italics) is as follows:

	£
Total of previous transfers brought forward	417,500
Less IHT at current lifetime rates on 161,000	*(32,200)*
Revised 'clock' ('B')	385,300
Net transfer to trustees	175,000
Less 50% BPR	*(87,500)*
Total net amount	472,800
Tax on the total net amount (¼ of excess over £285,000)	*46,950*
Net total of previous transfers from (B) above	417,500
Net current transfer	87,500
Total IHT	*46 950*
Less IHT brought forward	*(28,500)*
Current IHT	*18,450*
Clock carried forward: ((B) + 87,500 + 18,450)	491,250

Recalculation of IHT on death as a result of clawback:

	£
The first transfer:	
Previous clock	300,000
The transfer	150,000
Tax already paid	*23,750*
Total ('C')	473,750
Note: the BPR of £75,000 has now been lost.	
IHT on (C) above (40% on excess over 300,000)	69,500
Deduct previous transfers	300,000
Transfer remaining ((C) – 300,000):	173,750
Tax due on transfer	69,500
Deduct tax already paid	*23,750*
Top up clawback tax	45,750

As has been noted at **10.21**, this clawback charge fortunately does not alter the clock. There is, therefore, no need to recalculate the tax on the second transfer. The aggregation figure calculated in relation to the September Trust of £417,500 stays the same. Nevertheless, the complexity of this calculation might have been avoided if funds had not been released to Rachel.

Further difficulty: value-shifting

10.31   One aspect of clawback that may give difficulty is a transfer of value by a close company which is apportioned under *s 94* to the participators. The cause of the difficulty is that the charge in such a situation may well arise because the relative value of shareholdings has been affected by the transfer of rights in them. No person is actually the 'transferee' in such a situation, because the person who benefits is one who already holds shares which, by virtue of the waiver or other action, are more valuable than they had been previously.

As a result of this, strict compliance with the requirements to avoid clawback is impossible, because there cannot be a notional transfer by the transferee. The beneficiary of the value-shifting cannot point to an additional asset that he owns by virtue of the operation, so the notional transfer rules required for clawback and its avoidance cannot work in his favour. As a general rule, therefore, where there is a lifetime transfer by means of the shifting of value in close company shares, there is always a risk of clawback of BPR on the death of the participator within seven years.

COMPARISON OF POTENTIALLY EXEMPT TRANSFERS WITH IMMEDIATELY CHARGEABLE TRANSFERS

10.32   The treatment of potentially exempt transfers is almost the same as that of immediately chargeable transfers where BPR (or APR) is allowable at 100%. From the table that follows, it will be seen that, in certain circumstances, there can be an advantage in making an immediately chargeable transfer of property subject to 100% relief, rather than making a potentially exempt transfer.

Table 10.1 Clawback: effect on transfer of relevant business property

Property entitled to 100% relief: comparison of potentially exempt transfers with immediately chargeable transfers.

	PET Treatment	*CT Treatment*
1. Immediate charge to IHT?	No: a PET	No: value reduced to nil
2. Death within seven years of transfer: assets retained by donee	No IHT: full APR/BPR	No IHT: full APR/BPR
3. Death within seven years of transfer where clawback applies:	IHT charge (subject to nil rate band)	IHT charge (subject to nil rate band)

	PET Treatment	*CT Treatment*
(*a*) as to the transfer itself	On the full amount	On the full amount
(*b*) as to aggregation with the later transfers, eg on death	Full value is aggregated	Value is nil, so there is an advantage in making the transfer by CT
4. Transferor lives seven years from gift.	No IHT: transfer has become exempt	No IHT: falls out of cumulation

CLAWBACK: A LOOPHOLE?

10.33   One fundamental aspect of clawback is that it is largely limited to potentially exempt transfers: see the initial wording of *s 113A(1)*. Thus, a transfer which is for any reason a chargeable transfer falls mainly outside the clawback rules, except as to the tax rates.

FA 1996, s 184(4) amended the clawback rules. It changed the definition of shares or securities in *IHTA 1984, s 113A(3A)* so as to include not only securities of a company giving the transferor control but also the more general category in *s 105(bb)*, 'any unquoted shares in a company'.

Commentators have argued that this opens up a specific loophole. The reasoning is in the following stages. *Section 113A(3A)* is stated to apply to two classes of shares or securities namely:

●   shares that were quoted at the time of the PET that fails; or

●   shares that were quoted at the time of a chargeable transfer which, by virtue of *s 113A(2)*, qualified for BPR and was made within seven years of the death of the transferor.

The shares must then fall within *s 105(1)(b)* or *(bb)* in relation to that initial transfer and must remain unquoted from that transfer through to the death of the transferor. For this purpose, 'quoted' means 'listed', and 'unquoted' means 'not listed'. It has been argued that the planning opportunity arises because it does not matter that, at the time of the 'clawback event', the shares are no long relevant business property.

Example 10.23: imaginative use of the rules

Hetty has only one year to live and has consulted Geoff. She has a trading company, a care home. Her two sons do not work in the business and, at present, have no shares in it. The freehold is worth £500,000. It is not held within the company but is used by the company. As a result, BPR is available, but only at 50%. Hetty would like to transfer the property to the company in exchange for shares. Insofar as the issue of shares was not exact in value terms, ie equivalent to arm's length, there would be a chargeable transfer because it was a transfer to the company. The value transferred would not be great, because Hetty owns 85% of the company. The transfer would be within the nil rate band but, effectively, it would be chargeable because Hetty will not live seven years.

Hetty's plan is to transfer the property to the company, then to transfer the shares to her sons. The transfer of shares to the sons will be sheltered by 100% BPR. They will then sell the trade but keep the company as a mere investment vehicle. Geoff wondered if clawback would be a problem, so asked Melissa to research it. Melissa concluded that there would be no problem. There would be no clawback provided the sons keep the shares. In other words, the retained property need not continue to qualify for BPR, owing to the particular rules in *s 113A(3)(b)*.

To confirm this to Geoff, Melissa summarised the legislation. *Section 113A(1)* sets out the rule for clawback. *Section 113A(2)* provides that the tax has to be calculated without BPR where clawback applies. *Section 113A(3)(a)* imposes a condition that the original property was owned by the transferee from the transfer to the death, ie you must keep the property. *Section 113A(3)(b)* provides a general rule that the property is relevant business property and qualifies for BPR at the time of the death on the notional transfer made by the person who has received it.

There is, however, an exception to that particular rule, which was inserted by *FA 1987*. The effect of it is that the rule in *s 113A(3)(b)* does not apply in the circumstances provided by *s 113A(3A)*. The subsection itself has two limbs, and excludes from clawback shares that were quoted at the time of the original transfer which, to come within BPR, must have been part of a control holding. Equally, it excludes shares that were part of the old category of unquoted shares which, with other securities, gave control and which remained unquoted through to the death, or unquoted shares under the general rule in *s 105(1)(bb)* and which remained unquoted.

Geoff was doubtful. All the categories of property in *s 105(1)* are subject to the opening words of that section. That makes them subject to the rest of the section as a whole, with the result that the 'wholly or mainly' provision of *s 105(3)* will 'colour' the subject matter of a gift. If Geoff was right, effectively *s 105(1)(bb)* is subject to *s 105(3)*. That is why Geoff was not too sure that the planning opportunity did actually exist, so he warned Hetty accordingly.

Chapter 11

Woodlands

QUICK GUIDE

This is a 'Cinderella' relief: essentially, it is a relief by way of deferral of tax rather than relief from the tax itself.

First, this chapter examines aspects of the timber trade to establish whether an application for woodland relief will be appropriate or whether APR or BPR might be applicable instead – and in preference.

The conditions for the relief to apply are set out at **11.6**, with a flow chart as to the availability of the relief. The tax charge itself is examined at **11.11** onwards. There are several refinements to the calculations and reliefs from the tax, especially the 50% reduction under *IHTA 1984, s 127* noted at **11.11** and illustrated at **11.15**.

Given the rarity of its application and its complexity, woodland relief is for enthusiasts only. Any government serious about simplification of tax would abolish the relief.

COMMERCIAL OCCUPATION OF WOODLANDS: OVERVIEW OF TAX TREATMENT

11.1   This book is mainly concerned with reliefs from IHT. There is a special code for the tax treatment of woodlands, and an adviser on IHT planning should have some knowledge of the special treatment of woodlands for taxes other than IHT. Historically, tax was charged under Schedule B in respect of the occupation of woodlands managed on a commercial basis. That charge was abolished with effect from 6 April 1988. A person occupying land mainly for the purposes of husbandry might apply to have the assessment under Schedule B discharged if the profit from woodland management was less than the notional assessment. It was important for the Schedule B charge to identify the occupier.

The result of this regime was a fixed charge under Schedule B on one-third of the annual value, whilst any income from the sale of timber or from insurance claims or forestry grants was free of income tax. On the other hand, the fixed nature of the Schedule B charge meant that there could be no deduction for expenditure of a capital or of a revenue nature. It was therefore worthwhile to elect to be assessed under Schedule D at the early stage of growth of woodland, where expenditure was high, and to refrain from making that election later when the estate moved into profit. Overall, the commercial occupation of woodlands was under-taxed.

Abolition of Schedule B charge

11.2   With effect from 6 April 1988, the charge under Schedule B was abolished. The income now derived from the occupation of woodlands in the UK, which are managed on a commercial basis and with a view to the realisation of profits, is exempt from tax, either under Schedule D or under Schedule A with effect from 15 March 1988.

The corollary of this is that losses arising from the occupation of woodlands are not trading losses. They cannot be offset against any other income. There is no relief for revenue expenditure. Capital allowances are not available. There is no relief for interest paid and, where that interest is paid by a company whose business consists of the occupation of woodlands, that interest is not deductible as a charge on income. There is a proportionate restriction where the company is engaged partly in the management of woodlands and partly in other trades. That proportion will (see *FA 1988, Sch 6, para 3(5)(b)*) relate to the business of the whole of a group of companies where a woodland management company is part of the 51% group.

Is there a trade?

11.3   It is still relevant to identify the activities which amount to no more than the commercial occupation of woodlands and those which go further and are effectively the carrying on of a trade. Two cases are probably still good law. In *Christie v Davis* [1945] 1 All ER 370 the owner and occupier of a woodland estate set up a sawmill. Timber from the estate was used to produce fences and gates and the bark was sold. Timber was bought in from other estates for the same purpose. The owner was assessed to Schedule D, Case I. The General Commissioners dismissed the taxpayer's appeal. Slightly surprisingly, Wrottesley J held, on appeal, that working the sawmill was an ordinary method of making the timber marketable and that, to the extent that the timber came from the owner's estate, the profit was covered by the Schedule B assessment.

In *IRC v Williamson Bros* 1950 SC 391, timber merchants wished to ensure future supplies of timber and bought woodlands which were some distance from their sawmills. They cut the timber and carried it to their sawmills, where it was sold either to other commercial sawmills or direct.

11.3   *Woodlands*

Following the decision of the High Court in *Christie v Davis*, the Special Commissioners in *IRC v Williamson Bros* considered that they were bound by the ruling there and must exclude the felled timber from an assessment under Schedule D. On appeal to the Court of Session, it was held that the Special Commissioners should consider the whole facts of the case and must decide whether the operations of felling and sawing timber were part of the right of ownership or occupation or should be treated as separate trades. This was a borderline case: when the matter came back to the Court of Session, it appeared that the General Commissioners had decided that the timber was not cut up into planks before it was sent out to other sawmills. It was sent rough. The appeal by the Revenue was withdrawn.

Collins v Fraser [1969] 3 All ER 524 took the issue to new lengths of detail. The taxpayer again owned woodland and a sawmill (about 12 miles away). The timber was felled, stripped, trimmed, and reduced to cross-cut timber at the wood or was cut to five-foot lengths at the wood or at the mill. Once it reached the mill, the timber, if over five feet long, was reduced to that length and then turned into planking one inch or one and a half inches thick, converted into boards and made into boxes. The issue was how much of this entire operation could be said to be done so as to make the wood marketable in some shape or form. To that extent, the profit was covered by Schedule B. On appeal, the case was sent back to the Commissioners for them to decide what was done with the timber, up to and including the planking stage, which might extend beyond what could legitimately be regarded as normal preparation of timber for the market 'and disposing of the fruits of the taxpayer's land'.

That almost poetic image of husbandry is swept away by the curt terms of *FA 1988, Sch 6, para 2(1)*: 'The charge to tax under Schedule B in respect of the occupation of commercial woodlands is hereby abolished'. As a result, the proceeds of felling and selling the timber are free from income tax, and the value of growing timber is free from both income tax and CGT.

Are woodlands occupied for commercial purposes? In truth, many woods are retained mainly for amenity and sporting value. There is very little profit for the grower, only for the woodland and timber contractors. Whilst the question is no longer relevant to the income tax treatment, it is important to decide whether rollover relief from CGT will be available. The gain arising will be on the value of the land itself, not on the value of timber. Similarly, VAT may be chargeable on the sale of timber or on the grant of the right to fell timber if the woodlands are commercial. BPR should be available (see **11.8** below) on the basis that the woodlands constitute a business, if it can be shown that separate accounts are maintained for those woodlands which are commercial rather than those which are not.

Case commentary on timber: whether income or capital

11.4   Cases, examined in earlier editions of this work, arose on the deductibility in the computation of profits of a payment for the right to obtain trading stock, particularly where that stock was timber or growing crops. Readers are referred to *Kauri Timber Co Ltd v New Zealand Commissioner of Taxes* [1913] AC 771, where the Privy Council upheld the Revenue view that the transactions by the taxpayer under which the rights were acquired gave them an interest in possession of the land rather than the mere purchase of the timber.

In *Murray v IRC* (1951) 32 TC 238, the Court of Session confirmed the view of the General Commissioners that the profit on re-sale of the right to cut timber was part of the taxpayer's normal trade.

In *Hood Barrs v IRC* [1957] 1 All ER 832, the amounts that the taxpayer had paid for two lots of standing timber were capital and not deductible from his Schedule D, Case I trading profit.

The issue in *Hopwood v C N Spencer Ltd* (1964) 42 TC 169, where expenditure was incurred on the purchase of a wood to secure future supplies, was whether a transaction represented the purchase of stock in trade, rather than of a capital asset. The company provided the purchase price but the conveyance was taken in the name of the controlling shareholders. There was no formal agreement between the shareholders and the company, except a minute at a company meeting that the company was the owner of the timber in the wood and that the wood had been purchased to provide a reserve. The company expected the wood to be cleared within seven to ten years. It was held that the expenditure was incurred not on the purchase of a capital asset, but on buying stock in trade.

If any clear principle can be extracted from these cases, it does seem that failure to fell timber makes it easier to regard the transaction as a capital one. Thus, in *Chu Lip Kong v Director General of Inland Revenue* [1981] STC 653 a timber merchant bought land and sold it without taking any timber. The purchaser specialised in felling timber that belonged to other people. He was assessed on the basis that the profit from the sale of land was a trading profit. Although the Special Commissioners regarded the immediate sale as a fictitious transaction, the Privy Council held that the taxpayer had sold the land at a profit without separate exploitation of the timber on it. There was no evidence that the taxpayer had previously dealt in land. This was an isolated transaction. As a result, the land was purchased as a capital asset, and the subsequent sale gave rise to a gain of a capital, and not of an income, nature.

The former woodland relief

11.5   The policy of successive governments was to recognise the long-term nature of investment in forestry. The view of the people showed the present

Coalition government that their forests should not be sold off to save expense. There has for many years been a form of relief from IHT for woodland. The relief we have now applies to deaths after 12 March 1975. Under *Finance (1909–10) Act 1910, s 61(5)*, relief from estate duty was available for growing timber in respect of deaths on or before 11 March 1975. That relief exempted growing timber unless and until sale. The rules may still be relevant.

Supposing the timber is to be sold before there is a transfer of value of the land itself for IHT purposes (other than for an exempt transfer to a spouse), there will be a liability to estate duty. The transfer of the land brings to an end the liability for estate duty. If that transfer is made after 30 June 1986, it is affected by *FA 1986, Sch 19, para 46*. That paragraph provides that, notwithstanding anything in *IHTA 1984, s 3A*, a transfer of value which is made:

- on or after 1 July 1986; and

- which brings to an end the period during which estate duty is payable on the net monies received from the sale of timber etc by virtue of *FA 1975, s 49(4)*;

is not a PET.

That paragraph could give rise to injustice where, out of a transfer of a substantial piece of land, only a small part related to woodlands which were subject to the deferred estate duty charge. By ESC F15 ,the scope of the paragraph is restricted solely to that part of the value transferred which is attributable to the woodlands which are the subject of the deferred charge. The overall effect of this provision is that no liability arises to estate duty after 12 March 1975, unless money is received:

- from the sale of timber felled or cut after 12 March 1975; and

- at or before the time of the first transfer of the woodland concerned for IHT purposes (other than a transfer to a spouse).

RELIEF ON DEATH

11.6   An election may be made within two years of a death (or longer, see below) for the value of any trees or underwood (in this chapter called 'timber') on any land, whether in the United Kingdom or, since 22 April 2003, in any EEA state, to be left out of account in determining the value transferred on death. The extension to foreign woodlands was made by *FA 2009, s 122* where the tax or the last instalment of it would have been due on or after 22 April 2009 or was actually paid or due on or after 23 April 2003. The election will not be made where APR can be claimed. The election relates to the value of the timber, and not to the land itself. The claim must be made by the person liable for any part of the tax. The effect of the claim is to defer tax until a later disposal.

Under *IHTA 1984, s 125(2)(a)*, the value of timber is left out of account in fixing the value transferred on a death, subject to the other terms of the code contained in *ss 125–130*. The circumstances in which this relief may apply are:

- it is available on the occasion of death only (*s 125(1)(a)*);

- the estate of the person dying includes land in the United Kingdom or an EEA country;

- there must be timber on the land;

- the circumstances must be such that APR does not apply;

- the transferor must have owned the land for five years before death, or the transferor, if not owning the land for five years before death, must have become the owner otherwise than for consideration in money or money's worth;

- there must be an election by the person liable for the whole or part of the tax; and

- that election must be made within two years of the death or within such longer time as the Board may allow.

Most of the conditions enumerated above are straightforward and self-explanatory. The relief relates to the timber and not to the land. A flowchart follows that illustrates the steps to be satisfied. The tax becomes chargeable on a later disposal of the timber. It is thus necessary to establish the value of the underlying land excluding the timber.

The relief is not particularly common, since the representatives of the taxpayer will prefer, wherever possible, to claim the full relief of APR or BPR, as is noted in the flowchart on pages 272–273.

Note the required link between ownership of the timber and the bare land, which is stressed at IHMT04376. Once that link is severed, even though the trees still stand, relief is lost. For this reason, care should be taken, in setting up business structures such as partnerships or syndicates, to ensure that each participant owns directly the land that he is growing trees on. By the same token, relief may be available where ownership is deemed to persist through the operation of the 'gift with reservation' rules, as noted at IHTM04374.

11.6   *Woodlands*

Availability of Woodland Relief

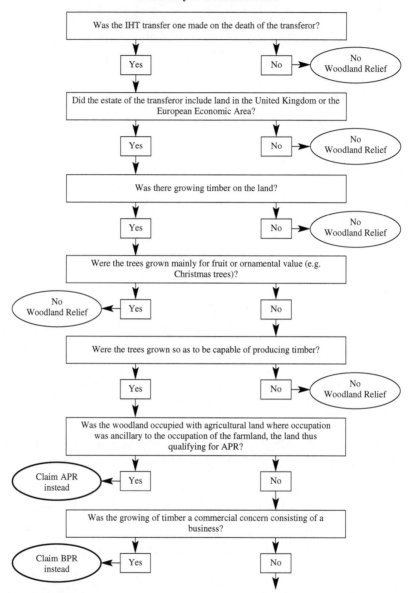

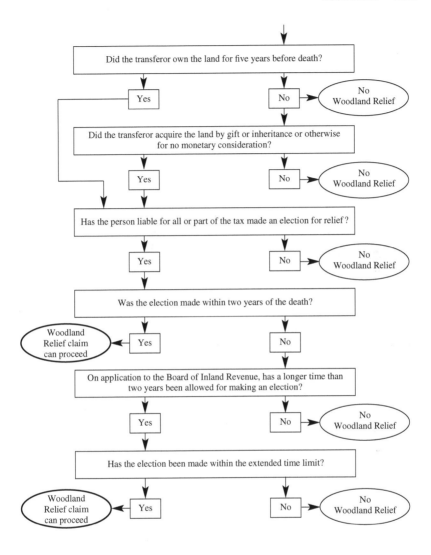

___

Example 11.1: stupid old man

David owned woodland as part of the family estate and, in October 2006, by two conveyances transferred the main house and parkland, and a large area of woodland nearby, to his daughter Jennifer as part of an IHT planning exercise. However, notwithstanding advice to the contrary, David continued to enjoy sporting rights over the estate.

David did not merely ride, or just take a gun when walking his dogs, which might (just) have been *de minimis* within RI 95. Instead, he would occasionally get a group of friends together for the purpose, so that on such days the woodland workers did not feel safe to carry out timber operations. Even though David made no money out of his hobby, the shooting did (to a very minor extent) restrict Jennifer's use of the land by interrupting timber management, so amounted to reservation of benefit out of the gift, at least as far as the woodland was concerned. That made him the deemed owner of the land for woodland relief.

Prior relief as agricultural property

11.7   The relief for woodland where ancillary to the occupation of agricultural land or pasture was considered in **Chapter 2**. The possibility of a claim for APR should be considered first. The District Valuer for HMRC will consider whether, under *s 115(2)*, APR is available.

Prior claim to BPR

11.8   Having eliminated the possibility of a claim to APR, the code for BPR may still apply to woodland which is part of a business which qualifies as relevant business property. BPR will be available in respect of the value of trees and underwood under *s 127(2)*. It is essential that the woodlands are part of a business which qualifies for BPR. This may be difficult to show where the woodlands are not part of a syndicate but merely part of a rural landholding and are so small in area as to be barely viable from a commercial point of view, and yet have high amenity or sporting value.

There is an overlap between woodlands relief, as it has been discussed earlier in this chapter, and business property relief. Where, for example, the estate of the deceased includes growing trees and underwood, the value of that timber can be left out of account under the general provisions for woodland relief in connection with the death. On subsequent disposal of the timber before any transfer of the land on which it is growing, the disposal gives rise to a charge on the timber; but, if that timber qualifies for BPR, a reduction may be made after deduction of the deferred tax which became payable in respect of the death.

An example of how the section works appears at the end of the chapter. The amount on which tax is charged under *s 126* (the postponement provision) is reduced by 50% where, if the value of the timber had not been left out of account under *s 126*, it would:

- have been taken into account for the purposes of a claim to BPR; or

- in relation to early cases, would have been taken into account for BPR if the *Act* had then been in force.

This later alternative will apply only where the relevant death occurred before 7 April 1976.

PROPERTY QUALIFYING FOR RELIEF

11.9   *IHTA 1984, s 125* applies only to woodlands held by the *deceased* in one capacity or another, and not to woodlands owned by a *company* in which the deceased held shares. There is, for woodlands relief, no parallel to the provision in APR under *s 119* by which occupation of land by a company controlled by the transferor is treated as occupation by that transferor himself.

Woodlands, for the purposes of this relief, do not include nurseries or orchards. As to orchards, note the failed attempt to claim APR in *Dixon v IRC*, considered at **2.6** above. As to nurseries, that issue has been tested for income tax purposes in *Jaggers (t/a Shide Trees) v Ellis* [1997] STC 1417. Whilst it may be that the case has little relevance to IHT (see below), it contains some definitions. Young conifers were planted on nine acres of land and the Special Commissioner had held that, as a matter of both fact and law, the land did not comprise woodland and was not in any sense being prepared for use for forestry purposes. It was a Christmas tree plantation. The taxpayer appealed.

The High Court held that 'woodland' and 'forestry' are not defined in *ICTA 1988*. Where the terms appear in other legislation, they are no help. No authority or legal textbook was any help. The Commissioner, with so little to guide him, had listened to the expert evidence and had decided that the site was used for growing Christmas trees, and not for producing timber.

By reference to *Brutus v Cozens* [1973] AC 854, the court held that the right approach is that:

'the meaning of an ordinary word of the English language is not a question of law ... it is for the tribunal which decides the case to consider, not as law but as fact, whether in the whole circumstances the words do or do not as a matter of ordinary usage of the English language cover or apply to the facts which have to be proved. If it is alleged that the tribunal reached the wrong decision ... the question would normally be whether their decision was unreasonable in the sense that no tribunal acquainted with the ordinary use of language could reasonably reach that decision.'

The Commissioner had been right in his decision. 'Woodlands' in *ICTA 1988, s 53(4)* meant 'land used for forestry purposes'. The Oxford English Dictionary defined 'woodland' as 'land covered with wood, ie trees; a wooded region or piece of ground', and 'forestry' as 'the science and art of forming and cultivating forests and the management of timber'.

The taxpayer had argued that the site was covered with trees and was therefore woodland. To accept that was to disregard age, size, type or appearance of trees, the way they were spaced or pruned, the age at which they were cut or removed, and the general appearance of the trees themselves. 'Woodland' meant a wood, a sizeable area of land to a significant extent covered by growing trees of some maturity, height and size. As a rule of thumb, the trees should be capable of being used as timber. It was a matter of impression and personal judgement. In the instant case, the site had not struck the Commissioner as woodlands and would not strike Lightman J for a moment as wood or woodlands. The trees looked more like bushes than timber trees, and the site looked more like a nursery than a wood. The appeal was dismissed.

The case is therefore more relevant to consideration of APR, by virtue of the exposition of the meaning of 'woodlands', than to woodland relief. That is because *s 125(1)* refers to land 'on which trees and underwood are growing', whereas the value of Christmas trees is as cut articles. A Christmas tree plantation will usually qualify for APR as a nursery. Likewise, a grower would benefit more from 100% BPR than from woodland relief.

THE CHARGE TO TAX ON DISPOSAL

11.10   Where:

- the value of timber has been left out of account by virtue of *s 125*; and

- any part of the timber is later disposed of;

then:

- if that disposal occurs before any part of the value transferred on the death of any other person 'is attributable to' the value of the land on which the timber grows;

- tax is, by *s 126(1)*, chargeable under *ss 127* and *128*.

An exception to the rule in *s 126(1)* is a disposal made by any person to a spouse. Where tax has been charged by *s 126* on the disposal of timber, tax is not charged again in relation to the same death on a further disposal of the same timber. The person entitled to the proceeds of sale (or who would be entitled if the disposal of the timber had been by sale) is liable for the tax. The form of account used to be C-5 (timber) although, in the recent reorganisation of IHT forms mentioned in **Chapter 22**, that form has become obsolete. A new form, IHT100f, must now be used in conjunction with new form IHT100, which has been remodelled so as to incorporate computation boxes. By virtue of *s 216(7)*, the account must be delivered by the person liable within six months of the end of the month in which the disposal occurs.

The basis of charge

11.11   Where a charge to tax arises under *s 126*, the amount on which that tax is charged is, by *s 127*, determined by the net proceeds of sale, where that sale is for full consideration; or by the net value of the timber at the time of disposal in any other case. That rule itself is subject to relief under *s 127(2)*. That relief applies where, if no claim had been made for relief under *s 125* on the occasion of the death:

● the value of the timber would have been taken into account for the purposes of BPR; or

● the value of the timber would have been taken into account if BPR had been available at the relevant time.

The relief under *s 127(2)* is at 50%.

The rate of tax

11.12   *Section 128* determines the rate of tax. The tax is charged at the rates at which it would have been charged on the death in respect of which the original claim was made, at the rate(s) applicable on that death as the top slice of the estate as enlarged by:

● the amount (net value or net proceeds of sale) fixed by *s 127*; and

● any amount on which tax was previously charged under *s 126* in relation to that death.

The reference here is to the last person to die in relation to which the relief has been claimed.

Net value: deduction of expenses

11.13   In calculating the net value of the timber or the net proceeds, the expenses may be deducted of:

● disposal of the timber;

● replanting to replace the trees within three years of a disposal (or such longer time as the Board may allow); and

● replanting, so far as not allowed on the previous disposal (see *s 130*).

11.14 *Woodlands*

The old Valuation Office Manual required the District Valuer to ignore any allowable expenses and any obligations to replant, and to value the 'net value' as the higher of:

● the value of the trees for sale for felling, including any underwood; and

● the value of the standing trees or underwood as part of the estate of the transferor;

but the array of manuals now available do not set out the guidance in the same detail. That valuation by the District Valuer will not include the value of the land itself. The valuation on the basis of standing trees will generally apply to estates containing young trees or trees with high value as amenity rather than simply for forestry.

Where deferred tax becomes chargeable following a reduction in IHT rates by substitution of a new table, the new rates will be used even though the death occurred when an old scale applied on which the rates were higher.

Credit for tax charged

11.14 Where a disposal occurs on which tax is chargeable under *s 126*, and that disposal is a chargeable transfer, the value transferred is calculated under *s 129* as if the value of the timber had been reduced by the *s 126* charge to tax.

Example 11.2: forestry operations continue

Algie, a widower whose late wife had used the nil rate band available to her, had himself made no chargeable transfers in his lifetime. On his death in February 2007, his estate was as follows:

	£
House, cash and investments	490,000
Woodlands	100,000
	590,000

The value of the bare land was £30,000 and of the trees £70,000. Algie left the whole of his estate to his sister Julia.

Julia elected under *s 125*. In November 2007, she had some of the trees cut down. In doing so, she incurred costs to fell of £17,000 and to replant of £13,000. The trees were worth £75,000.

Julia, who had exhausted her own nil rate band, had made a gift to a goddaughter of £15,000. She used up her annual exemptions in that year. She then gave the trees to her nephew, Jim. Julia died in August 2009.

On the death of Algie, the IHT had been charged as follows:

	£
Gross estate	590,000
Less s 125 claim value	(70,000)
Taxable estate	520,000
Less nil rate band	(285,000)
Chargeable transfer	235,000
Tax at 40%	94,000

By giving the trees to Jim, Julia triggered a further charge to IHT with reference to Algie's death. The basis of the transfer is:

	£
Gross value of trees	75,000
Less costs to fell	(17,000)
Less costs to replant	(13,000)
Net value of trees	45,000

An IHT charge on the disposal by Julia arises by reference to Algie's estate. It is calculated on £45,000, which is regarded as being part of an estate of (£520,000 + £45,000 =) £565,000. The tax is at 40% on the excess over the nil rate band, but using the rates in force as at November 2007, viz £300,000. The chargeable transfer is thus 265,000 × 40%, ie £106,000, of which £94,000 has already been paid. The original relief of £28,000 has been reduced by the deferred tax charge of £12,000.

IHT is also chargeable, on Julia's death, on the failed PET by Julia to Jim. The value transferred is:

	£
The value of the timber:	75,000
Less the deferred charge on Algie's estate	12,000
	63,000

That is chargeable as part of an estate amounting to (63,000 + 15,000) = 78,000, all of which exceeds the available nil rate band, so there is a second tax charge of £31,200.

The charge in respect of Algie's death is payable immediately but, by *s 229*, the instalment option is available in respect of the second charge of £4,800.

50% REDUCTION UNDER S 127

11.15   The operation of the 50% reduction under *IHTA 1984, s 127* can be illustrated as follows:

Example 11.3: settlement of woodland

Fred died in January 2007. His estate included timber valued at £50,000 ,which passed to Susan who made a claim under *s 125*. Having inherited the timber, Susan, who had used the nil rate band and any annual exemptions available to her, then transferred it to a discretionary trust when it was worth £55,000 and thereby triggered an 'entry charge'.

The result of this is that IHT becomes payable on the value at the time of passing into the discretionary trust, ie £55,000. The rate is that which would have applied to the estate of Fred as its top slice. If the timber would have qualified for BPR on Fred's death, the 50% reduction available under *s 127(2)* brings the value transferred down to £27,000, on which the tax would be £11,000.

The value therefore transferred to the discretionary trust is £55,000 less the deferred tax charge of £11,000, ie £44,000. On the assumption that the transfer of the timber to the trust qualifies for BPR, the exercise becomes somewhat academic, in that the whole of the £44,000 will qualify for 100% relief.

RELIEF FOR LIFETIME GIFTS

11.16   Essentially, woodland relief is a relief on death. For there to be any relief in respect of a lifetime transfer of woodland, the transferor must show that the transaction has the benefit either of APR or of BPR, as illustrated in the flowchart on pages 272–273, and as discussed earlier in this chapter and in the earlier chapters relating to each of those reliefs. Given the somewhat simpler treatment of property qualifying for 100% APR or BPR, there will be many instances where those reliefs are, from a practical point of view, more attractive than woodland relief.

Chapter 12

Overlap of APR and BPR

QUICK GUIDE

This chapter ought not to be necessary. Arguably, we do not need two reliefs that sit unhappily side by side: see **12.23**. However, for as long as we have two reliefs, it will be necessary for practitioners to become familiar with both of them. For a short list of the relative merits of each relief, see **12.6** and **12.7**.

HISTORICAL PERSPECTIVE

12.1   In respect of transfers before 9 March 1981, the relationship between APR and BPR was quite different from what it is now. Where APR was not available, BPR might in certain circumstances be claimed. It was seldom necessary to claim APR on transfers of value which took place after 26 October 1977 (and before 10 March 1981) because, by then, relief at 50% was available under BPR, and the qualifying conditions for APR were more difficult to satisfy. There was one actual disadvantage to APR because of the way in which exemptions applied: to claim APR, it was necessary first to deduct any available exemptions, and second to make the deduction for APR. For BPR, the order was the exact opposite, ie first deduct BPR and then set off the exemptions, which was altogether more beneficial for the taxpayer.

The importance of a knowledge of the rules was even greater where a person made more than one transfer in the same year, because the Revenue would set off the exemptions against the first eligible transfers in the year. As a result, the taxpayer was at a disadvantage if, during a tax year, the first gift was of agricultural property and the second of business property, because the exemptions were then applied in the least efficient manner. Fortunately, in respect of transfers and other events occurring after 9 March 1981, APR is applied in the same way as BPR. There were certain specific circumstances in which APR was advantageous but, unless a transferable nil rate band is in issue, it is unlikely that many practitioners will now need to examine transactions of this kind which took place before 9 March 1981.

12.2   *Overlap of APR and BPR*

The changes introduced by *FA 1981*, *s 96* and *Sch 14* reflected several factors. The way in which BPR was applied worked better than APR. Many owners of agricultural land were securing double discount by letting land to partnerships of which they were members. The old relief had too many anomalies. The way in which APR operated after reliefs was changed to conform with the more generous BPR structure.

Few busy practitioners will find the time to read through, at one sitting, the whole of the BPR code and APR code (although an opportunity to do so is provided by the appendices to this book). Those who do so will be struck by the similarity of the drafting of a number of the sections. This is particularly noticeable in the following areas:

- the way that each relief is applied to property in discretionary trusts;
- the fact that each relief works by reducing the value transferred by a transfer of value rather than by reducing the chargeable transfer itself;
- the way that replacement property is treated;
- the succession provisions;
- the treatment of property subject to a binding contract for sale;
- clawback provisions;
- the way that property is treated which is subject to a reservation; and
- the rates of relief themselves.

PRIORITY/ELECTION

12.2   The main statutory provision regulating the interaction of APR and BPR is *IHTA 1984*, *s 114*, which provides in *sub-s (1)* that:

- where any part of the value transferred by a transfer qualifies for agricultural relief; or
- would qualify for agricultural relief except for the rules as to successive transfers and in particular *s 121(3)*;

no BPR is allowable in respect of that part of the value.

By *s 114(2)*, double relief is again avoided in relation to woodland relief. This provision concerns the credit for tax charged which is allowed under *s 129* in respect of the value of trees or underwood left out of account under *s 126*. The value to which BPR may apply under *s 104* is the net value after taking the trees and underwood out of account. To this extent, therefore, there is no election for relief: if the relief is available, it will be given in the order in which the statute allows.

It was noted in **Chapter 1** that, in respect of transfers before 10 March 1981, it could be beneficial not to claim agricultural relief where the 'working farmer' limits might apply but to take advantage of business relief. That choice has now gone.

TERRITORIALITY

12.3   There is a clear distinction in this respect between APR and BPR. By *s 115(5)*, APR may apply only to agricultural property in the United Kingdom, the Channel Islands or the Isle of Man or an EEA state, whereas there is no corresponding restriction for BPR in *s 103*. For a list of EEA states, see **2.29**.

AMOUNT

12.4   Neither BPR nor, in its present form, APR is limited in amount. There was a limit, as has already been noted, to working farmer relief which could make it beneficial to elect for BPR instead. That distinction is becoming increasingly academic. In a different sense, there is a limitation in APR to the amount of the relief, because it relates to the agricultural value only of the property. BPR may be available in respect of the excess.

Example 12.1: agricultural land with hope value

Wilfred owns land which he farmed for many years until his retirement. The holding comprises agricultural land with a small farm bungalow. A significant aspect of the value of the holding is that it adjoins gravel workings which are now nearly exhausted. It is believed that further gravel deposits lie under Wilfred's land, and the operator of the adjoining quarry has expressed interest in purchase of the land for a sum which is naturally significantly in excess of the agricultural value.

Wilfred does not now enjoy good health and no longer lives on the farm, preferring (a preference which is fortunately shared) to live with his niece. Since 1 September 1995, the land has been occupied under a farm business tenancy for the purposes of agriculture. In his present state of health, Wilfred cannot realistically set up a new business so as to exploit the potential of the mineral deposits himself: indeed, his niece now has an enduring power of attorney for him.

The present position is therefore that, on Wilfred's death, APR should be available on the land, but that only with great difficulty can any claim be made out for BPR. The niece might, in her capacity as attorney, begin to take active steps to exploit the gravel deposits on her uncle's behalf, by arranging for soil tests and the like, and she might be able to enter into a joint venture agreement with the gravel operator to exploit the land in the hope that her uncle will survive by two years the date on which it can be shown that there is in being a business which might be recognised as such for BPR. During that two-year period, Wilfred would be the (long-term) owner of an asset used in a (new) business, so relief at 50% might become available immediately under *s 105(1)(d)*.

In this connection, it might help the niece to terminate the farm business tenancy so as to recover possession of the land and be recognised as the occupier of it, thereafter entering into farm contracting agreements over such part of the acreage as is not immediately required for gravel working. All this is clutching at straws: HMRC can be expected to deny BPR unless it can be shown that there really is a business in existence and not merely the taking of preliminary steps to establish a business. Merely walking the land, cleaning drinking troughs and the like did, just, amount to a business in *McCall v HMRC* [2009] NICA 12, but it was not a farming, but only an investment, business so did not qualify for BPR.

The issue of what constitutes a legal partnership was considered in *Khan v Miah* [1998] 1 WLR 477, where the Court of Appeal had to establish what, if any, business the parties had agreed to conduct. The case concerned a restaurant. The court held that an agreement to set up and carry on a business as a partnership was not proof that a partnership existed at that stage, any more than a mere statement by the parties that they were partners would on its own suffice to establish a partnership. If the court could establish what business the parties had agreed to conduct, it must then decide whether the business was being carried out by the partners at the material time.

REPLACEMENT ASSETS: SWITCHING

12.5   In RI 95, the Revenue considered the operation of *ss 113B* and *124B*, which were examined in **Chapter 10**. The issue is the availability of relief where agricultural property is replaced by business property (or the other way around). After preliminary observations as to the definition of a PET and the operation of BPR and APR, the Revenue noted qualifying conditions for relief and the rules which allow for the sale and replacement of qualifying property. In their view, where agricultural property which is a farming business is replaced by non-agricultural business property, the period of ownership of the original property will be relevant for applying the minimum ownership condition to the replacement property. BPR will be available on the replacement if all the conditions for that relief are satisfied. Where non-agricultural business property is replaced by a farming business, and that farming business is not eligible for APR, it may still be possible to claim BPR under *s 114(1)* if conditions for that relief are satisfied.

The Revenue (now HMRC) have in mind a situation where agricultural land is not part of a farming business, so that any replacement could qualify for BPR only if it satisfied the minimum ownership conditions in its own right. The Revenue felt that such cases were likely to be exceptional, and they are.

The effect of *s 124A(1)* is to deny APR on the value transferred by the PET where the donee of a PET of a farming business sells the business and replaces it with a non-agricultural business. As a result, *s 114(1)* does not exclude BPR if the conditions for that relief are satisfied. In the reverse situation, the farming business acquired by the donee can be 'relevant business property' for the purposes of *s 113B(3)(c)*.

One commentator has asserted that these provisions may give difficulty where the gift is of a tenanted farm that qualifies for APR. If sold, should it be replaced by other farmland, whether tenanted or owner-occupied, that will qualify for APR? Such a replacement clearly will qualify as 'APR property'. If the land originally given is occupied by the donee, there is less of a problem because the gift may qualify for BPR or for APR, giving the donee more scope on replacement.

WHERE APR IS AVAILABLE BUT BPR IS NOT

12.6   The few circumstances where APR is more generous than BPR include:

- land which the transferor does not farm;

- land belonging to a sole trader, which is transferred by itself without the business carried on there;

- land with the benefit of vacant possession used by a partnership where the transferor is a partner but where the land itself does not belong to the partnership;

- land farmed by a company, but not owned by it, where the transferor is a minority shareholder only;

- let land which is owned by a company which is controlled by the transferor; and

- a farmhouse occupied by the transferor.

THE SITUATIONS WHERE BPR IS MORE FAVOURABLE THAN APR

12.7   The circumstances where BPR is more favourable include:

- the assets of farming businesses other than land and buildings;

- non-controlling unquoted shareholdings in farming companies; and

- businesses or shares attributable to agricultural property where the ownership requirement is not yet sufficient for APR but which replace non-agricultural business assets (so that the assets qualify for BPR under the replacement property rules).

THE FARM: APPLICABILITY OF BPR

12.8 Where the owner of the farm is, as will often be the case, the person carrying on the farming activities, some of the difficulties noted in Example 12.1 may be avoided. The farming activity will constitute a business within *s 105(1) (a)*, one asset of which is the value of the farmland, insofar as not already relieved by APR under *s 114(1)*. Frequently, a part of the farm will have a special value which exceeds its agricultural value. It has already been noted that a farmhouse may have a premium value by virtue of its location. We now see that argument advanced, even in respect of farmland where there is a clear local demand for land, especially pasture, for non-agricultural use. Although, in general, a residence does not qualify for BPR whilst the farmhouse may qualify for APR, it may be possible to show that part of a 'premium' farmhouse is in fact used for the purposes of the business. Where that can be shown, the premium element, which would not have qualified for APR, may qualify for BPR.

Hope value

12.9 In the more common case of land used for farming which has planning potential, the unrealised or hope value of that potential will qualify for BPR where the land is an asset of the farming business. It is otherwise where the land with hope value is a 'mere asset', as has been noted in **Chapter 5**.

Sheltering proceeds of sale of a business through agricultural property

12.10 It is not uncommon for a successful entrepreneur to turn to agriculture late in life. The fondness of the English for farming as a pastime has been noted elsewhere in this book. Whilst the assets of the entrepreneur remain within his business, he may pass them to the next generation with the benefit of substantial relief. On a successful sale, perhaps sheltered in part by entrepreneurs' relief, the taxpayer faces a new problem. The substantial value which had been protected by BPR is represented by cash which, unless invested in qualifying property, will be taxed very heavily in the event that he dies without having distributed it among his family and survived seven years. This was precisely the situation that gave rise to the difficulties in *Swain Mason v Mills & Reeve* [2011] EWHC 410 (Ch).

An attractive option might seem the purchase of a landed estate including, typically, a home farm in hand, some let farms, and local facilities such as part of a village. The estate will be run as a composite whole. The question arises as to how far the entrepreneur has succeeded in reinvesting into favoured property. Generally, APR will be allowable but problems will arise in relation to those let properties which are not occupied for the purpose of agriculture. Depending on the location of the estate, such properties might command a premium value because of their setting. BPR will not be available on such properties if, taking the estate as a whole, *s 105(3)* applies to treat it as consisting wholly or mainly of making or holding investments.

The cases on this subject were considered in **Chapter 9**, notably *Farmer (Executors of Farmer Deceased) v IRC* and, more recently, *Brander (Executor of Balfour Deceased) v HMRC* [2009] TC 00069, examined at **9.14**. The decision has to be made looking at profits, turnover, the time spent and the value of the assets concerned. These all help to establish the fundamental nature of the business.

Why are you in the business of farming?

12.11   It might be reasonable to ask the holder of such a business whether his attitude to return on capital invested is the same in relation to the landed estate as it was when he managed the successful business which he has disposed of. Why is he in the business of running a landed estate? Is the business carried on otherwise than for gain, disqualifying it for relief under *s 103(3)*? How far can it be said that he pursues a business, and how far is it truer to observe that ownership of the estate provides him with, say, the opportunity to watch his granddaughters exercise ponies? The concept of 'zones' within a property was noted in **Chapter 9** in considering the *Hall* case. It might be argued that a composite enterprise, such as the ownership of a landed estate, should be analysed into its separate zones, and that those parts of the enterprise which, taking one year with another, consistently make losses should be disregarded for the purposes of allowing BPR.

In general, seeking the protection for an estate of APR or BPR has a great advantage for tax planning over the making of lifetime gifts where the life expectancy of the taxpayer is not great, because of the possibility of qualifying for the relief within two years. It should be noted, however, that BPR discriminates against companies. Whereas BPR is available under *s 105(1)(d)* in respect of a building which is occupied for business purposes by a partnership to which the owner of that building belongs, whether or not a rent is charged, no BPR at all is available in respect of a building occupied by a company in respect of which the owner of that building holds 50% or less of the shares.

Use a corporate 'wrapper'?

12.12   The difficulties that might be experienced by the owner of a composite asset, such as a landed estate, described above may be somewhat less where the assets are all owned through a company. This was noted in Example 7.4. As was noted there, there are two tests to be applied, first whether a company with mixed activities is mainly trading, and second whether the 'excepted assets' rules will apply. An asset is widely considered to be an 'excepted asset' only if it is not used in any of the activities of a company. That suggests that, by implication, a company can carry on a number of activities making up a single business. However, there must be a risk that the progressive increase in peripheral investments of this type may threaten the underlying (and more important) question whether the company is trading or whether it is fundamentally an investment company.

FAMILY LIMITED PARTNERSHIPS

12.13   Family limited partnerships (FLPs) have increased in popularity as structures to replace family trusts since the changes in *FA 2006*.

Example 12.2: how the structure arises

A family has substantial wealth which is, for some reason, sheltered neither by BPR nor APR, as where:

- land is merely grazed but has development value; or

- the investment content of a business now swamps the original business; or

- an existing business has been sold, converting sheltered assets into vulnerable cash; or

- relief is restricted to 50% or to the agricultural value only.

The value is large enough that a gift into trust of even a modest part would exceed the nil rate band and trigger an immediate IHT charge at 20%.

To address this, the family sets up a limited partnership in which one person is the general partner who runs the business. Cash is given to other relatives, who merely invest in the venture. The arrangement is transparent: it is a contract and may therefore appeal to those from civil law jurisdictions who have such trouble with the trust concept. The partnership is not an entity in itself and has no legal personality.

The main purposes of this structure are to protect assets and to trickle value down the generations. Since partners will often be quite young children who, on reaching the age of 18, can decide for themselves whether or not to repudiate the contract, they should be separately advised. At the age of 18, they may become more involved in the venture as an encouragement to leave value in, rather than dissipating it. This will be less of a problem where the children's money is already held by trustees.

Treatment of FLPs for law and tax

12.14 The partnership is transparent. If the funding of a child's interest is from a parent, the income profit share is assessable on the parent; but, if from a grandparent or as inheritance, the income is the child's. What the child (or his trustee) owns is the right to a share in the assets of the partnership, not to specific assets, over which there is no control. The limited partner cannot interfere in the management of the fund, save by withdrawing capital, as to which see below.

A gift of funds to be added to the partnership is a PET, whether the money is paid to the child who then invests it or is paid straight to the partnership bank account for his or her benefit. On the death of the child, the share is part of his or her estate. Meanwhile, unlike with a relevant property trust, there are no periodic IHT charges. The gift of an interest in the FLP may trigger a CGT charge, but not on the cash constituent of the share nor on any assets qualifying for holdover relief under *TCGA 1992, s 165*. That is better than the gift of certain trust interests since, in the family context, many will be settlor interested. Holdover is not possible on the transfer in, but may shelter a gain on the way out.

The general partner runs the partnership, making reserves for tax and expenses as necessary, and controls the flow of income. The enterprise must be run so as to make a profit; this is to show that this is a genuine partnership under general principles. Just holding property or investments together is not enough.

A well-drawn FLP will set out quite definite limits to capital withdrawal, for example:

- no withdrawal for any purpose for five years;
- no withdrawal until the partner has reached the age of 22 (and has completed his education);
- staged withdrawal thereafter for any purpose and (with consent of other partners) lump sum withdrawal for the purchase of a residence or of another business to be run separately from the FLP; and
- early withdrawal for other purposes and at other times only after deduction of penalties.

The general partner

12.15   The general partner may be an individual or could be corporate. That might help to limit liability and provide cover in the event of death. If the general partner is an individual of comfortable wealth, he or she may feel vulnerable to claims and require indemnities. The dividing lines of responsibility should be clear, especially if the FLP benefits an extended family.

If the general partner is corporate, control may be an issue, with the person who funds gifts to children wanting to own shares in the corporate body. On death, the founder's shares are important strategically. Do not let them pass to the limited partners as a group: that could make them owners of the whole structure, which might weaken asset protection.

We do not yet know, in the absence of cases strictly in point, how much the general partner may be paid for his work. Take care that the structure does not degenerate into a vehicle for the founder to milk the assets to supplement his pension, whilst hoping that capital value has left his estate. It can be seen how control may be reserved, but over that control hangs the spectre of reservation of benefit from gifts made to children if it appears that the money was, from the beginning, destined to be invested in an FLP.

Regulation and protection

12.16   The management of investments or dealing with and advising on them is regulated by the Financial Services Authority. The general partner will be promoting investment, so must be duly authorised. The FLP is a 'collective investment scheme'. There will be costs to registration as well as delays. Values must be substantial to justify all this.

Each partner owns a share, not the underlying assets. That may prove difficult to realise to meet liabilities, as in divorce proceedings. Some discount will be appropriate, but the courts will probably not let that get in the way of making an appropriate order. The share will be a 'resource' to which the court may look to provide for the other party to a marriage. This may be where restrictions on the withdrawal of capital requiring the consent of other partners will be helpful. Much will turn on recent management of the FLP: if it produces a steady income, an order might be made to use it to fund maintenance.

The level of protection is not so different from a discretionary trust, where there is a pattern of income or of capital distributions that a court may take into account in deciding to what extent to regard the partnership share as a resource. Some protection may perhaps be achieved by taking the FLP offshore. The foreign court might disregard an English court order and refuse to enforce it. Only if values are substantial will the extra compliance costs justify such a course. In practice, what will usually be most important is the location of the defendant who owns the share of the FLP. He will be made to pay, somehow, and his family will have to rally round to help him.

SHARE FARMING OR CONTRACT FARMING

12.17 These arrangements were described towards the end of **Chapter 3**. Given the valuable relief under BPR in respect of the non-agricultural value of farmland, it may be very important for the landowner to show that he qualifies for BPR rather than APR, as was attempted in *McCall v HMRC* [2009] NICA 12, examined in detail at **5.6**. The Country Land and Business Association model agreement may be a useful guide here.

As a side issue, it should be noted from the standpoint of the contractor (who might well be related to the landowner) that farmers' averaging relief is not available in respect of contracting income. Where contracting income forms a significant proportion of the income of a farming business, this may be a material consideration, particularly where the form of agriculture gives rise to cyclical variations.

Care should be taken in drawing the agreement. It is easy for it to slip into the nature of either a tenancy on the one hand or a partnership on the other, particularly since a partnership can be created for tax purposes at least, without the need for any actual deed. Where there is no deed, it may be argued that the landowner retains possession of the land, but that may in fact not follow from what the parties have agreed. HMRC consider that it is the availability of vacant possession, rather than the existence of any tenancy, that will decide whether relief is at 50% or at 100%.

Important aspects of the agreement, for it to achieve the desired purpose of leaving the landowner with CGT reliefs whilst allowing the contractor to undertake the risk of the farming operation, include an obligation that the landowner must provide the variable inputs and that he actually pays for them. The crops in the ground should remain the property of the landlord all the way through the farming cycle. It is therefore undesirable to give the contractor the right to sell any crops before harvesting. That might be regarded as giving the contractor occupation of the land. The occupation of the land by the contractor would be fatal to claiming that the landowner was a farmer.

Under share farming, both the landowner and the operator farm the land. Here, the operator will provide the working machinery and labour and will pay a proportion of the variable input costs. The same risk of slippage into partnership or tenancy exists as with contract farming. The tenancy problem is avoided if neither the landowner nor the operator has exclusive possession. The landowner needs to keep occupation of the land and of any buildings for CGT purposes. The operator should have a mere licence to occupy. The agreement should provide that the landowner can terminate the agreement within 12 months, subject to paying the contractor compensation. A difficulty will arise where, for example, animals on the land are owned by one party or the other to the agreement rather than in shares. The occupation of the land by the animals might lead to their owner being regarded as the occupier of the land.

The risk of inadvertent entry into partnership can be avoided by a careful definition of what each party receives from the agreement. Each will conduct a separate business. There should be separate bank accounts, except perhaps for one into which gross takings are paid which are then divided in agreed shares. Each party should keep their own books.

As with so many arrangements which test to the limits the available reliefs, part of the success will lie in the careful execution of the plan. Proper accounting procedures should be in place. Good companies specialising in this area 'know the form', and establish specific bank accounts for the trade, sometimes a separate account for each season's 'campaign'. If there are meetings, as there should be, to decide farm policy, there should be minutes of those meetings. Without such minutes, it may well be very difficult to show that the landowner has taken any active part in the farming operation at all.

Two factors in particular create difficulties: not enough good machinery, and too much bad paperwork. The farmer may have a great deal of practical farming knowledge, but the lack of expensive modern machinery may prevent him from carrying out personally many of the traditional farming operations. That leaves him only the care of hedges, and looking after livestock, which may also represent someone else's investment. Meanwhile, the greater part of many farming incomes arises not from the tending of any crops or animals, but from the completion of such forms as will secure the best government subsidies. It is very easy for the farmer in later life to delegate more and more of the work to the point where he is in truth no more than an investor, as if landlord of his own farm. If family leave home and cannot really work in partnership with the old man and take on what he can no longer do, there is every prospect that relief may be endangered.

Finally, take care of the basics. If, as is common, the agreement lasts for a limited period only, the practitioner should make a forward note in his diary to remind the farmer to renew when it expires. It is that kind of care that wins cases (and new clients).

GRANTING AGRICULTURAL TENANCIES

12.18   By *IHTA 1984, s 16* the grant of a tenancy of agricultural property in the United Kingdom, the Channel Islands or the Isle of Man for the use of agricultural purposes is not a transfer of value by the grantor if made for full consideration in money or money's worth. 'Grant' probably encompasses the coming into existence of the tenancy by any means. Usually, it will now mean the creation of a farm business tenancy.

What is 'full consideration'? HMRC have in the past argued that consideration should be a 'tender rent' rather than a mere 'rack rent', ie in areas where agricultural land is keenly sought after, it should not merely be the amount of rent passing on the recent review of the rent of similar land, but should be the premium rent that would be offered by a farmer in that area to secure the land in question. It will certainly be necessary to consider the surrounding circumstances, including any circumstances which have a value in money and which relate to the grant of the tenancy, such as terms agreed orally between the parties or the terms of any other transaction to which the grant of the tenancy is related.

It may also be relevant to look at the personal circumstances of the tenant, including his agricultural experience or the training that he has undergone or financial status. Because of the premium involved in establishing a tender rent, HMRC will not accept as evidence of full consideration new rents charged to existing tenants. The yardstick is the rent which would be expected to be obtained on the grant of the tenancy on the open market by a willing grantor to a willing grantee, but on the same terms as the actual tenancy, including provision as to rent reviews and obligations to repair and the like.

Security of tenure

12.19   By virtue of *Agricultural Tenancies Act 1995, s 4*, agricultural tenancies beginning after 31 August 1995 generally do not have security of tenure. That fact alone may have done much to narrow the gap between rack rents and tender rents, since it was the security of tenure which doubtless influenced the premium. It was the apparent intention of the Government, in introducing the change, to encourage a freer letting market in agricultural property which, if achieved, would as a by-product give the tax valuer more comparables. In the event, the state of the letting market has probably been influenced as much by other factors affecting the profitability of agriculture as a whole.

Even though the mere grant of a lease may not itself be a transfer of value through the operation of *IHTA 1984, s 16*, that grant may be part of a series of associated operations under *s 268* except (see *s 268(2)*) where more than three years elapse from the grant of the tenancy to the next 'operation'. The matter is now hopefully of academic interest, as *s 268(2)* also provided that no operation effected on or after 26 March 1974 is to be taken to be associated with an operation effected before that date.

Whilst the grant of tenancies was distinctly advantageous before 10 March 1981, the benefit of such grants has been progressively reduced. As the taxable value of tenanted land subject to APR at the lower rate became similar to the taxable value of the same vacant land, there was no material advantage. The introduction of APR at 100% for vacant land caused the advantage to go the other way, in that granting an agricultural tenancy could actually increase the taxable value, since APR on let land was available at 50% only. That imbalance has been removed in respect of transfers after 31 August 1995 where the tenancy began after that date. As a result, the arguments which used to arise as to the tax charge on the grant of a tenancy have gone. There is no reduction in the rate of APR where other conditions have been satisfied, making that relief available merely because a new tenancy is granted.

Agricultural Holdings Act 1986, s 1 gave security of tenure to agricultural tenancies where the whole of the land was let for use as agricultural land. Certain exceptions were allowed which might not, however, substantially affect the character of the tenancy. Tenancies or leases which covered the use of land, only part of which was agricultural, might not enjoy the statutory protection. Where the lease does not grant that protection and where it can be assigned, it can have a value and, insofar as the property demised is agricultural, APR may be available in respect of it. The valuation will not be straightforward, since it must be on the basis that the lease is assignable but that the assignee will be restricted to agricultural use of those parts which are so used for the assignment.

What should the discount be for the existence of a tenancy? This is very much a matter for negotiation with the District Valuer. Even where the tenancy has been created since 31 August 1995, such that the tenant does not have security, some discount should be allowable because of the delay in gaining possession (which can be up to two years). The valuation should also allow for any compensation payable to the tenant on leaving. Discounts seem to range from 20% to 50%. Valuation principles in general are considered in **Chapter 8**.

BPR ON AN AGRICULTURAL PROPERTY COMPANY

12.20   Agricultural property may be the underlying asset of a trading company. It may then qualify as relevant business property. The operation of *IHTA 1984, s 114(1)* will ensure that APR is applied automatically first, and BPR is applicable only to the value of the underlying asset unreduced by APR. APR will not be available in respect of a minority holding of shares in a farming company; but 100% BPR will, subject to the observation below, be allowable where the holding is, as will often be the case, in unquoted shares.

Similarly, a company may have owned business property which is disposed of and which is replaced by agricultural property. Where the agricultural property has not been owned long enough to qualify for APR, the combined period of ownership may be sufficient for BPR. This was examined at **12.5** in considering RI 95.

A significant limitation on BPR is that, where a company owns a tenanted farm, BPR will not be available because the company is not trading; it is 'wholly or mainly holding investments' within *s 105(3)*. A minority shareholding in such a company carries the benefit neither of BPR nor of APR, although the controlling shareholder will be better treated if it can be shown that the company has owned the farm for seven years, and if the controlling shareholder has likewise owned the shares for seven years. Then, 50% APR will be available.

FARMERS DIVERSIFYING INTO NON-AGRICULTURAL ENTERPRISES

12.21 It was noted earlier that many farming families are reluctant to give up their way of life, even though the acreage held is not viable from an economic point of view. The change in farming methods can frequently mean that buildings, both cottages and farm buildings, are no longer occupied for the purposes of agriculture. The height of farm buildings, which in the last century was perfectly adequate to house farm equipment and the horses which provided the main power on the farm, is totally inadequate for machinery of the size now commonly in use. Yet the farmer may not wish (or even be allowed) to dismantle attractive old farm buildings, particularly where they lie close to the farmhouse, to replace them with large modern structures.

An alternative use is to divide them into small workshops for craftsmen and the like. That, and the holiday industry in other forms, may provide the farmer with a much earlier, more certain, and more regular return of cash than is available from his crop and other stock. The difficulty is, of course, that, from the point of view of APR, the buildings will no longer be occupied for the purposes of agriculture; and, from the point of view of BPR, no relief will, subject only to the decision in *Farmer v IRC* [1999] STC (SCD) 321 (reviewed at **9.13**), be available in respect of the part of the business which is wholly or mainly holding investments, however active the farmer may be in managing the land and buildings producing the leisure-based or craft-based income.

Other difficulties arise from a planning point of view, in that the development of redundant farm buildings into a profitable portfolio of investment properties may render those properties far more valuable than their cost plus the cost of improvements. CGT is likely to be a significant factor in deciding whether the portfolio of 'leisure-based' buildings should be the subject of a gift. Commonly, the advice of the tax planner in these circumstances will be to recommend the creation of a lifetime trust (limited to amounts within the nil rate band) to which the assets can be transferred, with the gain being held over under *TCGA 1992, s 260*.

Care should be taken to establish the trust properly. It is no longer essential for the trust to be discretionary in nature: since *FA 2006*, the creation of almost any form of lifetime trust, other than for charity or for the disabled, is a chargeable transfer. Thus the old problem, that it was virtually impossible to argue that there was a discretionary trust where in substance there was one beneficiary only, perhaps the child of the settlor, has gone. It is no longer necessary, except for the purpose of avoiding reverter to the settlor, to ensure that there is a range of beneficiaries.

However set up, let the arrangement be genuine, notwithstanding the cost to the family in terms of professional time. Thus, the trustees should insist on meeting from time to time to consider the exercise of their discretion, and should be seen to exercise it and should minute that exercise. It is wrong that the minutes of meetings of trustees, like those of directors, should too closely resemble the Loch Ness Monster, in that while their existence is not doubted, it is seldom proved.

The problem of diversification might be considered within the context of incorporating the farm business. Probably on its own the tax planning point now mentioned would not be a sufficient argument for incorporation, but it has been noted elsewhere in this chapter and in **Chapter 7** that a 'hybrid' company, ie one with activities which encompass both trading and non-trading activities, may secure limited protection through BPR for activities which, taken by themselves, would not qualify for BPR but which do so within the context of being used for part of the trade of the company as a whole.

One reason for not incorporating the farming business in order to secure relief for a small part of the operation, such as the ownership of two holiday cottages, is the restriction on relief in respect of minority holdings of farming companies, which has been noted earlier in this chapter. Where, for example, it is intended to allow members of the family a share in the farming business, even though they are not actively engaged in the conduct of the farm, the tax adviser may find, on looking at all the circumstances, that partnership is a better vehicle for carving out an interest for a non-farming member of the family. Alternatively, farming assets may be the subject of a trust whose trustees farm the land in partnership with the other owners of farm assets.

Holiday lettings

12.22   One area of confusion is that holiday lettings are treated as a trade for income tax by virtue of *ITTOIA 2005, s 323(2)* and *(3)*, which set out a number of conditions that are relevant to income tax, namely:

- the property must be let on a commercial basis;

- with a view to the realisation of profits; and

- the tenant must be entitled to the use of furniture.

By *ITTOIA 2005, ss 325* and *326*, to be 'qualifying holiday accommodation' further conditions are imposed:

- it must be available generally as holiday accommodation for periods which amount to not less than 140 days in the year (the 'availability condition');

- it must actually be let for at least 70 days per year (the 'letting condition'); and

- for a period of at least 155 days in the year, it is not normally in the same occupation for a continuous period exceeding 31 days ('period of longer-term occupation').

ITTOIA 2005, s 326 sets out averaging rules and an election to deal with accommodation ('under-used accommodation') which would qualify as holiday accommodation if actually let 70 days per year.

For capital gains tax purposes, holiday cottages may be a trade, but in general terms the business of managing holiday cottages has not qualified either for APR or BPR in its own right. In the past, HMRC could consider the inclusion of the value of holiday cottages within a business; but, where the cottages were not part of the business, they did not qualify for any relief. The issue of BPR on holiday property was considered at **9.8**, in the light of the decision in *Brendan Peter James Furness*, and in the review at **9.11**; holiday lets were considered at **9.23**. HMRC did, for a time, recognise that the business of running furnished holiday lettings may be very similar to that of running a hotel or motel, but their attitude has hardened somewhat (see IHTM25278).

The latest view appears to be that, depending upon the incidents of the business itself, running furnished holiday lettings may be regarded as qualifying for BPR where:

- the lettings are short term (for example, weekly or fortnightly); and

- some person (it was formerly considered to be the owner himself or an agent) was substantially involved with the holiday maker(s) in terms of their activities on and from the premises, even if the lettings were for part of the year only.

As IHTM25278 shows, HMRC will now look closely at the level of services provided, rather than at the identity of the provider. Previously, only the more difficult cases were referred to the Litigation Group, such as those where:

- the lettings are longer term (including assured shorthold tenancies); or

- the owner had little involvement with the holiday maker(s) – for example, a villa or apartment abroad; or

- where the lettings were to friends and relatives only; or

- where it is clear that no services were provided to the holiday maker(s).

For the time being, whilst HMRC reconsider their attitude, all claims for BPR on holiday lets are to be referred to the Technical Team (Litigation). Such cases are strongly argued.

Do we really need two reliefs?

12.23 Any observer of rural matters over the last few years has seen that, for some at least, farming is no longer a viable commercial activity. Farmers are now in competition with producers of crops from other countries, although the current weakness of Sterling may help. There is nothing new about this: producers of tea and coffee know all too well the problems of producing a crop in competition with others, and the difficulties of agriculture as a sustainable activity. Workers in the textile trade and in electronics feel the difficulties of competing worldwide.

Why do we have the two reliefs? The official line is that:

'The purpose and scope of the two reliefs differ. Business relief is designed to encourage and protect investment in risk-taking family trading ventures generally whereas agricultural relief is focussed more specifically on farmland and buildings and includes letting of farmland. But the practical outcome is that most trading companies and farms get 100% exemption from Inheritance Tax.'

That is true as far as it goes, but the two reliefs sit uneasily side by side, both from the point of view of policy and of application.

There is, for example, no clear and logical distinction between the premises from which, say, a farrier carries on his trade where he happens also to live, and the premises enjoyed by his farmer customer, and yet the farmer gets relief from IHT on his residence, whereas the farrier does not. There is no clear and logical distinction between the sophisticated exploitation (for as long as it was still possible) of EEC subsidies from the comfort of a centrally heated office, which did qualify as 'farming,' and the careful exploitation of farm buildings to produce an alternative income which, in general terms, did not qualify as a business, whether farming or not.

It is in this context that the case of *Farmer v IRC* [1999] STC (SCD) 321 could offer the means of a very significant simplification of the law if extended into a statutory principle. Farming is a business that qualifies for BPR. The letting of, say, warehouses is not such a business, but developing land is. If, following the principle in *Farmer*, the management of land on an active basis could be regarded as a business for BPR, many of the difficult cases would be removed. The problem, as always, is where to draw the line. Under the law as it stands, farmers are leaving the land, or allowing it to lie fallow, because farming is not profitable. The existence of APR has not prevented that; it has merely persuaded that farmer to retain the asset, but not to put it to any good commercial use. To that extent, therefore, it could be argued that APR is not working.

Almost certainly, the existence of APR attracted to the purchase of farmland people who had 'money to burn' and who were simply seeking the equivalent, in IHT terms, of the protection afforded through ISAs in relation to income tax and CGT. That distorted the market and, for as long as it lasted, placed on agricultural land an artificial value that was so high that the farming operations ceased to be commercially viable. The decimation of jobs in financial services will have helped to reduce this problem, and the price of land is only one factor in the economics of farming. A courageous government could address this issue and achieve significant simplification of the law. Certain vested interests would be disappointed, although transitional reliefs could be devised to protect 'working farmers'. That might be an acceptable price for the country as a whole to pay.

Chapter 13

Tax shelters

QUICK GUIDE

An appreciation of the APR/BPR rules can shelter assets from IHT and, where a tenant farmer can buy the freehold reversion, exposure to very considerable tax can be saved overnight.

Shares listed on AIM and PLUS can offer very useful savings where the investor accepts the risks inherent in those markets.

Whilst investment properties will not normally qualify for BPR, there are group structures that may afford relief: see **13.16**.

INTRODUCTION

13.1   The use of the word 'shelter' may demonstrate a particular attitude to tax and tax planning. Indeed, to some the very term is offensive, as is the suggestion that any family blessed with assets equal to or exceeding two nil rate bands needs shelter from any kind of storm, financial or otherwise. The rise in value of domestic property in some areas has made IHT a regional tax. The author does not take sides in this debate, except to note that there are some solicitors and accountants in general practice who consider that their first and main duty is to ensure compliance with the law. To them, the whole edifice of tax planning is not merely intellectually challenging but artificial and, in its own way, morally wrong: see also the observations of Harman J in *Cancer Research Campaign v Ernest Brown* [1997] STC 1425 at 1430, when speculating as to the attitude of the testatrix, in his reference to 'something rather unattractive, to be indulged in by sharp people with connections in the City of London'.

That is not to say, however, that a well planned and executed scheme, in respect of which full disclosure is made, brings with it any risk of prosecution under the offence of tax fraud introduced by *FA 2000, s 144*. That offence is discussed at **22.11**. The emphasis should be on good execution, but meaning not merely good documents but careful adherence in practice, on the ground, to what those documents put in place. It is the sloppily executed transaction that is the easiest prey for the diligent tax inspector; see, for example, the *Dugan-Chapman* and *Vinton* cases referred to at **6.5**.

A GENERAL ANTI-AVOIDANCE MEASURE?

13.2   This is something of a political football, and is considered in Appendix 9 to this book. Successive governments have merely introduced legislation targeted at specific tax schemes. The legislation has not always achieved what might be hoped for it by HMRC and has required occasional revision. That makes projects such as simplification more urgent. It also illustrates the attractions of a general anti-avoidance measure to the tax gatherer: flexibility to meet new challenges and relative simplicity. For as long as legislation is targeted against specific schemes, there will be the incentive for tax practitioners to examine the legislation in minute detail and devise new ways round it. The intellectual challenge that was mentioned at **13.1** above is positively enjoyed by some practitioners.

The difficulty is, of course, that it makes more law for everyone else to learn. There is a risk that a practitioner may be deemed to be negligent because he has failed to exploit a scheme. The practitioner is in a difficult position: if he does advise the implementation of a scheme, he must take care to issue a health warning: see the decision of the Court of Appeal in *Grimm v Newman* [2002] STC 1388. It is probably not enough to include general words in the letter of engagement: the warning must probably be quite specific.

SHAM

13.3   Every tax practitioner has to guard against recommending structures that the clients then do not properly implement. One illustration of sham is *Hitch v Stone* [2001] STC 214, described in Appendix 9. One area where the issue of sham may often have applied to nullify a scheme which otherwise has intellectual attraction was the 'debt or charge' scheme, as regularly employed to make use of the nil rate band. That scheme is no longer relevant but is briefly described at **15.10**.

FARMS

As landlord

13.4   Commonly, the notion of a tax shelter implies that an event has arisen, giving rise to a liability to tax which can be mitigated or postponed by action taken after the event. In relation to IHT, the expression has a slightly different connotation, in that the liability to tax has normally not yet arisen, and action is being taken in order to protect from IHT assets which would otherwise suffer that charge.

The purchase of let farms may give that protection. The land is agricultural land or pasture within *IHTA 1984, s 115(2)* and occupied for the purposes of agriculture (subject to the discussion of the meaning of that phrase in **Chapter 3**). After ownership for seven years, the condition in *s 117(b)* is satisfied. APR is available in respect of the agricultural value either at 50% or, if the tenancy is one beginning on or after 1 September 1995, at 100%. Thus, the purchase of let farms does not give immediate relief but does give relief eventually.

Share-farming and contract farming

13.5   The nature of these farming arrangements was considered in both **Chapters 3** and **7**, where some of the difficulties were noted. Properly structured, the existence of a share farming or contract farming agreement may enable the owner of a farm to show that he is the 'paramount occupier' and thereby bring himself within *s 117(a)*, with the result that the minimum period of occupation or ownership required to earn relief is two years rather than seven. Such a valuable relief as APR is worth the effort required strictly to comply with the statutory requirements. The success of use of farmland as a tax shelter lies largely in the care with which arrangements are executed.

Tenant buying out landlord

13.6   An established tenancy, here meaning one created before 1 September 1995 and carrying security of tenure, may have considerable value. Part of that value is reflected in the possibility that the landlord may be willing to sell to the tenant on terms which give to the tenant part of the 'marriage value' arising when the tenant becomes the owner of the property with the benefit of vacant possession.

A point which greatly helps the tenant in this situation is that *s 117(a)*, in specifying a minimum period of occupation or ownership, does not require the transferor both to own and occupy the land to qualify.

Example13.1: death-bed purchase

Ben, a tenant, has occupied Low Farm for two years or longer. On purchase of the freehold, he immediately satisfies the test in *s 117(a)*. Before that purchase, Ben had substantial cash assets which would not qualify either for APR or BPR. Thus, even on his deathbed, where Ben gains the opportunity to buy the freehold of the farm he has rented, there is a chance, which from the tax planning perspective is not to be missed, of overnight securing 100% APR. The difficulty arises where, for example, Ben wishes to provide for family members who are not engaged in the family farm, since the purchase locks up the capital that could have been given to non-farmers.

These rules may, however, be part of an exercise to help non-farming members of the family.

Example 13.2: protecting the farming son

Father, in partnership with one of his sons, grants a tenancy which gives the son security under the *Agricultural Tenancies Act 1995*, perhaps until retirement age. He leaves the freehold to all his children equally, with the result that after his death they receive rent only until sale. On the sale, the son is bought out, unless his lease has expired. Entrepreneurs' relief may shelter the farming son's gain.

APR will be available to the farming son after two years, either by virtue of his occupation as a partner before the tenancy or under the tenancy, and to the other children after seven years from their inheritance. An interesting point might arise if 100% relief were in the future to be cut down: *IHTA 1984, s 163* operates to reduce the value of an asset in certain circumstances, although the grant of a lease by father's will would probably not be one of them, since *s 163(1)(a)* requires consideration to be given.

If all the children were willing to become partners with the farming son, they might earn the CGT benefits of roll-over relief and (subject to meeting all the tests) entrepreneurs' relief. In these circumstances, it may be better to keep the land outside the partnership but to grant the partnership a tenancy which itself would be a partnership asset. A disposal could then fall within *TCGA 1992, s 169I(8)(c)* as a material disposal of business assets.

A difficulty would arise in the use of a company structure because no shareholder without control would get BPR, and there is a risk that the company might be no more than an investment vehicle: this is considered at **12.16**. There would also be no relief under *IHTA 1984, s 105(1)(d)* owing to the absence of control.

BUSINESSES

PLUS companies

13.7　　PLUS is an unregulated trading facility for share dealing in certain companies, several of which are unquoted. A selection of PLUS-traded companies is listed in, for example, the *Financial Times*. Private investors may deal only through a stockbroker who is regulated by the FSA. If such an adviser can be found who will recommend specific companies as suitable for investment, PLUS can allow a means of sheltering from IHT an investment after only two years of ownership. However, the investor must take care: some PLUS companies are in fact listed, which deprives them of relief.

There are three practical difficulties. First, by the very nature of the market it is illiquid. Dealings in a number of the companies proceed only on a 'matched bargain' basis. It may, therefore, take some time to assemble a substantial shareholding and, following a death, the executors may find that there is a delay in liquidating the holding.

The second practical difficulty is in identifying stockbrokers willing to advise on unlisted securities. This is a specialist market where some of the stocks are fledgling companies with only a very short established track record. Among PLUS securities there are, however, some very well-kept secrets, in the form of companies of considerable quality with an established record, which would be an asset to a share portfolio even without the specific advantage of BPR.

The third difficulty is the commitment to hold the portfolio until death or until the relevant chargeable transfer.

AIM companies

13.8   It was noted, in relation to the clawback provisions at **10.4**, that the status of certain unquoted shares has not always remained the same. The Alternative Investment Market (AIM) is regarded as 'the second tier' of the Stock Exchange (see Romesh Vaitilingam's guide *Using the Financial Pages*). AIM was established in 1995 and trades shares that are not suitable for the main market. AIM has less onerous listing requirements than the main market, and is designed to encourage smaller, fast-growing businesses to seek a quotation. There is much less trading in AIM stock. Shares are less easy to buy and sell.

Difficulty and confusion arises because the definition of 'quoted', as was noted in **10.12**, has changed from time to time. *IHTA 1984, s 272* indicates that 'quoted' means 'listed on a recognised stock exchange or dealt in on the Unlisted Securities Market'. The Unlisted Securities Market or USM was the predecessor to AIM. For a time, USM shares were regarded as quoted, but the expression 'listed' was substituted with effect from 1 April 1996. Whilst AIM has succeeded USM, the definition in *s 272* has not been amended so as to treat AIM shares as 'quoted' or 'listed'. The test, as was noted at **6.20** onwards, is whether securities dealt in on a recognised stock exchange satisfy the tests both of:

- listing by a competent authority; and

- admission to trading on a recognised stock exchange.

Thus, subject to the caveat below, AIM securities still count as unlisted because they are not securities admitted to the Official List by the Financial Services Authority.

Not all AIM shares will qualify for BPR. All are capable of qualifying, but the exclusion of BPR by *s 105(3)* (wholly or mainly holding investments) can, it is submitted, apply just as much to an AIM company as to any other unquoted company. The majority of AIM companies, particularly those engaged in high technology industries, will have the characteristics of relatively high risk and relatively low cash resources that will qualify them as typical trading companies, investment in which BPR is intended to encourage.

The liquidity of AIM is restricted, but not as restricted as that of PLUS. More stockbrokers are willing to advise on AIM investments than on PLUS investments. As a result, AIM shares are a valuable element of the tax planner's arsenal.

Caveat: secondary market listings

13.9 Trading in shares is, of course, international. Stock exchanges are often not the property of governments but are themselves freely traded. Exchanges compete, and companies go shopping for the regulation regime and the pool of investors that suits them best. As a result, even a small company may be traded on several exchanges and, whilst it may be unquoted in the UK, it may have a listing in another country. This should be checked, since a listing anywhere in the world will deprive shares of BPR.

Fully private companies

13.10 The lack of a ready market, or in some cases of any market at all, in the shares of fully private companies may be enough to discourage any investor save a family member of the main executive directors of the company. Difficulties of valuation abound, of which only a handful of examples were given in the discussion of this subject in **Chapter 8**. Nevertheless, where there is sound commercial justification for an investment, or where for example a minority holding in a trading company is inherited and enjoys the benefit of an income stream from dividends, there can be good reasons for its retention. In particular, the simplification of *s 105(1)(bb)*, so as to afford 100% relief to unquoted shares regardless of the size of the shareholding, has greatly increased the attraction of keeping a minority holding.

Conversion of debt into equity

13.11   It is explained in **Chapter 14** in relation to unincorporated businesses that debt is not part of the value of the business, and that a transfer of a debt owed by a business from one person to another qualifies for no relief. There may be excellent commercial reasons, at the formation of the company, for an investment in a private limited company to be made by way of loan rather than by way of shareholding. In addition, the existence of a loan account offers the founder shareholder the opportunity of withdrawing funds from the company without suffering income tax on them. However, from the point of view of IHT, an equity holding is infinitely more attractive: it will qualify for 100% BPR under *s 105(1)(bb)*, assuming of course that the nature of the business carried on by the company is one which is not disqualified from BPR by *s 105(3)*.

The conversion of debt into equity will not in normal circumstances amount to a transfer, although it can do.

Example 13.3: good money after bad

Susan graduated from Warwick University in engineering and, although her full-time employment was in the energy industry, she pursued a hobby working on an invention that might eventually be marketable. A company was formed for the purpose and, when orders materialised, Susan lent the company money for development. The company ate cash at the development stage. The bank refused finance unless Susan agreed to convert half her loan account into shares, which she did.

Contracts were placed but the pricing was wrong, and the company came close to liquidation. Under pressure from the bank, a year later Susan converted the rest of her loan account into shares. Worry about the company distracted Susan while driving, and a momentary lapse in concentration caused her early death within a year of the second conversion. Her executors successfully claimed BPR (for what it was worth) on her original shareholding and on the shares resulting from the first conversion of loan account, which had been more than two years before death. They claimed that the shares resulting from the second conversion, which had not been held for two years, were of negligible value. The argument was put to them by HMRC that, when Susan agreed to the second conversion, she was throwing good money after bad and was, in effect, making a gift to the company.

Equally, such a conversion will seldom give rise to a chargeable gain. There will be expenses on the issue of shares but those costs will usually be small by comparison with the potential IHT saving. The conversion of debt into equity is, therefore, a useful device in suitable circumstances, particularly where the holder of the debt is considered likely to live for two years, but much less likely to live for seven years, from the transaction.

Conversion of cash into equity

13.12 A simple purchase of additional shares in an unquoted trading company achieves shelter only after two years. As originally envisaged (but not fully implemented) in *The Executors of Mrs Mary Dugan-Chapman & Another v Revenue & Customs Commissioners* [2008] SpC 666 a two-year period may be abridged where the company makes a rights issue which is taken up. This is in reliance on *IHTA 1984, s 107(4)* when read with the 'paper for paper' provisions of *TCGA 1992, ss 126–136*.

Buildings or machinery

13.13 A problem may arise where buildings or machinery are used by a family company but are not owned by the controlling shareholder. If the controlling shareholder settles all his shares on the owner of the buildings or machinery, it becomes possible for the owner of the buildings or machinery to make a gift of those assets with the benefit of 50% BPR. This is so, even if the shares then revert to the settlor free of IHT, provided that BPR continues to be available on those shares at 100%. Naturally, there may be CGT issues to address in such an arrangement, but it is likely that the buildings or machinery may in part constitute business assets qualifying for holdover relief and for business assets taper relief.

Nursing home businesses

13.14 These businesses have been singled out for a brief mention because, if well run, they used to represent, at least before recent changes in regulation and funding, an attractive investment for a taxpayer holding large funds not otherwise qualifying for APR or BPR. The operating of a nursing home business is not, in general terms, wholly or mainly one of making or holding investments. In the line of cases examined towards the end of **Chapter 9**, the distinction between the position of proprietors of caravan sites and of hoteliers was noted, in *Powell (Personal Representatives of Pearce deceased) v IRC* [1997] STC (SCD) 181. It was considered by the Commissioner that the services of hoteliers were business activities, and not 'holding investments'.

This proposition is consistent with the earlier case of *Griffiths (Inspector of Taxes) v Jackson* (1983) 56 TC 583, on which HMRC rely extensively (see IHTM25273 and 252777), even though it is not an IHT case. It concerned a couple of accountants who between them assembled a portfolio of 180 student lettings in Bristol and were arguing for income tax treatment under Schedule D

Case I rather than Case VI. It was there held that the deriving of income from the exercise of property rights was not income from carrying on a trade.

It is beyond doubt that the care of the elderly involves rather more than merely providing accommodation and charging a rent. Provided, therefore, that the investment content of a company which operates a nursing home is not excessive, ie that it can be shown that the business does not carry liquid resources which are far beyond the regular needs of the business, a nursing home business may be a very acceptable investment as a shelter securing 100% BPR. The attraction of this kind of business has in the past been that generally it was low risk, being substantially property-based. There was text in the old AIM Manual that suggested that BPR would usually be available, but IHTM25277 is much less encouraging, at least in relation to 'residential homes', so it will be for the taxpayer to press the argument as to the level of services. Note the comment there as to 'entrenched position': the taxpayer should prepare the ground well.

Lloyd's interests

13.15   Few taxpayers, given the experience of Lloyd's underwriters in recent years, would consider the prospect of shelter from IHT sufficiently attractive to persuade them to join a syndicate. Those who remain underwriters enjoy substantial relief because the investments or other assets which support the underwriting qualify for BPR at 100%, as was noted in **Chapter 5**. As was noted there, different rules apply to a Nameco. It follows that an underwriter wishing to retire faces a difficult choice. He may find, on an auction of his capacity, that he receives a very satisfactory payment for what is in effect the goodwill of his business. He must accept that, when he reduces his underwriting capacity, the release of assets from his deposit increases his exposure to IHT overnight. Immediate planning, perhaps including the making of substantial gifts, may well be appropriate.

INVESTMENT PROPERTIES

13.16   It has been noted at various points in this book that the holding of mere investments does not qualify for BPR. How can such a holding be sheltered from IHT? The long-term solution, noted elsewhere, may be the creation of a nil rate band discretionary trust of the investments, holding over any gain into the trust. There is one other possibility for relief, namely the holding of investment properties through the medium of a subsidiary of a group of companies. As was noted in **Chapter 8**, this stratagem is not without risk. The interaction of *IHTA 1984, ss 110* and *112* must be carefully observed. Properly structured, the holding of investment properties through a subsidiary, where the remainder of the group of companies do trade, may shelter those properties from IHT. Each case must be treated on its own merits.

SUPER SHELTERS

13.17   For a time, until its recent abolition, reinvestment relief when coupled with business property relief offered the chance of spectacular savings of tax, provided that the requirements of reinvestment relief were strictly observed. The code for the Enterprise Investment Scheme is now set out in *TCGA 1992, Sch 5B*, as amended by *FA 1998*. A consideration of the workings of the scheme, and its statutory modification from time to time, is well outside the scope of this book, save for the observation that the relief is available to a UK resident investor who incurs a chargeable gain on the disposal of any asset after 28 November 1994, or in whose hands a gain which had previously been deferred is brought back into charge by a chargeable event. Practitioners are referred to such works as Bloomsbury Professional's *Core Tax Annuals, Capital Gains Tax 2010/11*, Chapter 16, for a thorough and readable account of the legislation. EIS relief is limited to smaller companies, though not necessarily to unquoted ones; that extra limitation is needed for BPR to be allowed as well.

Chapter 14

General planning points

QUICK GUIDE

The complexity of APR and BPR rules creates hazards for the practitioner that are illustrated in this chapter. In general, reservation of benefit can be regarded as less of a problem where the asset qualifies for APR or BPR because, if the asset is still treated as part of the estate of the donor, it may still so qualify. Note, however, the detailed rules at **14.4** onwards.

One of the most important issues, considered at **14.6** onwards, is the deductibility of debts: it is possible to achieve considerable savings of tax overnight where an existing structure has the effect of limiting BPR or APR because of debt within the situation. Shift the debt and the relief can increase. There is no waiting period. Similarly, the 'cleansing' of an asset that has already been held for two years, so that obstacles to a claim for relief are removed, brings immediate reliefs: see **14.34**.

Generally, a contract for the sale of an asset robs it of APR or BPR. The specific rules and 'buy and sell' agreements and options are considered at **14.7** onwards.

Clients considering IHT planning are frequently elderly. Planning may occur at the time of retirement from business. That retirement, and especially sale, should be discouraged where a structure can be maintained that will preserve APR or BPR: see *Swain Mason and Others v Mills & Reeve* [2011] EWHC 410 (Ch), examined at **14.14**. In particular, there is immediate loss of relief where a partnership interest is converted to a mere loan to the partnership: see especially the *Beckman* case discussed at **14.11**. Clawback problems arise where the donee of property that has the benefit of APR or BPR wishes to dispose of it.

The concluding sections digress from strict APR/BPR situations to review other options to mitigate the burden of IHT.

UNFORTUNATE GIFTS

14.1   Often, planning advice will include a recommendation that the owner of business or agricultural property should make gifts. There are situations where the IHT effect of making a PET may be worse than if the assets concerned had been left in the estate of the transferor on death. As will be seen in **Chapter 15** on the double use of 100% relief in respect of property passing from transferor to children and repurchased by the spouse of the transferor, there may be other reasons not to make a gift.

Example 14.1: PET following chargeable transfer

Hugh, a widower whose late wife had used her nil rate band in full, made a gift of £400,000 to a discretionary trust on 17 June 2001. On 20 July 2005, he gave his son Ian a cheque for £160,000. On 11 October 2006, he completed the sale of his farm. When Hugh died on 1 July 2008, his estate was worth £500,000 and had the benefit neither of APR nor of BPR.

The chargeable transfer had taken place more than seven years before the death and therefore fell out of accumulation. The PET was less than three years before the death and therefore outside the scope of taper relief.

To calculate IHT on the PET, it is necessary to look at the situation on 20 July 2005. At that stage, Hugh's cumulative total was £400,000, more than the current nil rate band, so IHT on the failed PET is a straight 40%, ie £64,000.

The tax on Hugh's estate for probate purposes must include the estate of £500,000 and the failed PET of £160,000. The effect is to tax the failed PET again. After allowing for a single nil rate band at the rate in force on 1 July 2008 of £312,000, tax on the estate is £139,200.

Had Hugh not given Ian the cheque, and had he instead made equivalent provision for Ian by will, and assuming that the £160,000 was not spent but that the income of it was not saved, Hugh's estate at death might have been £660,000 on which the tax, as noted, would be £139,200. The tax charge on the failed PET would have been entirely saved. The moral is that someone in Hugh's position, who has made a substantial chargeable transfer, must weigh up quite carefully the advantages of early giving and the risk that a charge by virtue of *IHTA 1984, s 7(1)* may apply.

THE TAXATION OF RELEVANT PROPERTY TRUSTS OF RELIEVED PROPERTY

14.2   A full discussion of the taxation of relevant property trusts is outside the scope of this book; see, for example, *Inheritance Tax 2010/11* (Bloomsbury Professional), chapter 8 and the many examples there set out, but the practitioner should be aware of particular points relating to the present rates of relief for

14.2 *General planning points*

APR and BPR. The creation of a lifetime trust, other than for a disabled person or for charity, is a chargeable transfer. When the top rate of relief was 50%, it followed that a gift which exceeded the nil rate band by 100% triggered an immediate charge to IHT at the lifetime rates on the excess. *IHTA 1984, s 68(5) (a)* has the effect that, on any exit charge within the first ten years of the trust, the basis of calculation for IHT was the gross value rather than the value after relief.

This is in contrast to the rule under *s 68(4)(b)*, whereby the cumulative total of the settlor which applies when fixing the charge on a second chargeable transfer (perhaps to a further trust) is calculated on the value after relief. An alert mind will appreciate that, under these arrangements, a settlement might be made on day one of the amount of the nil rate band, on the following day of one half of that amount, and on the third day one quarter of that amount etc. Such an arrangement was always open to the risk of challenge that one gift was associated with another. The *Reynaud* and *Rysaffe* cases, both considered in this chapter, are a great encouragement to tax advisers.

In the days before 100% APR or BPR, the rules as to added property in *s 67* would operate quite harshly. The 'clock' of a settlement is increased to match that of the settlor on the day before any addition to the fund if that total is greater than the existing cumulative total of the settlement. It is to avoid that particular rule that advisers have recommended multiple settlements.

Whilst APR and BPR remain at 100%, it might seem that these particular rules may safely be ignored. To do so is to take a view on the likelihood that the relief will at any time in the future be cut down. In the event that a single settlement has been created with substantial funds, all qualifying at present for APR or BPR at 100%, and there is a change in the availability of reliefs, the charge either at the ten-year anniversary or on the appointment out of funds might be very considerable.

Crawford Settlement Trustees v HMRC [2005] SpC 473 illustrates the complexity of IHT treatment of relevant property trusts. Under a 1954 settlement, a beneficiary was due to become entitled to an interest at the age of 21. In 1989, aged 19, he assigned the whole of his presumptive interest to trustees of a discretionary trust. (This may have been done to achieve holdover for CGT under *TCGA 1992, s 260*.) Notice of determination was issued that the assignment was a chargeable transfer under *IHTA 1984, s 71(3)*. The trustees appealed. Held, *s 71(3)* did not apply. The trust property was the same after the assignment as before: one or more persons would, on reaching the age of 21, become entitled to an interest in possession in the fund. As a result, the requirements of *s 71(1)* were still satisfied, just as before, so the fund did not cease to be settled property, so there could be no charge under *s 71(3)*. The case has become academic with the ending of the transitional period following the fundamental *FA 2006* changes to the taxation of such trusts.

THE FAMILY HOME AND PRE-OWNED ASSETS TAX

14.3   The taxation of the family home in all its aspects is a subject in its own right. The practitioner is referred to specialist works on the subject. Before the introduction of transferable nil rate bands by *FA 2008*, introducing *IHTA 1984, ss 8A–8C* with effect from 9 October 2007, there were 'in play' a number of schemes relating to the family home which attempted to separate out different aspects of ownership, such as carving out a lease separate from the freehold reversion. Some of these schemes are still usable, but the combination of the availability of two nil rate bands and the sudden fall in house prices in 2008 has curtailed much planning in this area.

FA 1986, s 102 (gifts with reservation) was supplemented by *ss 102A–102C* specifically to counteract schemes based on the (eventually successful) litigation in *Ingram (executors of the estate of Lady Ingram, deceased) v IRC* [1999] STC 37.

Pre-owned assets tax ('POAT') was introduced by *FA 2004, Sch 15* to counteract the variants of the scheme that had escaped with *Lady Ingram* and threatened to impose a crushing and ongoing income tax burden on families that had tried to shelter the family from a tax for which there was, quite simply, no money to pay. In practice, POAT seems to have yielded hardly any tax. Many families that feared that it might apply have found, to their disappointment, that the arrangements that they had put in place had not achieved the savings for which they had hoped and that they were outside POAT because they were still caught by reservation of benefit, as described below.

GIFTS WITH RESERVATION

14.4   Where an individual disposes, by way of gift, of an interest in land on or after 9 March 1999, the gifts with reservation rules set out in *IHTA 1984, s 102(2)–(4)* apply where:

- at any time in the relevant period
- the donor or the spouse of the donor enjoys 'a significant right or interest' in relation to the land or
- is party to 'a significant arrangement' in relation to the land.

The definition of a right, interest or arrangement which is significant for this purpose is (see *s 102A(3)*) a right which entitles or enables the donor to occupy all or part of the land or to enjoy some right in relation to all or part of the land otherwise than for full consideration in money or money's worth. The rule in *s 102A* is made slightly less harsh by the exclusion in *s 102A(5)* of any right or interest granted or acquired seven years before the gift of the property.

If an individual, on or after 9 March 1999, disposes of an undivided share of an interest in land, the gift with reservation rules of *s 102(3)* and *(4)* will apply, except where the donor does not occupy the land or, if he does so, he occupies the land to the exclusion of the donee but pays full consideration in money or money's worth for doing so.

There was, under the exception widely used which was derived from comments in Parliament and known as the *Hansard* exception, some relaxation of the rule for the family that could share a large house. This was made statutory by *FA 1986, s 102B(4)* where the donor and donee together occupy the land and the donor receives no benefit, other than a negligible one, which is provided by or at the expense of the donee himself for some reason connected with the gift. By *FA 2004, Sch 15, para 11(5)(b)*, this is recognised for POAT purposes and excluded from that tax.

For the purpose of the new rules, 'the relevant period' means a period ending on the date of the death of the donor and beginning seven years before that date or, if it is later, on the date of the gift (see *s 102(1)*).

Example 14.2: starting all over again

Bernie owned a flat in Hendon where he lived with his wife Sheila and disabled son Leon. In 1990, he transferred ownership of the flat to Leon, entering into a lease back at £5,000 pa and agreeing to pay all the running costs of the property. Leon had no income apart from the rent. When POAT was introduced, Bernie was reassured by a friend that he was in no difficulty, because well over seven years had elapsed since the gift, so it was free and clear. He consulted Geoff, who was initially minded to agree but, since he was not up to speed with POAT, referred the case to Melissa.

Melissa explained that POAT would apply only if the scheme had succeeded in avoiding reservation of benefit. For that, the period Bernie must consider was the seven years preceding Bernie's death, ie the present. If any benefit had been reserved in the last seven years, a benefit had been reserved. London flats, even in the recession of 2008, are not to be had for £5,000 pa and certainly not in the better parts of Hendon; so, if Bernie were now to die, the flat would be treated as comprised in his estate unless it came within the exception in *Hansard* (because *s 102B* was not in force in 1990). Melissa debated whether the exception in *Hansard* had been less restrictive than the wording of *s 102B*, which is specific in describing a gift 'of an undivided share of an interest in land'. Bernie had given away the whole, not just a share. Discussion of the case over a skinny latte with Carol confirmed her view.

Melissa reluctantly advised Bernie, who was still in good health, and his family to start again. Leon could give the flat back to his father free of CGT, because it had been his only residence throughout. Bernie could then put the flat into joint names with Sheila and Leon, to comply strictly with *s 102B*. Although that gift would use Bernie's nil rate band, it was a PET and gave Leon back the security that his disability demanded.

Some specific aspects of the code of gifts with reservation are dealt with at **14.5** below. It has been argued that the reservation of benefit provisions cannot apply to transfers of value which qualify for relief at 100%, because the effect of 100% relief is to reduce the value transferred to nil. As a result, the value transferred does not exceed £250 and, where the gift is an outright one and the total transfers of value made by the transferor in the relevant tax year to the transferee do not exceed £250, the operation of *IHTA 1984, s 20* is that the transfer of value is exempt and that the gift with reservation legislation does not apply to a disposal of property by way of a transfer exempt under *s 20*.

Does this argument work? It assumes that a transfer of value, even though reduced to nil, remains a transfer of value. That much appears from *s 3(1)*. Once the amount of a transfer of value has been fixed, it is possible to apply the 100% relief so as to reduce that value to nil. To exploit the argument, it may be appropriate to ensure, by some means, that the value transferred is more than nil but does not exceed £250. That will not be easy in the case of a straightforward gift of an interest in a business. It might be possible with a holding of shares or securities. For example, the holder of shares wishing to make a gift of, say, 500 shares might purchase one share from another shareholder before making the gift, so that part of the gift did not qualify for BPR because the transferor had not held that particular share for two years. Nice points of identification of property arise under this argument. Generally, HMRC will not be drawn into a review of BPR where no, or virtually no, tax is in issue, just so that the taxpayer can then make a larger transfer with certainty. A limited system of rulings has been introduced (described at **5.27**) but has, it seems, so far been little used.

An argument also runs that, where the donor of property qualifying for 100% relief dies having reserved a benefit in that property, then provided the donee still holds the property, 100% relief will still be available by virtue of *FA 1986, Sch 20, para 8*. Clearly, there is a risk in deliberately setting up a gift with reservation in order to exploit this particular provision: the death of the donor must occur whilst the law remains as it is now. Not every taxpayer will accept the implications of the need to die before the next Budget.

Gifts with reservation: de minimis

14.5   In a case that must serve as a warning to all settlors, *Personal representatives of Lyon deceased v HMRC* [2007] SpC 616, it was held that the receipt of only £15,965 from a trust of £2,700,000 could be the reservation of a benefit so as to taint the gift. The settlor retained a right of revocation and was a potential beneficiary of the trust, and it was in that capacity that the benefits were received. The way the trust had been operated showed that possession and enjoyment of the property had not been assumed at the beginning of the relevant period.

Gifts with reservation: treatment where BPR is available

14.6   An IHT charge may arise on property which is subject to a reservation at the death of the donor, or which is at that date no longer subject to reservation but was subject thereto at some time within seven years of the death. BPR may be available but special rules apply. These operate as if the occasion, by reference to which the tax is charged, were a transfer of value by the donee rather than one made by the donor.

Outline of the rules

The main rules are set out in *FA 1986, Sch 20, para 8*. They apply (see *para 8(1)*) in any of the three following circumstances:

- there is a disposal by gift of property which qualifies for BPR in relation to the donor; or

- there is a disposal by way of gift of property which qualifies for APR under *IHTA 1984, s 116*; or

- there is a disposal of shares or securities which qualify for APR under *s 122(1)*, ie agricultural property of companies.

FA 1986, Sch 20, para 1A provides that the test as to whether shares qualify for BPR is fixed by considering them as if they were owned by the donor, and had continued to be owned by him since the gift. However, in deciding whether or not either BPR or APR is available, the percentage at which relief may be claimed is fixed, in relation to the property in the gift, as if the transfer of value were one made by the donee.

This applies if the property that is subject to the gift with reservation charge that applies on the death of the donor (or on the giving up of the reservation) is property that:

- was comprised in the gift with reservation which qualified for APR or BPR when the original gift was made; and

- qualifies for relief by reference to the donee.

It becomes necessary to look at the history of ownership of the donor at the time of the gift. As a result, it may be necessary to trace the ownership, applying the rules in *Sch 20* (see eg *para 2*). As will be seen, the second condition can also cause difficulty.

Tracing the subject matter of the gift

This is one of the areas where there is no complete 'mix and match' between agricultural property and business property, contrary to the more general rule noted at **10.26** and considered in more detail at **12.5**. It has been argued that the tracing provisions operate favourably where the original property qualified for APR and the later property for BPR. The rule is otherwise where the original property was shares qualifying for APR and the later property qualified for BPR only.

The authority for this is the combined effects of *FA 1986, Sch 20, para 8(1)* and *(3)*. It is hard to see the policy objective behind *para 8(3)*. Although perhaps the risk of a charge under the gift with reservation provisions in exactly these circumstances is slight, one may imagine a possible occasion of negligence. This could occur where, through company reorganisation or the like, the taxpayer is still very much within the spirit of the APR and BPR rules but happens to fall foul of this particular sub-paragraph.

The effect of these relieving provisions is, in other respects, entirely logical. They treat the donor as making the hypothetical transfer rather than the donee, since the donee would not normally be able to show that he had owned the relevant asset for two years before the deemed transfer to him. The result (see *para 8(2)*) is that the donee steps into the shoes of the donor and counts the donor's ownership of the asset prior to the gift as part of the ownership requirement of the donee.

Equally, occupation by the donor of property prior to disposal, and occupation by the donor after that disposal, is treated as occupation by the donee.

The position of the donee

The donee may receive the benefit of the donor's period of ownership as described above, but in other respects the clawback legislation, when linked to gifts with reservation, still looks to the notional transfer by the donee. Thus, if the requirements of BPR are not met, perhaps because the donee does not control the company that uses an asset he has been given, clawback may apply to a gift that otherwise satisfies the spirit or policy of the legislation, which seems unfair.

Further substitution rules affecting gifts with reservation

14.7   There are further substitution rules (see **Chapter 10**) where the donee has died. As far as any period up to the death of the donee is concerned, any reference in *FA 1986, Sch 20, para 8* to the donee is construed as being a reference also to the personal representatives of the donee or to the beneficiary of any will or intestacy affecting the donee.

Further rules relate to shareholdings which are the subject of gifts with reservation. These concern only the situation where control is in issue, for example under *IHTA 1984, s 105(1)(b), 105(1)(cc)* or *122(1)(b)*. Who must show control? The issue is decided on the hypothesis that the donor owned the shares even after the making of the gift. This will generally facilitate the claim to BPR.

Example 14.3: obstinate director

Owen owned 66% of Intellectual Resources Ltd, from which he drew a salary which far exceeded the commercial value of any work that he did for that company. On 30 June 2006, he gave 16% of the company to his friend Colin but insisted that his salary remained the same, notwithstanding the gift.

Colin kept the shares in the company, which is a non-farming company. Being a minority holding, those shares did not at that time, under the law as it then was, qualify in their own right for full BPR, because they did not give Colin sufficient votes in the company. The failure by Owen to reduce his salary to commercial levels was a reservation of benefit.

Owen' died in January 2008. Examination of the gift at that stage shows that Colin has held the shares for 18 months only. That is not a long enough period to qualify for BPR under *s 106*, but the rules operate to credit Colin with Owen's period of ownership by treating the shares as if still held by Owen. Further, it is accepted that the transfer is from a 66% controlling holding because the other shares retained by Owen are taken into account. As a result, 100% BPR is available.

Example14.4: negligence avoided in the nick of time

Denis formed a company in May 2003 to carry out farming activities. He kept 79% of the issued shares in the company, which the following month bought farmland. By October 2008, Denis' son Sam had joined him in the farming operation and Denis was considering a gift of shares to Sam. He consulted Geoff, explaining that he was really not in good health and that his doctors had given him ten months to live at the most. He wished to make a gift of the shares but still retain his (artificially high) salary as a director of the company. He was considering a gift of between 28% and, at the outside, 51% of the company, though he made it clear to Geoff that he did not really wish to part with control of the family business.

Geoff advised on the tax effect of the minimum gift by Denis, of 28% of the company to Sam. The fact that Denis retained a high salary would make the gift one with reservation. Geoff considered that this might not be fatal since, if Sam retained the shares, the rules would operate to credit Sam with his father's period of ownership and to treat the transfer as being from Denis' controlling shareholding.

Geoff argued that relief would be available on the gift with reservation at 100% and that, even if Denis were to die as early as August 2009, provided the shares had been retained by Sam, relief would still be available on the transfer at 100%.

Fortunately, before posting the letter, Geoff ran it past his assistant, Melissa. She observed that, although the situation might be considered to be similar to that of a gift in a non-farming company, there was actually a distinction between the rules for BPR and for APR. There was no provision for APR exactly parallel to *FA 1986, Sch 20, para 8(1A)*, which relates only to securities qualifying for BPR under *IHTA 1984, s 105(1)*. Melissa therefore considered that, although relief would be available at 100% on the gift with reservation, there would be no relief if Denis were to die, because the test would be the availability of relief on a hypothetical transfer *by Sam* of his shares in August 2009. Since the gift was proposed to be of 28% of the company only, it would not qualify for APR since minority shareholdings in farming companies do not so qualify. It would not be possible to 'borrow' control in this circumstance, as it would have been in relation to a non-farming company.

Melissa went on to argue that BPR, rather than APR, would be available, insofar as the shares qualified as being shares in a trading company. That would, however, force Sam to demonstrate that the company was indeed a trading company and that there were within the company no excepted assets. Melissa observed that not infrequently the trade of farming companies is carried on not by the companies themselves but by managers for the company or even tenants. Thus, the availability of BPR may be in doubt where the APR test is not satisfied, because it may sometimes be difficult to show that the company is carrying on a trade, or is wholly or mainly trading, rather than merely holding land that is farmed by others.

With this in mind, Melissa suggested that the gift by Denis to Sam should be of not less than 51% of the company. Since Denis was reluctant to abandon any of his present salary, he would not lose any income by making the larger gift. Melissa argued that, in the event of Denis' early death, relief would be available in respect of the gift, provided Sam retained the shares given to him. This was because:

- it was available on the original gift with reservation;

- Sam would have kept the subject matter of the gift;

- viewing the matter as at August 2009, it could be shown that Sam had a shareholding which controlled the company, thus satisfying the requirements of *s 123*; and

- the minimum period of ownership would be treated as satisfied by virtue of the rule in *FA 1986, Sch 20, para 8(3)* by reference to *para 8(1)(c)*.

Example 14.5: clawback avoided

Alan farmed in partnership with his son Barry and daughter-in-law Clare. When Alan's wife died he moved to a bungalow built on one of the fields, and Barry and Clare took over the farmhouse. Alan had owned the freehold of the farm for many years but did not charge the partnership a rent. On 6 June 2006, Alan gave the farmhouse and the farm buildings next to it to Barry with 15 acres of pasture adjoining. Alan retained 300 acres of farmland. There was no adjustment to the profit-sharing ratio at the time of the gift.

On 1 January 2008, there was an opportunity to buy 75 acres of land close to the farmhouse and, as part of a financing arrangement, Barry transferred the farmhouse and land that had been given to him by Alan into joint names with Clare, so that they could between them buy the extra 75 acres.

On 7 March 2011, Alan died and it became necessary to consider the rules both as to clawback and gifts with reservation. In this situation, there have been two transfers, each of which will be relevant to the tax analysis.

Alan's gift on 6 June 2006

Benefit may have been reserved out of the gift, even though Alan vacated the house, because part of the house may have served as the farm office, and the 15 acres may have contributed in some way to farm profits (if there ever were any) and there has been no change in the partnership shares of profit to recognise the fact that Alan had less capital in the business after the gift than before. (There is a contrary argument, namely that Alan did not reserve any benefit out of the gift because there was no direct benefit to him and because his profit share remained unchanged and was a fair share for the work that he did; but assume for the purposes of this example that benefit was reserved.)

The HMRC approach (see IHTM24201) is to test this gift for relief in 2006 and to test it again at the time of clawback, ie March 2011. Their procedure then requires (see IHTM24202) different treatment according to whether the clawback charge arises on the death of the original transferor or on a failed PET where the PET was the release of the benefit.

Where, as in this example, the clawback is (or may be) occasioned by death, HMRC consider whether, if the house and 15 acres had still been owned by Alan at the date of his death, relief would have been available. In this example, it may be assumed that the house and 15 acres, if considered on their own, might not have qualified for relief but, in the context of Alan's previous estate relief, might have been allowable.

Unfortunately, that is not the end of the matter. As was noted in the review of relief from clawback at **10.23**, it becomes necessary to apply the four additional conditions for lifetime transfers (see IHTM24173), namely that:

- Barry has owned all the property continuously from 2006 to 2011 (which he has not);

- the property is not being sold;

- it still qualifies for APR; and

- it has been occupied for agricultural purposes from the transfer to the date of death.

On the 'four tests' basis, clawback would apply.

There is some qualification to the rules, because the test as to whether the house and 15 acres still qualify for APR is by reference to Alan rather than by reference to Barry. That is helpful because, seen in the context of Barry, the house might be viewed in the context of only 90 acres (subject to the doubts that were expressed at **2.17**).

Barry's gift on 1 January 2008

Again, there has been no change in profit-sharing ratios and still no rent is charged, so it is arguable that there has been a reservation by Barry out of the gift to Clare. In the event of the death of Barry within seven years, *FA 1986, Sch 20, para 8* could be applied to Barry's gift. There is one intellectual difficulty here: BPR and APR serve only to reduce the value transferred. They therefore require a transfer to take place before they are in point. In relation to the gift in January 2008, no clawback charge arises on the death of Alan because, at that date, Barry is still alive. On that basis, the provisions that import relief from clawback are not relevant because clawback itself is not relevant to the gift in 2008 but only to the gift in 2006. Therefore, even though *Sch 20, para*

8 would operate to treat the house and 15 acres as still being part of Barry's estate on 7 March 2011 if he also had died on that date, those provisions can most unfortunately not be relied upon to deem the house and 15 acres still to be owned entirely by Barry for the purpose of preserving the earlier gift in 2006 from clawback.

Fortunately, in this situation, relief is preserved by *FA 1986, Sch 20, para 2(4)*. The point is recognised in IHTM14374 but could be clearer; in any case, it is for the adviser to work out reliefs and for HMRC to get on with the business of collecting tax. *Paragraph 2(4)* specifically addresses the possibility that has arisen here, namely that the donee makes a gift of property that was comprised in the gift to him. Since the gift is not back to Alan but is to Clare, Barry is treated as continuing to have possession and enjoyment of all of the house and 15 acres and not merely a half interest in it. Reading that back to Alan's gift, we can deem Barry still to own the entirety of what Alan gave him, so the 'four tests' are satisfied and clawback does not apply to Alan's gift.

Gifts with reservation: inter-spouse transfer

14.8   The case of *IRC v Eversden and Another* [2002] EWHC 1360 (Ch) illustrated the interpretation of *FA 1986, s 102(5)(a)* as it was before legislation overturned the decision of the courts, introducing *FA 1986, s 102(5A)* for disposals after 19 June 2003. As amended, the law now provides that even an exempt transfer is within the gift with reservation rules.

One significant aspect of the case was the failure of the Inland Revenue to argue that SP 7/79 should apply so as to deem the settlor to be a tenant for life. That failure must raise some doubts as to the legal authority of SP 10/79; there have been other opportunities since *Eversden* for the principle to be tested, which have not been taken.

A feature of *Eversden* that has survived the amended legislation in *s 102(5A)* is the subtle argument concerning the change of statutory basis for holding of property that has occurred by virtue of the enactment of *Trusts of Land and Appointment of Trustees Act 1996`*. Every co-owner of a house held on trust for sale under the *Law of Property Act 1925* had an equal right of occupation. The Special Commissioner in *Eversden* had so found on the authority of *Bull v Bull* [1955] 1 QB 234. On that basis, the settlor could occupy the whole house by virtue of the 5% share that did not pass to the substantive trusts for her husband and the other beneficiaries. She did not need to enjoy any benefit from the 95% given away. Those were the rules in force at the time of establishing the settlement but, by 1998, when the original property was sold and the replacement property purchased, *TLATA 1996* was in force, with the result that the High Court had to decide whether the settlor now had rights of occupation under the *1996 Act*.

Lightfoot J decided that the settlor did become entitled to occupy the land by virtue of *TLATA 1996, s 12(1)*. That section provides that a beneficiary who has an interest in possession is entitled to occupy land that is held in trust provided that:

- the purpose of the trust includes making the land available for his occupation or for the occupation of beneficiaries of a class of which he is a member; or
- the land is held by the trustees so as to be so available.

Lightfoot J considered the purposes for which the trust had been established. However, this examination of the *1996 Act*, while interesting academically, is *obiter*. Lightfoot J concluded, as already noted, that the entire settlement was protected by *s 102(5)*.

DEDUCTIBILITY OF DEBTS

14.9   The treatment of liabilities was considered in **Chapter 8**. The rescheduling of debt may be beneficial both in relation to BPR and APR, although the possibilities in respect of APR are greater.

As was noted in **Chapter 8**, an operation of this kind is not a PET. There is no need for seven years to expire. Similarly, the two-year rule for BPR does not apply; the effect is immediate. There may be expense in connection with the advice and the disposals, but there need not be any other substantial tax costs. In particular, it becomes important to examine the availability of liquid resources which can be used to discharge 'unnecessary' debts. Given the 'discrimination' against sole traders described in **Chapter 8**, repayment of debt can be particularly effective for sole traders.

It was also noted in **Chapter 8** that for APR, in the absence of the rules contained in *IHTA 1984, s 110, s 162* applies debts in an unrestricted way. A liability which is an encumbrance on a specific item of property is taken, as far as possible, to reduce the value of that property. APR will therefore be lost only in respect of qualifying assets subject to specific charges.

Example 14.6: debt-shifting

Brendan and Mary have farmed successfully for many years. On part of the farm, they have developed not merely a farm shop but virtually an out-of-town shopping centre. They have created franchises for the sale of goods which have no connection with farming. The farmland as a whole has been security for the purchase of land from time to time and for the development of the shopping centre.

They consult Carol, who advises that the level of involvement by the family in the sales of goods from the shopping centre is now so slight, by comparison with the work done by others, and the revenue from the farm shop is so small, by comparison with the franchise income, that, even though the management of the enterprise takes a considerable amount of time, there is a strong risk that it will not qualify for BPR, being regarded as 'wholly or mainly holding investments'. She therefore advises Brendan and Mary to reschedule the loans so as to charge them on the shopping centre rather than on the farmland, with an immediate increase in the overall amount of APR available to the family.

Example 14.7: further shifting of debt

Gerald, a widower whose late wife had used her nil rate band, has traded successfully as a printer for many years. He has learnt that he has contracted an illness from which he is unlikely to recover and that he has only six months to live. On a review of his estate by Carol, whom he consults for IHT purposes, it appears that he holds the following assets which are, to a greater or lesser extent, connected with his business:

	£
Unit 3, Welsford Trading Estate (print shop)	170,000
Unit 1a, Welsford Trading Estate (store)	35,000
17 Lyhart Street (shop premises)	70,000
The Chestnuts, Swardeston (residence)	300,000
Investments (mainly cash)	75,000
Heidelberg Printing Press	275,000
Other stock, plant and machinery	100,000

Gerald has never kept his non-trading activities entirely separate from the printing trade. The assets of each have supported the other. There are two loans outstanding: loan A, of £30,000; and loan B, of £100,000. Investigation shows that loan A, secured on Unit 3 (from which the business trades), was in fact applied in the purchase of the shop premises at 17 Lyhart Street, which have never been used for the purposes of the trade and in respect of which there was never any intention of such use. On the other hand, the proceeds of loan B, secured on the residence, can be traced specifically to the purchase of the Heidelberg Press.

A pro forma account for IHT planning purposes suggests the following calculation:

Personal or private assets (no BPR):	£	£
Investments	75,000	
The Chestnuts	300,000	
17 Lyhart Street	70,000	
		445,000

Business assets:	£	£
Unit 3	170,000	
Unit 1a	35,000	
Heidelberg Press	275,000	
Stock, plant and machinery	100,000	
Less loans	(130,000)	
		450,000
Estate before reliefs		895,000
BPR at 100%		(450,000)
Nil rate band (August 2011)		(325,000)
		125,000
Tax at 40%		50,000

Carol negotiates with the lenders for loan A to be rescheduled and charged specifically on the shop premises. Loan B is in part discharged from the surplus cash, with the balance being secured specifically on the Heidelberg Press. As a result, the cash and the non-business assets are reduced in value, but the amount of loan A, which could otherwise have reduced BPR, no longer does so. This results in a revised calculation:

	£	£
Investments (net of Carol's £500 costs)	44,500	
The Chestnuts	300,000	
17 Lyhart Street	70,000	
		414,500
Unit 3	170,000	
Unit 1a	35,000	
Heidelberg Press	275,000	
Stock, plant and machinery	100,000	
		580,000
Less loan B	(100,000)	
		480,000
Estate before relief		894,500
BPR at 100%		(480,000)
Nil rate band		(325,000)
Estate after reliefs etc		89,500
Tax at 40%		35,800

14.9 General planning points

	£
Net saving: reduction in tax	14,200
Less costs	500
Net saving	13,700

The effect of *IHTA 1984, ss 110* and *162* illustrated above is limited to property of the type in the illustration. For holders of other kinds of property, the scope for reducing IHT by moving debt may be slightly greater.

Example 14.8: another debt-shifting example

Quentin, a bachelor aged 86, holds the following assets:

	£
Shares in Neptune Ltd, traded on PLUS	75,000
Debt on purchase of shares	(25,000)
	50,000
Partnership share: Marine Chandlers	50,000
Unit 6 Quayside Trading Estate	75,000
Liability incurred on purchase	(30,000)
	45,000
Residence (free of mortgage)	350,000
Bank deposits	40,000
Quoted investments, ISAs	50,000

Unit 6 is occupied by Marine Chandlers. Quentin consults Geoff, who is a customer of Marine Chandlers. After some delay, Geoff produces the following pro forma account for IHT planning purposes:

	£	£
Residence		350,000
Cash		40,000
Investments		50,000
Unquoted shares	75,000	
Less liability	25,000	
Net value for BPR		50,000
Partnership share		50,000
Business premises	75,000	
Less liability	(30,000)	
Net value for BPR		45,000

	£	£
Estate		585,000
BPR claim:		
Shares	50,000	
Partnership share	50,000	
Premises*	45,000*	
Total claim		(145,000)
Estate after reliefs		440,000
Nil rate band, autumn 2011		(325,000)
Chargeable estate		115,000
Tax at 40%		6,000

* Regrettably, Geoff has missed the point that BPR on the business premises falls within *s 105(1)(d)* and is available at 50% rather than at 100%. The true liability is therefore £55,000. Apart from that, Geoff's basic advice is sound, which is to shift the debt away from the relevant business property.

Quentin renegotiates the loans. The £25,000 secured on the unquoted shares is reduced, as to £10,000 from cash resources with the balance being secured on the quoted investments, which Quentin is reluctant to sell in a bad market. The loan of £30,000 is re-secured, at a cost of £500, on the residence. Geoff's revised IHT calculation is as follows:

	£	£
Residence	350,000	
Loan secured on house	(30,500)	
		319,500
Cash		30,000
Investments	50,000	
Less loan	(15,000)	
		35,000
Unquoted shares		75,000
Partnership share		50,000
Business premises		75,000
Estate		584,500
BPR claim:		
Shares	75,000	
Partnership share	50,000	
Premises	75,000*	
Total claim		(200,000)

	£
Estate after reliefs	384,000
Nil rate band, autumn 2011	(325,000)
Chargeable estate	59,000
Tax at 40%	23,600
Tax saving, on Geoff's figures* (46,000 – 23,600):	22,400

*Geoff made the same mistake as before: had he correctly calculated the relief at £37,500, he would have realised that the chargeable estate amounted to £97,000, giving rise to a liability of £38,800. However, there is still a net saving (before Geoff's charges) on the exercise of £16,200.

RESTRICTION ON OFFSET OF DEBT

14.10   One situation where debt may not reduce the estate for IHT has been illustrated by *St Barbe Green v CIR* [2005] EWHC 14 (Ch), where the holder of an interest in possession had died. There was substantial value in two trust funds but the deceased himself, in his personal capacity, was insolvent. The trustees set the personal debts off against the trust funds. The Revenue rejected this treatment. Appeal to the High Court failed. Mann J held that the words 'except as otherwise provided by this Act' in *s 5(3)* qualified the principle that debts were deductible. The personal estate must be seen in isolation: once debts had reduced it to nil, there was no asset against which further debt could be set. The trust funds gained no benefit by way of offset.

Probably few settlors would want trust funds to be dissipated by advances to cover the debts of beneficiaries: that would defeat one of the main purposes of settling funds rather than making an outright gift. However, the *St Barbe Green* case shows that it could be useful for trustees to have a power to advance capital to a life tenant; and that, if that power were exercised seven years before death, the funds to be taxed would be less and (for those who care about such things) family honour might be saved by avoiding insolvency. Most trustees will simply preserve the trust fund to give the next generation a chance to dissipate it.

BUY AND SELL

14.11   The issue of whether or not there is a contract for the sale of property was considered in some detail in **Chapter 6** in relation to business property, where reference was made not only to SP 12/80 but to the ICAEW memorandum TR557 which considered 'buy and sell' agreements in some detail. TR557 specifically identified a number of provisions which might be found in partnership agreements and suggested the 'apparent effect' on which the Inland Revenue commented on 5 July 1982. The result of this can be seen in several situations:

- The partnership determines on the death or retirement of the partner and his share remains his asset: BPR is available both in respect of lifetime transfers and on death.

- On the death of a partner, the partnership continues but the share of the partner dying or retiring is free to be sold and, if not sold, passes to the personal representatives or a beneficiary: BPR is available both in respect of lifetime transfers and on death.

- The situation is as just described and the personal representatives have an option to sell and the continuing partners an option, but no obligation, to buy: BPR is available both in respect of lifetime transfers and on death.

- The partnership continues notwithstanding death or retirement, but the share of the outgoing partner automatically accrues to the continuing partners who must then pay for that share (usually according to a predetermined formula): no BPR is available in respect of the share, whether on a lifetime transfer or on death.

- The partnership continues as before and the partnership share passes to the personal representatives but those representatives are under an obligation to sell. Here the situation is finely judged and will depend on the particular circumstances. Even though there is, within the context of the partnership agreement, a contract to sell the partnership share on the happening of an event which has not yet occurred, BPR may be available in respect of a lifetime transfer if that transfer itself, within the terms of the partnership deed, does not trigger the automatic purchase provisions. In the event of death, however, no BPR will be available, because the automatic purchase provisions have, as a result, been triggered.

- The partnership continues on death or retirement and where there is no obligation within the partnership agreement to sell. Here, BPR will be available both in respect of lifetime transfers and on death, even though the outgoing partner may have executed a will directing the executors to sell. This is logical: the will itself could be revoked at any time and, in the absence of compulsion within the partnership deed, there is no reason, for the mere intention of the outgoing partner that the property should be sold, to deny him relief during his lifetime.

A way out, perhaps?

14.12   Occasionally, the practitioner will be faced with a situation where it seems that, through inadvertence, a partnership deed has been drawn up which, by including a binding contract for the sale of a partnership share, denies BPR to the outgoing partner. The practitioner should look carefully at the present constitution of the partnership. Not infrequently, it may be discovered that the partnership deed is of some antiquity and that there have been partnership changes since it was first signed. If, as is equally likely, there has been insufficient formality in the accession of later partners, there may well in fact be a partnership at will only. All the present partners have informally adopted the partnership agreement and the accounts have been prepared in a manner which is entirely consistent with it, without realising that any one of them at any time could retire from the partnership at will without being bound either as to any provisions as to notice or in relation to the offending obligations respectively to sell and to buy.

OPTIONS IN RELATION TO SHARES

14.13   Shares may have variable rights such that the entitlement to the distribution of profits or to assets in a winding up may differ in a future accounting period from the present one. The percentage of profits or assets for the current accounting period is the lower of:

- the percentage to which the parent company is entitled in the current accounting period; and

- the percentage to which it would be entitled in any later accounting period in which the rights had changed (see *ICTA 1988, Sch 18, para 5*).

Where the shares or securities are held within arrangements which might result in a change to entitlement, either to distributions or to assets at some future time, *ICTA 1988, Sch 18* assumes that effect would be given to those arrangements. Those arrangements are, however, confined to the variation of rights attaching to shares and securities; they do not include arrangements which could affect the ownership of shares (see *J Sainsbury plc v O'Connor* [1990] STC 516). The Court of Appeal there held, in a case which concerned group relief rather than IHT, that the mere existence of an option to purchase shares did not affect the beneficial ownership of those shares by the taxpayer company.

RETIREMENT

Consider alternatives to an immediate sale, especially where ill-health may be an issue?

14.14   The sale of a business can be a stressful affair and there will be many considerations apart from tax. The main shareholder in the family company may feel that it is his duty to see the sale through, to complete his life's work and to provide his family with lasting security. On the other hand, it may be better for him (usually it is 'he' rather than 'she' in this situation) to take a back seat and to let others resolve the problem whilst he retains a significant interest in the business through to his death. That way, he may save both CGT, through the uplift on death, and IHT, by retaining assets qualifying for BPR.

In *Swain Mason and others v Mills & Reeve* [2011] EWHC 410 (Ch), these issues were raised in a case that will be a warning to all practitioners and which merits close examination, even though at the time of writing it is not yet concluded. Mr Swain, a company director who was 61, overweight and who had previously suffered a heart attack, consulted solicitors in June 2006 about selling his controlling shareholding in the family company. He was by then spending most of his time in Thailand and had agreed in principle to sell the company to the current management. The solicitors advised in a letter in January 2007 about the tax consequences of the sale. A letter applying for certain tax clearances referred to Mr Swain's 'continuing weak health', to his heart attack and diabetes and to the fact that he would not return to active work. That letter also showed that Mr Swain, though still domiciled, resident and ordinarily resident in the UK, might cease to be so resident as soon as the 2007/08 tax year started, ie within a few weeks.

Mr Swain made an appointment for a hospital procedure to take place in Thailand on 17 February 2007 and told all relevant parties, including the solicitors (though in a somewhat oblique way), that this was his priority and that he would not be attending board meetings. The sale went ahead on 31 January 2007. Mr Swain died during the hospital procedure.

IHT on his estate was greater than it would have been had the sale been deferred, because BPR had been lost. CGT was also incurred that might have been avoided. Tax took about one-third of the sale proceeds. The daughters sued the solicitors, arguing that they should have advised delaying the sale until after the operation. The solicitors argued that the risk of death had been negligible: there was evidence that it was less than one chance in one thousand.

The case was dogged with difficulty over evidence, both expert and medical, and over pleading exactly what the family considered had gone wrong. One hearing had to be abandoned because a key witness was detained by the Iceland volcano and could not attend court. The pleadings were amended so as to claim that the January advice letter should have extended to advice on IHT and that, had it done, Mr Swain would have sought further advice before proceeding. It was only quite late in the proceedings that expert evidence was adduced, which suggested several courses of action that might have been put to the company director to mitigate the burden of taxes.

An important procedural issue was whether any solicitor dealing with this type of case must advise on the tax consequences of death intervening and possibilities for mitigation of that tax; or whether this case proceeded only on the basis that the solicitors knew their client's state of health. The family sought to amend the pleadings so as to allege that the solicitors should have advised on the tax consequences. The solicitors resisted the amendments but the judge ruled against them and allowed the case to proceed on the revised basis. The preliminary report of the expert witness, and more evidence from the family, were lodged. The solicitors applied to the trial judge to disallow the amendment. He (Peter Smith J) gave them short shrift, going so far as to describe them as playing 'pre-CPR games' and, later, their actions as 'an abuse of the process of the court'. As he predicted, the solicitors appealed.

The Court of Appeal was concerned with trial procedure rather than with the merits of the case. Peter Smith J had been dismissive ('dead in the water') of the claimants' case as originally pleaded, based on the medical evidence for the solicitors and his, the judge's, personal knowledge of the procedure that Mr Swain underwent. The court considered all aspects of the case, even suggestions of bias against the judge, and a little known but important case on procedure, *Worldwide Corporation Ltd v GPT Ltd* [1998] EWCA Civ 1894. They considered an expanded version of the pleading but decided that it had been brought to the case far too late. As a result, the case to be tried became narrower than the family would have liked, ie that negligence must be linked to knowledge of the hospital operation, and was directed to be tried by a different judge.

Thus the case came before Arnold J who examined carefully the extent of the solicitors' retainer. One issue was whether the clients were getting other tax advice elsewhere. The question was whether the solicitors had excluded tax advice as to the effect of the disposal. Arnold J held that they had, but by only a narrow margin, because the letter could have been more specific about IHT and CGT. He concluded:

> 'It would be entirely understandable if, at the end of this case, Claire, Abby, Gemma and Christa were left with a strong feeling that they had been ill-served by the legal profession. Nevertheless, for the reasons I have given, I conclude that the Claimants' claim must be dismissed.'

What can we learn from Swain Mason?

14.15   One principle underlies the entire text of this work: that we learn far more from those cases that go wrong than from a passive study of the statute. All the 'Geoff' examples are designed to support that theory. While the solicitors in *Swain Mason* may escape liability, the public may feel that they have done so on a technicality; if that is the feeling, the best interests of the profession will not have been served. Practitioners will take home from the case the following precepts:

- keep in touch with your client: do not 'steamroll' a transaction through;

- in a commercial case, remember the 'private client' issues: have regard to all taxes; but

- if sued, do not throw in the towel but use all means allowed by the court rules to defend your position.

That will be small comfort to clients, who may have hoped that judges like Peter Smith J would uphold their rights. They may remember that he heard the case of *RSPCA v Sharp* [2010] EWHC 268 at first instance and there made observations about another equally eminent firm of solicitors, but was overruled on appeal. Clients should learn these principles:

- get advice on all aspects of a proposed transaction;

- give full instructions;

- don't rush; and

- if things go wrong, research carefully before embarking on litigation and get all your evidence ready at the beginning.

More interestingly, how would we have advised Mr Swain? The expert in that case was Andrew Farley of Wilsons LLP, who considered that a competent solicitor would have recommended a shorrt delay. From 6 April 2007, Mr Swain could have claimed to be non-resident for CGT. It would, however, take three years to lose UK domicile but Mr Swain could have invested the proceeds in Free of Tax for Residents Abroad ('FOTRA') securities. These are exempt gilt-edged securities which are excluded from IHT within *IHTA 1984, s 6(2)*. Insofar as Mr Swain received payment in loan notes, FOTRA would be no help, but perhaps insurance cover for three years, until UK domicile had been shed, might have been possible. Would such delay have scuppered the deal? Would it have taken too long even to get tax advice? To cover that eventuality, Mr Farley suggested mutual, but not matching, options.

How good at their job are practitioners expected to be? This was discussed by Arnold J at para 146 and following, quoting with approval the statement of Oliver J in *Midland Bank Trust Co Ltd v Hett, Stubbs & Kemp* [1979] Ch 484 at 402, that the test is 'what the reasonably competent practitioner would do having regard to the standards normally adopted in his profession' The standard by which specialist or 'above average' practitioners will be judged in these circumstances is illustratedin *Swain-Mason,* where the defendants, a national firm whom many will consider to be of outstanding repute, were to be judged by the standard of competence of firms with specialist tax departments We did not see exactly how matters were resolved in *Vinton and others v Fladgate Fielder* [2010] EWHC 904 (Ch), although it seemed likely that that case might, at trial, go against the solicitors: see comment at **6.5**.

Inactive partner still a partner

14.16   *IHTA 1984, s 105(1)(a)*, as was noted in **Chapter 5**, allows relief in respect of property consisting of an interest in a business. There is no requirement in *s 105* that the owner of an interest in a business should be actively concerned in the furtherance of the trade. It has been noted that *s 103(3)* excludes from the definition of 'business' one which is 'carried on otherwise than for gain', but that is not taken to mean that the elderly partner who contributes very little which is positive to the running of the business (and may even obstruct or frustrate the efforts of younger partners, perhaps his own children) is carrying on the business otherwise than for gain so as to deny himself BPR.

In practical terms, there may be difficult decisions to make. If the elderly partner leaves the business, younger partners, able to make business decisions without having to consult the retiring partner, may be able to drive the business forward more successfully than before. On the other hand, the old partner will often have capital in the business which is substantial by comparison with the capital of the younger partners. For as long as the capital of the old partner remains as true capital, then, subject to the rules as to excepted assets which were examined in **Chapter 7**, BPR will be available on the interest of the old partner. From the standpoint of saving IHT, the old man should stay on (but fit in).

Leaving money in

14.17   In practical terms, it will often be impossible for the younger partners to introduce into the business capital equal to what the old partner holds. If the old partner is to take a less active role, the question arises how his interest should be treated in the accounts. Loans to a partnership are not part of a business, as was noted earlier in this chapter. It is therefore important that the interest of the elderly partner should not be converted from capital account to loan account, since the balance of any loan account will not qualify for BPR.

This issue was examined in *Beckman v IRC* [2000] STC (SCD) 59. Mrs H ('mother') was in partnership with her daughter Mrs B. Mother retired in 1993. There had been no partnership agreement but profits had been shared equally. Mother's capital account was £169,185 just before she retired. Four years later, it was down to £112,811 and it was the same figure at her death. The daughter argued that that was mother's interest in the business and that BPR ought to apply.

Whilst the Revenue agreed that mother had had an interest in the business up to the time of her retirement, they argued that her relationship with the business changed fundamentally when she retired. The money due to her was an unpaid debt representing the capital and undrawn share of profit. After she retired, she no longer had an interest in the business within *s 105(1)(a)*.

The Special Commissioner agreed with the Inland Revenue. Before her retirement, mother had enjoyed the rights of management and suffered the liabilities of a partner. After mother retired, her rights were like those of a creditor. The capital account did not represent an interest in the business within *s 105(1)(a)* after the retirement.

A gift of such a loan account, made by increasing the loan account of one partner and reducing that of another, attracts no relief. On the other hand, BPR may be available to shelter a transfer between the capital account of one partner and another, subject to the observations noted in Example 5.2 of transfers by Ellen (where it could be demonstrated that the interest which Ellen transferred had not been owned by her for the requisite period).

The partnership structure is well adapted to succession within a family, provided that arrangements are put in hand early enough. Where the younger generation are admitted to partnership with a fair share of profit, not all of which is drawn, there is the opportunity over many years for substantial capital accounts to be established by the younger generation and for the older partner or partners to draw fully their shares of profits, with any capital requirements of the business being provided by the younger partners. Difficulties arise where, as will commonly be the case, no proper arrangements for succession have been taken until the older partners are within a few years of retirement. In the case of farming businesses where the return on capital may have been low, the older partners will be quite happy to part with substantial assets as long as their income is not thereby diminished. One structure which may be appropriate is to divide profits in tranches, first recognising the time and other skills which each partner brings to the business, then the capital which each makes available to it.

All too often, the older partner will wish, notwithstanding, say, a gift of farmland, to enjoy the share of profits which should in commercial terms go to the donee of the gift of the land. It is at this stage sometimes argued that the older partner should accept a smaller share of profit but nevertheless continue to draw as much as he has done hitherto. This is on the basis that the younger partners, to whom a larger share of the profits have been credited, should refrain from drawing those profits precisely because the old partners have just taken out of the business the available liquidity.

The difficulty of such a scheme lies in the argument that there is a reservation of benefit by the older partner, in that the drawings policy has been fixed artificially so as to benefit him. A better structure is for drawings to be on a similar basis for all partners. If that puts the business under strain financially, and if specific capital expenditure is contemplated, then the younger partners may decide, as a transaction entirely separate from regular drawings, to introduce capital as and when it is needed.

MONEY BOX

What is possible?

14.18   Clearly, there is an advantage in holding assets within the favourable tax environment of a business, subject only to the normal commercial risks of investment. The limit of what may reasonably be held in such a business was examined in some detail in **Chapter 7** in relation to excepted assets. As was noted there, particularly in the flowchart on page 175, the test can be quite strict. Apart from the guidance contained in *IHTA 1984, s 112*, there is little authority on the subject other than observations in the HMRC Manual and a decision of the Special Commissioner in *Barclays Bank Trust Co Ltd v IRC* [1998] STC (SCD) 125, examined in some detail at **7.11**. Where a taxpayer seeks to shelter money by leaving it in a business, he should take steps to establish the records which will tend to show that the business either had an immediate need for that money or had a need of it in the reasonably near future for, as was noted in *Barclays Bank Trust Co Ltd v IRC*, some 'palpable business purpose'. The hallmark of money in a business which may very well not qualify for BPR is that it lies in an account undisturbed from one year's end to the next, save for the addition of interest.

The other important recent case on the issue is *Brown, Ralph Louis (executors of) v IRC* [1996] STC (SCD) 277, where the Special Commissioner had to consider whether the nature of a company's business had changed after the sale of the main asset of the business.

The deceased owned 99% of the issued share capital of an unquoted company, Gaslight Entertainments Ltd Company. In January 1985, an offer was accepted for the night-club run by the business. The proceeds of sale went onto short-term deposit whilst Mr Brown searched for an alternative night-club for the company to purchase. He died in November 1986, at which time most of the proceeds of sale were still on deposit. The case was brought by way of appeal from the claim of the Revenue that, following the sale of the night-club, effectively the business of the company was no more than holding investments and thus disqualified from BPR by *s 105(3)*.

It appeared to be agreed between the parties that the company was carrying on a business during 1985 and 1986; the question was the nature of the business. What the directors intended to do was not a full answer to that question; it was important to look at what the company was actually doing.

On the evidence, the Special Commissioner could not agree with the Revenue that the business consisted wholly or mainly of making or holding investments. Whilst acknowledging that the proceeds of sale were held in an account which produced income, they were available at short notice so that, when Mr Brown found a suitable alternative night-club, he could buy it. There was evidence to show what efforts he had made to find an alternative venture. But for his illness and death, he might well have made a purchase. The administration and marketing of the company went on throughout the interregnum.

Brown v CIR is a case on its own particular facts but it does show how, in suitable circumstances, money may be held within a business on deposit and yet qualify for BPR. When cases come before the Special Commissioner, the evidence is extremely important, since there are many instances where the higher courts on appeal have refused to overturn the decision of the Special Commissioner. It is for that reason that any taxpayer wishing to use a business as a 'money-box' should take great care to keep the records that will tend to show the purpose for which the money is being held. Short-term deposits are more likely to qualify for BPR than long-term fixed deposits.

VARIOUS STRUCTURES

Wholly or mainly

14.19   There was a lengthy examination, again in **Chapter 9**, of the line of cases which examine the test in *IHTA 1984, s 105(3)* as to whether a business consisted wholly or mainly of dealing in securities, stocks or shares, land or buildings; or making or holding investments. As was observed at the beginning of that chapter, this is a problem which can arise by stealth as the balance sheet of the business strengthens. With the exception of the recent case of *Brendan Peter James Furness* SpC 202 (noted at **9.8**), most of the decisions in this area have gone against the taxpayer, who should accordingly take care.

For the unincorporated business, there must come a point at which the holding of assets which have taken on the character of investments can threaten eligibility of much of the business to BPR at all. The question is one of degree, as was noted in the discussion of excepted assets in **Chapter 7**. The relevant factors are:

- the value of assets employed in each part of the business;
- the source of turnover;
- the source of profit; and
- the way the directors or partners spend their time.

One must then look at the business as a whole. Occasionally, where the holding of specific assets is borderline, it may be wise to extract from the balance sheet of the business those assets which are unlikely to qualify for BPR, so as to strengthen the argument that the remainder of the assets do qualify.

Dual/multiple company structure

14.20   **Chapter 7** also included an examination of the valuation principles which are applied where there are excepted assets, the view of HMRC as set out in the Shares Valuation Division Manual, and an illustration of a hybrid company.

Each company structure must be examined on its own. The operation of *ss 110(c)* and *112(2)* must be appreciated. Probably a trading company can, without threat to BPR, support a certain level of 'non-trading' investment. The difficulty is, as usual, in deciding how far to push that argument. There comes a point, which will be different for each trade, at which it has to be accepted that the bulk of the assets, income and activity of the company do not relate to trade and do not justify the protection of BPR. Before that point is reached, it may be helpful to remove from the group structure, if this can be done without serious tax charges in another connection, the investments or group companies which clearly are wholly or mainly holding investments.

USE OF RELEVANT PROPERTY TRUSTS TO SECURE 100% RELIEF

14.21   Several factors may encourage the owner of business or agricultural property to make a gift by way of lifetime trust. With limited exceptions, such as provision for the disabled, the creation of lifetime trusts has, since *FA 2006*, been a chargeable transfer. One reason for a discretionary trust is that the donor cannot make up his mind to whom to give the property among a group of potential beneficiaries such as children or grandchildren. Another is fear of dissipation by younger family members; another the fear of claims in matrimonial proceedings of younger family; a further and less positive factor may be the reluctance of the settlor to part with the asset save on terms that allow him to retain a degree of control or even, put bluntly, power over the asset and, by implication, over the beneficiaries.

In relation to non-business assets, there can be very good reasons to make a gift by way of a lifetime trust from which the settlor is excluded since, as a chargeable transfer, it allows holdover of gains under *TCGA 1992, s 260*. That argument is not as strong in relation to business assets, where *TCGA 1992, s 165* also gives (in relation to assets other than shares) relief by way of holdover from an immediate charge to CGT (provided the settlor retains no interest under the trust, which he should not do anyway, to avoid reservation of benefit). Given that a transfer to a relevant property trust is a chargeable one rather than a PET, the availability of 100% APR or BPR becomes highly relevant to the decision whether or not to make the gift at all. Frequently, a viable plan to mitigate the prospective burden of IHT is not implemented because it is recognised that there will be an immediate charge to tax, even though the payment of tax on the occasion of the gift can, in certain circumstances, earn for the transferor and transferee significant saving in tax at a later date.

AIM portfolio as a route to an investment trust?

14.22   A family may wish to pass wealth down a generation but may be unhappy with the risks inherent in holding unquoted shares in trading companies. The following strategy has been suggested.

Example 14.9: trustees averse to risk

Sarah, a serial entrepreneur, has £1,200,000 available from a successful business transaction and wishes to benefit her adult children Tanja and Uri. Using her established stock-picking skills, she invests in unquoted shares in trading companies. Insofar as this may represent reinvestment in assets qualifying for BPR, there may be no need to hold the shares for two years; but assume that she does hold them for that period. She then settles the shares, taking care not to reserve any benefit to herself. That is a chargeable transfer, greatly exceeding the nil rate band, so the availability of BPR must be tested. Assume that none of the AIM companies has a secondary listing on a recognised exchange and that BPR is allowed in full.

Clawback is not in point (see below). The trustees do not therefore need to retain the AIM shares; although, if they still hold them when the first ten-year charge falls due, that will reduce or eliminate the periodic charge. The trustees decide to limit their exposure to that charge by retaining part of the fund in assets that qualify for BPR, but liquidating as much of the fund as amounts from time to time to the current nil rate band. They then hold cash which they can use to help Tanja and Uri with advances or loans for house purchase.

One important aspect of such transfers is that the rules as to clawback are not relevant to fixing the IHT payable at lifetime rates on chargeable lifetime transfers. If the transferor dies within seven years, the 'top up' charge will apply unless the conditions are fulfilled which will save the transfer from clawback, for example in relation to agricultural property that the property remains agricultural property and is used as such. This was considered in some detail in **Chapter 10**. The availability of BPR, even at 50%, can greatly increase the value of the assets which a transferor is willing to settle on discretionary trusts. This particular point features strongly in the tax planning scheme, designed principally to save CGT, featured in the next section.

Associated operations: Reynaud v IRC

14.23   The structure adopted in *Reynaud v IRC* [1999] STC (SCD) 185 illustrates a particular form of planning which, when it came before the Special Commissioner, was successful.

The principle upon which the scheme rested is that the availability of relief depends upon the facts at the date of the transfer and the previous history, but not upon what happens afterwards. Thus the existence of a contract before a transfer causes relief to be lost, but a contract immediately after the transfer does not change the relief available at the instant of transfer itself.

Mr 'Reynaud' and his three brothers established discretionary settlements for, in each case, the benefit of family and charity (but excluding, in each case, the settlor and his wife). This took place on 27 April 1995. Shares in C Limited, a company wholly owned by the four brothers, were transferred to the trustees. On 28 April 1995, C Limited purchased some of its own shares with the aid of a bank loan. The remainder of the shares were then sold to M Limited.

On the day when the discretionary settlements were made, there was a real possibility that the sale to M Limited would not proceed. C Limited would not have purchased its own shares from the trustees if it was not certain that the sale of the remaining shares to M Limited would take place, since C Limited did not have enough funds of its own to satisfy the share purchase.

The Revenue argued that the transfer by Mr Reynaud of his shares to the discretionary trustees was a transfer of value under *IHTA 1984, s 3*. The Revenue also considered that the transfer of shares and the own share purchase by C Limited were associated operations within *s 268*. On that basis, those operations took place at the time of the latest of them, ie the date on which C Limited bought the shares. On that date, no BPR was available.

As an alternative, the Revenue argued that, under the principle in *Ramsay v IRC* [1981] 1 All ER 865, the transaction should be treated as a gift of cash to the trustees. It may have been the fact that each of the brothers entered into similar transactions that influenced the attitude of the Revenue to the transaction.

The taxpayers argued that the gift of shares to the discretionary trust was a transaction which stood alone, being complete at that stage. The purchase of the shares from the trustees by C Limited was not a 'relative associated operation'. That purchase did not contribute to any transfer of value represented by the initial gift to the trustees by virtue of which the estate of the taxpayer was reduced. BPR should therefore be available.

The Special Commissioner had to decide whether there was a disposition effected by associated operations. He found for the taxpayer. There was here only a single disposition. The operation which reduced the estate of each taxpayer arose solely through the transfer of the shares into the discretionary settlement. The disposition could not be treated as having taken place later than the date on which it had actually occurred. On that basis, BPR was available as claimed.

The Special Commissioner considered the principle of fiscal nullity under *Ramsay*. For that principle to apply, there must be a pre-ordained series of transactions or a single composite transaction. There must be steps inserted into the transaction which had no commercial, and no family or non-tax, purpose. The inserted steps were then ignored for fiscal purposes. In the present case, there were two transactions, namely the settlement of the shares and the purchase of those shares by the company from the trustees. The Commissioners held that those transactions were not part of a single composite transaction. The sale to the third party, M Limited, took place after a day of negotiations. There must have been some reasonable likelihood that the negotiations might fail.

Even if, which the Commissioner did not find, there had been a single, composite transaction, there was no inserted step which might be ignored so as to change the nature of the gifts into settlement from gifts of shares into a gift of cash. There was no way that a gift of shares could become a gift of cash. The Revenue had argued that, because the taxpayers knew that the shares were to become cash in some way, they had inserted the shares into a transaction which could have been made with cash. That was a wrong use of the principle of fiscal nullity. It was not open to the Revenue to alter the character of a particular transaction in a series, or to pick bits out of it and reject other bits. The principle of fiscal nullity did not apply. The notices of determination were discharged.

Advisers should not be over-jubilant at this result: a reading of IHTM14821– 14836 will show how closely such transactions are scrutinised. All the facts will be examined in a search for any formal linkage which may show that the subject matter of the gift is, in reality, not the favoured, relievable property but the proceeds of its sale. See also the next case, for an example of detailed scrutiny of transactions.

Associated operations: the Rysaffe case

14.24 The issue of associated operations was tested again in *Rysaffe Trustee Co (Channel Islands) Ltd v CIR* [2002] STI Issue 23, where initially the

Special Commissioner and eventually the Court of Appeal had to consider ten discretionary settlements, five made by each of two settlors in exactly the same form save for the date which, it appeared, had been inserted by the solicitors to the settlors after execution. Each was for £10, satisfied by a single payment from the settlor to the solicitors of £50 each.

The intention of the scheme had been that shares in a private company (of which the settlors were shareholders and directors) would be transferred to the trustee, in equal proportions to each settlement. It had been intended that deferred shares be issued, but most unfortunately that issue proved to be invalid; so, instead, the settlors took some existing ordinary shares, re-designated them as deferred shares, and transferred them to the trustee.

The issue of 'associated operations' arose in connection with the ten-year periodic charge on the settlements. Since that charge is affected, amongst other things, by the initial size of the transfer, the settlors had wanted each settlement to stand alone for the purposes of the computation. However, the Revenue argued that there was, in relation to each settlor, a single settlement. As a result, tax should be charged under *s 64* at the rate applicable to the total value, in relation to each settlor, of all five settlements. Alternatively, the five settlements in each case were 'dispositions of property' within the meaning of *s 43* and resulted in one settlement.

The trustee argued that the 'associated operations' rules did not apply or, even if they did, the settlements were not 'dispositions of property' as a result of which the property was held in trust, within the meaning of *s 43(2)*. The trustee required each settlement to be considered separately, because they were separate settlements under trust law. Even if there were a single disposition by associated operations, it could result in property being held on the trusts of five separate settlements.

The Special Commissioner had found in favour of the Revenue, though that decision was overturned on appeal. A study of the reasoning of the Special Commissioner helps an understanding of the issues. In an examination at first instance of the circumstances of the transaction, which may serve as a chilling warning to tax advisers to get the paperwork right first time, it was clear that the transfer of £10 was part of the establishment of each settlement and that each had been created to facilitate the later transfer of shares to the trustees. It did not matter that the original transfer failed because the issue of shares was invalid and that matters had to be put right later. The creation of each settlement and the later transfer to each of them of the shares were together associated operations.

The Special Commissioner found that all the settlements were treated in exactly the same way, both by the settlor and by the trustee. It was clear from *s 268(1)* and *(3)* that the operations might be carried out at different times.

It could not be clearly established when the sum of £50 was paid over and thus when each settlement commenced. For IHT, therefore, the settlements all began on the same date, regardless of the care with which they had all been dated differently. What was more important was not the date that the lawyers had put on the deeds but the fact that the 'pump priming' sum of £10 for each settlement was paid as part of a block payment for the group of trusts and that the deferred shares transferred to each of the settlements all came from one holding of shares. That was enough, in the view of the Special Commissioner, to link the five documents. The associated operations thus found within the scope of *s 268* comprised the establishment of the settlements, the transfers of £10, and the later transfers of deferred shares.

Next, the Special Commissioner considered the interpretation of *s 43(2)* and the definition of 'settlement'. She held that the associated operations were the establishment of the five settlements in each case and the later transfers of the shares. They were all within the definition, namely 'dispositions ... whereby the property is for the time being ... held in trust'. The trusts were the same. The property was comprised in 'a settlement' by means of a disposition which included all the dispositions which had been affected by the associated operations. That was enough to bring it within *s 43(2)*.

She further considered whether the five settlements comprised 'any disposition or dispositions of property' within *s 43(2)* in order to decide what property was referred to as property comprised in 'a settlement', ie in a single settlement rather than all five settlements. Since each settlement was identical in that, on the basis of the previous findings, each had:

- the same settlor;
- the same trustee;
- the same type of trust property;
- the same beneficiaries;
- the same commencement date;
- each was a disposition; and
- each was affected by reference to the other;

there was one settlement within the meaning of *s 43(2)*.

This had serious consequences for the original tax plan. It had been part of the structure of the shares that, at the time of settlement, they carried very limited immediate rights, though they were to have equal rights with ordinary shares 12 years later. If the plan had worked, the value of what was settled would have been low and, even at the time of the ten-year anniversary, the value would be moderate although, with the prospect of increased rights only two years later, there would doubtless be by then some 'hope value'.

On appeal to the High Court, it was held that it was actually not relevant that the five settlements were identical. There were, in fact, separate documents with separate dates. The settlor had intended to create five separate settlements. They could not be artificially amalgamated merely because their terms were similar.

On its true construction, *s 268* came into effect only insofar as the expression 'associated operations' was used elsewhere. It was not an anti-avoidance provision that could be invoked to nullify the tax advantages of any scheme. In the present case, the making of the five settlements was, for IHT purposes, a disposition. There was no reason to consider the associated operations rule. The associated operations rule had been designed to identify a disposition that had been made by several transactions and not by just one. Here, the making of each settlement was a single disposition and there was therefore no need for the associated operations provisions to apply. Each settlement was separate. The ten-yearly charge applied to each settlement separately. They were not to be amalgamated to calculate the ten-year charge.

The Revenue's appeal to the Court of Appeal also failed, on a strict interpretation of the charging section, ie *s 43*. Each of the five trusts was a 'settlement' within *s 43(2)(b)*. Having determined that, the charge applied to the assets within that settlement for the purposes of *s 43(1)*, so that the trusts were not aggregated. The Revenue arguments based on *s 268* were rejected: the court held that the IHT charge was arrived at on the plain words of *s 43*, without any need to ask whether a disposition was 'associated operations'. *Section 268* came into play in those cases where a dispute arose as to whether there was a 'disposition' at all for IHT purposes. The court approved the judgment of Park J in the lower court.

There are, however, lessons to be learned here. First, a scheme that had some intellectual attraction was very nearly spoilt through the lack of meticulous care in execution. This could have been avoided by variation of one settlement from another, not merely in respect of date, but by the choice of different beneficiaries or different trustees, and by establishing quite clearly different and distinct transfers of property to each.

Second, there is some intellectual difficulty in the argument that five transfers of shares from the same holding are linked, as if the shareholding itself could be a single asset. No authorities were quoted either for or against the argument. The Special Commissioner did draw a distinction between transfers of shares and transfers of cash. She was not willing to accept that the rules as to associated operations could extend to the payment of cash from the same bank account, but for some reason did not have the same difficulty in treating the shares as a single asset rather than as being fungible. For the time being, the issue is closed.

Associated operations: Smith

14.25   In *Smith and others v HMRC* [2007] SpC 605, something of a test case but unconnected with business or agricultural relief, the Special Commissioner had to decide whether life policies taken out by a husband and wife were connected with contemporaneous annuities issued by the same assurer, Equitable Life. The wife signed the illustration to show that she would enter into the plan, under which a trust was established of some endowment assurances for her children. HMRC's Statement of Practice E4 was reviewed, which provided that policies would not be regarded as connected where there was full medical evidence of the health of the assured and evidence (which there was) that the policy would have been issued on the same terms even if the annuity had not been bought from the same provider.

The Commissioner determined that full medical evidence had not been provided within SP E4, and held that the purchase of the annuities and the issue of the life policies were associated. It was not necessary for the one expressly to refer to the other. The purchase and the insuring were more than just elements of an overall scheme. The documentation established contractual relationships between Equitable Life, the wife and the husband. For one thing to facilitate another (as required by *s 268(1)(b)*), there need be no contractual link, merely that one thing made another easier. The receipts from the annuity made it easier for the wife to pay the premiums on the life policies, and so facilitated those policies.

On appeal, the High Court held that it was not enough that a policy was issued on the basis of a health questionnaire. Statement of Practice E4 was to protect HMRC, not the insurer, and required full medical evidence, not merely enough to satisfy the insurer's purposes when issuing the life policy and the annuity. The appeal was dismissed.

Discounted gift schemes

14.26   These schemes do not directly impact on business or agricultural property, but are mentioned as structures that are commonly used to achieve IHT savings late in life. They might be used, for example, by taxpayers who had sold their business and, like Mr Swain described earlier, had thereby lost BPR. In brief, there is a gift of a bond out of which certain rights are retained or carved, so that the gift is of the difference between the amount invested and the retained rights. HMRC consider that, where the purchaser of the scheme is very old, the retained rights have virtually no value because no purchaser would pay anything for them, so the whole sum involved is a gift that, in the event of death within seven years, fails as a PET.

That was made clear in a technical note published on the HMRC website on 1 May 2007, but even clearer by their arguments in *Bower v HMRC* [2008] EWHC 3105. HMRC were not wholly successful: the Commissioner held that the retained rights did have a value, albeit low. HMRC later successfully appealed.

Shearing operation?

14.27   It has been suggested that income and capital can, within the same structure, be separated and that a taxpayer may settle, say, the nil rate band on terms that a life interest, with no power to advance capital, is reserved for himself but with the capital remainder to his children. This is, in a way, a 'DIY' variant of the discounted gift scheme. The trustees buy residential property and the settlor draws the rents. This being a trust set up after *FA 2006*, it cannot create an 'old style' interest in possession that would cause the value of the fund to be aggregated with the settlor's free estate on death. If it worked, the asset in the estate of the settlor would reduce in value with age. POAT would not be in issue because the trust fund is let property rather than intangible assets.

Practitioners may decide that such a structure should be attempted only with extreme care and should be accompanied by a 'health warning' that it may not work: it has all the hallmarks of reservation of benefit and is extremely vulnerable to challenge by HMRC. The greatest difficulty would be in achieving the separation of the two interests, so that nothing was reserved out of the gift of capital.

Sale of asset in return for debt

14.28   Another scheme canvassed occasionally involves the sale of an asset, not qualifying for relief, in return for a debt which is then disposed of by outright gift and not by settlement. There is some risk to the donor, because the donee can call in the loan at any time and is not hampered by any trustees, who might wish to favour the settlor/borrower. The sale is to a spouse or civil partner, allowing continued but indirect enjoyment of the asset, whilst triggering no CGT and avoiding reservation of benefit. *FA 1986, s 102(5)(a)* is qualified as to gifts between spouse or civil partners by *s 102(5A)* and *(5B)*. However, *s 102(5A)(a)* relates only to settled gifts, being specifically targeted to scotch *Eversden*-type arrangements. *Section 102(5B)* applies only where *s 102(5A)* is in point.

Does it work? Again, it is provocative and would very likely be attacked by HMRC on discovery. The first line of attack might well be to disallow the debt, either under *IHTA 1984, s 5(5)*, insofar as not incurred for money's worth, or under *FA 1986, s 103*: careful drafting would be needed to avoid these challenges.

Transfer between settlements

14.29   The effect of *IHTA 1984, s 81* should be noted in relation to transfer of assets from one settlement to another. Suppose that trust A, a relevant property trust now just over two years off its ten-yearly charge, has cash, and that trust B, which provides for similar beneficiaries, holds property qualifying for BPR. What is the effect of acquisition by the A trustees of BPR assets from the B trustees, who would not otherwise be interested in transferring to anyone? Will that give the A trustees relief from the ten-yearly charge? The problem is that *s 81* treats the property as being still comprised in trust B, unless a person becomes entitled to the property itself, and not merely to a life interest in it.

The maiden aunt

14.30   In the same way that excluded assets may accumulate late in a business as it matures, so holdings of shares in a private family company can become aggregated in the hands of a single person who may not, at his or her death, have available the benefit of the spouse exemption or of transferable nil rate band. On the one hand, the family as a whole may greatly benefit, since such a person may make few demands on the business and may build up capital which the younger (and sometimes not so young) members of the family can cheerfully dissipate later. On the other hand, in planning transfers, whether by lifetime gift or by will, the practitioner should have regard to the possibility that a controlling shareholding may build up in the hands of the 'wrong' member of the family for IHT purposes.

CGT planning: exploiting ss 191 and 179

14.31   The effect of an election under either *IHTA 1984, s 191* or *s 179* is to revalue assets on sale for IHT purposes. The revised value will have been 'ascertained' for IHT purposes, which triggers revaluation for CGT under *TCGA 1992, s 274*. In the, perhaps fairly common, situation that the family home is eventually sold for more than probate value, the effect may be modest, unless an exemption or relief applies (for example, where the family home is occupied by a major beneficiary). CGT will be payable at 18% or at 28% instead of IHT at 40%. There may be a further saving, in that the expenses of the sale will be allowable against the gain, whereas IHT is chargeable on the gross value. The advantage arises where relief from IHT is available either because the asset is within the nil rate band or it is covered by the spouse exemption or it attracts APR or BPR at 100%.

The argument was for a time put forward that, where an asset, perhaps farmland attracting 100% APR, is sold by the personal representatives for development, it may be possible to claim APR at 100% on the agricultural value and BPR at 100% on the planning premium; but that the base cost is deemed to be the sale price by virtue of the operation of *TCGA 1992, s 274* and *IHTA 1984, s 191*. Such a benign result does not appear to have been contemplated by the legislation, which is concerned with a relief from IHT. That was certainly a strong argument in favour of the Revenue in the slightly different circumstances of *Stonor (executors of Dickinson deceased) v IRC* SpC 288, [2001] SWTI 1501, considered below. Clearly, the strict requirements of *s 191*, in particular *sub-s (3)*, must be observed. There is no provision for the withdrawal of a disadvantageous claim, neither is there a special time limit for making the claim.

The tax avoidance possibilities of the legislation have not been overlooked by HMRC. The Capital Gains Manual at CG32234 argues that a claim under *s 191(1)* will fail because such a claim can be made only by 'the appropriate person'. *Section 190(1)* defines such a person as 'the person liable for [capital transfer tax] attributable to the value of that interest'. In the second edition of this book, the writer was not aware of any reported case in which the issue had been tested, even at Special Commissioner level. Given the trend over recent years to adopt a purposive interpretation of statute, the attempt to use the 'fall in value' relief in this way is perhaps the preserve of the brave and the wealthy.

Stonor (executors of Dickinson deceased) v IRC

14.32   That was proved right in *Stonor*. Mrs Dickinson held freehold properties, valued at the time of her death in 1992 at £582,000. Her will left some chargeable gifts, but they were within the nil rate band. The residue was left to charity. Within the time limits prescribed by *s 191*, the executors sold the properties for £918,457, informing the Revenue and asking for the gross sale prices to be accepted as the amended probate values.

No IHT turned on the point, so the Revenue declined to investigate the values. The executors then made a formal claim under *s 191*, hoping thereby to use the higher values at sale as the base values for CGT. The Revenue replied with a notice of determination. There was no 'appropriate person' to make a claim. The executors on the other hand considered that, had the residuary beneficiaries not all been charities, they would have been liable for tax on the estate or would have been so liable if the chargeable transfers had exceeded the nil rate band.

The Special Commissioner dismissed the appeal. The purpose of *s 191* was to grant relief from IHT, not to reduce liability to CGT on a later disposal. Whilst the section did not state that it could not apply where there had been an increase in values after the death, any claim must be made by the 'appropriate person', ie one liable for IHT. That tax was charged on a chargeable transfer, one which was not an exempt transfer. Here, the transfers were exempt, and so there was no tax chargeable. Since no tax was payable, there was no liability for tax. There was no person liable to pay the tax.

More specifically, *s 190(1)* provided that, if there is more than one person liable for the tax and one of them is in fact paying the tax, it is that person who is the 'appropriate person'. In the light of this, there was in the instant case clearly no 'appropriate person', so the claim must fail.

Correcting errors: Hastings-Bass and related cases

14.33 Such is the complexity of the taxation of trusts that the order in which events occur can significantly alter the tax treatment. The trustees may be under pressure to make a distribution, and may pay out too soon, as in the frightening case of *Frankland v IRC* [1997] STC 1450, or may exercise one of their powers in some other way, only to discover that it has produced unforeseen results. The best the trustee can do in these cases is to seek the help of the court. Thus, in *Re Hastings-Bass* [1975] Ch 25 it was held that the trustees must show that they would have acted differently had they fully appreciated the consequences of their actions. The same principle was expressed in *Re Mettoy* [1991] 2 All ER 513 that:

'Where a trustee acts under a discretion given to him by the terms of the trust, the court will interfere with his action if it is clear that he would not have acted as he did had he not failed to take into account considerations which he ought to have taken into account.'

Breadner v Granville-Grossman

Trustees hoped to rely on that principle in *Breadner v Granville-Grossman* [2001] Ch 523, a case concerning a time limit which the trustees missed by one day. Park J refused to apply Hastings-Bass. He did not feel that the rule could be used so as, in effect, not to declare a decision of the trustees void, but to declare that they should be treated as having exercised their power but as having exercised it at some other time. He felt, somewhat firmly, that:

'It cannot be right that whenever trustees do something which they later regret and think that they ought not to have done, they can say that they never did it in the first place.'

Abacus

The trustees were more successful in *Abacus Trust Co (Isle of Man) Ltd v National Society of the Prevention of Cruelty to Children* [2001] STC 1344, again a case concerning dates. That particular case was brought in relation to the timing of a disposal which triggered a liability on the whole of the trust fund under *TCGA 1992, s 86*, but situations may be imagined where it would be equally relevant to time limits for IHT, such as sales triggering clawback of BPR or APR. Counsel had advised that the relevant appointment should not be made before 6 April 1998. In fact, the deed of appointment was executed three days earlier. The court held that, in exercising powers of appointment, trustees must have regard to the fiscal consequences of their actions. Where it could be shown that proper consideration of those consequences would have led to a particular appointment not being made, the court could and should treat such exercise of the power as invalid.

The tax implications of the exercise of powers by trustees were an essential part of the financial consequences of such exercise. If the effect of a proposed appointment was that the trust fund or the beneficiaries were likely to be exposed to a significant tax charge, the trustees must consider the tax charge when deciding to make the appointment. This showed that tax was relevant to the exercise of powers, and that failure to take tax into account could nullify the exercise of the power, unless it could be shown that the trustees would have gone ahead with that exercise regardless of the tax consequences.

Here, the trustees made the appointment without properly taking into account the advice of leading counsel in connection with the date on which the appointment should be made. The exercise of the power of appointment was invalid and of no effect. It would seem that, in relation to tax matters, the courts have not yet exhausted the possibilities of relief. Whilst it was originally thought that the remedy was available only where there was mistake as to the nature of a document, rather than as to its effect, the present trend is towards relief, even where the terms of the document are clear but it does not achieve the tax savings its maker hoped for.

Wolff and Wolff v Wolff

The courts do seem to be willing to use the principle in a variety of circumstances. This was illustrated in *Wolff and Wolff v Wolff and others* [2004] STC 1633, where a married couple had owned a freehold property. They wanted to avoid inheritance tax, and the solicitor in 1997 recommended entering into a reversionary lease of the property in favour of their daughters, to begin in 2017. The parents later began to realise that they would have nowhere to live after 2017 and applied to the court to set aside the lease. Mann J in the Chancery Division described the document as 'manifestly defective as a piece of drafting' and said that the solicitor 'did not fully understand the implications of what he had brought about'. It was clear from the evidence that the parents 'did not know that the effect of the lease was to deprive them of their right to occupy the property in 2017'. The judge set aside the lease, applying the observation by Millett J in *Gibbon v Mitchell* [1990] 1 WLR 1304 that:

'wherever there is a voluntarily transaction by which one party intends to confer a bounty on another, the deed will be set aside if the court is satisfied that the disponor did not intend the transaction to have the effect which it did.'

Ogden v Griffiths

We cannot know when our allotted span on this earth is up, a problem that afflicted the family of Ronald Ogden who, having used the nil rate band, made in February 2004 a PET of £2,600,000. In the autumn of that year, he was diagnosed with cancer and died in April 2005. Mr Ogden's wife was somewhat younger than he: with hindsight, it would have been better for him to have done nothing, left the money to her exempt, and perhaps for her to have made gifts. This was unfortunately an example of just the situation that is illustrated at **14.1** and Example 14.1. In *Ogden and another v Trustees of the RHS Griffiths 2003 Settlement* [2008] STC 776, the executors applied to the High Court to have the gift set aside, arguing that there had been a mistake: had Mr Griffiths known of his true state of ill-health, he would not have entered into the settlement. (HMRC were not party to the action; they have indicated that, in future, they may seek greater involvement where tax is in issue: see *Tax Bulletin* 83, 13 October 2006.)

Held:

- The gift would be set aside.
- It was just possible that Mr Griffiths was suffering from the cancer in February when he made the gift and then had a life expectancy of less than three years.
- A gift may be set aside only where the donor was under a mistake so serious that it would be unjust for the donee to keep the gift.
- There was a distinction between the effect of a transaction and its consequences, allowing setting aside where the mistake was as to the effect, not merely the consequences.
- The early death, not the tax charge, was unexpected.
- The mistake must be such that, had the truth been known, the gift would not have been made.

Pitt v Holt; Futter v Futter

Practitioners should bear in mind the above potential limitations of the *Hastings-Bass* principle. Rectification requires a court order, fully argued in court, and not merely a consent order. That has costs implications. HMRC reviewed the situation in Revenue Interpretation 278, June 2006, becoming more ready to be party to litigation where tax is in issue. They feel that the principle in that case has been pushed too far, and suggest that commentators agree; some certainly do.

It has long been thought that the *Hastings-Bass* principle cannot be relied upon to rectify a mistake as to the tax consequences of a particular course of action (see eg *Allnutt and another v Wilding and others* [2007] EWCA Civ 412). The ability of trustees to set a transaction aside was considered in *Ogden and another v Trustees of the RHS Griffiths 2003 Settlement*, noted above.

These principles were examined recently in the CGT case of *Futter and Another v Futter and Others* [2010] EWHC 449 (Ch), where trustees, having triggered stockpiled gains, and having overlooked *TCGA 1992, s 2(4)*, sought relief by avoiding the transaction. HMRC as defendants argued that the rule in *Hastings-Bass* had been carried to absurd lengths. They wished the court to distinguish between the 'effects' and the 'consequences' of an action, on the basis that unintended tax consequences were not, of themselves, good reason to set aside. Norris J did not agree: after reviewing many authorities, he quoted with approval the decision of Patten J in *Abacus Trust v NSPCC* [2001] STC 1344 that 'the financial consequences for the beneficiaries of any intended exercise of a fiduciary power could not be assessed without reference to their fiscal implications'.

HMRC next argued that relief should be denied unless the mistake was 'objectively significant'. The case concerned more than one settlement; in one, the gains were small and did not merit relief. Norris J held that: 'No doubt there is no general principle that a trustee must be familiar with the personal tax position of every intended recipient of funds on a distribution from or dealing with a trust fund', an observation that will be a relief to many trustees. In the present case, however, the tax effect on the beneficiary was highly relevant, as any tax would fall on the trust fund: 'Trustees ought in general to take into account the impact upon the trust fund of an intended distribution'.

Finally, HMRC argued that the trustees had, in fact, gone 'to great lengths to take advice upon that very matter. The problem was that the advice was wrong. The "Hastings-Bass principle" did not exist to enable advisers to be relieved from the consequences of bad advice'.

Again, Norris J, while acknowledging that principle, found for the trustees. What was important was not saving the advisers but protection of the beneficiaries from an invalid exercise by the trustees of their powers. One must look at the failure to take a particular factor into account and how that failure affected the proper use of the power. The deeds would be set aside.

HMRC appealed successfully to the Court of Appeal in this case and another, together heard as *Pitt v Holt* [2011] EWCA Civ 197, which found a clear distinction between:

- the existence and extent of a trust power; and

- the manner of its exercise.

A disposition was void if it was a misapplication of property; but it was not void if it was within the power, even if there was a fault in the exercise, as where tax had not been properly taken into account. Any case to set aside must show breach of fiduciary duty. Such a claim would normally be made against the trustee, not by him. The upshot is that, in future, beneficiaries may simply claim against professional advisers in negligence rather than try to unscramble transactions that have gone wrong. The lack of the 'escape route' previously employed will no doubt concentrate the mind of advisers but may also lead to yet more extensive exculpation clauses in trust documents.

DEATH BED PLANNING

14.34   *IHTA 1984, s 106* requires ownership of relevant business property for at least two years before the transfer of value. Curiously, the section does not require that the property must have been relevant business property throughout that two-year period. In the case of land or buildings, machinery or plant that qualifies for BPR under *s 105*, the use must continue throughout the two years that immediately precede the transfer of value, subject to replacement property rules. However, a different rule can apply to shares in a company.

Example 14.10: fundamental but urgent change to activity

An elderly shareholder, or perhaps one suffering from a terminal illness, might own shares in an investment company. It may be possible to change the character of the business carried on by the company such that, at the time of death, it is in truth a trading company. The actual mechanics of achieving such a change would be difficult to arrange and might involve the disposal of investments and the acquisition of trading assets, so the idea may be more academic than practical; but, if it could be achieved, there would be a substantial saving.

Example 14.11: asset switch to earn relief

There could be a transfer of assets to a trading company which the trading company then used in its business. Subject to the discussion of this point at **7.5** above, it might be possible by this method to shelter from IHT the assets so transferred. However, given the purposive advice in the Shares and Assets Valuation Manual reviewed at **7.9**, such transfers might well be regarded as provocative. There could easily be issues of capital gains tax on the transfer to the company.

GIFTS BY ATTORNEYS

14.35   Advisers are often faced with the difficult situation where a wealthy estate owner is no longer capable of looking after his or her own affairs and has appointed an attorney, perhaps a family member, whose perspective on wealth management and tax mitigation may be different from that of the estate owner. It may seem more urgent to the attorney that the estate owner should make lifetime gifts than was of concern to the estate owner. A senior member of the judiciary once observed, though not in relation to any particular individual and not in the course of a judgment, that, when the old lady signed an enduring power of attorney, she did not thereby agree that her estate might be administered as if she were already dead. The attorney may wish to establish a pattern of regular gifts for mitigation purposes.

The difficulties of such a situation were examined in *Executors of McDowall deceased v IRC* [2004] STI Issue 3. Mr McDowall, a Scot, gave his son-in-law power of attorney which included various powers but no express powers to make gifts. Following the mental deterioration of Mr McDowall, the attorney considered the financial position and decided to continue an existing pattern established by Mr McDowall of making gifts to family members. He thought that he was in the position that Mr McDowall would have been in, had he been capable of managing his own affairs. In the seven years before Mr McDowall's death, the attorney made a number of substantial gifts, although none of them were actually ratified by Mr McDowall because of his physical and mental condition. The Revenue issued notices of determination to the executors that none of the gifts were deductible from the estate for IHT purposes, and to the executors and trustees of a settlement that had been made by the deceased in his lifetime that five of the relevant gifts were not exempt transfers under *IHTA 1984, s 21* as normal expenditure out of income.

On appeal to the Special Commissioner, it was argued for the taxpayer that, because five years had elapsed from some of the gifts, they could no longer be challenged and must be regarded as validly made; and that the five gifts with which the trust was concerned had been made from money that had retained its character as income and had been made with the intention of making regular payments on a settled pattern. The Special Commissioner held that the attorney had no express powers to make gifts. As a result, right up to his death, Mr McDowall had the right to recover the gifts made by his attorney. That right of recovery was part of his estate and time did not run against it. Whilst the five gifts, if they had been valid, would have been exempt, the same rule applied to them as to the other gifts. The entire value of all the transfers made under the power of attorney was effectively represented by the right of recovery. The appeals were dismissed.

JOINT ACCOUNTS

14.36   As people get older, they often arrange for signing facilities on bank accounts by family members that stop short of a full power of attorney. The new formalities associated with lasting powers of attorney may increase that trend. It is sometimes later argued that this amounts to a gift. In *Taylor and another v HMRC* [2008] SpC 704, the deceased put two building society accounts into joint names with her brother-in-law and herself, either to sign, the proceeds to pass to the survivor. Within the family, it was widely known that the money would go to grandchildren. The deceased left her estate to her daughters. No IHT was paid on the building society accounts, but HMRC issued notice of determination that the accounts were part of the estate, or that a benefit had been reserved out of the gift. The executors appealed on the basis that the brother-in-law could at any time have closed the accounts by drawing all the money out.

Held, the deceased did not hold the accounts as trustee. She could have disposed of the money in the accounts. Most of the withdrawals were in fact made by the deceased. There were not separate shares in the account as tenants in common. The accounts were not enjoyed to the entire exclusion of the deceased, so she was treated as entitled to the proceeds of the accounts at the date of her death.

Chapter 15

Will planning

QUICK GUIDE

Major difficulties arise through the attribution rules, which can have the effect of wasting APR or BPR on gifts that, being exempt, need no relief. Much of this chapter is devoted to the difficult subject of the allocation of reliefs and the horrors of double grossing. The simplest and probably best advice must be to avoid these complexities if at all possible.

Successful will planning involves the use of the reliefs and deciding whether to use the nil rate band on the first death or to transfer it under the new rules in *FA 2008*. This is illustrated in an extended example at **15.9**, and in a review of the use of the nil rate band at **15.10–15.12**.

At the moment, a spouse is, still, a person who is legally married, and not one who lives as man and wife. That much appears from *Holland*, discussed at **15.19**.

The use of a will in planning to mitigate the prospective burden of IHT is a large subject, part of which is outside the scope of this book. For a more general approach, the practitioner might consider, for example, *Ray & McLaughlin's Practical Inheritance Tax Planning* (Bloomsbury Professional). This chapter concentrates on the use of APR and BPR to mitigate the IHT burden.

THE NIL RATE BAND

Infinite nil rate band

15.1 This heading is, of course, a misnomer. Only where all the property concerned qualifies for 100% APR or BPR can there be said to be a nil rate band which, in suitable circumstances, may encompass the whole estate. As was noted (or rather not noted) in the illustration of the advice of Geoff in **Chapter 7** in relation to categories of business property, regard must always be given to the distinction between those assets which qualify for the full relief and those which do not. Nevertheless, one of the cardinal principles of IHT will planning used to be the use of the nil rate band to avoid or to reduce the aggregation of estates as between husband and wife on the death of the survivor of them. There will often be individual family circumstances which thwart the intentions of the tax planner; but, in general terms, assets which do not qualify for relief are suitable for transfer to exempt beneficiaries such as the surviving spouse or a charity, whilst assets qualifying for APR and BPR can, with advantage, be left to children and other beneficiaries where the transfer is not exempt.

Double nil rate band

15.2   This is not a reference to the transferable nil rate band. The same asset may, by agreement between the family and with suitable planning, be used to earn relief twice over. Where the finances of the family permit, assets qualifying for APR or BPR are left to the children and other assets to the surviving spouse. The surviving spouse applies his or her inheritance in purchasing the business assets from the children. If the spouse survives two years (this not being a case where the rules as to succession can apply), APR or BPR will be earned for a second time.

Partly exempt transfers: interaction with APR and BPR

15.3   The transfer by a person of his estate on death is, for IHT, a single gift of the whole estate which may be wholly taxable, where it passes to children or more distant relatives, or wholly exempt, where for example it passes to a charity. Problems arise where the estate passes partly to taxable beneficiaries and partly to those who are exempt. The rules to regulate the problem are contained in *IHTA 1984, ss 36–42*. It is necessary to attribute exemptions among the various gifts, making distinctions between, on one hand, the residuary estate and, on the other hand, all other gifts, which are called 'specific gifts'.

Taking first the specific gifts, they may or may not be exempt; but, where they are not exempt, it becomes necessary to establish whether they bear their own tax. This will in turn depend on the terms of the will (if there is one) of the deceased. Gifts of residue may likewise, of course, be exempt or not; but, where a gift of residue is not exempt, it will always bear its own tax.

Non-exempt 'gross' legacy

15.4   What is the value, for IHT, of a non-exempt specific gift? Is it necessary to gross up the specific gift? The answer will depend on whether any non-exempt specific gift bears its own tax or not, and on what other gifts there may be in addition to that specific non-exempt gift.

Example 15.1: gift bearing its own tax

Joanna, a widow whose late husband had used his nil rate band, died on 16 April 2011 leaving an estate of £600,000, having made no lifetime chargeable transfers. She (somewhat unusually) left her son £100,000 not free of tax but subject to IHT, and split the rest of her estate between a charity and her daughter.

The residue is £500,000 and the daughter's share is £250,000. The tax on death is charged on £350,000. The tax is (£350,000 – £325,000) × 40% = £10,000. Of this, the share of the son *pro rata* is £2,857 and that of the daughter £7,143.

Non-exempt 'free of tax' legacy

15.5   Where a legacy is left, as will very often be the case, free of tax, the complications of grossing up may be involved.

Example 15.2: simple grossing

Kylie died on 17 April 2011 having made no prior chargeable lifetime transfers. Her estate is £700,000 of which she has left £350,000 to Luke, her boyfriend, and the residue to her husband. She is treated as having made a net transfer on death of £25,000 over and above the nil rate band of £325,000. IHT on that net £25,000 is £16,666, making the provision for Luke £366,666. That leaves exempt residue for the husband of £333,334.

This example illustrates the effect of *s 38(3)*. The grossing up attributes to the specific gift:

- the amount of the gift itself; and
- the tax that would be chargeable if the value of the gift equalled the gift plus its tax.

A mixture of legacies, with exempt and non-exempt shares of residue

15.6   The situation becomes yet more complicated where there are non-exempt specific gifts which do not bear their own tax and where those gifts are not the only chargeable gifts because, as well, there may be non-exempt specific gifts which bear their own tax and, as a further complication, gifts of residue which are taxable. This situation brings into play, under *s 38(5)*, 'the assumed rate'.

It is highly likely that, if the legislation were being enacted now under the excellent drafting principles of the Tax Law Rewrite, it would be accompanied by worked examples. The legislation explains that the assumed rate is found by dividing the assumed amount of tax by a portion of the value transferred which would be charged on the transfer after making a hypothesis, namely that:

- the amount which corresponds to the value of the specific gifts not bearing their own tax is equal to the aggregate already identified in *s 38(3)*, which has been illustrated above; and

- the parts of the value transferred attributable to specific gifts and to gifts of residue or shares in residue are determined accordingly.

The assumed amount of tax is the amount that would be charged on the value transferred on that hypothesis. The following worked example breaks the calculation into its constituent parts. Accountant readers are asked to be patient: each element of the calculation is set out in full for the benefit of those who find multi-step calculations somewhat daunting.

Example 15.3: double grossing

Tanya died on 10 April 2011 with an estate worth £850,000. In her lifetime, she made transfers, all chargeable, of £280,000. Her will gives a net legacy of £70,000 to her son Wayne, and the residue to her daughter Cherie and to her husband Jason in equal shares. We are therefore concerned with total transfers of £1,130,000.

All grossing up must start from a net amount of transfers, in this case £280,000, which is part of Tanya's nil rate band of £325,000, leaving unused £45,000.

Stage 1: calculating the gift to Wayne and residue

Of the legacy to Wayne, £45,000 is within the nil rate band, leaving £25,000 to be grossed up. The appropriate rate on the net fraction is two-thirds, so the tax is £16,667. That grosses up Wayne's legacy from £70,000 to £86,667. That is the basic 'stage one' grossed-up value of the legacy, used to identify the residue of the estate, part of which is exempt and part chargeable.

The residue is found by taking:

	£
The estate	850,000
And deducting the grossed up legacy	86,667
To leave	763,333
Of that, Cherie's half share is chargeable	381,667

Taking the provision for Wayne and Cherie together, the gross chargeable transfer is thus:

	£
Legacy, grossed up	86,667
Plus share of residue	381,667
	468,334

Stage 2: calculating the 'assumed rate'

What is the IHT chargeable on £468,334? That will produce the 'assumed rate' for revising the grossing up of the legacy:

	£
We must now take the lifetime transfers	280,000
Add the gross transfer on death, just established	468,334
This gives us a chargeable transfer of	748,334
Deduct the nil rate band	(325,000)
	423,334
Tax on that at 40% is	169,334

This produces 'the assumed rate', ie the proportion which the tax on death bears to the chargeable transfers on death. It is:

$$\frac{169,334}{468,334} = 36.15\%$$

Stage 3: re-grossing in the context of the whole estate

We must now review the legacy to Wayne. The sum is:

$$\frac{£70,000 \times 100}{(100 - 36.15)} = £109,632$$

The result is a sharp increase in the tax, by some 26.5%. The new grossed-up value of Wayne's legacy is greater because it is now seen in the context of an estate half of which is subject to tax.

Stage 4: recalculating residue after re-grossing Wayne's legacy

We must now re-examine the transfer on death as a whole and recalculate the residue:

	£
The gross estate at death was	850,000
Deduct the new grossed-up legacy of	109,632
Residue becomes	740,368
Half passes to Cherie	370,184

Thus, the value passing to chargeable beneficiaries is now:

	£
Legacy to Wayne	109,632
Share for Cherie	370,184
Total	479,816

This transfer is the one that is taxed, not forgetting the lifetime transfers which must also be brought into the computation. The calculation is:

	£
Chargeable transfers on death	479,816
Failed PETs	280,000
Total for rate	759,816
Deduct nil rate band	(325,000)
Left in charge to tax	434,816
Tax at 40%	173,926

Who actually pays the tax?

So far, the computation has served only to establish the tax to be charged. The nature of a gift of residue is such that both Cherie and Jason must, from their inheritance, find the legacy for Wayne and the tax on it. Once that has been established, Jason takes the rest of his inheritance tax free, whilst Cherie suffers tax on her share. At this point, it is also necessary to consider what administration costs there may have been. In the present example, the costs and disbursements amount to £17,000, of which half attracted VAT at the old rate of 17.5% and the balance at 20%, so a total bill of £20,188.

First, calculate the residue:

	£
Estate	850,000
Deduct legacy	(70,000)
Deduct tax	(173,926)
Pay the costs and VAT	(20,188)
Residue	585,886

The way that the tax is calculated on the legacy is actually non-statutory. The basis commonly adopted is to assume that the proportion of tax attributable to Wayne's legacy is calculated by reference to the gross value. Returning, therefore, to 'stage 4' of the double grossing calculation, the gross legacy was £109,632 and the total transfer on death £479,816. The proportion of tax attributable to the gross legacy is:

$$\frac{£109,632}{£479,816} \times £173,926 = £39,739.92$$

The total that may be distributed has already been established at £585,886.

The tax payable on death of £173,926 may be apportioned:

	£	£
Attributable to Wayne	39,740	
Attributable to residue	134,186	
Residue as calculated		585,886
Add back the 'non-Wayne' tax		134,186
Estate available for division between Cherie and Jason		720,072
Of this, Jason receives half free of any deduction, ie		360,036
From her half, Cherie must suffer the tax of £134,186, leaving		225,850

Summary:

	£
Husband	360,036
Daughter	225,850
Son	70,000
Lawyers	20,188
HMRC	173,926
Donees of failed PETs	280,000
Total disposed of	1,130,000

The estate may occasionally not be large enough to satisfy all the gifts made, with the result that they must abate. By *s 37(1)*, where a gift would be abated and without regard to any tax chargeable, it is treated for the purposes of the 'double-grossing' code as being abated before the code applies. The gifts are treated as reduced as far as is necessary to fit the size of the estate. The reduction is made in the order in which it would apply under the terms of the will, or under any rule of law which determines abatement in the absence of a specific term of the will.

Difficulties arising under s 41(b)

15.7   In the illustration set out in the previous paragraph, it was provided that none of the tax attributable to the value of the property comprised in residue should, in accordance with *IHTA 1984, s 41(b)*, fall on any gift of a share of residue if, or to the extent that, the transfer was exempt with respect to the gift. That provision was examined in *Lockhart v Harker (Re Benham's Will Trusts)* [1995] STC 210, where the court had to consider the effect of the apparent intention of the testator to override *s 41(b)*. For a time, this decision caused very great concern to practitioners. The rules tended to work in favour of the chargeable beneficiaries and against charitable beneficiaries. Charities took a very strong line even though, in some respects, the decision in *Re Benham*, inconvenient though it may have been, probably did reflect what the average testator would want, ie to achieve the same net inheritance for exempt and non-exempt beneficiaries alike. The difficulty was that the calculation which resulted in *Re Benham* actually increased the tax payable overall.

For two reasons, this may now no longer be of such great concern to practitioners. First, IRCT published their view (see *Tax Journal* of 5 September 1996) that:

> 'generally speaking the court is concerned in such cases to establish the intention of the testator or testatrix from the wording of the will and admissible extrinsic evidence. If the will is drafted in common form with the direction to ascertain residue after payment of funeral and testamentary expenses and debts followed by a bequest of that residue then it is focusing on the ascertainment and division of disposable residue rather than on what each residuary beneficiary is to receive. Accordingly wills so drafted would not appear to involve *Benham*-style grossing up computations.'

Second, the situation was, for most practitioners, put beyond doubt by the decision of the High Court in *Holmes v McMullen (Re Ratcliffe deceased)* [1999] STC 262 (reported first in the *Tax Journal* of 1 March 1999 at p 5). There, the testatrix left one half of her estate to relatives and the other half to four charities. Mindful of the decision in *Re Benham's Will Trusts*, the executors issued a summons for a declaration as to the correct method of administering the net residuary estate.

The court held that the half shares were to be calculated for the payment of IHT due in respect of the shares passing to the relatives. The net amount received by the relatives would be less than the net amount received by the charities. An equal division of the residue between the charities and the relatives was bound to mean that the IHT attributable to the share of the relatives had been borne by that share. To subject the share of the charities to any part of the burden was prohibited by *s 41(b)*.

The court naturally considered the decision in *Re Benham's Will Trusts* but did not follow it, finding that it did not establish a principle which need be followed. By implication, that decision was not approved. Nevertheless, practitioners need to be aware of the case.

The impact of the proposed additional charity relief

15.8   At the time of writing, the details are not yet fully known but, as part of the Budget announcement 2011, the Chancellor indicated that, in respect of deaths occurring on or after 6 April 2012, where at least 10% of a net estate is given to charity, the rate of IHT applied to the estate will be reduced from 40% to 36%. There will be consultation before implementation. Any reduction in tax is, of course, to be welcomed. Even so, the complexity of calculations such as that set out in Example 15.3 could be exacerbated by applying a different rate. The practitioner is asked to advise, even to forecast, what would be the tax impact of suggested provisions for a will. Given the variables, including fluctuation values, this becomes very difficult.

The gift of a share of residue to charity might seem the obvious solution, but for two issues. The first is that it may commit the executors to the double grossing calculation in Example 15.3. The second difficulty is, frankly, more sinister, and concerns the worries that many practitioners have about giving shares of residue to charities in any circumstances. Charities can be quite demanding beneficiaries. There is nothing wrong in that, as a professional executor should be willing to: answer questions as to the administration of the estate; produce timeous reports and accounts; and manage the estate so that, as far as consistent with the executors' duty to all beneficiaries, charities are not disadvantaged by tax rules. However, it may seem to the lay executor that charities are intrusive, even hectoring, in their approach. Further, as was illustrated in *RSPCA v Sharp and Others* [2010] EWCA Civ 1474, any error or ambiguity in the terms of the will is likely to be litigated where the charity beneficiary has deep pockets.

There is certainly a view, probably more widely held since the victory of the charity in the Court of Appeal in that case, that any gift to a charity is best made by way of fixed legacy. That would certainly have avoided the difficulties in the *RSPCA* case. Where the gift to an exempt beneficiary, be it spouse, civil partner or charity, is fixed, calculation of relief is simple: the amount given is exempt. The rest of the estate is chargeable, so grossing up and double grossing are avoided. A testator (and this will include most) who is uncertain how much they will leave at death, but who wishes to take advantage of the new 36% rate, will be able to leave a fixed amount to charities, with residue to chargeable beneficiaries, but only after also including a discretionary trust of a sum that effectively 'tops up' the charitable giving to at least 10% of the estate at death. The following example is hypothetical, because the details of the new relief are not yet known. It may, however, illustrate the principle.

Example 15.4: large gift to the church

Diana is widowed. Her late husband did not use his nil rate band and she has made no chargeable lifetime gifts. She has a son, Fergus, now well set up in life, and two grandchildren: there will be no more. She is a keen supporter of her local church, which is about to undergo major restoration, and she heads the appeal committee.

Her estate comprises:

	£
Residence	300,000
Shares in family trading company	400,000
Quoted shares	200,000
Let properties	640,000
Total	1,540,000

Diana assumes that the nil rate band will not be increased, so there will be £650,000 available to her executors. The family shares qualify for BPR at 100%, so may be inherited free of tax. Fergus runs the company, so Diana wishes to leave him the shares. The let properties have been valued recently and the figure of £640,000 may be relied upon. Diana wants her grandchildren to have them tax free. Diana therefore makes her will as follows:

●   specific bequest of shares to Fergus;

●   specific devise of let properties, free of tax, to a trust for the grandchildren;

●   legacy to the church restoration fund of £125,000;

●   legacy to a discretionary trust of £100,000 to be held for the grandchildren and the church, with a letter of wishes explaining that Diana would like the total gift to the church to be at least 10% of her net estate; and

●   residue to Fergus.

Assuming that Diana dies on 7 April 2012, at a time when all the values are the same except that the quoted shares are worth £250,000, and subject to the caveat mentioned above, the tax calculation might become:

	£
Residence	300,000
Shares in family trading company	400,000
Quoted shares	250,000
Let properties	640,000
Total	1,590,000

	£
Deduct BPR	(400,000)
Deduct legacy to church	(125,000)
Chargeable estate	1,065,000
Deduct nil rate band	(650,000)
Chargeable estate	415,000
Primary charge to IHT at 40%	166,000

If the trustees exercise their discretion after 8 July 2012 but before 6 April 2014 to increase the legacy to the church, that will be read back under *IHTA 1984, s 144*. If they act promptly, as soon as the extent of the estate is known, the deed of appointment of extra funds to the church can be lodged with Form IHT400 to secure immediate relief. There is still no grossing up: it is a simple increase from £125,000 to, say, £160,000. The chargeable estate is reduced to £1,030,000 and the estate taxed is reduced to £380,000. If the executors then secure the 36% IHT rate, the tax payable will become £136,800, a saving of £29,200. It is understood that the charity, rather than the family, enjoy that extra 4% benefit, but that is a matter to be clarified.

Will planning for an elderly couple

15.9   An extended example.

Example 15.5: how reliefs play out over time

Jack and Jill are in their seventies. They made their money in farming and, a few years ago, secured planning permission on part of the land for a golf course. They sold all of the rest of the acreage, except for the farmhouse and just under two acres enjoyed with it, which they still own and occupy jointly. Jill's share of the proceeds is now represented by a portfolio of stocks and shares worth £600,000, of which £200,000 is a holding in a regional brewery where the shares are traded on PLUS but are not 'listed'. Jack, a golfer himself, invested his share of the proceeds in Driver Ltd, the unquoted company which now operates the golf course. That investment is worth £400,000. Jack has other investments of £300,000.

Jack and Jill have two children, now in their forties, and five grandchildren. They wish to make tax-efficient provision for the whole family. Driver Ltd pays Jack fees, as a non-executive director, which form part of his pension and dividends of £20,000 per year. Their present wills provide that the entire estate passes to the survivor, with the usual gifts over to the children and grandchildren. Carol is a member of the club (and a director of Driver Ltd) and they consult her.

Carol's pro forma IHT computation of the prospective liability to IHT is based on Jill's comment that, with all the golf he plays, Jack is reckoned to be the better life of the two. Neither has made any lifetime gifts of any substance, although Jack was wondering if he should give away some of his Driver Ltd shares because the club is doing well and the company might soon develop land that is not needed. The computation is as follows.

Jill (assumed to die first):

	£
Portfolio	600,000
Share of house	200,000
Contents (share)	25,000
Personal effects	10,000
	835,000

Under the present will, all is exempt, passing to Jack.

Jack (assumed to survive Jill):

	£
Driver Ltd	400,000
Portfolio	300,000
Share of house and contents	225,000
	925,000
Inheritance from Jill	835,000
Less probate costs	(15,000)
	1,745,000
Less BPR on Driver Ltd	(400,000)
Less BPR on PLUS	(200,000)
	1,145,000
Less nil rate band allowed @200%	(650,000)
	495,000
Tax at 40%	198,000

Carol naturally advises Jill that no APR is available on the farmhouse, now shorn of its farmland. Carol advises that it is no longer necessary to use the nil rate band on the first death, but that Jill should consider a gift of her brewery shares to her children on the basis that that gift will be sheltered by BPR and that, after her death, Jack may buy the shares back from the children (who probably need cash more than a long-term investment). If Jack survives that purchase by two years and still holds the shares at his death, they will qualify for BPR a second time. There is, so long as 40% is the top rate of IHT, little advantage in causing an immediate charge to IHT by making legacies to the children or grandchildren (of assets not qualifying for relief) any greater than the nil rate band, unless it is considered that the asset will appreciate very quickly and it is desired that that appreciation be taken in the names of the younger generation.

Carol advises that, in the light of *IRC v Lloyds Private Banking* [1998] STC 559, there is little to be achieved by attempting to pass a half share in the house to the next generation for so long, at least, as Jack as the survivor will need to live there.

Jack should not make an inter vivos gift of the Driver Ltd shares, since (*a*) BPR will almost certainly be available on his death (if the law remains unchanged), and (*b*) the shares yield useful income, leaving Jack free, if he wishes, to make gifts from other funds. Carol considers that the land on which Driver Ltd might get planning permission is, for the time being, still used by the club for parking and for a practice range; so, although the club might sell it, it is not an 'excepted asset' within *IHTA 1984, s 112*, and so BPR is not at risk. To allow for the possibility that he might die first, Jack should in his will leave the Driver Ltd shares to his children on the basis that Jill will have enough, with her own securities and what she inherits from him, to 'recycle' BPR in the same way, by buying his Driver Ltd shares back so as to give the children cash and hold the BPR assets until the second death.

On this basis of Jill's instructions, Carol's revised IHT computation is:

	£
Jill's estate (as before)	835,000
Distributed to children	(200,000)
Residue (to Jack)	635,000
No IHT payable	

Jack's estate (assuming he survives Jill by two years):

	£
Portfolio of 300,000 (less cost of PLUS shares and, say, CGT of 10,000)	90,000
Driver Ltd	400,000
PLUS shares	200,000
Share of house and contents	225,000
Inheritance from Jill (net of costs of 15,000)	635,000
	1,550,000

	£
Less BPR on Driver Ltd and PLUS	(600,000)
Less nil rate band (200%)	(650,000)
	300,000
Tax at 40%:	120,000

Carol shows Jack that, although he will have incurred some CGT, he may achieve a useful saving of IHT with these plans.

Jack tells Carol that he is happy with her advice, except for two points. On (or rather in) 'The 19th Green', he has heard advice to the effect that a discretionary trust may be used so as to avoid the aggregation of the estates of husband and wife whilst still allowing the surviving spouse access to all the income in the discretionary trust fund. That seems to him to give him the best of both worlds, in that Jill need not actually leave anything to the children at this stage. Could he not sever the joint tenancy in the house, so that Jill's share went into a trust? The other point is that he has met a (very persuasive) financial adviser in the bar who recommends the use of borrowing to fund lifestyle and lifetime gifts. If the Driver Ltd shares are doing well, might they be good security for such a scheme?

Carol urges caution. How did Jack imagine that such a discretionary trust might work? Would he want to be one of the trustees? Would he want to regard the income of the trust fund as being his, in all but name? What if, for example, following Jill's death, he were to sell the house as being too large for him on his own: would he expect the trustees to buy a smaller house and, in the exercise of their discretion, allow him to live in it? Did he think that, if he lived in a house belonging to a discretionary trust, the proceeds of sale might later be realised free of CGT?

Jack nodded approval to all these propositions until Carol pointed out that, specifically, there would be a serious risk that Jack would be regarded as the tenant for life of a trust fund if he did indeed have significant control over the destination of the income, and particularly if the income were, for reasons of convenience, to be mandated to his bank account. If Jack really felt that he could not live in retirement without the benefit of the income from Jill's securities, then he must accept that, on his death, IHT would be chargeable on the fund that had supported his lifestyle.

Further, Carol pointed out to Jack the effect of SP10/79, by which the exercise by the discretionary trustees of a power to allow a beneficiary to occupy a dwelling house might well cause that house to be regarded as subject to an interest in possession in favour of the occupier.

If Jack wanted the proceeds of resale of such a property to be tax free, as would be the case if the trustees could bring themselves within *TCGA 1992, s 225*, then it would follow that, on Jack's death, there would be a charge to IHT on the fund; whereas, if Jack could show that he was not the only occupier of the property, had no actual right to live there, and that the trustees from time to time went so far as to take away from him the benefit of occupation and in their discretion gave it to someone else, such that he was not regarded as having a life interest, then on resale *s 225* would not apply and a CGT charge might be levied.

Carol advised Jack that discretionary trust arrangements which are intended to give a surviving spouse benefits from a fund, without aggregation of that fund with the free estate of the surviving spouse, must be transparent in their operation. The trustees must have full discretion to make provision for beneficiaries other than the surviving spouse, and for such an arrangement to stand any chance of success the trustees must, as a matter of course, no matter how tedious and expensive the operation, meet from time to time for the purpose of exercising their discretion. It greatly helps in such a situation if the surviving spouse is not one of the trustees. If Jack lived in a 'trust house', he should pay the trustees for the use of any part of it that he did not own.

Carol was not keen on the idea of borrowing, and definitely not on the security of the shares, since that would cut down BPR which was so valuable here. With the inescapable, if unpalatable, logic of an accountant, she said that, if the family home was too big, they should 'downsize' and release equity that way. Jack had had enough of a lecture by this time. He graciously observed that clubroom chat made no mention of SP10/79 or of BPR, and accepted Carol's advice.

DRAFTING POINTS – THE USE OF A CAP

15.10   It was, for many years, common practice for wills to include a legacy of a sum equal to the nil rate band at the date of death of the testator. The advent of the transferable nil rate band has had the effect that, for most families, this will no longer be much use: most families do not hold assets qualifying for APR or BPR. The nil rate band is still useful for 'put together' families, where each spouse has children from an earlier marriage and they wish to find a balance between providing for each other and satisfying the reasonable expectations of their children. In recent years, as the size of the nil rate band was being increased sharply, there was the risk that a government might increase the size of the nil rate band by more than inflation, and that the use of a clause of this type could result in provision for members of the family other than the surviving spouse which is wholly inappropriate and which is, frankly, more than the estate can afford. That risk has receded, for the time being at least.

The simple solution is to take a will precedent (such as the excellent one prepared by James Kessler) and limit the definition of 'the nil rate sum' to an amount which both husband and wife agree is appropriate in relation to the overall assets of the family. There is clearly a risk that the adviser will be found to be negligent if he fails to point out the (relatively) unlimited nature of a simple gift of a nil rate band legacy. Particular care should be taken where the estate includes assets qualifying for APR or BPR, since a 'slack' draft could result in a gift of all such property within the nil rate sum. James Kessler is, of course, alert to the problem.

DRAFTING POINTS: DEFINING THE LEGACY

15.11   Ambiguity had dreadful results in *RSPCA v Sharp* [2010] EWCA Civ 1474, where it was not clear whether a particular gift was intended to fall within the nil rate band, the residue passing to charity; or was in addition to a prior gift of the nil rate band, so that it must be grossed up and residue became much smaller. The rights and wrongs of the hearings and judgments are aired fully elsewhere: for our present purposes, it is enough to say that the whole problem could have been avoided by clear drafting. To return to James Kessler QC: his draft makes it clear that the gift of the nil rate band is of a sum arrived at after taking account of other gifts, in lifetime or within the will itself.

DRAFTING POINTS: THE 'UNTRANSFERABLE' NIL RATE BAND

15.12   In *Drafting Trusts and Will Trusts* (10th edition), at 18.8, James Kessler and Leon Sartin highlight a particular issue that does not directly concern BPR or APR, so is not explored in detail here: the 100% limit on transferable nil rate bands that can affect couples who marry but who had previously been widowed and who, by marriage, in effect lose some IHT flexibility. Whilst acknowledging that '*it is not immediately obvious what is the best form of will*', the writers go on to make good suggestions, such as giving an amount equal to two nil rate bands to a discretionary trust, with residue passing to surviving spouse, either absolutely or on IPDI trust, to make sure that the double nil rate band is actually used.

THE DEBT OR CHARGE SCHEME

15.13   It was noted in Example 15.4 that the gift of a half share in the family home to the next generation can, in certain circumstances, be regarded as creating an interest in possession for the surviving spouse. Whilst this book concentrates on property qualifying for special property reliefs, the practitioner will often find that, for one reason or another, no relief attaches to the family home. It may well be the most valuable single asset, and the will draftsman may look in vain for suitable assets to pass to the next generation so as to use the nil rate band of the first to die of husband and wife.

The debt or charge scheme served for a time to shelter estates from IHT. For most families, the availability of the transferable nil rate band makes the scheme wholly redundant. A trust for the next generation will now commonly be used only where there are 'spare' assets to go into it. The real urge to save IHT was highest when it threatened the family home. Many homes in England now are worth somewhat less than £650,000, so that urgency is diminished.

Attribution rules

15.14   *FA 1986, s 106* introduced, with respect to transfers of value after 17 March 1986, *IHTA 1984, s 39A* to determine the way in which value should be attributed to specific and to residuary gifts. It was considered that an anomaly arose where an individual made a PET, some or all of the value transferred by which related to property qualifying for APR or BPR. *Section 39A* added provisions to clarify the situation.

Example 15.6: how the rules used to work

Julienne has made no previous chargeable transfers. (This example is old, for reasons that will become clear.) At her death in February 1986, her estate includes:

	£
Residence	100,000
Personal effects	20,000
business assets qualifying for 50% BPR	600,000
	720,000

Julienne's will gives to her husband Bernard the house, the contents and half the shares. The residue was given to their son Alphonse.

Under the old rules, it could be argued that the transfer was partly exempt because some of the property passed to Bernard (and was therefore exempt) while the rest passed to Alphonse (this transfer was potentially chargeable). Special provisions in *IHTA 1984, Part II, Chapter III* (ie *ss 36–42*) applied. BPR reduced the value transferred by the transfer of value in question. There was nothing in the legislation requiring a specific gift made out of property qualifying for, in this case, BPR to be taken into account in fixing the value of the gift. The application of the rules could work either for or against the taxpayer. In the present example, the total value transferred by Julienne after BPR was:

	£	£
Property without reliefs		
Residence	100,000	
Chattels	20,000	
		120,000
Business property	600,000	
Less BPR	300,000	
		300,000
		420,000

It could be argued that the value of specific gifts by Julienne to Bernard was £420,000, ie £120,000 non-business property and £300,000 drawn from the value of the shareholding. It could therefore be argued that all of the value being transferred was attributable to Bernard and therefore exempt. Alphonse therefore received, free of (in those days) CTT, property worth £300,000.

Had Julienne made a specific gift to Alphonse of the non-relievable non-business assets and given the remainder (including all the business assets) to Bernard, the rules would have worked the other way. The business relief would have been wasted, because the transfer to Bernard was exempt anyway.

THE EFFECT OF S 39A

15.15   *Section 39A(2)* requires the value of any specific gifts of relevant business property or of agricultural property to be taken to be their value after relief. Actually, in each case the relief reduces the value transferred by a transfer, rather than the value of the property, but that is the way the legislation is framed.

Section 39A(3) requires the value of any specific gifts which do not qualify for relief to be 'the appropriate fraction' of their value. 'The appropriate fraction' is defined in *s 39A(4)* as being one where:

- the numerator is the difference between the value transferred and the net value of any gifts qualifying for relief as reduced; and

- the denominator is the difference between the unreduced value transferred and the gross value of gifts without the value of relief.

The effect of *s 39A(3)* can be to attribute part of the APR or BPR to an exempt transfer. This causes wastage of the relief.

Example 15.7: how the rules now work

Applying the rules to Example 15.6 above:

	£
Value of specific gifts to Bernard:	
Shares	300,000
House and contents: 120,000 multiplied by:	

$$\frac{(420,000 - 150,000)}{(720,000 - 430,000)}$$

ie $\dfrac{270,000}{290,000} \times 120,000$ — 111,724

411,724

As a result, the value transferred at Julienne's death of £720,000 is attributed as follows:

Bernard   £411,724

Alphonse   £380,276.

The gift to Alphonse is chargeable (in so far as it exceeds the nil rate band).

There is a trap for the will draftsman in these provisions.

Example 15.8: loose giving

Chantalle's farm is worth £600,000. It qualifies for APR at 100%. She has made no chargeable lifetime gifts. She has life policies which, by virtue of bad management, will fall into her estate amounting to £320,000. Her present will gives the residue to her husband Algernon, subject to a legacy of the nil rate band to her friend Shaun. The will has been drafted in such a way that the legacy consists of the value of the farm after relief, such that Shaun inherits the entire farm (having a nil chargeable value after APR) and all the policy proceeds. Algernon gets nothing.

Supposing that, according to the way the will is drafted, the farm assets are not specifically allocated to the legacy. The legacy is treated as coming partly from the value of the farm and partly from the policy proceeds and, to that extent, BPR may be wasted. The sum is:

	£
The legacy (based on the nil rate band in 2011)	325,000
Divided by the estate	920,000
Multiplied by the legacy	325,000
To produce a figure of	114,809

Shaun's legacy is treated for IHT as coming, as to £114,809, from the value of the farm and, as to the balance, from the policy proceeds.

Avoiding the difficulties of s 39A

15.16   For the general practitioner the moral is simple: take care to avoid grossing up and to avoid *s 39A*. After an explanation of the principles involved, many clients will wish to avoid the complexities of the legislation and will be willing to identify more precisely the gifts which they wish to pass to exempt beneficiaries.

If a chargeable specific gift is made of an asset that qualifies for relief, that fixes the availability of the relief.

Example 15.9: much improved will

Kenneth, who has made no chargeable transfers nor PETs in the last seven years, owns the following assets:

	£
Residence	300,000
Savings: quoted shares	400,000
Business property qualifying for 50% relief	200,000
	900,000

His present will leaves the house and the business assets to his widow Leonie and the quoted shares to his daughter Marie. That is inefficient, triggering a charge to IHT on death at 40% on the excess of the gift over the nil rate band, currently £325,000, so tax of £30,000. His will should be varied (or a deed of variation entered into following his death) to give Marie the business assets and (possibly) £200,000, with residue to Leonie. That way, for family purposes, £400,000 will still be attributed to the specific gift to Marie but, after deducting BPR of £100,000, all the value will be within the nil rate band. Later, mother and daughter might think about a second transaction, to re-use BPR on the business assets in the way already described earlier in this chapter.

As an alternative, the will might have been drawn, or might after death be varied, so as to give Marie only some quoted shares, equal to the nil rate band of

£325,000. There will be no charge on death, though there will be no further nil rate band, at least from Keith, to transfer on the widow's death. Leonie, taking the residue, might consider a simple gift to Marie of the unquoted shares. There would be no charge on Keith's death. If done promptly, there might be no gain on the shares, so no CGT. If Leonie made a lifetime gift of the unquoted shares but failed to survive that gift by seven years then, subject to clawback, BPR would be available by virtue of the succession provisions of *IHTA 1984, s 108*. Clearly, care would be required to avoid, in the case of a variation, any understanding that Leonie would make the gift to avoid the suggestion within *s 142(3)* that there had been any consideration for the making of the variation.

Sometimes, a conscious effort is needed to avoid *s 39A*. The practitioner needs to be aware of the rule in order to give appropriate advice when taking will instructions.

Example 15.10*: not seeing the wood for the trees**

Maud lived in modest circumstances with her friend Winifred. The house belonged to Maud, who also held stocks and shares worth £300,000, including a holding worth £75,000 of shares in the company which her father had founded many years ago and which was now run by more distant relatives. The shares in the family company are unquoted.

In consulting Geoff about a new will, Maud made it clear that, in the event of her death, she would want Winifred to be able to go on living in the house for as long as she might want. In fact, Winifred was not in terribly good health and it seemed quite likely that, in the event of Maud's death, Winifred would move into sheltered housing. To tide Winifred over, Maud wanted to ensure that there was a suitable sum of money available tax free. Subject to that, Maud wished her estate to pass, as far as possible, in equal shares to three charities and to a niece and nephew.

Geoff was very concerned to avoid the '*Re Benham*' problem, not being aware of the more recent decision in *Re Ratcliffe* which might have afforded him some reassurance. By concentrating exclusively on avoiding wording which might fall precisely within the difficulties of *Re Benham*, Geoff overlooked one or two other points.

On Maud's death, it appeared that the house was rather more valuable than Geoff had appreciated, having the benefit of an area of land to the rear with planning potential. For a time, it seemed that Winifred would be happy to continue to live there and, in his capacity as executor, Geoff saw no reason to encourage her to move on. In accordance with the power given to him by the will, Geoff earmarked £15,000 (the limit allowed by the will) as the 'cushion' to tide Winifred over.

Geoff was both surprised and concerned to receive a letter from HMRC Capital Taxes raising with him the operation not only of *s 39A* but also of SP10/79, of whose existence he had previously been blissfully unaware. The HMRC argument was that the power in the will to allow Winifred to continue to occupy the dwelling house, even though she had no formal interest in possession, amounted to such an interest with the result that, in calculating IHT, the value of the house (and the land to the rear which Winifred was also, in effect, occupying) fell to be regarded as a transfer to a non-exempt beneficiary.

Further, the clause in the will allowing up to £15,000 to be made available for Winifred was a gift free of tax. Since there was no chargeable specific gift of an asset qualifying for relief, the gift of the £15,000 must be treated as 'spread' across the property qualifying for BPR, the shareholding in the family company, and the remainder of the estate. Clearly, as a result, some of the available BPR was thus wasted. It also became necessary, because of the distribution of residue between exempt and non-exempt beneficiaries, to carry out a full exercise of the double grossing calculation after applying the attribution and allocation rules.

A deed of variation was needed to put things right. Fortunately, the nephew and niece were of full age and Winifred decided to move into sheltered housing after all. It therefore became possible to remove the offending provisions of the will, in particular the quasi-life interest, such that the remaining gift of £15,000 fell entirely within the nil rate band. Grossing up of that gift could be avoided.

These principles should be borne in mind when considering the form of will, often used, that creates a nil rate band discretionary will trust. The beneficiaries of such a trust will often be the surviving spouse, children and grandchildren. Unless there is a *specific* gift of property that qualifies for APR or BPR, the relief in respect of that property will be spread across the whole of the estate including the residue, which may perhaps be exempt as passing to the surviving spouse. It is not enough for the personal representatives merely to appropriate certain assets to the discretionary trust. That will not satisfy the requirement of *s 39A* for a specific gift unless there is, in the circumstances, no choice as to the assets to be appropriated. An alternative, and more flexible, will would create a discretionary trust not merely of the nil rate band but over residue. The trustees could then make the necessary appointments (at least three months after the death but less than two years thereafter) which would constitute specific gifts for the purposes of *s 39A*.

ROUTING THROUGH NON-EXEMPT BENEFICIARIES

15.17 Frequently, will planning is geared towards skipping a generation in order, perhaps through the medium of a trust, to get property down to grandchildren. There are advantages to the children in that, whilst income (over the first £1,000) is taxed in the hands of the trustees at 50% where beneficiaries have no other income, that tax may be recovered, save insofar as it is notional tax on dividends. On the other hand, there is one circumstance in which exactly the opposite tactic is helpful: this concerns woodland.

Example 15.11: elderly aunts have their uses

Suppose the testator owns woodlands which, owing to the age and nature of the trees, are now very valuable. The testator may have a relative who, although elderly, might nevertheless survive the testator. If the woodlands are given by the will to the elderly relative, there is perhaps little chance of a disposal during the lifetime of that relative. An election might then be made to leave the value of the timber out of account when fixing the tax on the death of the testator, on the basis that the tax would be chargeable on any later disposal but, since the elderly relative would (it is hoped) not dispose of the timber, that relative's death would frank the IHT charge on the first death.

Securing, for tax planning purposes, such a combination of deaths 'at the right time and in the right order' may be beyond the office facilities available to the average tax planner. Explaining the scheme and putting in place safeguards to ensure that the elderly relative does not sell the timber may be quite difficult. The whole scheme may therefore be of somewhat academic interest.

In the more normal situation, where the testator has 'cashed in' the value of his woodlands and has only recently replanted them, he may wish to transfer them to a young beneficiary. In such a situation, the value of timber at the time of the death of the testator may be quite low because the trees are still young. In these circumstances, the tax charge may be small. It will not be worth making an election for woodlands relief since there is a risk that, when the deferred tax comes to be payable (it is hoped not until many years later), the woodlands may have increased considerably in value. Similarly, it will not be worth making the election for woodlands relief where the transfer of the woodlands is exempt, as for example to a spouse or to charity. The tax planner must look at the circumstances and compare the possibility of avoiding the payment of tax on the death of the will beneficiary with the cash flow advantages just outlined.

GIFTS OF BUSINESSES

15.18   Often, a simple tax planning scheme will involve the gift, on the one hand, of assets that qualify for neither APR nor BPR to the surviving spouse and, on the other hand, of assets that do qualify for such relief to other beneficiaries, perhaps in the next generation. A difficulty can arise where there is a specific legacy of an interest in a business, particularly an underwriting business at Lloyd's. It was noted at **5.22** that there is some question as to whether there can be succession for the purposes of BPR to the business of a Name, in that underwriting is in some respects personal to the Name. It is, however, clear that personal representatives may continue the underwriting business so, whilst the rules as to succession in *IHTA 1984, ss 108* and *109* may not apply, the business may be the subject matter of a gift.

Supposing the gift to be of 'all my Lloyd's business', there can be a distinction between what is defined as the business itself and the value that will attract relief, ie between the value on the 'commercial' basis and on the 'relief' basis, discussed in **Chapter 5**. This is not a problem specific only to Lloyd's Names: there is the same difficulty in relation to the gift of a farmhouse which enjoys premium valuation by virtue of its situation. Nevertheless, the will draftsman must take care to define with precision what the legatee gets. This will be particularly important where relations between the beneficiaries are strained. In particular, it will be difficult to decide what assets pass under a gift of 'such of my property as shall be eligible for business property relief' or of 'such interest in my [farmhouse] as shall be eligible for agricultural property relief'. The executor will have to decide with some precision what value attracts relief. It is in the nature of the asset that an early transfer to the beneficiary will be essential, so that the business can be run and directed efficiently; and yet the executor may need to take from the beneficiary some undertaking or other security for the return of value if there has been, with hindsight, an error in the calculation of relief or the basis on which it should be claimed.

It is in this context that the executor should consider the decision in *Hardcastle (executors of Vernede deceased) v IRC* [2000] [STC] 532 (SCD), examined in some detail at **5.20**, and HMRC's review of that decision, which they consider not to be of general application.

One concern with the decision in *Hardcastle* might be that the ordinary liabilities incurred in the running of the business would not go to reduce the value of the business for BPR purposes, and that that itself might be a general principle. It would seem, although the matter is yet to be clarified, that it is these wider implications of *Hardcastle* that HMRC do not accept.

THE MEANING OF 'SPOUSE'

15.19 The law adapts to changing social circumstances. A challenge was mounted in *Holland (Executor of Holland Deceased) v IRC* SpC 350, [2003] STI Issue 2. The appellant had not been married to the deceased, but had lived with him as man and wife for 31 years until his death on 17 April 2000. She claimed that the property that passed to her on his death should be exempt from IHT under *s 18*. She argued that the word 'spouse' in that section was not restricted to those who were legally married but included those who lived together as husband and wife. In the alternative, she argued that her rights to respect for private and family life and to peaceful enjoyment of her possessions were infringed by discrimination based on status. That claim was under the *Human Rights Act 1998, s 3*, which required *IHTA 1984, s 18* to be read in a way which would remove that discrimination.

The Special Commissioner disagreed. The meaning of a word must accord with the understanding of the ordinary man using the word in its popular sense at the relevant time. Whilst the meaning of the word 'family' had changed over time, the meaning of the word 'spouse' had not. There was authority for that both in *Dyson Holdings Limited v Fox* [1976] QB 503 and *Fitzpatrick v Sterling Housing Association Limited* [2001] 1 AC 27 (HL).

When Parliament used the word 'spouse', whether in *IHTA 1984* or other provisions of the tax code generally, it intended to mean only married persons. That could be inferred unequivocally as an intention of Parliament from the Official Report of 5 February 1975. This is reinforced, though not mentioned at this point of the judgment, by the fact that 'or civil partner' has been added after 'spouse' in the legislation with effect from 5 December 2005.

The *Human Rights Act 1998* did not apply. The case was concerned with the law as at the date of death, so *HRA 1998, s 3(1)* would not apply. Further, the Commissioners could not declare that *HRA 1998* required a wider interpretation of the word 'spouse'. They must read primary legislation in a way that was compatible with convention, but only insofar as it was possible to do so.

In the light of conflicting decisions of UK higher courts, the Commissioner must take account of the decisions respectively in *Lindsey v UK* (1986) (Commission Decision 1 November 1986) DR 49 p 181 and *Shackell v UK* EHCR decision of 27 April 2000 which established the principle that married persons were not in a situation analogous to that of non-married persons. Whilst the Court of Appeal had held, in *Mendosa v Ghaiden* [2002] EWCA Civ 1533, that a person in a same-sex relationship was living with another as husband and wife, that did not mean that non-married couples could be equated with married couples. People living together as husband and wife were not in the situation of married people. It was not possible by virtue of the *HRA 1998, s 3* to read *IHTA 1984, s 18* so as to give the word 'spouse' any meaning other than a person who was legally married.

Chapter 16

APR and BPR: the new regime

QUICK GUIDE

The IHT regime for business and agricultural property has remained relatively stable for several years now. Elsewhere in this book, the writer has argued for an amalgamation of the two reliefs but, despite the recent push for simplification, there is no sign of significant work in this field. The key question for the practitioner advising on IHT planning is whether the present rates can safely be relied upon for the next few years. If they can, **16.7** shows why it may be prudent to retain assets in the hands of the older generation. If the present rates are not to be relied upon, **16.5** and **16.6** put the arguments for taking action now.

WHAT NEW REGIME?

16.1   It was noted earlier that taxpayers and their advisers feared that a Labour Government might introduce a harsh new regime. Owners of property who for years had delayed in making gifts finally resolved to do so. The actual experience under Labour was not as bad as feared. Whilst the Liberal Democrats have become the loudest campaigners for redistribution of wealth, they lack the power to move the present coalition far in that direction. The constant changes in CGT and the work on aligning the powers of the old Inland Revenue and (even older) Customs & Excise will no doubt have occupied a great deal of policy-making time. That may have delayed any changes to IHT.

Most of the changes to IHT have been targeted anti-avoidance measures rather than full reappraisals of the tax. Any restriction of APR or BPR to achieve redistribution of wealth could, at the highest levels, hit a few people disproportionately hard: those who have great fortunes tend not to invest them in bank current accounts but in land, especially farmland, and in businesses; so the reliefs are fundamental to the decision whether or not to keep a store of wealth in this country. Such people know no territorial boundaries, and a significant change would result in economic migration; we have seen it happen in relation to family trusts and the 50% trust tax rate.

Excluded property settlements

16.2   Is any reform really necessary? The creation of excluded property settlements by foreigners who have lived happily in this country for nearly 17 out of the last 20 years does seem to warrant some attention. There is an important issue here, namely whether a settlement within *IHTA 1984, s 6* (and thus excluded property) is outside the scope of IHT, such that the gifts with reservation code cannot apply. This has long been accepted as a view and remains the present law, but it appears that it may now be under review.

For the time being, it would seem that *s 6* takes priority; but the issue is unresolved, and we have seen more movement in the taxation of 'non doms' than in many other areas, so watch this space. Practitioners were reassured that any change would be brought to their attention, and would not be introduced by stealth. The consultation document on domicile noted the 'interesting and generous results' of placing certain property within a trust to exclude it from the burden of IHT, but was merely stating existing practice. Most of the domicile issues are, however, outside the scope of this book.

Shadow directors

16.3   One issue in this area, which concerns primarily income tax but which may have knock-on effects for capital tax planning, is the extent to which a shadow director may be subject to a charge under *ITEPA 2003, Chapter 5* in respect of living accommodation. That was one of the issues raised in *R v Dimsey* and *R v Allen* [1999] STC 846 before the Court of Appeal. There was some tightening up of CGT in relation to offshore trusts, and it would be consistent with those CGT changes for the IHT regime to be made slightly harsher.

Reform

16.4   Each new government appears to wish to be 'friendly' to industry. Reliefs for risk-taking by investing in business or acting as a 'business angel' are being made more generous. It is acknowledged that farming is undergoing very serious financial difficulties, partly as a result of the strength of sterling. Politically, therefore, a major tightening up of APR and BPR seems no more attractive than when this book was first published 11 years ago.

There are one or two possible areas which might be regarded as reforms by the general public, though not by those who would suffer the changes. The first might be a return to some form of 'working farmer' relief. In the view of the popular voter, there may well be a distinction between the reliefs which should be accorded to a family who draw all of their income from farming, and those which should be available to, for example, a prosperous accountant who wisely invests part of his capital in a farm which he operates through a contracting agreement.

Another possible change, in keeping with the view of some who do not live in the country, might be making entitlement to APR conditional upon the agreement of the landowner to much greater rights of access for the public than at present. In other words, APR would have to be 'earned' by positively encouraging access, including suitable provision for parking, provision of stiles, signposts and the like.

For some reason, the politics of envy seem to find fewer targets among non-farming business people. Nonetheless, there may be environmental considerations which could impinge on BPR. For example, BPR could be made conditional upon compliance with safety and environmental standards or, at a more idealistic level, upon achieving a six-sided contract with society as well as owners of the type envisaged by Charles Handy (*The Empty Raincoat* at p 131). That would be consistent with some noises from the present coalition. At the moment, we see increased measures to tax and combat pollution, but not the much graver sanction of withdrawal of such a valuable relief as APR or BPR.

USE OF 100% RELIEFS WHILE THEY LAST

16.5   The fact remains that the present regime is benign. This book has, it is hoped, highlighted the many intricacies and difficulties of APR and BPR, and has shown that there are occasions when the existence of the relief actually makes it better to retain assets qualifying for the relief rather than to transfer them. Overall, however, where the assets are substantial and where members of the family can be trusted to look after family assets, there is much merit in encouraging large transfers of property subject to 100% relief. Where a gift is made early enough and without reservation, such that the transferor survives by seven years, all the complications of clawback can be avoided.

Interesting situations arise where planning opportunities are currently available which could easily be lost by changes to the rates of relief.

Example 16.1: careful use of company structure

Cedric established a successful business. A few years ago, his company obtained a stock exchange quotation. The capital is now £15,000,000, divided into £7,500,000 ordinary shares (which are unquoted) and an equal number of

'A' ordinary, which are quoted. All shares carry equal votes. Cedric still holds all the unquoted ordinary shares. He holds 2,000,000 of the quoted shares and now wishes to establish a trust for charitable purposes.

The unquoted ordinary shares qualify for BPR at 100%, coming within *IHTA 1984, s 105(1)(bb)*. The quoted shares fall within *s 105(1)(cc)*. They do not give control in their own right but, by virtue of Cedric's holding of unquoted shares, the quoted shares give him control. BPR is available at 50%.

Cedric had in mind to transfer some of the unquoted shares to the charity. That would be an exempt transfer and, for the purposes of CGT, would give rise to no chargeable gain by virtue of *TCGA 1992, s 257*. However, a gift of unquoted shares, if sufficiently large to take Cedric's holding below a control holding, would cause the loss of the 50% BPR on the quoted shares.

Subject to company and commercial considerations, such as the difference in value between the ordinary and the 'A' ordinary shares, a gift of the quoted shares to the charity would leave in Cedric's hands assets all of which still qualify for BPR at 100%.

Since very little legislative effort would be required to reduce the present 100% rate for BPR to 50% and to reduce the existing 50% to, say, 30%, it makes sense to do the transaction now.

LOCKING INTO THE 100% RATE EVEN ON FAILED PETS

16.6   A feature of the legislation which may help the tax planner was noted in **Chapters 3** and **6**: in respect of deaths and other chargeable events occurring after 9 March 1992, APR became available for certain categories of property at 100%. This was by virtue of *F (No 2) A 1992, s 73* and *Sch 14*. The commencement provisions were set out in *Sch 14, paras 8* and *9*. By *para 9(1)*, the new rates apply to a PET which fails and to the top-up charge on death in respect of a lifetime chargeable transfer. For the purposes of *IHTA 1984, ss 113A* and *113B*, relating to the clawback provisions and the savings provisions for clawback in respect of replacement property, it is to be assumed that:

- the new and more generous rates of relief came into effect at the time that the transfer was made; and

- in relation to the charge that would otherwise have applied to top up the tax from the lifetime rate to the death rate, the portion of the value transferred which would have qualified for relief at the new rates does so qualify.

Where shares qualified for BPR within *s 105(1)(b)*, it was possible to disregard the amendments in respect of relief in deciding whether or not the shares were affected by *s 113A(3A)*, ie shares which were quoted at the time of the chargeable transfer or were unquoted shares or securities within *s 105(1)(b)* or *(bb)* and stayed unquoted throughout the period from the date of the chargeable transfer to death of the transferor.

A similar provision in *FA 1996* at *s 184(6)* enlarged the relief in relation to any transfers of value on or after 6 April 1996. *Section 184(6)(b)(ii)* made it clear that the new rates also had effect for the purposes of any charge to tax by reason of any event occurring on or after 6 April 1996 in relation to transfers of value before that date.

The effect of the rule on a PET which fails is therefore, at present, that 100% APR or BPR is available so that, provided the conditions are observed which will save the PET from clawback, the transferor and transferee would seem to have secured the relief, regardless of changes that might take place to reduce that relief. Is that actually how the legislation would work if the government considered that a 100% rate was too generous? Possibly not: it would not be difficult to reverse the effects of *F (No 2) A 1992, Sch 14* and *FA 1996, s 184(6)* in relation to events occurring after the enactment of the harsher rule, if so desired.

Whilst it may therefore be argued that, on the present law, it is possible to 'lock into' the 100% rate, it may be over-optimistic to suggest that such an action would render the transaction immune from legislative change. It would no doubt be argued, in representations after the draft legislation was published, that such changes were retrospective and threatened transactions which had been entered into in reliance on the earlier law. A government with a strong majority that was committed to simplifying the law might disregard such arguments on the ground that, in relation to PETs which at the date of enactment had not yet failed, there was still the possibility that the transferor might survive the gift by seven years. Both *F (No 2) A 1992* and *FA 1996* introduced provisions as part of a trend not only towards simplification but towards increasing the reliefs: new legislation to withdraw the reliefs could easily adopt a much harsher line.

Therefore, practitioners should use the reliefs for as long as they last, recognising that the present provisions for 'lock in' are as vulnerable as the reliefs themselves.

The effect of a potentially exempt transfer that is relieved at 100% is very similar to that of an immediately chargeable transfer. That can be seen from the Table that follows, which gives a comparison of potentially exempt transfers with immediately chargeable transfers:

	PET Treatment	*CT Treatment*
1. Immediate charge to IHT?	No: a PET	No: value reduced to nil
2. Death within 7 years of transfer: assets retained by donee	No IHT: full APR	No IHT: full APR
3. Death within 7 years of transfer where clawback applies	IHT charge (subject to nil rate band)	
(a) as to the transfer itself	On the full amount	On the full amount
(b) as to aggregation with the later transfers, eg on death	Full value is aggregated	Value is nil, so an advantage in making the transfer by CT
4. Transferor lives 7 years from gift	No IHT: transfer has become exempt	No IHT: falls out of cumulation

LOSS OF CGT FREE UPLIFT ON DEATH

16.7   Practitioners with long memories will remember the charge to CGT that applied on death. Complaint was made that the combination of CGT and IHT was punitive. The existence of free uplift on death is very valuable as a feature of tax planning, but does force the taxpayer to consider volunteering to pay tax at the time of a transfer in order to save a greater charge later.

For example, the owner of freehold investment property qualifies neither for APR nor BPR nor for holdover relief under *TCGA 1992, s 165*. Any gift of the property may trigger a charge to CGT save a gift to a discretionary trust, where holdover is available under *TCGA 1992, s 260*. At present, relief is available under *s 260* because the transfer to a discretionary trust is a chargeable transfer, even though the charge may be at 0% because the transfer is within the nil rate band.

One aspect of the new regime, not directly affecting APR and BPR, might be the withdrawal of the right to holdover under *s 260*, save where there is a charge to IHT at a positive rate. An even harsher rule might provide mere set-off of one tax against the other, so as to ensure a 'tax take' of up to 40% of the funds transferred. That would be exceptionally harsh but would affect non-business property and, as such, might be doctrinally acceptable to a cash-strapped government committed to redistribution of wealth.

For the time being, the tax practitioner must, in trying to mitigate the burden of IHT, bear in mind that a gift of business assets subject to holdover under *s 165* will leave the donee liable to pay the tax on the gain held over.

Example 16.2: failure to advise fully?

Sally, an elderly widow whose late husband had used his nil rate band, was concerned about the burden of IHT on her estate. She owned shares in the family trading company that qualified for BPR at 100% and that stood at a significant gain over acquisition value. She also wanted to encourage her daughter Lucy to greater efforts as manager of the company, so consulted Geoff about transferring shares to Lucy.

Geoff advised that BPR should be available and put the share transfer in hand, remembering (at the last moment, just before Sally signed the forms) to advise Sally that there might be CGT implications and that it might be possible to hold over the gain on the shares. He also acted for Lucy and warned her about the clawback provisions of *IHTA 1984, s 113A*. Lucy regarded the shares as a long-term investment.

Sally unexpectedly died only months later. Lucy still held the shares, so IHT was not in issue (as it would have been if BPR had not been available) but, with hindsight, Sally should not have made the transfer, because tax-free uplift on death, for CGT purposes, had been lost. There was, however, no claim in negligence against Geoff: he had mentioned CGT at the time, and Sally seemed to be in good health, and likely to live for some time, when the transfer took place.

THE LAST RESORT: LIFE ASSURANCE

16.8   To regard life assurance as 'the last resort' betrays perhaps an unfair attitude towards the financial services industry. Whilst it is fair to comment that, occasionally, taxpayers will have purchased insurance policies to fund tax liabilities which need not have arisen if proper planning had been put in place, life assurance can of course be a considerable help to the tax planner.

It was noted in Example 4.3 that there are specific occasions when, for technical reasons, APR may not be available for a time. Life assurance in these circumstances is no more than prudent management. Similarly, Examples 4.8 relating to successive transfers and 4.5 and 4.6 relating to inherited ownership, show various conditions which must be complied with. Insurance might be appropriate to cover the risk of a death at a time of non-compliance. Exactly the same position may arise in relation to clawback where, through outside forces, a sale takes place of property which had qualified for BPR and, for commercial reasons, it is difficult immediately to reinvest the funds in qualifying property so as to preserve the situation from clawback. The use of insurance was considered in *Swain Mason v Mills & Reeve* [2011] EWHC 410 (Ch), although only in a limited context.

There is one other specific use for life assurance which is relevant to all entrepreneurs in business, but perhaps to farmers most of all. It concerns provision for those members of the family who do not work on the farm or in the business. Farmers will seldom admit to having enjoyed a good year; but, when there is a trading surplus, the farmer will far more readily apply the funds in the purchase of land and machinery than in making provision for the non-farming son or, regrettably even more so, non-farming daughter.

If the tax adviser can persuade the farmer to set aside insurance premiums each year for a policy written specifically for the benefit of the non-farming relative, the situation of the farmer late in life, and of his children after his death, may be infinitely easier than would otherwise have been the case. Similarly, where the inheritance structure is such that the farming son inherits the live and dead stock and a share only in the land, leaving him with the obligation of buying out his brothers and sisters at market value, life assurance taken out by a son may provide him with at least part of the funds that he needs to raise in order to carry on farming after his father has died.

Chapter 17

Heritage property: what qualifies, undertakings and access

QUICK GUIDE

There are six categories of heritage property:

- pre-eminent chattels;
- pre-eminent collections;
- outstanding land;
- outstanding buildings;
- amenity land; and
- associated chattels.

The qualitative tests of heritage property are considered at **17.4** onwards. In general terms, applications in respect of new property since 31 July 1998 face higher hurdles than the continuation of old heritage status. There are broadly four tests:

- history and national life;
- artistic interest;
- educational importance; and
- historic association.

Public access is fundamental and, in relation to 'new' applications, will be considered before qualitative vetting of the property itself. Under the old rules, the requirement of public access could be satisfied on a 'by appointment only' basis. That system fell into disrepute following certain investigative journalism and is almost disregarded as a form of access under the new rules. What may be considered reasonable access is outlined at **17.13**. Publicity is also fundamental to the scheme, through the register of conditionally exempt works of art and the other measures of disclosure described at **17.19** onwards.

OVERVIEW

17.1   Unlike BPR and APR, the relief for heritage property is not absolute. Unlike woodland relief, the relief for heritage property may be one of deferral for an indefinite time. The regime for heritage property allows the owner, or a succession of owners, to escape IHT for so long as certain undertakings, once given, are complied with. A major feature of the regime is the scheme for 'clawback' (the author's term for the event) of the exemption in the event of non-compliance.

As a separate matter devised by government for the support of heritage property, the transfer of assets to an approved trust fund, established for the maintenance of a qualifying heritage building, will also escape IHT for as long as the funds are applied for the approved purpose. Although this book is principally concerned with IHT, it should be noted that there are parallel reliefs from CGT in respect of heritage property which, for completeness, are considered where relevant to the discussion of IHT.

Another feature of heritage property is that, in appropriate circumstances, it may be used in satisfaction of a liability to tax on negotiated terms which can be favourable to the owner. In few other areas of tax law is the purpose of the relief so clearly focused. It is, quite simply, that there is a trade-off between the burden of tax on the owner of heritage property, on the one hand, and access to that property for the general public on the other. To be relieved of the burden of the tax that would otherwise be due, the owner must assume obligations to the public. As with all tax, this creates a tension between the desire to save the tax and the desire to minimise public intrusion into personal privacy. As will be seen, the regime was, until recently, fairly benign, but the coming into force of rules under *FA 1998* has forced HMRC to reappraise the old arrangements and to seek the agreement of the owners of heritage property to a new regime.

FINDING THE LAW

17.2   There is relatively little modern case law, but see the examination of the case on access at **18.15**. The statutory code is mainly in *IHTA 1984, ss 30–35A*. There is substantial guidance in Official Notes, as noted below though (as befits the subject, perhaps) few of these documents seem to be available, or significantly referred to, online. A pre-2009 HMRC document (hmrc.gov.uk/cto/national-heritage.pdf) states that 'We will not be publishing a new edition of IR67 as a separate publication. Instead, updated and revised guidance on public access will be published on our website next year. The 'Access Notes' are now set out as an annex to IHTM. Hard copies of the following guidance are available from the Department for Culture, Media and Sport at 2–4 Cockspur Street, London SW1Y 5DH,:

- The register of conditionally exempt works of art: this is now available online at www.hmrc.gov.uk/heritage/index.htm;

- April 1982 'Works of Art: A basic guide to Capital Taxation and the National Heritage', in this book called 'the Basic Guide';

- April 1984 'Works of Art: Guidance on *in situ* offers in lieu of capital taxation', in this book called 'the *in situ* Guidelines';

- November 1986 'Works of Art: Private Treaty Sales', in this book called 'the Private Treaty Notes';

- December 1986 'Capital Taxation and the National Heritage', in this book called 'IR67' (but see below);

- January 1999 'Capital Taxes – relief for Heritage Assets: Notes on the changes made by the *Finance Act 1998*', in this book called 'the 1999 Notes'; and

- August 2006 'Guidance Notes on Public Access', in this book called 'the Access Notes'.

It is understood that HMRC are updating their Manual and that, perhaps before the end of 2011, we shall see a revised version of IR67.

HERITAGE PROPERTY: WHAT QUALIFIES

17.3   *IHTA 1984, s 31* allows designation of property by the Treasury. Until 25 July 1985, administration of the scheme for conditional exemption of property lay with the Treasury but, by *FA 1985, s 95*, the responsibility for conditionally exempt transfers, whether under the *Act* or under earlier legislation, was transferred to the Board of Inland Revenue. Thus, any authorisations, designations or other acts by the Treasury have the same effect as if made or done by the Board.

Section 31(1) identifies six categories of heritage property:

(*a*)   objects which are pre-eminent for national, scientific, historic or artistic interest (in this book called 'pre-eminent chattels');

(*aa*) collections or groups of objects which taken as a whole are pre-eminent for national, scientific, historic or artistic interest ('pre-eminent collections');

(*b*)   land of outstanding scenic or historic or scientific interest ('outstanding land');

(*c*)   a building for the preservation of which special steps should be taken because of its outstanding historic or architectural interest ('outstanding buildings');

(*d*)   land essential for the protection of the character and amenities of a building as above ('amenity land'); and

(*e*)   any object historically associated with a building as above ('associated chattel').

The names used above relate to heritage property under the present regime, and not to the (similar) categories that previously applied.

By *s 31(1A)*, the quality of heritage property is judged by reference to the circumstances that exist after the death of the transferor. This provision was enacted with reference to transfers of value made after 17 March 1986 by *FA 1986, s 101(3)* and *Sch 19, para 8*.

The quality of heritage property: rules after 31 July 1998

17.4   Following adverse press comment, the scheme for conditional exemption was revised by *FA 1998* such that, for claims for conditional exemption made on or after 31 July 1998, objects qualified for exemption only if meeting new and higher standards. The property must now be either:

● of pre-eminent national, scientific, historic or artistic interest, taking into account any significant association that the property might have with a particular place; or

● historically associated with a building which is itself of outstanding historical or architectural interest.

'Pre-eminence' means, in general terms, that the property is certainly of 'museum quality', ie that a national or local authority, university or independent museum would regard the property as a pre-eminent addition to its existing collection. It is here that the question of place may be relevant, in that the association of the property or group of items with a particular place may enable property to be pre-eminent where, without that association, the article might not pass the test.

Equally, in relation to chattels, the condition of the article will be highly relevant. Unfortunately, practitioners cannot obtain an official opinion in advance. Appeal lies to the Special Commissioner. As far as land is concerned, anything not already classified as being within a National Park, SSSI, part of the Heritage Coast etc will probably fail to qualify. It must be of national importance and recognised as such. Buildings will probably be listed Grade II* or higher if they are to qualify. Amenity land need not meet such a stringent test: it merely supports the main property.

The 'Waverley' criteria

17.5   HMRC have long had the power, with the agreement of the Secretary of State, to accept property in satisfaction of tax itself. This is considered in detail at **Chapter 23**. The administration of that power, under *IHTA 1984, s 230*, has developed standards for the property so accepted that they are now applied in interpreting *s 31(1)*. Guidance was originally established by the Museums and Galleries Commission (MGC), but responsibility passed to the Museums, Libraries and Archives Council (MLA), and in April 2012 is to move again, this time to to The National Archives (TNA) MLA has operated a 'Designation' scheme, but that concerns public collections rather than heritage assets still in private ownership.

Practitioners should view the 'Acceptance in Lieu Guidance Notes' (available on the MLA website which, although geared to acceptance in lieu, is also relevant to applications for conditional exemption. As this guidance explains, the Acceptance in Lieu Panel will make a recommendation to the Secretary of State. This is not, incidentally, a 'one way bet': the panel seek the right price and will, on occasion, recommend a higher price for public acquisition than the owner demanded. This guidance concerns pre-eminent chattels rather than outstanding land. There are four broad tests of pre-eminence applied by the AIL Panel, which will gather advice when considering whether property is 'pre-eminent' and will consult widely where the object has local significance. Further advice is available from the Acquisitions, Export and Loans Unit, MLA, currently housed at Wellcome Wolfson Building, 165 Queen's Gate, London SW7 5HD. When functions are transferred, some staff may move to Birmingham, but this work is likely to stay in London, perhaps moving to Great Peter Street; details will be posted on the MLA website when known.

Test 1: History and national life

The first test is whether the object has an especially close association with 'our' history and national life. *Section 230(5)* explains that 'national interest' includes interest within any part of the United Kingdom. That does not mean that the work must necessarily be British. Gifts from foreign sovereigns (if any such remain) or foreign governments may count. So may objects that, as the guidance delicately puts it, 'have been acquired abroad' in circumstances closely associated with the history of the United Kingdom. Note in this connection that any application should include full provenance, in particular details of ownership between 1933 and 1945. The property might be associated with a particular part of the United Kingdom or with the development of one of its institutions or industries. Some property may well be below national importance but may qualify through local connections.

Test 2: Artistic interest

Some property is clearly of such quality that any national museum or gallery would be glad to accept it. The category here includes not only famous works but those items which may not be pre-eminent in a national museum but would pass that test from the standpoint of smaller galleries, such as those maintained by local authorities, universities or independent galleries. The test of quality is, theoretically at least, to be judged separately from any undertaking (see below) as to public access.

Take, for example, a minor work of a member of the Norwich School of Painters that flourished in the late 18th and early 19th centuries. The Castle Museum at Norwich has a fine collection of such works, such that 'one more Cotman' might not be regarded there as a pre-eminent addition, whilst to some other local authority gallery the work might be more highly prized.

It is understood that the AIL Panel, and indeed ministers, are keen to promote the enjoyment of fine works of art, not just in London but at a more local level. Whilst by far the majority of applications come through the main auction houses, the Annual Acceptance in Lieu Report shows that the panel is trying to encourage smaller estates to apply. The 2009/2010 Report lists acquisitions of great range, from Seaton Delaval Hall, at £4,883,599, down to a very rare woodcut, 393mm x 500mm, by Karl Schmidt-Rottluff valued at £4,900. There was evidence in the Report that other work by Schmidt-Rottluff had previously been declined by major British museums and ended up in Germany; this woodcut was fairly priced and clearly too good to lose.

Test 3: Educational importance

Another test applied by MLA includes a wide variety of objects, not necessarily works of art. These may be important for the study of, for example, a particular scientific development. This category can also include objects which form part of a series or collection and which need not be in one place. It may be a 'virtual collection', in that its components may be dispersed across the whole of the United Kingdom. Here, the test is somewhat similar to the 'twelfth chair' criterion, ie is the group of objects impaired if one particular item is removed from it? Does the lack of a particular object affect the unity of the collection or of the series?

Test 4: Historic association

The fourth MLA test is whether an object has an especially close association with a particular historic setting. The kind of property that will qualify includes manuscripts, works of art, furniture or other items that are pre-eminent by virtue of the specific contribution that they make to the understanding of an outstanding historic building. Examples are of furniture specially commissioned for a particular house, or paintings commissioned for a house, or a group of paintings which have an association with a particular location. Note, in particular, that, under this head, value is not a determining factor. Items of modest worth, that reflect the taste of the relevant time, may qualify for exemption.

Preliminary approach

17.6   For most practitioners, the first port of call for advice is likely to be the HMRC website, which has much relevant material. It is perhaps rare that HMRC say 'we're here to help', but that is precisely the attitude of the Heritage Team on 0115 974 2514. If the application is in respect of a chattel, HMRC will refer it to MLA.

Public access and publicity

17.7   As will be seen from the consideration (see **Chapter 18**) of the procedure for application for conditional exemption, and the events that can cause that exemption to be lost, it is fundamental to the heritage property scheme that there be an agreement between the owner, or family of the owner, of property that escapes taxation and the public, whereby the public gain rights of access in return for the tax forgone (and therefore, by implication, carried in some small part by them). This right of access is governed by undertakings which were the subject of the adverse press comment referred to earlier. There was initially considerable debate between HMRC and the professions with specific reference to *IHTA 1984, s 35A*, which (see below) provides a mechanism for the variation of undertaking as to access already given, but the procedure seems to have settled down. Owners now know what the requirements are. This has reduced the quantity of applications.

Difficulties arose because taxpayers were keen to enjoy exemption from taxation without equal enthusiasm for the disturbance to their personal arrangements that could or might arise from giving access to the general public. Thus, any register of heritage property that clearly identified not only the property but its location was perceived to be a 'burglar's charter'. Access to the objects was gained by application made to an agent of the owner and, it appears, owners occasionally made it quite difficult even for genuine students of art and history to inspect heritage property. There is now a procedure to curb abuse.

NEW UNDERTAKINGS

Chattels

17.8   *IHTA 1984, s 31(2)* specifies the undertakings to be given in return for conditional exemption where the heritage property is a pre-eminent chattel or pre-eminent collection. The undertakings are as follows:

- the property will be kept permanently in the United Kingdom;

- the property will not leave the United Kingdom temporarily except for a purpose, and a period, approved by HMRC;

- steps must be taken as agreed between HMRC and the person giving the undertaking for the preservation of the property; and

- steps must also be taken as above to secure reasonable access to the public.

A form of undertaking is set out in the Access Notes.

Certain documents may be excluded from an undertaking under a power given to HMRC in *s 31(3)* where those documents contain information which ought to be treated as confidential, either for personal or other reasons.

Land and associated chattels

17.9   Where the heritage property is outstanding land, buildings or an associated chattel, the undertakings required are as follows:

- in the case of outstanding land, for its maintenance and the preservation of its character;

- in the case of any other property, for its maintenance, repair and preservation and, if it qualifies as an associated chattel, an undertaking to keep it associated with the building concerned; and

- in either case, for reasonable access.

In practice, the undertaking will incorporate a detailed plan for the management of the land, negotiated between the taxpayer (or his agent) and the agency representing HMRC. Access does not mean free right to roam over the entire site: it will commonly be limited to existing and new permissive rights of way, with appropriate extension to suit the needs of (horse and cycle) riders.

Amenity land

17.10   Where land qualifies as heritage property, not in its own right but because it protects the character and amenities of a heritage building, a further undertaking is required that specified steps will be taken for the maintenance, repair and preservation of the land and for access. Those 'specified steps' will be agreed between HMRC and the person giving the undertaking, and will be set out in the undertaking (see *s 31(4A)*). Different people may give different undertakings where the relevant property is held by separate people.

The rules as to amenity land apply to property falling within the definition in *s 31(4C)*. The property affected may be either:

- a building for the protection of whose character and amenities the land is essential in the opinion of the Treasury (*s 31(4C)(a)*); or

- any other area of land which serves that purpose and which lies between the amenity land and the building itself or is, in the opinion of the Treasury, physically closely connected with the relevant land or building (*s 31(4C)(b)*).

This amenity land (also called '*section 31(4A)* land') is the subject of its own particular code of undertakings. Where *s 31(4A)* requires an undertaking for the maintenance, repair, preservation and access of property, that undertaking is required even though some other effective undertaking may exist for its maintenance, repair, preservation and access (see *s 31(4D)*). Any undertaking given pursuant to *s 31(4A)* is given with respect to the relevant land, and it is for the person who seeks exemption of the amenity land by designation to secure that any undertaking necessary under *s 31(4A)* is given. The 'specified steps' in *s 31(4A)* must ensure that access to the amenity land is not confined 'by appointment only' to access.

It is the nature of exemption of amenity land that it rests on exemption of the principal property, which may well be in separate ownership. This gives rise to complicated inter-property and inter-taxpayer arrangements to secure exemption for all parties.

Publicity of the terms of undertakings

17.11   The undertaking that accompanies an application for conditional exemption will include provisions to secure reasonable access to the public. It may include matters such as the publication of the terms of the undertaking itself and any other information relating to the property which, but for *s 31(4FB)*, would be treated as confidential. However, *s 31(4FB)* is itself subject to the 'privacy' qualification of *s 31(3)*.

PUBLIC ACCESS UNDER THE 'NEW' RULES

17.12   The 'by appointment only' system of public access had the result that assets might escape IHT even though only one or two members of the public might actually exercise their right to view. That is no longer acceptable. Public access can no longer be restricted in that way. This does not mean that, even for new applications for exemption, the giving of access by appointment has altogether been abolished. What has changed is that the option of giving access only by appointment is unacceptable for new undertakings. All owners of heritage property that is subject to a condition of public access must now provide some measure of open access. Where the heritage property is particularly delicate, for example where it consists of manuscripts, watercolours and the like, it may be possible to negotiate relatively restricted open access combined with access by appointment. Even under new undertakings, the public will not be able to demand '24/7' access. Access will be limited to the terms agreed between the owner and HMRC, as set out in the undertaking.

What amounts to reasonable access

17.13   *IHTA 1984, s 31(4FA)* requires the access to the public that is agreed between the owner and HMRC to be 'reasonable'. What is reasonable will, in the case of any particular asset, be what has been agreed and is set out in the undertaking. The measure of open access that HMRC will seek has been outlined in the 1999 Notes. The level of access will be determined by:

- the nature of the asset;
- the type of asset; and
- the preservation and maintenance needs of the asset.

Originally, HMRC set out what they considered to be the *minimum* number of days of access per year. The Access Notes are more flexible. There must be a serious intention to provide good access. Owners fall into three broad categories:

- existing exhibitors;
- major private collectors; and
- minor private collectors.

Existing exhibitors

These are claimants whose works of art are already on public display. Access is probably satisfied, so the claim can be referred to MLA for 'pre-eminence' vetting.

Major private collectors

These claimants have several items but they are not yet displayed. Access proposals should be well formulated by the time the claim is made.

Minor private collectors

Here, access may be a problem, because HMRC will want the items to be displayed permanently or regularly in a public building. The owner must therefore 'line up' a museum, historic house or gallery that is willing to take the item. Not every such institution wants items on periodic loan. The alternative is '*in situ*' access, ie much like the old scheme before 1998, but the requirements are strict. Isolation of the site is a relevant factor: less will be demanded in respect of a windswept Scottish island accessible only at low tide than in respect of a mansion ten minutes' drive from a motorway. The old criteria were:

Category of heritage property	Minimum days per year
Exempt chattels not located in a heritage building	5–100
Exempt chattels in a heritage building	25–156
Historically associated chattels	25–156
Amenity land for exempt buildings	25–156
Exempt buildings	25–156
Exempt land	All year*

* Where access is given in respect of land all the year round, there may be agreed periods of temporary closure for the purpose of either land management or nature conservation. Note, in the consideration of breach of undertakings later in the work (see **19.2**) and, for example, the relaxation of the rules during the outbreak of foot and mouth disease a few years ago.

HMRC wish to promote open access through European Heritage Open Days. These are organised by the Civic Trust but occur only rarely and will not by themselves satisfy even the minimum requirement, since HMRC would generally expect a minimum of one month per year.

One possibility is a 'heritage buddy' scheme, to display one's valuables at the premises of one's friend whose house is open to the public. Some sharing of overhead costs may be appropriate. It would depend on the friend. Items need not be on permanent display: for instance, historically associated objects might be stored in the 'heritage house' in bookcases or in suitable furniture. Unless exempted in the higher category, *viz.* pre-eminent chattels, such storage may be acceptable. Problems can arise where the owner has no control over the display building; default provisions should be included in the undertaking.

Access: the chattel, not the owner

17.14 The personal circumstances of the owner are irrelevant. The Access Notes establish some principles then illustrate them with examples. The principles are these:

399

- display may be of part of a set, for example one place setting of silver, crockery etc rather than all 12;

- archives should be catalogued and a copy deposited with the National Archives;

- owners of manuscripts or drawings should be willing to display part, for example one page, for short periods;

- it is good enough to see the spine of a book on a shelf, with more access by appointment; and

- the 'Heineken' rule, namely that 'below stairs' items may qualify, if there is good reason not to allow access to the part of the house where they are kept, but special (well publicised) tours should give access.

The following example illustrates the law as it currently stands.

Example 17.1: Bateman nerd

During a long career as a solicitor, Roger established two collections. The first was of silver from the family workshop of: Hester Bateman; Peter and Anne Bateman; Peter, Anne and William Bateman; Peter and Jonathan Bateman; William Bateman (the elder); and his son of the same name. In the course of amassing this collection, Roger secured, as a second collection, a number of original records of the family that together supplement information on the workshop and go well beyond what collectors can find in *Jackson*, or in the pages of '*Silver Studies*' (the Journal of the Silver Society), or other specialist works.

The expense of all that collecting prevented Roger from living in a particularly grand style in any other respect. The collection is stored in a fairly unassuming private house. On Roger's death in May 2001, his housekeeper and lifetime companion, Mary, seeks conditional exemption of the collection of silver and manuscripts. Gout and other disabilities make it difficult for Mary to have strangers tramping through the house all the time to look at the collection. She, therefore, seeks to restrict access to five days per year.

This will not be acceptable in respect of the collection of silver. Mary may be able to negotiate restricted access to the Bateman workshop records, on the ground that frequent handling will damage them, by offering to get them catalogued and lending them to the local county record office. Unless Mary can agree a minimum period of access to the silver itself, conditional exemption will be refused (see examples (c) and (f) in the Access Notes).

Example 17.2: official example (1)

The Access Notes describe, in their example (a), pictures in a Scottish property that is open for only 25 days per year with good advance publicity. That is satisfactory, but items not on the visitor route should be available to special tours or on request.

Example 17.3: official example (2)

Again taken from the Access Notes, their example (d), although fictitious, has a ring of truth about it. D lives with a relative and has provisionally agreed with two local authority art galleries for occasional display of pictures; the National Trust will take one picture on 'permanent loan', and a local auctioneer will display one picture for the foreseeable future. Whilst some of the plan is good enough, the arrangement with the auctioneer needs clarification, and a 'back up' facility needs to be put in place for the picture to go to a public gallery for a month a year or three months every three years.

Example 17.4: official example (3)

Practitioners are referred to example (h) in the Access Notes, which is too detailed to summarise here but which shows an imaginative and flexible approach to the problem.

Means of access

17.15   Heritage chattels (and perhaps their government administrators!) will seldom benefit from being constantly on the move. A decision must be made by the owner as to where the chattel will be kept and displayed. HMRC have in the past made six broad suggestions:

- the owner's residence;
- the place where the owner normally keeps the chattel;
- a museum or gallery open to the public;
- a public building such as the local Record Office;
- Heritage Open Days organised by the Civic Trust; or
- a regional or touring exhibition.

As to Open Days, see www.heritageopendays.org.uk for details, published in about July for the open season of four days in the autumn.

These are not exclusive, and HMRC will consider alternative suggestions by the owner. Where an object is provided on loan for display in the public collection of a national institution, local authority or university, it will usually count as open access, provided that arrangements are in place for viewing when the item is not on public display. Presumably, this will also be true even where the article forms part of the reserve collection of the national institution, though the fact that the article is not permanently on display may give some indication that it is not of 'pre-eminent' quality.

Damage to chattels

17.16 The government have instituted an indemnity scheme, which is intended to provide cover against loss or damage in respect of objects loaned. Subject to that, the owner of heritage property should have sufficient personal resources such that, in the event of loss or damage, he can reinstate the heritage property.

Other access details: charges, limited numbers of visitors and guided tours

17.17 The owner may charge for providing access but that charge must be reasonable, not from the point of view of the owner but from the point of view of the public at large. Subject to agreement with HMRC, the owner may limit the number of visitors at any one time and may restrict the open access to guided tours. The owner may, and probably will, forbid photography of the items. What the owner may not do is restrict access to pre-eminent chattels to the old 'by appointment' arrangement on the ground that the owner can neither find a suitable venue for open access nor afford to provide one. Under the new rules, there must be a measure of open access as a condition of securing the exemption. Access may be on pre-booked tours, perhaps for quite small numbers of visitors. If visitors, having booked, fail to visit, that will not count as 'non-access'. Access may not be 'virtual'. Owners may ask the public for identification, such as passport, but should make that clear in advance.

Venue for provision of access

17.18 This must be specified in the undertaking, and will be obvious where the chattels are historically associated with a building or are located in a private building which is open to the public. Equally, where items are on long-term loan to public collections, the gallery or museum premises will be the nominated building. There may be situations where it is not practicable to specify the location of the chattel. The owner and HMRC must agree. The principle behind undertakings under the new rules is that the owner must both agree where the articles will be displayed and publicise it, well in advance of the specified period, so that the public are aware of when and where the heritage property may be seen. Such an arrangement may be combined with access by appointment.

Example 17.5: Bateman silver on display

To continue Example 17.1: after negotiation with HMRC, Mary agrees to provide Roger's collection of Bateman silver to her local museum and art gallery. The quality and range of the collection is such that the gallery is happy to set aside one small room for its display. There is no particular connection between the Bateman family and the locality, but Roger himself, whilst not being immensely popular in the local community, was at least well known, and many local people are curious to see the collection that had driven him to a lifetime of parsimony.

Mary secures an immediate advantage, in being relieved of the not inconsiderable cost of insuring the silver as part of the contents of the home. As a separate matter, Mary deposits a catalogue of the Bateman records with the local reference library and agrees that, for two months a year, the Bateman workshop records themselves should be deposited at the museum to provide open access and that, for the rest of the year, the public may see the records at Mary's home by appointment only.

PUBLICITY

17.19   The level of publicity that is appropriate will in part depend on the nature of the heritage asset. For example, in February 1987 the then Chancellor of the Exchequer, Norman Lamont, in reply to a parliamentary question, set out the norm for property other than chattels by indicating that publicity would normally include some or all of five procedures:

- Owner to inform the British Tourist Authority or, where appropriate, the Scottish Tourist Board and the Highlands and Islands Development Board, of the opening arrangements and of subsequent changes.

- Owner to advertise the opening arrangements in one or more suitable publications with national circulation.

- Owner to display a notice outside the property giving details of the opening arrangements.

- Owner to agree that the advisory body or bodies (and its/their agents), who confirmed that the relevant property was eligible for relief and with whom the owner had negotiated detailed management agreements, might divulge the access arrangements to anyone who enquired about them.

- Owner to agree to such other publicity as the advisory body or bodies considered to be appropriate. That could include displaying a notice in some public place in the locality – for example, the local post office (in the days when they still existed), the local library, the local tourist office or town hall – or in the newsletter of a local preservation society.

The Chancellor indicated that the management agreement would normally also provide scope for other agreements between the owner and the advisory body.

The register of conditionally exempt works of art

17.20   The starting point for any member of the public seriously wishing to inspect heritage property is, however, probably not the notice board in what used to be the local post office. He or she will begin with what used to be called 'the V and A list' but is now on the HMRC website accessed via www.ir.gov. uk/heritage, which is pleasantly set out and easy to search, whether by location or by type of article. This is the register of conditionally exempt works of art available for viewing by appointment with the owners.

What the owner need not disclose to the public

17.21   An owner of a heritage chattel need not disclose to the public everything contained in the undertaking negotiated with HMRC. Personal information, not relevant to public access, may be excluded. For example, the name of the owner and the value of the asset need not be shown. The private address of the owner need not be shown, except where it is relevant for public access, perhaps because the house is itself heritage property or because that house is also the venue for access to other exempt items. In this context, it will be possible to conceal the usual location of an exempt chattel, either for security or other reasons, except where the chattel is in a building that is or will be open to the public. Whilst the value of the asset, as already noted, need not be disclosed, nor indeed the amount of tax that has been deferred, other details of the asset itself must be shown. Specifically, the owner is expected to disclose, through the website, certain basic information, according to the nature of the asset. Examples of entries appear at the end of the Access Notes.

Disclosure: pre-eminent chattels and pre-eminent collections

17.22   The website must show the following:

- a brief description of each object;

- the full address of the building and the opening times (where the chattel is in a building that is open to the public); and

- where the chattel is not in a building open to the public, the periods when open access will be available, and the name, address and telephone number of the person who will give details of actual opening days and venues. That person might be the owner or might be an agent.

Disclosure: outstanding buildings and amenity land

17.23 The website must show the full address of the building and the opening times.

Disclosure: land

17.24 The requirements are twofold:

- where the land is – for example, the name of the estate and the nearest town or village; and

- the name, address and telephone number of the person who can give further details on request.

In addition to the 'V and A list', the owner, in accordance with Norman Lamont's indication to Parliament, will normally be required to give details of access to local tourist offices and, in the case of buildings, to advertise in one of the annual Heritage Guides.

Footnote: foreign-owned works of art

17.25 A work of art that is normally kept overseas can become liable to IHT on the death of its owner merely because it happens to be in the United Kingdom at the relevant date. By Extra Statutory Concession F7, the liability to IHT will be waived if the work of art had been brought to the United Kingdom solely for public exhibition or for cleaning or for restoration. If the work of art is held by a discretionary trust, or is otherwise comprised in settled property in which there is no interest in possession, the charge to tax that would otherwise arise under *IHTA 1984, s 64* will be waived.

HM Treasury announced in March 2003 an extension to this concession to cover the case where a work of art, which would otherwise have left the United Kingdom to be kept overseas, is kept here solely for the purposes of cleaning, restoration or exhibition.

Chapter 18

Heritage property: application for exemption and variation of undertakings

QUICK GUIDE

A claim must be made within two years. Where the circumstances warrant it, a protective or provisional claim should be made on the basis set out at **18.4**. The full claim should contain the information mentioned at **18.5**.

The most important single issue, namely the variation of undertakings under *IHTA 1984, s 35A*, is discussed at **18.10**. The test case on *s 35A* does seem to have cleared the air. Things are settling down.

THE OLD LAW

18.1   Understanding the old provisions is important in this field. Before the changes introduced by *FA 1998*, there was no specified time limit for claiming the exemption, which might be claimed in respect of chattels, outstanding land, buildings of outstanding interest and their amenity land and associated chattels. As noted in **Chapter 17**, the definition of those assets that will now qualify for exemption has been tightened up considerably.

Prior to the changes in *FA 1998*, an undertaking was required for the preservation of chattels, to keep them permanently in the United Kingdom, to maintain them and preserve their character, to secure reasonable public access and to publicise the availability of that access. The undertaking, once agreed with the Revenue, could not later be altered. The obligation to publicise the availability of access was qualified. The owner did not have to disclose any information that might be considered confidential. Where a new undertaking was given to continue an existing exemption, it was only necessary to repeat the terms of the previous undertaking.

As previously seen in **Chapter 17**, under the old law there could be quite considerable restriction to public access, and use was made of the 'by prior appointment' limitation.

REQUIREMENTS UNDER THE NEW LAW: THE TIMING OF THE CLAIM

18.2   In relation to transfers made, and deaths occurring, on or after 17 March 1998, a claim to conditional exemption must be made (see *IHTA 1984, s 30(3BA)*) no more than two years after the date of the transfer or, where the transfer itself was a death, the date of death. There is some possibility for the extension of this period, since *sub-s (3BA)* does go on to provide, 'or (in either case) within such longer period as the Board may allow'. Any late claim will be considered, but the Board will exercise their discretion only in exceptional circumstances. Specifically, any mistake by the tax adviser, and the failure to make the claim on time, is no reason to allow a later claim. Not realising that a claim may be made, or simple neglect, will be no excuse.

Although there may at present be little 'track record' to go on, a parallel may be seen with the experiences of practitioners in relation to the two-year time limit in respect of deeds of variation under *s 142*. In the early days of the legislation, there was some leniency whilst advisers grew accustomed to it, but eventually the Revenue took the view that the existence of the time limit was (or ought to be) so widely known that no excuses could be accepted. Even though the ability to make claims for conditional exemption is a more specialised area of law than the ability to vary dispositions within two years of death, it must now become standard practice, on taking instructions in connection with the administration of an estate, to consider whether there might be any heritage property in respect of which a claim should be made.

The best guidance we have at present is partly that contained in IHT Newsletter, April 2001, in which it was noted that the Revenue has a discretion to allow a longer time than two years. They will consider a late claim on its merits. Merely overlooking the need to make a claim will not be a good enough reason, nor the failure to claim some other relief such as APR or BPR, nor the delays attendant upon putting in place a post-death variation. The Revenue would normally expect such matters as the entitlement to APR or BPR to be resolved within two years of the death or of the transfer. There is also the 'don't waste our time' warning in paragraph 12 of the Access Notes, that HMRC will discontinue negotiations, and will charge tax instead, where:

- more than six months have elapsed from receiving the exemption claim, but even rudimentary access proposals have not been settled; or

- more than six months have elapsed since agreement that the item was pre-eminent, yet detailed access had not been agreed.

Where a practitioner believes that he will not know, within the two-year period, whether or not APR or BPR applies, there is the facility available of making a protective claim. Such claims are considered at the end of this section.

However, this should not encourage the making of a 'frivolous' claim, merely to delay collection of IHT. That could attract penalties just as easily as the making of a claim to APR or to BPR that cannot, in truth, be supported by the facts of the case.

Heritage property in discretionary trusts

18.3   *IHTA 1984, s 79* sets out the procedure for discretionary trusts. Where heritage property is included in the trust and there has been a conditionally exempt transfer, either on the occasion of the settlement or earlier, the ten-year charge that would otherwise be imposed under *s 64* will not take effect on any ten-year anniversary that falls before a charge is triggered by a chargeable event in respect of the property. The nature of that charge is described in **Chapter 20**. Where the property is comprised in the trust and there has been neither a charge nor a disposal:

- the property is designated as heritage property;

- the appropriate undertaking has been given by the 'appropriate person'; and

- the property is 'relevant property' within the code for the taxation of discretionary trusts.

Whilst *s 79(3)* does not make the point blindingly obvious, not only must the claim to exemption be made before the date of the charge; it must be made long enough before the date of the charge for the claim to be processed and for the heritage property to be designated as such, all before the date on which the charge will otherwise fall due.

Heritage maintenance funds are considered in **Chapter 21**. A claim in respect of a heritage fund is referred to in *IHTA 1984, Sch 4, para 1*, and the wording of *para 1(2)* is guidance that the claim should be made in advance of setting up the settlement.

In no other situations can a claim be made in advance of the taxable event.

Protective or provisional claims

18.4   A claim to exemption may be protective or provisional. For administrative convenience, HMRC expect the claimant to pursue the matter 'without undue delay'. If the claim is not ultimately proceeded with, HMRC may charge tax on the basis that the claim has been abandoned. This will, however, be done only after proper notice to the taxpayer, as explained in the Access Notes, para 12.

A formal or protective claim must include the following elements:

- a statement that the exemption is being claimed, specifying the event to which the claim relates;
- confirmation that there is no present intention to sell the asset or assets;
- particulars of each asset or group of assets covered by the claim; and
- a brief statement why each asset is considered to qualify for exemption, including confirmation that proposals will be made for public access.

In addition, particulars of any previous exemption should be supplied, showing the date of the death or event, official reference, tax rate applicable, and details of the asset. For chattels, update the old official exemption list for any disposals. For land, supply a plan and copies of any old undertakings. The 'no intention to sell' issue is discussed at **18.6** below.

THE CLAIM ITSELF

18.5   Interestingly, there is as yet no prescribed form, perhaps because conditional exemption can apply to such a wide variety of property. The application should, however, cover certain prescribed information. HMRC guidance sets out the following requirements:

- Full description of the asset.
- Location of the asset.
- Where associated chattels are included in the claim, the exact location of those associated chattels within the building concerned.
- Confirmation that there is at present no intention to sell the asset.
- Previous tax history, ie particulars of any previous occasion of conditional exemption, whether from estate duty, capital transfer tax, IHT or CGT. In each case, any reference from HMRC should be quoted.
- Contact details, ie the name, full address and telephone number of the person whom HMRC or its advisers should contact to inspect the asset.
- Estimated market value of the asset at the date of the taxable event in respect of which the claim is made.
- The owner's proposals as to maintenance and preservation of the asset.
- The proposals for providing public access to the asset.
- The proposals for publicising arrangements for public access to the asset.
- Name, address and telephone number of owner.

- Confirmation of authority to the Inland Revenue to disclose or publicise information and undertakings relating to the exemption.

- A brief statement, in respect of all assets other than chattels, of why each item qualifies as heritage property.

- A statement, in respect of a building or amenity land or historically associated chattels, confirming that all appropriate undertakings will be given, regardless of who owns the land or chattels.

- In respect of pre-eminent chattels, a statement of why each item is 'pre-eminent' and each qualifies as heritage property.

- For chattels, three coloured photographs of each item.

- For chattels, confirmation that the owner will not take them out of the United Kingdom without prior approval from HMRC.

- For associated chattels, confirmation that that association with the building concerned goes back at least 50 years; that the chattels will stay in that building; and will stay in the place specified in that building as mentioned in the claim.

In practice, other information will also be relevant to support the claim. It may not be possible for the claimant to gather all the information required within the two-year period. In that case, the recommendation is to make the claim as fully as possible, indicating when the balance of the information will be available.

Unfortunately, however, the claim is not valid for the purposes of the two-year time limit within *IHTA 1984, s 30(3BA)* until all the information has been received. The claim will not be processed by HMRC until it is complete in all respects. Above all, the claimant must show commitment to providing public access.

No intention to sell

18.6   A new claim, ie one in respect of which no previous undertaking has been given, cannot succeed, in HMRC's view, if there is any intention to sell the heritage property. Suitable assurances must be given, when demanded, that no sale is in prospect. Some such condition may be implied from the requirements of *s 31(2)(b)* as to the undertakings that are to be given. When the claim is for the renewal of old undertakings, rather than the negotiation of new ones, a slightly less harsh attitude seems to have been taken by HMRC, in the past at least, as was noted in earlier editions of this work. As will be seen in **Chapter 19,** heritage property may be subject to very high historic rates of estate duty. It could therefore be good planning to seek a fresh undertaking, at current rates, only to break it later and in effect substitute the new rate of tax for the old. This merely illustrates what many tax advisers will (happily) confirm: when the rate of tax goes above 40%, clients will devote ever greater effort, expense and ingenuity to its avoidance.

Triggering a chargeable transfer on which to hang a claim

18.7   A feature of the heritage property code just noted is that property may be burdened with an estate duty liability that may be clawed back. To prevent this, it may be helpful to achieve a transfer on death under the IHT rules, which will 'wash' the old estate duty liability, and to apply for exemption on death. Where the death triggers a transfer that is exempt, for example to the surviving spouse, there can be no application for exemption.

The solution is a deed of variation redirecting the heritage property to a non-exempt beneficiary. That enables an application for conditional exemption to be made.

Example 18.1: timeous variation of a will

Harry died in 1942. The top rate of estate duty on his estate was 60%. Harry left his daughter, Joyce, a fine serpentine chest of drawers on which Joyce obtained conditional exemption. Joyce died in December 2009 leaving the item, then worth £20,000, to her husband Cyril for life, with the remainder to her son Richard.

The estate is administered by Cyril's old friend and adviser, Geoff, who soon has all the formalities out of the way and who does not consider that any particular action need be taken with regard to the contents of the home left to Cyril: after all, no tax is due.

Richard, however, consults Carol. Richard is no lover of antiques and thinks that, in a few years' time, the old chest will translate into school fees for his children. Carol advises that a sale will trigger massive tax charges. For example, if the trustees were now, with Cyril's consent as tenant for life, to sell the piece for its present value of £30,000, there would be a 28% CGT charge on the gain price since 2009, and 60% estate duty charge on the proceeds.

Far better, Carol advises, to vary Joyce's will. There is still (just) time. Transfer the chest of drawers to Richard. Richard, who is not yet in need of the funds for school fees, can honestly say he does not immediately intend to sell.

On eventual sale, the tax charge will be by reference to Joyce's estate. Estate duty will no longer be in point. The IHT charge will be at 40%, a saving of 20%. In any case, Richard might consider a private treaty sale to a heritage body.

Claims processing

18.8   Although HMRC have specialist teams to advise on chattels, they will in most cases discuss with specialist advisers the proposals for the maintenance and preservation of the assets or management, where land is concerned, and, in particular, will discuss with relevant authorities the proposals for the provision and publicity of public access. Obtaining that advice can take HMRC about a year. A report will be prepared and submitted to the claimant in draft. This will include a draft of their terms of the undertakings. Once those terms are agreed, HMRC will formally designate the assets under *IHTA 1984, s 31*. The procedure is similar in respect to that of an approved heritage maintenance fund, save that, for such a fund, HMRC must also be satisfied as to the terms of the trust documents, that the assets to be transferred to the fund are appropriate, and that the amount is suitable to cover the projected maintenance expenditure for which the fund is set up.

Supervision of owners' compliance with undertakings

18.9   HMRC take steps to ensure that owners comply with the undertakings given. This is done on three bases: a five-year programme; an annual programme; and spot checks. During the five-year programme, advisers to HMRC inspect land and buildings, and ask the taxpayer whether there have been any disposals of exempt assets and for confirmation that all undertakings have been, and are being, observed. The annual programme requires owners of outstanding land or outstanding buildings (with amenity land and associated chattels) to make an annual report to the advisers. The report must detail the maintenance and preservation of the assets and the provision of public access. HMRC will check that these annual reports are made.

The programme that does not fall into any particular time scale is that which requires owners or their personal representatives to inform HMRC of any disposals of exempt assets, including any transfer occurring on death, since such a disposal is a breach of the undertaking. Random inspections are made by HMRC of heritage chattels to ensure compliance with undertakings.

Variation of undertakings

18.10   The most significant change introduced by *FA 1998* is contained in *IHTA 1984, s 35A*. If allowed to take effect without challenge, this section gives HMRC very significant power to tighten up (considerably) the existing regime in respect of heritage chattels. *Section 35A(1)* provides that an existing undertaking made to secure conditional exemption may be varied from time to time by agreement between the Board of Inland Revenue and the person who is bound by the undertaking, and covers an undertaking whether given under:

- *s 30* – the general section relating to conditional transfers;
- *s 32* – an undertaking given in respect of a chargeable event (see *s 32(5) (b), (5AA)*, as described in **Chapter 19**); or
- *s 32A* – the 'associated properties' rule.

There is nothing controversial in the varying of any undertaking by agreement. The controversy, and the possibility of challenge to the legislation, arose under *s 35A(2)*, which gives a Special Commissioner power to vary the undertaking. The conditions specified under *s 35A(2)* are that:

- the Board have made a proposal to vary an undertaking and have put it to the person who is bound by the existing undertaking;
- the person bound by the undertaking has not, within six months of that proposal, agreed to the variation; and
- it is just reasonable, in all the circumstances, for the variation to be made.

The Commissioner may direct that the existing undertaking is to have effect, from a date that he specifies, as if the person bound by the undertaking had actually agreed to the HMRC proposals. The Special Commissioner, when making his ruling, must specify a date for the variation to come into force that is not less than 60 days from the date of his decision. That 60-day period can be used by HMRC and by the person who is bound by the undertaking to negotiate. By *s 35A(4)*, the direction of the Special Commissioner will not take effect if, before the date specified in that direction, the taxpayer and HMRC can agree different terms.

That time limit does not, however, apply to relief from CGT (as to which, see below). Equally, this requirement does not affect the tax that is chargeable on a transfer of value that occurs before 18 March 1986 in respect of a death or other event occurring after 17 March 1986. This follows from the general transitional provision in *FA 1986, Sch 19, para 40(1)*, that nothing in the amendments to the *1984 Act* brought about by *FA 1986* is to affect the tax chargeable on a transfer of value that occurs before 18 March 1986.

As will be seen when considering occasions of charge, an exemption may arise in respect of heritage property held in a discretionary trust so as to spare the trust the burden of tax on the ten-yearly charge. That is provided by *s 79*. The new two-year time limit does not affect any claim for relief under *s 79*.

MANAGING CHANGE: THE TRANSITION FROM THE OLD REGIME TO THE NEW

18.11 There was correspondence between HMRC and heritage owners and their representatives in 1999 to negotiate open access to conditionally exempt heritage objects. HMRC were concerned, wherever possible, to reach agreement with owners, but reminded owners that they could take the matter to a Special Commissioner, which they eventually did (see below). HMRC made it clear that 'by appointment only' access should continue only 'in exceptional circumstances, where there are overriding conservation reasons why the heritage object should not be placed on open display'.

The correspondence highlighted the considerations that will always be relevant in relation to heritage property. For example, where an object may not be suitable for a national collection, an appropriate period of access might be in the range 5–25 days, but 'clearly the nearer to national collection standard [the] object is, the more days' open access we shall expect [the owner] to offer'. In other words, conditional exemption will now be granted only in respect of high quality heritage property and, given that high quality, a substantial measure of open access will be required.

The conservation argument is restated in the annex to the letter noting that, in the case of a library, the public might have open visual access but arrange a more detailed inspection by appointment. In the case of an archive, access would normally be by appointment and be supervised. In this context, the attitude of the National Trust, as reported recently, is interesting. From a conservation viewpoint, it may be better to leave books covered with dust for a few years than to take them down each year for cleaning. *A fortiori* it cannot do the books much good to be handled (especially without gloves) by members of the public exercising a right of access to them.

There was evidence in *Undertakings of A and B* [2004] SpC 00439 (see **18.15**) that very little use had been made of the 'by appointment' viewing arrangements. There had also been few loans of chattels to public exhibitions. The tax deferred under the exemptions, taking the two owners together, was about £33,356,400. The point does not appear from the report of the case but, from 6 September 2004, inheritance tax unpaid attracted interest at 4%, putting the cost to the general public of the deferral relief in those particular cases at £1,334,256 in a full year. Given the sums involved, it is understandable that HMRC sought a change to the undertaking.

There was reference in those cases to the burden on the estate owner of agreeing to open access, and it was recognised that the proposals that the Special Commissioner was reviewing would impose substantial additional obligations, costs and disadvantages on the owners without any compensation as such. The Special Commissioner observed, 'Parliament no doubt saw the burdens, financial or otherwise, placed on the owner as a *quid pro quo* for continuing deferral of IHT'. He concluded that part of his enquiry by holding that, 'I do not regard the absence of compensation to be a feature of the 1998 Act regime that necessarily requires me to conclude that [varying the undertaking] will inevitably and always be unjust and unreasonable.'

Museum quality properties

18.12   Under the old rules, an item could qualify as heritage property even though it was not 'pre-eminent', either because it was historically associated with an eligible building or because it was of 'museum' quality and yet not outstanding. In this chapter, property of this kind is referred to as 'museum quality property'. Museum quality property can be transferred without loss of an existing exemption. The new owner may keep the exemption that had already been given in respect of museum quality property, by replacing an undertaking that had been given by the previous owner.

Unfortunately, that does not mean that there will be no tax to pay on the present transfer itself. Unless the present transfer is exempt from tax for some other reason, perhaps because it is being transferred to the spouse of the owner or to a charity, the effect of retaining the exemption will be only to avoid a charge, described below as the 'clawback' charge, that would otherwise apply on the transfer of heritage property without undertaking. The new owner may claim new conditional exemption; but, if the article is of museum quality only, there is of course the strong possibility that it will fail the new 'pre-eminent' test. Still, one tax charge is better than two.

On the transfer of heritage property under the new rules, the undertaking to be given by the new owner will have to meet different tests according to whether the existing exemption relates to estate duty, to capital transfer tax or to IHT. The detail of the legislation is set out at Appendix 8 below but, in summary, where the existing exemption relates to estate duty, the new undertaking will reflect the relevant provisions of the law for estate duty and will not be subject to the new requirements as to public access. On the other hand, where the existing exemption is in respect of capital transfer tax or IHT, the new undertaking must comply with rules in force at the time the new undertaking is given, with the result that open access will be required for the future, even where it was not previously given.

Sales of heritage property

18.13   Where the transition from the old regime to the new causes loss of conditional exemption, for whatever reason, the owner may want to consider a sale of the property. This may be particularly relevant to property which is of museum quality only. There is no guarantee that such property will be accepted in satisfaction of tax. The Secretary of State has the power to decline to accept even property which is of pre-eminent quality, so the owner of museum quality property will face an uphill struggle. The fact that the property once qualified for relief under the old rules is absolutely no guarantee that it can now be used to satisfy a tax liability. For use in satisfaction of tax, the chattel must qualify under the new rules, which will normally involve the pre-eminent quality test.

Review and variation of undertakings

Old undertakings

18.14   Two categories of existing undertaking are exempt from the provisions of *FA 1998* (see *Sch 25, para 10*). These are:

(*a*)   undertakings that were given when estate duty was in point; and

(*b*)   undertakings given under *FA 1975, s 31(2)*.

This second category (*b*) concerned the exemption from capital transfer tax of chattels transferred on a death occurring before 7 April 1976. The regime applicable before 7 April 1976 is examined in Appendix 8.

Other undertakings

All other undertakings may be subject to review. There are no circumstances under which a 'new' undertaking, ie one given on or after 31 July 1998, may not be varied. The variation will be by agreement or with the consent of a Special Commissioner. More important, perhaps, are changes of 'old' undertakings that fall outside the exclusions mentioned above. The change sought must relate either to the preservation and maintenance of the asset or to the provision of reasonable public access. In relation to an old undertaking, as already noted, the chief change will be the securing of open access rather than access by appointment only; although of equal importance will be the publicity arrangements, the requirements for which are more stringent than hitherto. Usually, an undertaking will be left undisturbed for at least five years.

Undertakings of A and B

18.15   The regime for seeking variation did not proceed quickly. It was argued that 'a deal is a deal', that the government was bound by old undertakings and had no right, by the enactment of *IHTA 1984, s 35A*, to renege on those agreements.

A test case emerged, *Undertakings of A and B* [2004] SpC 00439. Any practitioner faced with a proposal to vary an undertaking should read the report in full. The case decided two issues:

●   whether it is just and reasonable in all the circumstances to require the proposed variation of an undertaking to be made; and

●   if so, whether a direction to that effect should be made.

In brief, the Commissioner concluded that *s 35A* did not interfere with the rights of owners so as to produce substantial injustice nor violate human rights, but that, in the particular circumstances of the two cases, no direction should be made to give effect to the proposed variation.

The case was very fully argued. It gave an airing to many arguments that affect the general law. The practitioner will also need considerable detail from the report of the decisions of the Special Commissioner to assess the merits of any case. It is therefore worth examining the facts, the arguments and the decision in *Undertakings of A and B* at moderate length, not least because the decision has not since been challenged.

A was born in the 1950s and lived with his wife and family at A house, a Grade I listed house set in a large park close to a city. On the death of the previous owner, conditional exemption was granted for about 150 items, or pairs or sets of items, which had been valued by Christies at £20.89 million. In view of the grant of conditional exemption, those values were not examined but, if correct, the IHT deferred was £8,356,400. A could have claimed that A house itself was heritage property, but instead paid IHT on the house and grounds, so no public access obligations arose in respect of the house itself. In considering whether or not to claim conditional exemption, A judged that the practical and administrative burden of access 'would be manageable and would not, as he saw it, interfere unduly with his family life'. Only 13 days after the designation of the 150 items for conditional exemption, the budget day press release of 17 March 1998 announced the proposed changes to the exemption regime.

B, born in the 1960s, was the owner of B house, where he lived with his wife and family. B house is Grade I listed, set in a large park, also Grade I listed, which are at the heart of a substantial estate which includes a number of important historical sites. On the death of the previous owner, B had to decide whether to claim conditional exemption in respect of the house itself as heritage property. In response to B's claim HMRC stipulated a minimum of 28 open days per year. B considered that would cause him and his family undue inconvenience and disturbance, so he withdrew the heritage claim in respect of the house and parkland, preferring to pay the tax. Christies advised B that nearly 780 chattels could qualify for heritage relief, so B applied for conditional exemption.

HMRC did their homework. They considered the insurance and security implications of extended access and the implications of the *Disability Discrimination Act 1995*. They visited other heritage sites to see how many visitors might be attracted to A house and to B house if the undertakings were to be reviewed. They chose fewer numbers of days of access than they would require in respect of new claims for conditional exemption to reflect the transitional and quasi-retrospective nature of the powers given them by *s 35A*. In relation to owner A, they took account of the tax at stake and of the fact that A had been admitting tours to the family home over the years. They also noted that a room in A house had occasionally been used for functions to raise funds for charities. They took expert advice as to the quality of the items to be included as 'Part 1 objects', ie being of outstanding artistic and/or historic interest. Their proposal identified 49 Part 1 objects for owner A. A local museum and art gallery was interested in exhibiting some of the Part 1 objects, although the Special Commissioner later observed that 'the local museum and gallery's curator had been enthusiastic about taking a few great paintings from A house but had had to back-pedal once the costs and implications were realised'.

In the same way, HMRC looked at B house. The estate within which B house stood had the benefit of conditional exemption. Very little use had been made of the 'by appointment' viewing arrangements. There had been few loans of chattels to public exhibitions. HMRC received expert advice that chattels were pre-eminent quality and lendable to museums as an alternative to admitting the public to B house itself. They identified 51 Part 1 objects.

All of this preparatory work was very relevant to the consideration by the Special Commissioner of the procedural fairness with which HMRC had acted. He had paid tribute to 'the careful and painstaking work carried out by Mr Cushing and his team in the preparation and support of the proposals. The whole exercise calls for sensitivity and patience and these characteristics have been fully demonstrated by their approach'.

A house had been in the family for centuries and contained important items recorded on A's database, most of the paintings being family portraits. The other items were rugs, carpets, tapestries, china, furnishings, books and sculptures spread throughout the house. Keeping the collection was 'a constant and burdensome commitment'. The pictures had been in the family for between 250 and 450 years. Since 1998, there had been from one to five visitors to A house per year. A had lent items to museums and galleries. Significantly, special interest groups visited A house. Here, the numbers were larger: as many as 215 individuals in 2002.

Following his tour of A house, the Special Commissioner summarised his impressions:

> 'It is a family house. There are no facilities for the disabled. Were the public to be admitted and the numerous stealable objects (other than the Part 1 objects) to be placed out of sight or in some other way concealed, an extensive removal task would have to be undertaken. There is no obvious place to stow they away. Paintings could be removed and transferred to more accessible places but this would be at the risk of damage to the paintings on panels and to all the frames of the portraits. The great townscapes in the long hall could be moved, but this would leave unsightly marks. Because the children occupy the only downstairs rooms where there are no Part 1

objects, it would not be practicable to lock the stealable objects away in those rooms on open days. All in all, the reorganization of the household furnishings and paintings to meet the open access proposals would, on each occasion, take a great deal of time.'

The circumstances at B house were slightly different. Numerous items, great and small, of significant value, were spread throughout the house, including many exempt carpets and smaller rugs, all of which were delicate. There were many tapestries. As with taxpayer A, there was no suggestion that any of the chattels had been bought for their potential as investments. As already noted, after negotiation, B pursued a claim for exemption in relation to the estate but not the house, on which he paid IHT. B had received threatening letters in the past which he took seriously. He was concerned that, if B house were open to the public, there would be an increased risk to himself, his family, the house and its contents. That increased risk was corroborated by the county police force. The collection of sculpture was in a separate building. The family used every room in B house save one. There were private possessions and photographs everywhere. Most of the portraits were in fine frames that might be damaged if not moved with professional care.

Previous viewing

18.16   At house B, there had been little use of the 'by appointment' viewing arrangement since the grant of conditional exemption. On one day in 2000, there were visits by two special interest groups. There was evidence from B that, if it had been suggested that open access would be required, he would have considered his application for exemption in a different light, and would have considered selling certain of the chattels to pay the bulk of the tax on the rest of them. He was concerned about the personal security of his wife and children, which had been increased by recent publicised thefts from open houses. Opening the house would force on him a complete review and upgrade of security measures. It would increase wear and tear of the fittings and soft furnishings. There were no normal visitor facilities, such as toilets. The facilities relating to access for the disabled were limited.

Were the proposals for variation of the undertakings just and reasonable in all the circumstances?

The Special Commissioner held that he was required to act fairly and to decide whether the expectations of the owners, in giving the existing undertakings, were such that it would be an abuse of power to disappoint those expectations. He must then also decide whether there is an overriding public interest that would justify the disappointment of those expectations. He concluded that HMRC were not the creators of the new access and publicity policy: they were doing what Parliament had told them to do. He therefore considered that the argument of the owners was misconceived and that the only matter he must decide was whether, in all the circumstances, the proposals for variation of the undertakings were just and reasonable.

It was agreed that the Part 1 objects were of outstanding quality and most of them satisfied the new 'pre-eminent' quality test. The owners argued that the proposals to vary the undertakings ('the Proposals') were not justified simply because few people had taken advantage of viewing the chattels by appointment. He concluded that there was nothing inherently wrong with the 'by appointment' viewing system. He reviewed the public interest considerations in the context of any greater exposure to crime that might be involved. He concluded that the Proposals would expose the taxpayers to greater security risks, which was a negative factor in the balance; and that open access would involve extra security requirements that would make viewing the chattels a less rewarding experience; but that that was only a minor point and did not displace any overriding public interest in making the chattels available for public viewing.

Is it unreasonable to force upon owners proposals which they will find unacceptable?

This issue is likely to be the most important for the future. The taxpayers argued that the Proposals would bring taxpayers generally to the 'breaking point' at which they prefer not to accept the demands for public access but instead to pay the tax involved, probably by selling part of the collection. Thus, it was argued, the public interest suffers in two ways: there is a loss to the integrity of the collection; and a loss of any existing public access to the entire collection. On the evidence, the Special Commissioner was not satisfied that the breaking point had been reached in either case.

There is no compensation to the owner

It was argued that the lack of compensation to the owner who was given an existing undertaking, but is affected by the Proposals, was interference with his rights without compensation. HMRC disagreed: the owner was compensated in each case. The specific requirements under consideration were that the owner must grant access on specified days between 1 April and 31 October without prior appointment. They must notify HMRC of open days by 31 October in the previous year. They must arrange conducted tours to cover the rooms in which the Part 1 objects were on display, a minimum of four tours per day in the first year. They must keep all the exempt items in an appropriate room if normally located there before the opening.

The alternative option was to lend every one of the Part 1 objects to a public gallery or museum for a continuous period of at least three months in every 39 months, notifying HMRC of the arrangements three months before the loan. They must: allow publicity on the HMRC website; provide a copy of the undertaking to the public on reasonable request; provide reasonable details to local tourist information centres; and provide images of the Part 1 objects and notification of the availability of those objects for loan to certain specified galleries.

Cost

The taxpayers would probably incur additional costs and suffer disruption as a result of all these requirements. Specifically, there was evidence that the cost of providing barrier posts and rope throughout the houses would be £47,000 at A house and £36,000 at B house. There would be a labour cost in preparing the houses for open access; the price of druggets, etc was put at £12,540 at A house and £6,000 at B house.

Security and risk

There was evidence as to the security risk (and, in particular, to a handful of Irish travelling families, of whom it was said that they are 'violent towards each other, [but] not generally violent to members of the public although they do threaten violence ... they would leave [the owner's] wives and children alone because this was part of their "code"'). Those houses already had security systems and good security staff and alarm systems. Evidence was heard of arrangements made by the National Trust. The Commissioner was satisfied that variation of the undertakings would expose the owners, their families and their households to additional security risks. Whilst those risks might not be as acute as the taxpayers feared, 'their reasonable apprehensions must be taken into account in assessing the reasonableness of the Proposals'.

Retrospectivity

The Special Commissioner accepted that *s 35A* did involve an element of retrospectivity but that that was intended by Parliament; and that no taxpayer can have a legitimate expectation that is immune to the possibility of subsequent statutory alteration.

Double taxation

The taxpayers argued that, in certain circumstances, the sale of a chattel to fund IHT payable on a breach of an undertaking that had been required by the variation would give rise to a double tax charge. However, the Special Commissioner was not convinced by the logic of the comparison given in argument. There was no necessary connection between the sale by a taxpayer of a particular asset and the breach of the IHT undertaking that had been given in relation to it. The possibility of two tax charges was 'not a consideration of any compelling weight, to be taken into account in applying the statutory test of whether it is just and reasonable to make the direction under *s 35A*'.

Intrusion

Another specific issue was the extent to which the impact on the family life of the taxpayer and enjoyment of his house should count against the interest of the public in access to the heritage property. After a review of the evidence, the Commissioner concluded that the Proposals were:

> 'onerous and intrusive. The time required to prepare the house for open access viewing, to remove and store away vulnerable chattels on the viewing route and to lay out druggets and roped barriers will, I expect, subtract from the days when the house is suitable for normal family life. Overall the proposals will involve a real disruption to the lives of the families.'

The loan alternative

The Commissioner found several problems with this alternative arrangement. Unless the owner can arrange to lend every one of the Part 1 objects, there will be intrusion and risk of much the same nature as if the open access option were to be adopted. More specifically, one large painting at B house would be difficult to move and to place in a public gallery. The paintings on wooden panels at A house and at B house could be damaged through movement to a new location. HMRC argued that purpose-built homes for those items could be constructed, but it was accepted that the maintenance costs would be great.

Whilst museums and galleries expressed enthusiasm for exhibiting items, there were difficulties. A curator had given thought to issues such as safe transport, invigilation, security and insurance of paintings that might be borrowed from A house. The curator thought that they could be contextualised by information given on their historic and social backgrounds in ways that would allow many members of the public to appreciate them. A Museums Officer for the county in which B house was situated was interested in various paintings and portraits for loans for between two and five years. Within that time frame, the very large investment that would be made in security, transport and hanging would become worthwhile. However, a sizeable amount of lottery funding would be required for the venue that the officer had in mind for the B house paintings. The venue would need upgrading.

However, it had to be accepted that, at the moment, the public facilities were quite inadequate for the proposed loans. Both in relation to A and B, the relevant authorities had had to withdraw from the idea of loans once the cost implications were revealed. The Commissioner therefore concluded that the museum/gallery option could not be regarded as a reasonable condition for continued conditional exemption of the chattels.

Taking all the circumstances into account, the Commissioner considered that the burdens placed on each owner would so outweigh the benefit to the public as to make it neither just nor reasonable for him to direct that the variation proposals should take effect. He therefore did not make any direction requiring the existing undertakings to be varied.

Appeal

18.17　There is no right of appeal from the decision of the Special Commissioner in the heritage property legislation. Such right of appeal, if any, as may exist will be under the general law in respect of judicial review of the Special Commissioner's ruling.

Preserving earlier exemption: replacement undertakings

18.18　The regime for 'clawback' of exemption is considered in the next chapter, but it is appropriate here to consider the kind of undertaking that will be effective not to shelter an existing transfer from tax, but to preserve an earlier exemption. An undertaking given for that purpose is in this book called a 'replacement undertaking'. A replacement undertaking given on or after the coming into force of the rules on 31 July 1998 must comply with the rules on undertakings that were in force on the date the replacement undertaking is given (except, as already noted, where the rules concerning estate duty apply). Effectively, this means that the new owner is bound by the new rules relating to the maintenance and preservation of the property, public access, publicity about the exemption and the rules as to review and variation. As already noted, a transfer of 'museum quality' chattels may not attract conditional exemption under the new rules, but a replacement undertaking may save those chattels from the clawback charge. This is a fairly narrow field: it is understood that HMRC receive about one new case per month.

Does the system work?

18.19　Anecdotal evidence suggests that, for those who accept the full limitations of public access, the regime as now administered does work and preserves for the nation assets that might otherwise be sold away. Claimants now better understand their obligations. As the Access Notes put it at para 24, 'Access is for the general public, not just for specialists and enthusiasts'. There is significant flexibility in the Access Notes.

Perhaps the only improvement might be some 'democratisation' of the process by which provincial practitioners and their clients, owners of smaller estates, become more closely involved. At present, nearly all the work centres upon the leading auction houses, which may lead to a concentration of fine objects in London, whose public places are already well endowed with fine things. The scope for close examination of fine heritage objects is more difficult in economically deprived areas, where perhaps their civilising effect might be much appreciated. Perhaps we need yet more Margates and Wakefields.

Chapter 19

Heritage property: loss of the exemption

QUICK GUIDE

Either a breach of undertaking, or death, or a disposal will trigger a clawback of the relief previously given. In relation to a composite holding of heritage property, sale or breach of undertaking in respect of any constituent part can endanger relief on the whole. The rules are complicated, and it is hoped that the flowcharts at **19.5** and **19.6** will help the practitioner through the maze.

Before calculating the charge to tax, define 'the relevant person' by applying the rules in **19.9**. Then, establish whether it will be the lifetime rate or the death rate that is to apply, using the rules at **19.10** onwards. Finally, place the event in its context. There is guidance in the examples at **19.13** and **19.14**.

THE GENERAL RULE

19.1   The legislation (see *IHTA 1984, s 32(1)*) uses the expression 'chargeable event' to describe the circumstances that trigger the loss or clawing back of the exemption that had previously been given, subject to conditions. Where the transfer of the property was a PET, the chargeable event will occur on or after the death of the transferor, since the survival by the transferor of a PET by seven years would cause it to be exempt, regardless of any conditional exemption.

Breach of undertaking under s 32

19.2   The failure, in any material respect, to observe the terms of the undertaking given in respect of heritage property is a chargeable event. For example, the question arose, during the outbreak of foot and mouth disease, as to whether owners of heritage land would be in breach of access undertakings if their property fell into an exclusion zone at a time when access should have been given. Other examples could be imagined where local conditions or government guidelines made it impractical for the public to have access. In Tax Bulletin special edition 'Foot and Mouth Disease', issued on 9 May 2001, the Revenue stated that they would not regard it as a breach of the undertaking for the owner to decide, after judging the risks, that access or visits should be suspended. Where there was a commitment to allow visits on a number of prearranged days in each year, the Revenue would not insist, for tax compliance purposes, that the days missed should be made up later in the year.

Breach may easily occur where the terms of the undertaking as to access have not been observed. The Access Notes, Part III, describe good practice where access is by prior appointment (see paras 18–26). Basically, the owner or his agent should facilitate access, not frustrate it. Thus:

- Appointments should be made as soon as asked, rather than the agent asking for a telephone request to be re-made in writing.

- Agents should not be off-putting.

- Owners should not discriminate against a potential visitor who may seem 'unwholesome because of the [visitor's] gauche or semi-literate style': access is for the public, not just specialists. Access for such Bohemians may be arranged at some other location. (The Access Notes do not say so in as many words but, if access is at the house, such a person would presumably not wish to enter other than through the servants' quarters: there would be no objection to that.)

- Owners must ensure that their agent is helpful and does not fob the public off.

- Articles may be moved, for example for renovation or short-term loan; if so, the owner should notify the public where the article is and when it will be back.

- Holidays should be accommodated: a member of the public may be able to visit only because holidaying in the area, which should be allowed for. Make arrangements in advance and keep them unless absolutely impossible.

Where a member of the public notifies HMRC via the website that access has been frustrated, the assertion will be examined carefully. If there has been a breach of undertaking, HMRC will seek its remedy. If that cannot be done, or if this is not the owner's first offence, HMRC will claim tax on the current value of the item concerned. That could be the entire contents of a house, but more likely only the article that the member of the public wanted to see. If the owner was just obstructive, it might be the whole collection.

Example 19.1: enthusiasts together

The writer, a silver enthusiast, noted from the website a collection of household goods. He happened to know the owner's agent personally, so rang him and was without delay put in touch with the owner. The owner invited him to lunch and to see and handle the artefacts, which were of the finest quality. It was a privilege, rather than the exercise of a taxpayer's right, to be welcomed into the home in that way. All the owner asked in return was a letter acknowledging that the visit had taken place, as evidence for his 'access' file, which the writer gladly sent soon afterwards.

Death or disposal

19.3   The chargeable event occurs where the person beneficially entitled to heritage property dies (see *s 32(3)(a)*) or if the heritage property is disposed of by any means (*s 32(3)(b)*). However, this rule is subject to qualification. Thus, there will be no chargeable event, whether arising by death or by disposal, if:

- there is a transfer of the settled property by the personal representatives of the deceased, or the trustee of settled property, or the person next becoming entitled to settled property to a 'heritage body', as defined below; or
- the heritage property is accepted by HMRC in satisfaction of tax.

Section 32(4) imposes one further condition, by providing that a death or disposal of the property after transfer to a heritage body is not a chargeable event with regard to that heritage property unless there has, after the disposal, been a further conditionally exempt transfer of it. It is not immediately clear how there can again be a conditionally exempt transfer of heritage property after it has been accepted by HMRC in satisfaction of tax or after it has been sold to a heritage body. Neither the legislation nor established commentaries on the legislation are any help in imagining how this part of *s 32(4)* comes into play. Some guidance was suggested by previous HMRC guidance, now superseded, explaining that *s 32(4)* can cover the possibility that the heritage body might sell the property to a private individual. It is understood that a new section of the Manual is in the course of preparation, which may explain this further.

Neither death nor a disposal of the heritage property is a chargeable event where further conditions are satisfied. The first of these (see *s 33(5)(a)*) is where the transfer, which would otherwise be a chargeable event, is itself conditionally exempt. The second is similar and is provided by *s 32(5AA)*, which was inserted into the legislation in respect of undertakings given on or after 31 July 1998. This provides that death or disposal is not a chargeable event where a person whom HMRC consider to be 'appropriate' gives an undertaking under *s 31*, or where the property is amenity land within *s 31(1)(d)* and appropriate undertakings are given under *s 31*.

The composite heritage estate: 'associated properties' under s 32A

19.4   Heritage property may commonly be held by several different persons, perhaps members of the same family, or it may be held partly by family members and partly by trustees. There may be, for example, a house, fine contents and amenity land (ie land within *s 31(1)(d)* which is essential

427

to the protection of the character and amenities of the house). These separate entities are 'associated properties' for the purposes of *s 32A(1)*. *Section 32A*, in general terms, seeks to hold associated properties together, and makes the exemption granted in respect of any element of the composite property conditional upon observance of the conditions and undertakings in respect of the whole. The workings of *s 32A* are complicated, being a set of rules adapted to different circumstances. The rules are illustrated in the series of flowcharts that appear on pages 428–431.

IHTA 1984, s 32A : Associated properties

section 32A(1): general principles

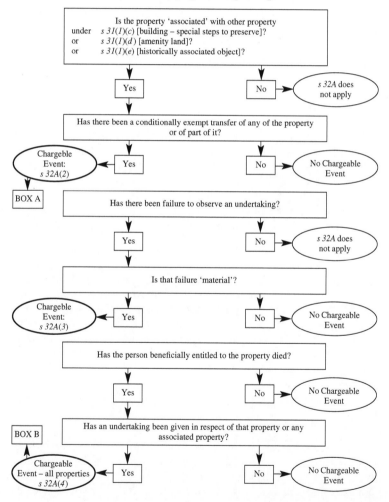

Is the property 'associated' with other property

under *s 31(1)(c)* [building – special steps to preserve]?

or *s 31(1)(d)* [amenity land]?

or *s 31(1)(e)* [historically associated object]?

section 32A(1): **general principles (continued)**

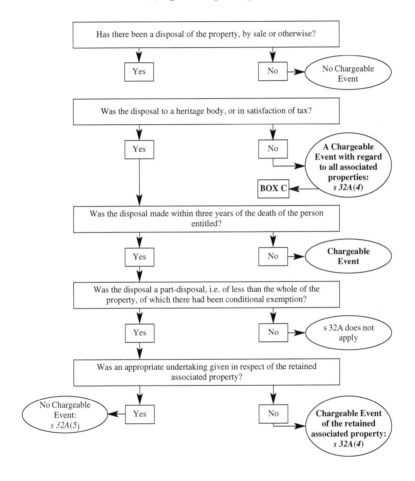

section 32(8): **death or disposal (not by sale)**

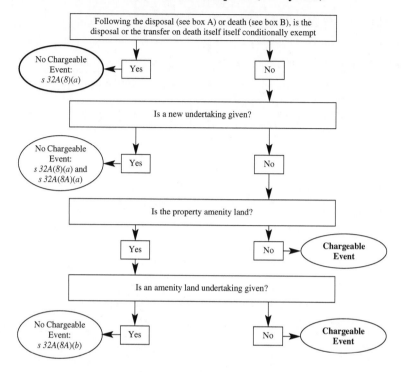

section 32A(9): **sale of part**

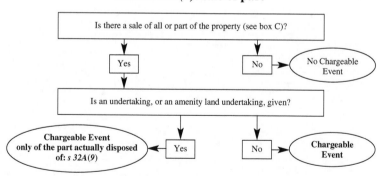

section 32A(10): **keeping the property repaired**

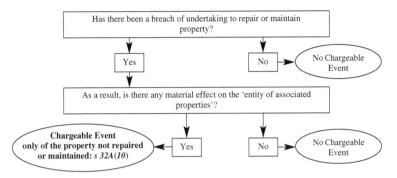

Selling (only) the family silver

19.5   The potential charge under *s 32A* can extend to the whole of the property in respect of which exemption was granted, even though the bulk of it has been retained (but see the *de minimis* exception under *s 32A(10)* described below and illustrated in the flowchart above). The chargeable event can also occur in respect of the breach of an undertaking in respect of any part of the composite estate. The death of a person entitled to associated property, or its disposal by sale or gift or otherwise, triggers a chargeable event in respect of all the associated properties. This is with the exception of the situation where the personal representative of the deceased or the trustees or the next person entitled to the property dispose of the asset concerned to a heritage body or it is accepted in satisfaction of tax. This part disposal affects all the associated properties, unless appropriate undertakings are given in respect of the associated properties that are not disposed of.

It would seem that, by this means, there is the opportunity of refreshing the undertakings given in respect of associated property, even where the actual article, in respect of which the undertaking is given, has not been disposed of, but instead some other associated item. Generally speaking, this will not be an onerous burden for the owners of heritage property, because the kind of undertaking that is given, for example with regard to chattels, is likely to provide for a measure of open access where the chattels qualify for conditional exemption, perhaps not in their own right as being pre-eminent, but by virtue of the connection with the house that qualifies for exemption.

Nevertheless, from an administrative point of view, the disposal of one of the elements of a composite heritage estate will cause considerable administrative work in the refreshing of all the undertakings given in respect of all the associated properties that are not disposed of.

'RELEVANT DISPOSAL'

19.6 *IHTA 1984, s 32A(7)* mirrors the wording of *s 32(4)*. It is concerned with the death of a person entitled to heritage property or part of heritage property following a 'relevant disposal'. For this purpose, a relevant disposal is one that complies with *s 32A(5)(a)* or *(b)*, ie a sale by private treaty to a heritage body or disposal in satisfaction of tax. The death is not a chargeable event with respect to the property concerned, unless there has been a conditionally exempt transfer of that property after the relevant disposal. In the same way, the disposal is not in itself a chargeable event, unless there has again been a conditionally exempt transfer. Given that the disposal, to qualify under *s 32A(5)*, is to a heritage body or in satisfaction of tax, it is not immediately clear how the circumstances envisaged under *s 32A(7)* could arise, nor is there any official guidance on the point.

Section 32A(8) and *(8A)* largely follow the wording already noted in *s 32(5)* and *(5AA)*. They provide that the death of a person entitled to property, or its disposal otherwise than by sale, is not to be a chargeable event if the transfer itself is conditionally exempt or if the *s 32A(8A)* conditions are satisfied, ie the giving of appropriate undertakings. These are illustrated in the flowcharts.

Part disposals: effect limited to the item sold

19.7 The general scheme of *s 32A*, if rigorously applied, would restrict the proper management of heritage estates. This is because any disposal of any part of the estate could cause a clawback of all of the relief granted. Sometimes, this will not be a problem. Members of the National Trust will know that, on more than one occasion, property may have been frozen in time with assets left undisturbed for many years following the death of their owner. The most notable example is Mr Straw's House at 7 Blyth Grove, Worksop, the interior of which has remained unchanged since the 1930s, with contemporary wallpaper, Victorian furniture and household objects. Occasionally, this situation can give a quite remarkable snapshot of life and times long gone.

Equally, however, many fine estates that qualify as heritage property are living entities for which time does not stand still. Trees may have been planted at the time of Capability Brown that now, instead of enhancing a view, obscure it. (This is particularly true of some of the vistas enjoyed by Turner, as an inspection will reveal of his depiction of Richmond Castle and Town, published in 1820. See, for example, 'In Turner's Footsteps' by David Hill, published by John Murray.) A property may contain artefacts that are of intrinsic value, but which cannot be publicly displayed because of shortage of space. Land on the edge of an estate may be taken for road widening. To address these issues, *s 32A(9)* allows for undertakings to be given in respect of property so as to preserve the estate as a whole from the chargeable event, and so as to provide that the disposal is a chargeable event only with respect to the part that is actually disposed of.

HMRC also have the power to apply a *de minimis* provision where it appears to them that the heritage entity as a whole has not been materially affected by the happening of what would otherwise be a chargeable event, such as the disposal of one of the associated properties. Where so satisfied, HMRC may direct that the disposal or breach of undertaking is a chargeable event only in relation to the property so disposed of, or in respect of which the undertaking has been broken.

However, these provisions do not really allow 'dynamic' collecting.

Example 19.2: a living collection

Josiah's (fairly) fine collection of silver passed on his death to his daughter Anastasia, who cherished it and gave undertakings to secure heritage relief, which she observes. She wished to weed out a few pieces that were not well hallmarked and replace them with better examples of the work of the same goldsmiths . To do so would enhance the collection but trigger breach of the undertaking. Only if Anastasia can afford to buy the new items mainly out of new money, and meanwhile pay the tax on the items sold, will she be able to carry on the collecting that her father established. There is no 'rollover' relief except in cases of loss (see below).

Loss or destruction of heritage property: not a chargeable event

19.8   The general rule used to be that the loss or destruction of heritage property was not an occasion for an IHT charge, even where insurance monies had been received. The situation would be different where a clear breach of an undertaking has caused the loss. However, where the building has not been completely destroyed, any sale of it other than to an approved heritage body will be a chargeable event.

Current practice is somewhat harsher. Where items are missing, HMRC now assume that a sale took place at some time since the item was last clearly seen 'where it should have been'. A mid point in time is assumed. The value must then be agreed as at that date. No allowance is made for CGT. Interest is due on the tax charged from the assumed time.

CGT rule

For CGT, the rules are different, since the loss of an asset is normally treated as a disposal giving rise to a chargeable gain where any compensation received is greater than the acquisition cost (see *TCGA 1992, s 23*). The old concession in this respect, ESC D19, is now the statutory code in *s 23(6)–(8)*. If the destruction of the building is irreparable and all the insurance money is laid out in acquiring a replacement building on other land, then the old building and the new building are regarded as an asset which is separate from the land, and the old building is treated as lost or destroyed.

Replacement of chattels, etc

HMRC guidance in respect of heritage property indicates that there is some flexibility in the interpretation of the replacement facility. Thus, in the case of loss of furniture, purchase of other furniture to serve the same function in relation to the heritage property would be acceptable; or if works of art are lost, purchase (insofar as that might be possible) of other similar works of art would be acceptable. Thus, applying the rules in *TCGA 1992, s 23*, and the 'functional' test above, heritage property could be replaced by a modern building which would not be suitable for designation as heritage property in its own right. That would not be relevant for CGT purposes.

Associated objects

As is nearly always the case, a separate code applies to property which, though not heritage property itself, supports it. As Practice Note IR67 reasonably observes, if a building is totally destroyed by fire, most, if not all, of the historically associated objects are likely to have gone up in flames with it, leaving essential amenity land potentially affected. Where the conflagration does not arise from a breach of an undertaking, the receipt of insurance monies is not a disposal to trigger an IHT charge on the supporting property. Provided the original undertakings continue to be observed, the ancillary property is unaffected. A fine estate may yet exist without the palace that used to grace it: see, for example, Clumber Park, or Lady Jane Grey's home at Bradgate Park, Leicestershire.

Breach of undertaking accompanied by destruction

If, for any other reason, there is a breach of undertaking, the IHT charge will apply in the normal way. The loss of the principal heritage property may naturally mean that the ancillary land loses its claim to heritage relief, not being heritage property in its own right. Thus, through the passing of time a further occasion of charge may arise when the undertaking falls to be renewed and the conditions no longer apply for re-designation as heritage property.

Similarly, for CGT no immediate charge applies to amenity land on the destruction of the subject land until loss of conditional exemption is triggered through other circumstances.

The destruction of heritage property can naturally affect maintenance funds, which are considered in **Chapter 21**. It is likely that, with no heritage property to maintain, the Direction by the Treasury under *IHTA 1984, Sch 4* that supported the maintenance fund will be withdrawn. At that point, the trustees must consider how they apply the fund, since application of the fund to endow another property or resettlement of new maintenance trusts would avoid the charge.

The charge to tax

19.9   *IHTA 1984, s 33* employs the expression 'the relevant person', which is defined in *s 33(5)*. There are three rules set out in *section 33(5)*, and these are dealt with in turn.

Rule 1: simple cases

Where there has been only one conditionally exempt transfer of the property before the chargeable event, the relevant person is the one who made the transfer.

Rule 2: two or more conditional transfers, one going back 30 years

In these more complex cases, it is necessary to consider the ownership of the property for the period of 30 years leading up to the chargeable event. Where the most recent transfer of the property was more than 30 years ago, the person who made that transfer is the relevant person.

Where there have been several transfers, but one has taken place in the last 30 years, that transferor is the relevant person.

Rule 3: two or more conditional transfers, both recent

Where, in the last 30 years, there have been two or more transfers, 'Russian roulette' applies. HMRC may choose whichever they please of the transferors as the relevant person. The reason for this last rule is to prevent avoidance of tax by channelling of heritage property through, perhaps, members of the family who do not have taxable estates to ensure that, in the event of a chargeable event, the charged tax would be as low as possible.

These rules contain traps for executors and trustees, who may have to retain sums to pay tax clawed back on breach of undertaking without knowing how much may be involved. Practitioners facing this issue may wish to read *Re Bedford, Russell v Bedford* [1960] 3 All ER 756 and *Re Scott* [1916] 2 Ch 268.

THE RATE OF IHT APPLIED: LIFETIME TRANSFERS

19.10   Where the relevant person is alive at the time of a chargeable event, lifetime rates apply. This could occur where:

- there was a lifetime transfer made before 18 March 1986; or

- an immediately chargeable transfer was made after 17 March 1986,

because it is not possible to claim conditional exemption in respect of PETs until they fail by reason of the death of the transferor within seven years; there is, of course, no need for conditional exemption in respect of a PET that does not fail.

Where, therefore, the lifetime rates apply, the value of the property in respect of which the charge is applied is added to the 'clock', already established, of chargeable lifetime transfers thus far made by the relevant person. This rule is applied by looking only at the seven years that led up to the chargeable event.

No allowances

19.11   Whilst the nil rate band is available to reduce the charge to tax, there is no scope for claiming personal exemptions such as annual allowances. The rates used are those in force at the time of the chargeable event. There are too few signposts in the legislation, which would benefit from the Tax Law Rewrite. The last proposition just put forward, for example, appears not from the context of the conditional exemption legislation in *IHTA 1984, s 33* but from *Sch 2, para 5*, which provides that where:

- tax is chargeable under *s 32* or *32A* on a chargeable event that occurs after a reduction in the rates generally; and

- the rate of tax is to be fixed under *s 33(1)(b)(ii)* by reference to a death which occurred before that reduction took place,

the provisions of *s 33(1)(b)(ii)* apply by reference to the most recent table in force.

Neither APR nor BPR is available to reduce the clawback charge.

Taper relief under *s 7* is not available to reduce the clawback charge.

Transfers on death

19.12   The rules are more complicated where the relevant person is dead. Where the conditionally exempt transfer was made in the lifetime of the relevant person, the tax is charged at lifetime rates. The amount on which the charge is levied is treated as if it were the top slice of the estate on death. However, even that statement of the rule is not complete. Where the chargeable event occurs after 17 March 1986, which will perhaps be in the majority of cases for readers of this book, but the death itself was before 18 March 1986, the lifetime rates that apply are those in force after 17 March 1986. This is by virtue of the transitional provisions in *FA 1986, Sch 19, Part II* (specifically *para 41*).

Where the conditionally exempt transfer was made on the death of the relevant person, special rules apply if the conditionally exempt transfer was also a gift with reservation. Then, by virtue of *s 33(2)*, the lifetime transfer rules apply but the tax is charged at the death rates as the top slice of the estate of the transferor. If the transfer was by way of settlement, of which the relevant person was the settlor, the death rates will be used if the settlement was created on death; otherwise, lifetime rates will be used. The benefit of any reduction in the rates of tax can apply here, because the rates that are applied are the most recent ones in force at the time of the chargeable event.

Example 19.3: progressive sales

George owned a library of rare manuscripts worth £350,000, which he gave to his grandson Stephen in March 1992, having in that year, as in previous years, used up his annual exemption. On his death in June 1994, the remainder of his estate is left to George's niece Mary, and is valued at £200,000.

To avoid an IHT charge on the failed PET, Stephen lodged the collection with his university, claiming conditional exemption. Had he not done so, the tax charge on the collection and on the estate could have been:

	£
George's estate at death	200,000
Value of failed PET	350,000
	550,000
Nil rate band	150,000
IHT on PET (40% on 200,000) – payable by Stephen	80,000
IHT on the estate (40% on 200,000) – payable by Mary	80,000

Many years later, however, changes in government policy on education and Stephen's own need for cash resulted in the return to Stephen of the manuscripts, which he sold at auction in June 2010 for £425,000. That is a chargeable event.

The IHT charge on £425,000 at the rates applicable in June 2010:

	£
George's estate at death	200,000
Sale proceeds	425,000
	625,000
Nil rate band	325,000
	300,000
IHT at 40% payable by Stephen	120,000

As a result, Mary's inheritance escaped IHT, but Stephen paid more.

INCREASING RATES OF IHT

19.13   Since 15 March 1988, the rate of IHT above the nil rate band has been a flat one, although occasionally there is the suggestion that multiple rates will be introduced. The effective rate of IHT increases progressively with the size of an estate, as practitioners who have to calculate charges on discretionary trusts will be aware. The rate of tax on successive chargeable events attributable to the same 'relevant person' thus increases progressively. The first transfer to trigger a chargeable event is at a lower rate of tax than later ones.

The effect of this is that an early breach of an undertaking may bring about a lower charge to IHT than a later one. The owner of conditionally exempt property should bear in mind the transfers that the relevant person has made or is likely to make. In particular, a chargeable event affecting conditionally exempt property will attract a lower charge before the death of the relevant person and before any substantial lifetime transfers by the relevant person. The difficulty for the owner of conditionally exempt property is in knowing who actually is the relevant person at any one time, since the way the rules work, as described at **19.9** above, demonstrates that the identity of that person changes according to a retrospective test.

Example 19.4: early sales taxed lower

On her death in May 2004, the estate of Fiona, a widow, included:

(*a*)   a collection of early twentieth century Lalique glassware, worth £25,000, bequeathed to Jason who sold it all in September 2005 for £40,000;

(*b*) a bronze statue worth £75,000 bequeathed to Sharon, who sold it in June 2006 for £90,000;

(*c*) scientific instruments used in an 1850 geographical survey worth £50,000, bequeathed to Simon and sold by him in May 2007 for £70,000; and

(*d*) a painting worth £200,000, bequeathed to Tom, who is considering its sale in March 2012. It is likely to fetch £400,000.

Fiona's estate at death was worth £200,000. She had made no lifetime transfers. Conditional exemption was claimed on all the gifts.

Jason's sale in 2005 attracts no IHT: it is £40,000 in the band £200,000–£240,000 at a time when the nil rate band is £275,000.

Sharon's sale is in the band £240,000–£330,000. By June 2006, the nil rate band is £285,000, so £45,000 of the proceeds attract an IHT charge of £18,000.

When Simon sells, the nil rate band is £325,000, all of which has been eaten up by previous events. All of the proceeds of £70,000 are chargeable at 40%, yielding IHT of £28,000 and taking the total of transfers to £400,000.

As a result, it might be thought that Tom should be advised that a sale on the open market will attract an IHT charge on all the proceeds. However, by now, the provisions for the transferable nil rate band apply and, under *s 8C(1)(b)*, the unused nil rate band of Fiona's husband(s) may be taken into account.

SET-OFF AND CREDIT

19.14 The circumstances that trigger a chargeable event may also be a chargeable transfer. When that happens, the IHT on the chargeable transfer is allowed as a credit against the IHT payable in respect of the chargeable event. This will not apply to a failed PET, however. Where a chargeable transfer is not itself a chargeable event, the tax paid in respect of the chargeable transfer stands as a credit that may be used by way of set-off against the IHT liability on the next chargeable event to occur. The credit may be set off either against IHT or against capital transfer tax. The set-off may apply even where the conditional exemption arose under the estate duty rule, or under the rules for relief before 7 April 1976 or those that applied thereafter.

Example 19.5: the tax credit in practice

Lucy had made no lifetime transfers. Her estate, on her death in February 1992, comprised the value of her house and cash totalling £250,000, plus a collection of rare china worth £100,000. The china was left to her sister Margaret, who claimed conditional exemption on it.

Margaret, a widow whose husband had used his nil rate band, died in July 2010. By virtue of publicity, the china was now worth £125,000. Margaret's other estate totalled £375,000 and passed to her son Fred. He had no wish to retain the old china and did not claim conditional exemption. Margaret had made no lifetime transfers.

Margaret's death is a chargeable event. The tax charge on Lucy's estate would normally be calculated as follows:

	£
Lucy's estate	250,000
Value of china (July 1992)	125,000
	375,000
Less nil rate band	150,000
	225,000
Charge as a result of sale @ 40% on 125,000	50,000

However, there is a chargeable transfer on Margaret's death. Her estate comprises:

	£
Value of china	125,000
Other estate	375,000
	500,000
Less nil rate band	325,000
Chargeable	175,000
Total tax charge at 40%	70,000

Of this £70,000, 125,000/500,000 or 25%, is attributable to the china, a tax charge of £17,500. That sum is allowed as a credit against the charge in respect of Lucy's estate, reducing it to £32,500.

Set-off can apply in a different way too. Suppose that there has been a PET of property that is already conditionally exempt. At the time of the making of the PET, the conditions and the undertaking may be honoured, with the result that there is no chargeable event. If, however, the PET fails or a chargeable event occurs after the PET and before the death of the transferor, chargeable event tax becomes payable although, at that time, it is not known that the PET will fail. When the PET does in fact fail, the tax on the chargeable event is allowed as a credit against the tax on the failed PET.

Example 19.6: set-off of tax against later charge

Henry managed a family business situated in premises which are part of the national industrial heritage. He died in May 2004, leaving his daughter

Sylvia an estate worth £350,000, including the heritage site worth £200,000. Conditional exemption is claimed by Sylvia, who for a time continues both to retain the site and to run the business.

Sylvia, a widow whose husband had used his nil rate band, gave the site and the business to her son Sean in November 2005. By then, the business was worth £100,000 and the site £300,000. Sean did not give the undertakings nor claim the exemption. Instead, he wound up the business and sold the premises for £375,000 in August 2007.

Sylvia died in December 2009.

There is a chargeable event on the gift by Sylvia to Sean in relation to the previous transfer by Henry to Sylvia:

	£
Henry's estate other than the site	150,000
Value of the site at time of gift	300,000
	450,000
Nil rate band, November 2005	275,000
	175,000
'Event charge' on the site: 300,000 in the band	100,000
150,000–400,000, ie 250,000 at 40%	

The gift by Sylvia to Sean was a PET when made, but it becomes chargeable. Clawback applies to negate any BPR that might have reduced the values, because Sean has sold everything before Sylvia's death. There is no IHT taper relief: the death is too soon.

	£
Failed PETs:	
Business	100,000
Heritage site	300,000
	400,000
Less nil rate band	325,000
Chargeable at 40%	75,000
IHT on failed PET	30,000
Attributable to business (¼)	7,500
Attributable to heritage site (¾)	22,500
Set off: tax on the PET of the site	22,500
Less 'event charge' credit	100,000
IHT now payable on the failed PET	NIL

THE 'CLOCK' OF CHARGEABLE TRANSFERS

19.15   There is adjustment of the cumulative total of chargeable transfers of a person who has made the last conditionally exempt transfer before the chargeable event if that person is still alive. The hypothesis is that the transferor, whether or not he is the 'relevant person', has made a transfer of value of the amount chargeable on the chargeable event at the time of his transfer. That amount is added to his own cumulative total of transfers of value. The rate of tax chargeable on all later transfers made by the transferor will, therefore, be increased.

The legislation that provides for this is *IHTA 1984, s 34(1)* and *(2)*, as varied by the particular circumstances set out in *sub-s (3)*, namely where:

- the person who made the last conditionally exempt transfer of the property before the relevant event is *not* the relevant person in relation to that event;

- the property is, or has been at any time within the last five years, comprised in a settlement;

- the settlement was made within the 30 years immediately preceding the event; and

- the settlor has made a conditionally exempt transfer of the property within those 30 years.

Where these four conditions are satisfied, it is the settlor who is treated as having made a transfer of the value that is chargeable on the chargeable event. The value in respect of which the chargeable event is triggered is added to the cumulative total of the settlor. The effect is to increase the rate of IHT chargeable on later transfers by that settlor. However, where the relevant person is *not* the last person to make a conditionally exempt transfer of the property, the calculation of the clawback charge will not affect cumulation of tax on his own estate (although the amount may affect the clawback charge). Equally, previous chargeable, non-exempted, charges are unaffected: there is no extra charge on such transfers.

The old rules in relation to heritage property

19.16   As will have been realised from this review of the existing legislation, it is in the nature of heritage property, and claims in respect of it, that the history not only of the property but of tax transactions relating to it can go back a considerable time. For that reason, it may be important to the practitioner to have available to him an account of the rules that were in force under estate duty and capital transfer tax. For a full account, the reader is directed towards specialist works such as *Foster* (eg at sections G5.21 and following) and *Tolley's Administration of Estates*, section G5. A summary of the relevant rules may be found at Appendix 8.

Transferable nil rate band

19.17   There was reference in Example 19.4 to the effect on the normal charge of the extension of the nil rate band by *IHTA 1984, ss 8A–8C*, a subject of sufficient difficulty and rarity that it is perhaps best left to the end of this account, which draws heavily on *Ray & McLaughlin's Practical Inheritance Tax Planning* (9th edition, Bloomsbury Professional), to which reference should be made for a fuller account of the treatment of the transferable nil rate band.

As already noted, under certain circumstances it becomes necessary, in relation to both heritage relief and woodland relief, to look back to an earlier death to establish the tax charge. The availability of the nil rate band can affect that tax charge. *Section 8C* takes account of this, where a heritage or woodland clawback charge applies.

Clawback of heritage relief whilst surviving spouse still alive

19.18   If the event triggering the charge happens before the death of the surviving spouse, it becomes necessary to recalculate the available (or used) nil rate band. To apply the legislation:

- first, find the nil rate band for the first spouse to die, defined in *s 8A(4)* as 'NRBMD';

- next, find the current nil rate band, ie that in force at the time of the event triggering the charge. This is defined by *s 8C(2)* as 'NRBME';

- next, establish 'E'. This is the excess of the nil rate band over the chargeable transfer at the first death; effectively, the unused nil rate band; and

- finally (for this stage of the computation), calculate 'TA': this is the amount on which the clawback is charged.

Then apply the fraction

$$\left(\frac{E}{NRBMD} - \frac{TA}{NRBME} \right) \times 100$$

to discover the percentage of the nil rate band in respect of which a claim may be made.

Example 19.7: desecration of an iconic vehicle

Lady Penelope's pink Rolls Royce, worth £100,000, was the subject of an undertaking under *s 30* when she died in November 2007. Her son had the car re-sprayed in May 2009, which destroyed the essential character of the vehicle and which was in breach of the undertaking, triggering a *s 32* charge. Lady Penelope had made chargeable lifetime transfers of £25,000 and left her estate, apart from the car, to Parker, whom she had married late in life.

Nil rate band – November 2007 (NRBMD): £300,000

Nil rate band – May 2009 (NRBME): £325,000

Unused nil rate band, November 2007:

Applying the formula in *s 8A(2)* and *(4)*

(E) amounts to £275,000, *viz*

M = £300,000

VT = £25,000

E = (M – VT) = £275,000

TA: £100,000

Computation:

$$\left(\frac{£275,000}{£300,000} - \frac{£100,000}{£325,000} \right) \times 100 = 60.8975\% \text{ of the nil rate band}$$

If there is more than one breach of undertaking, or where there are several clawback charges, the nil rate band that may be transferred is reduced by the proportion of the nil rate band clawed back by all the deferred charges, ie by the aggregate of TA/NRBME in respect of each triggering event (see s 8C(3)).

Clawback of heritage relief after the second death

19.19   If a deferred charge is triggered after the nil rate band has been transferred, *s 8C(4)* reduces the nil rate band of the first spouse to die. The mechanics of the adjustment are set out in *s 8C(5)*. The nil rate band of the first to die of the spouses or civil partners is first adjusted by applying *Sch 2* (the uprating provisions that give the benefit of any reduction in the tax that applies because the nil rate band has been increased over time).

That uprated nil rate band is then potentially both increased and decreased: the increase can apply where the first spouse to die might have more than one nil rate band available, perhaps being a widow or widower; the reduction is the amount of any increase in that band by virtue of the nil rate band transfer rules. The language of the legislation is rather convoluted; it was with greater optimism than truth that the Explanatory Note to the *Finance Bill 2008* suggested that *s 8C(5)* 'makes [it] clear' at all; but the following example, which is optimistic, may illustrate it.

Example 19.8: interaction of clawback and transferable nil rate band

Sir James was first married to Zuleika who became UK domiciled in 1975 and who left her estate to Sir James when she died in March 1991. Zuleika did not use her nil rate band. In 1997, Sir James married Sally and, on his death in November 2009, he left her his estate, having made only one chargeable transfer of £50,000 (a failed PET). The family seat qualified as heritage property, but a sale of amenity land for £200,000, to meet Lady Sally's debts after her death in September 2013, triggers a clawback charge under the 'associated property' provisions of *s 32A*.

The nil rate band in 1990/91 was £128,000 but none of it was used. In November 2009 it was £325,000, so the total nil rate band available to Sir James's executor is (£325,000 – £50,000 = £275,000 + £325,000) = £600,000. The nil rate band at Sally's death is, say, £375,000. The clawback charge is on £200,000. The reduction under *s 8C(5)* is of the increase in the nil rate band from Sir James's death to that of Sally (£375,000 – £325,000), ie £50,000. Thus, Sir James's executor has available a reduced (double) nil rate band of (£600,000 – £50,000 – £200,000) = £350,000.

Note that, if a Scottish law claim to 'legitim' is made after a claim to transfer unused nil rate band following the death of the second parent, HMRC may adjust the claim in respect of the unused nil rate band accordingly (see *s 147(10)* and IHTM43041).

Compliance

19.20   Compliance generally is discussed later in this book. Where conditional exemption is lost, the owner must deliver an account in form IHT100 within six months of the end of the month in which the 'loss event' arose. HMRC indicated, in their May 2003 Special Edition Newsletter, that delay will trigger penalties. Slightly less stringent rules apply for capital transfer tax and estate duty recapture charges than for IHT.

Chapter 20

Heritage property: the regime for relevant property trusts

QUICK GUIDE

As may be expected, the combination of rules for 'relevant property' or discretionary trusts and for heritage property makes for some fine distinctions and difficult computations. Few practitioners will still need to know the old law set out in **20.1** to **20.4**. If 'clawback' arises, identify the 'relevant person' (except where the choice lies with HMRC). Apply the computation rules in **20.11**, taking note of the anti-avoidance rule described at **20.12**. The tax return in form IHT100 is a considerable improvement on the previous form. The calculation guide will assist.

The changes in *FA 2006* have the result that there will, in future, be fewer beneficiaries in the position of tenant for life of a settlement for IHT purposes, but such as remain are in the same position as an individual as far as heritage property is concerned by virtue of *IHTA 1984, s 49*, which treats them as being beneficially entitled to the property. This chapter is concerned with relevant property trusts only, although most new trusts will fall into that category. The capital transfer tax regime is described at **20.1** to **20.4**; at **20.5** onwards, the present regime is examined. Given the extended duration of both relevant property trusts and matters relating to heritage property, a long perspective is appropriate here.

THE OLD LAW: THE CAPITAL TRANSFER TAX CODE

20.1 A code of taxation for the charging of capital transfer tax on relevant property trusts existed until 9 March 1982, but is outside the scope of this work. Practitioners with cases still unresolved from that era should consult specialist works such as *Foster* at Division E10. The possibility of a charge to capital transfer tax arose in respect of events after 6 April 1976. That was the date from which, for the first time, the regime for heritage property was extended so as to include property in relevant property trusts. Whilst the main legislation on relevant property trusts, as now applicable, is to be found in

446

IHTA 1984, ss 78, 79 and *79A*, the rules that applied before 9 March 1982 are to be found only in *FA 1976, ss 79–81*.

The scheme contemplated the giving of an undertaking by an appropriate person in respect of heritage property comprised in a relevant property trust for six years. The trustees must own the heritage property itself, not merely some interest in it. Where the appropriate undertakings were given, an event that would otherwise be subjected to an exit charge escaped that charge as a 'conditionally exempt distribution'.

Where the beneficial owner of the heritage property died, and no new application for conditional exemption was made or accepted, capital transfer tax became payable (as it did where the property was sold, or where there was a capital distribution or other trigger for an exit charge without fresh conditional exemption). Likewise, the breach of an undertaking in respect of such property was a chargeable event. A later distribution payment of capital distribution would normally be conditionally exempt, save where the person becoming entitled to an interest in the property was unwilling to give the undertaking. The old rules involved a more extended concept of cumulation than now applies.

The charge to tax

20.2   Where an exit charge was appropriate under the normal rules by reference to a chargeable event, capital transfer tax was fixed on the basis of the chargeable event that triggered the exit charge. If that brought the trust to an end, the rate for the exit charge was calculated on the assumption that there was a capital distribution when the settlement ceased to exist. The distribution was added to the cumulative total of capital distributions that had by then actually been made. The new rates that would apply were lower than the old: see *FA 1978, s 62(6)*, which applies by virtue of *FA 1980, Sch 15, para 5*.

The effect of treating the chargeable event as a distribution payment was only to assist the calculation of capital transfer tax that became payable in the event of the breach of an undertaking or death by the person who received the proceeds of sale or the person for whose benefit the property was disposed of. The deemed capital distribution was not itself a distribution payment. It did not enter into the cumulative total of the settlement under the general rule, but only in the particular circumstances set out below.

Exclusion of cumulation

20.3   *FA 1976, s 81(5)* provided that, where the last conditionally exempt transfer or distribution before the chargeable event was made by the trustees, the chargeable event did not operate for cumulation as if it were a distribution payment.

Example 20.1: Paul Klee painting sold

The Joskins Discretionary Trust owned, amongst other things, an early Klee, which the trustees released to one of the beneficiaries, Hilda Joskins, who applied for exemption in respect of the distribution. Hilda later sold the painting, triggering a chargeable event. The distribution to Hilda was the last conditionally exempt distribution before the chargeable event but there is no cumulation.

If, on the other hand, Hilda had died and a further application had been made for conditional exemption on her death, that would prevent the distribution from the discretionary trust from being the last conditionally exempt event before the occurrence of the chargeable event. In such a circumstance, for example the sale by Hilda's son following conditional exemption on Hilda's death, that sale would be treated as a distribution payment. This is so, whether or not the Joskins trustees are also liable to capital transfer tax, because some other person is to be regarded as the relevant transferor.

Further exception to the rule

20.4   Even where the last conditionally exempt transfer to arise before the chargeable event was made by the trustees, there was one other circumstance where it would not be regarded as a deemed distribution payment. For this exception to apply, the following conditions must be satisfied:

- the trustees must not be treated as the relevant transferor;

- at the time of the chargeable event, the property must be comprised in a settlement made not more than 30 years before the chargeable event;

- within the last five years, the property must have been comprised in a settlement made not more than 30 years before the event; and

- the settlor has made a conditionally exempt transfer within those 30 years.

As to the last of these conditions, the conditionally exempt transfer affected would normally be the one by which the property came into the settlement. Where these conditions were satisfied, there would be no cumulation within the settlement. Instead, cumulation would apply to the settlor rather than to the settlement itself. This was difficult legislation, as is so often the case with an anti-avoidance provision. The purpose was apparently to discourage a settlor from using the settlement to create separate cumulation whilst leaving his own 'clock' undisturbed.

TREATMENT OF RELEVANT PROPERTY TRUSTS: RULES APPLICABLE AFTER 8 MARCH 1982

20.5   *IHTA 1984, s 78* sets out the regime by which there can be conditional exemption from an exit charge. The conditions are that:

- the property has been comprised in the settlement throughout the six years ending with the transfer of it, or with any other event that would otherwise have given rise to an exit charge; and

- the property is designated by the Board under the *s 31* regime; and

- the appropriate *s 31* undertaking is given by such person as HMRC consider to be appropriate in the circumstances; or

- in the case of amenity land falling within *s 31(1)(d)*, the appropriate undertaking for amenity land is given with regard to the amenity land by such person(s) as HMRC consider appropriate.

As was noted at **18.2**, any claim under *s 78(1)* must be made not more than two years after the date of the transfer or other event, or within such longer period as HMRC allow. The regime in *s 78(1)* relates to events happening after 8 March 1982, regardless of the regime under which the original conditional exemption was granted.

The regime for relevant property trusts links directly to the requirements of *ss 32, 32A, 33(1), (3)–(7)* and *35(2)*. The charging provisions under *ss 32* and *32A* also apply directly. The effect of this is that relevant property trusts are affected by the following requirements in respect of designation and of undertakings on or after 31 July 1998:

- chattels must be pre-eminent;

- undertakings must ensure that there is a measure of open public access;

- undertakings must satisfy the new requirements for greater publicity;

- information about conditionally exempt property must satisfy the new higher standards;

- the new rules as to varying undertakings apply; and

- the rules in *s 35A* apply directly to property in a relevant property trust so as to affect undertakings that were given before the coming into force of *FA 1998*.

CLAWBACK CHARGE ON RELEVANT PROPERTY TRUSTS

20.6   It follows from the importation into the trust regime of the general rules for heritage property that IHT can become payable, unless the occasion of the event is not itself conditionally exempt, where:

- an undertaking is broken in some material respect; or

- the heritage property is sold; or

- the heritage property is disposed of otherwise than by sale, including on an occasion which triggers an exit charge under the normal regime for taxing relevant property trusts.

Calculating the tax charge

20.7   As in so many other respects, relevant property trusts have their own regime for calculating the tax charge.

Start with the date on which the property became comprised in the settlement (whether or not that was the date on which the settlement itself began). If the chargeable event happens within ten years of the date on which the heritage property joined the trust, the rate of tax is 30% of what it would otherwise be (see *s 78(4)(a)*).

If the chargeable event occurs more than ten years after the heritage property joined the trust but before the second ten-year anniversary of it so joining, the rate of tax is 60% of what it would otherwise have been. In either case, the 'death' rates of *s 7(1)* apply and not the lifetime rates of tax under *s 7(2)*. The rule observed previously, relating to the reinstatement of the cumulative total of transfers or 'clock' of the transferor, does not apply to trustees under this regime.

THE 'RELEVANT PERSON' AND SPECIAL RULES

20.8   Usually, the settlor of a relevant property trust will be the relevant person. If there is more than one settlor, HMRC may choose which of them is to be relevant. If the relevant person died before 13 March 1975, *IHTA 1984, s 78(5)* introduces a special rule. The rate of tax to be applied is whichever rate would have applied to the value of the heritage property at the time of the chargeable event, where three conditions apply (see below). The charge to tax is at the lifetime rates, unless the conditionally exempt transfer was made on death and was not a transfer being a gift with reservation. In either of these last two cases, the charge is at the death rates (see *s 33(2)*).

The conditions are these:

- the settlor had died when the chargeable event occurred;

- the value transferred on his death was equal to the amount on which estate duty was chargeable when he in fact died; and

- the value of the property now being charged had been added to the estate on death and formed the top slice of it.

This is the effect of *s 78(5)*, which substitutes *s 33(1)(b)(ii)* for these particular circumstances.

To understand *s 78(5)*, the practitioner requires a knowledge of the rest of the legislation. For this particular purpose, *s 33(1)* reads as follows:

'33 Amount of charge under section 32

(1) Tax chargeable in respect of any property under section 32 or 32A above by reference to a chargeable event shall be charged–

(*a*)   on an amount equal to the value of the property at the time of the chargeable event; and

(*b*)   at the following rate or rates–

    (i)   if the relevant person is alive, the rate or rates that would be applicable to that amount in accordance with section 7(2) above if it were the value transferred by a chargeable transfer made by the relevant person made at that time;

    (ii)   the rate or rates that would have applied to that amount ("the chargeable amount") in accordance with the appropriate provision of section 7 above if the relevant person had died when the chargeable event had occurred, the value transferred on his death had been equal to the amount on which estate duty was chargeable when he in fact died, and the chargeable amount had been added to that value and had formed the highest part of it.'

Example 20.2: charges on selling silver

In August 1983, Michael established a relevant property trust, to which he transferred cash of £100,000. He transferred a collection of silver worth £40,000 to the trustees in January 1989, by which time his personal 'clock' of transfers over the previous seven years amounted to £135,000.

The trustees claimed and received conditional exemption on the silver. In February 1995, finding the obligations of insurance and protection burdensome, they appointed the silver *in specie* to a beneficiary, Nellie, who also claimed exemption. The collection was by this time worth £50,000.

Michael died in January 2000, leaving an estate of £200,000. He had made lifetime transfers totalling 150,000.

Nellie had only kept the silver so as not to hurt Michael's feelings. She hated cleaning it and the intrusion of the requirements of conditional exemption. She sold it all in March 2000 for £75,000.

The IHT charges are as follows:

- On transfer to the trust, nil. Conditional exemption applies.

- On the ten-year anniversary of the trust in August 1993, nothing in respect of the collection.

- On release of the collection to Nellie in 1995, nil. The trustees had held the silver for (just) six years. Exemption again applies.

- On the sale, a charge on Nellie, as the relevant person. This being the second decade of the trust, 60% of the rate will apply. The gift of the silver was a lifetime one, even though Michael had died by the time of the chargeable event

	£
Sale proceeds	75,000
Michael's 'clock'	150,000
Michael's estate	200,000
Upper end of range	425,000
Transfer in the range 350,000–425,000:	
Tax at 20% on 75,000 would be	15,000
Charge becomes 60% of this, ie	9,000

Exemption from the ten-year periodic charge

20.9 The legislation is to be found in *s 79*. Exemption from the periodic charge will apply where:

- there was conditional exemption on the transfer of the property into the trust; and

- there has been a chargeable event in relation to the heritage property since receipt by the trustees.

Exemption will also apply where the disposal of the trust property qualified for relief from CGT under *TCGA 1992, s 258(4)* (the regime for relief of heritage property from CGT) and there has been no chargeable event in relation to it since that exempt disposal.

Two exemption regimes

20.10   There is slightly different treatment within the trust according to whether the exemption arises from freedom from IHT or from CGT. In relation to property conditionally exempt from IHT, the exemption continues until there is a chargeable event. In relation to property exempted for CGT, that exemption continues until the property is treated as sold under the CGT regime or there is a breach of the undertaking. Either way, at the next ten-year anniversary of the trust, the usual regime for taxing relevant property trusts will apply and, at that point, the cumulative total applicable to the trust will be used, unaffected by exemption on any previous ten-year anniversaries.

The rules arise where there has been neither a conditionally exempt transfer nor a CGT-relieved disposal in favour of the trust on the transfer into the settlement or before it. Where the usual undertakings are given, and designation by HMRC is achieved before the ten-year anniversary, the property can be relieved from the ten-year charge. It is here that some forward planning is necessary, in that the claim for exemption and designation must be made sufficiently in advance of the ten-year anniversary for the process to have run its course in time. It would seem appropriate to allow not less than three years for the process. Fortunately, in view of this, it is not necessary for the property to have been held in the settlement for six years (see *s 79(3)*), as was illustrated in Example 20.2.

In such a case, a charge to tax arises on the first chargeable event that would occur under the general regime but for conditional exemption. That charge, otherwise applied by virtue of *s 79(4)*, will not arise if, between the date of the settlement and the date of the notional chargeable event, there has been an occasion which is conditionally exempt. This is because, in those circumstances, the normal rules for taxing relevant property trusts would give rise to a charge. There would be a real event giving rise to a full charge.

CALCULATING THE RATE OF IHT ON NEW HERITAGE PROPERTY IN A RELEVANT PROPERTY TRUST

20.11   First, find the appropriate 'start date' for the period to which the rates will apply. This will be the latest of:

- 13 March 1975; or

- the commencement of the settlement; or

- the last ten-year anniversary of the trust that occurred before the day on which the heritage property came to the trust.

20.11   *Heritage property: the regime for relevant property trusts*

The period, from the last of the three days just identified to the date of the event that triggers the charge, is 'the relevant period' under *IHTA 1984, s 79(7)*. That period must now be divided into complete successive quarters (of a year) under *s 79(6)*. A rate is charged that, over a period of 50 years, reaches a maximum of 30%. It is illustrated (in whole years) in the table that follows and is applied as follows:

- first 40 quarters: 0.25%

- next 40 quarters: 0.2%

- next 40 quarters: 0.15%

- next 40 quarters: 0.1%

- next 40 quarters: 0.05%.

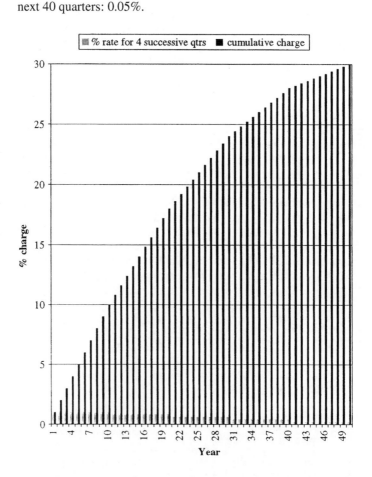

Section 79(5) charges the tax on its value at the time of the event, but subject to the 'market value' rule which provides for substitution of the sale price where the sale was not at full market value.

Liability for tax in relation to conditional exemption is discussed more fully later in this book. In relation to relevant property trusts, *s 207(3)* provides that the persons liable for tax charged under *s 79(3)* are:

- the trustees of the settlement; and
- any person for whose benefit any of the property, or income from it, was applied at or after the time of the event triggering the clawback charge.

Anti-avoidance: prevention of the purchase of heritage property to keep down periodic charges

20.12   *Section 79(9)* provides rules for calculating the tax charge under *s 64*, the general rule. The value of any consideration given for heritage property when it comes to the settlement is treated, for the purposes of *s 66(5)(b)* (ie for the calculation of the amounts on which charges to tax are imposed in respect of the settlement in the ten years before the current ten-year charge), as if the price paid for the heritage property were an amount on which a charge to tax arose in respect of the settlement at the time the heritage property joined the trust under the rules in *s 65* for exit charges. This affects the IHT for the periodic charge on any other property in the trust at the first ten-year anniversary charge after the acquisition of the heritage property where that anniversary is within ten years of the claim for exemption.

Chapter 21

Maintenance funds

QUICK GUIDE

Relief is available on funds set aside for the maintenance of heritage property. The various reliefs are catalogued at **21.2**. The trust must be:

● of an acceptable wording;

● with acceptable trustees;

● holding acceptable property;

● for the maintenance of suitable heritage property.

An acceptable use is the maintenance of heritage property rather than expenditure on capital items.

Once established and authorised, rules apply to supervise the fund and its accounts. A flowchart at **21.12** charts the progress of the procedure. Anti-avoidance rules abound, including those as to 'excess value' and 'purchase' noted at **21.16**. Further anti-avoidance rules are summarised at **21.18** and illustrated thereafter.

Relief is clawed back where the fund is used for unacceptable purposes, such as:

● the release of capital;

● dispositions by trustees;

● the loss of heritage status in respect of the property for which the fund was established; or

● the withdrawal of the Treasury Direction: see **21.24**.

The subject of maintenance funds is too rarefied for professional examinations. If it were not, the intricacy of the '*paragraph 13*' and '*paragraph 14*' calculations described in **21.25** would surely form the basis of a compulsory question. Where funds were previously in a discretionary trust, a somewhat simpler calculation applies: see **21.28**. There is a regime for CGT for maintenance funds; for completeness, it is outlined at **21.32**.

OUTLINE OF THE SCHEME

21.1   Any honest yachtsman will confirm that it is not the original expense of the boat that breaks him but the upkeep. So, too, with some heritage property, leading to the loss of many fine properties, as was catalogued and vividly displayed in an exhibition at the Victoria and Albert Museum concerned with the destruction of the English country house. That loss to the national heritage is the focus for the funds described in this chapter. The legislation is designed to encourage the settlement of funds that are to be used towards the cost of upkeep of qualifying heritage property. As originally conceived, the provisions did not allow the assets to be used for any purpose other than such maintenance or transfer to a national heritage body. The conditions were strict and it appears, from the record in the Standing Committee of the House of Commons in June 1980, that only two funds were ever set up under the old legislation.

As will be seen, the code for maintenance funds contains strict provisions to curb abuse, leading to considerable complexity which will, in itself, be enough to deter many advisers from recommending the establishment of maintenance funds. Nevertheless, under the scheme as it now exists, assets can eventually be returned to the settlor or applied for non-heritage purposes, subject to an appropriate tax charge. Equally, the scope of the exemption has been enlarged so that maintenance funds may be used to benefit a wide range of heritage property. Even so, there are few such funds.

The main relieving provisions in *IHTA 1984* that trigger an examination of the code relating to maintenance funds are:

- *s 27* (the general provision in respect of exempt transfers to maintenance funds);
- *s 57A* (a section inserted into the regime for taxing interest in possession trusts);
- *s 58* (the section that defines 'relevant property' for the IHT regime for discretionary trusts, the definition of which specifically excludes property passing to maintenance funds); and
- *s 77*, which introduces the code for maintenance funds in *Sch 4*.

Where the owner of heritage property wishes to set up a trust fund to provide for the maintenance, repair or preservation of the property, and for the provision of reasonable public access to it, exemption will be granted from various forms of taxation. As already noted, there is very little case law on heritage property, but the official guidance is substantial. IR67, 'Capital Taxation and the National Heritage', is the starting point for interpretation of many of the aspects of the legislation. At chapter 8, it summarises the relief. It is understood that IR67 is being revised but that the changes are unlikely to be substantial.

Summary of the relief

21.2   Listed below are the main points of the relief:

- No capital transfer tax to be paid when property is put into the fund.

- No IHT to be paid when property is put into the fund.

- The charge to CGT which might otherwise arise when property is put into the fund may be deferred.

- No capital transfer tax ten-yearly charge.

- No IHT ten-year charge.

- At the option of the trustees (which will not be exercised whilst present rates persist), the income of the fund is not to be treated as that of the settlor but suffers tax at the rate applicable to trusts.

- At the option of the trustees, cash paid from the fund for heritage purposes is not to be treated, as might otherwise be the case, as the income of a person by virtue of that person's occupation of the heritage property.

- Whether or not the trustees so elect, cash paid from the fund for heritage purposes is not to be treated as the income of a person by virtue of his occupation of the heritage property, provided that the income of the fund is treated for tax purposes as being the income of the settlor of the fund.

- No charge to capital transfer tax or IHT where capital is taken from the fund for heritage purposes, including resettlement into a new maintenance fund.

- CGT deferral where assets are transferred from the maintenance fund to another trust, including a maintenance fund or to an individual.

- stamp duty land tax liability restricted to the single fixed conveyance duty.

- 'As you were' tax provisions apply where any part of the maintenance fund is used for a purpose not connected with heritage. In particular, under these provisions, depending on who receives the money, there may be charges to capital transfer tax or IHT. There will be an income tax charge at up to 30% on any of the fund income that has been taxed only at the rate applicable to trusts and not been used for heritage purposes. Normal CGT rules apply, such that holdover relief under *TCGA 1992, s 260* will be available in respect of a transfer from a discretionary trust. Stamp duty can be payable in certain circumstances.

CONDITIONS FOR THE RELIEF

21.3   The legislation is mainly to be found in *IHTA 1984, Sch 4*, and the conditions for the relief are set out in *paras 2–4*. Where those conditions are satisfied and a claim has been made, HMRC give a direction under *para 1*. The direction may in fact be given in advance of the establishment of the settlement, where HMRC are satisfied that they would be obliged to give a direction once the property was so comprised. Transitional relief is allowed under *para 1(3)* in respect of property comprised in a settlement as a result of transfer of value that was exempt under *FA 1976, s 84* and made before *FA 1982, s 94* came into force.

The conditions relate to:

- the wording of the trusts of the maintenance fund;
- the trustees of the fund;
- the property in the fund; and
- the property to be maintained.

The first condition: the trust instrument

21.4   Drafting the maintenance fund trust is critical to the success of the application. As is noted elsewhere in this chapter, it may take time to arrive at a form that is acceptable both to the party wishing to set up the fund and to the 'other side', as represented by HMRC. One suitable precedent is to be found in *Practical Trust Precedents* (February 2001, Bloomsbury Professional), precedent F2. That draft contains paragraphs to deal with the following matters:

- definitions;
- retention or sale of trust fund;
- power of accumulation;
- maintenance trusts;
- default trusts of income for qualifying charities;
- powers of appointment and ultimate default trusts;
- power of investment;
- powers in relation to real property;
- power to borrow;
- trustee charging clause;
- power to enter into transactions with the trustees;

- power to appoint nominees;
- appointment of new trustees;
- provision of accounts; and
- stamp duty certificate.

Like other precedents in that volume, F2 is admirable for its clarity and brevity. An alternative precedent, settled by Robert Ham QC and Emily Campbell of counsel, was set out in full in *Christie's Bulletin* (vol 7, no 2, pp 27–32). That precedent follows broadly similar ground. It came with the benefit of a commentary by the authors on both the requirements of HMRC in relation to such trusts and the extent to which counsel felt bound to update the precedent to meet those requirements.

The six-year rule

Schedule 4, para 3 sets out the terms of a trust that will be acceptable for a maintenance fund. The first is 'the six-year rule'. This is that (see *para 3(1) (a)*) none of the property held on the trusts can at any time in the period of six years, beginning with the date on which that property came to the maintenance fund, be applied for a 'non-heritage purpose'. Acceptable purposes for the use of the property are basically two:

- the maintenance of heritage property; or
- the making of that property available to a heritage body or qualifying charity.

More specifically, *para 3(1)(a)(i)* identifies a number of uses as acceptable for property in a maintenance fund. These uses are all in relation to the heritage property for the maintenance of which the fund has been established.

In this chapter, that property is called 'qualifying property', the name given to it by *para 3(2)*, and the funds or assets set aside for the maintenance of qualifying property are called the 'trust property'. *Paragraph 3(4)* contains another definition, useful to be noted at this stage, namely that of a 'qualifying charity'. Such a charity is one that exists wholly or mainly for the maintaining, repairing or preserving for the public benefit of either buildings of historic or architectural interest, land of scenic, historic or scientific interest, or objects of national, scientific, historic or artistic interest. 'National interest' includes interest within any part of the United Kingdom. The acceptable uses for the trust property are, in relation to qualifying property:

- maintenance, repair or preservation of qualifying property;
- provision for public access to qualifying property;

- maintenance, repair or preservation of the trust property;

- improvement of the trust property where such improvement is reasonable, having regard to the purposes of the trusts of the maintenance fund; and

- paying the expenses of trustees in relation to the trust property.

Alternative use of the income of the fund under para 3(1)(a)(i)

The second limb of *para 3(1)(a)* is the alternative provision where the trust property is not used for the maintenance etc of the qualifying property. This second limb will be appropriate where the qualifying property is, for example, sold. The second limb allows for the application of surplus income of the maintenance fund to a qualifying charity or to a heritage body as defined in *Sch 3*. *Schedule 3* is set out in full in Appendix 1 to this book.

Alternative use of the income or capital of the fund under para 3(1)(b)

The second main condition that must be included in the trusts of an acceptable fund is that none of the property can, within the period of six years from the establishment of the trust or within the lifetime of the settlor if he dies less than six years after the making of the trust, go otherwise than to a heritage body or qualifying charity.

There is a rider to this rule, as will be seen later, where a maintenance fund is established following an interest in possession in a trust. This particular situation is covered by *para 15A*, which came into force in respect of events after 16 March 1987. The code is considered at **21.17** below. Where that code applies, the effect of *para 3(5A)* is to apply a further condition to *para 3(1) (b)*. Thus, the condition becomes that none of the property can, on ceasing to be held on the maintenance trusts at any time in the six-year period or, if the tenant for life dies within that period, at any time before the death of the tenant for life, devolve otherwise than to a heritage body or a qualifying charity.

As to income, the rule is absolute. That income, unless accumulated, must be used only for the qualifying purposes set out at the beginning of this section. That rule applies not merely for the first six years but for the entire duration of the fund. Any maintenance fund trust must, by its drafting, satisfy this rule.

Qualifications to the first condition

21.5   The rules just set out are varied where property was previously comprised in another settlement and is transferred to the maintenance fund under circumstances that qualify for exemption under the rules in *Sch 4*. The condition as to income still applies, namely that it may be applied only for the maintenance purposes set out above. In these circumstances, it is assumed that the six-year period will already have expired at some time in relation to the previous settlement. Where that period has not expired, the six-year period begins not with the date on which the property comes to the new, ie present, maintenance fund, but with the date on which it was comprised in the earlier settlement. These adjustments to the general rule are contained in *Sch 4, para 4.*

Maintenance of heritage property

21.6   A distinction is drawn between:

- repairs to the qualifying property; and
- alterations.

Essentially, the fund may be used only for repairs. The provision of a new roof for a house would generally qualify, but the acquisition of new property would not. By way of illustration of running repairs and maintenance costs that will qualify, see the guidance in IR67, divided into categories of qualifying property. It may be summarised as follows.

Buildings

- preserving stonework and fabric;
- internal redecoration;
- general maintenance;
- heating costs where necessary to maintain or preserve the building;
- heating costs where necessary to preserve qualifying contents; and
- heating costs where necessary for the purpose of public access.

Qualifying land

- bracken control;
- scrub clearance;
- woodland management;
- replacement of mature trees, for example in parkland;
- fencing;
- maintenance of hedges, hedge-banks and walls; and
- upkeep of ditches and drainage.

Gardens

- the cost of seeds and plants, materials and implements;
- the repair and heating costs of greenhouses; and
- wages for gardeners.

Historically associated objects

- cleaning and restoration of pictures;
- repairs to tapestries, curtains and carpets; and
- repairs to clocks, furniture and similar objects.

Public access requirements

21.7   Here, the appropriate expenditure may be either capital or income in nature. The main illustrative categories of appropriate expenditure are:

- provision and maintenance of car parks;
- provision and maintenance of public lavatories;
- wages of guides and attendants;
- special fire precautions;
- lighting, heating and security costs where necessary for public access; and
- maintenance of roads and drives where necessary for public access.

The property within the maintenance fund itself will often need management. It may, for example, consist of a landed estate that supports a stately home. All expenses necessary for the proper and 'prudent' management of the assets of the fund will qualify. The trustees may spend either capital or income on repairs and maintenance to property in the fund. In a similar way, the property in the heritage fund may be improved so as to generate a higher income. This could involve the purchase of extra farmland or other expenditure which will assist good management of the trust assets. All of this is, however, subject to the qualification that these improvements must be 'reasonable having regard to the purposes of the trust'. The maintenance of the qualifying property is the priority: improving the property in the fund must take second place.

Expenses and other items

21.8   Professional fees, any rates and taxes in respect of the capital or income of the fund and certain other expenses are properly payable from the fund. In particular, insurance of the qualifying property itself is a proper expense, as is the cost of public liability insurance in relation to public access.

The second condition: the trustees

Status

21.9   By *Sch 4, para 2(1)(b)*, the trustees must be approved by HMRC, formerly by the Treasury. They must include either a trust corporation or a solicitor or an accountant or a member of such other professional body as HMRC may allow. For this purpose, an accountant means, see *Sch 4 para 2(3)*, a member of an incorporated accountants, and a trust corporation means one so defined for the purposes of the *Law of Property Act 1925* or *Administration of Estates (Northern Ireland) Order 1979, art 9*.

Residence

The trustees must be resident in the United Kingdom at the time that HMRC make the direction under *para 1* that effectively approves the maintenance fund. *Paragraph 2(2)* defines residence in the United Kingdom of trustees for this purpose as being satisfied where the general administration of the trusts is ordinarily carried on in the United Kingdom, and the trustees or a majority of them are resident in the United Kingdom. Where there is more than one class of trustees, a majority of each such class must be resident in the United Kingdom. The residency of a trust corporation is determined as for the purposes of corporation tax, involving the test of where the central management and control of the trust corporation resides.

The third condition: the content of the maintenance fund

21.10   The third principal condition to be satisfied is that the property transferred, or to be transferred, to the maintenance fund is 'of a character and amount appropriate for the purposes of those trusts'. The official guidance in IR67 points out that assets which provide little or no income are, on the face of it, unsuitable for a maintenance fund, particularly if these assets themselves will require money to be spent on them for their maintenance. Equally, the amount of property transferred to the fund should not be excessive in relation to the likely burden of expenditure on the fund. After all, for the trust to be acceptable, the income of the fund is locked into the heritage maintenance purpose. The fund need not be established all at once. It is possible for a small initial fund to be established, provided that it is clear that further assets will be added to the maintenance fund later.

Further condition: anti-avoidance 'charity' rules

21.11   A further condition applies before transfer to a maintenance fund can attract relief. This is a condition which is not specific to maintenance funds, but applies to several forms of exempt transfer, and first appears in *IHTA 1984, s 23(2)* in relation to gifts to charities. Transfers of value to charities are not exempt (see *s 23(2)*) where the transfer:

- takes effect only on the termination of some interest or period after the transfer of value; or

- depends on some condition which is not satisfied within 12 months after the transfer; or

- is defeasible.

For this purpose, a disposition which has not in fact been defeated on the first anniversary of the transfer, and is not defeasible after that time, is treated as not being defeasible – in other words, a 'wait and see' rule applies which can exempt the transfer.

The second limb of the qualification in respect of gifts to charities is that exemption shall not apply (see *s 23(3)*) in relation to property carved out of other property where:

- the interest so carved out is less than the full interest of the donor to charity; or

- the interest so carved out is given for a limited period only.

These sections in relation to gifts to charities are applied to transfers of maintenance funds by *s 27(2)*. That subsection also imports *s 24(4)*, which further qualifies *s 23(2)–(5)*. It is here that IR67 is particularly helpful, in summarising the effect of *s 27(2)*. The tax reliefs for a maintenance fund will not apply where the transfer into an existing maintenance fund results in the trustees acquiring a reversionary interest only by purchase. Equally, the tax reliefs will not apply where property is transferred to the maintenance fund in exchange for a reversionary interest which does not form part of the estate of the person who acquires it.

PROCEDURAL POINTS

21.12   The application for exemption should be made to the designated property section of HMRC Capital Taxes, Heritage Section, Ferrers House, PO Box 38, Castle Meadow Road, Nottingham, NG2 1BP. It must be made within two years of the transfer although, by *IHTA 1984, s 27(1)(a)*, HMRC may allow a longer period. Where the application is made after the trust has been set up, HMRC must give the direction if satisfied that the conditions mentioned in this chapter have been satisfied. Where the property has not yet been settled, HMRC have a discretion as to whether or not to give a direction. *Section 27(1A)* disapplies *s 27(1)* where a direction is given after the transfer is made, unless the claim is made within two years or such longer period as HMRC allow.

Satisfying the condition as to timing may present personal representatives with significant problems. Where no 'pilot' trust has been established, it will naturally take time to agree the terms of the trust instrument so as to comply with the points made earlier in this chapter. Assuming that this hurdle is overcome, it may be that the personal representatives hold property on discretionary trusts that are established by the will they are administering, and that they are keen to exercise their discretion within two years of the date of death, so that the property is treated as passing to the maintenance fund 'straight from the death'. Equally, there may be issues involving preparation and agreement of a deed of variation, again with a two-year time limit.

The best practical advice is to contact the Heritage Section of HMRC soon after the death, to discuss possible solutions so that, if the personal representatives find that they are running out of time, an application to HMRC to exercise its discretion can be considered in good time and in a spirit of cooperation. The flowchart on pp 467–470, outlining the procedure, may perhaps be used as a checklist.

Supervision of the fund

21.13   Once the trust is established and a direction has been made, HMRC have certain powers of supervision. HMRC may withdraw the direction if they consider that the trustees are exercising their powers in a manner that is inconsistent with the purposes of the maintenance fund. IR67 shows that, in these circumstances, HMRC will normally give the trustees an opportunity to put matters right before taking the step, which they may under *Sch 4, para 5*, of withdrawing the benefit of the tax relief on the fund itself. In the event that the direction is withdrawn in this way, the tax charges, set out later in this chapter, would apply.

Accounts

21.14   HMRC may revoke the direction if such revocation is warranted by circumstances affecting any property or its administration. The Board can call for the accounts of the maintenance fund. The trustees should provide appropriate accounts and information concerning the fund itself, and should maintain records of any income accumulated during the lifetime of the

'Subject property' means the property to be supported and maintained by the fund.

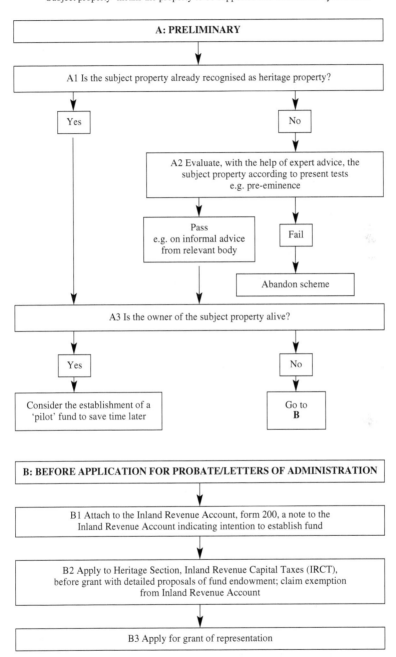

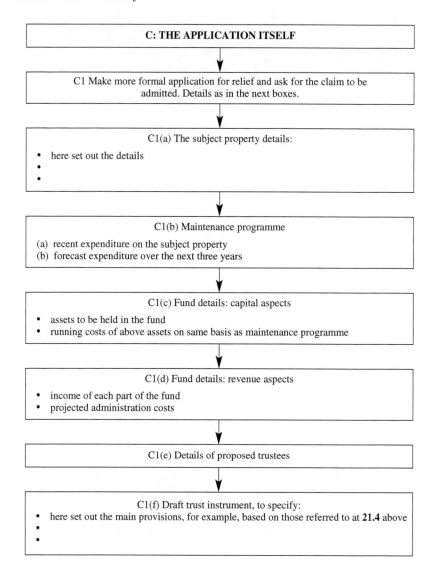

C: THE APPLICATION ITSELF

C1 Make more formal application for relief and ask for the claim to be admitted. Details as in the next boxes.

C1(a) The subject property details:

• here set out the details
•
•

C1(b) Maintenance programme

(a) recent expenditure on the subject property
(b) forecast expenditure over the next three years

C1(c) Fund details: capital aspects

• assets to be held in the fund
• running costs of above assets on same basis as maintenance programme

C1(d) Fund details: revenue aspects

• income of each part of the fund
• projected administration costs

C1(e) Details of proposed trustees

C1(f) Draft trust instrument, to specify:
• here set out the main provisions, for example, based on those referred to at **21.4** above
•
•

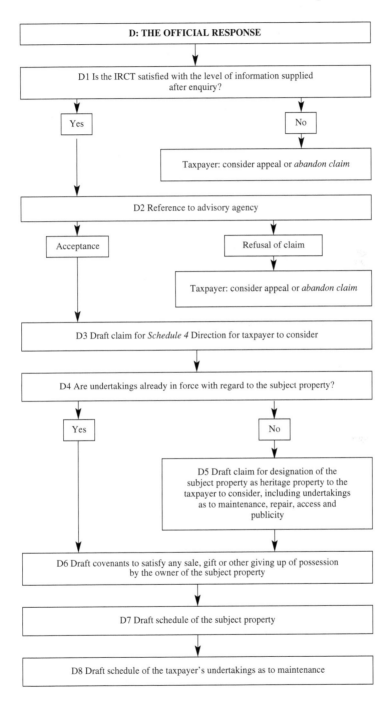

D: THE OFFICIAL RESPONSE

D1 Is the IRCT satisfied with the level of information supplied after enquiry?

Yes

No

Taxpayer: consider appeal or *abandon claim*

D2 Reference to advisory agency

Acceptance

Refusal of claim

Taxpayer: consider appeal or *abandon claim*

D3 Draft claim for *Schedule 4* Direction for taxpayer to consider

D4 Are undertakings already in force with regard to the subject property?

Yes

No

D5 Draft claim for designation of the subject property as heritage property to the taxpayer to consider, including undertakings as to maintenance, repair, access and publicity

D6 Draft covenants to satisfy any sale, gift or other giving up of possession by the owner of the subject property

D7 Draft schedule of the subject property

D8 Draft schedule of the taxpayer's undertakings as to maintenance

469

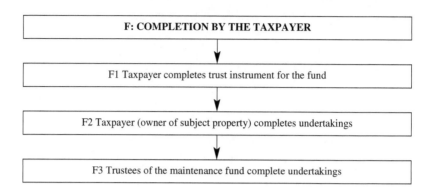

E: NEGOTIATION BETWEEN IRCT AND TAXPAYER

F: COMPLETION BY THE TAXPAYER

F1 Taxpayer completes trust instrument for the fund

F2 Taxpayer (owner of subject property) completes undertakings

F3 Trustees of the maintenance fund complete undertakings

G: CONFIRMATION BY THE REVENUE

G1 IRCT issue letter of confirmation
• that the subject property is 'qualifying property' within *Sch 4 para 3* (2)
• of a Direction under *Sch 4 para 1 (1)*
• that the maintenance fund is exempt IHT under *IHTA 1984, s 27 (1)*

fund. HMRC will expect annual audited accounts with a balance sheet and a statement of income and expenditure, plus an annual report on the activities of the fund describing what the trustees have done during the year. This is because, as will be seen below, a charge to tax may arise when property is withdrawn from the fund for non-heritage purposes. At that point, it would be necessary to show how the income of the fund had been taxed, what part of the fund was accumulation of income, and what part of the income had been applied for maintenance of the heritage property. By *Sch 4, para 7*, HMRC are given all the rights and powers of a beneficiary in relation to the enforcement of the trusts of the maintenance fund, and in relation to the appointment, removal and retirement of trustees.

Entry of property to the fund

21.15   Property may become comprised in a maintenance fund either:

- by straightforward transfer exempted under *s 27*, for example by an individual or a company; or

- by a transfer from a 'new style' interest in possession trust (see below), where the exemption will arise under *s 57* or *57A* (in respect of transfers after 16 March 1987); or

- where the property has been 'relevant property within a discretionary trust' before being transferred to the maintenance fund, in which case exemption arises through the operation of *s 65* and *Sch 4, para 16(1)*.

By 'new style' interest in possession trust is meant one of the few remaining categories of trust that is not a relevant property trust (see *s 57A(1A)*, introduced by *FA 2006*), such as:

- an IPDI;

- a disabled person's trust; or

- a transitional serial interest; or

- a trust coming within the narrow category of '*s 5(1B)* interests' (see below).

As to *s 5(1B)* interests, the amendment was introduced by *FA 2010* where the person became entitled to the interest on or after 9 December 2009. The issue here is of countering avoidance schemes where a person became entitled to an interest in possession by virtue of a 'no benefit' transaction, ie one that was not a transfer of value because, under *s 10*, it was not intended to confer gratuitous benefit, ie a purchased life interest. The idea was that:

- A had made the settlement on B for life, remainder to C and D;

- B then bought the trust fund from A;

- so neither A nor B made a transfer of value because it was a commercial transaction. B however enjoyed the interest in possession, but for the anti-avoidance provisions of *s 53*; and

- C or D bought their interests for full value.

Such arrangements were intended to get property into a relevant property trust without suffering the 'entry' charge to IHT. The amendment in *FA 2010* works by applying the relevant property regime to an interest in possession where a person became entitled by virtue of a commercial transaction.

The transfer to the fund will be exempt insofar as the value transferred to the fund becomes comprised in the settlement at, or immediately after, transfer and there is in force a direction in respect of the maintenance fund either at or after the transfer. As was noted in the previous section, the anti-avoidance provisions that relate to exempt transfers to a charity apply here with equal force. Specifically, where property transferred to the fund is an interest in possession in property comprised in a settlement, that settlement must come to an end in relation to the property transferred when it moves to the maintenance fund (see *s 56(3)(a)*).

Contributions to maintenance funds from discretionary trusts: anti-avoidance rules

'Excess value'

21.16   The transfer of funds from a relevant property trust to a maintenance fund would normally attract the exit charge, because the funds then cease to be relevant property. Relief from that charge is given subject to qualifications in *Sch 4, para 16*. The first difficulty concerns what is known as 'excess value', as that value is determined by *para 16(2)*. It is possible for the transfer, and even the tax that would have been charged on the funds before APR or BPR and before grossing up, to be greater than the value of the property itself that reaches the fund (after deduction of any money received by the trustees of the relevant property trust in respect of the property). This test is applied immediately after the transfer of the property to the fund. Consider the following example.

Example 21.1: transfer between trusts

The Myers Discretionary Trust holds 72% of the issued share capital of Myers Engineering Ltd, a private trading company whose net asset value is £300,000. The trust holding is considered to be worth £183,600.

Myers Hall Preservation Trust has been established for the protection and maintenance of heritage property in North London. The trustees of the Discretionary Trust transfer a 20% holding in the family company to the Hall trustees: the holding is valued at £15,000. The 52% retained holding is valued at £124,800.

The fall in value of the trust fund is £58,800. The value received by the Hall trustees is £15,000. The difference, £43,800, is prima facie taxable.

On one view of *Sch 4, para 16(2)*, there is a reduction in value of the property transferred to the fund, viz. ($^{20}/_{72}$ × 183,600), ie 51,000 − 15,000 = 36,000. Applying *s 65*, under general principles, the loss in value is greater, ie £43,800 as calculated above. Either way, the sum would have to be grossed up.

However, where BPR applies, as it would seem to do here, there may in fact be no liability.

'Purchase rule'

The further limit on exemption from the tax charge on transfer to a maintenance fund, again an anti-avoidance provision, arises where the trustees of the maintenance fund buy an interest from a relevant property trust and pay for that interest in money or money's worth. Another version of the transaction which the legislation seeks to avoid is one where the trustees of the maintenance fund distribute property to a person for a consideration. In these artificial situations, the relief on transfer to the maintenance fund does not apply.

Equally, the exemption that would normally apply in respect of the exit charge on a relevant property trust will be excluded where, within 30 days of property leaving the relevant property trust, an individual transfers that property to the maintenance fund but the person making the transfer had acquired the transferred property for money or money's worth. This could also apply where the transferor became entitled to the property through transactions which involved purchase. This might apply where, for example, the trustees of a relevant property trust had no power to appoint property to a maintenance fund. They could appoint it to an individual, however, who would in turn transfer it to a maintenance fund, but the 'excess value' rule would apply.

It is in this context that *Raikes v Lygon* [1988] 1 All ER 884 is relevant. This concerned an application to the court to decide whether the trustees could transfer property to a maintenance fund to maintain a historic property. The property itself was part of the trust. It was acknowledged that, by *Settled Land Act 1925, s 64*, the trustees could enter into transactions which were for the benefit of the beneficiaries or of the settled land. The difficulty for the trustees was that the trusts of the maintenance fund, to comply with the statutory requirements that have already been described in this book, would have to include a charity or national museum as default beneficiaries if the primary purposes of the trust were to be exhausted (see **21.4** above). Such beneficiaries were not beneficiaries of the existing trust.

The tax advantages of the proposed action were put to the court, which held that those advantages themselves justified the proposed transfer to a maintenance fund. The transfer was for the benefit of the settled land itself and of the existing beneficiaries. The charity and museums were introduced only as part of the price of obtaining the tax advantage, a consideration that did not invalidate the proposal as an exercise by the trustees of their power.

Property entering a maintenance fund from an interest in possession trust

21.17 The original legislation was too restrictive. In relation to deaths after 16 March 1987, *FA 1987* inserted *IHTA 1984, s 57A* to provide relief, subject to anti-avoidance provisions, where:

- a person dies who, immediately before his death, was the tenant for life of trust property; and

- that property enters a maintenance fund within two years of the death.

For this purpose, it does not matter whether the trusts of the maintenance fund are the same settlement as that in which the tenant for life had an interest, or are some other trust (see *s 57A(1)(a), (b)*). Where the conditions of *s 57A(1)* are satisfied, the exemption for property entering a maintenance fund applies as if the property had entered the maintenance fund on the death of the tenant for life, even though there may have been a delay of up to two years before the transfer of the property. No disposition or other event occurring between the date of the death and the date on which the property enters the maintenance trust is a transfer of value, nor is it an occasion for a charge to IHT.

By *s 57A(3)*, one extra year is allowed prior to the transfer, where court proceedings are necessary, before the property can move from the interest in possession trust in which it had been held to the maintenance fund. Proceedings under the *Variation of Trusts Act 1958* would fall within what is contemplated in *s 57A(3)*. Practitioners may feel that the extension of one year only is ungenerous. It is also not entirely beyond doubt that proceedings of the type described above in the account of *Raikes v Lygon* would fall within the subsection, since it is arguable, as indeed the court there found, that the proposal to transfer to a maintenance fund was within the powers of the trustees.

ANTI-AVOIDANCE RULES

21.18   The anti-avoidance provisions that have been noted in relation to outright transfers to maintenance funds apply again here, namely that:

- relief will not be allowed (see *s 57A(4)*) in respect of a conditional or defeasible transfer to a maintenance fund; nor

- where the interest transferred to the fund is no more than a life interest in trust property; nor

- where the trustees buy an interest under a settlement which contained the property immediately before the death of the tenant for life; nor

- where the property entering the maintenance fund is purchased or has at any time since the death of the tenant for life been purchased.

There is a further restriction on the relief. Property, such as minority shareholdings in unquoted companies, may have more than one value, according to the context in which it is held. This was the case with Myers Engineering Ltd in Example 21.1. The operation of the related property rules in *s 161* is but one example of this. If the value of the property transferred to the maintenance fund, when seen in isolation, is lower than the value of that same asset when considered as part of the deemed transfer on death of the tenant for life, relief is granted only in respect of the lower value.

Example 21.2: very limited relief

Thomson Fabrication Ltd was formerly an engineering company, but in 2002 holds only a portfolio of industrial units by virtue of which, following the rule in *Moore v IRC* 1995] STC (SCD) 5, BPR is no longer available. The net asset value of the company is £880,000. *Section 161(2)(b)* (related property) is not satisfied here.

Edwin Thomson holds 40% of the shares, his wife Sally 20%, with the remainder held by the trustees of the Thomson 1990 Life Interest Trust. Edwin's shares on their own would be subject to a discount of, say, 30% at £246,400 but, when considered with Sally's holding, a discount of only 20% might be appropriate, valuing his holding at £281,600.

Edwin transfers a holding representing 10% of the capital, ie one quarter of his holding, to a maintenance fund. In the hands of the fund's trustees, the shares are only worth £6,000 (after applying an 80% discount), but the fall in Edwin's estate is from part of a 60% holding (when taken with Sally's shares) to part of a 50% holding: a much greater figure.

Relief will be on £6,000 only.

The final anti-avoidance provision is *s 57A(6)*, which merely provides, for completeness, that a person is treated as buying the property if he becomes entitled to it as a result of transactions which include:

- any disposition for any consideration;
- either of that or other property; and
- whether to that person or to some other person.

The scheme of anti-avoidance provisions is rather like those in *s 142* relating to deeds of variation, where again any consideration for the variation is vital to securing the favourable tax treatment sought.

Schedule 4, para 15A contains provisions to bring the treatment of maintenance funds that arise following an interest in possession trust into line with other maintenance funds. In the main, the provisions of *para 15A* are relevant when considering property leaving a maintenance fund and will be considered later in this chapter.

PROPERTY LEAVING THE MAINTENANCE FUND

21.19   The favourable tax treatment of maintenance funds was summarised at the beginning of this chapter. Provided that funds are applied for the purposes of the protection of heritage property, those tax advantages can be preserved. Where, however, the trustees no longer apply the fund to maintain heritage property and take action to return it to the settlor or to release it to the other beneficiaries of the trusts that were established for the maintenance fund, a charge arises – particulars of which are set out at *IHTA 1984, Sch 4, para 8*.

It may, however, be helpful first to consider the consequences of the 'proper' use of heritage funds, ie use for the purpose of which the funds were established. Application of the funds in this way secures exemptions from charge which are provided for by *Sch 4, paras 9* and *10*. Essentially, the exemptions from charge are these:

- reverter to settlor;

- use for heritage purposes;

- transfer to a new maintenance fund; and

- transfer to a suitable purpose, namely charity, a political party, a heritage body or another non-profit making body.

Reverter to settlor

21.20   There is no charge to tax where property leaves a maintenance fund and again becomes property to which the settlor is beneficially entitled or to which his wife or her husband (or civil partner in either case) is so entitled or, where the settlor has died in the two years preceding the withdrawal of property from the maintenance fund, the settlor's widow or widower is entitled to *(Sch 4, para 10(1))*. There are qualifications to this rule: the 'excess value' rule and the 'purchase' rule, both outlined at **21.16** above.

The specific legislation covering these points is to be found in *Sch 4, para 10(2), (4)* and *(5)*. Further restrictions apply. The exemption from charge is not available unless the person who becomes beneficially entitled to the property is, at the time that he receives the property, domiciled in the United Kingdom (see *para 10(8)*). Further, it will be remembered that the relief in respect of maintenance funds is available only where the six-year rule applies, as described in **21.4** above. To prevent circumvention of that rule, the tax charge on 'non-heritage' use of property in a maintenance fund is not available where that property came to the maintenance fund, either directly or indirectly, from a discretionary trust or another maintenance fund. That is the effect, although it may not be immediately apparent on first reading, of *para 10(6)* and *(7)*.

Use for heritage purposes

21.21 The use by the trustees of the property in the maintenance fund for heritage purposes will not trigger any charge. Specifically, the purposes that qualify for this treatment are those set out in *para 3(1)(a)(i)* or *(ii)*, which were examined at **21.4** above, ie broadly, use for maintenance, repair or preservation, securing access in respect of the property, or transfer to a heritage body or qualifying charity.

Transfer to another maintenance fund

21.22 The transfer of property from one maintenance fund to another does not trigger any clawback of relief, provided that the property reaches the new fund in normal circumstances within 30 days. Up to two years is allowed when the settlor has died and his death would, but for the transfer to the new heritage fund, be an occasion of charge. As before, this exception is not available where the 'purchase rule' applies, and the exception is subject to the 'excess value' restriction already noted at **21.16** above.

Other acceptable uses

21.23 *IHTA 1984, s 76* contains a general relief, which applies equally to a maintenance fund, in respect of property that comes to be held for charitable purposes. These are defined in *s 76(1)* as:

● property held for charitable purposes only;

● the property of a political party qualifying for exemption under *s 27*; and

● the property of a *'Schedule 3'* body, ie one of the heritage bodies identified in *IHTA 1984, Sch 3*.

Until its repeal in respect of transfers of value made after 17 March 1998, *IHTA 1984, s 26* allowed for gifts for public benefit. It should be noted, however, that *s 26A* was introduced in respect of transfers of value made after 17 March 1986. It provides that a PET is exempt to the extent that the value transferred by it has been designated as heritage property or could be so designated and which has been disposed of by private treaty sale to a *Schedule 3* body or has been transferred to a *Schedule 3* body otherwise than by sale or has been accepted in satisfaction of tax under *s 230*. These procedures are described in **Chapter 23**.

Relief under *s 76* is subject to the 'excess value' restriction and to the 'purchase' rule, both noted at **21.16** above.

Events giving rise to clawback of relief

21.24   There are several events that can give rise to the loss of relief that arose when a direction was given in respect of a maintenance fund under *Sch 4, para 1*. These occasions of charge arise where the exemptions mentioned above do not apply. They are as follows:

- payment of capital to anyone other than the persons, or for the purposes, mentioned above;
- dispositions by the trustees, including depreciatory transactions or omissions:
- loss of heritage status in respect of the subject property; and
- withdrawal of the Treasury Direction.

Each of these sections is examined below.

Release of capital

The general charging section is *Sch 4, para 8(2)(a)*, which imposes the charge where settled property leaves the maintenance fund without being applied for the 'heritage' purposes for which the fund was established, ie those provided by *para 3(1)(a)*, namely the maintenance, repair or preservation of the 'subject' property. The charge to IHT is on the amount by which the value of the property in the maintenance fund is reduced as a result of the event that gives rise to the charge. If the tax is paid out of the assets that remain in the fund, the amount is grossed up. The tax charge is at 'the appropriate rate'. The rate is identified from the various circumstances set out below.

Transactions by the trustees

When the trustees of a maintenance fund do something, or deliberately fail to exercise a right, which in either case reduces the value of the property in the maintenance fund, a charge to IHT arises under *para 8(2)* except where:

- the property was applied for a heritage purpose; or
- it was a commercial transaction and thus was not a transfer of value because it was not a disposition intended to confer gratuitous benefit and is, therefore, exempt under *s 10*; or
- it was the grant of an agricultural tenancy for full value falling within the exceptions to transfers of value in *s 16*.

The statutory authority for these occasions of charge is *para 8(3)*, which applies the rules in *s 70*. *Section 70* itself is concerned with property leaving temporary charitable trusts. A signpost to that legislation and the charging code under *s 70* might have improved the clarity of *Sch 4*.

Loss of heritage status

Since the maintenance fund is set up to support heritage property, the loss of heritage status in respect of the property that is the subject or purpose of the maintenance fund will trigger a charge to tax on the fund itself. Thus, when the subject property no longer qualifies for conditional exemption, any event that would trigger the loss of exemption through the failure to comply with *Sch 4, para 3* triggers the IHT charge on the maintenance fund itself.

Withdrawal of Treasury Direction

It was noted that the making of the Treasury Direction under *Sch 4, para 1* was the basis for exemption of the maintenance fund. It follows that the withdrawal of that direction under the power in *Sch 4, para 5* triggers the charge under *para 8*.

The rate of tax: general cases

21.25 *Schedule 4, para 8(4)* defines the tax rate as being whatever results from a consideration of *paras 11–15*. There is a special code under *para 11* for property that came to a maintenance fund from a relevant property trust, considered at **21.28** below. This section of the book is concerned with the rate of charge that will apply in all other circumstances. It is the higher of two rates. The first rate is that determined by *Sch 4, para 13*, and the second is that determined by *para 14*.

The first or 'para 13' rate

This is the rate that was described at, and illustrated in the table immediately following **20.11**. The rate of charge is relatively high in the early years and, although the cumulative rate increases over time, the increments get smaller in the later years. The time charged (see *para 13(2)*) relates to the period starting from the day on which the property first became subject to the maintenance fund regime to the day before the event that gives rise to the charge. That period is varied where there has been a previous taxable event. In that case, the time-related charge runs from the previous taxable event, and the period from entry to the fund to that taxable event is disregarded (see *para 13(3)*). However, that rule itself is subject to an exception in respect of an 'excess value' charge under *para 9(4)* (see *para 13(4)*).

479

The second or 'para 14' rate

The rate charged depends on the tax position of the settlor or of the tenant for life. The rate depends on whether or not that person is alive at the time of the charge. *Paragraph 14(1)* imposes a charge:

- at the effective rate at which tax would be charged on the relevant amount;
- if that were the value transferred by a chargeable transfer;
- made by him on the date of the present charge to tax;
- in accordance with the lifetime rates in *s 7*.

The lifetime rate is applied (see *para 14(9)*) even if the death of the settlor occurs within seven years of the occasion of charge on the maintenance fund. The effective rate is more easily calculated than the rates that apply to periodic and exit charges in respect of relevant property trusts. It is simply the tax chargeable as a percentage of the amount on which it is charged (see *para 14(8)*).

Example 21.3: adoption of the higher tax rate

Hubert, who had made no previous chargeable transfers, established the Huntsman Preservation Trust in June 1994, transferring to it £150,000 for the upkeep of Grade 1 listed kennels and other property on the Huntsman estate.

Not all citizens admire either the architecture of the buildings or the purpose for which they were erected and used. Vandalism in 2001, in support of parliamentary change, caused major destruction of the kennels. The trustees, considering the buildings to be beyond repair, applied £100,000 in January 2002 for the support of field sports generally, which is not a charitable purpose.

Under the table of rates, the tax chargeable at the *para 13* rate would be 7.5%, or £7,500. Under *para 14*, the rate is fixed by reference to Hubert's circumstances. The trust was within the nil rate band when established. It has not reached the first ten-year periodic charge. The exit charge under general principles is, therefore, nil. The *para 13* rate is higher and will thus be applied.

Schedule 4, para 15A imports charging rules in respect of maintenance funds that follow interest in possession trusts. Thus, the reference to the settlor in *para 14(1)–(3)* is reinterpreted as being a reference to the tenant for life, and there are appropriate amendments to the remainder of *para 14* wherever necessary.

Death of tenant for life

21.26   Where the settlor is dead and, which will presumably be in virtually all such cases, where the chargeable event occurs on the death of the tenant for life, the rate of charge will again depend on the particular circumstances of the establishment of the fund. The full 'death' rate of tax will apply if the settlement was made on death. If the settlement was a lifetime one but the settlor has since died, even if the death occurred within seven years of the making of the settlement, the rate for lifetime transfers is used. Having found the rate of tax to be applied, it is then necessary to determine the effective rate, whether the settlor or the life tenant has died. This is the rate at which tax would have been charged if the amount now taxable had been the top slice of the estate on death. The combined effect of *para 14(2)* and *(9)* is that this top slice of estate is charged:

- at the lifetime rates in respect of property settled by a lifetime transfer; or
- at the death rates if settled on death.

If the death of the settlor occurred before 13 March 1975, the charge to IHT is calculated as the top slice of the estate on which estate duty had been charged (see *para 14(3)*). However, that reference to the amount on which estate duty was chargeable does not import the old estate duty rates; it only fixes the size of estate with which the charge is concerned, because the effective rate is that which would have been charged in accordance with *s 7. Schedule 2, para 6* comes to the aid of the fund here. By that paragraph, where:

- tax is chargeable under the 'clawback' provisions now being considered; and
- the charge arises after any reduction in the general rates of IHT,

the appropriate rate is the most recent reduction in force.

Schedule 4, para 14(4) and *(5)* address the situation where property in a maintenance fund was previously comprised in another maintenance fund. HMRC have an option to base tax by reference to:

- the settlor of the present fund; or
- the settlor of the previous fund; or
- the tenant for life of either fund.

Paragraph 14(6) and *(7)* create a form of cumulation of charge. Where property in a maintenance fund has been withdrawn on some previous occasion, giving rise to a charge to tax under these clawback provisions, any further clawback event within seven years (see *para 14(6)(a)*) triggers aggregation of the amount that was charged on the first occasion with the present clawback charge.

Example 21.4: withdrawal of funds for the family

Sebastian made only one chargeable transfer in his life, namely of shares in his residential property management company. On 1 December 1995, he transferred a majority shareholding worth £300,000 to maintenance fund trustees.

On 16 June 2004, the trustees released part of the holding to Sebastian's daughter, Rachel. The value of their remaining holding, which fell below the control threshold, was diminished by £200,000. The shares transferred were worth £75,000. Sebastian died in May 1997. His estate was worth £150,000.

In January 2011, the trustees released the remainder of the shares, now worth £550,000, to Jonathan, Sebastian's son.

	£
Tax charge on the event in June 1995:	
Value lost by the trust	200,000
Value received by Rachel	75,000
Excess value to be charged	125,000
Paragraph 13 calculation:	
34 complete quarters: 01.12.95–16.06.04, so	
$34 \times 0.25\% = 8.5\% \times 125{,}000 =$	10,625
Paragraph 14 calculation:	
Transfer on 16 June 2004: 125,000 in the bracket 0–125,000: within nil rate band	
Tax therefore	NIL
Therefore, charge under *para 13* =	10,625
Tax charge on the event in 2011	
Paragraph 13 calculation:	
Value of transfer	550,000
60 complete quarters: 01.12.95–January 2011	
$40 \times 0.25\% = 10\%$	
$20 \times 0.2\% = 4\%$, so 14% in all:	77,000

£

Paragraph 14 calculation:

Transfer by Sebastian:

lifetime transfer	75,000
estate at death	150,000
value transferred	550,000
	775,000

A lifetime settlement by Sebastian, so use lifetime rates:

550,000 in the bracket 225,000–775,000:

nil rate band, May 2005	275,000
balance in charge	500,000
charge at 20%	100,000
fraction 100,000/550,000, ie 18.18%	

The *para 14* rate is higher than the *para 13* rate

Tax charge is therefore   100,000

Note: the seven-year period was originally longer; in respect of events that occurred before 17 March 1986, the period was ten years.

Special property reliefs

21.27   The nature of the clawback charge is that it is a charge on a transfer of value. As has been noted, a transfer which is exempt under the general provisions escapes the clawback. In the same way, APR and BPR may be available in appropriate circumstances to shelter the transfer of property from a maintenance fund. Perhaps, not infrequently, agricultural land may have been introduced to a maintenance fund some years ago when the reliefs were less generous than they are now. It would not be unusual for a heritage house to be supported by agricultural land. The normal tests will apply for APR. The guidance at IR67 suggests that BPR will be available 'if the trustees are themselves running a business', which would seem to be a somewhat restrictive interpretation of BPR, although it must be remembered that IR67 was published in December 1986 when the rules were considerably tighter than they are now. This is, of course, also true of the supplement to IR67, produced to take account of the changes that were introduced by the *Finance Acts* of that year.

Calculation of the clawback charge where property was previously comprised in a discretionary trust

21.28   Contrary to the general run of the legislation, where the computation of tax in connection with discretionary trusts is infinitely more complex than that relating to other transfers, the clawback charge that arises on a maintenance fund in respect of property that came to it from a discretionary trust is simple. It is a time-related charge on the scale set out in *Sch 4, para 11(2)*, with which readers are already familiar from the table set out at **20.10** above. The starting point for the time charge is determined by *para 11(3)*. It is the latest of the following dates:

- 13 March 1975;

- the last ten-year anniversary of the 'originating' trust; and

- the day, or the most recent day where there is more than one, on which the property that is now subject to the clawback became subject to a discretion in the originating trust before it ceased to be subject to that discretion (or, where the property has slipped in and out of discretion, where it last ceased to be subject to a discretion).

One may imagine practical difficulties arising where the records of the originating trust are incomplete or imprecise, or where it is not immediately apparent which assets were subject to a discretion and which were, for example, comprised in a separate settled fund for a beneficiary in respect of which there was an interest in possession. The fear here is that the cost of research and of computing the tax charge may at least equal the charge itself.

The period in respect of which the clawback charge applies runs from the last of the three dates extracted from the description just mentioned to the day before the clawback event. It has already been noted that there can be a period during which property is not in a maintenance fund but comes to be comprised in one. This may be up to two years following the death of the settlor or the life tenant, or up to 30 days in any other situation. This is a reference to 'the permitted period' identified in *para 9(2)*. That permitted period is counted as part of the period for the calculation of clawback (see *para 11(4)*).

THE IMPACT ON MAINTENANCE FUNDS OF OTHER TAXES

Income tax

'One estate'

21.29   For many years, a special rule applied to landed estates by which expenses relating to one part of the estate, such as the mansion, could be deducted from income in respect first of that part of the estate and then from other income, such as rents, of the rest of the estate. This was the 'one estate' election. However, as part of the review of Schedule A that coincided with the introduction of self-assessment, the ability to profit from the one estate election, which had existed for many years, was brought to an end, with effect from 1 April 2001. The rules, which had applied to heritage property also, were brought to an end on the same date.

Sea defences

A more specific relief for property maintenance does, however, continue. It may become increasingly relevant with global warning. Relief is still available for capital expenditure on the making of a sea wall or embankment to protect premises against the encroachment or overflowing of the sea or of any tidal river. This relief was amended for income tax purposes from 1995/96 onwards, and for corporation tax purposes from 1 April 1998. Broadly, the effect is to spread the cost of the wall over 21 years and treat it as an expense of the Schedule A business (see *ICTA 1988, s 30*).

Income tax treatment of maintenance funds

21.30   The main income tax code for maintenance funds is *ITA 2007, Chapter 10, ss 507–517*, formerly *ICTA 1988, ss 690–694*. Under *ITA 2007, s 508*, the trustees may elect for income not to be treated as that of the settlor (see *ITA 2007, s 508(3)*). Where that happens, no money applied for heritage purposes is treated as being the income of any person either because he was the settlor or because he has an interest in the heritage property or occupies it. The result is that the income is taxed at the rate applicable to trusts.

Since that is now 50%, whereas many individuals are taxed at a lower rate, the election is, for most purposes, useless. Where any income arises for which no election is made and that income is treated as income of the settlor, any funds not used for maintenance of the heritage property will be treated as the income of the settlor by virtue only of the retained interest of the settlor through his interest in, or occupation of, the heritage property.

Elections under *ITA 2007, s 508* are by notice in the form approved by the Board and must be made by 31 January following the year of assessment to which they relate, ie the date on which the trust and estate tax return should be filed. Split year treatment is allowed under *ITA 2007, s 509* where, for example, the direction under *IHTA 1984, Sch* comes to an end during the year.

A different rule applies where income from a maintenance fund is treated as income of the settlor and is paid to the settlor to reimburse him for expenditure that he has incurred for heritage purposes. If the expenditure is deductible from the profits of a trade or UK property business carried on by the settlor or would be so deductible, but for the reimbursement, *ITA 2007, s 511* avoids double taxation by providing that that income is not treated as reducing the heritage expenditure and is not treated as income of the settlor except for the purposes of the maintenance fund code. In a complicated situation, where a trust comprises both settled property which is part of a maintenance fund and other property, those funds are treated as separate settlements for the purposes of this code.

The benefit of the election under the income tax code for maintenance funds lasts only as long as those funds are used for heritage purposes. If property in a maintenance fund reverts to the settlor, or for any other reason comes to be applied other than for heritage purposes, the benefit of the election is lost. A charge is levied on the income of the fund that has not been used for heritage purposes. The legislation, as rewritten in *ITA 2007, s 512*, sets out four main situations where this may happen:

- property used otherwise than for property maintenance – Case A;

- property not used for property maintenance, nor accumulated, nor paid to a heritage body – also Case A;

- property leaves the settlement but does not pass to a heritage body – Case B;

- heritage direction no longer applies – Case C; and

- property leaves the settlement and goes to a heritage body – Case D; or

- property leaves the settlement and an interest in the heritage fund itself is acquired by a heritage body – also Case D.

Thus, even where income is applied by payment to a heritage body or other qualifying body, it will not escape the charge, levied under *ITA 2007, s 512*, where the heritage or other qualifying body has purchased an interest in the fund, unless that purchase is from a heritage body. The charge is on all of the income in 'the relevant period' (see *ITA 2007, s 513*), namely since the creation of the settlement or since the previous charge under this legislation.

The rate actually applied by *ITA 2007, s 515* is equivalent to the additional rate of income tax for the year of assessment (currently 50%) but reduced by the trust rate for that year (also currently 50%), and so for the moment is nil. The tax charge, when it is a positive rate, is in addition to any other tax charged on the fund income under any other provision.

Stamp duty and stamp duty land tax

21.31   *FA 1980, s 98* provides that stamp duty is not to be chargeable on any document by virtue of which property comes out of a settlement if, as a result of that property becoming comprised in another settlement, there is no IHT charge on the property. The situations that will qualify for this relief are

486

the '30-day' resettlement or the 'two year on death' situations, noted at **21.28** above. Where part only of the property goes into the new maintenance fund, stamp duty on the remainder of the property is unaffected.

To take advantage of *s 98(1)*, it is still necessary to obtain a 'denoting' stamp under *Stamp Act 1891, s 12* that the document is not chargeable with any duty or is duly stamped.

There is no corresponding provision for SDLT, only an exemption under *FA 2003, s 69* where the property is sold to:

- The Historic Buildings and Monuments Commission for England;

- The National Endowment for Science, Technology and the Arts;

- The British Museum;

- The National Heritage Memorial Fund; or

- The National History Museum.

As Matthew Hutton noted when reviewing this legislation in his work *Hutton & Anstey: Stamp Duty Land Tax*, the National Trust is not mentioned. However, there is other provision in *FA 2003, Sch 8* for charities, but the definition of 'charitable trust' in *Sch 8, para 4* has not been widened, as it might have been, to include maintenance funds.

Capital gains tax

21.32   *TCGA 1992, s 260(2)(b)(iii)* allows holdover on transfer of property to a maintenance fund, by carrying forward the CGT base cost of the transferor. This holdover is available even where property passes to a maintenance fund from an interest in possession. Likewise, it can apply where the '30-day' or 'two year on death' situations arise, noted at **21.28** above.

The question arises whether holdover relief is available where property moves directly from one maintenance fund to another, being separate settlements. One leading work, *Foster on Inheritance Tax*, at G5.46, footnote 8, considers that, this not being an occasion of charge, none of the provisions of *TCGA 1992, s 260* will be relevant. Is that actually correct? Certainly, *s 260* bears the heading 'Gifts on which inheritance tax is chargeable etc', but the occasions under which holdover is permitted under *s 260(2)* are stated as being in the alternative: note the word 'or' at the end of *s 260(2)(e)*. The writer, therefore, considers that holdover should be available even in cases of direct transfer between separate settlements which are maintenance funds.

There used to be a trap in the legislation where the settlor retains an interest under the trust under old *TCGA 1992, s 77*, by which the gains of the trustees were charged as if made by the settlor. That rule was circumvented by an election under the legislation that became *ITA 2007, s 508*, particulars of which have been noted at **21.30** above. The difficulty was that, until there had been a direction under the heritage legislation, the fund could not benefit from an election. That mattered less for income tax, where split year treatment was available (see **21.30**) than for CGT, where split year treatment was never available. Fortunately, this complication died with the repeal of *TCGA 1992, s 77* by *FA 2008* with effect for 2008/09 and later years. The following example illustrates the problem: readers will need to study it if they share the writer's fear that rates for CGT may change over the years, and that we may again see *TCGA 1992, s 77* or something similar.

Example 21.5: gain on trust cottages

In August 2000, Hector indicated to HMRC, through his advisers, that he wished to set up a maintenance fund for the family estate and to transfer to it some cottages. He hoped to reduce the value of his estate for IHT. Setting up the trust took time, but it was in place by July 2001. In August 2003, Hector told HMRC that he might add more property to the trust and, a month later, HMRC told him that a Treasury direction would be needed under *Sch 4, para 1*.

The cottages were transferred into the maintenance fund in October 2003 and, soon after, were sold by the trustees. Hector was assessed to tax on the gain and paid it. Work on the annual report for the trust a year later reminded the trustees that there was no direction in place, although that did arrive in October 2004, whereupon the trustees made the election under (what was then) *ICTA 1988, s 691*.

This was rejected by HMRC, as far as the gain was concerned: at the time that the trustees made their gain, there was no direction in place, so they could not elect. Split year treatment could not apply. The trustees had to accept that. What also worried the trustees was whether reimbursement to Hector of the tax he had paid would be a wrongful use of money in a heritage fund. However, *TCGA 1992, s 78* gave a right to reimbursement, which reassured them.

Chapter 22

Compliance

QUICK GUIDE

In line with other areas of taxation, steps have been taken to enforce greater compliance. Personal representatives and those advising them must go to much greater lengths than hitherto to establish accurately the size of the estate.

Estimates are acceptable only within certain limits, noted at **22.5**. Values should be fair and not artificially depressed.

The penalties for non-compliance are set out at **22.11** to **22.17**.

Nearly all IHT forms have, within the last few years, been overhauled. The most relevant forms are considered at **22.18** onwards.

CHARGEABLE LIFETIME TRANSFERS

22.1   It is sometimes imagined by practitioners that the creation of a chargeable transfer which is chargeable at the nil rate, for example the establishment of a nil rate band discretionary trust, need not be disclosed to HMRC at the time. It is assumed that it will be sufficient, if death occurs within seven years of the transfer, to include particulars of the settlement in the HMRC account at that stage.

That is wrong. *IHTA 1984, s 216(1)(a)* requires 'every person' who is liable as a transferor for tax on the value transferred by a chargeable transfer, 'or would be so liable if tax were chargeable on that value', to deliver an account. Significant changes have arisen since the last edition of this work and the current regulations are now:

- the *Inheritance Tax (Delivery of Accounts) (Excepted Estates) Regulations 2004, SI 2004/2543*;

- the *Inheritance Tax (Delivery of Accounts) (Excepted Transfers and Excepted Terminations) Regulations 2008, SI 2008/605*; and

- the *Inheritance Tax (Delivery of Accounts) (Excepted Settlements) Regulations 2008, SI 2008/606.*

Compliance with these regulations is now enforced by a raft of legislation, which has arisen in part from the amalgamation of the former HM Customs & Excise and Inland Revenue. It seeks to rationalise their powers so that the same team of officers can enforce compliance across all taxes. The main legislation is:

- *FA 2007, Sch 24*: Penalties;
- *FA 2008, Sch 36*: Information and Inspection Powers;
- *FA 2008, Sch 37*: Record Keeping;
- *FA 2008, Sch 38*: Disclosure of Tax Avoidance Schemes;
- *FA 2008, Sch 39*: Time Limits; and
- *FA 2008, Sch 40*: Penalties.

Although not all of these provisions originally affected IHT, they have gradually been extended to that tax. This work is concerned only with the details of compliance as it affects APR, BPR, and woodland and heritage reliefs. For a more general review of the legislation, the reader is referred to *Ray & McLaughlin's Practical Inheritance Tax Planning* (9th edition, Bloomsbury Professional), Chapter 2, or to the *Core Tax Annuals*, especially *Inheritance Tax 2010/11* (Bloomsbury Professional), Chapter 6.

DUTY OF THE PERSONAL REPRESENTATIVE

22.2 It would appear that the quality of the completion of HMRC accounts is somewhat uneven. There is not, frankly, much excuse for this. Guidance has always been available: forms were published to help completion of forms IHT 100 or 400 or their predecessors. They are supplemented by worksheets to take the practitioner or the individual through the process. Where relevant to the reliefs discussed in this book, these are examined at **22.18** onwards.

Some personal representatives will delay the filing of an account until they have, for example, audited accounts of the business in which the deceased had an interest up to the date of death. Others take a much broader view and rely heavily on estimates. HMRC have now published a 'toolkit' to help executors to avoid the commonest errors and to address the aspects of compliance perceived as carrying the greatest risk. The guidance is practical, for example in urging personal representatives not to rush the forms but to take enough time to do a proper job; but still to file on time.

All this is not without its difficulties. For example, in *Re Sir Malcolm Arnold Deceased, Day v Harris and others* (2010) (unreported), the first defendant, a chartered tax adviser, mindful of the issues mentioned at **22.3** below, felt it to be his duty as executor to make searching enquiries into lifetime transactions carried out by the plaintiff, also an executor, who had been attorney for the deceased. The tax adviser called for, and reported on, transactions in the last years of the life of the deceased, and caused the IHT 400 to be qualified in part to reflect his researches. The plaintiff sought the removal of the first defendant from office as executor, both on the ground of partiality towards other beneficiaries and for spending too much time and cost on the compliance aspects of the estate. His application failed, leaving the tax adviser to continue his work.

HMRC guidance

22.3   HMRC official guidance is not wholly impartial, being instructions to its own officers, but forms a clear and useful starting point for anyone unsure of the accepted attitude to particular tax issues. Put another way, if you decide to disregard the guidance, you can be fairly sure that your case will be referred to a senior inspector and, if you persist, that your client may lend his or her name to a case before the First-tier Tribunal. There is a great deal of information on the HMRC website: apart from the text of the Manual, there is, for example, specific help in completing the forms at www.hmrc.gov.uk/inheritancetax/ iht400-notes.pdf. Executors and those advising them should make enquiries into the history of lifetime transfers by the deceased.

The level of enquiry which is appropriate will depend on the facts and on the knowledge by the personal representative of the financial affairs of the deceased in his lifetime. A thorough search should be made of the deceased's papers, such as the records kept for self-assessment or copy tax returns. In practice, there will seldom be proper records, and there may well be surprises for those members of the family who were treated less generously than others by the deceased. If gifts come to light even after the personal representatives have made reasonable enquiries, particulars should be supplied to HMRC, who may make enquiry of the personal representatives to find out whether they either knew, or should have found out, about the gift. Where there is prompt disclosure, the only 'penalty' suffered is likely to be that the correct tax is paid. Where there is evidence of a more serious nature, a clearance certificate, if one has previously been issued, may be set aside, and HMRC can then pursue additional tax and, possibly, penalties.

Property details

22.4   *IHTA 1984, s 216(3)* specifies the details of the property to be shown in the return. It is subject to the rules, now set out in *s 216(3A) and (3B),* introduced by *FA 1999* and discussed below. Where the personal representatives take out a full grant, they must show all property which formed part of the estate of the deceased immediately before his death, other than the property which would not form part of the estate except for the gift with reservation provisions.

The requirement to show 'all property which formed part of the estate of the deceased immediately before his death' was examined in *Daffodil (administrator of Daffodil Deceased) v IRC* SpC 311, [2002] STI Issue 20. Mr and Mrs Daffodil had owned a bungalow as tenants in common. He died intestate in 1994. Although Mrs Daffodil could have applied for a grant of representation in her husband's estate, she did not do so. She went on living in the bungalow until her death in February 2000. Her son, as administrator of his mother's estate, obtained a grant of letters of administration in August 2000. The value of the entire estate was something over £320,000, including the bungalow at £95,000. IHT was paid.

The son then wanted to sell the bungalow, but his lawyer advised him that his father's share had not passed to his mother by survivorship on death, because it had been held by them as tenants in common, and that the son must therefore apply for a grant of letters of administration of his father's estate to complete the title. He did this.

A notice of determination was issued by IRCT stating that the interest of Mrs Daffodil in the estate of her late husband formed part of Mrs Daffodil's estate for IHT. The son disagreed. He said that, because his late mother had not taken out a grant of letters of administration to the estate of his late father, his mother was not entitled to property that had belonged to his father at the date of her death.

IRCT disagreed. At the date of her death, Mrs Daffodil had the right to require the whole of the estate of Mr Daffodil to be transferred to her. That right was 'property' within *s 272*. The half share of the bungalow owned by Mr Daffodil was therefore part of the estate of Mrs Daffodil.

The Special Commissioners agreed with IRCT. The estate of Mrs Daffodil included the value of the estate of her late husband as at her death which, under *s 5(1)*, formed part of her estate.

A similar issue arose in *Thompson (Thompson's Executor) v CIR* SpC 429. A widow had died in 1971, leaving her house to her daughter who, in turn, died in 2002. It appeared that the daughter had never signed any document accepting title to the house. On appeal from a notice of determination charging IHT on the value of the house, the Special Commissioner held that the daughter was the sole owner of the house, despite her inaction, and it was part of her estate for IHT.

The use of estimates

22.5   *Section 216(3A)* is the statutory authority for the inclusion in the account of estimates. This is often an issue where the deceased owned a business or an interest in one. It is sufficient to make use of a provisional estimate of the value, provided that:

- the return contains a statement to the effect that an estimate has been used; and

- the personal representatives undertake to deliver a further account as soon as the value has been ascertained.

Section 216(3B) is the authority for the Board of HMRC to control the use of estimates. HMRC expect personal representatives to make a thorough search of the deceased's papers. There is no absolute duty to make enquiries of any particular person, but HMRC consider it reasonable to expect the personal representatives to think about making enquiries of any professional advisers who may have dealt with the affairs of the deceased, such as solicitors, accountants, stockbrokers, financial advisers and banks.

Robertson v IRC

22.6   The use of estimates was considered by the Special Commissioners in *Robertson v IRC* [2002] STI 19. Mrs Stanley had died on 10 October 1999, owning both a house and contents in Scotland and a property in England. The executor was a solicitor, Mr Robertson, who considered that a valuation of the Scottish house and contents was required. He had no direct knowledge of the property in England, save a letter indicating that it was occupied by longstanding tenants at a rent of £260 per annum, and a photograph showing what appeared to be a small cottage. What Mr Robertson did not then appreciate was that the English property was set in five acres of grounds.

With commendable speed, Mr Robertson submitted to the Inland Revenue an inventory of Mrs Stanley's estate, showing an estimated value of the Scottish house of £60,000, its contents at £5,000, and the English cottage at £50,000. IHT of over £400,000 was payable on lodging the account. Soon afterwards, confirmation was issued. After submission of the inventory, Mr Robertson received valuation of the contents of the Scottish house in the sum of £24,845. The sale of the Scottish house went ahead rapidly, with missives concluded before Christmas, at a sale price of £82,000. The following month, Mr Robertson received a valuation of the English property in the sum of £315,000. Very shortly afterwards, Mr Robertson submitted a corrective inventory to the Inland Revenue and paid the additional IHT then due of nearly £120,000.

The Inland Revenue were not impressed with Mr Robertson's actions. They considered that the disparity between the original estimates and the later figures showed that he had not fulfilled his obligation under *s 216(3)* to make the fullest enquiries that were reasonably practicable in the circumstances. They imposed a penalty of £9,000. Mr Robertson objected.

The Special Commissioner held that Mr Robertson had made the appropriate statutory statement, because it was to be inferred from the form of account as completed that it was compiled to the best of the knowledge and belief of the person signing it. An executor was required to make the fullest enquiries that were reasonably practical in the circumstances. The executor had been to the home of the deceased. He put in estimates, but disclosed them for what they were. In the particular circumstances, it had been prudent to go ahead on the basis of estimates only: that enabled the executor to obtain confirmation rapidly, so as to be able to sell the house in Scotland. Mr Robertson was not negligent in delivering an incorrect account. The account was not incorrect. He had followed acceptable legal practice. He had complied with his common law duties as an executor and was not liable to any penalty.

A chorus of articles in the professional press supported Mr Robertson's actions, sometimes with a touch of righteous indignation. Perhaps prompted by that, IRCT issued a special newsletter in May 2002 on the subject, noting that the particular form that Mr Robertson had used, Cap A3, did not contain an express declaration to the effect that, where estimates are supplied, the personal representative undertakes to provide exact valuations as soon as practicable. That form has now been replaced by IHT 200, which incorporates a declaration along the lines suggested by the Special Commissioner.

The Revenue stressed, in that newsletter, its willingness to help personal representatives to fulfil their obligations without incurring penalties. They will normally expect the exact value of property to be given, and not merely an estimate. If there is a *proven need* to obtain a grant urgently (author's italics), personal representatives may feel they need to submit an estimated account of the value of a particular item. Even in such circumstances, the executors must make the fullest enquiries that are reasonably practicable before using a mere estimate. The estimate itself should be as accurate as possible. A personal representative who employs a professional to value the property should ensure that the estimate is a reasonable one. The May Newsletter lays down a fairly high standard of compliance, which will upset some practitioners, but is perhaps to be expected of the tax-gathering authority.

HMRC deprecate the practice of 'special' valuations for probate, for example that a house is worth £200,000 'but for probate the value is £175,000'. Use of the lower value in such a case can trigger a claim for penalties: if the valuation baldly shows a lower figure 'for probate', HMRC may seek penalties from the valuer for assisting in the furnishing of an incorrect return.

Robertson v IRC (No 2)

22.7   The sequel to Mr Robertson's first hearing before the Special Commissioners concerned the issue of costs. In *Robertson v IRC (No 2)* [2002] STI 25, Mr Robertson pressed home that advantage of his earlier success and claimed costs. Costs, the Revenue argued, were not allowable (see *Special Commissioners (Jurisdiction and Procedure) Regulations 1994, reg 21*) unless the Commissioners were satisfied that a party to the proceedings had acted 'wholly unreasonably' in connection with the hearing.

The Special Commissioner held that neither the evidence presented by the Inland Revenue nor the agreed statement of facts showed any rational basis for bringing the proceedings against Mr Robertson. The Revenue had not addressed the issue of negligent furnishing of an account nor the issue of what was reasonably practicable in the circumstances of the case. What Mr Robertson did was in accordance with standard practice. It was not negligent. What he did amounted to making the fullest enquiries that were reasonably practicable in the circumstances. The Revenue had therefore acted wholly unreasonably. Mr Robertson got his costs.

Where it seems likely that property will qualify for APR or BPR at 100%, personal representatives may be reluctant to go to the expense of a full valuation. If relief is allowed at 100%, the value of the asset as returned for IHT will not be 'ascertained' within the meaning of *TCGA 1992, s 274*. However, HMRC in their Newsletter of April 2004 indicated that under no circumstances should nominal or ill-considered values be used. If it later transpires that relief is not due, penalties could arise if a substantial uplift in value is appropriate. The issue of relief can often be resolved, even without getting in touch with the practitioner, where the return has been completed and, in particular, forms D13 and D14 have been fully completed so as to allow HMRC to review the claim for relief.

VALUATION: COMPLIANCE ISSUES

22.8   HMRC perceive valuation as a key area of risk. Penalty issues can and do arise where an incorrect valuation included in a return results in an IHT liability being understated, if there has been a lack of reasonable care in that valuation. HMRC's Inheritance Tax & Trusts Newsletter (August 2009) featured a report on its Annual Probate Section Conference indicating that, if instructions for the valuation of a property had been given on the correct basis, any uplift in value subsequently agreed was 'unlikely' to attract a penalty. The 'correct basis' is defined as:

> '... a hypothetical sale in the open market under normal market conditions and marketed properly with no discounts for a quick sale or the time of year etc.'

To show that 'reasonable care' had been demonstrated, the executor should obtain three valuations from different estate agents or a professional (ie Royal Institution of Chartered Surveyors) valuation if a definitive valuation was necessary. HMRC will look at what steps were actually taken, and consider:

- Was professional advice sought?

- Were instructions given on the correct basis?

- Was the valuer's attention drawn to particular features of the property (eg development potential)? and

- Was anything unusual about the valuation questioned?

Clearly, this implies a high standard of care.

Cairns v HMRC

22.9   In *Cairns v Revenue & Customs* [2009] UKFTT 00008 (TC), HMRC had imposed a penalty on Mr Cairns, a solicitor acting as a personal representative. The penalty related to a valuation of £400,000 in respect of the deceased's residence, as returned on form IHT200. This was a valuation by chartered surveyors in January 2004, which was stated to be an '... arbitrary figure pending investigations as to costs involved in upgrading'. The valuation was heavily qualified, due to the poor state of the property. Mr Cairns was uncertain of the property's value, but considered that the existing valuation was sufficient in the meantime. The District Valuer subsequently valued the property at £600,000 as at the date of death, which was also the amount for which the property was sold. The Special Commissioner was asked to consider whether Mr Cairns submitted an incorrect IHT account, and whether he had acted negligently.

The Special Commissioner held: '... the mere failure to obtain another valuation when it has not been established that a second valuation would have led to a different figure being inserted in the statutory form does not constitute negligent delivery of an incorrect account'. He added: 'On the evidence before me, even if it were concluded that an incorrect account was delivered or furnished, it is simply not possible to conclude that it was negligently delivered or furnished except in one minor respect'. The 'minor matter' referred to concerned the fact that the valuation obtained had been heavily qualified, and was a provisional estimate. Mr Cairns had not disclosed this in the IHT account. The omission to do so was a careless error. However, the Commissioner added that '... it was minor, technical and of no consequence whatsoever'.

The Commissioner concluded that there had been a 'narrow, technical failure ...'. The account was incorrect. The sum of £400,000 should have been described as a provisional estimate. Whilst that failure was negligent, it was held to be a 'failure of the merest technicality'. Mr Cairns was held to have acted 'perfectly sensibly and reasonably throughout'. The summons against Mr Cairns was dismissed. The Commissioner added that, even if he had been wrong to dismiss it, he would have reduced the penalty to a nominal amount or recommended that it be so reduced.

That case pre-dates the new penalty regime, but nevertheless may offer some comfort to the personal representatives of a deceased person's estate on the circumstances in which penalties can be imposed for an incorrect IHT return. However, it also provides a warning as to the degree of disclosure required in respect of provisional valuations and estimates, to avoid an accusation by HMRC of careless behaviour. In general, provision of good, detailed information in support of values will often achieve earlier agreement with HMRC.

PERSONAL APPLICATIONS FOR GRANTS OF REPRESENTATION

22.10   It is increasingly common to find that application has been made for a grant of representation in a substantial estate without the use of a solicitor. Commonly, this will be a 'personal application' where family members are confident of their ability or where an executor, not being a solicitor, has the relevant experience, perhaps as a member of the Society of Trust and Estate Practitioners (STEP). All professional agents assisting with preparation of HMRC accounts are expected to make 'reasonable yet searching enquiries', so that the person actually signing the declaration in the account is making a true and complete return. All the information known to professional agents at the time of delivery of the account should be reflected in that account.

PENALTIES: THE NEW REGIME

22.11   For a full account of the penalty regime, the reader is referred to *Ray & McLaughlin's Practical Inheritance Tax Planning* (9th edition, Bloomsbury Professional), from which some of the following material is taken. Penalties may be incurred for failing to deliver an account, make a return or comply with a notice seeking information. Fraud or negligence in the provision of information or accounts and returns may also be penalised. Any penalty is in addition to tax and interest. *FA 2007* applied, in *Sch 24*, the penalty regime for taxes other than IHT. *FA 2008, Sch 40* took that further. The changes apply with effect for all chargeable events occurring on or after 1 April 2009.

A penalty of up to £100 may be charged under *IHTA 1984, s 245(2)* for a failure to deliver an IHT account. If the account has still not been delivered within six months following the filing date and no proceedings for declaration of the failure have commenced, there is a liability to a further penalty of up to £100. These penalties are restricted in total to the IHT liability if the taxpayer can prove that the tax liability is lower. There is a further penalty of up to £60 for each day following that on which the failure has been declared by a court or the First-tier Tribunal and before the day on which the account is delivered. If a person has a reasonable excuse for failing to deliver the account, he is not liable to a penalty if he delivers the account without unreasonable delay after the excuse has ceased (*s 245*).

The penalty is not imposed where the taxpayer can show reasonable excuse, by completing a simple form setting out the circumstances, but the penalty will be charged unless the taxpayer delivers the account without unreasonable delay after the excuse has ceased (see *s 245(7)*). The mere fact that the estate is complicated is not itself a factor; there must be some other element. A person who fails to comply with a notice under *s 219A* requiring the production of documents, accounts or particulars is liable to a penalty of up to £50, plus a further penalty of up to £30 for every day after that on which the failure has been declared and before the day on which the notice is complied with. Daily penalties can be avoided by remedying the failure before the proceedings are commenced. Any person who has a reasonable excuse for failing to deliver an account or comply with a notice is not liable to a penalty, provided that he complies without unreasonable delay after the excuse has ceased (*s 245A*).

A person not liable for the tax (eg an agent or adviser) who fraudulently or negligently supplies any incorrect document or information in connection with a chargeable transfer is liable to a penalty of up to £3,000. A person who assists in or induces the supply of any account, information or document he knows to be incorrect is liable to a penalty of up to £3,000 (see *s 247(3), (4)*).

A person may have supplied an account, information or document without fraud or negligence but later discover that it is 'materially' incorrect (ie where the tax in issue is £1,000 or more). Such a return is treated as having been negligently supplied unless the error is remedied without unreasonable delay. If another person (eg an agent or adviser) supplied the account, information or document and the person liable to the tax discovers that it is incorrect, he must inform the Board of the error without unreasonable delay. Otherwise, he is liable to a penalty as if he personally had negligently supplied the incorrect account, information or document (*s 248*).

Overview of the penalty provisions

22.12   Whereas other aspects of the modernisation of penalties do not specifically concern IHT, that tax is included in *FA 2008, ss 122–123* and *Sch 40*. The intention of the new legislation is to address five areas of concern:

- incorrect returns;
- failure to notify a new taxable activity;
- late filing and late payment;
- failure to keep records, and powers to seek information; and
- other regulatory failures.

The rules do not yet address failure to submit returns at all, as where all property, though part of a taxable estate, is held jointly or in some form of trust. This may be a significant issue. We are seeing fewer applications for grants of representation by lawyers, whilst the number of personal applications is steady. Does this mean that fewer are dying, or is there a more sinister explanation, that might generate penalties later?

FA 2007, Sch 24 is amended and extended by *FA 2008, Sch 40* so as to include:

- accounts under *IHTA 1984, ss 216* and *217*;
- information or documents required by *s 256*; and
- statements or declarations in connection with deductions, exemptions or reliefs.

In IHT situations, there is often shared responsibility for information gathering, most obviously in relation to lifetime gifts. The new rules apply to errors on returns for tax events and periods beginning on or after 1 April 2009, where the filing date is 1 April 2010 or later (although, if information or a document is produced under *s 256* from 1 April 2009, the tax period must begin on or after that date).

There is no penalty in the case of an 'innocent error' (ie broadly where a person has taken reasonable care in completing the return, and has taken reasonable steps to notify errors if appropriate). The deceased's personal representatives will have taken reasonable care where they:

- follow the guidance provided about filling in forms such as the IHT 400 and IHT 205/207/C5;
- make suitable enquiries of asset holders and other people (as suggested in the guidance) to establish the extent of the deceased's estate;
- ensure correct instructions are given to valuers when valuing assets;
- seek advice about anything they are unsure of;
- follow up inconsistencies in information they receive from asset holders, valuers and other people; and
- identify any estimated values included on the form.

Where an agent is acting, HMRC expect the personal representatives to check through the form before signing it and to question anything that does not accord with what they know about the deceased. Simply signing an account completed by an agent is not taking reasonable care. The use of the toolkit may be regarded as the taking of reasonable care. If IHT is payable other than on death, HMRC expect the transferor (or trustees) to deliver a full and complete return of the transaction concerned, and to have sought professional advice as necessary.

Levels of penalty

22.13   There are three degrees of culpability:

- The lowest level of culpability, described as 'careless', is where the taxpayer fails to take reasonable care in completing the return.

- The 'middle' level of culpability is 'deliberate but not concealed', where the return is wrong and results from the deliberate action of the taxpayer, but the taxpayer makes no arrangements to conceal the inaccuracy.

- Finally, the most serious level of wrongdoing is that which is 'deliberate and concealed', where the taxpayer has deliberately sent in a wrong return and deliberately tries to conceal the parts of the return that are wrong, for example by submitting false evidence in support of false figures.

The following maximum levels were established by *FA 2007, Sch 24*, but their scope was extended by *FA 2008*:

- The 30% rate: 30% of the potential lost revenue, where the taxpayer was careless.

- The 70% rate: 70%, where the action of the taxpayer was deliberate but not concealed.

- The 100% rate: 100%, where the action of the taxpayer was deliberate and concealed. This can apply in two circumstances. Under *FA 2007, Sch 24, para 4(1)(c)*, the full penalty could apply to 'deliberate and concealed action'. That penalty is extended to cover 'third party' acts. The collection of tax lost through third party inaccuracy is extended to include any inaccuracy resulting from the supply of false information or the withholding of information.

Careless inaccuracies are corrected before deliberate inaccuracies; and deliberate but not concealed inaccuracies are corrected before deliberate and concealed inaccuracies. In calculating the lost tax, account is taken of any overstatement in any document given by the taxpayer that relates to the same tax period.

The tax in issue on death can greatly exceed what an ordinary family person would be likely to incur in respect of any other tax or on any other occasion. Preparation of IHT 400 should fully reflect the tax in issue and the professional risks involved.

FA 2007, Sch 24, para 4 sets bands of penalties, and *para 9* allows reduction within the bands but not total reduction in the more serious cases. *FA 2008* updates *FA 2007, Sch 24, paras 9–12*. The penalty is reduced where a person, including a third party, discloses inaccuracy in a tax document. Where the disclosure is made by the taxpayer at a time when he has no reason to believe that HMRC have discovered or are about to discover the inaccuracy, that disclosure is classified as 'unprompted'. The effect of this is that an unprompted disclosure of a careless error can reduce the penalty to nil.

Mitigation of 30% penalties

22.14   Where the disclosure is prompted, a careless error, attracting a penalty of 30%, may be reduced, but not below 15%. However, the mechanism of valuation in deceased estates relies on disclosure which, in turn, includes answering the question whether the property is to be offered for sale. The value of the property is routinely referred to the Valuation Office. If it is known that a property is to be sold within a reasonably short time after the death, then it is quite common for the gross sale proceeds to be taken as the value at the date of death.

Mitigation of 70% penalties

22.15   Where the action of the taxpayer was deliberate but not concealed, the starting point for penalties is 70%, but it may be reduced under *FA 2007, Sch 24, para 10(3)* to a minimum of 20%. The mitigation will depend on the 'quality' of the disclosure, to include timing, nature and extent. Under *FA 2007, Sch 24, para 10(4)*, a penalty that is otherwise chargeable at 70% cannot be reduced below 35% if the disclosure is prompted.

Mitigation of 100% penalties

22.16   Similar rules apply to errors that fall into the 100% regime, but they are harsher. For unprompted disclosure, the minimum penalty is 30%; but, where the disclosure arises only after HMRC have raised questions, the penalty cannot be less than 50%. There is facility in *FA 2007, Sch 24, para 11* for 'special reduction' of a penalty if HMRC think it right because of 'special circumstances', but that does not include inability to pay, nor the fact that the increased liability of one taxpayer may reduce the liability of another. There is a 100% cap on penalties (see *FA 2007, Sch 24, para 12(4)*) to cover the situation where a penalty could be charged against both the taxpayer and a third party.

Penalties will not be claimed from a deceased person who had not been compliant, but that in no way exonerates delinquent personal representatives.

THE CRIMINAL OFFENCE OF TAX FRAUD

22.17   *FA 2000, s 144* brought in a new and specific criminal offence, punishable by up to seven years in prison. It is aimed at tax fraud but applies only to the fraudulent evasion of income tax and not to other taxes. It can be tried either summarily or before a jury. The essence of the new defence is dishonesty, such conduct to be judged by what is considered dishonest by the ordinary standards of reasonable and honest people. There is no need for any positive act of deception. Refraining from notifying a chargeability to tax, which could easily happen in the administration of an estate, whether by a lay personal representative or, it must be said, by a professional, could come within the offence.

The distinction between avoidance and evasion has not, in the opinion at least of HMRC, been changed by the introduction of the new offence. If a scheme has a sound technical basis, and if there is no concealment of the true facts, a criminal offence has probably not been committed.

FORMS AND PROCEDURES

22.18   Good practice starts with careful preparation. It is too late, days before a hearing, to be taking witness statements. Most APR/BPR cases before the First-tier Tribunal turn on the particular facts. Good work, therefore, starts with the forms that accompany the returns. The most relevant of these for the purposes of this book are:

- IHT405: Houses, land, buildings and interests in land;

- IHTD36: Land, buildings and interests in land (lifetime chargeable transfers);

- IHT412: Unlisted stocks and shares, and control holdings;

- IHT413: Business and partnership interests and assets;

- IHTD38: Business relief, business or partnership assets (lifetime chargeable transfers);

- IHT414: Agricultural relief;

- IHTD37: Agricultural relief (lifetime chargeable transfers); and

- IHT420: National Heritage assets – Conditional exemption and offers in lieu of tax.

Agricultural relief

22.19   Usually, form IHT405 or D36 (lifetime transfers) will be required in respect of any land held. Show the agricultural value claimed in column F or E as appropriate. It is frequently claimed by HMRC that the agricultural value is lower than open market value but, in the case of bare land, this should be resisted (see **3.1**). The factors that may affect value are more fully described in IHT 405 than in D36, which is an older form.

To claim the relief, form IHT414 or D37 will also be needed. The IHT400 Notes, 'Guide to completing your Inheritance Tax account', Schedule IHT414 explain the detail expected when filling in these forms. In particular, details are needed of the actual agricultural activities carried on, whether by the owner or another. That involves finding any letting agreements, or other agreements as to the use of the land, if not occupied by the owner.

Farmhouses and farm cottages are a major source of contention. Fill in the claim carefully to justify the claim. Similarly, bear in mind the observation *obiter* in *Antrobus No 2* [2006] 1 EGLR 157 as to the use of farm buildings to repair cars, which was not an agricultural purpose.

Business relief

22.20   Often, form IHT412, unquoted shares, will be relevant. See the brief comments in Schedule IHT412 in the Guide. Then move to IHT413 or D38 to claim the relief. The forms force the taxpayer or agent to identify an interest in the business separately from a mere asset in the business because, of course, the tax treatment differs. The notes in the Guide are far too brief to help anyone to fill in the form satisfactorily without further research, as for example reading this book. IHT413 asks for three years' accounts: these will normally be only what is already available, not accounts prepared to the date of death or specially prepared for the return. These forms take time to complete: the questions are short but the answers, or the research to produce them, may be very demanding.

Woodland relief

22.21   There is no separate form to claim this relief. Instead, note the claim on form IHT405, column F, or on D36, column E.

Heritage relief

22.22   Use form IHT420 and Schedule IHT420 in the Guide. This form differs from the others in that it is used not only to claim relief when submitting a return in form IHT400 but also when negotiating an offer in lieu of tax, as described in the next chapter. The Guide is brief, and good on that account, but many taxpayers will need to do some homework or get specialist advice before completing the return. Again, to answer the simple questions may involve hours of research, in particular to track down old papers relevant to the claim.

Chapter 23

Payment of IHT

QUICK GUIDE

Part of the IHT on an estate has always been payable before obtaining the grant. For unrepresented taxpayers, the funding of that tax has been made easier by the procedure outlined in **23.4**.

Illiquid assets of certain categories qualify for an instalment facility outlined at **23.5**. As will be seen at **23.8**, care should be taken to observe the rules relating to instalment. Even greater care should be taken when releasing assets from an estate before all the tax has been paid.

The scheme by which heritage property may be used in satisfaction of tax is considered in detail at **23.11** onwards, noting especially the discount arrangements or 'douceur' at **23.12**.

THE GENERAL RULES

23.1   Subject to a contrary intention in the will, the IHT for which the personal representatives are liable is treated as part of the administration expenses of the estate (see *IHTA 1984, s 211(1)*). As a result, by the operation of *Administration of Estates Act 1925, s 34(3)* and *Sch 1, para 8*, tax is chargeable against the assets of the estate in the order set out in *AEA 1925, Sch 1*. *IHTA 1984, s 211* limits the applicability of this rule to the value of property in the United Kingdom which:

- vests in the personal representatives of the deceased; and

- was not, immediately before the death, comprised in a settlement.

Where the amount of tax paid by the personal representatives on the value transferred by a chargeable transfer made on the death does not fall to be borne as part of the testamentary and administration expenses of the estate within the rules in *s 211(1)*, that tax, where appropriate, should be repaid to them by the person in whom the property is vested to which the value of the tax is attributable. This can give the executor a right of action, although HMRC acknowledge that their responsibility ends there. Where the executor has become liable for IHT that should have been paid by the donee, HMRC have commented that 'there is really nothing we can do directly. The problem lies with the executor to take legal action against the donee of the gift'.

'Free of tax' legacies

23.2 Where a will expresses some gifts to be 'free of tax' but not others, all the gifts in question being specific rather than residuary, the question arises whether those gifts not expressed to be free of tax should bear their own tax. The better view is that, if the testator wishes a gift of UK property to bear its own tax, he should say so. On the other hand, a gift of foreign property without reference to tax will have to carry its own IHT. The problem arises where a pecuniary legacy is payable and the assets out of which it is to be paid include both UK and foreign property. *Dymond* is authority for the view that the foreign property will bear a proportion of the IHT unless the will expresses that the foreign property be given free of tax.

Many of the cases in this area are of some antiquity, examining phrases such as 'free of estate duty' and 'free of CTT'. *IHTA 1984, Sch 6, para 1* effectively updates all such references to earlier capital taxes on death so as to apply to IHT. Such a clause will, however, normally relate only to the liability to tax on the death of the testator. It was held in *Re Pattersons Will Trusts, Lawson v Payn* [1963] 1 All ER 114 that a gift of property free of tax to A for life, with remainder to B, will relate in normal circumstances only to tax payable on the death of the testator and not to any charge to tax on the death of A or on the transfer arising by disposal by A of his interest in his lifetime. *Re Owers* [1940] 4 All ER 225 established the rule that an instruction that residue should carry testamentary expenses does not include payment of tax on foreign property.

Payment of tax on failed PETs

23.3 *IHTA 1984, s 199(1)* places the liability for the 'top up' charge on:

- the transferee;
- any person in whom the property is vested (whether or not beneficially);
- any person beneficially entitled to an interest in possession; and
- any person for whose benefit the property or income is supplied where the property has become settled.

The transferee is the first person liable. If the transferee does not pay, the personal representatives may become liable under *s 204*. This naturally has caused practitioners some concern, which was discussed between the Law Society and HMRC, who indicated that they will not normally assess IHT on personal representatives, provided that:

- the executors have made the fullest enquiries that are reasonably practicable to discover the existence of lifetime transfers;

- the executors have done all they can to make full disclosure of lifetime transfers to IRCT;

- the executors or other personal representatives have obtained a clearance certificate; and

- the estate has been distributed before the existence of the chargeable transfer comes to light.

A special rule applies under *s 208* for woodlands, in that the person liable for tax chargeable under *s 126* in relation to a disposal of timber is the person who is entitled to the proceeds of sale (or would be entitled to those proceeds if the disposal were a sale).

Due date for payment

23.4 The normal payment date is six months from the end of the month in which the transfer takes place. In relation to failed PETs, this is six months after the month in which the death occurred (see *s 226(3A)*). Special rules apply where a lifetime transfer is made after 5 April and before October in any year. Tax on transfers falling within that period is due (see *s 226(1)*) at the end of April in the next year.

Interest was traditionally charged at a lower rate on IHT (and, before it, CTT) than on other taxes and, on the whole, changed less frequently than was the case with other taxes. That changed with effect from 21 July 2009, by virtue of *FA 2009, s 105*, which aligned the interest rates for IHT with those for other taxes.

It has long been difficult for unrepresented applicants to obtain funding to pay IHT on delivery of the HMRC account. Although building societies have long been helpful, banks have not, in the past, been willing to accept undertakings from the general public. To ease this difficulty, HMRC introduced the direct payment scheme, by which the financial institution that holds funds for the deceased is asked to pay the tax direct to HMRC. Most banks have now agreed to participate in the scheme, which came into effect on 31 March 2003. The scheme is voluntary, so the practitioner should check with the relevant financial institution whether they participate in the scheme, which applies only to accounts in the sole name of the deceased. If the deceased had several accounts with the same bank or building society, including loan or credit card accounts, it is likely that only the net amount will be available to pay tax. Where there are several accounts, it will naturally be necessary for inter-account transfers to be made to the account from which the payment of IHT itself is made. Withdrawal of funds will be subject to normal banking rules, including requirements as to notice.

The procedure is simple. First, get an IHT reference for the estate, either online through the HMRC website or using form IHT422. Then download form IHT423 from the HMRC website, fill it in and send it, not to HMRC, but to the institution holding the money. A separate form IHT423 must be completed for each financial institution from which the personal representatives wish to transfer money to pay the tax. All this will take rather longer than if the tax had been paid by cheque, but most personal representatives will consider that the extra time is well worth the trouble.

Payment of tax by instalments

23.5   *IHTA 1984, s 227* provides that, on an election by the person paying the tax, that tax may be paid by ten equal yearly instalments, where the tax is payable on the value transferred by a chargeable transfer which is attributable to the value of 'qualifying property' and conditions are satisfied. 'Qualifying property' means:

- any land, anywhere;
- '*s 228*' shares or securities (the meaning of which is described below); and
- a business or an interest in a business.

The conditions of eligibility for the instalment option are:

- the transfer is made on death; or
- the tax is being paid by the person who benefits from the transfer; or
- the transfer comes within the settled property regime and either the tax is borne by the beneficiary or the property stays in the settlement.

The instalment option is not available in respect of tax payable on the value transferred by a failed PET, nor on the top-up charge to tax when a PET fails, except insofar as the tax is attributable to the value of property which satisfies one of two conditions set out in *s 227(1C)*, namely:

- the property was owned by the transferee throughout the period beginning with the date of the chargeable transfer and ending with the death of the transferor (or, if earlier, the death of the transferee); or

- for the purposes of determining the tax or 'top up' tax arising because of the death of the transferor, the property qualifies for APR or BPR; in other words, the clawback charge.

Where the property consists of unquoted shares or unquoted securities, further conditions apply under *s 228(3A)*, ie that the shares or securities remained unquoted throughout the period beginning with the date of the transfer and ending with the death of the transferor (or the earlier death of the transferee). The usual definitions of 'unquoted' apply, as have been discussed elsewhere in this book.

'Section 228 shares'

23.6   *IHTA 1984, s 228* applies to four categories of shares or securities of a company, namely:

- those which, immediately before the chargeable transfer, gave control of the company to the deceased, the transferor or, within the trust regime, the trustees;
- unquoted shares, where the chargeable transfer is made on death and the condition is satisfied in *s 228(2)*, ie that at least 20% of the tax chargeable on the value transferred is tax for which the person paying the tax attributable is liable in the same capacity and is tax attributable to the value of the shares or securities or other tax qualifying for instalment relief under *s 227*;
- unquoted shares where the Board are satisfied that the tax attributable to their value cannot be paid in one sum without undue hardship. For this test to apply, it is assumed, in the case of a chargeable transfer not made on death, that the shares will be retained by the person liable to pay the tax; and
- shares of a company not falling within the first bullet point above, ie not control holdings which are unquoted where conditions are satisfied, set out in *s 228(3)*, namely the value of the transfer is over £20,000 and:
  - the nominal value of the shares is at least 10% of the nominal value of all the shares of the company at the time of transfer; or
  - the shares are ordinary shares and their nominal value is at least 10% of the nominal value of all of the ordinary shares of the company at that time.

'Ordinary shares' means (see *s 228(4)*) shares carrying a right to dividends not restricted to those at fixed rate, or shares with a right to conversion to shares carrying such a right.

By *s 229*, the instalment option is available in respect of woodlands under the charge in *s 129*. The tax may be paid by ten equal yearly instalments, the first being payable six months after the end of the month in which the transfer within *s 129* is made.

Interest on instalments

23.7   *IHTA 1984, s 234* sets out the rules. Where the instalment option is available, the tax, for the purposes of interest to be added to each instalment, is treated as carrying interest from the date at which the instalment is payable. That rule, in *s 234(1)*, is limited by the operation of *s 234(2)*. The limitation relates to companies dealing in securities, to holding companies whose business likewise consists in dealing in securities, and to market-making companies. The rule as to interest on instalments does not apply to dealing in investing companies, unless they are also holding companies or market-makers within *s 234(3)(b)* or *(c)*. 'Market maker' is defined in *s 234(4)*.

Termination of the right to pay tax by instalments

23.8   Even though an election may have been made under *s 227*, any tax unpaid and interest on it may be paid at any time. Likewise (see *s 227(4)*), if at any time the whole or any part of the property qualifying for the instalment option is sold, the right to instalments ceases forthwith and the tax unpaid becomes payable. Where part only has been sold, a proportionate part of the tax is payable. Where the sale takes place before the date on which the first instalment is payable, tax is payable on that first instalment date.

There are two traps hidden in *s 227(4)*. Whilst the subsection blandly indicates that 'the tax for the time being unpaid, with interest to the time of payment, may be paid at any time', it does not make clear the interpretation of HMRC that there is no 'half election'. In other words, if the executors elect to pay tax by instalments and subsequently, finding themselves substantially in funds which are earning little interest, wish to make a payment on account, that payment on account has the effect of causing all the remaining instalments to become due. This situation is unsatisfactory for the executors, who may not have sufficient funds to achieve complete finality, and yet wish to put the liquidity in their hands 'in a safe place'.

The second trap is contained in *s 213*. Where a person, say the executor, has paid tax over in one lump sum which might have been paid by instalments, and he is entitled to recover it from any person, as for example a beneficiary, the beneficiary is entitled to refund the tax to the executor by only the same instalments as were available to the executor, even if he paid by one lump sum. If the executor pays over without seeking the instalment option, he cannot compel repayment at once; he must wait.

A striking example of the difficulty is illustrated in *Howarth's Executors v IRC* [1997] STC (SCD) 162. The will of the deceased was proved by the son, his wife and an employee of the firm of solicitors who dealt with the administration of the estate. The lawyer was not a beneficiary (save, possibly, in respect of a charging clause). The executors elected to pay the tax, which was then CTT, by instalments. The amount was £34,380. At the request of the family, the lawyer agreed that the assets of the estate might be transferred out of the names of the executors and into the names of the beneficiaries.

To begin with, all went well. The beneficiaries made the payments of instalments. The son was then made bankrupt. At this stage, the tax outstanding plus interest amounted to £8,084. The Revenue served a notice of determination on each of the executors, who appealed. None appeared at the appeal. The lawyer was absent due to ill health. On his behalf, it was argued that the Revenue should have registered their charge (arising under *s 237*) against the property. That registration would have protected the interests of the lawyer when the land was sold.

The lawyer had not been told by the Revenue that there had been any problem with payment of instalments until almost two years after he had retired owing to ill health. He suffered from high blood pressure and diabetes. Attending court would have caused a further deterioration in his health, as indeed would enforcement proceedings to recover from him the outstanding tax that the family should have paid. Not being a beneficiary, he had received nothing from the estate.

The Special Commissioners held that a charge in favour of the Revenue in relation to unpaid tax and interest was created under *s 237(1)*. The property itself ceased to be subject to that charge when sold, 'but the property for the time being representing it shall be subject to it', according to *s 238(1)*. The Inland Revenue charge thus moved from the property of the deceased to the proceeds of sale. There was no need for the Revenue to register the charge.

Should the Revenue have acted earlier to approach the lawyer? They could not be criticised, in the view of the Special Commissioner. The son was not made bankrupt until after the date of notification by the Inland Revenue. He was still making monthly payments, which continued after the notification of the problem to the lawyer.

There was some sympathy for the lawyer, but he was the author of his own misfortune. In his capacity as an executor, he had agreed to pay the tax by instalments. He had agreed to the transfer of the assets out of the names of the executors and into the names of the beneficiaries. He took a chance. CTT was a personal liability of each executor or personal representative. It was not easy to shed that responsibility, as had been noted in *IRC v Stannard* [1984] STC 245.

The Commissioner had no alternative but to uphold the notices which had been issued.

The Inland Revenue charge

23.9   Mention was made, in the discussion of *Howarth's Executors v IRC*, of the Inland Revenue charge under *s 237(1)*. Where tax charged on the value transferred by a chargeable transfer is unpaid, a charge is imposed by *s 237(1)* in favour of HMRC on any property to the value of which the value transferred is wholly or partly attributable.

The charge is also imposed on any property comprised in a settlement where the chargeable transfer is the making of the settlement or is made under the settled property regime. 'Property' includes any property directly or indirectly representing it (*s 237(2)*).

Section 237(3), as originally enacted, excluded from the Inland Revenue charge personal or moveable property situated in the United Kingdom which was beneficially owned by the deceased immediately before his death and vested in his personal representatives. The definition of 'personal property' previously included leaseholds as well as undivided shares in land held on trust for sale, whether statutory or not. That has been changed by *FA 1999*, such that personal property now does not include leaseholds.

Section 237(3A) applied to failed PETs. Property (or an interest in it) disposed of to a purchaser before the death of the transferor is not itself subject to the Inland Revenue charge but:

- property which has been disposed of by any other means; and
- property which at the death of the transferor represents either the original property or any interest in it,

is subject to that charge. The new *s 237(3C)* imposes a charge in favour of HMRC in respect of unpaid tax. The tax concerned is any charge under:

- *s 32* (chargeable events relating to conditionally exempt transfers);
- *s 32A* (charge in relation to associated properties);
- *s 79(3)* (exemption from the ten-yearly charge);
- *Sch 4, para 8* (the charge to tax where property leaves maintenance funds); or
- *Sch 1, para 5* or *Sch 3, para 5* (the charges on the failure of conditional exemption in respect of objects and buildings).

The charge under *s 237(3C)* will apply except where the event giving rise to the charge was a disposal to a purchaser of the property or object in question and,

512

in such a case, on any property for the time being representing that property or object.

PURCHASE OF OWN SHARES BY AN UNQUOTED TRADING COMPANY

23.10   Sometimes, families who run businesses as a company plough back a considerable amount of the profit. BPR encourages retention of liquidity within the family company, subject only to the rules as to excepted assets considered in **Chapter 7**. The general rule is that any payment by an unquoted trading company for the purchase of its own shares will be treated as a taxable distribution for corporation tax, save for those exceptions where the requirements of *ICTA 1988, s 219* are met.

During the lifetimes of the shareholders, the exceptions most commonly encountered are those where the transaction is for the benefit of the trade of the company and is not for the avoidance of tax. Specifically, however, *s 219(1)(b)* allows the purchase of own shares by an unquoted trading company *not* to be treated as a distribution where:

- the proceeds of that purchase are all, or nearly all, used to pay inheritance tax; and
- the transaction is completed and the tax paid within two years of the death.

The rule is itself subject to an exception, which extends its application. Whilst, in general, the proceeds of the sale of shares must be applied in paying IHT, those proceeds may also be applied in paying CGT arising on the disposal of the shares to the company.

This relief may be relied on, in IHT cases, only where it is shown that the IHT could not be paid by any other means without undue hardship. *Corporation Tax Act 2010, s 1044* allows for advance clearance of payments under this code. The application must be in writing and must set out particulars of the relevant transactions (*CTA 2010, s 1045(1)*). It is more likely to succeed if it demonstrates the hardship on which the application is based. The Board have 30 days in which to respond (*CTA 2010, s 1045(5)*). There is no appeal from their decision.

PUBLIC PURCHASE OF HERITAGE PROPERTY BY PRIVATE TREATY SALES: OUTLINE

23.11   On a sale in the open market of property that has been the subject of conditional exemption, that previous exemption, whether for estate duty, capital transfer tax or IHT, is lost. It is also quite likely that the sale will give rise to a gain on which CGT is chargeable. Although it is common practice for auctioneers to charge a 'buyer's premium', which may have the result of reducing the other charge that is made against the seller on the hammer price, the sale charges may be considerable but will be allowable against the gain for computation of CGT.

However, private treaty sales were, until 1998, less attractive to acquiring institutions than transfers to heritage bodies, because acceptance in lieu of tax involved some contribution from central government, which was not the case on a private treaty sale. This difficulty was removed in 1998 and now, in effect, HMRC just write off the tax involved. That avoids long delays. Items are reviewed by the Museums, Libraries and Archives Council (MLA) where the Acquisitions, Export and Loans Unit will refer them to the Acceptance in Lieu Panel. The AIL Panel seeks the true market value of the item and, in 10% to 15% of cases, will actually recommend a higher figure than was proposed by the owner. Given the limited funds currently available to museums, the AIL scheme is very important to them.

A sale by private treaty to a '*Sch 3*' body, ie a heritage body within *IHTA 1984, Sch 3* does not trigger clawback of conditional exemption, nor does it give rise to a CGT charge. That tax exemption comes, however, at a price. The vendor is asked to accept a lower price than he would get in the open market. The principles behind this are those recommended by the Waverley Committee (1952 Report of the Committee on the Export of Works of Art). The sweetener or, to use its somewhat archaic technical name, the 'douceur', to encourage the owner of heritage property to sell to the nation, is an administrative arrangement. It benefits both parties.

There is a secondary saving. The clawback of exemption from IHT or its predecessors can involve, as has been explained earlier, not only a charge in relation to the event that triggers the clawback but also a tax charge found by reaching back to the cumulative total of transfers made by the last person in respect of whom conditional exemption was given. Thus, the clawback charge may affect not only the value of the heritage property itself, but also the value of other family wealth. Sale by private treaty to the public leaves the calculation of tax on other family property undisturbed. It can also benefit the tax 'clock' of a person who has settled heritage property and is still alive.

IHTA 1984, s 230(1) refers to 'the application of any person liable to pay tax or interest'. That suggests not merely that only such a person may make the application, but that an application may be made only in respect of property in which the applicant has a beneficial interest or which he holds as personal representative of the deceased former owner. Thus, a beneficiary liable to pay tax might offer property that he already owns or might offer property coming to him by an inheritance, which was the trigger for the liability to tax. What such a person, presumably, may not do is offer other property which he holds in some other capacity, as, for example, the trustee of a family trust. Equally, an executor can offer property in the estate that he administers but cannot, according to IRCT, offer his personal property unless he is not only an executor but also a beneficiary in the estate.

'Douceur'

23.12   The calculations assume agreement of the value of the heritage property on the principles described earlier in this book. A calculation is made of the net of tax value, after taking account of CGT on the sale itself and clawback of IHT or its predecessors. Costs of sale are not taken into account in this notional tax calculation even though, as noted above, they may be considerable. The 'douceur' is then applied. The net of tax value is enhanced. The starting figure for 'douceur' is 25%, although that may be increased on low value objects or reduced on high value objects. It is always reduced on land, generally to 10%. Douceur is not allowed on amenity land: for this point, see IR67 at para 11.

The institution that makes the purchase must be aware of the full facts. The taxpayer should authorise HMRC to disclose his potential liability to tax. When the figures are agreed, the buyer pays the special price, ie the net of tax market value, plus the 'douceur'.

Example 23.1: an official illustration

The illustration given in Appendix 11 to IR67, reproduced here, is now somewhat out of date in relation to the tax rates, but is a useful starting point for understanding the mechanism. It is there assumed that a work of art is likely to fetch £100,000 gross at auction and that such a sale would realise a gain of £40,000. CGT is charged at 30%, yielding £12,000. It is also assumed that, the property having benefited from previous conditional exemption, an open market sale would trigger loss of the exemption and a tax charge at 60% on the market value after deducting CGT.

The clawback charge thus arrived at is:

	£
Sale price	100,000
Less CGT assumed	12,000
	88,000
60% assumed tax charge	52,800
Proceeds net of CGT and IHT	35,200
Douceur at 25% of notional tax (12,000 + 52,800)	16,200
Special price (35,200 + 16,200)	51,400

Example 23.2: another official illustration

Applying similar principles, the illustration set out in Appendix 12 to IR67 is in respect of land, showing the lower level of douceur:

	£
Assumed market value of the land	100,000
Assumed gain	50,000
Assumed CGT at 30%	(15,000)
Assumed clawback of IHT at 60% on 85,000	(51,000)
Net proceeds	
Net value after tax:	34,000
Douceur: 10% of the tax (15,000 + 51,000):	6,600
Special price: (34,000 + 6,600)	40,600

The 'other side' of each of these calculations is that HMRC write off the total tax (£64,800 in the illustration relating to the work of art, and £66,000 in the illustration relating to land). The public end up paying the special price: thus, it is easily seen why the purchasing body must know 'the full story'. Whilst, in the IR67 examples, it simplifies the calculations, in that the expenses of sale are ignored, many owners and their advisers will in effect rework the calculations to take into account expenses, not least because there will be some expense for professional advice sought to negotiate a private treaty sale to the public.

Stamp duty and stamp duty land tax

23.13   No duty is payable on any transfer of property accepted in satisfaction of tax (*National Heritage Act 1980, s 11*). The acquisition of an interest that is chargeable to SDLT by a charity is exempt from SDLT under *FA 2003, s 68* and *Sch 8*. Acquisition by certain heritage bodies is exempt under *s 69*, as mentioned at **21.31**.

Value added tax

23.14   It is possible, but perhaps unlikely, that property offered in lieu of tax could be subject to a VAT charge on disposal. This could apply to property that had been exhibited in a house open to the public, or property that had been used for some business purpose. The impact of VAT on works of art is governed by *VATA 1994, Sch 9, Group 11*. The disposal of property in satisfaction of tax under *s 32(4)* or *32A(5)* or *(7)* is not chargeable (see *Group 11, Item 3*). The corresponding item for CGT is *Item 4*, with additional *Items 1* and *2* respectively for estate duty and claims under *IHTA 1984, Sch 5*. Transfer of property to the state is not treated as a 'supply'.

Interest and the valuation date option

23.15   The value of heritage property fluctuates. Since 17 March 1987, the basis for acceptance of property in satisfaction of tax is the value on the date of offer rather than what the value might be at the date the property is actually accepted. In times of inflation, this rule could work against the owner. On the other hand, interest on the tax in issue ceases to run from the date of the offer rather than from the date of acceptance, even though, in effect, the owner may have had the use and enjoyment of the property meanwhile.

This rule is not absolute. By SP 6/87, there is a facility to opt for revaluation as at the date on which the property is accepted. Where that option is taken, interest on the unpaid tax runs until acceptance. By para 5 of SP 6/87, where the 'offer date' option remains open and is chosen by the owner, interest on the tax to be satisfied by the item will cease to accrue from that date rather than from the date of acceptance.

As a separate matter, the date of completion of the offer of chattels and their acceptance will be important to the issue of risk. Such risk remains with the owner of the chattel until the Secretary of State has nominated the institution that will take charge of the item, either on a temporary or on a permanent basis, and that institution has collected the object. Thus, any insurance that the owner of the item maintains should be kept in force until the item is delivered in this way. Different conditions should apply where the item is already on loan to a public museum. In such a case, the owner should try to negotiate that risk passes at an earlier stage, ie when the 'memorandum of acceptance' has been agreed and exchanged between the parties. The risk in respect of land passes only on completion of the assurance by way of conveyance or transfer to the body nominated to receive it.

'Supermarket' heritage offer

23.16   A problem arises if an offer of property fails. Tax becomes payable, plus interest, even though a new offer may later succeed. Where an owner holds many items of heritage property, together worth far more than the liability to tax that must be satisfied, the owner may 'set his stall out' by making a multiple offer. This allows HMRC to self-select the items they most want. That way, the owner reduces his risk of exposure to an interest charge.

Offers 'in situ'

23.17   In 1997, changes were indicated, by the Department for Culture, Media and Sport, to the previous scheme for offers of property *'in situ'*. In essence, such an offer is made by the owner on the basis that the chattel, which must be pre-eminent and not merely associated, remains at the private property where it has, in effect, always been. The ownership of the chattel passes to the state and is allocated to a public museum. A loan agreement is set up between the owner and the museum. Present procedure is that the offeror must find a museum that will take ownership of the article and lend it back to the owner before the *in situ* offer is submitted to HMRC, so the owner must do a fair amount of leg-work first. Although there was previously in use a model form of *in situ* agreement, it is now likely that HMRC may not regard it as correct. In outline, the agreement will cover at least the following issues:

- *Public access*: the building where the item remains must be open to the public. The minimum access likely to be required is 100 days per year.

- *Preservation*: had the item been in a museum, there would have been in place environmental controls and measuring devices. If it is to remain in the present property, standards of environmental control must be appropriate. This will be fixed by the MLA and by the museum which becomes the owner of the chattel. The owner must pay.

- *Future conservation*: the museum that becomes the owner of the chattel will be responsible for these arrangements.

- *Security*: again, the MLA will advise. The owner must stand the initial cost of the security arrangements, but later upgrades will be met by the museum that owns the chattel.

- *Insurance*: the museum to which the chattel is allocated may seek a government indemnity for up to 99% of the 'special price', as determined in accordance with the principles discussed earlier in this chapter. The owner covers the other 1%.

- *Future owners*: an *in situ* agreement runs for the lifetime of the owner of the chattel who puts it into effect, but is terminated if that person leaves the property at which the chattel is kept. Under the latest scheme for agreements of this kind, any attempt to achieve automatic succession as between one member of the family and the next is excluded. A successive occupier of the heritage property may indicate that he or she wishes to enter into a new *in situ* agreement; but, if the museum owning the chattel is not happy with that, new arrangements must be made. Such matters should be referred to arbitration, as indeed should any provision that allows the museum to raise the issue of whether it is still appropriate for the chattel to remain at the property once 21 years have elapsed from the date of the original agreement.

- *Exhibition*: the museum must have the right to remove the chattel occasionally for short periods of public exhibition or for conservation purposes. Equally, if the former owner of the chattel no longer observes the terms of the agreement, the museum must have power to remove it.

Appendix 1

Legislation

Note: in this Appendix the sections are not set out in numerical order but are grouped by broad subject matter, dealing first with the main codes for BPR and APR, then woodland relief. There then follows the Heritage Property Code with its associated schedules relating to Heritage Bodies, Maintenance Funds and Acceptance in Lieu, with and the Income Tax code for maintenance funds. Next are set out the provisions relating to 'double grossing'. Finally section 267A is included, relating to Limited Liability Partnerships. Although it is believed that this version takes account of all amendments, to keep the text simple the actual dates of amendments are not shown. The practitioner should refer to official copies when involved in litigation.

INHERITANCE TAX ACT 1984

Part V   Miscellaneous Reliefs

Chapter I   Business Property

103   Preliminary
(1) In this Chapter references to a transfer of value include references to an occasion on which tax is chargeable under Chapter III of Part III of this Act (apart from section 79), and:
  (a)   references to the value transferred by a transfer of value include references to the amount on which tax is then chargeable, and
  (b)   references to the transferor include references to the trustees of the settlement concerned.

(2) For the purposes of this Chapter a company and all its subsidiaries are members of a group, and 'holding company' and 'subsidiary' have the meanings given by section 1159 of and Schedule 6 to the Companies Act 2006.

(3) In this Chapter 'business' includes a business carried on in the exercise of a profession or vocation but does not include a business carried on otherwise than for gain.

104   The relief
(1) Where the whole or part of the value transferred by a transfer of value is attributable to the value of any relevant business property, the whole or that part of the value transferred shall be treated as reduced—

  (a) in the case of property falling within section 105(1)(a)(b) or (bb) below, by 100 per cent;

  (b) in the case of other relevant business property, by 50 per cent,

but subject to the following provisions of this Chapter.

(2) For the purposes of this section, the value transferred by a transfer of value shall be calculated as a value on which no tax is chargeable.

105   Relevant business property

(1) Subject to the following provisions of this section and to section 106, 108, 112(3) and 113 below, in this Chapter 'relevant business property' means, in relation to any transfer of value,—

  (a) property consisting of a business or interest in a business;

  (b) securities of a company which are unquoted and which (either by themselves or with other such securities owned by the transferor and any unquoted shares so owned) gave the transferor control of the company immediately before the transfer.

 (bb) any unquoted shares in a company;

 (cc) shares in or securities of a company which are quoted and which (either by themselves or together with such other shares or securities owned by the transferor) gave the transferor control of the company immediately before the transfer;

  (d) any land or building, machinery or plant which, immediately before the transfer, was used wholly or mainly for the purposes of business carried on by a company of which the transferor then had control or by a partnership of which he then was a partner; and

  (e) any land or building, machinery or plant which, immediately before the transfer, was used wholly or mainly for the purposes of a business carried on by the transferor and was settled property in which he was then beneficially entitled to an interest in possession.

(1ZA) In relation to subsection (1) above 'quoted', in relation to any shares or securities, means listed on a recognised stock exchange and 'unquoted', in relation to any shares or securities, means not so listed.

(2) Shares in or securities of a company do not fall within subsection (1)(cc) above if—

  (a) they would not have been sufficient, without other property, to give the transferor control of the company immediately before the transfer, and

  (b) their value is taken by virtue of section 176 to be less than the value previously determined.

(3) A business or an interest in a business, or shares in or securities of a company, are not relevant business property if the business or, as the case may be, the business carried on by the company consists wholly or mainly of one or more of the following, that is to say, dealing in securities, stocks or shares, land or buildings or making or holding investments.

(4) Subsection (3) above—

  (a) does not apply to any property if the business concerned is wholly that of a market maker or is that of a discount house and (in either case) is carried on in the United Kingdom, and

  (b) does not apply to shares in or securities of a company if the business of the company consists wholly or mainly in being a holding company of one or more companies whose business does not fall within that subsection.

(5) Shares in or securities of a company are not relevant business property in relation to a transfer of value if at the time of the transfer a winding-up order has been made in respect of the company or the company has passed a resolution for the voluntary winding-up or is in the process of liquidation, unless the business of the company is to continue to be carried on after a reconstruction or amalgamation and the reconstruction or amalgamation either is the purpose of the winding-up or liquidation or takes place not later than one year after the transfer of value.

(6) Land, a building, machinery or plant owned by the transferor and used wholly or mainly for the purposes of a business carried on as mentioned in subsection (1)(d) or (e) above is not relevant business property in relation to a transfer of value, unless the business or the transferor's interest in it is, or shares or securities of the company carrying on the business immediately before the transfer are, relevant business property in relation to the transfer.

(7) In this section 'market maker' means a person who—
(a) holds himself out at all normal times in compliance with the rules of The Stock Exchange and is willing to buy and sell securities, stocks or shares at a price specified by him, and
(b) is recognised as doing so by the Council of the Stock Exchange.

106 Minimum period of ownership
Property is not relevant business property in relation to a transfer of value unless it was owned by the transferor throughout the two years immediately preceding the transfer.

107 Replacements
(1) Property shall be treated as satisfying the condition in section 106 above if—
(a) it replaced other property and it, that other property and any property directly or indirectly replaced by that other property were owned by the transferor for periods which together comprised at least two years falling within the five years immediately preceding the transfer of value, and
(b) any other property concerned was such that, had the transfer of value been made immediately before it was replaced, it would (apart from section 106) have been relevant business property in relation to the transfer.

(2) In a case falling within subsection (1) above relief under this Chapter shall not exceed what it would have been had the replacement or any one or more of the replacements not been made.

(3) For the purposes of subsection (2) above changes resulting from the formation, alteration or dissolution of a partnership, or from the acquisition of a business by a company controlled by the former owner of the business, shall be disregarded.

(4) Without prejudice to subsection (1) above, where any shares falling within section 105(1)(bb) above which are owned by the transferor immediately before the transfer would under any of the provisions of sections 126 to 136 of the 1992 Act be identified with other shares previously owned by him his period of ownership of the first-mentioned shares shall be treated for the purposes of section 106 as including his period of ownership of the other shares.

108 Successions
For the purposes of sections 106 and 107 above, where the transferor became entitled to any property on the death of another person—

Appendix 1   *Legislation*

(a) he shall be deemed to have owned it from the date of his death, and
(b) if that other person was his spouse or civil partner he shall also be deemed to have owned it for any period during which the spouse or civil partner owned it.

109   Successive transfers
(1) Where—
  (a) the whole or part of the value transferred by a transfer of value (in this section referred to as the earlier transfer) was eligible for relief under this Chapter (or would have been so eligible if such relief had been capable of being given in respect of transfers of value made at that time), and
  (b) the whole or part of property which, in relation to the earlier transfer, was relevant business property became, through the earlier transfer, the property of the person or the spouse or civil partner of the person who is the transferor in relation to the subsequent transfer of value, and
  (c) that property or part, or any property directly or indirectly replacing it, would (apart from section 106 above) have been relevant business property in relation to the subsequent transfer of value, and
  (d) either the earlier transfer was, or the subsequent transfer of value is, a transfer made on the death of the transferor,

the property which would have been relevant business property but for section 106 above shall be relevant business property notwithstanding that section.

(2) Where the property which, by virtue of subsection (1) above, and is relevant business property replaced the property or part referred to in paragraph (c) of that subsection, relief under this Chapter shall not exceed what it would have been had the replacement or any one or more of the replacements not been made, but section 107(3) above shall apply with the necessary modifications for the purposes of this subsection.

(3) Where, under the earlier transfer, the amount of the value transferred which was attributable to the property or part referred to in subsection (1)(c) above was part only of its value, a like part only of the value which (apart from this subsection) would fall to be reduced under this Chapter by virtue of this section shall be so reduced.

110   Value of business
For the purposes of this Chapter—
  (a) the value of a business or of an interest in a business shall be taken to be its net value;
  (b) the net value of a business is the value of the assets used in the business (including goodwill) reduced by the aggregate amount of any liabilities incurred for the purposes of the business;
  (c) in ascertaining the net value of an interest in a business, no regard shall be had to assets or liabilities other than those by reference to which the net value of the entire business would fall to be ascertained.

111   Value of certain shares and securities
Where a company is a member of a group and the business of any other company which is a member of the group falls within section 105(3) above, then, unless either—
  (a) that business also falls within section 105(4), or
  (b) that business consists wholly or mainly in the holding of land or buildings wholly or mainly occupied by members of the group whose business either does not fall within section 105(3) or falls within both sections 105(3) and 105(4),

the value of shares in or securities of the company shall be taken for the purposes of this Chapter to be what it would be if that other company were not a member of the group.

112 Exclusion of value of excepted assets
(1) In determining for the purposes of this Chapter what part of the value transferred by a transfer of value is attributable to the value of any relevant business property so much of the last-mentioned value as is attributable to any excepted assets within the meaning of subsection (2) below shall be left out of account.

(2) An asset is an excepted asset in relation to any relevant business property if it was neither—
  (a) used wholly or mainly for the purposes of the business concerned throughout the whole of the last two years of the relevant period defined in subsection (5) below, nor
  (b) required at the time of the transfer for future use of those purposes:
but where the business concerned is carried on by a company which is a member of a group, the use of an asset for the purposes of a business carried on by another company which at the time of the use and immediately before the transfer was also a member of that group shall be treated as used for the purposes of the business concerned, unless that other company's membership of the group falls to be disregarded under section 111 above.

(3) Subsection (2) above does not apply in relation to an asset which is relevant business property by virtue only of section 105(1)(d) above, and an asset is not relevant business property by virtue only of that provision unless either—
  (a) it was used as mentioned in that provision throughout the two years immediately preceding the transfer of value, or
  (b) it replaced another asset so used and it and the other asset and any asset directly or indirectly replaced by that other asset were so used for periods which together comprised at least two years falling within the five years immediately preceding the transfer of value;
but in a case where section 105 above applies this condition shall be treated as satisfied if the asset (or it and the asset or assets replaced by it) was or were so used throughout the period between the earlier and the subsequent transfer mentioned in that section (or throughout the part of that period during which it or they were owned by the transferor or the transferor's spouse or civil partner.

(4) Where part but not the whole of any land or building is used exclusively for the purposes of any business and the land or building would, but for this subsection, be an excepted asset, or, as the case may be, prevented by subsection (3) above from being relevant business property, the part so used and the remainder shall for the purposes of this section be treated as separate assets, and the value of the part so used shall (if it would otherwise be less) be taken to be such proportion of the value of the whole as may be just.

(5) For the purposes of this section the relevant period, in relation to any asset, is the period immediately preceding the transfer of value during which the asset (or, if the replacement business property is an interest in a business, a corresponding interest in the asset) was owned by the transferor, or, if the business concerned is that of a company, was owned by that company or any other company immediately before the transfer of value was a member of the same group.

(6) For the purposes of this section an asset shall be deemed not to have been used wholly or mainly for the purposes of the business concerned at any time when it was used wholly or mainly for the personal benefit of the transferor or of a person connected with him.

113   Contracts for sale

When any property would be relevant business property in relation to a transfer of value but a binding contract for its sale has been entered into at the time of the transfer, it is not relevant business property in relation to the transfer unless—

(a) the property is a business or an interest in a business and the sale is to a company which is to carry on the business and is made in consideration wholly or mainly of shares in or securities of that company, or

(b) the property is shares in or securities of a company and the sale is made for the purpose of reconstruction or amalgamation.

113A   Transfers within seven years before death of the transferor

(1) Where any part of the value transferred by a potentially exempt transfer which proves to be a chargeable transfer would (apart from this section) be reduced in accordance with the preceding provisions of this chapter it shall not be so reduced unless the conditions in subsection (3) are satisfied.

(2) Where—

(a) any part of the value transferred by any chargeable transfer, other than a potentially exempt transfer, is reduced in accordance with the preceding provisions of this Chapter, and

(b) the transfer is made within seven years of the death of the transferor,

then, unless the conditions in subsection (3) below are satisfied, the additional tax chargeable by reason of the death shall be calculated as if the value transferred had not been so reduced.

(3) The conditions referred to in subsections (1) and (2) above are—

(a) that the original property was owned by the transferee throughout the period beginning with the date of the chargeable transfer and ending with the death of the transferor: and

(b) except to the extent that the original property consists of shares or securities to which subsection (3A) below applies that, in relation to a notional transfer of value made by the transferee immediately before the death, the original property would (apart from section 106 above) be relevant business property.

(3A) This subsection applies to shares or securities—

(a) which were quoted at the time of the chargeable transfer referred to in subsection 1 or subsection 2 above; or

(b) which fell within paragraph (b) or (bb) of section 105(1) above in relation to that transfer and were unquoted throughout the period referred to in subsection (3) (a) above.

(3B) In subsection (3A) above 'quoted', in relation to any shares or securities, means listed on a recognised stock exchange and 'unquoted', in relation to any shares or securities, means not so listed.

(4) If the transferee has died before the transferor, the reference in subsection (3) above to the death of the transferor shall have effect as a reference to the death of the transferee.

(5) If the conditions in subsection (3) above are satisfied only with respect to part of the original property, then,—
- (a) in a case falling within subsection (1) above, only a proportionate part of so much of the value transferred as is attributable to the original property shall be reduced in accordance with the preceding provisions of this Chapter; and
- (b) in a case falling within subsection (2) above, the additional tax should be calculated as if only a proportionate part of so much of the value transferred as was attributable to the original property had been so reduced.

(6) Where any shares owned by the transferee immediately before the death in question—
- (a) would under any of the provisions of sections 126 to 136 of the 1992 Act be identified with the original property (or part of it); or
- (b) were issued to him in consideration of the transfer of a business or interest in a business consisting of the original property (or part of it),

they shall be treated for the purposes of this section as if they were the original property (or that part of it).

(7) This section has effect subject to section 113B below.

(7A) The provisions of this Chapter for the reduction of value transferred shall be disregarded in any determination for the purposes of this section of whether there is a potentially exempt or chargeable transfer in any case.

(8) In this section—
'the original property' means the property which was relevant business property in relation to the chargeable transfer referred to in subsection (1) or subsection (2) above: and
'the transferee' means the person whose property the original property became on that chargeable transfer or, where on the transfer the original property became or remained settled property in which no qualifying interest in possession (within the meaning of Chapter III of Part III of this Act subsists, the trustees of the settlement.

113B   Application of section 113A to replacement property
(1) Subject to subsection (2) below, this section applies where—
- (a) the transferee has disposed of all or part of the original property before the death of the transferor;
- (b) the whole of the consideration received by him for the disposal has been applied by him in acquiring other property (in this section referred to as 'the replacement property').

(2) This section does not apply unless—
- (a) the replacement property is acquired, or a binding contact for its acquisition is entered into, within the allowed period after the disposal of the original property (or, as the case may be the part concerned); and
- (b) the disposal and acquisition of both made in transactions at arm's length or on terms such as might be expected to be included in a transaction at arm's length.

(3) Where this section applies, the conditions in section 113A(3) above shall be taken to be satisfied in relation to the original property (or, as the case may be, the part concerned) if—
- (a) the replacement property is owned by the transferee immediately before the death of the transferor; and

(b) throughout the period beginning with the date of the chargeable transfer and ending with the death (disregarding any period between the disposal and acquisition) either the original property or the replacement property was owned by the transferee; and

(c) in relation to a notional transfer of value made by the transferee immediately before the death, the replacement property would (apart from section 106 above) be relevant business property.

(4) If the transferee has died before the transferor, any reference in subsections (1) to (3) above to the death of the transferor shall have effect as a reference to the death of the transferee.

(5) In any case where—

(a) all or part of the original property has been disposed of before the death of the transferor or is excluded by section 113 above from being relevant business property in relation to the notional transfer of value referred to in section 113A(3)(b) above; and

(b) the replacement property is acquired, or a binding contract for its acquisition is entered into, after the death of the transferor but within the allowed period after the disposal of the original property or part; and

(c) the transferor dies before the transferee,

subsection (3) shall have effect with the omission of paragraph (a), and as if any reference to a time immediately before the death of the transferor or to the death were a reference to the time when the replacement property was acquired.

(6) Section 113A (6) above shall have effect in relation to the replacement property as it has effect in relation to the original property.

(7) Where a binding contract for the disposal of any property is entered into at any time before the disposal of the property, the disposal shall be regarded for the purposes of subsections (2)(a) and (5)(b) above as taking place at that time.

(8) In this section 'the original property' and 'the transferee' have the same meaning as in section 113A above and 'allowed period' means the period of three years or such longer period as the Board may allow.

114   Avoidance of double relief

(1) Where any part of the value transferred by a transfer of value is reduced under Chapter II of this Part of this Act by reference to the agricultural value of any property, or would be so reduced but for section 121(3), such part of the value transferred as is or would be so reduced under that Chapter shall not be reduced under this Chapter.

(2) Where the value transferred by a transfer of value is reduced under section 129 below by reference to the tax chargeable on the disposal of any trees or underwood, the value to be reduced under section 104 above shall be the value as reduced under section 129 (but subject to section 104(2) above).

Chapter II   Agricultural Property

115   Preliminary

(1) In this Chapter references to a transfer of value include references to an occasion on which tax is chargeable under Chapter III of Part III of this Act (apart from section 79) and—

(a) references to the value transferred by a transfer of value include references to the amount on which tax is then chargeable; and

(b) references to the transferor include references to the trustees of the settlement concerned.

(2) In this Chapter, 'agricultural property' means agricultural land or pasture and includes woodland and any building used in connection with the intensive rearing of livestock or fish if the woodland or building is occupied with agricultural land or pasture and the occupation is ancillary to that of the agricultural land or pasture; and also includes such cottages, farm buildings and farmhouses, together with the land occupied with them, as are of a character appropriate to the property.

(3) For the purposes of this Chapter the agricultural value of any agricultural property shall be taken to be the value which would be the value of the property if the property were subject to a perpetual covenant prohibiting its use otherwise than as agricultural property.

(4) For the purposes of this Chapter the breeding and rearing of horses on a stud farm and the grazing of horses in connection with those activities shall be taken to be agriculture and any buildings used in connection with those activities to be farm buildings.

(5) This Chapter applies to agricultural property only if it is in
   (a) the United Kingdom, the Channel Islands or the Isle of Man, or
   (b) a state, other than the United Kingdom, which is an EEA state (within the meaning given by Schedule 1 to the Interpretation Act 1978) at the time of the transfer of value in question.

116 The relief
(1) Where the whole or part of the value transferred by a transfer of value is attributable to the agricultural value of agricultural property, the whole or that part of the value transferred should be treated as reduced by the appropriate percentage, but subject to the following provisions of this Chapter.

(2) The appropriate percentage is 100 per cent if—
   (a) the interest of the transferor in property immediately before the transfer carries the right to vacant possession or the right to obtain it within the next twelve months; or
   (b) the transferor has been beneficially entitled to that interest since before 10th March 1981 and the conditions set out in subsection (3) below are satisfied; or
   (c) the interest of the transferor in the property immediately before the transfer does not carry either of the rights mentioned in paragraph (a) above because the property is let on a tenancy beginning on or after 1st September 1995;

and, subject to subsection (4) below, it is 50 per cent in any other case.

(3) The conditions referred to in subsection (2)(b) are—
   (a) that if the transferor had disposed of his interest by a transfer of value immediately 10th March 1981 and duly made a claim under paragraph 1 of Schedule 8 of the Finance Act 1975, the value transferred would have been computed in accordance with paragraph 2 of that Schedule and relief would not have been limited by paragraph 5 of that Schedule (restriction to £250,000 or 1,000 acres); and
   (b) that the transferor's interest did not at any time during the period beginning with 10th March 1981 and ending with the date of the transfer carry a right

mentioned in subsection (2)(a) and did not fail to do so by reason of any act or deliberate omission of the transferor during that period.

(4) Where the appropriate percentage would be 100 per cent but for a limitation on relief that would have been imposed (as mentioned in subsection (3)(a) above) by paragraph 5 of Schedule 8 to the Finance Act 1975 the appropriate percentage shall be 100 per cent in relation to a part of the value transferred equal to the amount which would have attracted relief under that Schedule and 50 per cent in relation to the remainder.

(5) In determining for the purposes of subsections (3)(a) and (4) above whether or to what extent relief under Schedule A of the Finance Act 1975 would have been limited under paragraph 5 of that Schedule, that paragraph shall be construed as if references to relief given under that Schedule in respect of previous chargeable transfers included references to—
  (a) relief given under this Chapter by virtue of subsection (2)(b) or (4), above, and
  (b) relief given under Schedule 14 to the Finance Act 1981 by virtue of paragraph 2(2)(b) or (4) of that Schedule,

in respect of previous chargeable transfers made on or after 10th March 1981.

(5A) Where, in consequence of the death on or after 1st September 1995 of the tenant, or as the case may be, the last surviving tenant of any property, the tenancy—
  (a) becomes vested in a person, as a result of his being a person beneficially entitled under the deceased's will or other testamentary writing or his intestacy, and
  (b) is or becomes binding on the landlord and that person as landlord and tenant respectively,

subsection (2)(c) above shall have effect as if the tenancy so vested had been a tenancy beginning on the date of the death.

(5B) Where in consequence of the death on or after 1st September 1995 of the tenant or, as the case may be, the last surviving tenant of any property, a tenancy of the property or of any property comprising the whole or any part of it—
  (a) is obtained by a person under or by virtue of an enactment, or
  (b) is granted to a person in circumstances such that he is already entitled under or by virtue of an enactment to obtain such a tenancy, but one which takes effect on a later date, or
  (c) is granted to a person who is or has become the only or only remaining applicant, or the only or only remaining person eligible to apply, under a particular enactment for such a tenancy in the particular case.

subsection (2)(c) above shall have effect as if the tenancy so obtained or granted had been a tenancy beginning on the date of death.

(5C) Subsection (5B) above does not apply in relation to property situate in Scotland.

(5D) If, in a case where the transferor does on or after 1st September 1995,—
  (a) the tenant of any property has, before the death, given notice of intention to retire in favour of a new tenant, and
  (b) the tenant's retirement in favour of the new tenant takes place after the death but not more than thirty months after the giving of the notice,

subsection (2)(c) above shall have effect as if the tenancy granted or assigned to the new tenant had been a tenancy beginning immediately before the transfer of value which the transferor is treated by section 4(1) above as making immediately before his death.

(5E) In subsection (5D) and this subsection—
'the new tenant' means—
  (a) the person or persons identified in a notice of intention to retire in favour of a new tenant as the person or persons who it is desired should become the tenant of the property to which that notice relates; or
  (b) the survivor or survivors of the person so identified whether alone or with any other person or persons;

'notice of intention to retire in favour of a new tenant' means, in the case of any property, a notice or other written intimation given to the landlord by the tenant, or (in the case of a joint tenancy or tenancy in common) all of the tenants, of the property indicating, in whatever terms, his or their wish that one or more persons identified in the notice or intimation should become the tenant of the property;

'the retiring tenant's tenancy' means the tenancy of the person or persons giving the notice of intention to retire in favour of a new tenant;

'the tenant's retirement in favour of a new tenant' means—
  (a) the assignment, or (in Scotland) assignation, of the retiring tenant's liability to the new tenant in circumstances such that the tenancy is or becomes binding on the landlord and the new tenant as landlord and tenant respectively; or
  (b) the grant of a tenancy of the property which is the subject of a retiring tenant's tenancy, or of any property comprising the whole or part of that property, to the new tenant and the acceptance of that tenancy by him;

and, except in Scotland, 'grant' and 'acceptance' in paragraph (b) above respectively include the deemed grant, and the deemed acceptance, of a tenancy under or by virtue of any enactment.

(6) For the purposes of this Chapter the interest of one of two or more joint tenants or tenants in common (or, in Scotland, joint owners or owners in common) shall be taken to carry a right referred to in subsection (2)(a) above if the interests of all of them together carry that right.

(7) For the purposes of this section, the value transferred by a transfer of value shall be calculated as a value on which no tax is chargeable.

(8) In its application to property outside the United Kingdom, the Channel Islands and the Isle of Man, this section has effect as if any reference to a right or obligation under the law of any part of the United Kingdom were a reference to an equivalent right or obligation under the law governing dispositions of that property.

117 Minimum period of occupation or ownership
Subject to the following provisions of this Chapter, section 116 does not apply to any agricultural property unless—
  (a) it was occupied by transferor for the purposes of agriculture throughout the period of two years ending with the date of the transfer, or
  (b) it was owned by him throughout the period of seven years ending with that date and was throughout that period occupied (by him or another) for the purposes of agriculture.

118 Replacements
(1) Where the agricultural property occupied by the transferor on the date of the transfer replaced other agricultural property, the conditions stated in section 117(a)

above shall be treated as satisfied if it, the other property and any agricultural property directly or indirectly replaced by the other property were occupied by the transferor for the purposes of agriculture for periods which together comprised at least two years falling within the five years ending with that date.

(2) Where the agricultural property owned by the transferor on the date of the transfer replaced other agricultural property, the conditions stated in section 117(b) shall be treated as satisfied if it, the other property and any agricultural property directly or indirectly replaced by the other property were, for periods which together comprised at least seven years falling within the ten years ending with that date, both owned by the transferor and occupied (by him or another) for the purposes of agriculture.

(3) In a case falling within subsection (1) or (2) above relief under this Chapter shall not exceed would it would have been had the replacement or any one or more of the replacements not been made.

(4) For the purposes of subsection (3) above changes resulting from the formation, alteration, or dissolution of a partnership should be disregarded.

119   Occupation by company or partnership
(1) For the purposes of section 117 and 118 above, occupation by a company which is controlled by the transferor shall be treated as by the transferor.

(2) For the purposes of section 117 and 118 above, occupation of any property by a Scottish partnership shall, notwithstanding section 4(2) of the Partnership Act 1890, be treated as occupation of it by the partners.

120   Successions
(1) For the purposes of section 117 above, where the transferor became entitled to any property on the death of another person—
  (a) he shall be deemed to have owned it (and, if he subsequently occupies it, to have occupied it) from the date of the death, and
  (b) if that other person was his spouse or civil partner he shall also be deemed to have occupied it for the purposes of agriculture for any period for which it was so occupied by his spouse or civil partner, and to have owned it for any period for which his spouse or civil partner owned it.

(2) Where the transferor became entitled to his interest on the death of his spouse or civil partner on or after 10th March 1981—
  (a) he shall for the purposes of section 116 (2)(b) above be deemed to have been beneficially entitled to it for any period for which his spouse or civil partner was beneficially entitled to it;
  (b) the conditions set out in section 116(3)(a) shall be taken to be satisfied only if it satisfied in relation to his spouse or civil partner; and
  (c) the conditions set out in section 116(3)(b) shall be taken to be satisfied only if it satisfied both in relation to him and in relation to his spouse or civil partner.

121   Successive transfers
(1) Where—
  (a) the whole or part of the value transferred by a transfer of value (in this section referred to as the earlier transfer) was eligible for relief under this Chapter (or would have been so eligible if such relief had been capable of being given in respect of transfers of value made at that time), and

(b) the whole or part of the property which, in relation to the earlier transfer, was or would have been eligible for relief became, through the earlier transfer, the property of the person (or of the spouse or civil partner of the person) who is the transferor in relation to a subsequent transfer of value and is at the time of the subsequent transfer occupied for the purposes of agriculture either by that person or by the personal representative of the transferor in relation to the earlier transfer, and

(c) that property or part of any property directly or indirectly replacing it would (apart from section 117 above) have been eligible for relief in relation to the subsequent transfer of value, and

(d) either the earlier transfer was, or the subsequent transfer of value is, a transfer made on the death of the transferor,

the property which would have been eligible for relief but for section 117 above shall be eligible for relief notwithstanding that section.

(2) Where the property which, by virtue of subsection (1) above is eligible for relief replaced the property or part referred to in paragraph (c) of that subsection, relief under this Chapter shall not exceed what it would have been had the replacement or any one or more of the replacements not been made, but section 118(4) shall apply for the purposes of this subsection as it applies for the purposes of section 118(3).

(3) Where, under the earlier transfer, the amount of the value transferred which was attributable to the property or part referred to in subsection (1)(c) was part only of its value, a like part only of the value which (apart from this subsection) would fall to be reduced under this Chapter by virtue of this section shall be so reduced.

122 Agricultural property of companies

(1) Where the whole or part of the value transferred is attributable to the value of shares in or securities of a company it shall be taken for the purposes of this Chapter to be attributable (as far as appropriate) to the agricultural value of agricultural property if and only if—

(a) the agricultural property forms part of the company's assets and part of the value of the shares or securities can be attributed to the agricultural value of the agricultural property, and

(b) the shares or securities gave the transferor control of the company immediately before the transfer.

(2) Shares or securities shall not be regarded for the purposes of subsection (1)(b) above as giving the transferor control of a company if—

(a) they would not have been sufficient, without other property, to give him control of the company immediately before the transfer, and

(b) their value is taken by virtue of section 176 below to be less than the value previously determined.

(3) Where subsection (1) above applies—

(a) the references in section 116(2)(a) and (3)(b) above to the transferor's interest shall be construed as references to the company's interest, and

(b) section 123(1) below shall apply instead of section 117 above.

123 Provisions supplementary to section 122

(1) Section 116 above shall not apply by virtue of section 122(1) above unless—

(a) the agricultural property—

(i) was occupied by the company for the purposes of agriculture throughout the period of two years ending with the date of the transfer, or

(ii) was owned by the company throughout the period of seven years ending with that date was throughout that period occupied (by the company or another) for the purposes of agriculture, and

(b) the shares or securities were owned by the transferor—

(i) in a case within paragraph (a)(i) above, throughout the period there mentioned, or

(ii) in a case within paragraph (a)(ii) above, throughout the period there mentioned.

(2) Subsections (1) and (2) of section 118 above shall apply in relation to the conditions stated in subsection (1)(a) above as they apply in relation to the conditions stated in section 117 taking references to the transferor as references to the company.

(3) Where the shares or securities owned by the transferor on the date of the transfer replaced other eligible property (that it is to say, agricultural property or shares or securities the value of which is wholly or partly attributable to the value of such property) the conditions stated in subsection (1)(b) above shall be treated as satisfied if the shares or securities, the other eligible property which they replaced and any eligible property directly or indirectly replaced by the other eligible property were owned by the transferor for periods which together comprised—

(a) in a case within subsection (1)(a)(i) above, at least two years falling within the five years ending with that date, or

(b) in a case within subsection (1)(a)(ii) above, at least seven years falling within the ten years ending within that date.

(4) Subsection (3) and (4) of 118 above shall have effect in relation to a case falling within subsection (2) and (3) above as they have effect in relation to a case falling within subsection (1) and (2) of that section.

(5) For the purposes of subsection (1) above, a company shall be treated as having occupied the agricultural property at any time when it was occupied by a person who subsequently controls the company.

124   Contracts for sale

(1) Section 116 above shall not apply to agricultural property if at the time of the transfer the transfer transferor has entered into a binding contract for its sale, except where the sale is to a company and is made wholly or mainly in consideration of shares or securities of the company which will give the transferor control of the company.

(2) Section 116 above shall not apply by virtue of section 122(1) above if at the time of the transferor has entered into a binding contract for the sale of the shares or securities concerned, except where the sale is made for the purpose of reconstruction or amalgamation.

124A   Transfers within seven years before death of transferor

(1) Where any part of the value transferred by a potentially exempt transfer which proves to be a chargeable transfer would (apart from this section) be reduced in accordance with the preceding provisions of this Chapter, it shall not be so reduced unless the conditions in subsection (3) below are satisfied.

(2) Where—

(a) any part of the value transferred by any chargeable transfer, other than a potentially exempt transfer, is reduced in accordance with the preceding provisions of this Chapter, and

(b)   the transfer is made within seven years of the death of the transferor,

then, unless the conditions in subsection (3) below are satisfied, the additional tax chargeable by reason of the death shall be calculated as if the value transferred had not been so reduced.

(3) The conditions referred to in subsections (1) and (2) are—
  (a)   that the original property was owned by the transferee throughout the period beginning with the date of the chargeable transfer ending with the death of the transferor (in this subsection referred to as 'the relevant period') and it is not at the time of the death subject to a binding contract for sale; and
  (b)   except in a case falling within paragraph (c) below, that the original property is agricultural property immediately before the death and has been occupied (by the transferee or another) for the purposes of agriculture throughout the relevant period; and
  (c)   where the original property consists of shares in or securities of a company, but throughout the relevant period the agricultural property to which section 116 above applied by virtue of section 122(1) above on the chargeable transfer was owned by the company and occupied (by the company or another) for the purposes of agriculture.

(4) If the transferee has died before the transferor, the reference in subsection (3) above to the death of the transferor shall have effect as a reference to the death of the transferee.

(5) If the conditions in subsection (3) above are satisfied only with respect to part of the agricultural property, then—
  (a)   in a case falling within subsection (1) above, only a proportionate part of so much of the value transferred as is attributable to the original property shall be reduced in accordance with the preceding provisions of this Chapter, and
  (b)   in a case falling within subsection (2) above, the additional tax shall be calculated as if only a proportionate part of so much of the value transferred as was attributable to the original property had been so reduced.

(6) Where any shares owned by the transferee immediately before the death in question—
  (a)   would under any of the provisions of sections 126 to 136 of the 1992 Act be identified with the original property (or part of it); or
  (b)   were issued to him in consideration of the transfer of agricultural property consisting of the original property (or part of it),

his period of ownership of the original property shall be treated as including his period of ownership of the shares.

(7) This section has effect subject to section 124B below.

(7A) The provisions of this Chapter for the reduction of value transferred shall be disregarded in any determination for the purposes of this section of whether there is a potentially exempt or chargeable transfer in any case.

(8) In this section—
  'the original property' means the property which, in relation to the chargeable transfer referred to in subsection (1) or subsection (2) above, was either agricultural property to which section 116 applied or shares or securities of a company owning agricultural property to which that section applied by virtue of section 122(1) above; and

'the transferee' means the person whose property the original property became on that chargeable transfer or, where on the transfer the original property became or remained settled property in which no qualifying interest in possession (within the meaning of chapter III of part III of this Act) subsists, the trustees of the settlement.

124B   Application of section 124A to replacement property

(1) Subject to subsection (2) below, this section applies where—
    (a) the transferee has disposed of all or part of the original property before the death of the transferor; and
    (b) the whole of the consideration received by him for the disposal has been applied by him in acquiring other property (in this section referred to as 'the replacement property').

(2) This section does not apply unless—
    (a) the replacement property is acquired, or a binding contract for its acquisition is entered into, within the allowed period after the disposal of the original property (or, as the case may be, the part concerned); and
    (b) the disposal and acquisition are both made in transactions at arm's length or on terms such as might be expected to be included in a transaction at arm's length.

(3) Where this section applies, the conditions in section 124A(3) above shall be taken to be satisfied in relation to the original property (or, as the case may be, the part concerned) if—
    (a) the replacement property is owned by the transferee immediately before the death of the transferor and is not at that time subject to a binding contract for sale; and
    (b) throughout the period beginning with the date of the chargeable transfer and ending with the disposal, the original property was owned by the transferee and occupied (by the transferee or another) for the purposes of agriculture; and
    (c) throughout the period beginning with the date when the transferee acquired the replacement property ending with the death, the replacement property was owned by the transferee and occupied (by the transferee or another) for the purposes of agriculture; and
    (d) the replacement property is agricultural property immediately before the death.

(4) If the transferee has died before the transferor, any reference in subsections (1) to (3) above to the death of the transferor shall have effect as a reference to the death of the transferee.

(5) In any case where—
    (a) all or part of the original property has been disposed of before the death of the transferor or is subject to a binding contract for sale at the time of the death, and
    (b) the replacement property is acquired, or a binding contract for its acquisition is entered into, after the death of the transferor but within the allowed period after the disposal of the original property or part, and
    (c) the transferor dies before the transferee,

subsection (3) above shall have effect with the omission of paragraph (a) and (c), and as if any reference to a time immediately before the death of the transferor were a reference to the time when the replacement property is acquired.

(6) Section 124A (6) shall have effect in relation to the replacement property as it has effect in relation to the original property.

(7) Where a binding contract for the disposal of any property is entered into at any time before the disposal of the property, the disposal shall be regarded for the purposes of subsections (2)(a) and (5)(b) as taking place at that time.

(8) In this section 'the original property' and 'the transferee' have the same meaning as in section 124A above and 'allowed period' means the period of three years or such longer period as the Board may allow.

124C   Land in Habitat Schemes

(1) For the purpose of this Chapter, where any land is in a habitat scheme—
   (a) the land shall be regarded as agricultural land;
   (b) the management of the land in accordance with the requirements of the scheme shall be regarded as agriculture; and
   (c) buildings used in connection with such management shall be regarded as farm buildings.

(2) For the purposes of this section land is in a habitat scheme at any time if—
   (a) an application for aid under one of the enactments listed in subsection (3) below has been accepted in respect of the land; and
   (b) the undertakings to which the acceptance relates have neither been terminated by the expiry of the period to which they relate nor been treated as terminated.

(3) Those enactments are—
   (a) Regulation 3(1) of the Habitat (Water Fringe) Regulations 1994;
   (b) The Habitat (Former Set-Aside Land) Regulations 1994;
   (c) The Habitat (Salt-Marsh) Regulation 1994;
   (d) The Habitats (Scotland) Regulations 1994, if undertakings in respect of the land have been given under Regulation 3(ii)(a) of those Regulations:
   (e) The Habitat Improvement Regulations (Northern Ireland) 1995, if an undertaking in respect of the land has been given under Regulation 3(i)(a) of those Regulations.

(4) The Treasury may by order made by statutory instrument amend the list of enactments in subsection (3) above.

(5) The power to make an order under subsection (4) above shall be exercisable by statutory instrument subject to annulment in pursuance of a Resolution of the House of Commons.

(6) This section has effect—
   (a) in relation to any transfer of value made on or after 26th November 1996; and
   (b) in relation to transfers of value made before that date, for the purposes of any charge to tax or to extra tax which arises by reason of an event occurring on or after 26th November 1996.

Chapter III   Woodlands

125   The relief

(1) This section applies where—
   (a) part of the value of a person's estate immediately before his death is attributable to the value of land in the United Kingdom on which trees or underwood are growing but which is not agricultural property within the meaning of Chapter II of this part of this Act, and

(b)   either he was beneficially entitled to the land throughout the five years immediately preceding his death, or he became beneficially entitled to it otherwise than for a consideration in money or money's worth.

(1A)   But this section applies only if the land is in the United Kingdom or another state which is an EEA state (within the meaning given by Schedule 1 to the Interpretation Act 1978) at the time of the person's death.

(2)   Where this section applies and the person liable for the whole or part of the tax so elects—

(a)   the value of the trees or underwood shall be left out of account in determining the value transferred on the death, but

(b)   tax shall be charged in the circumstances mentioned in section 126 below.

(3)   An election under this section must be made by notice in writing to the Board within two years of the death, or such longer time as the Board may allow.

126   Charge to tax on disposal of trees or underwood
(1)   Where under section 125 above the value of any trees or underwood has been left out of account in determining the value transferred on the death of any person, and the whole or any part of the trees or underwood is disposed of (whether together with or apart from the land on which they are growing) then, if the disposal occurs before any part of the value transferred on the death of any other person is attributable to the value of that land, tax shall be charged in accordance with sections 127 and 128 below.

(2)   Subsection (1) above shall not apply to a disposal made by any person to his spouse or civil partner.

(3)   Where tax has been charged under this section on the disposal of any trees or underwood tax shall not again be charged in relation to the same death on a further disposal of the same trees or underwood.

127   Amount subject to charge
(1)   The amount on which tax is charged under section 126 above on a disposal of trees or underwood shall be—

(a)   if the disposal is a sale for full consideration in money or money's worth, an amount equal to the net proceeds of the sale, and

(b)   in any other case, an amount equal to the net value of the trees or underwood at the time of the disposal.

(2)   Where, if the value of the trees or underwood had not been left out of account in determining the value transferred on the death of the person in question—

(a)   it would have been taken into account in determining the value of any relevant business property for the purposes of relief under Chapter I of this Part of this Act in relation to the transfer of value made on his death, or

(b)   it would have been so taken into account if this Act had then been enforced, the amount on which tax is charged under section 126 above shall be reduced by 50 per cent.

128   Rate of charge
Tax charged under section 126 above on an amount determined under section 127 above shall be charged at the rate or rates at which it would have been charged on the death first mentioned in section 126 if—

(a) that amount, and any amount on which tax was previously charged under section 126 in relation to that death, had been included in the value transferred on death, and

(b) the amount on which the tax is charged had formed the highest part of that value.

129 Credit for tax charged

Where a disposal on which tax is chargeable under section 126 above is a chargeable transfer, the value transferred by it shall be calculated as if the value of the trees or underwood had been reduced by the tax chargeable under that section.

130 Interpretation

(1) In this Chapter—

(a) references to the value transferred on a death, or references to the value transferred by the chargeable transfer made on that death;

(b) references to the net proceeds of sale or the net value of any trees or underwood are references to the proceeds of sale or value after deduction of any expenses allowable under this chapter so far as those expenses are not allowable for the purposes of income tax; and

(c) references to the disposal of any trees or underwood include references to the disposal of any interest in the trees or underwood (and references to the disposal of the same trees or underwood shall, where the case so requires, be construed as referring to a disposal of the same interest).

(2) The expenses allowable under this chapter are, in relation to any trees or underwood the value of which has been left out of account on any death,—

(a) the expenses incurred in disposing of the trees or underwood; and

(b) the expenses incurred in replanting within three years of a disposal (or such longer time as the Board may allow) to replace the trees or underwood disposed of; and

(c) the expenses incurred in replanting to replace trees or underwood previously disposed of, so far as not allowable on the previous disposal.

INHERITANCE TAX ACT 1984

Part II   Exempt Transfers

Chapter II
Conditional Exemption

30   Conditionally exempt transfers

(1)   A transfer of value is an exempt transfer to the extent that the value transferred by it is attributable to property—

(a) which, on a claim made for the purpose, is designated by the Treasury under section 31 below, and

(b) with respect to which the requisite undertaking described in that section is given by such person as the Treasury think appropriate in the circumstances of the case or (where the property is an area of land within subsection (1)(d) of that section) with respect to which the requisite undertakings described in that section are given by such person or persons as the Treasury think appropriate in the circumstances of the case.

(2) A transfer of value exempt with respect to any property under this section or under section 76 of the Finance Act 1976 is referred to in this Act as a conditionally exempt transfer of that property.

(3) Subsection (1) above shall not apply to a transfer of value other than one which under section 4 above a person makes on his death unless—

    (a) the transferor or his spouse or civil partner, or the transferor and his spouse or civil partner between them, have been beneficially entitled to the property throughout the six years ending with the transfer, or

    (b) the transferor acquired the property on a death on the occasion of which there was a transfer of value under section 4 above which was itself a conditionally exempt transfer of the property.

(3A) The provisions of this section shall be disregarded in determining under section 3A above whether a transfer of value is a potentially exempt transfer.

(3B) No claim may be made under subsection (1) above with respect to a potentially exempt transfer until the transferor has died.

(3BA) A claim under subsection (1) above must be made no more than two years after the date of the transfer of value to which it relates or, in the case of a claim with respect to a potentially exempt transfer, the date of the death, or (in either case) within such longer period as the Board may allow.

(3C) Subsection (1) above shall not apply to a potentially exempt transfer to the extent that the value transferred by it is attributable to property which has been disposed of by sale during the period beginning with the date of the transfer and ending with the death of the transferor.

(4) Subsection (1) above does not apply to a transfer of value to the extent to which it is an exempt transfer under section 18 or 23 above.

31   Designation and undertakings

(1) The Treasury may designate under this section—

    (a) any relevant object which appears to the Board to be pre-eminent for its national, scientific, historic or artistic interest;

    (aa) any collection or group of relevant objects which, taken as a whole, appears to the Board to be pre-eminent for its national, scientific, historic or artistic interest;

    (b) any land which in the opinion of the Treasury is of outstanding scenic or historic or scientific interest;

    (c) any building for the preservation of which special steps should in the opinion of the Treasury be taken by reason of its outstanding historic or architectural interest;

    (d) any area of land which in the opinion of the Treasury is essential for the protection of the character and amenities of such a building as is mentioned in paragraph (c) above;

    (e) any object which in the opinion of the Treasury is historically associated with such a building as is mentioned in paragraph (c) above.

(1A) Where the transfer of value in relation to which the claim for designation is made is a potentially exempt transfer which (apart from section 30 above) has proved to be a chargeable transfer, the question whether any property is appropriate for designation under this section shall be determined by reference to circumstances existing after the death of the transferor.

(2) In the case of property within subsection (1)(a) or (aa) above, the requisite undertaking is that, until the person beneficially entitled to the property dies or the property is disposed of, whether by sale or gift or otherwise—

    (a) the property will be kept permanently in the United Kingdom and will not leave it temporarily except for a purpose and a period approved by the Treasury, and

    (b) such steps as are agreed between the Treasury and the person giving the undertaking, and are set out in it, will be taken for the preservation of the property and for securing reasonable access to the public.

(3) If it appears to the Treasury, on a claim made for the purpose, that any documents which are designated or to be designated under subsection (1)(a) or (aa) above contain information which for personal or other reasons ought to be treated as confidential, they may exclude those documents, either altogether or to such extent as they think fit, from so much of an undertaking given or to be given under subsection (2)(b) above as relates to public access.

(4) In the case of other property within subsection (1) above, the requisite undertaking is that, until the person beneficially entitled to the property dies or the property is disposed of, whether by sale or gift or otherwise, such steps as are agreed between the Treasury and the person giving the undertaking, and are set out in it, will be taken—

    (a) in the case of land falling within subsection (1)(b) above, for the maintenance of the land and the preservation of its character, and

    (b) in the case of any other property, for the maintenance, repair and preservation of the property and, if it is an object falling within subsection (1)(e) above, for keeping it associated with the building concerned;

and for securing reasonable access to the public.

(4A) In the case of an area of land within subsection (1)(d) above (relevant land) there is an additional requisite undertaking, which is that, until the person beneficially entitled to property falling within subsection (4C) below dies, or it is disposed of, whether by sale or gift or otherwise, specified steps will be taken for its maintenance, repair and preservation and for securing reasonable access to the public; and 'specified steps' means such steps as are agreed between the Treasury and the person giving the undertaking, and are set out in it.

(4B) Where different persons are entitled (either beneficially or otherwise) to different properties falling within subsection (4C) below, subsection (4A) above shall have effect to require separate undertakings as to the maintenance, repair, preservation and access of each of the properties to be given by such persons as the Treasury think appropriate in the circumstances of the case.

(4C) The following property falls within this subsection—

    (a) the building for the protection of whose character and amenities the relevant land is in the opinion of the Treasury essential;

    (b) any other area (or areas) of land which, in relation to the building, falls (or fall) within subsection (1)(d) above and which either lies (or lie) between the relevant land and the building or is (or are) in the opinion of the Treasury physically closely connected with the relevant land or the building.

(4D) Where subsection (4A) above requires an undertaking for the maintenance, repair, preservation and access of property, such an undertaking is required notwithstanding that some other undertaking for its maintenance, repair, preservation and access is effective.

(4E) Any undertaking given in pursuance of subsection (4A) above is for the purposes of this Act given with respect to the relevant land.

(4F) It is for the person seeking the designation of relevant land to secure that any undertaking required under subsection (4A) above is given.

(4FA) For the purposes of this section, the steps agreed for securing reasonable access to the public must ensure that the access that is secured is not confined to access only where a prior appointment has been made.

(4FB) Subject to subsection (3) above, where the steps that may be set out in any undertaking include steps for securing reasonable access to the public to any property, the steps that may be agreed and set out in that undertaking may also include steps involving the publication of—
  (a) the terms of any undertaking given or to be given for any of the purposes of this Act with respect to the property; or
  (b) any other information relating to the property which (apart from this subsection) would fall to be treated as confidential;

and references in this Act to an undertaking for access to any property shall be construed as including references to so much of any undertaking as provides for the taking of steps involving any such publication.

(4G) In a case where—
  (a) the transfer of value in question is a potentially exempt transfer which (apart from section 30 above) has proved to be a chargeable transfer, and
  (b) at the time of the transferor's death an undertaking by such a person as is mentioned in section 30(1)(b) above given under paragraph 3(3) of Schedule 4 to this Act or under section 258 of the 1992 Act is in force with respect to any property to which the value transferred by the transfer is attributable,

that undertaking shall be treated for the purposes of this Chapter as an undertaking given under section 30 above.

(5) In this section—
'national interest' includes interest within any part of the United Kingdom; and 'relevant object' means—
  (a) a picture, print, book, manuscript, work of art or scientific object, or
  (b) anything not falling within paragraph (a) above that does not yield income;

and in determining under subsection (1)(a) or (aa) above whether an object or a collection or group of objects is pre-eminent, regard shall be had to any significant association of the object, collection or group with a particular place.

32 Chargeable events
(1) Where there has been a conditionally exempt transfer of any property, tax shall be charged under this section on the first occurrence after the transfer (or, if the transfer was a potentially exempt transfer, after the death of the transferor) of an event which under this section is a chargeable event with respect to the property.

(2) If the Treasury are satisfied that at any time an undertaking given with respect to the property under section 30 above or subsection (5AA) below has not been observed in a material respect, the failure to observe the undertaking is a chargeable event with respect to the property.

(3) If—
  (a) the person beneficially entitled to the property dies, or
  (b) the property is disposed of, whether by sale or gift or otherwise.

the death or disposal is, subject to subsections (4) and (5) below, a chargeable event with respect to the property.

(4) A death or disposal is not a chargeable event with respect to any property if the personal representatives of the deceased (or, in the case of settled property, the trustees or the person next entitled) within three years of the death make or, as the case may be, the disposal is—
  (a) a disposal of the property by sale by private treaty to a body mentioned in Schedule 3 to this Act, or a disposal of it to such a body otherwise than by sale, or
  (b) a disposal in pursuance of section 230 below,

and a death or disposal of the property after such a disposal as is mentioned in paragraph (a) or (b) above is not a chargeable event with respect to the property unless there has again been a conditionally exempt transfer of it after that disposal.

(5) A death or disposal otherwise than by sale is not a chargeable event with respect to any property if—
  (a) the transfer of value made on the death or the disposal is itself a conditionally exempt transfer of the property, or
  (b) the condition specified in subsection (5AA) below is satisfied with respect to the property.

(5AA) The condition referred to in subsection (5)(b) above is satisfied if—
  (a) the requisite undertaking described in section 31 above is given with respect to the property by such person as the Board think appropriate in the circumstances of the case, or
  (b) (where the property is an area of land within section 31(1)(d) above) the requisite undertaking described in that section are given with respect to the property by such person or persons as the Board think appropriate in the circumstances of the case.

(5A) This section does not apply where section 32A below applies.

32A Associated properties
(1) For the purposes of this section the following properties are associated with each other, namely, a building falling within section 31(1)(c) above and (to the extent that any of the following exists) an area or areas of land falling within section 31(1)(d) above in relation to the building and an object or objects falling within section 31(1)(e) above in relation to the building; and this section applies where there are such properties, which are referred to as associated properties.

(2) Where there has been a conditionally exempt transfer of any property (or part), tax shall be charged under this section in respect of that property (or part) on the first occurrence after the transfer (or, if the transfer was a potentially exempt transfer, after

the death of the transferor) of an event which under this section is a chargeable event with respect to that property (or part).

(3) If the Treasury are satisfied that at any time an undertaking given under section 30 above or this section for the maintenance, repair, preservation, access or keeping of any of the associated properties has not been observed in a material respect, then (subject to subsection (10) below) the failure to observe the undertaking is a chargeable event with respect to the whole of each of the associated properties of which there has been a conditionally exempt transfer.

(4) If—
  (a)   the person beneficially entitled to property dies, or
  (b)   property (or part of it) is disposed of, whether by sale or gift or otherwise,

then, if the property is one of the associated properties and an undertaking for its maintenance, repair, preservation, access or keeping has been given under section 30 above or this section, the death or disposal is (subject to subsections (5) to (10) below) a chargeable event with respect to the whole of each of the associated properties of which there has been a conditionally exempt transfer.

(5) Subject to subsection (6) below, the death of a person beneficially entitled to property, or the disposal of property (or part), is not a chargeable event if the personal representatives of the deceased (or, in the case of settled property, the trustees or the person next entitled) within three years of the death make or, as the case may be, the disposal is—
  (a)   a disposal of the property (or part) concerned by sale by private treaty to a body mentioned in Schedule 3 to this Act, or to such a body otherwise than by sale, or
  (b)   a disposal of the property (or part) concerned in pursuance of section 230 below.

(6) Where a disposal mentioned in subsection (5)(a) or (b) above is a part disposal, that subsection does not make the event non-chargeable with respect to property other than that disposed of unless—
  (a)   the requisite undertaking described in section 31 above is given with respect to the property (or part) not disposed of by such person as the Board think appropriate in the circumstances of the case, or
  (b)   (where any of the property or part not disposed of is an area of land within section 31(1)(d) above) the requisite undertakings described in that section are given with respect to that property (or that part) by such person or persons as the Board think appropriate in the circumstances of the case;

and in this subsection 'part disposal' means a disposal of property which does not consist of or include the whole of each property which is one of the associated properties and of which there has been a conditionally exempt transfer.

(7) Where, after a relevant disposal (that is, a disposal mentioned in subsection (5)(a) or (b) above made in circumstances where that subsection applies), a person beneficially entitled to the property (or part) concerned dies or the property (or part) concerned is disposed of, the death or disposal is not a chargeable event with respect to the property (or part) concerned unless there has again been a conditionally exempt transfer of the property (or part) concerned after the relevant disposal.

(8) The death of a person beneficially entitled to property, or the disposal of property (or part) otherwise than by sale, is not a chargeable event if—
  (a)   the transfer of value made on the death or the disposal is itself a conditionally exempt transfer of the property (or part) concerned, or

(b) the condition specified in subsection (8A) below is satisfied with respect to the property (or part) concerned.

(8A) The condition referred to in subsection (8)(b) above is satisfied if—

(a) the requisite undertaking described in section 31 above is given with respect to the property (or part) by such person as the Board think appropriate in the circumstances of the case, or

(b) (where any of the property or part is an area of land within section 31(1)(d) above) the requisite undertakings described in that section are given with respect to the property (or part) by such person or persons as the Board think appropriate in the circumstances of the case.

(9) If the whole or part of any property is disposed of by sale and—

(a) the requisite undertaking described in section 31 above is given with respect to the property (or part) by such person as the Board think appropriate in the circumstances of the case, or

(b) (where any of the property or part is an area of land within section 31(1)(d) above) the requisite undertakings described in that section are given with respect to the property (or part) by such person or persons as the Board think appropriate in the circumstances of the case,

the disposal is a chargeable event only with respect to the whole or part actually disposed of (if it is a chargeable event with respect to such whole or part apart from this subsection).

(10) If—

(a) the Treasury are satisfied that there has been a failure to observe, as to one of the associated properties or part of it, an undertaking for the property's maintenance, repair, preservation, access or keeping, or

(b) there is a disposal of one of the associated properties or part of it,

and it appears to the Treasury that the entity consisting of the associated properties has not been materially affected by the failure or disposal, they may direct that it shall be a chargeable event only with respect to the property or part as to which there has been a failure or disposal (if it is a chargeable event with respect to that property or part apart from this subsection).

33 Amount of charge under section 32

(1) Tax chargeable in respect of any property under section 32 or 32A above by reference to a chargeable event shall be charged—

(a) on an amount equal to the value of the property at the time of the chargeable event; and

(b) at the following rate or rates—

(i) if the relevant person is alive, the rate or rates that would be applicable to that amount in accordance with section 7(2) above if it were the value transferred by a chargeable transfer made by the relevant person at that time;

(ii) if the relevant person is dead, the rate or rates that would have applied to that amount in accordance with the appropriate provision of section 7 above if it had been added to the value transferred on his death and had formed the highest part of that value.

Appendix 1 *Legislation*

(2) For the purposes of subsection (1)(b)(ii) above the appropriate provision of section 7 above is—

    (a) if the conditionally exempt transfer by the relevant person was made on death (but the property was not treated as forming part of his estate immediately before his death only by virtue of section 102(3) of the Finance Act 1986), subsection (1) of section 7 and

    (b) in any other case, subsection (2) of section 7.

(2A) The rate or rates of tax determined under subsection (1)(b)(i) above in respect of any chargeable event shall not be affected by the death of the relevant person after that event.

(3) Where the chargeable event is a disposal on sale and the sale—

    (a) was not intended to confer any gratuitous benefit on any person, and

    (b) was either a transaction at arm's length between persons not connected with each other or a transaction such as might be expected to be made at arm's length between persons not connected with each other,

the value of the property at the time of the chargeable event shall be taken for the purposes of subsection (1)(a) above to be equal to the proceeds of the sale.

(4) Where by virtue of section 30(4) above the conditionally exempt transfer extended only to part of the property, the amount mentioned in subsection (1)(a) above shall be proportionately reduced.

(5) The relevant person in relation to a chargeable event in respect of any property is—

    (a) if there has been only one conditionally exempt transfer of the property before the event, the person who made that transfer;

    (b) if there have been two or more such transfers and the last was before, or only one of them was within, the period of thirty years ending with the event, the person who made the last of those transfers;

    (c) if there have been two or more such transfers within that period, the person who made whichever of those transfers the Board may select.

(6) The conditionally exempt transfers to be taken into account for the purpose of subsection (5) above in relation to a chargeable event do not include transfers made before any previous chargeable event in respect of the same property or before any event which apart from section 32(4) above would have been such a chargeable event or, where the property has been disposed of as mentioned in section 32A(5) above, before any event which apart from section 32A(5) would have been such a chargeable event.

(7) Subject to subsection (8) below where after a conditionally exempt transfer of any property there is a chargeable transfer the value transferred by which is wholly or partly attributable to that property, any tax charged on that value so far as attributable to that property shall be allowed as a credit—

    (a) if the chargeable transfer is a chargeable event with respect to the property, against the tax chargeable in accordance with this section by reference to that event;

    (b) if the chargeable transfer is not such a chargeable event, against the tax chargeable in accordance with this section by reference to the next chargeable event with respect to the property.

(8) Where after a conditionally exempt transfer of any property there is a potentially exempt transfer the value transferred by which is wholly or partly attributable to that property and either—

   (a) the potentially exempt transfer is a chargeable event with respect to the property, or

   (b) after the potentially exempt transfer, but before the death of the person who is the transferor in relation to the potentially exempt transfer, a chargeable event occurs with respect to the property,

the tax charged in accordance with this section by reference to that chargeable event shall be allowed as a credit against any tax which may become chargeable, by reason of the potentially exempt transfer proving to be a chargeable transfer, on so much of the value transferred by that transfer as is attributable to the property; and subsection (7) above shall not apply with respect to any tax so becoming chargeable.

34 Reinstatement of transferor's cumulative total

(1) Where tax has become chargeable under section 32 or 32A above by reference to a chargeable event in respect of any property ('the relevant event') the rate or rates of tax applicable to any subsequent chargeable transfer made by the person who made the last conditionally exempt transfer of the property before the relevant event shall be determined as if the amount on which tax has become chargeable as aforesaid were value transferred by a chargeable transfer made by him at the time of the relevant event.

(2) Where the person who made the last conditionally exempt transfer of the property before the relevant event—

   (a) is dead, and

   (b) is for the purposes of section 33 above the relevant person in relation to a subsequent chargeable event,

section 33(1)(b)(ii) shall have effect as if the value transferred on his death were increased by the amount on which tax has become chargeable on the occasion of the relevant event.

(3) If—

   (a) the person who made the last conditionally exempt transfer of the property before the relevant event is not the relevant person for the purposes of section 33 above in relation to that event, and

   (b) at the time of that event or within the previous five years the property is or has been comprised in a settlement made not more than thirty years before that event, and

   (c) a person who is the settlor in relation to the settlement has made a conditionally exempt transfer of the property within those thirty years,

subsections (1) and (2) above shall have effect with the substitution for references to the person who made the last conditionally exempt transfer before the relevant event of a reference to any such person as is mentioned in paragraph (c) above.

(4) The conditionally exempt transfers to be taken into account for the purposes of subsection (3)(c) above in relation to the relevant event do not include transfers made before any previous chargeable event in respect of the same property or before any event which apart from section 32(4) above would have been such a chargeable event or, where the property has been disposed of as mentioned in section 32A(5) above, before any event which apart from section 32A(5) would have been such a chargeable event.

Appendix 1 *Legislation*

35 Conditional exemption on death before 7th April 1976
(1) Schedule 5 to this Act shall have effect with respect to certain cases where, by virtue of sections 31 to 34 of the Finance Act 1975 the value of any property was left out of account in determining the value transferred on a death before 7th April 1976.

(2) Where there has been a transfer of value in relation to which the value of any property has been left out of account under the provisions of sections 31 to 34 of the Finance Act 1975 and, before any tax has become chargeable in respect of that property under those provisions, there is a conditionally exempt transfer of that property, then, on the occurrence of a chargeable event in respect of that property—
- (a) if there has been no conditionally exempt transfer of the property on death, tax shall be chargeable either—
  - (i) under section 32 or 32A above (as the case may be), or
  - (ii) under Schedule 5 to this Act, as the Board may elect;
- (b) if there has been such a conditionally exempt transfer, tax shall be chargeable under section 32 or 32A above, (as the case may be) and not under that Schedule.

(3) In section 33(7) and (8) above, references to a conditionally exempt transfer of any property include references to a transfer of value in relation to which the value of any property has been left out of account under the provisions of sections 31 to 34 of the Finance Act 1975 and, in relation to such property, references to a chargeable event or to the tax chargeable in accordance with section 33 above by reference to a chargeable event include references to an event on the occurrence of which tax becomes chargeable under Schedule 5 to this Act, or to the tax so chargeable.

35A Variation of undertakings
(1) An undertaking given under section 30, 32 or 32A above or paragraph 5 of Schedule 5 to this Act may be varied from time to time by agreement between the Board and the person bound by the undertaking.

(2) Where the tribunal is satisfied that—
- (a) the Board have made a proposal for the variation of such an undertaking to the person bound by the undertaking,
- (b) that person has failed to agree to the proposed variation within six months after the date on which the proposal was made, and
- (c) it is just and reasonable, in all the circumstances, to require the proposed variation to be made,

the Commissioner may direct that the undertaking is to have effect from a specified date as if the proposed variation had been agreed to by the person bound by the undertaking.

(3) The date specified by the tribunal must not be less than sixty days after the date of the tribunal's direction.

(4) A direction under this section shall not take effect if, before the date specified by the tribunal, a variation different from that to which the direction relates is agreed between the Board and the person bound by the undertaking.

230 Acceptance of property in satisfaction of tax
(1) The Board may, if they think fit, and the Secretary of State agrees, on the application of any person liable to pay tax or interest payable under section 233 below, accept in satisfaction of the whole or any part of it any property to which this section applies.

(2) This section applies to any such land as may be agreed upon between the Board and the person liable to pay the tax.

(3) This section also applies to any objects which are or have been kept in any building—

    (a) if the Board have determined to accept or have accepted that building in satisfaction or part satisfaction of tax or of Estate Duty, or

    (b) if the building or any interest in it belongs to Her Majesty in right of the Crown or of the Duchy of Lancaster, or belongs to the Duchy of Cornwall or belongs to a Government department or is held for the purposes of a Government department, or

    (c) if the building is one of which the Secretary of State is guardian under the Ancient Monuments and Archaeological Areas Act 1979 or of which the Department of the Environment for Northern Ireland is guardian under the Historic Monuments and Archaeological Objects (Northern Ireland) Order 1995, or

    (d) if the building belongs to any body within Schedule 3 to this Act,

in any case where it appears to the Secretary of State desirable for the objects to remain associated with the building.

(4) This section also applies to—

    (a) any picture, print, book, manuscript, work of art, scientific object or other thing which the Secretary of State is satisfied is pre-eminent for its national, scientific, historic or artistic interest, and

    (b) any collection or group of pictures, prints, books, manuscripts, works of art, scientific objects or other things if the Secretary of State is satisfied that the collection or group, taken as a whole, is pre-eminent for its national, scientific, historic or artistic interest.

(5) In this section—

    'national interest' includes interest within any part of the United Kingdom;

and in determining under sub-section (4) above whether any object or collection or group of objects is pre-eminent, regard shall be had to any significant association of the object, collection or group within a particular place.

231 Powers to transfer property in satisfaction of tax

(1) Where a person has power to sell any property in order to raise money for the payment of tax, he may agree with the Board for the property to be accepted in satisfaction of that tax in pursuance of section 230 above; and except as regards the nature of the consideration and its receipt and application, any such agreement shall be subject to the same provisions and shall be treated for all purposes as a sale made in the exercise of the said power, and any conveyance or transfer made or purporting to be made to give effect to such an agreement shall have effect accordingly.

(2) The references in subsection (1) above to tax include references to interest payable under section 233 below.

(3) This section shall not affect paragraph 1(4) or 3(4) of Schedule 5 to this Act.

FINANCE ACT 1980

Stamp Duty

98 Maintenance funds for historic buildings

(1) No Stamp Duty shall be chargeable on any instrument whereby property ceases to be comprised in a settlement if as a result of the property or part of it becoming

comprised in another settlement (otherwise than by virtue of the instrument itself) by virtue of paragraph 9(1) or 17(1) of Schedule 4 to the Capital Transfer Tax Act 1984 there is no charge to Capital Transfer Tax in respect of the property ceasing to be comprised in the settlement or a reduced charge to that tax by virtue of paragraph 9(4) or 17(4) of that Schedule; but where any part of the property becomes comprised in the other settlement this subsection shall not affect the Stamp Duty chargeable on the instrument by reference to the other part.

(2) An instrument in respect of which Stamp Duty is not chargeable by virtue only of this section or in respect of which the duty chargeable is reduced by virtue of this section shall not be treated as duly stamped unless it is stamped in accordance with section 12 of the Stamp Act 1891 with a stamp denoting that it is not chargeable with any duty or that it is duly stamped.

INCOME TAX ACT 2007

Heritage Maintenance Settlements

Introduction

507   Overview of chapter

(1) This chapter makes provision about income arising from heritage maintenance property comprised in a heritage maintenance settlement.

(2) In this chapter—
> 'heritage body' means a body or charity of a kind mentioned in paragraph 3(1)(a)(ii) of Schedule 4 to IHTA 1984 (Maintenance Funds for Historic Buildings etc),
> 'heritage direction' means a direction under paragraph 1 of that Schedule,
> 'heritage maintenance property' means any property in respect of which a heritage direction has effect,
> 'heritage maintenance settlement' means a settlement which comprises heritage maintenance property, and
> 'property maintenance purpose' means any of the purposes mentioned in paragraph 3(1)(a)(i) of that Schedule.

(3) If a settlement comprises both heritage maintenance property and other property, the heritage maintenance property and the other property are treated as comprised in separate settlements for the purposes of chapters 2 to 8 of this Part and the following provisions—
> (a)   Sections 64 to 66 and sections 75 to 79 (trade loss relief against general income),
> (b)   Sections 83 to 88 (carry-forward trade loss relief) and
> (c)   Chapter 5 of Part 5 of ITTOIA 2005.

Trustees' election in respect of income etc

508   Election by trustees

(1) The trustees of a heritage maintenance settlement may elect for this section to have effect for a tax year.

(2) If an election under subsection (1) has effect for a tax year, the rules in subsections (3) and (4) apply.

(3) Income arising in the year from a heritage maintenance property comprised in the settlement, which would otherwise be treated as income of the settlor under chapter 5 of Part 5 of ITTOIA 2005, is not to be so treated.

(4) Any sum applied out of the heritage maintenance property in the year for a property maintenance purpose, which would otherwise be treated for income tax purposes as the income of a person—
- (a) because of the person's interest in (or occupation of) the property in respect of which the sum is applied, or
- (b) under section 633 of ITTOIA 2005 (capital sums paid to settlor by trustees of settlement), is not to be so treated.

(5) An election under subsection (1) must be made on or before the first anniversary of the normal self-assessment filing date for the tax year to which it relates.

509 Change of circumstances during a tax year

(1) If a change of circumstances arises during a tax year—
- (a) the part of the year before the change and the part of the year after the change are to be treated as separate tax years for the purposes of section 508, this section and section 510, and
- (b) separate elections under section 508(1) may be made for each part.

(2) A change of circumstances arises if conditions A and B are met.

(3) Condition A is that for any part of the tax year—
- (a) a heritage direction has effect, and
- (b) income arising from the heritage maintenance property comprised in the settlement is treated as income of the settlor under chapter 5 of Part 5 of ITTOIA 2005.

(4) Condition B is that for the remaining part of the year one or both of the following paragraphs applies—
- (a) no Heritage Direction has effect, and
- (b) no income arising from property comprised in the settlement is treated as income of the settlor under chapter 5 of Part 5 of ITTOIA 2005.

510 Sums applied for property maintenance purposes

(1) This section applies if—
- (a) income arises from the heritage maintenance property comprised in a heritage maintenance settlement in a tax year in respect of which no election is made under section 508,
- (b) the income is treated under chapter 5 of Part 5 of ITTOIA 2005 as income of the settlor, and
- (c) a sum in excess of the income is applied for a property maintenance purpose in the year.

(2) Any such sum which is so applied in that year, which would otherwise be treated for income tax purposes as the income of a person—
- (a) because of the person's interest in (or occupation of) the property in respect of which the sum is applied, or
- (b) under section 633 of ITTOIA 2005 (Capital sums paid to settlor by trustees of settlements),

is not to be so treated.

Appendix 1 *Legislation*

511 Prevention of double taxation: reimbursement of settlor

(1) This section applies to income arising from heritage maintenance property if—
  (a) the income is treated under Chapter 5 of Part 5 of ITTOIA 2005 as income of the settlor,
  (b) the income is applied in reimbursing the settlor for expenditure incurred by the settlor for a property maintenance purpose, and
  (c) the expenditure is deductible in calculating the profits of
     (i) a trade, or
     (ii) a UK property business,
  carried on by the settlor.

(2) Any such income—
  (a) is not to be brought into account as a receipt in calculating the profits of that trade or business and
  (b) is not to be treated as income of the settlor otherwise than under Chapter 5 or for Part 5 of ITTOIA 2005.

512 Charge to tax on some settlements

(1) Income tax is charged in respect of a heritage maintenance settlement on any of the occasions described in cases A to D subject to sections 516 and 517.

(2) Case A is where any of the property comprised in the settlement (whether capital or income) is applied otherwise than—
  (a) for a property maintenance purpose, or
  (b) as respects income not so applied and not accumulated, for the benefit of a heritage body.

(3) Case B is where any of that property, on ceasing to be comprised in the settlement, devolves otherwise than on a heritage body.

(4) Case C is where the heritage direction ceases to have effect in respect of the settlement.

(5) Case D is where any of the property comprised in the settlement, on ceasing at any time to be comprised in the settlement—
  (a) devolves on a heritage body, and
  (b) at or before that time an interest under the settlement is or has been acquired for a consideration in money or money's worth by that or another such body.

(6) For the purposes of subsection (5)(b) any acquisition from another such body is to be ignored.

513 Income charged

(1) Tax is charged under section 512 on the whole of the income—
  (a) which has arisen in the relevant period from the property comprised in the settlement, and
  (b) which has not been applied (whether or not it has been first accumulated) for a property maintenance purpose or for the benefit of the heritage body.

(2) In this section 'relevant period' means—
  (a) if tax has become chargeable under section 512 in respect of the settlement on a previous occasion, the period since the last occasion, and
  (b) in any other case, the period since the settlement took effect.

(3) Tax charged under section 512 is in addition to any tax otherwise chargeable.

(4) All the provisions of the Income Tax Acts relating to assessments and to the collection and recovery of Income Tax (so far as applicable) are to apply to that charge.

514 Persons liable
The persons liable for any tax charged under section 512 are the trustees of the settlement.

515 Rate of tax
Tax is charged under section 512 at the rate found by—
   (a) taking the additional rate for the tax year during which the charge arises, and
   (b) reducing it by the trust rate for that year.

516 Transfer of property between settlements
(1) This section applies if the whole of the property comprised in a settlement becomes comprised in another settlement because of a tax-free transfer.

(2) The occasion of charge under section 512, which would otherwise occur at the time of the transfer, occurs when tax first becomes chargeable under that section in respect of any settlement comprising the transferred property ('the chargeable settlement').

(3) For the purposes of section 513(1) as it applies to the chargeable settlement, the relevant period is adjusted so that it begins—
   (a) on the occasion when tax last became chargeable under section 512 in respect of any previous settlement from which the property was transferred, or
   (b) if there has been no such occasion, when such previous settlement (or the first of them) took effect.

(4) In this section 'tax free transfer' means a transfer of property from one settlement to another in either of the following cases—
   (a) where paragraph 9(1) of Schedule 4 to IHTA 1984 provides (or, but for paragraph 9(4) of that Schedule, would provide) an exception from charge in respect of the property, or
   (b) where, both immediately before and immediately after the transfer, the property is heritage maintenance property.

517 Exemption for income treated as income of settlor
(1) Tax is not chargeable under section 512 in respect of income which is treated under section 624 or 629 of ITTOIA 2005 as income of the settlor.

(2) If such income arises in a tax year, any sums applied in the year—
   (a) for a property maintenance purpose, or
   (b) for the benefit of a heritage body,

are to be treated as paid first out of that income and, so far as there is any excess, out of income that does not fall within subsection (1).

SCHEDULE 3

GIFTS FOR NATIONAL PURPOSES ETC

SECTIONS 25, 32, 230 ETC

The National Gallery.
The British Museum.
The National Museums of Scotland.

The National Museum of Wales.

The Ulster Museum.

Any other similar national institution which exists wholly or mainly for the purpose of the public benefit or collection of scientific, historic or artistic interest and which is approved for the purposes of this schedule by the Treasury.

Any museum or art gallery in the United Kingdom which exists wholly or mainly for that purpose and is maintained by a local authority or university in the United Kingdom.

Any library the main function of which is to serve the needs of teaching or research at a university in the United Kingdom.

The Historic Buildings and Monuments Commissioner for England.

The National Trust for Places of Historic Interest or Natural Beauty.

The National Trust for Scotland for Places of Historic Interest or Natural Beauty.

The National Art Collections Fund.

The Trustees of the National Heritage Memorial Fund.

The National Endowment for Science, Technology and the Arts.

The Friends of the National Libraries.

The Historic Churches Preservation Trust.

Nature Conservancy Council for England.

Commission for Rural Communities.

Natural England.

Scottish Natural Heritage.

Countryside Council for Wales.

The Marine Management Organisation.

Any local authority.

Any government department (including the National Debt Commissioners).

Any university or university college in the United Kingdom.

A health service body, within the meaning of section 986 of the Corporation Tax Act 2010.

SCHEDULE 4

MAINTENANCE FUNDS FOR HISTORIC BUILDINGS, ETC

SECTIONS 27, 58, 77 ETC

PART I
TREASURY DIRECTIONS

Giving of directions

1—(1) If the conditions mentioned in paragraph 2(1) below are fulfilled in respect of settled property, the Treasury shall, on a claim made for the purpose, give a direction under this paragraph in respect of the property.

(2) The Treasury may give a direction under this paragraph in respect of property proposed to be comprised in a settlement or to be held on particular trusts in any case where, if the property were already so comprised or held, they would be obliged to give the direction.

(3) Property comprised in a settlement by virtue of a transfer of value made before the coming into force of section 94 of the Finance Act 1982 and exempt under section 84 of the Finance Act 1976 shall be treated as property in respect of which a direction has been given under this paragraph.

Conditions

2—(1) The conditions referred to in paragraph 1 above are—
- (a) that the Treasury are satisfied—
  - (i) that the trusts on which the property is held comply with the requirements mentioned in paragraph 3 below, and
  - (ii) that the property is of a character and amount appropriate for the purposes of those trusts; and
- (b) that the trustees—
  - (i) are approved by the Treasury,
  - (ii) include a trust corporation, a solicitor, an accountant or a member of such other professional body as the Treasury may allow in the case of the property concerned, and
  - (iii) are, at the time the direction is given, resident in the United Kingdom.

(2) For the purposes of this paragraph trustees shall be regarded as resident in the United Kingdom if—
- (a) the general administration of the trusts is ordinarily carried on in the United Kingdom, and
- (b) the trustees or a majority of them (and, where there is more than one class of trustees, a majority of each class) are resident in the United Kingdom;

and where a trustee is a trust corporation, the question whether the trustee is resident in the United Kingdom shall, for the purposes of paragraph (b) above, be determined as for the purposes of corporation tax.

(3) In this paragraph—
'accountant' means a member of an incorporated society of accountants;
'trust corporation' means a person that is a trust corporation for the purposes of the Law of Property Act 1925 or for the purposes of Article 9 of the Administration of Estates (Northern Ireland) Order 1979.

3—(1) The requirements referred to in paragraph 2(1)(a)(i) above are (subject to paragraph 4 below)—
- (a) that none of the property held on the trusts can at any time in the period of six years beginning with the date on which it became so held be applied otherwise than—
  - (i) for the maintenance, repair or preservation of, or making provision for public access to, property which is for the time being qualifying property, for the maintenance, repair or preservation of property held on the trusts or for such improvement of property so held as is reasonable having regard to the purposes of the trusts, or for defraying the expenses of the trustees in relation to the property so held;

553

(ii) as respects income not so applied and not accumulated, for the benefit of a body within Schedule 3 to this Act or of a qualifying charity; and

(b) that none of the property can, on ceasing to be held on the trusts at any time in that period or, if the settlor dies in that period, at any time before his death, devolve otherwise than on any such body or charity; and

(c) that income arising from property held on the trusts cannot at any time after the end of that period be applied except as mentioned in paragraph (a)(i) or (ii) above.

(2) Property is qualifying property for the purposes of sub-paragraph (1) above if—

(a) it has been designated under section 34(1) of the Finance Act 1975 or section 77(1)(b), (c), (d) or (e) of the Finance Act 1976 or section 31(1)(b), (c), (d) or (e) of this Act; and

(b) the requisite undertaking has been given with respect to it under section 34 of the Finance Act 1975 or under section 76, 78(5)(b) or 82(3) of the Finance Act 1976 or under section 30, 32(5)(b), 32A(6), (8)(b) or (9)(b) or 79(3) of this Act or paragraph 5 of Schedule 5 to this Act; and

(c) tax has not (since the last occasion on which such an undertaking was given) become chargeable with respect to it under the said section 34 or under section 78 or 82(3) of the Finance Act 1976 or under section 32, 32A or 79(3) of this Act or paragraph 3 of Schedule 5 to this Act.

(3) If it appears to the Treasury that provision is, or is to be, made by a settlement for the maintenance, repair or preservation of any such property as is mentioned in subsection (1) (b), (c), (d) or (e) of section 31 of this Act they may, on a claim made for the purpose—

(a) designate that property under this sub-paragraph, and

(b) accept with respect to it an undertaking such as is described in subsection (4), or (as the case may be) undertakings such as are described in subsections (4) and (4A), of that section;

and, if they do so, sub-paragraph (2) above shall have effect as if the designation were under that section and the undertaking or undertakings under section 30 of this Act and as if the reference to tax becoming chargeable were a reference to the occurrence of an event on which tax would become chargeable under section 32 or 32A of this Act if there had been a conditionally exempt transfer of the property when the claim was made and the undertaking or undertakings had been given under section 30.

(3A) Section 35A of this Act shall apply in relation to an undertaking given under sub-paragraph (3) above as it applies in relation to an undertaking given under section 30 of this Act.

(4) A charity is a qualifying charity for the purposes of sub-paragraph (1) above if it exists wholly or mainly for maintaining, repairing or preserving for the public benefit buildings of historic or architectural interest, land of scenic, historic or scientific interest or objects of national, scientific, historic or artistic interest; and in this sub-paragraph 'national interest' includes interest within any part of the United Kingdom.

(5) Designations, undertakings and acceptances made under section 84(6) of the Finance Act 1976 or section 94(3) of the Finance Act 1982 shall be treated as made under sub-paragraph (3) above.

(5A) In the case of property which, if a direction is given under paragraph 1 above, will be property to which paragraph 15A below applies, sub-paragraph (1)(b) above shall have effect as if for the reference to the settlor there were substituted a reference to either the settlor or the person referred to in paragraph 15A(2).

4—(1) Paragraphs (a) and (b) of paragraph 3(1) above do not apply to property which—

(a) was previously comprised in another settlement, and

(b) ceased to be comprised in that settlement and became comprised in the current settlement in circumstances such that by virtue of paragraph 9(1) below there was no charge (or, but for paragraph 9(4), there would have been no charge) to tax in respect of it;

and in relation to any such property paragraph 3(1)(c) above shall apply with the omission of the words 'at any time after the end of that period'.

(2) Sub-paragraph (1) above shall not have effect if the time when the property comprised in the previous settlement devolved otherwise than on any such body or charity as is mentioned in paragraph 3(1)(a) above fell before the expiration of the period of six years there mentioned; but in such a case paragraph 3(1) above shall apply to the current settlement as if for the references to that period of six years there were substituted references to the period beginning with the date on which the property became comprised in the current settlement and ending six years after the date on which it became held on the relevant trusts of the previous settlement (or, where this sub-paragraph has already had effect in relation to the property, the date on which it became held on the relevant trusts of the first settlement in the series).

Withdrawal

5 If in the Treasury's opinion the facts concerning any property or its administration cease to warrant the continuance of the effect of a direction given under paragraph 1 above in respect of the property, they may at any time by notice in writing to the trustees withdraw the direction on such grounds, and from such date, as may be specified in the notice; and the direction shall cease to have effect accordingly.

Information

6 Where a direction under paragraph 1 above has effect in respect of property, the trustees shall from time to time furnish the Treasury with such accounts and other information relating to the property as the Treasury may reasonably require.

Enforcement of trusts

7 Where a direction under paragraph 1 above has effect in respect of property, the trusts on which the property is held shall be enforceable at the suit of the Treasury and the Treasury shall, as respects the appointment, removal and retirement of trustees, have the rights and powers of a beneficiary.

PART II
PROPERTY LEAVING MAINTENANCE FUNDS

Charge to tax

8—(1) This paragraph applies to settled property which is held on trusts which comply with the requirements mentioned in paragraph 3(1) above, and in respect of which a direction given under paragraph 1 above has effect.

(2) Subject to paragraphs 9 and 10 below, there shall be a charge to tax under this paragraph—
  (a) where settled property ceases to be property to which this paragraph applies, otherwise than by virtue of an application of the kind mentioned in paragraph 3(1)(a)(i) or (ii) above or by devolving on any such body or charity as is mentioned in paragraph 3(1)(a)(ii);
  (b) in a case in which paragraph (a) above does not apply, where the trustees make a disposition (otherwise than by such an application) as a result of which the value of settled property to which this paragraph applies is less than it would be but for the disposition.

(3) Subsections (4), (5) and (10) of section 70 of this Act shall apply for the purposes of this paragraph as they apply for the purposes of that section (with the substitution of a reference to sub-paragraph (2)(b) above for the reference in section 70(4) to section 70(2)(b)).

(4) The rate at which tax is charged under this paragraph shall be determined in accordance with paragraphs 11 to 15 below.

(5) The devolution of property on a body or charity shall not be free from charge by virtue of sub-paragraph (2)(a) above if, at or before the time of devolution, an interest under the settlement in which the property was comprised immediately before the devolution is or has been acquired for a consideration in money or money's worth by that or another such body or charity; but for the purposes of this sub-paragraph any acquisition from another such body or charity shall be disregarded.

(6) For the purposes of sub-paragraph (5) above a body or charity shall be treated as acquiring an interest for a consideration in money or money's worth if it becomes entitled to the interest as a result of transactions which include a disposition for such consideration (whether to that body or charity or to another person) of that interest or of other property.

Exceptions from charge

9—(1) Tax shall not be charged under paragraph 8 above in respect of property which, within the permitted period after the occasion on which tax would be chargeable under that paragraph, becomes comprised in another settlement as a result of a transfer of value which is exempt under section 27 of this Act. (2) In sub-paragraph (1) above 'the permitted period' means the period of thirty days except in a case where the occasion referred to is the death of the settlor, and in such a case means the period of two years.

(3) Sub-paragraph (1) above shall not apply to any property if the person who makes the transfer of value has acquired it for a consideration in money or money's worth; and for the purposes of this sub-paragraph a person shall be treated as acquiring any property for such consideration if he becomes entitled to it as a result of transactions which include a disposition for such consideration (whether to him or another) of that or other property.

(4) If the amount on which tax would be charged apart from sub-paragraph (1) above in respect of any property exceeds the value of the property immediately after it becomes comprised in the other settlement (less the amount of any consideration for its transfer received by the person who makes the transfer of value), that sub-paragraph shall not apply but the amount on which tax is charged shall be equal to the excess.

556

(5) The reference in sub-paragraph (4) above to the amount on which tax would be charged is a reference to the amount on which it would be charged apart from—

(a)   section 5(5)(b) of this Act (as applied by paragraph 8(3) above), and

(b)   Chapters I and II of Part V of this Act;

and the reference in that sub-paragraph to the amount on which tax is charged is a reference to the amount on which it would be charged apart from section 70(5)(b) and those Chapters.

10—(1) Tax shall not be charged under paragraph 8 above in respect of property which ceases to be property to which that paragraph applies on becoming—

(a)   property to which the settlor or his spouse or civil partner is beneficially entitled, or

(b)   property to which the settlor's widow or widower or surviving civil partner is beneficially entitled if the settlor has died in the two years preceding the time when it becomes such property.

(2) If the amount on which tax would be charged apart from sub-paragraph (1) above in respect of any property exceeds the value of the property immediately after it becomes property of a description specified in paragraph (a) or (b) of that sub-paragraph (less the amount of any consideration for its transfer received by the trustees), that sub-paragraph shall not apply but the amount on which tax is charged shall be equal to the excess.

(3) The reference in sub-paragraph (2) above to the amount on which tax would be charged is a reference to the amount on which it would be charged apart from—

(a)   section 70(5)(b) of this Act (as applied by paragraph 8(3) above), and

(b)   Chapters I and II of Part V of this Act;

and the reference in sub-paragraph (2) above to the amount on which tax is charged is a reference to the amount on which it would be charged apart from section 70(5)(b) and those Chapters.

(4) Sub-paragraph (1) above shall not apply in relation to any property if, at or before the time when it becomes property of a description specified in paragraph (a) or (b) of that sub-paragraph, an interest under the settlement in which the property was comprised immediately before it ceased to be property to which paragraph 8 above applies is or has been acquired for a consideration in money or money's worth by the person who becomes beneficially entitled.

(5) For the purposes of sub-paragraph (4) above a person shall be treated as acquiring an interest for a consideration in money or money's worth if he becomes entitled to the interest as a result of transactions which include a disposition for such consideration (whether to him or to another person) of that interest or of other property.

(6) Sub-paragraph (1) above shall not apply in respect of property if it was relevant property before it became (or last became) property to which paragraph 8 above applies and, by virtue of paragraph 16(1) or 17(1) below, tax was not chargeable (or, but for paragraph 16(2) or 17(4), would not have been chargeable) under section 65 of this Act in respect of its ceasing to be relevant property before becoming (or last becoming) property to which paragraph 8 above applies.

(7) Sub-paragraph (1) above shall not apply in respect of property if—

(a)   before it last became property to which paragraph 8 above applies it was comprised in another settlement in which it was property to which that paragraph applies, and

(b) it ceased to be comprised in the other settlement and last became property to which that paragraph applies in circumstances such that by virtue of paragraph 9(1) above there was no charge (or, but for paragraph 9(4), there would have been no charge) to tax in respect of it.

(8) Sub-paragraph (1) above shall not apply unless the person who becomes beneficially entitled to the property is domiciled in the United Kingdom at the time when he becomes so entitled.

Rates of charge

11—(1) This paragraph applies where tax is chargeable under paragraph 8 above and—
- (a) the property in respect of which the tax is chargeable was relevant property before it became (or last became) property to which that paragraph applies, and
- (b) by virtue of paragraph 16(1) or 17(1) below tax was not chargeable (or, but for paragraph 16(2) or 17(4), would not have been chargeable) under section 65 of this Act in respect of its ceasing to be relevant property on or before becoming (or last becoming) property to which paragraph 8 above applies.

(2) Where this paragraph applies, the rate at which the tax is charged shall be the aggregate of the following percentages—
- (a) 0.25 per cent for each of the first forty complete successive quarters in the relevant period,
- (b) 0.20 per cent for each of the next forty,
- (c) 0.15 per cent for each of the next forty,
- (d) 0.10 per cent for each of the next forty, and
- (e) 0.05 per cent for each of the next forty.

(3) In sub-paragraph (2) above 'the relevant period' means the period beginning with the latest of—
- (a) the date of the last ten-year anniversary of the settlement in which the property was comprised before it ceased (or last ceased) to be relevant property,
- (b) the day on which the property became (or last became) relevant property before it ceased (or last ceased) to be such property, and
- (c) 13th March 1975, and ending with the day before the event giving rise to the charge.

(4) Where the property in respect of which the tax is chargeable has at any time ceased to be and again become property to which paragraph 8 above applies in circumstances such that by virtue of paragraph 9(1) above there was no charge to tax in respect of it (or, but for paragraph 9(4), there would have been no charge), it shall for the purposes of this paragraph be treated as having been property to which paragraph 8 above applies throughout the period mentioned in paragraph 9(1).

12—(1) This paragraph applies where tax is chargeable under paragraph 8 above and paragraph 11 above does not apply.

(2) Where this paragraph applies, the rate at which the tax is charged shall be the higher of—
- (a) the first rate (as determined in accordance with paragraph 13 below), and
- (b) the second rate (as determined in accordance with paragraph 14 below).

13—(1) The first rate is the aggregate of the following percentages—
- (a) 0.25 per cent for each of the first forty complete successive quarters in the relevant period,

(b) 0.20 per cent for each of the next forty,
(c) 0.15 per cent for each of the next forty,
(d) 0.10 per cent for each of the next forty, and
(e) 0.05 per cent for each of the next forty.

(2) In sub-paragraph (1) above 'the relevant period' means the period beginning with the day on which the property in respect of which the tax is chargeable became (or first became) property to which paragraph 8 above applies, and ending with the day before the event giving rise to the charge.

(3) For the purposes of sub-paragraph (2) above, any occasion on which property became property to which paragraph 8 above applies, and which occurred before an occasion of charge to tax under that paragraph in respect of the property, shall be disregarded.

(4) The reference in sub-paragraph (3) above to an occasion of charge to tax under paragraph 8 does not include a reference to—
(a) the occasion by reference to which the rate is being determined in accordance with this Schedule, or
(b) an occasion which would not be an occasion of charge but for paragraph 9(4) above.

14—(1) If the settlor is alive, the second rate is the effective rate at which tax would be charged, on the amount on which it is chargeable, in accordance with the appropriate provision of section 7 of this Act if the amount were the value transferred by a chargeable transfer made by him on the occasion on which the tax becomes chargeable.

(1A) The rate or rates of tax determined under sub-paragraph (1) above in respect of any occasion shall not be affected by the death of the settlor after that occasion.

(2) If the settlor is dead, the second rate is (subject to sub-paragraph (3) below) the effective rate at which tax would have been charged, on the amount on which it is chargeable, in accordance with the appropriate provision of section 7 of this Act if the amount had been added to the value transferred on his death and had formed the highest part of it.

(3) If the settlor died before 13 March 1975, the second rate is the effective rate at which tax would have been charged, on the amount on which it is chargeable ('the chargeable amount'), in accordance with the appropriate provision of section 7 of this Act if the settlor had died when the event occasioning the charge under paragraph 8 above occurred, the value transferred on his death had been equal to the amount on which estate duty was chargeable when he in fact died, and the chargeable amount had been added to that value and had formed the highest part of it.

(4) Where, in the case of a settlement ('the current settlement'), tax is chargeable under paragraph 8 above in respect of property which—
(a) was previously comprised in another settlement, and
(b) ceased to be comprised in that settlement and became comprised in the current settlement in circumstances such that by virtue of paragraph 9(1) above there was no charge (or, but for paragraph 9(4), there would have been no charge) to tax in respect of it.

then, subject to sub-paragraph (5) below, references in sub-paragraphs (1) to (3) above to the settlor shall be construed as references to the person who was the settlor in relation to the settlement mentioned in paragraph (a) above (or, if the Board so determine, the person who was the settlor in relation to the current settlement).

(5) Where, in the case of a settlement ('the current settlement'), tax is chargeable under paragraph 8 above in respect of property which—

    (a)   was previously comprised at different times in other settlements ('the previous settlements'), and

    (b)   ceased to be comprised in each of them, and became comprised in another of them or in the current settlement, in circumstances such that by virtue of paragraph 9(1) above there was no charge (or, but for paragraph 9(4), there would have been no charge) to tax in respect of it,

references in sub-paragraphs (1) to (3) above to the settlor shall be construed as references to the person who was the settlor in relation to the previous settlement in which the property was first comprised (or, if the Board so determine, any person selected by them who was the settlor in relation to any of the other previous settlements or the current settlement).

(6) Sub-paragraph (7) below shall apply if—

    (a)   in the period of seven years preceding a charge under paragraph 8 above (the 'current charge'), there has been another charge under that paragraph where tax was charged at the second rate, and

    (b)   the person who is the settlor for the purposes of the current charge is the settlor for the purposes of the other charge (whether or not the settlements are the same and, if the settlor is dead, whether or not he has died since the other charge);

and in sub-paragraph (7) below the other charge is referred to as the 'previous charge'.

(7) Where this sub-paragraph applies, the amount on which tax was charged on the previous charge (or, if there have been more than one, the aggregate of the amounts on which tax was charged on each)—

    (a)   shall, for the purposes of calculating the rate of the current charge under sub-paragraph (1) above, be taken to be the value transferred by a chargeable transfer made by the settlor immediately before the occasion of the current charge, and

    (b)   shall, for the purposes of calculating the rate of the current charge under sub-paragraph (2) or (3) above, be taken to increase the value there mentioned by an amount equal to that amount (or aggregate).

(8) References in sub-paragraphs (1) to (3) above to the effective rate are to the rate found by expressing the tax chargeable as a percentage of the amount on which it is charged.

(9) For the purposes of sub-paragraph (1) above the appropriate provision of section 7 of this Act is subsection (2), and for the purposes of sub-paragraphs (2) and (3) above it is (if the settlement was made on death) subsection (1) and (if not) subsection (2).

15 Where property is, by virtue of paragraph 1(3) above, treated as property in respect of which a direction has been given under paragraph 1, it shall for the purposes of paragraphs 11 to 14 above be treated as having become property to which paragraph 8 above applies when the transfer of value mentioned in paragraph 1(3) was made.

Maintenance fund following interest in possession

15A—(1) In relation to settled property to which this paragraph applies, the provisions of this Part of this Schedule shall have effect with the modifications set out in the following sub-paragraphs.

(2) This paragraph applies to property which became property to which paragraph 8 above applies on the occasion of a transfer of value which was made by a person beneficially entitled to an interest in possession in the property, and which (so far as the value transferred by it was attributable to the property)—

    (a)   was an exempt transfer by virtue of the combined effect of either—

        (i)   sections 27 and 57(5) of this Act, or

        (ii)   sections 27 and 57A of this Act, and

    (b)   would but for those sections have been a chargeable transfer;

and in the following sub-paragraphs 'the person entitled to the interest in possession' means the person above referred to.

(3) Paragraph 9(2) shall have effect as if for the reference to the settlor there were substituted a reference to either the settlor or the person entitled to the interest in possession.

(4) Paragraph 10 shall not apply if the person entitled to the interest in possession had died at or before the time when the property became property to which paragraph 8 above applies; and in any other case shall have effect with the substitution in sub-paragraph (1) of the following words for the words from 'on becoming' onwards—

    '(a)   on becoming property to which the person entitled to the interest in possession is beneficially entitled, or

    (b)   on becoming—

        (i)   property to which that person's spouse or civil partner is beneficially entitled, or

        (ii)   property to which that person's widow or widower or surviving civil partner is beneficially entitled if that person has died in the two years preceding the time when it becomes such property;

but paragraph (b) above applies only where the spouse or civil partner, widow or widower or surviving civil partner would have become beneficially entitled to the property on the termination of the interest in possession had the property not then become property to which paragraph 8 above applies.

(5) Paragraph 11 shall not apply.

(6) Sub-paragraphs (1) to (3) of paragraph 14 shall have effect as if for the references to the settlor there were substituted references to the person entitled to the interest in possession.

(7) Sub-paragraph (4) of paragraph 14 shall have effect with the insertion after paragraph (b) of the words 'and

    (c)   was, in relation to either of those settlements, property to which paragraph 15A below applied,',

and with the substitution for the words from 'settlor shall' onwards of the words 'person entitled to the interest in possession shall, if the Board so determine, be construed as references to any person who was the settlor in relation to the current settlement.'

(8) Sub-paragraph (5) of paragraph 14 shall have effect with the insertion after paragraph (b) of the words 'and

    (c)   was, in relation to any of those settlements, property to which paragraph 15A below applied,', and with the substitution for the words from 'settlor shall' onwards of the words 'person entitled to the interest in possession shall, if the Board so determine, be construed as references to any person selected by them who was the settlor in relation to any of the previous settlements or the current settlement.'

(9) Except in a case where the Board have made a determination under subparagraph (4) or (5) of paragraph 14, sub-paragraphs (6) and (7) of that paragraph shall have effect as if for the references to the settlor there were substituted references to the person entitled to the interest in possession.

(10) Sub-paragraph (9) of paragraph 14 shall have effect with the substitution for the words '(if the settlement was made on death)' of the words '(if the person entitled to the interest in possession had died at or before the time when the property became property to which paragraph 8 above applies)'.

PART III
PROPERTY BECOMING COMPRISED IN MAINTENANCE FUNDS

16—(1) Tax shall not be charged under section 65 of this Act in respect of property which ceases to be relevant property on becoming property in respect of which a direction under paragraph 1 above then has effect.

(2) If the amount on which tax would be charged apart from sub-paragraph (1) above in respect of any property exceeds the value of the property immediately after it becomes property in respect of which the direction has effect (less the amount of any consideration for its transfer received by the trustees of the settlement in which it was comprised immediately before it ceased to be relevant property), that sub-paragraph shall not apply but the amount on which tax is charged shall be equal to the excess.

(3) Sub-paragraph (1) above shall not apply in relation to any property if, at or before the time when it becomes property in respect of which the direction has effect, an interest under the settlement in which it was comprised immediately before it ceased to be relevant property is or has been acquired for a consideration in money or money's worth by the trustees of the settlement in which it becomes comprised on ceasing to be relevant property.

(4) For the purposes of sub-paragraph (3) above trustees shall be treated as acquiring an interest for a consideration in money or money's worth if they become entitled to the interest as a result of transactions which include a disposition for such consideration (whether to them or to another person) of that interest or of other property.

17—(1) Tax shall not be charged under section 65 of this Act in respect of property which ceases to be relevant property if within the permitted period an individual makes a transfer of value—
    (a)   which is exempt under section 27 of this Act, and
    (b)   the value transferred by which is attributable to that property.

(2) In sub-paragraph (1) above 'the permitted period' means the period of thirty days beginning with the day on which the property ceases to be relevant property except in

a case where it does so on the death of any person, and in such a case means the period of two years beginning with that day.

(3) Sub-paragraph (1) above shall not apply if the individual has acquired the property concerned for a consideration in money or money's worth; and for the purposes of this sub-paragraph an individual shall be treated as acquiring any property for such consideration if he becomes entitled to it as a result of transactions which include a disposition for such consideration (whether to him or another) of that or other property.

(4) If the amount on which tax would be charged apart from sub-paragraph (1) above in respect of any property exceeds the value of the property immediately after the transfer there referred to (less the amount of any consideration for its transfer received by the individual), that sub-paragraph shall not apply but the amount on which tax is charged shall be equal to the excess.

18 In paragraphs 16(2) and 17(4) above the references to the amount on which tax would be charged are references to the amount on which it would be charged apart from—
  (a) paragraph (b) of section 65(2) of this Act, and
  (b) Chapters I and II of Part V of this Act;

and the references to the amount on which tax is charged are references to the amount on which it would be charged apart from that paragraph and those Chapters.

NATIONAL HERITAGE ACT 1980

Property accepted in satisfaction of tax

9 Disposal of Property accepted by Commissioners
(1) Any property accepted in satisfaction of tax shall be disposed of in such manner as the Secretary of State may direct.

(3) Where the Secretary of State has determined that any property accepted in satisfaction of tax is to be disposed of under this section to any such institution or body as is mentioned in subsection 2 (above) or to any other person who is willing to accept it, he may direct that the disposal shall be effected by means of a transfer direct to that institution or body, or direct to that other person instead of being transferred to the Commissioners.

(4) The Secretary of State may in any case direct that any property accepted in satisfaction of tax shall, instead of being transferred to the Commissioners, be transferred to a person nominated by the Secretary of State; and where property is so transferred the person to whom it is transferred shall, subject to any directions subsequently given under subsection (1) or (2) above, hold the property and manage it in accordance with such directions as may be given by the Secretary of State.

(7) References in this section to the disposal or transfer of any property include references to leasing, sub-leasing or lending it for any period and on any terms.

INHERITANCE TAX ACT 1984

THE 'DOUBLE GROSSING' PROVISIONS: ALLOCATION OF EXEMPTIONS

Chapter III   Exempt Transfers

36   Preliminary

Where any one or more of sections 18, 23 to 27 and 30 above apply in relation to a transfer of value but the transfer is not wholly exempt—

    (a) any question as to the extent to which it is exempt or, where it is exempt up to a limit, how any excess over the limit is to be attributed to the gifts concerned shall be determined in accordance with sections 37 to 40 below; and

    (b) section 41 below shall have affect as respects the burden of tax.

37   Abatement of gifts

(1) Where a gift would be abated owing to an insufficiency of assets and without regard to any tax chargeable, the gifts shall be treated for the purposes of the following provisions of this Chapter as so abated.

(2) Where the value attributable, in accordance with section 38 below, to specific gifts exceeds the value transferred the gifts shall be treated as reduced to the extent necessary to reduce their value to that of the value transferred; and the reduction shall be made in the order in which, under the terms of the relevant disposition by the rule of law, it would fall to be made on a distribution of assets.

38   Attribution of value to specific gifts

(1) Such part of the value transferred shall be attributable to specific gifts as corresponds to the value of the gifts; but if or to the extent that the gifts—

    (a) are not gifts with respect to which the transfer is exempt or are outside the limit up to which the transfer is exempt, and

    (b) do not bear their own tax,

the amount corresponding to the value of the gifts shall be taken to be the amount arrived at in accordance with subsections (3) to (5) below.

(2) Where any question arises as to which of two or more specific gifts are outside the limit up to which a transfer is exempt or as to the extent to which a specific gift is outside that limit—

    (a) the excess shall be attributed to gifts not bearing their own tax before being attributed to gifts bearing their own tax, and

    (b) subject to paragraph (a) above, the excess shall be attributed to gifts in proportion to their value.

(3) Where the only gifts with respect to which the transfer is or might be chargeable are specific gifts which do not bear their own tax, the amount referred to in subsection (1) above is the aggregate of—

    (a) the sum of the value of those gifts; and

    (b) the amount of tax which would be chargeable if the value transferred equalled that aggregate.

(4) Where the specific gifts not bearing their own tax are not the only gifts with respect to which the transfer is or might be chargeable, the amount referred to in subsection

(1) above is such amount as, after the deduction of tax at the assumed rate specified in subsection (5) below, would be equal to the sum of the value of those gifts.

(5) For the purposes of subsection (4) above—
  (a) the assumed rate is the rate found by dividing the assumed amount of tax by that part of the value transferred with respect to which the transfer would be chargeable on the hypothesis that—
      (i) the amount corresponding to the value of specific gifts not bearing their own tax is equal to the aggregate referred to in subsection (3) above, and
      (ii) the part of the value transferred attributable to specific gifts and to gifts of residue or shares in residue are determined accordingly; and
  (b) the assumed amount of tax is the amount that would be charged on the value transferred on the hypothesis mentioned in paragraph (a) above.

(6) For the purposes of this section, any liability of the transferor which is not to be taken into account under section (5) above or by virtue of section 103 of the Finance Act 1986 shall be treated as a specific gift and, to the extent that any liability of the transferor is abated under the said section 103, that liability shall be treated as a specific gift.

39   Attribution of value to residuary gifts
Such part only of the value transferred shall be attributed to gifts of residue or shares in residue as is not attributed under section 38 above to specific gifts.

39A   Operation of sections 38 and 39 in cases of business or agricultural relief
(1) Where any part of the value transferred by a transfer of value is attributable to—
  (a) the value of relevant business property, or
  (b) the agricultural value of the agricultural property, then, for the purpose of attributing the value transferred (as reduced in accordance with sections 104 or 116 below), to specific gifts and gifts of residue or shares of residue, sections 38 and 39 above shall have effect subject to the following provisions of this section.

(2) The value of any specific gifts of relevant business property or agricultural property shall be taken to be their value as reduced in accordance with sections 104 or 116 below.

(3) The value of any specific gifts not falling within subsection (2) above shall be taken to be the appropriate fraction of their value.

(4) In subsection (3) above 'the appropriate fraction' means a fraction of which—
  (a) the numerator is the difference between the value transferred and the value, reduced as mentioned in subsection (2) above, of any gifts falling within that subsection, and
  (b) the denominator is the difference between the unreduced value transferred and the value, before the reduction mentioned in subsection (2) above, of any gifts falling within that subsection;

and in paragraph (b) 'the unreduced value transferred' means the amount which would be the value transferred by that transfer but for the reduction required by sections 104 and 116 below.

(5) If or to the extent that specific gifts fall within paragraphs (a) and (b) of subsection (1) or section 38 above, the amount corresponding to the value of the gifts shall be arrived at in accordance with subsections (3) to (5) of that section by reference to their value reduced as mentioned in subsection (2) or, as the case may be, by subsection (3) of this section.

Appendix 1 *Legislation*

(6) For the purposes of this section the value of a specific gift of relevant business property or agricultural property does not include the value of any other gift payable out of that property; and that other gift shall not itself be treated as a specific gift of relevant business property or agricultural property.

(7) In this section—
  'agricultural property' and 'the agricultural value of agricultural property' have the same meaning as in Chapter II of Part V of this Act; and 'relevant business property' has the same meaning as in Chapter I of that part.

40 Gifts made separately out of different funds
Where gifts taking effect on a transfer of value take effect separately out of different funds the preceding provisions of this chapter shall be applied separately to the gifts taking effect out of each of those funds, with necessary adjustments to the values and amounts referred to in those provisions.

41 Burden of Tax
Notwithstanding the terms of any disposition—
  (a) none of the tax on the value transferred will fall on any specific gift if or to the extent that the transfer is exempt with respect to that gift, and
  (b) none of the tax attributable to the value of the property comprised in residue shall fall on any gift of a share of residue if or to the extent that the transfer is exempt with respect to the gift.

42 Supplementary
(1) In this Chapter—
  'gift, in relation to any transfer of value', means the benefit of a disposition or rule of law by which, on the making of the transfer, any property becomes (or would but for any abatement become) the property of any person or applicable for any purpose;
  'given' should be construed accordingly;
  'specific gift' means any gift other than a gift of residue or of a share in residue.

(2) For the purposes of this Chapter a gift bears its own tax if the tax attributable to it falls on the person who becomes entitled to the property given, or (as the case may be) is payable out of property applicable for the purposes for which the property given becomes applicable.

(3) Where—
  (a) the whole or part of the value transferred by a transfer of value is attributable to property which is the subject of two or more gifts, and
  (b) the aggregate of the values of the property given by each of those gifts is less than the value transferred or, as the case may be, that part of it,

then for the purposes of this chapter (and notwithstanding the definition of a gift in subsection (1) above) the value of each gift shall be taken to be the relevant proportion of the value transferred or, as the case may be, that part of it; and the relevant proportion in relation to any gift is the proportion which the value of a property given by it bears to the said aggregate.

(4) Where on the death of a person legal rights under the law of Scotland are claimed by a person entitled to claim them, they should be treated for the purposes of this chapter as a specific gift which bears its own tax; and in determining the value of such legal rights, any tax payable on the estate of the deceased shall be left out of account.

INHERITANCE TAX ACT 1984

267A Limited liability partnerships

For the purposes of this Act and any other enactments relating to Inheritance —

(a) property to which a limited liability partnership is entitled, or which it occupies or uses, shall be treated as property to which its members are entitled, or which they occupy or use, as partners,

(b) any business carried on by a limited liability partnership shall be treated as carried on in partnership by its members,

(c) incorporation, change in membership or dissolution of a limited liability partnership shall be treated as formation, alteration or dissolution of a partnership, and

(d) any transfer of value made by or to a limited liability partnership shall be treated as made by or to its members in partnership (and not by or to the limited liability partnership as such).

Statutory Instruments

SI 1992 NO 3181

THE INHERITANCE TAX (MARKET MAKERS) REGULATIONS 1992

Interpretation

(2) In these regulations 'subsection (7)' and 'subsection (4)' means subsections (7) of section 105 and subsection (4) of section 234 respectively of the Inheritance Tax Act 1984.

Modification of Subsection (7) and Subsection (4)

(4)   Subsection (7) and subsection (4) shall have effect as if—
  (a) the reference to The Stock Exchange in paragraph (a) of each of those subsections were a reference to either of The Stock Exchange and LIFFE (Administration and Management) (both being recognised investment exchanges within the meaning of the *Financial Services Act 1986*), and
  (b) references to the Council of The Stock Exchange in paragraph (b) of each of those subsections were a reference to the investment exchange concerned.

Appendix 3

Extra Statutory Concessions

F7   FOREIGN OWNED WORKS OF ART

This has become statutory: *IHTA 1984, s 64(2)* now reads:

> (2) For the purposes of subsection (1) above, a foreign-owned work of art which is situated in the United Kingdom for one or more of the purposes of public display, cleaning and restoration (and for no other purpose) is not to be regarded as relevant property.

F15   WOODLANDS

Finance Act 1986, Sch 19, para 46 denies potentially exempt transfer treatment for Inheritance Tax purposes to all property comprised in a single transfer any part of which, however small, is woodlands subject to a deferred Estate Duty charge. By concession the scope of this paragraph will henceforth be restricted solely to that part of the value transferred which is attributable to the woodlands which are the subject of the deferred charge.

F16   AGRICULTURAL PROPERTY AND FARM COTTAGES

On a transfer of agricultural property which includes a cottage occupied by a retired farm employee or their widow(er), the condition in *IHTA 1984, ss 117* and *169* concerning occupation for agricultural purposes is regarded as satisfied with respect to the cottage if either
- the occupier is a statutorily protected tenant, or
- the occupation is under release granted to the farm employee for his/her life and that of any surviving spouse as part of the employee's contract of employment by the landlord for agricultural purposes.

F17   RELIEF FOR AGRICULTURAL PROPERTY

- On a transfer of tenanted agricultural land, the condition in *IHTA 1984, s 116(2)(a)* is regarded as satisfied where the transferor's interest in property either

- carries a right to vacant possession within 24 months of the date of the transfer, or
- is, notwithstanding the terms of the tenancy, valued at an amount broadly equivalent to the vacant possession value of the property.

Appendix 4

Inland Revenue Statements

STATEMENTS OF PRACTICE

SP 12/80 Business Relief 'Buy and Sell' Agreements

The Board understands that it is sometimes the practice for partners or shareholder directors of companies to enter into an agreement (known as a 'Buy and Sell' Agreement) whereby, in the event of the death before retirement of one of them, the deceased's personal representatives are obliged to sell and the survivors are obliged to purchase the deceased's business interest of shares, funds for the purpose being frequently provided by means of appropriate life assurance policies.

In the Board's view such an agreement, requiring as it does a sale and a purchase and not merely conferring an option to sell or buy, is a binding contract for sale within *section 113* of *IHTA 1984*. As a result the inheritance tax business relief will not be due on the business interest or shares. (*Section 113* of *IHTA 1984* provides that where only property would be relevant business property for the purpose of business relief in relation to a transfer of value but a binding a contract for its sale has been entered into at the time of the transfer, it is not relevant business property in relation to that transfer.)

SP 18/80 Securities dealt in on the Stock Exchange Unlisted Securities Market: Status and valuation for tax purposes

Obsolete: the USM is closed.

SP 6/87 Acceptance of property in lieu of Inheritance Tax, Capital Transfer Tax and Estate Duty (8 April 1987)

1. The Commissioners for HMRC, with the agreement of the Secretary of State for Culture, Media and Sport (and, where appropriate, other ministers), accept heritage property in whole or part satisfaction of an inheritance tax, capital transfer tax or estate duty debt and any interest payable on the tax.

2. No capital tax is payable on property that is accepted in lieu of tax. The amount of tax satisfied is determined by agreeing a special price. This price is found by establishing an agreed value for the item and deducting a proportion of the tax given up on the item itself, using an arrangement known as the 'douceur'. The terms on which property is accepted are a matter for negotiation.

3. *FA 1987, s 60* and *F (No 2) A 1987, s 97* provide that, where the special price is based on the value of the item at a date earlier than the date on which it is accepted, interest on the tax which is being satisfied may cease to accrue from that earlier date.

4. The persons liable for the tax which is to be satisfied by an acceptance in lieu can choose between having the special price calculated from the value of the item when they offer it or when the Commissioners for HMRC accept it. Since most offers are made initially on the basis of the current value of the item, HMRC consider them on the basis of the value at the 'offer date', unless the offeror notifies them that he wishes to adopt the 'acceptance date' basis of valuation. The offeror's option will normally remain open until the item is formally accepted. But this will be subject to review if more than two years elapse from the date of the offer without the terms being settled. The Commissioners for HMRC may then give six months' notice that they will no longer be prepared to accept the item on the 'offer date' basis.

5. Where the 'offer date' option remains open and is chosen, interest on the tax to be satisfied by the item will cease to accrue from that date.

REVENUE INTERPRETATIONS

RI 95 (December 1994) Inheritance Tax — business and agricultural relief

The Inheritance Tax (IHT) legislation provides relief for transfers of agricultural property and for business property. We have been asked for our views on the availability of relief—

- where agricultural property is replaced by business property (or vice versa) shortly before the owner's death; and
- on the donor's death, where the donee of a potentially exempt transfer of agricultural property has sold it and reinvested the proceeds in a non-agricultural business (or vice versa).

A 'potentially exempt transfer' (PET) is a lifetime transfer which only becomes chargeable to IHT if the donor dies within seven years of the transfer.

All statutory references in this article are to *Inheritance Tax Act (IHTA) 1984*.

IHT business and agricultural relief reduces the value of the relevant business property, or the agricultural value of agricultural property, by either 50 or 100 per cent. The rate of relief depends on the nature of the property and interest held.

The qualifying conditions for the relief include requirements of a minimum period of ownership and, in the case of agricultural property, of occupation of the property for agricultural purposes immediately before the transfer. If, and to the extent that, the same property may qualify for relief to both agricultural property and business property, *s 114* prevents double relief.

There are also rules which allow for the sale and replacement of qualifying property. The replacement is qualifying property only if it, and the original qualifying property, have together been owned (and in the case of agricultural property, occupied) for a combined minimum period.

In the Revenue's view, where agricultural property which is a farming business is replaced by non-agricultural business property, the period of ownership of the original property will be relevant for applying the minimum ownership condition to the replacement property. Business property relief will be available on the replacement if all the conditions for that relief are satisfied. Where non-agricultural business property is replaced by a farming business, if the latter is not eligible for agricultural property relief, *s 114(1)* does not exclude business property relief if conditions for that relief are satisfied.

There could be cases where, for example, agricultural land is not part of a farming business, so any replacement could only qualify for business property relief if it satisfied the minimum ownership conditions in its own right. However, our experience suggests such cases are likely to be exceptional.

Where the donee of a PET of a farming business sells the business, and replaces it with a non-agricultural business, the effect of *s 124A(1)* is to deny agricultural property relief on the value transferred by the PET. Consequently, *s 114(1)* does not exclude Business Property Relief if the conditions for that relief are satisfied; and in the reverse situation, the farming business acquired by the donee can be 'relevant business property' for the purposes of *s 113B(3)(c)*.

RI 110 (April 1995) Inheritance Tax — Valuation of assets at the date of death

Where the value of an asset is ascertained for Inheritance Tax (IHT) purposes on the owner's death, this is also taken as the beneficiary's acquisition value for Capital Gains Tax (CGT) purposes. The Revenue have been asked to say whether they will ascertain the value of the estate assets using IHT principles, where either:
- the asset is wholly exempt or relieved from IHT; or no IHT is payable on the deceased's estate,

- in order to provide a value for any other Revenue purpose, in particular the CGT acquisition value.

The value of an asset for IHT purposes is usually the price it would realise if sold on the open market. In certain circumstances special rules may apply to give a different value. For example, under the related property provisions of the *IHT 1984, s 161*, property held jointly by husband and wife is treated as a single unit in arriving at the value of their respective interests.

IHT is charged on the assets of a person's estate on death if their value together with the value of any chargeable lifetime gifts exceeds the IHT 'threshold' £154,000 for deaths and other chargeable events occurring on or after 6th April 1995. There are various exemptions and reliefs. These include the exemption for assets given to a surviving spouse and up to 100 per cent relief for agricultural business property.

If an asset is wholly exempt of relief from IHT, neither the personal representative of the deceased nor the Revenue can require the value of that asset to be ascertained for IHT purposes.

Where it is evident that any possible increase or decrease in the value of the chargeable assets of the estate, as included in an Inland Revenue account, will leave the total value of the estate below the IHT threshold, it will not be necessary to ascertain the value of all of the individual assets for IHT purposes. In some cases, particularly where the estate is close to the threshold, values may be considered but not necessarily 'ascertained'.

For example, the value included in the Inland Revenue Account for a holding of shares in an unquoted company might appear to the Revenue's Shares Valuation Division (SVD) to be too high. In this situation, as no IHT is at stake, SVD is unlikely to negotiate an ascertained value for IHT. On the other hand, if the value included seems too low, SVD may negotiate an ascertained value if the likely amount of IHT at stake warrants this.

If the value of an asset is not ascertained for IHT, the normal rules of *TCGA 1992, s 272* will apply to determine the CGT acquisition value of the beneficiary.

The Revenue have also been asked how they will approach the valuation of a holding of shares in a unquoted company where not all of the company's assets qualify for IHT Business Property Relief, so that the shares are not wholly relieved. Again, SVD's approach will depend very much upon whether in any event IHT is payable and, if so, the amount of tax involved. SVD is unlikely to negotiate an ascertained value for the holding if very little or no tax is at stake.

RI 121 (August 1995) Inheritance Tax — relief for untenanted agricultural land
Inheritance Tax — relief for tenanted agricultural land — FA 1995, section 155

FA 1995, s 155 increased the rate of Inheritance Tax relief for transfers of tenanted agricultural land from 50 per cent to 100 per cent. The full relief applies to transfers, made on or after 1st September 1995, of agricultural land which is let on a tenancy starting on or after that date. The purpose of full relief is, as indicated in the Revenue Press Release of 27th January 1995, to boost the government's reforms of the law on agricultural tenancies, now contained in the *Agricultural Tenancies Act 1995*. *ATA 1995* applies to England and Wales and not to Northern Ireland or Scotland.

Application of Inheritance Tax for Relief

The Revenue have received enquiries asking whether the increased relief will apply only where the tenancy in question is within the provisions of *ATA 1995*.

The relief will apply to all agricultural tenancies, throughout the UK, starting on or after 1st September 1995, provided that all the statutory conditions for relief are met. In particular, a tenancy starting on or after that date by reason of statutory succession to an existing tenancy is not excluded from the full relief.

RI 210 Bookmakers' Pitches and capital gains tax

(Extract)

A pitch will also be 'property to which (the deceased) is beneficially entitled', *IHTA 1984, s 5(1)*, and where it formed part of the deceased's business its value may qualify for inheritance tax business property relief at 100% if the statutory conditions are met, *IHTA 1984, ss 103–114*.

Appendix 5

Revenue and other press releases

10 MARCH 1975 HANSARD: CTT — ASSOCIATED OPERATIONS

The Chief Secretary to the Treasury (Mr Joel Barnett):

> 'I want to explain the reason for the clause [now *IHTA 1984 section 268*]. As I said in Committee, it is reasonable for a husband to share capital with his wife when she has no means of her own. If she chooses to make gifts out of the money she has received from her husband, there will be no question of using the associated operation provisions to treat them as gifts as made by the husband and taxable as such.
>
> In a blatant case, where a transfer from a husband to wife was made on condition that the wife should at once use the money to make gifts to others, a charge on her gift by the husband might arise under the clause. The hon Gentleman fairly recognized that.
>
> I want to give an example of certain circumstances that could mean the clause having to be invoked. There are complex situations involving transactions between husband and wife and others where, for example, a controlling shareholder with a 60% holding in a company wished to transfer his holding to his son. If he gave half to his son, having first transferred half to his wife, and later his wife transferred her half share to the son, the effect would be to pass a controlling shareholding from father to son. The Revenue would then use the associated operations provisions to ensure that the value of a controlling holding was taxed.
>
> There are ordinary, perfectly innocent transfers between husband and wife. For example, when a husband has the money and the wife has no money — or the other way around, which happens from time to time — and the one with the money gives something to the other to enable the spouse to make a gift to a son or a daughter on marriage, that transaction would not be caught by the clause. It would be a reasonable thing to do. I have made that clear in Committee upstairs, and I make it clear again now.'

9 JUNE 1976 INLAND REVENUE LETTER

Normal expenditure out of income (*IHTA 1984, section 21*):

> 'The statute does not lay down a precise definition of income for the purposes of this exemption. We would therefore take the view that the word has to be interpreted in accordance with normal accountancy rules. This implies taking income net of tax; as regards taking into account the tax on a wife's income, I think it implies adopting a factual test — i.e. looking to see what tax has been borne by the spouse concerned. Of course this is an area in which it is difficult to lay down an inflexible rule, and the circumstances of individual cases will doubtless be diverse.'

Letter from Inland Revenue, *Law Society's Gazette*, 9 June 1976

2 NOVEMBER 1983 HANSARD

Blood Stock Industry (taxation)

Mr Latham asked the Chancellor of the Exchequer on what authority the Capital Taxes Office indicated that horse owners and breeders will not be permitted 50[now 100]% agricultural relief on capital transfer tax and also, in certain circumstances, not be permitted 50[now 100]% business relief; and if he will instruct the office to reverse this decision.

Mr Moore: Under the provisions of the Capital Transfer Tax, agricultural relief is given for agricultural property occupied for agricultural purposes. Business relief is given if the business is carried on for gain. Whether any particular property qualifies under these provisions is a matter of the proper interpretation of the law in relation to the fact of the particular case. If the taxpayer does not accept the view of the Inland Revenue he may appeal.

19 SEPTEMBER 1984 ICAEW

Memorandum TR557: CTT: 'buy and sell agreements'

[This memorandum is of considerable length and has not been set out. It is referred to at **6.14** and **14.11**.]

21 APRIL 1986 LAW SOCIETY'S GAZETTE

Assets used for life tenant's business: Business Property Relief

Under the Code in *IHT 1984, sections 103 to 114*. Business Property Relief is given at either [50]% or [100]% by adjusting the valuation of 'relevant business property' as defined in *section 105*. In *Featherstonehaugh v IRC* [1984] STC 261, it was decided that relief at what is now the [100]% rate was available for land on which a sole trader was life tenant and on which he had carried on a farming business prior to the transfer on his death.

The Inland Revenue's understanding of this decision is that, where there is a transfer of value of a life tenant's business or interest in a business (including assets of which he was life tenant which were used in that business), the case falls within *section 105(1)(a)* and the [100]% relief is available. Where, by contrast, the transfer of value is only of any land, building, machinery or plant used wholly or mainly for the purposes of a business carried on by the life tenant and in which he had an interest in possession under a settlement, the relief is only available at the rate of [50]% if the transfer takes place in circumstances in which the business itself is not being disposed of.

Thus, if land in a settlement has been used for the purpose of the life tenant's business, the 100% relief is only available if the transfer of value is one of his business as a whole (or an interest in it), including the property in which he has a life interest.

19 FEBRUARY 1987 INLAND REVENUE LETTER

Gifts with reservation: directors' remuneration

You are concerned about the possible effects of the provisions concerning gifts with reservation in a case where a company director or employee makes a gift of shares in a company, but stays in the company as a director or employee in return for a salary or other benefits that are no greater than what might reasonably be provided under an arm's-length deal between unconnected parties. The application or otherwise of these provisions to any given arrangement would, as you know, be a matter for determination in the light of the relevant facts and law of the date of the donor's death.

That said, I am pleased to tell you that the Revenue would accept that the continuation of reasonable commercial arrangements in the form of remuneration and other benefits for the donor's services to the business entered into prior to the gift would not, by itself, amount to a reservation provided that the benefits were in no way linked to or affected by the gift. For completeness, I might add that if in your example the gift of the shares was into trust and the settlor was also a trustee of that trust and a director or employee of the company, the fact that the terms of the trust empowered trustees to retain directors' fees would not, of itself, amount to a reservation of benefit. In this context too, the Revenue will need to be satisfied that the remuneration and other benefits were on a reasonable commercial basis. What is 'reasonable' would of course depend on the facts of the case.

Where, however, as part of the overall transaction, including the gift, new arrangements are made, it will be necessary to examine all the relevant facts to determine whether the remuneration package amounts to a reservation of benefit to the donor by contract or otherwise.

5 MARCH 1987 INLAND REVENUE LETTER

Gifts with reservation: Director's remuneration

I confirm that a downward adjustment made at the time of the gift to a director's pre-existing remuneration to bring the arrangement into line with the level no higher than would be commercially justifiable will not be regarded as giving rise to a reservation of benefit.

18 MAY 1987 INLAND REVENUE LETTER

IHT: Gifts with reservation

I am now able to write to you about the points concerning the provisions on gifts with reservation.

It does not seem realistic to think in terms of precise and comprehensive guidance on how the gifts with reservation provisions will be interpreted and applied since so much will turn on the particular facts of individual cases. However, as the provisions are similar to those adopted for estate duty, the relevant estate duty case law and practice provide a helpful guide to the interpretation and application of the IHT legislation. That said, may I turn to your specific concerns.

Gifts of Land
   (1) Consistent with the assurance given last year by the Minister of State and Standing Committee G (Hansard, 10 June 1986, col 425) the estate duty practice on the treatment of gifts involving a share in a house where the gifted property is occupied by all the joint owners including the donor will apply. The donor's retention of a share in the property will not by itself amount to a reservation. If, and for so long as, all the joint owners remain in occupation, the donor's will not be treated as a reservation provided the gift is itself unconditional and there is no collateral benefit to the donor. The payment by the donee of the donor's share of the running costs, for example, might be such a benefit. An arrangement will not necessarily be jeopardised merely because it involves a gift of an unequal share in the house.
   (2) In other cases the donor's occupation or enjoyment of the gifted land will only be disregarded if the occupation is for full consideration in money or monies worth as provided in *FA 1986, Sch 20 para 6(1)(a)* or if it is by way of reasonable 'care and maintenance' provision within

579

para 6(1)(b). Whether an arrangement is for full consideration will of course depend on the precise facts. But among the attributes of an acceptable arrangement would be the existence of a bargain negotiated at arm's-length by parties who were independently advised and which followed the normal criteria in force at the time it was negotiated.

(3) ...

Gifts involving family businesses or farms

(4) A gift involving a family business or farm will not necessarily amount to a gift with reservation merely because the donor remains in the business, perhaps as a director or partner. For example, where the gift is of shares of a company, the continuation of reasonable commercial arrangements in the form of remuneration for the donor's ongoing services to the company entered into before the gift will not of itself amount to a reservation provided the remuneration is in no way linked to or beneficially affected by the gift. Note in this connection the Inland Revenue letters of 19 February and 5 March 1987, both reproduced in Appendix 5 at 20.1.6 and 20.1.7. Similar considerations will apply in the case where the gift is into trust which empower the trustees, who may be the donor, to retain director's fees etc for his own benefit: see the letter of 19 February 1987.

(5) The 'Munro' principle will also be relevant in determining the tax treatment of gifts affecting family farms where the donor and the donee continue to farm the land in pursuance of arrangements entered into prior to and independently of the gift. In cases where this principle does not apply, the test of 'full consideration' for the purposes of *para 6(1) (a)* will need to be satisfied with regard to the donor's occupation of the land. In applying that test we shall take account of all the circumstances surrounding the arrangement including the sharing of profits and losses, the donor and the donee's interests in the land, and their respective commitment and expertise.

Gifts of chattels

(6) ...

Settlor's retention of reversion

(7) ...

17 MARCH 1988 HANSARD

IHT and Family companies

Viscount Mackintosh of Halifax asked whether, given their stated aim of creating a climate where family companies can flourish, it is their intention that clearance under [*ICTA 1988, s 219(2)*] will in all cases be refused on the death of a controlling shareholder where sufficient dividends can be voted by the executors to enable the Inheritance Tax liability to be met by instalments on the basis that hardship would not arise as the executors control the company and thus control the flow of dividends.

Lord Brabazon of Tara: I understand that there have been very few cases of the kind in question. However, where the company has surplus funds sufficient to discharge the inheritance tax liability, the Revenue take the view that there would be no hardship since the liability could be met by dividend payments from the company.

11 SEPTEMBER 1991

Inheritance Tax Act 1984, section 98(1) — deferred shares

Following recent legal advice, the Revenue's interpretation of *IHTA 1984, section 98* has changed.

Until now the Capital Taxes Offices have taken the view that when deferred shares come to rank equally with another class of shares there would be no alteration in the rights of the shares within the meaning of *IHTA 1984, section 98(1)(b)*, but there would be an alteration in the company's share capital within the meaning of *IHTA 1984, section 98(1)(a)*.

The Board of Inland Revenue has now been advised that an alteration of rights, within the meaning of *IHTA 1984, section 98(1)(b)*, occurs when deferred shares come to rank equally with another class of shares. Accordingly, claims for Inheritance Tax will be raised where deferred shares, issued after 5 August 1991, subsequently come to rank equally, or become merged, with shares of another class.

18 MARCH 1992

Valuation of agricultural tenancies

[This records an agreed summary of a meeting between representatives of the Law Society of England and Wales, the Law Society of Scotland and the Inland Revenue held on 3 February 1992 to discuss the specific issue of valuation of agricultural tenancies. The note is of some length and is not set out here: it appears in *Tolleys Yellow Tax Handbook,* for example *2010–11*, Part 3 at p 350.]

FEBRUARY 1993 INLAND REVENUE TECHNICAL BULLETIN

Milk Quota

For inheritance tax purposes, where agricultural land, or an interest in agricultural land, is valued and the valuation of the land reflects the benefit of milk quota, agricultural relief is given on that value.

Where milk quota is valued separately, it will normally constitute an asset used in the business, within *IHTA 1984, s 110*, so that business relief under *IHTA 1984, s 105(1)(a)* may be available.

Other press releases in this area that may be of interest to the practitioner but which are not set out here, many being freely available on HMRC website.

Business relief:
- Extension of non-statutory clearances service for HMRC business customers: 1 May 2008

Heritage property:
- Leasehold Enfranchisement of conditionally exempt property: 7 May 1993
- 'Heritage property: *IHTA 1984, s 30*: December 1995
- The Register of conditionally exempt works of art: 16 January 1996

Compliance:
- Simpler payment scheme for IHT: 27 March 2003

Appendix 6

Forms used in IHT100 and 400

The forms are no longer reproduced here, as in previous editions, because they are readily available from HMRC website (see below) and they change frequently. It used to be the practice, the author recalls from the 1970s, to keep a stock of forms. Do not do that: instead download a fresh form each time, to ensure that you are using the latest edition. Do not use supplemental pages from IHT100 for IHT400 or vice versa. They differ slightly, so use those designated for each return. The most common forms relevant to this book are mentioned in **Chapter 22** and are set out below.

LIFETIME TRANSACTIONS AND DISCRETIONARY TRUSTS

D36: Land, buildings and interest in land

D37: Agricultural relief

D38: Business relief, business or partnership interests

TRANSFERS ON DEATH

IHT405 Houses, land, buildings and interests in land

IHT412: Unlisted stocks and shares, and control holdings

IHT413: Business and partnership interests and assets

IHT414: Agricultural relief

IHT420: National Heritage assets conditional exemption and offers in lieu of tax

IHT400 Notes, especially the schedules relating to the above forms:

see www.hmrc.gov.uk/inheritancetax/iht400-notes.pdf

Appendix 7

Immensee farm: a case study

(with acknowledgment to the Novelle, or 'long short story', by Theodor Storm)

BACKGROUND

Reinhard Weber could hardly believe what he was reading. He had discovered that Immensee Farm was for sale and had now received the agents' particulars. He scarcely needed to refer to the plan (to be found at the end of this Appendix). The memory of the place was as vivid now as when, as a child sixty years before, he had walked in the little wood near Manor Cottage with Elizabeth searching for wild strawberries. He must try to buy the farm, for sentimental if not for tax reasons.

There might well be good tax reasons anyway. Reinhard, despite his name, was a domiciled Englishman. He and his brother Max had inherited from their father a publishing business. Max, like Reinhard but for different reasons, had never married. On his retirement five years ago, Max had given his shareholding to Reinhard. Max was still alive but not in good health. Reinhard, as well as being a publisher, was qualified as an accountant and had familiarised himself with certain IHT rules applicable to his situation.

Two and a half years ago, Reinhard received an offer, both for the publishing side of the business and for his own personal copyrights as a minor poet and writer of fairy tales, which he really could not resist. He had sold up. The last of the consideration had just come through. As to his own interest, he was aware that his copyrights might not have qualified for BPR even if he had retained them; and though he had neither wife nor children to provide for, he was not keen for his estate to become a sitting target for HMRC.

Reinhard was aware that, since he now no longer held Max's former shareholding, the death of Max within seven years of his gift to Reinhard could cause the clawback rules to bite. He knew that he must, within three years of the sale, a date now fast approaching, put all of the money representing the gift, to comply with the strict requirement of *IHTA 1984, s 113B(1)(b)*, into a replacement business or risk a clawback charge on the share of the business representing his late brother's interest. Although not trained as a farmer, he had had an abiding interest in agriculture and had access to professional help and advice.

PARTICULARS OF THE PROPERTY

The particulars showed that the total area of 45.86 hectares, or just over 110 acres, comprised several houses, as he remembered, and a relatively small acreage of arable land:

- Immensee House was vacant. Grade II listed, it had six bedrooms (of which four now, despite the listing, had en suite facilities) and several reception rooms. By virtue of being within easy commuter reach of London, it would clearly command a premium as a residence if offered with a small acreage, say enough for a paddock. At present, it stood in about 1.6 acres (see Area 1 below).
- Manor Cottage was vacant, following the retirement of the farm manager. It stood in 1.25 acres and had three bedrooms, one reception room and a further downstairs room which had been fitted out as the farm office with all the now usual electronic gadgetry (see Area 2 below).
- Hilltop Bungalow, with a small garden of 0.17 acres, was occupied by the remaining farm worker (see Area 3 below).
- Immensee Bungalow, with only 0.21 acres, was excluded from the sale and was to become the home in retirement of the previous farmer's widow, none other than Elizabeth Storm herself (see Area 3 below).
- Numbers 3 and 4 Railway Cottages, together amounting to 0.54 acres, were available for holiday lets (see Area 4 below).

THE VENDOR'S POSITION

Taking his courage in both hands, Reinhard arranged through the agents to inspect the farm and to meet Elizabeth, whom he had not seen since her marriage to Erich whilst he, Reinhard, had been away at university. He remembered, with a twinge of regret, that the farm had been a gift to Erich from his, Erich's, father. He now learned that Immensee House itself, though offered as part of the sale, had been transferred to joint names of husband and wife whilst the remainder of the estate was held by Erich Storm Limited.

After Erich's death a few years ago, Elizabeth had carried on farming until the manager retired. She now had to sell. She had been advised that any purchaser would insist on buying assets rather than the shares in the company, to avoid the risk of any problems with the past tax history of the company. She had not yet put the company into liquidation and was in a position to sell either the shares or the land. She hoped that main residence relief would shelter the now substantial gain on Immensee House. She was concerned that, owing to certain technicalities, entrepreneurs' relief might not be available to her, and that a sale of the land by the company followed by its liquidation could give rise to a double CGT charge.

Appendix 7   *Immensee farm: a case study*

THE OFFER

Reinhard's offer was for the freehold of Immensee House and for the shares, on the basis that he would continue to employ the remaining farm worker. He would buy as a going concern. He was willing to buy the shares, because he was offered comprehensive warranties and wished to help his childhood friend. He had considered RI 95. He knew that, where a non-agricultural business is replaced by a farming business and for any reason the farming business is not eligible for APR, BPR may still be available. He had in mind that the fairly full price that he had agreed to pay might well represent a premium over agricultural value, such that APR might be restricted anyway. Contracts were exchanged within three weeks.

One other factor had influenced his decision: he had noticed that the adjoining farm was for sale through another agent. It had no house, but a good range of buildings.

THE BEST USE OF THE PROPERTY

Reviewing his purchase, Reinhard decided as follows:
1.   He would, in due course, sell Immensee House. He was currently selling his own suburban home, on which he would realise a large tax-free gain, to move to Immensee Farm, but Manor Cottage was ample for his needs and he did not particularly wish to occupy Erich's old place. He reasoned that, unless he unified the ownership of Immensee House and the farmland in some way, he would face *Starke* problems. The House, if he added to it the five-acre field which lay between it and the road, would command far more than mere agricultural value. It might fund the next purchase of farmland.
2.   There was no need to hurry. Reinhard was only 70 and in good health. If he sold Immensee House too quickly, and at too great a profit, he would fall foul of the 'residence' test mentioned by the Court of Appeal in *Goodwin v Curtis (Inspector of Taxes)* [1998] STC 475. It would take him a year to refurbish Manor Cottage anyway. That should be long enough: he was not, as such, buying Immensee House wholly or partly for the purpose of realising a gain from it, so as to bring himself within *TCGA 1992, s 224(3)*. The eventual gain might be his hope, or even his expectation, as described in *Jones v Willcock* [1996] STC (SCD) 389, but it would not be his 'purpose'. Merely adding a field to the land enjoyed with the house would not amount to trading: it fell well short of the tests of the 'badges of trade' examined in *Lynch v Edmondson (HMIT)* [1998] STC (SCD) 185.
3.   He would also put with Immensee House, on resale, some of the now redundant farm buildings. They had been suitable years ago for stock keeping, and might still do as stables, but Reinhard would not himself be occupying them for the purposes of agriculture, so one of his aims, to

secure BPR or APR, would not be advanced by keeping them. He knew from *Harrold v IRC* that a mere intention to occupy at some future date was not enough.

4. For the same reason, he would sell Railway Cottages and put the proceeds towards the purchase of adjoining land if he succeeded in buying it.

5. He would definitely keep the small wood on the same side of the road as Manor Cottage. It was, now as sixty years ago, occupied with the agricultural land, and that occupation was ancillary to the occupation of the farm as a whole.

This would leave him with Manor Cottage, owned by the company and occupied with the land. He felt confident that it would qualify as a farmhouse for APR, both as being no larger than was reasonable and being in fact the place from which, for some years past, the farm had actually been administered. Under *IHTA 1984, s 119(1)*, by his ownership of a controlling shareholding in the company, he was deemed to be in occupation of the land, including the cottage, from the date of purchase.

By exchanging contracts within three years of the sale of the publishing business, he retained the protection of *s 113B(2)(a)*: Elizabeth might well have been the only love of his long life, and celebrated in the many poems he had shown her when he was a student, in which she had shown little interest at the time, but the terms of Reinhard's purchase were, within *s 113B(2)(b)*, at arm's length.

THE IHT ANALYSIS

Reinhard was also confident of the basic IHT analysis: he had not farmed before, but he was keeping the farm worker on and was planning to run the enterprise substantially as it had been run before, except that it would not be burdened by the overheads of Immensee House. This was not a mere investment exercise by a successful businessman on retirement. *Section 105(3)* would not apply. The only dwellings left would qualify as agricultural property. The company had vacant possession of the land within *s 122(3)*. As soon as Reinhard had owned the shares for two years, he would qualify for relief under *s 123(1)(b)*.

THE FUTURE

That left him with just one project to consider. The field near the road contained the 'Pit (disused)' marked on the plan. What scope was there now for reopening the workings? Was there a workable quantity of dolomite, or industrial limestone, there? Reinhard knew that, whilst limestone for use as aggregates was relatively plentiful, industrial limestone was scarce and worked in only a few sites in the country. Nothing in the local Development Plan seemed totally to rule out the possibility of quarrying. He resolved to commission a mineral reserves report and to take steps, if the report were favourable, to demonstrate that a part of his business was the exploitation of the mineral reserves of the land as well as of the topsoil. After all, any hope value would not qualify for APR, so he would do well to demonstrate that BPR ought to apply.

Immensee Farm: the plan

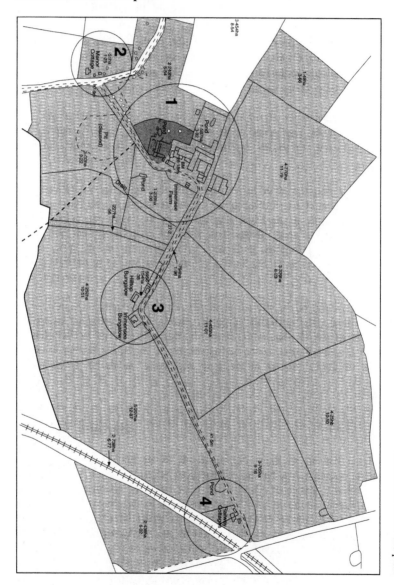

Area 1: Immensee Farm

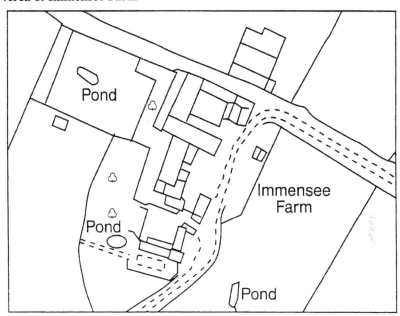

Area 2: Manor Cottage

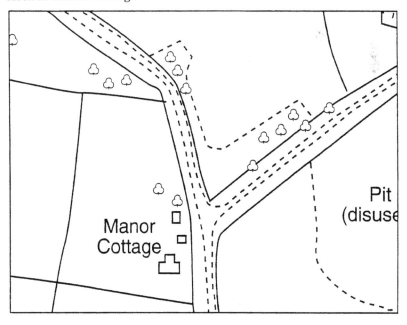

Appendix 7 *Immensee farm: a case study*

Area 3: Hilltop and Immensee Bungalows

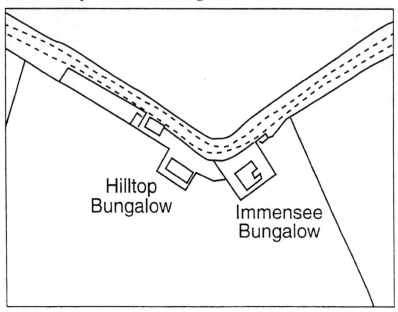

Area 4: Railway Cottages

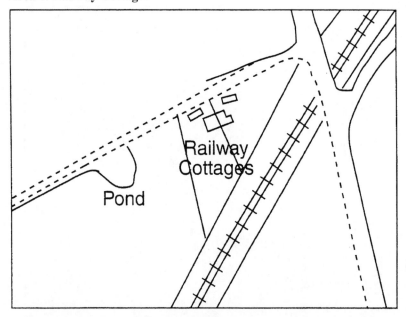

Heritage property: the old rules

These are retained, not merely as an academic museum piece, but to provide the context in cases that go back to an earlier set of rules, such as can still be relevant in this field.

DEATHS BEFORE 7 APRIL 1976

Conditional exemption from the charge to capital transfer tax (CTT) could be available in respect of heritage property so as to reduce the charge on a death before 7 April 1976. The Treasury could designate heritage property. Whilst the tests for qualification as heritage property fell into the same categories as they do now, there was no requirement that chattels be 'pre-eminent'. Conditional exemption was available in respect of property which either belonged to a person immediately before his death or was comprised in a settlement in which the deceased had an interest in possession. Property comprised within the discretionary trust did not qualify. The value of heritage property was excluded from the value deemed to be transferred on the death of the deceased.

Undertakings had to be given, but they were in many respects less demanding than the undertakings now required, as has been noted in **Chapters 17** and **18**. The Treasury had discretion to exclude confidential material from an undertaking. The early rules in respect of heritage property included the association of properties where one was a building of outstanding historic or architectural interest and the other was land or historically associated objects in relation to the building. On the breach of an understanding, capital transfer tax became chargeable. Where that breach occurred after 31 December 1984, the charge was made under *IHTA 1984, Sch 5*. As with the present code for heritage property, relief was available in respect of CGT, although that would apply only in respect of lifetime disposals.

The charge to capital transfer tax

A breach of an undertaking in respect of a death before 7 April 1976 triggered a charge to capital transfer tax on the previously exempted property. If the property was a building, or land adjoining it that was essential for the preservation of

Appendix 8 *Heritage property: the old rules*

its character, or an object historically associated with it, a charge to CTT also arose in respect of that other associated property. The charge arose under *FA 1975, s 32* on chattels or under *FA 1975, s 34* on land or buildings. For a charge arising after 31 December 1984, the appropriate legislation is *IHTA 1984, Sch 5*.

The person who would be entitled to receive the proceeds of sale (or income from the property) at the time of the chargeable event for capital transfer tax was the person liable for that tax. There was, under the old rules as now, an escape from the charge to capital transfer tax where the property was sold to a heritage body or, if not sold, transferred to a person who gave a fresh undertaking. In respect of those chargeable events, as now, acceptance by the Revenue of property in lieu of tax was not treated as a disposal of the property and did not, therefore, trigger a charge. Theft or loss or destruction of heritage property without the consent of the owner did not trigger a charge to capital transfer tax, as long as the terms of the undertaking had been complied with.

It might happen that heritage property was acquired by a heritage body, not in satisfaction of tax but by purchase at auction, perhaps where agreement could not be reached between the owner and the heritage body as to its value. Where that happened, capital transfer tax was chargeable on the disposal. Where the property concerned had been exempted on more than one death before 7 April 1976, the charge to tax was by reference to the last death: see *IHTA 1984, Sch 5, paras 1(ii)* and *3(ii)*.

Under the old rules, as now, a *de minimis* provision applied where the failure to comply with an undertaking did not materially affect the heritage property as a whole. That provision (see *Sch 5, para 3(iii)*) allowed for a charge to capital transfer tax on only the particular part of the property affected by the undertaking.

APPLICATION OF THE NEW RULES

The new rules may apply in certain circumstances, and will apply in others. The situation affected is one where tax would become payable under the old estate duty rules or the capital transfer tax rules but, before that tax becomes payable, there has been a conditionally exempt transfer of the same property after 6 April 1976 under the new regime that applies with effect from that date. Where this happens, HMRC can elect to charge under the new rules or the old if there has been no conditionally exempt transfer of property on death. Where, on the other hand, there has been a conditionally exempt transfer on death, capital transfer tax becomes chargeable only under the new rules.

Administration

In the event of a breach of undertaking, sale or gift, a person who is liable for the capital transfer tax that then arises should make a return within six months of the end of the month in which the event occurred. HMRC may withdraw the exemption by issuing a notice of determination. Such a notice, as with other notices of determination, may be challenged by an appeal to the Special Commissioners.

Calculation of the charge: event within three years of death

In calculating the charge to capital transfer tax, it is first essential to determine whether the occasion of charge occurs within three years after a death or at some later time. The charge arises through disposal of the property or failure to observe an undertaking. Where the event occurred within three years of death, the capital transfer tax, otherwise chargeable by reference to that death, was recalculated as if the exempted heritage property had been part of the estate. This rule can apply only in respect of deaths occurring before 6 April 1979. As a result, surely, most of the relevant estates will now have been fully administered.

Once the capital transfer tax has been recalculated, part of it is apportioned, by value, to the main estate and part of it to the heritage property. A sale, or a breach of undertaking such as a disposal, can trigger a liability to CGT. Here, there is a curious 'one way set-off' rule. The liability to CGT may be allowed against the capital transfer tax, but there is no allowance for the capital transfer tax liability against any liability to CGT.

Computations: chargeable event more than three years after the death

Once three years have elapsed from the death, the calculation of capital transfer tax due on the estate as at that death is not disturbed by the happening of a chargeable event. Instead, there is a recalculation of the amount of the capital transfer tax that would have been chargeable according to the rules set out below. This is charged on the property itself. The assumptions made are that:
- no exemption applied to the property; and
- the value of the property at the time of death was its value at the time of the chargeable event; or, where the property has been sold, the value of the property at the time of death was the proceeds of sale.

This causes a recalculation of the total capital transfer tax that would have been payable on the estate. A proportion is then charged with respect to the heritage property by reference to the value of the asset, calculated as above, as a proportion of the value of the estate as recalculated.

For this purpose, the figure used is that for the sale only where it is the true value, ie where:

- the sale was not intended to confer any gratuitous benefit on any person; and was either
- at arm's length between unconnected persons; or
- such as might be expected if it had been at arm's length.

For this, see *IHTA 1984, Sch 5, paras 2(2)(b), 4(b)* and *6*. Where those conditions do not apply, the open market value is used in substitution for sale price. This calculation applies only to the charge on the property that is sold; the tax on the estate itself is not changed.

Net proceeds, not gross

Fortunately (and somewhat exceptionally) the charge to tax is on the net proceeds after deducting any costs of sale and after deducting any CGT chargeable by reason of the sale. The authority for the first of these propositions is an old one, *Tyser v A-G* [1938] Ch 426, naturally a case on estate duty. For the second rule, the authority is *TCGA 1992, s 258(8)*.

Recalculation for each event

This recalculation in respect of chargeable events that occur more than three years after the death is applied separately with regard to each sale that takes place. The effect is not cumulative. For instance, where the property sold is one of several objects which did not constitute a set, the sum must be completed separately each time. It may be that this even applies where two separate items, not constituting a set, are sold from the same collection at the same time.

Special rules for sets of objects

The rule is different where:

- the items did form a set at the time of death; and
- two or more of them qualified for conditional exemption; and
- two or more of the components of the set attract a charge to capital transfer tax through the happening of chargeable events at different times.

IHTA 1984, Sch 5 is applied as if these events occurred when they first originated. If that was within three years of the death, the tax chargeable on the aggregate value of the transfer on death must be adjusted for each of the later events. If the first chargeable event occurred more than three years after the death, there is a re-adjustment of the charge in respect of each object as a result of the chargeable event on each later component of the set (see *Sch 5, para 2(3)*).

However, by *Sch 5, para 2(4)*, this tiresome rule will not apply where:
- there are two or more chargeable events;
- by disposals to different persons,

and it can be shown that:
- those persons do not act in concert; and
- are not connected with each other.

ESTATE DUTY

The statutory authority for conditional exemption from estate duty was *FA 1930, s 40*. Those provisions continue to operate under *IHTA 1984, Sch 6, para 4*, where property which qualified under the old estate duty rules remains subject to conditional exemption and, for example, has still not been sold or, which perhaps is increasingly rare, has not since been the subject of a transfer, either under the rules for capital transfer tax or those for IHT.

Breach of undertaking: estate duty cases

The scheme of *FA 1930, s 40* was similar to the present regime in many respects. Thus, the breach of an undertaking or the disposal of property triggered a chargeable event for estate duty. Again, the market value rule was applied in respect of a chargeable event by way of sale that was not at arm's length. By *IHTA 1984, Sch 6, para 4(3)*, the estate duty charged is a credit against the IHT.

As noted before, with use of the expression 'Russian roulette', this is an instance where HMRC are presented by the legislation with a wide choice. Where there is a disposal of conditionally exempt property triggering a charge under *FA 1930, s 40*, HMRC may charge tax either under that section, or under *IHTA 1984, s 32* or *32A*. Where, however, death has intervened and conditional exemption has been allowed on that death, HMRC are restricted to such charge as they may make under *IHTA 1984, s 32* or *32A* and may not make any estate duty charge.

Where it can still be applied, the estate duty is charged at the rate which applied to the estate of the last person to die in relation to whose death relief was obtained; that, at least, is the apparent effect of *FA 1930, s 40*. By *FA 1969, s 39*, if the death was after 15 April 1969, the proceeds of sale, or value at the time of the breach of undertaking, of the heritage property is aggregated with the estate, and the rate recalculated in the way described in **Chapter 19**.

LOSS OF TAPER RELIEF ON GIFTS

If the heritage property had been subject to a lifetime gift, and relief had been given in respect of it, it becomes necessary to refer to the Inland Revenue press release of 3 May 1984 for assistance in the calculation. It was noted here that, by *FA 1960, s 64*, taper relief could, in general cases, be applied to property given away within a certain period before the death. However, HMRC will not allow *s 64* taper relief to reduce the charge that arises on the chargeable event. The charge must apply to the full value or sale proceeds.

Appendix 9

A general anti-avoidance rule?

This is a political football. Early in the term of the (then) new Labour Government, the Chancellor had said:

'The tax burden avoided by the few falls on the many … I have also instructed the Inland Revenue to carry out a wide-ranging review of areas of tax avoidance, with a view to further legislation in future Finance Bills. I have specifically asked them to consider a general anti-avoidance rule. The principle of fairness in taxation will guide all my Budget decisions.'

Practitioners had feared that there would be numerous changes to IHT in *FA 1997* but were spared them.

In 1997 the Institute for Fiscal Studies (IFS) published the Report of the Tax Law Review Committee into Tax Avoidance. That report asked whether current methods of dealing with tax avoidance were adequate or satisfactory and, if not, what might be done. It considered the place in tax legislation of a GAAR in the context of legislation which is difficult to understand. Whilst there might be general agreement that legislation should be made more simple, controversy surrounded the subject of tax avoidance. Some doubted whether there was even a 'problem' at all, but in November 1997 it seemed to be very important to the new government. For the time being, any GAAR seems unlikely to be introduced, although apparently it still features in HMRC thinking.

Tax avoidance is seldom simply defined, but the IFS Report noted the reference, in *IRC v Willoughby* [1997] STC 1995, to 'a course of action designed to conflict with or defeat the evident intention of Parliament'. The House of Lords had observed:

'The hallmark of tax avoidance is that the taxpayer reduces his liability to tax without incurring the economic consequences that Parliament intended to be suffered by any taxpayer qualifying for such reduction in his tax liability. The hallmark of tax mitigation, on the other hand, is that the taxpayer takes advantage of a fiscally attractive option afforded to him by the tax legislation, and genuinely suffers the economic consequences that Parliament intended to be suffered by those taking advantage of the option.'

ENGINES OF REFORM

No-one knows how much the public purse is depleted by tax avoidance. The Tax Law Review Committee felt that there were already in place three engines of reform which would in future cut down on avoidance, ie:

(i)   the attitude of the courts, as seen in the then recent case of *IRC v McGuckian* [1997] STC 908;

(ii) the development of the decisions in *Ramsay* and in *Furniss*; and

(iii) the rewriting of tax law in simpler language, accompanied by notes explaining the purpose of the law.

Against this background, the Tax Law Review Committee were concerned that new GAAR measures should not extend the power of HMRC unnecessarily and should not unduly fetter ordinary commercial or personal transactions.

It was felt that the courts had worked hard to counter many tax avoidance schemes. One architect of such schemes (including that in *McGuckian*), Mr TPD Taylor, suffered another defeat in the Court of Appeal, as follows.

SHAM: HITCH V STONE

In *Hitch v Stone* [2001] STC 214, the scheme concerned the grant of a lease for 999 years of a farm, by the family that owned it, to a company controlled by Mr Taylor. That company in return would pay a rent immediately and would pay an annuity to arise at a future date, the amount of which was to be calculated by reference to the development value of the farm. HMRC considered that two documents in the scheme, an agreement in April 1984 and a deed completed in June of that year, were shams. They concealed a financial arrangement between the family and Mr Taylor that went beyond the terms of the documents. HMRC considered that family members released the rents that were due to them and received other benefits instead, including the provision of houses, a business investment and the acquisition of property abroad.

The Special Commissioners noted that the 1984 agreement contained numerous errors and blanks that had never been completed. Some of the terms were not acted upon, some were unusual, and some unexplained, as where the amount payable for the development land could be as much as £100 million, whilst the family argued that they were entitled only to a rent of £100,000 and the possibility of indemnity payments later.

In the Court of Appeal, the argument centred on whether a document could be part sham, and the court concluded that it could. Otherwise, it would be easy for anyone setting up a sham to avoid difficulty merely by inserting certain valid matters into the document. The Special Commissioners had not made a specific finding of fact that certain clauses were shams. It was, the court held, open to it to make such a finding The court found in favour of HMRC.

On the one hand, of its very nature a decision on a tax scheme by the court is extremely well targeted, in that it addresses precisely the events which have happened, something which is difficult for a statutory code to achieve. On the other hand, the court process is uncertain. The result of a judgment is to declare the law 'as it has always been', so that it is in effect retrospective. This makes it difficult for the taxpayer to know how to report transactions, particularly under self-assessment.

NECESSARY FEATURES OF A GAAR

For these reasons, the Tax Law Review Committee was in favour of a GAAR only if such a rule had certain specific features:

- the scope of operation should be limited to transactions which, judged as a whole, had tax avoidance as a main purpose or, in the case of multi-step transactions, when a particular step in the transaction had tax avoidance as its sole purpose;
- transactions which are consistent with the intention of Parliament should be excluded insofar as that intention appears from the legislation taken as a whole;
- action to invoke the rule should be initiated by HMRC Head Office, not by local Inspectors;
- there must be a clearance system, so that both taxpayers and their agents can discover the attitude of HMRC to a proposed transaction; some delay is acceptable but must be minimised;
- there should be a single-stage appeal process available in respect of clearance applications to an independent tribunal where clearance is refused;
- if HMRC consider that a transaction comes within the GAAR, they must first show why the transaction is of such a nature that the rule applies; and
- as part of the procedure for invoking the GAAR, HMRC must state the alternative transaction which it considers should be substituted for the actual transaction which has taken place as the basis for assessing tax. If, in fact, more than one permitted alternative transaction is possible, the one that attracts the least tax should be adopted.

The Tax Law Review Committee thought that many taxpayers and their advisers would take note of the existence of such a rule and would be cautious, perhaps more cautious than hitherto. One result might be a flood of clearance applications on practically every case which might conceivably come within the ambit of such a rule, as might well happen if the rule were too widely drawn. The Committee felt that there must be a proper administrative framework with safeguards for taxpayers; without that, there should be no GAAR. The rule should be implemented in a consistent manner, with regular reporting by HMRC to Parliament on the way the rule was working.

A SUGGESTED FORM OF GAAR

What would a GAAR look like? Most helpfully, the Tax Law Review Committee set out an illustration of a provision which might, if enacted, serve their requirements. This, despite later developments, is still the best written document on the subject.

The rule would state its purpose. The basic rule would be:

'(a)   Where a person carries out a tax-driven transaction, he shall be taxed as if he had carried out the normal transaction.

(b)   If because the tax-driven transaction does not have any non-tax objective, there is no normal transaction then he shall be taxed as if it did not take place.'

The rule is then excluded in relation to what is described as a 'protected transaction', ie one encouraged by the legislation, or coming within a specific exemption, or one which does not defeat the purpose of the legislation. The burden of proof would be on HMRC.

The rule defines the key expressions such as 'tax-driven transaction', 'tax', 'avoidance of tax', 'transaction', 'multiple step transactions', and 'normal transactions'. Of these, perhaps most interesting is the last, for which the suggested definition is:

'the "normal transaction" is the transaction that it would be reasonable to assume would, if the avoidance of tax had not been a purpose of the tax-driven transaction, have been carried out to obtain the same or similar commercial or other non-tax objectives as the tax-driven transactions intended to achieve. If there are two or more alternative transactions that satisfy the description, then the transaction that would be least burdensome to the taxpayer in terms of tax shall be taken as the normal transaction.'

One of the most telling comments, in referring to the draft GAAR, appears in paragraph 5.3 of the report: 'we have not drafted it as a clause to be read as legislation for enactment. We do not pretend that it is in the language or form that Parliamentary Counsel would adopt were he instructed to draft for some future Finance Bill a General Anti-Avoidance Provision that adopted our approach'. This comment, made on behalf of a committee of lawyers and parliamentary experts, might at first glance appear to reflect no more than reasonable deference to the skills of eminent counsel. A reading of the report and of the illustrative clause does, however, tempt the practitioner to reflect that there may have been more than a note of resignation about paragraph 5.3. One suspects that no government would allow the enactment of a clause so transparent in its meaning and intent. The Committee continued: 'it is not for us to say whether the Government should adopt a statutory general anti-avoidance rule or what form such a rule should take. These are political decisions'.

Where does that leave the practitioner? It was clear from the work of the Tax Law Review Committee that a GAAR was unworkable unless the Government were prepared to commit substantial resources to the clearance procedure. The resources of HMRC are already well stretched. It seemed for a time that a policy decision had been taken not to pursue a GAAR, at least until HMRC resources were available. Meanwhile, specific rules continued to be introduced, as for example those in *FA 1999* strengthening the provisions of *FA 1986, s 102* by introducing *FA 1986, ss 102A–C*, in order to counteract lease carve-out schemes, and the legislation to reverse the effect of *Melville* schemes, noted in an earlier edition of this book but not relating specifically to business or agricultural property.

DOTAS GUIDANCE

Although the Budget 2011 promised reform, for the time being practitioners will be more concerned with measures that are already in force. In particular, the rules for disclosure of tax avoidance schemes were extended to inheritance tax with effect from 6 April 2011. Details are available in official guidance at www.hmrc.gov.uk/aiu/disclosure-avoidance.htm, and include a flowchart, details of the test of a scheme and how to proceed after receiving a scheme number.

The key test is whether the scheme allows property to become 'relevant property', as for example comprised in a discretionary trust, without incurring the usual IHT entry charge.

There is a 'white list' of transactions that need not be disclosed as avoidance schemes. Specifically, for the purposes of this book:
- the purchase of business or agricultural assets, with a view to transferring them to a trust two (or seven) years later, is not a disclosable scheme (see examples C and D in the guidance); and
- transfers of heritage property are not disclosable (see example O in the guidance).

Most readers will therefore not be concerned with the further guidance on the use of scheme numbers.

Index

[References are to paragraph numbers and appendices]

Index